The Routledge Handbook of the Welfare State

'The welfare state' in all its many forms has had a profound role in many countries around the world since at least the Second World War. *The Routledge Handbook of the Welfare State* explores the classical issues around the welfare state, but also investigates its key concepts, along with how these can be used and analysed.

Over forty contributions from renowned international specialists in the field provide readers with expert analysis of the core issues related to the welfare state, including regional depictions of welfare states around the globe. The book combines essays on methodologies, core concepts and central policy areas to produce a comprehensive picture of what 'the welfare state' means around the world. In the midst of the credit crunch, the *Handbook* addresses some of the many questions about the welfare state.

It will be an invaluable reference book for students and scholars throughout the social sciences, particularly in sociology, social policy, public policy, international relations, politics, and gender studies.

Bent Greve is professor in Social Science at the Department of Society and Globalisation, University of Roskilde, Denmark. He studies the welfare state, often in a comparative perspective. His main research interests include the welfare state, social policy, labour market policy and financing the welfare state.

The Routledge Handbook of the Welfare State

Edited by
Bent Greve

LONDON AND NEW YORK

First published 2013
by Routledge
2 Park Square, Milton Park, Abingdon, Oxon OX14 4RN

Simultaneously published in the USA and Canada
by Routledge
711 Third Avenue, New York, NY 10017

Routledge is an imprint of the Taylor & Francis Group, an informa business

British Library Cataloguing in Publication Data
A catalogue record for this book is available from the British Library

Library of Congress Cataloging in Publication Data
The Routledge handbook of the welfare state / edited by Bent Greve. -- 1st ed.
p. cm.
Includes bibliographical references and index.
1. Public welfare. 2. Welfare state. I. Greve, Bent. II. Title: Handbook of welfare state.
HV31.R766 2013
330.12′6--dc23
2012016380

ISBN: 978-0-415-68292-3 (hbk)
ISBN: 978-0-203-08422-9 (ebk)

Typeset in Bembo
by Taylor & Francis Books

Printed and bound by CPI Group (UK) Ltd, Croydon, CR0 4YY

Contents

Illustrations

Figures

Tables

Contributors

Christian Aspalter is Professor of Social Policy and Former Founding Head of Social Work and Social Administration Programme, Beijing Normal University-Hong Kong Baptist University United International College, Zhuhai, China. He has published 18 books, including *Conservative Welfare State Systems in East Asia, Discovering the Welfare State in East Asia, Securing the Future for Old Age in Europe* (with Alan Walker), *Understanding European Social Policy* (with Peter Abrahamson), *The State of Social Welfare in Asia* (with Adel Aldosary et al.), *Debating Social Development* (with Surendra Singh), *Welfare Capitalism Around the World, The Welfare State in Emerging Market Economies, Neoliberalism and the Australian Welfare State*, as well as *Health Care Systems in Europe and Asia* (with Yasuo Uchida and Robin Gauld). His journal publications include e.g. 'The East Asian Welfare Model' (*International Journal of Social Welfare*); 'The Welfare State in Cross-Cultural Perspective' (*International Social Work*), 'Analyzing the Welfare State in Poland, Czech Republic, Hungary and Slovenia: An Ideal-Typical Perspective' (*Social Policy and Administration*), as well as 'Developing Ideal-Typical Welfare Regime Theory' (*International Social Work*).

Clare Bambra is Professor of Public Health Policy, Wolfson Research Institute, Durham University, UK. She studied political science and comparative social policy before moving into public health research. Her research is highly inter-disciplinary, applying theories and methods from the social sciences to epidemiology and public health. Her research focuses on health inequalities and the social determinants of health. She has three main areas of interest: (1) labour markets and the relationships between work, worklessness and health; (2) the influence of welfare state policies and political structures on international variations in public health and health inequalities; (3) Tackling health inequalities by addressing the wider social determinants of health.

Janeen Baxter is currently Australian Research Council Professorial Fellow and Professor of Sociology in the School of Social Science and the Institute for Social Science Research at the University of Queensland. She has research expertise in gender inequality, the changing demography and experience of families and households, wellbeing, life course transitions and the design and analysis of longitudinal surveys. She is a Fellow of the Academy of Social Sciences in Australia and Chair of the External Reference Group for the Households, Income and Labour Dynamics in Australia project. She has published widely in sociology journals and has a co-edited a volume forthcoming with Springer titled *Negotiating the Life Course: Stability and Change in Life Pathways*.

Jos Berghman was researcher in Southampton (UK) and in Antwerp (BE) where he took his PhD and became director of the Centre for Social Policy. Afterwards he became professor of social security studies and dean of the social faculty at the University of Tilburg (NL). Now he is full professor of social policy at the University of Leuven (BE) where he chairs the Centre for Sociological Research. He is president of the European Institute of Social Security and vice-president of the CEPS/INSTEAD research institute (LU). In cooperation with the latter institute he directs the International Master Programme in Social Policy Analysis IMPALLA. His main research interests are social security, (European) social policy, social inclusion and pension data analysis and policies. His most recent publications include the co-editing of *Social security in transition* (Kluwer Law International, 2002); and 'The Lisbon Agenda on social policy: revitalizing the European social model' in *Europe, Globalization and the Lisbon Agenda* (Edward Elgar, 2009).

Alfio Cerami has been research associate at the Centre d'études européennes at Sciences Po, Paris. He has also been a lecturer or visiting lecturer at the University of Erfurt (Germany), at Sciences Po Paris, at the Centre for German and European Studies of the State University of St. Petersburg (Russia), at Schiller International University (Paris Campus), at Southern Methodist University (Paris Campus) and Assistant Professor at the American Graduate School of International Relations and Diplomacy (AGSIRD). His research concentrates on the ways political, economic, and social transformations influence the process of democratization and of consolidation of democratic institutions. His most recent publications include *Migration and Welfare in the New Europe* (together with E. Carmel and T. Papadopoulos, 2011, Bristol: The Policy Press), *Post-Communist Welfare Pathways* (together with P. Vanhuysse, 2009, Basingstoke: Palgrave Macmillan), and *Social Policy in Central and Eastern Europe* (2006, Berlin: LIT Verlag).

Daniel Clegg is Senior Lecturer in Social Policy at the University of Edinburgh, UK. His main research interests are the politics of unemployment and labour market policy reform in developed welfare states, especially in Continental European countries. He has published widely on these themes, including the book *Regulating the Risk of Unemployment: National Adaptations to Post-Industrial Labour Markets in Europe* (co-edited with Jochen Clasen, Oxford University Press, 2011).

Robert Henry Cox is Professor and Co-Director of the European Union Center at the University of Oklahoma. He also served as co-editor for *Governance*, an interdisciplinary journal widely read by political scientists and scholars of public administration. He is the co-editor of two books that were published in 2011, *The Role of Ideas in Social Science Research*, (Oxford University Press) and *Social Policy in the Smaller European Union States*, (Berghahn Books).

Annelies Debels is Doctor in the Social Sciences and was a post-doctoral research fellow at CEPS/INSTEAD (Luxembourg) and at the Centre for Sociological Research of the University of Leuven (Belgium). She has written a PhD on labour market flexibility and its consequences for income and poverty dynamics. Other research interests include social security and pension protection, cross-national comparisons of labour markets and welfare states and panel data methodology. She published 'Transitions out of temporary jobs: consequences for employment and poverty across Europe' in *Flexibility aand Employment Security in Europe* (Edward Elgar, 2008). With Peeters, H. and R. Verpoorten 'Excluding institutionalized elderly from surveys. Consequences for old age research' in *Social Indicators Research* (online, 2011).

David Denney is Professor of Social and Public Policy at Royal Holloway, University of London. He has researched in the areas of race and criminal justice, violence against professionals as part of the ESRC Violence Research Project. He has also written on theories of risk (*Risk and Society*, Sage, 2005) and recently edited a collection which examined the impact of fear on the development of social policy in the UK in the post 9/11 7/11 world (*Living in Dangerous Times* (Wiley-Blackwell, 2009). He currently Chairs the Editorial Board of the international journal *Social Policy and Administration.*

Kevin Farnsworth is Senior Lecturer in Social Policy at the University of Sheffield. His primary research interests concern power and politics, class struggle and public policy, and the political economy of welfare systems. He is author of *Corporate Power and Social Policy* (Policy Press, 2004), *Social Policy in Challenging Times: Economic Crisis in Welfare Systems* (with Zoe Irving, Policy Press, 2011), *Corporate versus Social Welfare* (Palgrave, 2012).

John Gal is full professor and Dean at the Paul Baerwald School of Social Work and Social Welfare at the Hebrew University of Jerusalem. His fields of interest include social policy in Israel and in the Mediterranean region, and policy-practice in social work. Prof. Gal has published extensively in academic journals and has been very much involved in social policy formulation in Israel. Recent books include a study on income maintenance in Israel, a study of the history of unemployment policy in Israel, an edited volume on access to social justice (with Mimi Ajzenstadt), a volume on children and families in the Mediterranean welfare states (with Mimi Ajzenstadt), and *Professional Ideologies and Preferences in Social Work: A Global Study* with Idit Weiss and John Dixon. A book on policy practice in Israel, written jointly with Idit Weiss-Gal, was published in July 2011.

Ian Greener is Professor in the School of Applied Social Sciences at Durham University, as well as being Director of the ESRC North-East Doctoral Training Centre there. He has published three sole-authored books on research methods, public management and healthcare, and over fifty peer-reviewed journal articles, mostly concerned with health policy. Ian has research interests in the use of evidence in policy, in healthcare reorganisation and the means by which policymaking can become more evidence-driven.

Bent Greve is Professor in Social Science with an emphasis on welfare state analysis at the University of Roskilde, Denmark. His research interest focuses on the welfare state, and social and labour market policy, often from a comparative perspective. He has published extensively on social and labour market policy, social security, tax expenditures, public sector expenditures and financing of the welfare state. He is regional and special issues editor of *Social Policy & Administration*. Recent books include *The Times they are Changing* (2012), *Happiness* (2011), *Choice* (2010), *Social Policy and Happiness in Europe* (2010) and *Occupational Welfare* (2007).

Virginie Guiraudon is Research professor at the National Center for Scientific Research working at the Sciences Po Center for European Studies (CEE) in Paris, France. She holds a PhD from the Harvard Government Department. Her research focuses on comparative public policy with a focus on European integration and transnational collective action. She is currently conducting research on the nexus between social policy and migration. She is the author of 'Including Foreigners in National Welfare States: Institutional Venues and Rules of the Game' in Bo Rothstein and Sven Steimo (eds), *Restructuring the Welfare State: Political Institutions and Policy Change* (Palgrave, 2002). She recently edited two books on public policy in French (Presses de Sciences PO, 2008 and 2010) and *The Sociology of European Union* (Palgrave, 2010).

Michael Hill is Emeritus Professor of Social Policy of the University of Newcastle. He has written on many aspects of social policy and the policy process. He is author of *The Public Policy Process, Implementing Public Policy* (with Peter Hupe), *Social Policy in the Modern World and Understanding Social Policy* (with Zoë Irving). In 2009 he was given the Social Policy Association's lifetime award.

Karl Hinrichs is Senior Research Associate at Bremen University's Centre for Social Policy Research (since 1990) and Professor of political science at Humboldt University in Berlin. He received his PhD (1987) from the University of Bielefeld where he also worked (1980–89) as researcher and later as Assistant Professor. In 1989/90 he was John F. Kennedy Memorial Fellow at Harvard University (Center for European Studies) and in 2003 Guest Professor at the Norwegian University of Science and Technology (NTNU) in Trondheim. His main research focus is on comparative welfare state analysis, the development of social policy in Germany, and the study of old-age security policies and politics in ageing societies. The latest book publication is *Labour Market Flexibility and Pension Reforms: Flexible Today, Secure Tomorrow?*, edited together with Matteo Jessoula (Palgrave Macmillan, 2012).

Ine van Hoyweghen is assistant professor at the Department of Health, Ethics & Society (HES), Maastricht University. She holds a PhD in Social Sciences from the University of Leuven (Belgium), which was published as a book, *Risks in the Making. Travels in Life Insurance and Genetics* (Amsterdam University Press, 2007). Her work focuses on the social and political implications of biomedicine and biomedical technologies, with research interests in sociology of biomedicine, science and technology studies (STS), and social theory. Her empirical research covers the field of European life and health insurance. She has guest edited a special issue of *New Genetics & Society* (2010, vol. 29, 4) on genetic technologies in private and social insurance and its consequences for performing solidarity. With Van Hoyweghen, I. and Horstman, K. published 'Constructing access in predictive Medicine Comparing Classification for hereditary breast cancer risks in England, Germany and the Netherlands', in *Social Science and Medicine*, (2011, 72(4): 553–59). With Horstman K. 'European Practices of Genetic Information and Insurance: Lessons for the Genetic Information Nondiscrimination Act' (JAMA, 2008, 300(3) 326–27).

Bjørn Hvinden is Professor, PhD (Sociology), Head of Research; NOVA, Oslo and Leader, Nordic Centre of Excellence 'REASSESS' (2007–12). Areas of research are social citizenship, comparative welfare policy, disability policy, poverty, social exclusion and the agency of marginal groups. He published 'Redistributive and regulatory disability provisions: incompability or synergy?' in Quinn, G. and Waddington, L. *European Yearbook of Disability Law.*

Zoë Irving is Lecturer in Comparative Social Policy at the University of Sheffield. Her current research interests focus primarily on social policies in small island states and size as a factor in comparative analysis. She has previously published in the area of gender and employment, and is co-editor of *Social Policy in Challenging Times: Economic Crisis in Welfare Systems* (with Kevin Farnsworth, Policy Press, 2011) and co-author of *Understanding Social Policy* (with Michael Hill, Wiley-Blackwell, 2009).

Rana Jawad is a lecturer in social policy in the Department of Social and Policy Sciences at the University of Bath. She specialises in the welfare regimes of the Middle East with particular emphasis on the Arab countries and Islamic welfare practices. She also works on the role of religion generally in social policy and has published both on the Middle East and the UK. She is currently directing an ESRC research grant on social policy in the Middle East. Past publications include *Social Welfare and Religion in the Middle East: A Lebanese Perspective* and forthcoming publications include *Religion and Faith-based Welfare: From Wellbeing to Ways of Being*, both published by The Policy Press.

Olli Kangas is Professor and Research Director at Kela – the Social Insurance Institution of Finland and affiliated Professor at the Centre for Welfare State Research, University of Southern Denmark. His research interests include comparative welfare studies, the institutional set-ups of welfare programs, the political and structural factors behind the welfare states and the consequences of social policy in terms of income distribution and poverty, legitimacy and collective action.

Kees van Kersbergen is professor of comparative politics at the Department of Political Science and Government of Aarhus University, Aarhus, Denmark. His main research interests lie in comparative politics, political economy, and political sociology. One particular field of interest concerns the development and reform of the welfare state. He has published widely on these topics in major journals. He is the editor (with Philip Manow) of *Religion, Class Coalitions, and Welfare States* (Cambridge University Press, 2009) and he is currently completing a book titled *Comparative Welfare State Politics: Development, Opportunities, and Reform* (co-authored with Barbara Vis).

Jon Kvist is Professor of Comparative Social Policy at the Centre for Welfare State Research at the University of Southern Denmark. Kvist is active in various research networks, boards and projects on welfare state reforms in Europe often with a focus on the Nordic countries. He has published widely on the Nordic welfare model, the European Union and social policy, comparative labour market policy and social policy, and on issues in comparative methodology.

Bingqin Li is a lecturer in Social Policy. She is also a research associate of CASE, the Centre for Analyses of Social Exclusion at LSE. In the past five years, she had collaborated with researchers from China, Korea, Japan and the United States to examine the social exclusion faced by rural to urban migrants, long term unemployed people and informally employed people. Her research work has covered coastal and inland cities. She has lectured on international housing and social economics. She has been invited to give talks in universities, government agencies in China, Japan, Singapore and Germany regarding urban social exclusion in China and the history and trend in social welfare reform in China.

Peter Lloyd-Sherlock is Professor of Social Policy and International Development in the School of International Development, University of East Anglia. He is currently a Senior Research Fellow at the UK Government Department for International Development. His main research interests are health policy and social policies for older people in developing countries. His current research includes a study of the social and economic impact of care dependency on poor households in Peru, Mexico, China and Nigeria.

Claude Martin is research professor at the National Center for Scientific Research and director of the 'Research unit on political action in Europe' at University of Rennes, France. He has a chair on social care at the EHESP school of public health. He received his PhD in sociology from University of Paris 8 and his Accreditation to supervise research from University of Paris Descartes. His research focuses on comparative welfare state analysis mainly in the field of family, childhood and long-term care policies. He edited with Bruno Palier, *Reforming Bismarkian Welfare Systems* (Blackwell, 2008) and with Robert Castel, *Changements et pensées du changement* (Changes and thinking changes) (La découverte, 2012). He is the author of 'The Reframing of Family Policy in France: Actors, Ideas and Instruments', *Journal of European Social Policy*, (vol. 20, issue 5, December 2010, p. 410–421) and with B. Le Bihan, 'Reforming Long-term Care Policy in France: Public/Private Complementarities' *Social Policy and Administration*, (vol. 44, 4, 2010, p. 392–410).

Manos Matsaganis is Assistant Professor of Social and Employment Policy at the Athens University of Economics and Business. He studied economics at the Athens University of Economics (1986), health economics at the University of York (MSc 1988) and health econometrics at the University of Bristol (PhD 1992). His employment record includes jobs as research officer at the London School of Economics (1990–93), and as special adviser to the Prime Minister of Greece (1997–2001). His main research interests are in the political economy of welfare reform, tax-benefit models, and the economic analysis of public policy. In 2011 he published 'The welfare state and the crisis: the case of Greece' (*Journal of European Social Policy*), 'Pathways to a universal basic pension in Greece' (*Basic Income Studies*, with Chrysa Leventi) and *Social Policy at Hard Times: Economic Crisis, Fiscal Austerity and Social Protection* (a full-length book, in Greek).

Nathalie Morel is research associate at the Centre d'Etudes Européennes at Sciences Po, Paris. Her main research interest is in comparative European social policy, with a special focus on care policies. Her current research is focused on social investment policies, on the politics of 'free choice' in welfare provision, and on the political economy of domestic work in France and Sweden. She has recently co-edited *Towards a Social Investment Welfare State? Ideas, Policies and Challenges* (Policy Press, 2012), with B. Palier and J. Palme.

Janet Newman is Emeritus Professor in the Faculty of Social Science at the Open University. Her research interests include new formations of governance, political and organisational change, and the remaking of publics and publicness. Publications include *Working the spaces of power feminism, activism and neo-liberalism* (Bloomsbury, 2012); *Summoning the Active Citizen: Responsibility, Choice and Participation* (with E. Tonkens: Amsterdam University Press, 2011); *Publics, Politics and Power: Remaking the Public in Public Services* (with John Clarke: Sage, 2009); *Power, Participation and Political Renewal* (with M. Barnes and H. Sullivan: Policy Press, 2007); *Creating Citizen Consumers* (with John Clarke et al., Sage, 2007); and *Modernising Governance: New Labour, Policy and Society* (Sage, 2001).

Madelene Nordlund obtained a PhD in 2010 at the department of Sociology, Umeå University, where she studied individual long term effects of active labour market policies. She is now a researcher and lecturer at the same department and is at present involved in a research project studying multidimensional welfare consequences due to unemployment, seen over the life course.

Gregg M. Olsen is a Professor in the Department of Sociology at the University of Manitoba in Winnipeg, Manitoba, Canada, where he has taught since 1989. His main areas of interest and research include social inequality and comparative social policy. He is the author of numerous journal articles and books, including *Power and Inequality: A Comparative Introduction* (Oxford University Press, 2011), and *The Politics of the Welfare State: Canada, Sweden and the United States*

(Oxford University Press, 2002; 2nd edition forthcoming). He is currently working on a cross-national study of poverty and homelessness and another on the politics of music.

Joakim Palme is Professor of political science at Uppsala University. He has a background in comparative welfare state research, not least old-age pensions. In his past position as Director of the Institute for Futures Studies, he worked on the future funding of welfare states in ageing societies. Currently, his research is focused on the interface between welfare states and labour markets as well as on social investment and social inclusion.

Frans Pennings is professor of labour and social security law at Utrecht University, the Netherlands. He is also guest professor at Tilburg University (Netherlands) and Gothenburg University (Sweden). In addition he is judge at the Central Appeals Court of the Netherlands. His main research interests are European labour law and social security law; international labour law and social security law (ILO, Council of Europe); the law of unemployment benefits; incapacity for work benefits. Publications include *European Social Security Law* (Antwerp, Intersentia), 5 editions, and *International Social Security Standards. Current Views and Interpretation Matters* (Antwerp, 2007).

Bram Peper is Assistant Professor in Sociology at the Erasmus University Rotterdam, the Netherlands. His main area of expertise is cross-national research regarding work–family arrangements in organizations in different welfare state regimes. He is co-editor of a number of books: *Flexible Working, Organizational Change and the Integration of Work and Personal Life* (Edward Elgar, 2005), and *Diversity, Standardization and Social Transformation. Gender, Ethnicity and Equality in Europe* (Ashgate, 2011). He also co-wrote a Dutch introduction to sociology (Pearson, 2010). His current research interests include the well-being of employees, the work-life balance and role of managers, and boundary management in relation to work-life issues. He participated in the EC research project 'Gender, Parenthood and the Changing European Workplace: young adults negotiating the work-family boundary' (TRANSITIONS).

Maria Petmesidou is professor of Social Policy at Democritus University of Thrace and Fellow of CROP/ISSC (International Social Science Council). She holds a degree from Aristotle University of Thessaloniki; a postgraduate dipl. from University College London; and a PhD from Oxford University. She served as head of the Department of Sociology of Crete University and of the Department of Social Administration of Democritus University. She published a number of books and numerous articles in journals and collective volumes on social development, social stratification and social policy issues in Greece and comparative social protection systems in South Europe and the Mediterranean area. Her books include *Poverty & Social Deprivation in the Mediterranean: Trends, Policies & Welfare Prospects in the New Millennium* (with C. Papatheodorou, Zed Books, 2006) and *Social Policy Developments in Greece* (with E. Mossialos, Ashgate, 2006).

John Pierson has taught social policy for many years at Staffordshire University where he is currently visiting lecturer in the Creative Communities Unit. He has been a consultant and evaluator in the fields of neighbourhood management, urban renewal and Sure Start local programmes and is the author of *Tackling Social Exclusion*.

Caroline de la Porte is associate professor at the centre for welfare state research of the department of political science, University of Southern Denmark. Her research interests are EU and national social policy, new modes of governance, the open method of co-ordination. Recent publications include: 'Principal-agent theory and the Open Method of Co-ordination: the case of the EES', *Journal of European Public Policy* (2011, vol 18, no. 4, pp. 485–503) and with Jacobsson, K. 'Social investment or recommodification? Assessing the employment policies of the EU member states' in Morel, N. Palier, B. and Palme, J. (eds) *Towards a Social Investment Welfare State? Ideas, policies and challenges*, Policy Press, 2012, pp. 117–152.

Martin Powell is Professor of Health and Social Policy at the Health Services Management Centre, University of Birmingham. He has research interests in contemporary and historical social and health policy, including citizenship, consumerism, equality and partnerships. His publications on New Labour and the Third Way include his edited 'New Labour trilogy' (*New Labour, New Welfare State*? 1999, *Evaluating New Labour's Welfare Reforms*, 2002, *Modernising the Welfare State*, 2008, all Policy Press) and chapters in subsequent editions of *The Student's Companion to Social Policy* (P. Alcock et al., eds, Blackwell).

Chiara Saraceno is former professor of sociology at the University of Turin. From 2006 until June 2012 she was Research Professor at the Wissenshaftszentrum Berlin für Sozialforschung (WZB). Corresponding fellow of the British Academy, her research interests concern families and family policies, gender and intergenerational relations, poverty and welfare state arrangements.

Peter Saunders was the Director of the Social Policy Research Centre from February 1987 until July 2007, and now holds a Research Chair in Social Policy in the Centre. His recent books include *The Poverty Wars, Reconnecting Research with Reality* and (with James Walter) *Ideas and Influence. Social Science and Public Policy in Australia* (both published by UNSW Press in 2005). He was elected a Fellow of the Academy of the Social Sciences in Australia in 1995, and is currently the President of the Foundation for International Studies on Social Security (FISS) and in 2009 was elected the first President of the Australian Social Policy Association.

Steven Saxonberg got his PhD in political science at Uppsala University in Sweden and is now professor of sociology at the Department of Social Policy and Social Work at the Masaryk University in Brno, Czech Republic. He has published articles in international scientific journals and anthologies on the topic of post-communist social policies, family policies, attitudes toward social policies and attitudes toward gender. He also has a forthcoming book with Palgrave on gendering post-communist family policies.

Sheila Shaver's main research interests are in comparative social policy and studies of the welfare state, poverty and social inequality, gender and social policy, community services, and social and political theory. With Julia O'Connor and Ann Orloff, she is the author of *States, Markets, Families: Gender, Liberalism and Social Policy in Australia, Canada, Great Britain, and the United States* (Cambridge University Press, 1999). Her most recent publication is 'Culture, Multiculturalism and Welfare State Citizenship', *La Rivista delle Politiche Sociali/Italian Journal of Social Policy* 8(1) (2008). Sheila Shaver is a Fellow of the Academy of the Social Sciences in Australia. She is currently Conjoint Professor at the Social Policy Research Centre at the University of New South Wales, Australia.

Adrian Sinfield, Professor Emeritus of Social Policy, The University of Edinburgh, has worked on social security, poverty, unemployment and the social division of welfare. Chair and president of the Social Policy Association, receiving its first lifetime achievement award; co-founder of the Unemployment Unit and chair for its first ten years; vice-chair of the Child Poverty Action Group for eight years. Publications include: *The Long-term Unemployed* (1968); *Which Way for Social Work?* (1969); *What Unemployment Means* (1981); *The Workless State* (co-edited, 1981); *Excluding Youth* (co-authored, 1991); *Comparing Tax Routes to Welfare in Denmark and the United Kingdom* (co-authored, 1996).

Paul Spicker is Professor of Public Policy at the Robert Gordon University, Aberdeen, Scotland. His research has included studies related to poverty, benefit delivery systems, the care of old people, psychiatric patients and housing management. He has been a consultant on social welfare in practice, having done work for a range of agencies at local, national and international levels. His books include *Principles of Social Welfare* (1988), *The Welfare State: A General Theory* (2000) and *Social Policy: Themes and Approaches* (2008).

Frank Tros is sociologist and works as researcher at the Amsterdam Institute for Advanced Labour Studies (AIAS) at the University of Amsterdam. His publications focus on comparative studies on employment relations, activating labour market policies and older workers in labour markets and organizations in European countries. His article, written with Ton Wilthagen, about the concept of 'flexicurity' as an approach to regulating employment and labour markets in *Transfer* (2004) is broadly cited. Besides his position at AIAS, Frank Tros is affiliated to ReflecT, the Research Institute for Flexicurity, Labour Market Dynamics and Social Cohesion at Tilburg University.

Barbara Vis is Associate Professor of Comparative Politics, Department of Political Science, VU University Amsterdam. Barbara Vis's main research interests are comparative politics, especially comparative welfare state research, and comparative methodology, especially configurational comparative approaches. Her monograph *Politics of Risk-Taking: Welfare State Reform in Advanced Democracies* was published in 2010 by Amsterdam University Press. In 2012, her book co-authored with Kees van Kersbergen, *Comparative Welfare State Politics: Development, Opportunities, and Reform* will appear with Cambridge University Press.

Aïchetou Wagué is an economic analyst by training with more than two decades of experience in economic development. She has a twenty-year multi-faceted career that includes ten years of high-level economic policy analysis requiring constant interaction with key policy-makers, business leaders and civil society representatives grappling with crucial questions of government social and economic policies and reforms. She has spent the past six years working directly with local development leaders and beneficiaries' representatives on the design, implementation, monitoring and evaluation of poverty reduction and sustainable human development strategies and projects in several regions of Mauritania. She is a true believer in bottom-up sustainable development that puts the key beneficiaries at the center of the policy design and implementation. She has contributed or supervised several publications related to economic and social development in Mauritania and wrote Papers on (i) the decision making process on macroeconomic issues at the Ministry of Planning, and (ii) the impact of public investments on economic growth in Mauritania.

Claus Wendt, MA, PhD, a 2008–9 J. F. Kennedy Fellow at Harvard's Center for European Studies and Harkness Fellow of Health Policy & Practice at Harvard School of Public Health, is professor of sociology of health and healthcare systems at Siegen University. He is also an external fellow at the Mannheim Center for European Social Research at the University of Mannheim. Wendt's research interests include institutional theory, political sociology, international comparisons of welfare states and healthcare systems, and the sociology of health. He has published four books and four edited volumes, including *Reforming Healthcare Systems* (with Ted Marmor, Edward Elgar, 2011), and has written more than 30 peer-reviewed journal articles. He was awarded the prize for the best JCPA article 2010 for his article (Translating Monetary Inputs into Health Care Provision) (with Jürgen Kohl). Wendt holds a PhD *summa cum laude* in sociology and a master's degree in political science, sociology, and economics from Heidelberg University.

Ton Wilthagen holds a chair in institutional and legal aspects of the labour market at Tilburg University, in the Netherlands. He is also the Director of the multidisciplinary and inter-faculty research Institute ReflecT. Wilthagen is, among other things, a member of the International Board of the *British Journal for Industrial Relations* and of the Editorial Board of the *Dutch Tijdschrift voor Recht en Arbeid*. He is a member of several academic networks and bodies, including the European Flexicurity Network, the network on Reconciling Work and Welfare and the European Labour Law Network. Wilthagen was first to develop the concept of flexicurity. He has published intensively on issues related to flexicurity.

Mara A. Yerkes is Senior Research Fellow at the Institute for Social Science Research at the University of Queensland in Brisbane, Australia. She has research expertise in comparative social policy and the welfare state, the combination of work and care, industrial relations and gender and employment, in particular the prevalence of part-time work. Along with publications in *Community, Work and Family*; *European Journal of Industrial Relations*; *Gender, Work and Organization*; *Journal of Comparative Social Welfare*; *Journal of Social Policy*; *Policy & Politics*; and *Social Policy and Administration*, Yerkes is the author of *Transforming the Dutch Welfare State* (Bristol: The Policy Press), published in 2011.

Introduction

Bent Greve

The welfare state has been a contested term for a long time. Despite this, the welfare state has had a profound role in its many varieties at the least since the Second World War. This international Handbook on the welfare state covers many and varied aspects of the welfare state and tries to do it in such a way that not only the classical issues are covered, but that central and key concepts are also covered, while exploring how they can be used and analysed. This is further combined with typologies and methods to analyse existing welfare arrangements, changes in these, and the diversity in approach around the world. Given that welfare and welfare states are often connected with the more affluent countries around the globe they have a more central position in the presentation; however, it has also been seen as important to cover a wider geographical area including, for example, Africa, Southern America, China, and the Middle East. Finally, the welfare state is not only important due to an understanding of what it is and how it works, but also because the welfare state through central policy areas has an impact on the daily life and living conditions in many countries and has done in some countries for more than 100 years. The welfare state is thus not just a new buzz-word, but is seemingly an important institution that has been gradually developed, and also changed over time. The welfare states are still changing, and, as also shown in this book, many and varied interpretations and alterations take place.

The book is divided in four parts with the last part only containing one chapter, asking the still very important question of whether the welfare state has a future, and, if so, what type of future.

The first part of the book focuses on key concepts in the analysis of the welfare state alongside key aspects in relation to the understanding and interpretation of the welfare state. The section opens with chapters dealing with the definition of welfare and the Titmuss understanding – the classical way to welfare (e.g. public, fiscal, and occupational welfare). It then probes into classical issues such as how to prevent social contingencies from occurring, and how principles, such as citizenship, can have implications for the access to welfare benefits and services. The focus then shifts to what the outcome of welfare states, for example, in relation to reducing poverty and change in social inclusion/exclusion, might be. Principles of benefits and the interaction between benefits in kind and in cash are then followed by an often-discussed issue: gender and how this influences societies. Recent years have increasingly focused not only on what happens during one year or perhaps several years, but at the life-cycle perspective for individuals, and, also, the possible role for the welfare state in relation to this. Another still more important issue in many countries has been the way the labour market works. This is then our final focus, especially relating to active labour market policy and how to understand flexicurity.

The second part of the book focuses on typologies and methods. It thus follows the traits of Esping-Andersen, but has a broader view including a discussion of whether typologies are useful at all. This is then followed by a presentation of welfare states around the world, with the exception of the presentation of China, clustered into subsections. Naturally, not all the countries in the world are covered, but it should enable the reader to have a clear view on peculiarities and differences around the world, and how the use of typologies helps in the broader understanding of how welfare can be interpreted and developed given different economies, different histories, and different ideological backgrounds for welfare state development. Using the typology in a specific, but central welfare area – health – as a starting point, several chapters present and discuss how to analyse welfare states, welfare state typologies, why they change, drivers having an impact on the change, and how the recent fiscal crises have had an impact on the welfare states and their development.

The third part then looks into central policy areas (such as social security, healthcare, housing, disability, family, and old age including pensions). The section also looks into new risk and management of crime, and further how a supranational institution such as the EU has or might have an impact on the welfare state in a nation. Finally, the question of how to finance the welfare state is discussed, as well as a debate on evaluation as a new type of steering of the welfare state.

Part I
Key concepts

1

What is welfare and public welfare?

Bent Greve

Introduction

The concept of welfare needs to be defined before one is able to analyse the welfare state and understand its nature (cf. Chapter 2). The development of and changes in the concept of welfare have also had implications for our understanding of what a welfare state and a welfare society are (Greve, 2008). What welfare is also relates to the philosophical and historical underpinnings of what welfare states are, have been, and will be. Moreover, as most welfare state analysis deals with the public sector and its spending on welfare issues, it is important to know and understand what the public sector spending is, and its implications for a variety of issues. These issues include the organization of the public sector as well as central and decentral ways of organizing the welfare states (Barr, 2004). Furthermore, this might also have implications for what public welfare will have to deliver and finance, and thereby on what public welfare is.

Core concepts

The core question to be answered here is: What is welfare? This includes a more specific discussion of what public welfare is as this may have consequences of our understanding and analyses of welfare states and societies, various types of public interventions in the market, and how we draw the borderlines between state, market, and civil society.

Welfare can be defined as:

> [. . .] the highest possible access to economic resources, a high level of well-being, including the happiness of the citizens, a guaranteed minimum income to avoid living in poverty, and, finally, having the capabilities to ensure the individual a good life.
>
> *(Greve, 2008, p. 50)*

In the following section these aspects will be discussed, but first we need to see how we can understand this concept. It should be borne in mind as a starting point that the term 'welfare' derives from *wel* and *fare*, that is it has originated from '*well* in its still familiar sense and *fare*, primarily understood as a journey or arrival but later also as a supply of food' (Williams, 1976, p. 281). Welfare is thus a concept relating to aspects of central importance for individuals' lives. Additionally it involves an understanding, albeit implicitly, of how a good society which has many individuals and who have a variety of preferences can be developed. This involves the question of what role the public sector should play.

Public welfare thus to a large degree revolves around an understanding of what the public sector finances and most often also what it delivers in terms of income transfers and services. Public welfare is therefore not just the support given through the tax system (cf. Chapter 3), or welfare fully or partly paid by the labour market partners (cf. Chapter 4). It can be argued that the public sector does not always deliver all the services as they might be purchased from private providers, or money might be transferred to individuals as vouchers, for example, giving individuals the rights to buy or get certain social services offered by private providers including, in some cases, the voluntary sector, which may include families. The voluntary sector is normally also seen as being outside the public sector, notwithstanding that the boundaries can be blurred, and the public sector might provide the framework within which the voluntary sector can provide social services. In national accounts, the public sector is defined in terms of the delivery of welfare goods or finance of at least 50 per cent of expenditures related to the provision of the service. The implication being that in principle a fully private company which aims to create the highest level of profit while delivering care can be seen as part of the public sector as far as the national accounts are concerned. This makes the borderlines between the different sectors very unclear and consequently the statistical data about who is providing what type welfare and with what type of outcome are sometimes unclear.

This plethora of possible institutional combinations also indicates why comparative analysis is often very difficult and sometimes gives misleading conclusions as some small details might change how we are to interpret and understand national welfare systems.

Presentation and analysis of the elements of welfare

This section will discuss and analyse what can be included in the study of welfare and public welfare, as welfare concerns both the micro- and macro-levels. At the macro-level it can include the overall wealth of a society – we know that citizens in richer countries, at least to a certain level, are happier than individuals in poorer countries. The level of spending on public welfare thereby also has an impact on people's happiness. On the micro-level, individuals' happiness has an impact on the number of people living in poverty as well as the degree of social cohesion and ability to live a secure and stable life. Recent research on happiness has also had an impact on how we perceive welfare, what we know influence individuals' well-being, and the impact of various types of interventions on daily life. However, the issue of happiness will receive limited attention in this book (cf. instead Greve, 2011).

Welfare has been discussed in many and very varied disciplines. Economists talk about utility, sociologists about well-being, and philosophers have focused on the good life. There has thus, in reality, never been one unanimous definition of what welfare is and how this can be measured.

In **economic theory** it has often been seen as central to examine what individuals' perceptions or utilities of an available bundle of goods and services are. Individuals' decisions on how to combine and use their money are, it has been argued, the best way to maximize societal welfare. The best way to measure and compare outcomes has been seen as being in terms of gross domestic product (GDP) per capita as it allows for international comparisons and reflects individuals' choices. Thus in mainstream economic theory, the market has a central role. Recent developments within behavioural economics have shown an increased interest in other approaches, including non-monetary aspects, and how they influence our welfare and the decisions we take (Wilkingson, 2008).

Sociology has been more preoccupied with aspects related to social cohesion and well-being in a broader sense. Well-being could thus be achieved in various ways, and consequently there are various ways of measuring it, including the use of social indicators such as being alone or having a decent living standard. A distinction between objective and subjective well-being indicators is also made. Recent years have seen an upsurge in publications with data trying to reflect more than the classical measure of GDP per capita (cf. for example, the Organisation for Economic Co-operation and Development (OECD)'s *Society at a Glance* publications or *How's Life, Measuring well-being*).

Giddens (1998) has focused on what he labelled positive welfare by emphasizing the welfare state as a social investment state, focusing on elements such as active health, autonomy, education, and well-being. This is in line with welfare research underlining the possible positive impact of the welfare state, for example affordable and high-quality day care not only benefits children, but also ensures a more equal access to and participation in the labour market for both men and women.

Welfare can also be based upon needs, for example Allardt states 'the amount of welfare is defined by the degree of need-satisfaction' (Allardt, 1976 p. 228). He also points out that by focusing on needs welfare can be seen to have two levels: one dealing with the living standard and the other with the quality of life. This implies that one has to take into consideration both material and impersonal resources as well as human relations to each other and to society, thus focusing on having, loving, and being (Allardt, 1976).

Another approach related to the quality of life has focused on capabilities. The concept of capabilities has been promoted by the Nobel Laureate Amartya Sen (Nussbaum and Sen, 1993). Capabilities' centre of attention is on the individual's options and possibilities to be able to choose among a set of options. In this way this also relates to the ability to be socially included in society (cf. Chapter 8), and have abilities to choose among a certain set of possible outcomes.

John Mill's understanding of utility has also given rise to indications of what happiness is, such as that 'Happiness is intended pleasure, and, the absence of pain' (Mill,[1] 1972, p. 6) and also the moral approach when he states, 'To do as you would be done by, and to love your neighbour as yourself, constitutes the ideal perfection of utilitarian morality' (Mill, 1972, p. 16).

Approaches to welfare can and have been influenced by left, right, and middle ways of thinking, but have also been influenced by, for example, environmental and gender inspired approaches. Thus the emphasis on different elements of welfare reflects upon our understanding of what welfare is. Ideology can thereby influence the understanding of what welfare is and how one perceives the need for public sector intervention. Still, the analysis of welfare and definitions thereof can help in clarifying what welfare is. The meaning of the word welfare connected to issues such as state, systems, etc. therefore has as implications that we often overlook the more direct meanings of the concept of welfare, and instead focus on the role of the state, the institutional systems, etc.

The understanding of welfare can and has thereby presumably also been influenced by the development of more global markets, and increased regional integration. Despite this, there is seemingly also room for national interpretations of what is more important in one country than in another in terms of welfare. This may be affected, among other things, by different weather conditions, for example in some countries the need for shelter is more important than in others.

When analysing welfare one is forced to be aware of a variety of different ways of understanding the concept, and also that, at the end of the day, it is important to use an empirical approach in order to grasp and understand the consequences of different welfare policies (cf. Chapters 31–40). Furthermore, the welfare of individuals can be influenced not only by the public sector, but also the private and voluntary sectors, and the ability to have a job and be on the labour market. Therefore the mix between public, private, and market-based welfare and the borderline, sometimes labelled the welfare mix, is an important aspect of modern welfare states.

For individuals it need not be a specific or important issue as to whether or not welfare is delivered by the public or private sector, or even by the family, rather the central issue is access to services, who finances the services, and under what conditions the individual can get access to benefits.

Thus the welfare mix (Evers and Laville, 2004) can be an important analytical device as it might show who has the main responsibility for different aspects of welfare, and thereby can influence the options for access to services and benefits which might have an impact on the individuals' welfare.

Historically the establishment of the first social indicators in the 1960s and the examination of subjective and objective aspects of well-being can be seen as the beginning of measuring life satisfaction, well-being, or happiness in another way than just accepting the overall level of the value of production (measured by GDP). Recent years have seen a further upswing in the measurement of welfare including OECD social indicators, various national governments looking at ways to measure happiness, and the European Union (EU)'s attempt to establish indicators showing the quality of life in different countries. There has also been a tendency to look at human beings not only as individuals maximizing utility (the classical analysis), but as social animals (Brooks, 2011).

The focus within the EU, for example, has also been on trying to integrate the impact based upon an understanding of social and environmental issues as well as economic conditions. The quality of life, or life satisfaction, seems to be higher in the Nordic welfare states than liberal and central European welfare states, and lowest in Southern and Eastern Europe. A variety of studies of European countries and also around the world, (cf. Chapters 15–25) show that people in more affluent countries and more developed welfare states often have a higher level of satisfaction than others in terms of well-being.

Understanding welfare thus needs to embrace a variety of factors including knowledge concerning the four issues mentioned above (wealth, public spending on welfare, poverty, and happiness). This is also the reason for discussing these issues somewhat further.

Spending on welfare, and, in this context, public sector spending on welfare, can have an impact on the individual's level of welfare by giving them options that are otherwise not available. Spending on welfare can have a variety of purposes from trying to support the most vulnerable, to investing in future jobs and ensuring a higher degree of equality. Barr argues that the welfare state has to deal with three specific issues: efficiency, equity and administration. This can further be divided into issues of efficiency (macro- and micro-incentives), supporting living standards (poverty relief, insurance, consumption smoothing), the reduction of inequality (vertical equity, horizontal equity), social inclusion (dignity, social solidarity) and administrative feasibility (intelligibility, absences of abuse) (Barr, 2004). Naturally understanding the way to implement these three specific issues, also because they have contradictory elements, is influenced by ideological preferences and understandings of how different approaches work. Nevertheless, a good analysis of how, when, and why the public sector should be the core provider of welfare should include efficiency, equity, and administration in the analysis. The balance between these elements can vary and a central discussion might be whether it is possible to include and measure all these issues. Finally, whether we risk to spend more money and time on administrative issues than actually on the delivery of the expected welfare when evaluating interventions is an empirical question.

A historical and still central reason for public sector intervention, which needs to be included in the analysis, is market failure. Markets can fail for many and different reasons, and even if there is no complete agreement on the extent of market failure, the existence of monopolies, externalities, and elements related to equity and employment can be reasons for public intervention to ensure a higher level of welfare.

Still, the issues listed above indicate that public sector spending can have a central role in relation to welfare, given that this can influence living standards, how and if people can avoid living in poverty, and the degree of inequality. At the same time they might have an impact on macro-efficiency, which also implies a focus on and pressure for maximizing societal income. A higher level of income at the macro-level seems to have an impact, at least to certain degree, on the level of happiness, and, as both happiness and income also are components in relation to welfare it will thereby have an impact on societal level of welfare. In this way the concepts are interlinked.

A core discussion regarding the welfare state has been whether one needs a state or whether the market, regulated to ensure perfect competition, could ensure and cover the same types of needs. A good reason for having a welfare state is that in some areas individual coverage would be too expensive both for society and individuals. A good example of this is long-term care (Barr, 2010). It is not possible for the individual to know for how long and how much he or she will need care when elderly, and individual savings to cover old age would therefore need to be very large. Individual actuarial insurance is difficult to use due to information problems, and therefore in principle only two options are available: a system financed out of general taxation; or mandatory social insurance. These two options involve risk-sharing without the problems of moral hazard and adverse selection.

The public delivery and financing of welfare or systems enacted by the state (for example compulsory insurance) can thus be an important instrument with regard to how to ensure equality in access and efficiency in the use of scarce resources. However, one needs at the same time to be aware that the public sector is also efficient in its way of delivering and dealing with the services they will have to provide.

This also implies that the borderlines between public and private welfare, public and occupational welfare, and public and welfare delivered by civil society need to be analysed and discussed case by case. In some instances public welfare will be natural, such as the long-term care as discussed above, in others a more specific and concrete analysis needs to be done in order to establish what policy will give the best societal outcome.

At the same time, public policies have an impact on the overall level of income in a society and can have an impact on individuals' welfare. Wealth as understood by GDP per capita thus, for example, has an impact on welfare. Sudden changes in the level of GDP can further have both negative and positive impacts. A sudden negative drop in GDP, as in the wake of the financial crisis, will, all other things being equal, have a negative impact on happiness, whereas at the same time a sudden increase will increase happiness.

Poverty is also mentioned as a specific issue related to welfare, and again there is an overlap between public sector spending and its poverty impact, given that public welfare spending can be used to alleviate poverty by either income transfer benefits, or giving free or cheaper access to low income earners to central welfare aspects, such as health, care, and education (cf. Chapter 9). The combination of public sector spending and the impact of the tax and duty system (cf. Chapter 38) can thereby imply that the degree of inequality measured, for example, by the gini-coefficient will be reduced after public sector intervention. The ability to reduce the degree of inequality can be seen as an indicator of a welfare state's efficiency.

A high level of inequality seems to have a negative impact on societies' welfare, or, at least, more egalitarian societies have greater welfare and have a higher level of well-being than more unequal societies (Wilkinson and Pickett, 2010). Wilkingson and Pickett also show that in societies with higher levels of equality (like the Nordic countries and Japan) there is less crime, more social cohesion, higher levels of trust, people are healthier, and people, in general, live longer than in other countries. Their analysis does not inform us about the exact level of inequality at which the positive benefits of a more equal society can be achieved. Still, the data are a clear indicator of the fact that welfare and different aspects of welfare have an impact on everyday life and life satisfaction, and further that specific measures can be more important than others. In this respect, the degree of inequality seems to be one of the central issues that needs examination. There might even be a win/win situation in the sense that an increase in the degree of equality can reduce the pressure on public sector spending in relation to crime and combatting crime. Given, further, that happy people are more productive (Greve, 2011) there is a clear indication that a well-functioning society that increases welfare will be a more equal society.

Whether the welfare state can help in increasing the level of welfare and happiness is often disputed, with arguments ranging from claims that a focus on happiness can inform policy makers about the best instruments, to claiming that this is an individual matter and therefore intervention would distort policy making (Greve, 2011; Layard, 2005; Johns and Ormerod, 2007). Still, research on the quality of life, well-being, and happiness can give data that can be used by policy makers to inform them on how different choices will have an impact not only on classical economic issues, but also more generally the welfare of the population.

A further reason for discussing and analysing these issues relates to the fact that issues of happiness, utility, or welfare have for a long time been part of the discussion of what a good life, and, thereby what a good society, is. The OECD has, for example, in 2011 published a compendium dealing with well-being indicators, including life satisfaction in different countries (OECD, 2011). The full list of well-being indicators includes not only elements of subjective well-being, but also elements related to income, jobs, health, etc. The overview shows, as in several other studies, that the Nordic welfare states are at the top, as are countries including Canada, Switzerland, and The Netherlands. Those countries with the lowest life satisfaction include China, Hungary, Portugal, India, and Estonia – a more mixed group of countries.

The emergence of these new types of measurement is an acceptance of the fact that GDP is not the only measure of a society's welfare and that other aspects need to be included in order to understand it fully. This applies at the individual level too. The combination of various types of measures, social indicators, and other approaches points to the importance of having a broader set of indicators in order to know about both society's and the individuals' level of welfare.

It has been argued that taxation might have implied distortions in people's choice between different bundles of goods and services, and might also imply a trade-off between work/leisure and spending/saving. Therefore, it is argued that this has a negative impact on welfare by reducing the ability of individuals to achieve a specific level of utility. However, this type of analysis rests upon the assumption that individuals' preferences are always superior to others, and, further, that the analysis does not take into account the effect and impact of the redistribution of resources the welfare state is able to ensure.

Different ways of financing the welfare state can have a clear and systematic impact on several parameters that influence the welfare of individuals, for example the ability to finance public services and income transfers, as can the ability to redistribute consumption possibilities among different groups in society. The public sector's ability to reallocate, and preferably with as few as possible distortions, can imply a higher level of welfare in many countries. This impact of different types of public sector spending in combination with higher taxes will naturally need to be analysed not only theoretically, but also empirically.

Conclusion

Welfare is an ambitious concept that often means different things and is therefore ambiguous. The concept is often used in connection with other terms such as state, society, policy, and work, and is often understood as something in which the public sector has a role. This is despite the fact that many of the issues relate to increasing well-being or happiness, and, thereby are often also seen as welfare. This has something to do with our everyday lives and how we are able to cope with many and different aspects of them. Still more aspects related to the third sector, civil society, or the market have an impact on our welfare.

Welfare has therefore also been approached from many different angles and not always by using the word 'welfare'. Economists, sociologists, psychologists, philosophers, and political scientists have all, in one way or another, been involved in discussions of what welfare is, how it can be achieved, and how the consequence and outcomes related to welfare can be understood.

Recent years have seen a growing interest in non-monetary aspects which have an impact on our daily lives and how we perceive (including issues of well-being and happiness) our lives. Therefore knowledge on what promotes and what does not promote an improved level of welfare has been increasingly at the heart of the analysis of welfare states. At the same time, this type of analysis crosses the borderline between the use of objective data and the use of the individual's subjective evaluation of their life satisfaction, happiness, and the like. Social indicators, measures, and indexes of well-being, as well as think tanks focusing on elements other than traditional economic measurement, have been more and more at the centre of attention for analysis.

Public welfare refers specifically to the welfare decided and mainly financed by the public sector. In this way welfare can be public even if there is a private provider, given that the state is the main source of finance, and given that the state sets the rules for those who can have access to the benefits and services, and determines under which conditions. There is a borderline between public, fiscal, occupational, and pure private welfare. This borderline also implies that what the welfare state can achieve or not achieve will be influenced by the rules and systems, and the way they interact. Public welfare is thus only one way for the welfare state to influence the capabilities and outcomes for individuals, using the tax system, or supporting the voluntary sector, companies, and families.

The role of the state has over the years been disputed and discussed (cf. Chapter 2) given that in order to finance the welfare state it is necessary to ensure income to the public sector through, in particular, taxes and duties. The level and areas of the public sector intervention and supply is therefore also often contested. The literature when discussing the impact of market failures alone points to reasons for intervention without more precisely showing what type and what size of intervention is needed.

The need for combining material as well as non-material aspects of welfare has also increased in debates on sustainable development, implying that the concept of welfare and all it includes has become even more central, and, that data and analysis need to examine and combine different theoretical approaches.

Note

1 John Stuart Mill first published this book in *Fraser's Magazine* in 1861 and in book form in 1863. He died in 1873 and the quote used here is from reprint of the book as it was published in 1910.

References

Allardt, E. (1976), Dimensions of welfare in a Comparative Scandinavian Study. *Acta Sociologica*, vol. 19, no. 3., pp. 227–39.

Barr, N. (2004), *The Economics of the Welfare State*. Oxford: Oxford University Press.

——(2010), Long-term Care: A Suitable Case for Social Insurance, *Social Policy & Administration*, vol. 44, no. 4, pp. 359–74.

Brooks, D. (2011), *The Social Animal: The Hidden Source of Love, Character, and Achievement.* New York: Random House.
Evers, A. and Laville, J. (eds) (2004), *The Third Sector in Europe.* Cheltenham: Edward Elgar.
Giddens, A. (1998), *The Third Way.* Cambridge: Polity Press.
Greve, B. (2008), What is Welfare? *Central European Journal of Public Policy*, vol. 2, no. 1, pp. 50–73.
——(2011), *Happiness. Key Text.* Abingdon: Routledge.
Johns, H. and Ormerod, P. (2007), *Happiness, Economics and Public Policy.* London: The Institute of Economic Affairs.
Layard, R. (2005), *Happiness. Lessons from a New Science.* London: Penguin.
Mill, J. S. (1972), *Utilitarianism, Liberty, Representative Government.* London: J.M. Dent & Sons Ltd.
Nussbaum, M. and Sen, A. (eds) (1993), *The Quality of Life.* Oxford: Clarendon Press.
OECD (2011), *Better Life Compendium of OECD Well-being Indicators.* Paris: OECD.
Wilkingson, N. (2008), *A Introduction to Behavioral Economics.* Houndsmills: Palgrave.
Wilkinson, R. and Pickett, K. (2010), *The Spirit Level. Why Greater Equality Makes Societies Stronger.* New York: Bloomsbury Press.
Williams, R. (1976), *Keywords: A Vocabulary of Culture and Society.* Glasgow: Fontana.

2
What is a welfare state?

Michael Hill

Introduction

The object of this chapter is to explore how the concept of the welfare state is used. It identifies an area of confusion, deriving from the evidence that whilst there is a popular view that the welfare state is in some sense a socialist project the reality is that all economically advanced societies have developed welfare institutions. It suggests that it is helpful to look separately at issues about how societies, and accordingly their states, differ in respect of orientations to welfare and about how they differ in respect of the role given to the state. This enables identification of contemporary trends embodying not just welfare cut-backs but also changes to the roles played by the state in respect of welfare.

Core concepts

We have here an expression in which two nouns are used, with the first functioning adjectivally in relation to the second, in which the meanings of the two separate words need some consideration. The concept of welfare has been explored in the previous chapter. It has been shown that our welfare depends upon many things – our family, our work, our friendships, our environment, and so on – as well as upon, in some cases, specific support from the state.

On the other hand it may be argued that, at least in the modern world, without the state many of these other sources of welfare may function with difficulty. This is an aspect of what Gough and Wood (2004) identify as 'in/security regimes', many of them in what journalists have talked of as 'failed states', where individuals and their families struggle to survive. More generally we may consider that the maintenance of peace is fundamental for welfare, a topic on which nation states have (for better or worse) a role to play. The very notion of a failed state implies something to be rectified. And then, more controversially, there are questions to consider about the extent to which modern states make efforts to sustain employment regardless of their stances in relation to more direct ways of providing welfare.

As far as the concept of the state is concerned the study of stateless societies is today consigned to historical anthropology. While there are still places where the impact of a state is minimal (as noted above) there is general acceptance that nation states form the key building blocks of the contemporary world order. The word state is used casually in many contexts. What is important here is that it is seen as an institutional configuration, in the words of Max Weber: 'an administrative and legal order subject to change by legislation' claiming 'binding authority …

over all action taking place in the area of its jurisdiction' (Weber, 1947, p. 156). That captures nicely a point put by many writers that, although it is not synonymous with the government, it is subject to change by government. That is important for our topic, since we are concerned – in the context of the importance of welfare for the modern state – with a web of institutions that are nevertheless subject to change. There is a need to beware the tendency of some writers to treat the state as a powerful and fixed autonomous entity. We will come back below therefore to issues about kinds of states and the ways they may change.

Max Weber's definition implicitly gives a territorial location to the area of authority of the state. He might want to modify that point today. However, while we may want in some analyses of social policy to go to a more global level and recognise the role supra-national institutions play together with the impact of inter-relationships between nations upon welfare (George and Wilding, 2002), the study of formal welfare institutions still focuses primarily upon nation states.

The welfare state: a necessary conjunction?

Conceding, as stated above, that state action is likely to have an impact upon welfare, we need to move on from the expression created by using the two concepts together. The questions are then: to what extent can we identify states that are recognisably 'welfare states'? How do we identify such states? And, more controversially, is an advanced modern state – meaning one with a high standard of living and a stable system of government – necessarily a welfare state?

Recourse to a popular – and by no means small – modern dictionary on the author's shelves produced a highly contentious answer to the question 'what is a welfare state':

> A social system or state in which socialist principles have been put into effect with the purpose of ensuring the welfare of all who live in it, e.g. by paying unemployment benefits, old age pensions etc. and by providing other social services.
>
> *(Chambers Dictionary, 1998)*

That statement is open to challenge on the grounds there is good evidence that both the welfare state and the specific institutions itemised do not necessarily operate in terms of socialist principles, have been promoted by non-socialists, and have been seen as important for the smooth running of capitalist systems.

The *Chambers Dictionary* entry represents a popular view widespread in the mid-twentieth century that many Western countries experienced a social democratic compromise between capital and labour, in which the 'socialist' demand for greater equality had been fulfilled by the provision of social welfare benefits rather than by any fundamental change in the characteristics of capitalism. The probable British origin of the expression 'welfare state' is indicative. Briggs noted it as 'first used to describe Labour Britain after 1945' and then making 'its way round the world' (Briggs in Schottland, 1967, p. 25). But he also went on to add an historical perspective which helps us to see how misleading it is to approach this issue in this Anglo-centric way, drawing attention in particular to the role of Bismarck in the development of social insurance in Germany. Briggs defines a welfare state as one in which 'organised power is deliberately used … in an effort to modify the play of market forces' (p. 29). While he goes on to give specific examples we may follow that central point to note:

> There are many different ways this may happen, with many different ends in view. That modifying the play of market forces is a very widespread activity by modern governments (regardless of political ideology).

Hence that only leads us to note that all advanced states are in some sense welfare states (early comparative theory emphasised convergence in this respect, see, for example, Rimlinger, 1971; Flora and Alber, 1981). The alternative to doing that is to try to identify some way in which – in a context of extensive state spending, much of it on social welfare in some respect – we may distinguish welfare states in terms of the particular characteristics of their policies (particularly in respect of outputs and outcomes).

The development of the welfare state: different trajectories

It is perhaps unfortunate, at least for an unpartisan analysis of the welfare state, that the usage originates from Britain and is particularly linked to the achievements of the 1945–51 Labour government. Britain is peculiar in having had a well-established minimalist state but a strong economy since before the ninteenth century. In the context of the *laissez-faire* ideology that influenced the role of the state (outside the Empire) Britain also saw the development of voluntaristic welfare institutions: friendly societies, building societies, and charities. Participation in two major wars rather than the development of welfare as such played a key role in state development. So the state played a reluctant role in the development of welfare institutions, perhaps a more reluctant role than in some other Western European nations. It was in recognising the cautious nature of British welfare development that a leading advocate of more active welfare (and the founder of the systematic study of social policy in the UK) Richard Titmuss drew a distinction between different models of social welfare (1974). Building on his work Furniss and Tilton (1979) described the British state as a 'social security state' in contrast to Sweden as a 'social welfare state'. It is worth noting that they gave the United States another label indicating it was even further behind on the road of welfare development: a 'positive state'. This line of analysis led on to much contemporary comparative analysis.

So, of course, one can go on from there to draw distinctions between states in terms of their contributions to welfare. Variations in expenditure are obviously indicative here (there are very big differences, for example, in respect of overall public expenditure on welfare between the United States and Japan at one extreme, and the Scandinavian countries and France at the other). Or we may reach for more sophisticated measures, as discussed in Chapters 14; 27–29. This represents the main approach to recognising welfare state differences: with a strong emphasis upon the determinants of the politics of welfare. There are, however, questions to be raised about the way this approach emphasises politics rather than institutional configurations.

The coincidence of state growth and welfare growth

Despite these clear differences between states it has been generally the case that state growth and welfare growth have gone hand in hand. After the Second World War the idea of shifting the concerns of the now strengthened state towards a 'welfare state' rather than 'warfare state' was advanced with quasi-religious fervour (see Barnett's attack on 'the dream of the new Jerusalem' in chapter one of his *The Audit of War,* 1986). It is pertinent to view as coming together a social liberal position (often presented as the Keynes/Beveridge model) seen as able to 'save' capitalism from the consequences of market failure which seemed to be threatened in the 1930s and a democratic socialist position in which the state could advance socialist ideas without a direct attack upon capitalism. But since its emergence questions have arisen about the extent to which these views – implicitly advancing welfare without transforming the economic order – are unrealistic. They were rooted in a view of the welfare state as a national institution able to control the economy and redistribute increments of growth.

In this respect the neo-Marxist literature is pertinent (see in particular O'Connor, 1973; Wolfe, 1977; Gough, 1979). In the first place it challenges the view that the welfare state can be seen as a social democratic accommodation with capitalism. Rather it is suggested that in various respects capitalism needed welfare policies to reduce its inefficiencies and to legitimise it. In that sense the Left could be seen as 'pushing against an open door' between 1945 and 1970. But this literature then goes on to suggest that this generated a crisis in the long run: capitalism needed social expenditure but not to the point at which it threatened productivity. Of course when Marxist theory uses the concept of crisis it implies the start of a dramatic (revolutionary?) change process. There is little evidence of that, rather we may argue that capitalists (using that expression very loosely to embrace all those who control modern economic life) have learnt that they have less need of the welfare state as industrial employment has declined, working class organisations have been weakened, the globalisation of the economy has complicated social relationships and the mass media has grown more skilled at opinion manipulation.

State and welfare: an inevitable coupling?

As noted earlier a view that social welfare might be advanced without a strong state role can be seen as emergent towards the end of the nineteenth century. Twentieth-century events then seemed to shift the state into a dominant role. In examining to what extent states in advanced industrial societies are welfare states it is necessary to consider variations in views about the state's role.

Mainstream comparative theory, particularly the work of Esping-Andersen (1990), point us towards differences in the politics of different countries, particularly the relative power of political movements on the Left. Therefore, inasmuch as what we see in this phenomenon is ideological choice, the *laissez-faire* ideology so important for British and American capitalism may be seen as significant, as operating as a break on welfare growth despite state growth. Accordingly, given that it is the social policy agenda that dominates the public expenditure agenda, commitments to roll back the state and to limit welfare come together logically in many right wing agendas.

But when we look at the role mobilisation for war played both in state growth and in welfare policy growth (see 'War and Social Policy', Chapter 4 of Titmuss, 1958) it is pertinent to ask whether that conjunction still applies in nations committed to playing large roles on the international stage. There is a sense today in which we can see the United States, and to a lesser extent the UK, as societies where there is the maintenance of a strong central state at the same time as there is a weakening of the welfare state. However, what is characteristic of contemporary international conflict is the way in which a succession of wars has been waged without total mobilisation of the population. As Skocpol (1994) shows in United States that right back to the late nineteenth century a specific state welfare systems for veterans alone has been sustained in the absence of general state welfare development. In the UK today welfare decline is accompanied by a special concern for the needs of soldiers and their dependants.

Institutional perspectives on the state's role

There are, however, other questions to be raised about explanations of differences between states than those resting simply upon ideological or political differences. Institutional theory suggests that there will be differences between states in the ways in which they approach policy problems. A loose formulation of this speaks of 'weak' and 'strong' states, focusing on state capacity for problem solving (Katzenstein, 1977; Atkinson and Coleman, 1989). Another body of work raises question about different 'policy styles' (Richardson, 1982; Bovens, Hart, and Peters 2001; van Waarden, 1999). Richardson and his colleagues identify two dimensions in this respect: the extent to which styles are anticipatory rather than reactive, and the extent to which decisions are arrived at consensually as opposed to imposed (Richardson, Gustaffson, and Jordan, Chapter 1 of Richardson, 1982). This work is still rather under-developed, and one crucial problem it identifies is that styles may vary according to the policy issue. However, this approach may be relevant to the explanation of variations in state approaches to welfare. The maintenance of an effective welfare state seems to rest upon anticipation of policy problems. The point about consensual decision making raises an issue to which we return below.

A now rather old study is particularly forthright on seeing in some states (Germany in fact in his study):

> a widespread sense of the legitimacy of public action ... and ... a willingness to define 'public power' as distinctive and to exercise it authoritatively.
>
> *(Dyson, 1980, p. 256)*

But that is still to some extent a proposition about ideology. The widely discussed work of Lijphart provides another way of looking at differences between states. Lijphart is concerned with institutional (indeed generally constitutional) differences. Lijphart's initial distinction was between majoritarian systems (the 'Westminster model') and consensual democracies (often operating through corporatist policy-making processes). But in later work he introduced variations along another dimension: that between strong federalism at one extreme and high degrees of unification at the other (1999).

There is a need to be careful about Lijphart's analysis. The Westminster model is widely seen to facilitate decisive government (note Dunleavy writing of the fastest government in the west, 1995), but that has implications both for the enactment of policies and their reversal. Lijphart draws a rather different lesson from his contrast between majoritarian and consensual democracies: that it is the latter that will be particularly effective at social problem solving. He specifically argues:

> ... the consensus democracies do clearly outperform the majoritarian democracies with regard to the quality of democracy and democratic representation as well as with regard to what I have called the kindness and gentleness of their public policy orientations.
>
> *(Lijphart, 1999, p. 301)*

That is a strong claim, based on Lijphart's empirical analysis. However, what this work points us towards is questions about the extent to which some national systems have institutional characteristics which may be important for the way they handle welfare issues. The wider question is then about the extent to which an overall consensual approach leads to institutional design in respect of welfare policy which is less directive and relies more upon local arrangements and partnerships. In this respect the issues about federalism are less fully theorised. A comparative study of federalism and the welfare state (Obinger, Leibried, and Castles, 2005) explores issues about the extent to which federalism may be a brake upon change, hence restraining the growth of what they call 'the old welfare state' but curbing the cuts associated with the 'new welfare state'. But they admit that their cases do not support such easy generalisation. Clearly, as in the Lijphart model, federalism has to be considered alongside other variables. Furthermore, as Lane and Ersson (2000, Chapter 4) show federalism comes in a range of varieties.

The welfare state today: against welfare or against the state?

The central issue about the welfare state today is set out in the discussion above, where the notion of crisis was introduced. The interesting thing about the Marxist theory of crisis is that it has a counterpart in neo-liberal critiques of the welfare state (a classic example of this was Bacon and Eltis, 1976). The big state, taxing heavily in order to provide social programmes, is seen as damaging the economy. Also the fact that workers are protected by benefit systems makes them resistant to policies endeavouring to reduce the price of labour. Those arguments have gained strength from evidence of the difficulties the Western economies have in competing with the emergent economies of the East. Comparativists (Pfaller, Gough, and Therborn, 1991; Esping-Andersen, 1999) have challenged the cruder versions of this thesis, pointing out that there is no simple equation between the size of a welfare state and its economic competitiveness. Much has been made of the value of a secure well trained labour force as a national economic asset (Esping-Andersen, 2002). However, even that argument suggests that only some kinds of social policies contribute to competiveness, shifting the thrust of policies in even the strongest welfare states towards a more selective approach to who is supported and leading to the development of a much tougher line on the need to enforce labour market participation. In that sense the classic notion of the welfare state must be seen as changing, even if not disappearing.

But the other interesting feature of changes to the way the welfare state is regarded today is embodied in the possibility that we may be seeing (or could see) changes in the role of the state but not at the same time reductions in welfare. Here we are talking of a mixture of actual contemporary changes and change aspirations. In respect of these issues the points above about institutional arrangements and policy styles may be pertinent.

The arguments for these changes come from various places in the ideological spectrum. From the Right (loosely speaking as some of these ideas spread well across the political spectrum) there are two themes. There has been some distinct looking back to the nineteenth century, arguing the case for welfare as something to be dealt with by smaller scale participative organisations rather than by the state (Green, 2009). Forms of self help and mutual insurance are advocated. In the UK the current Prime Minister's notion of 'the big society' embodies an aspiration of this kind, though he is far from clear how he is going to secure this ideal (see Ellison, 2011). In the United States the image of the undesirability of 'bowling alone' (Putnam, 2000) stresses the need for individuals to have 'social capital' upon which they can draw in time of need. It should be added that there is often in both countries also an emphasis on the importance of 'real capital'. Ironically the 2008 crash was to a considerable extent engendered by efforts to extend home ownership as capital for lower income people.

The other theme here is much more into the mainstream in many countries – but with again the United States and UK in the lead – the privatisation of welfare systems. There is a distinction to be drawn here between forms of privatisation that involve a withdrawal of the state and those that generate hybrid systems. The slogan in respect of the latter – used indeed by members of Tony Blair's Labour Government in respect of health service privatisation (see Leys and Player, 2011) – is that it does not matter who provides so long as the government pays. The question raised by critics of this development is about how stable such developments will be, in respect of government payment.

However, this development – however much it may be driven by private sector aspirations to have roles in public services – rides on the back of a much wider critique of the classic welfare state. This is the argument that it is undesirable to have the state as a monopoly provider. It is argued that there is a need for choice. A distinction may be drawn here between privatisation and marketisation. But this argument has also been given a more distinctly libertarian flavour, with the powerful state being seen as an authoritarian force. This theme is developed by writers with a strong commitment to welfare, who would certainly not see themselves as endorsing either simple self help or privatisation. The Swedish scholar Bo Rothstein asks 'What are the conditions for persuading citizens to give over their money, their time ... and possibly themselves ... to the state?' (1998, p.140). He identifies as crucial conditions: the fairness of policy programmes, a just distribution of burdens and procedural justice in their implementation. He accepts the paternalist thrust of the classic welfare state and explores how services may move away from paternalism. He defends diversity, not from a market perspective but from one which explores how the state can fund and regulate mixed, including private, services which offer citizens a measure of choice. This he argues has to involve tackling problems of accountability at the local level, in terms of relationships between 'autonomous citizens' and 'quasi-autonomous' institutions.

But Rothstein draws a distinction between services and cash benefits, seeing explicit entitlements to the latter as crucial for citizen autonomy. This takes us back to a central element in the conception of the welfare state particularly developed by Titmuss in the 1960s; universal social insurance benefits available as of right. There is a paradox here: the conception of the welfare state as liberating us (even from the control of the state) has been transformed into one that sees it as constraining us. That view has always rested to some extent upon the perspective of those more likely to be contributors than beneficiaries. Then in more recent times the attack upon the welfare state has involved restrictions to benefit entitlements ('welfare rights') and an increased stress upon behavioural requirements (in particular job search). In that sense the *state* dimension of the welfare state has become more intrusive.

Rothstein thus actually offers a defence of a notion of the welfare state which is compatible with a distrust of the state. In much of Western Continental Europe that can still be seen as a defence of the centrality of social insurance in the welfare state design. What is particularly important about social insurance in several Western European countries is that it involves a partnership between the state and other organisations. In terms of the arguments developed here this is a product of, and a reinforcer of, consensual decision making, reducing the naked power of the state (Béland, 2001).

In the UK this is not the case. Unilateral government action has undermined what was always a limited insurance scheme. In the context therefore of what is now probably a lost cause another line of argument has developed: in favour of 'citizens' incomes' to achieve the same ideal (this issue has been explored in Bill Jordan's work – for a recent contribution see his 2006 book). The particular point about this idea is that where the social insurance system rests upon an expectation of labour market participation as the norm, basic income systems can accommodate to a world in which work may be much less readily available. But of course while it is very much an ideal scheme propagated by experts, it lacks a societal coalition to put it forward and defend it. It depends on the state having a positive orientation to welfare, putting the emphasis within the expression welfare state back upon *welfare*.

Conclusion

The problem that this chapter has struggled with is the difficulty in drawing a distinction between describing all economically advanced states as welfare states, since all have experienced welfare expenditure and welfare institutions growth as they have grown, and recognising, *in the terminology used*, a distinction between the characteristics of welfare within that group of nations such that it may be said 'this state is a welfare state and that is not'. If we look at variations in state institutions we are offered possibilities for ways of looking at this issue that complement conventional comparative analysis. This involves drawing a distinction between ideas about welfare and the role of the state. It also enables us to identify how, in modern times, whilst distinct back-tracking in terms of welfare (Taylor Gooby, 2001) is to different degrees on many national political agendas, there are other ideas on the agenda about which entail some disconnection between ways to enhance welfare and the expectation that the state should play a central role in that respect.

References

Atkinson, M. M. and Coleman, W. D. (1989), Strong states and weak states: Sectoral policy networks in advanced capitalist economies. *British Journal of Political Science*, 19, pp. 47–67.

Bacon, R. and Eltis, W. (1976), *Britain's Economic Problem: Too Few Producers*. London: Macmillan.

Barnett, C. (1986), *The Audit of War*. London: Macmillan.

Béland, D. (2001), Does Labor Matter? Institutions, Labor Unions, and Pension Reform in France and the United States. *Journal of Public Policy*, vol. 21, no. 2, pp. 153–72.

Bovens, M., Hart, P. and Peters, B.G. (eds) (2001), *Success and Failure in Public Governance*. Cheltenham: Edward Elgar.

Briggs, A. (1967), 'The Welfare State in Historical Perspective', in Schottland, C.I. (ed.), *The Welfare State*. New York: Harper Torchbooks.

Chambers Dictionary, The (1998), Edinburgh: Chambers.

Dunleavy, P. (1995), Policy disasters: Explaining the UK's record. *Public Policy and Administration*, vol. 10, no. 2, pp. 52–69.

Dyson, K. H. F. (1980), *The State Tradition in Western Europe: A Study of an Idea and Institution*. New York: Oxford University Press.

Ellison, N. (2011), 'The Conservative Party and the Big Society', in C. Holden, M. Kilkey and G. Ramia (eds), *Social Policy Review 23*. Bristol: Policy Press.

Esping-Andersen, G. (1990), *Three Worlds of Welfare Capitalism*. Cambridge: Polity Press.

——(1999), *Social Foundations of Post-Industrial Economies*. Oxford: Oxford University Press.

Esping-Andersen G. (ed.) (2002), *Why we need a New Welfare State*. Oxford: Oxford University Press.

Flora, P. and Alber, J. (1981), 'Modernization, Democratization and the Development of Welfare States in Western Europe', in P. Flora and A. J. Heidenheimer (eds), *The Development of Welfare States in Europe and America*. New Brunswick, NJ: Transaction.

Furniss, N. and Tilton, T. (1979), *The Case for the Welfare State*. Bloomington: Indiana University Press.

George, V. and Wilding, P. (2002), *Globalisation and Human Welfare*. Basingstoke: Palgrave.

Gough, I. (1979), *The Political Economy of the Welfare State*. London: Macmillan.

Gough, I. and Wood, G. (2004), *Insecurity and Welfare Regimes in Asia, Africa and Latin America: Social Policy in Development Contexts*. Cambridge: Cambridge University Press.

Green, D. G. (2009), *Individualists Who Co-operate: Education and welfare reform befitting a free people*. London: Civitas.

Jordan, B. (2006), *Social Policy for the Twenty-First Century: New Perspectives, Big Issues*. Cambridge: Polity Press.

Katzenstein, P. (1977), Conclusion: Domestic Structures and Strategies of Foreign Economic Policy, *International Organisation*, vol. 31, no. 4, pp. 879–920.

Lane, J.-E. and Ersson, S. (2000), *The New Institutional Politics*. London: Routledge.

Leys, C. and Player, S. (2011), *The Plot Against the NHS*. Pontypool: Merlin Press.

Lijphart, A. (1999), *Patterns of Democracy*. New Haven, CT: Yale University Press.

Obinger, H., Leibfried, S. and Castles, F. G. (eds) (2005), *Federalism and the Welfare State*. Cambridge: Cambridge University Press.

O'Connor, J. (1973), *The Fiscal Crisis of the State*. New York: St Martin's Press.

Pfaller, A., Gough, I. and Therborn, G. (1991), *Can the Welfare State Compete?* Basingstoke: Macmillan.

Putnam, R. D. (2000), *Bowling Alone: The Collapse and Revival of American Community*. New York: Simon & Schuster.

Richardson, J. (ed.) (1982), *Policy Styles in Western Europe*. London: Allen and Unwin.

Rimlinger, G. (1971), *Welfare Policy and Industrialisation in Europe, America and Russia*. New York: Wiley.

Rothstein, B. (1998), *Just Institutions Matter: The Moral and Political Logic of the Universal Welfare State*. Cambridge: Cambridge University Press.

Skocpol, T. (1994), *Social Policy in the United States*. Princeton, NJ: Princeton University Press.

Taylor-Gooby, P. (ed.) (2001), *European Welfare States under Pressure*. London: Sage.
Titmuss, R. M. (1958), *Essays on the Welfare State*. London: Allen and Unwin.
——(1974), *Social Policy: An Introduction*. London: Allen and Unwin.
Waarden, F. van (1999), 'Ieder land zijn eigen trant?', in W. Bakker and F. van Waarden (eds), *Ruimte rond regels: Stijlen van regulering en beleidsuitvoering vergeleken*, pp. 303–39. Amsterdam: Boom.
Weber, M. (edited by Parsons, T.) (1947), *The Theory of Social and Economic Organization*. New York: Oxford University Press.
Wolfe, A. (1977), *The Limits of Legitimacy*. New York: The Free Press.

3

Fiscal welfare

Adrian Sinfield

Arguments rage about the welfare state – who gets what, to what effect, and at whose cost? But there is still little attention to an alternative, expensive, and largely hidden 'tax welfare state'. This also conveys considerable benefits on many, reinforcing their efforts to achieve social and economic security, encouraging and supporting particular activities such as saving for retirement, bringing up children, or buying a home, while leaving others, generally on lower incomes, with higher taxes and fewer services.

Like the public welfare state, the tax system is not only government controlled and organised but its workings also effectively shift resources among different groups in society. However, who benefits from these tax benefits and who pays for them can differ dramatically from public welfare benefits, and it has very different visibility and accountability. It is all the more relevant to social policy analysis since it can assist governments in reducing public social spending by financially encouraging the use of alternative private provision without having to account publicly for the costs of doing so. This can undermine the welfare state and invisibly reinforce or widen inequalities, but it is by no means inevitable that this should happen.

Fiscal welfare and tax expenditure

The term *fiscal welfare* was first explicitly used in 1955 by Richard Titmuss, the first professor of social administration in the UK, to indicate benefits available through tax systems (Titmuss, 1958; and in Alcock, 2001). The 'social division of welfare' challenged the conventional wisdom of substantial redistribution in modern British society. The use of the term 'the welfare state', Titmuss argued, encouraged a limited view of the extent and impact of 'all collective interventions to meet certain needs of the individual and/or to serve the wider interests of society' (Titmuss, 1958, p. 42), and this led to mistaken assumptions about the role of the state and the extent of welfare provision across society. In particular it helped to conceal the impact of both the state's directing of resources through its tax systems and the value of occupational welfare through employment (see Chapter 4).

Fiscal welfare, Titmuss argued, deserves as much analysis as public spending on social services and benefits. 'Allowances and reliefs from income tax, though providing similar benefits [to public spending] and expressing a similar social purpose in the recognition of dependencies, are not, however, treated as social service expenditure. The first is a cash transaction; the second an accounting convenience. Despite this difference in administrative method, the tax saving that accrues to the individual is, in effect, a transfer payment' (Titmuss, 1958, pp. 44–5). As a result tax is foregone that would otherwise have been collected for public spending. The main forms of tax relief are:

- Tax allowances – amounts deducted from gross income for particular reasons, such as caring for a child, to arrive at taxable income.
- Tax exemptions – incomes excluded from the tax base and so not subject to income tax because paying interest on a home loan or contributing to a pension when some or all of that pension may later be taxed.
- Preferential tax rates – incomes taxed at lower rates applied to income from particular sources or used for specific purposes such as savings.
- Tax credits – similar to allowances but deducted from tax liability, not from gross income. They may be 'refundable', 'non-wastable' or 'non-refundable', 'wastable'. With the former any excess of credit over tax liable is paid to the taxpayer, and this has been used to help low income families and workers.

Related to and overlapping fiscal welfare is *tax expenditure*. This term was deliberately introduced to contrast with public expenditure to indicate the cost in lost revenue resulting from tax reliefs by a tax lawyer, Stanley Surrey, when he was US Assistant Secretary for Taxation Policy from 1961 to 1968 (Surrey, 1973). By 1974 the concept had been incorporated into a law requiring the US government to publish a tax expenditure list as a supplement to the annual federal budget. The term is now generally used in the accounting of ways in which tax systems operate as another form of intervention, 'running spending programs through the tax system' (McDaniel and Surrey, 1985, p. 6).

Tax expenditures are 'provisions of tax law, regulation or practices that reduce or postpone revenue for a comparatively narrow population of taxpayers relative to a benchmark tax' (Anderson, 2008, in Organisation for Economic Co-operation and Development (OECD), 2010, p. 12). Many exist in areas that are not welfare while much fiscal welfare is not recognised as tax expenditure. Because of much disagreement over what constitutes a benchmark tax, what is openly accounted for as fiscal welfare in one country remains less visible, or invisible, in others, so limiting comparative analysis. It is still important to recognise that these arrangements do represent an allocation or redirection of resources, whether officially identified as tax expenditures or not. However, tax expenditures cannot be ignored since most governments only estimate the cost of a tax relief when it is so recognised.

According to one OECD study 'accounting in many countries suggests the use of tax expenditures is pervasive and growing' (OECD, 2010, p. 14), but it was only able to make comparisons of their costs across seven of the ten countries surveyed. Including reported expenditure in any tax, and not just income tax, it ranked the UK highest at 13% gross domestic product (GDP), then Canada at 7%, the United States at 6% and Spain at 5% with Korea and the Netherlands at 2%, and Germany less than 1% (OECD, 2010, Table II.29, data between 2004 and 2009). Measured against 'relevant tax revenue', Canada and the United States were the highest tax spenders, both at 59%, UK at 39%, Spain at 28%, Korea at 25%, Netherlands at 10%, and Germany at 9% (OECD, 2010, Table II.31). How much of this could be identified as fiscal welfare, and how much of fiscal welfare is included, is not clear.

The scale of tax expenditure related to social policy can be substantial and can also take up a significant part of all tax spending. The UK's own published data for 2010–11 showed social tax benefits made up 96% of the main 25 purely income tax reliefs listed (excluding the basic personal allowance). Their cost in revenue foregone was equivalent to 21% of the total income tax collected (HMRC, 2011, Table 1.5). There were other significant tax reliefs in capital gains tax, value-added tax, and the excise duties.

Tax breaks for social purposes (TBSPs)

The development of the analysis of *tax breaks for social purposes (TBSPs)* by Willem Adema and colleagues at OECD provide more evidence on fiscal welfare, although by no means a comprehensive accounting. They have developed the category in using the OECD social expenditure database to reach 'net total social expenditure'.[1] TBSPs are 'those reductions, exemptions, deductions or postponement of taxes, which: *a)* perform the same policy function as transfer payments which, if they existed, would be classified as social expenditures; or *b)* are aimed at stimulating private provision of benefits' (Adema, Fron, and Ladaique, 2011, p. 110).

In 2007 the greatest providers of TBSPs among the 27 OECD member countries taking part in the study were the United States at 2.1% of GDP at factor cost, Germany at 1.8% and Canada at 1.6%. France, Mexico, Portugal, Australia, and the Netherlands were around 1%. The only other significant spenders were Korea and Spain at 0.7%, Belgium and Japan at 0.6%, the Czech Republic, Ireland, and the UK at 0.5%, and Italy at 0.3%. The remaining 11 countries were shown as providing 0.1% or nothing (ibid., p. 33, Table 1.4).

Although a valuable addition to knowledge, these analyses lack important elements of fiscal welfare needed for a full comparison. First, Adema and colleagues exclude tax breaks on state benefits such as child benefits, whether they are taxed more lightly or not at all, to avoid double counting because they are included earlier in a different form (ibid., p. 110). This removes a significant area of fiscal welfare in many countries: however, tax allowances and tax credits for children are included as TBSPs.

Next, tax and other reliefs to private pensions are omitted from the full analysis although the authors admit that they are 'arguably the most important' TBSPs (ibid., p. 29 and see below). 'Because of conceptual issues and gaps in data availability', these are only listed at the bottom of tables as a 'memorandum item' and not included in totals (ibid., p. 33, note c).

Despite its often substantial cost, fiscal welfare for married couples is also omitted because it is not 'considered as social in all OECD countries' (ibid., p. 112), virtually confining TBSP support 'for families' to that for children. In addition, TBSPs provided by sub-national agencies are excluded: in Canada these would increase the total by some 50% (ibid., p. 111, note 1). Finally, other subsidies equivalent to TBSPs, such as exemptions from social security contributions, appear to have been omitted.

There is enough and increasing evidence to indicate that fiscal welfare can be very significant despite the omissions. Yet this and other forms of tax spending continue to escape the regular scrutiny by parliamentary and other bodies to which public spending is subject. Given concerns to reduce, if not avoid, budget deficits, neglect of the scale of tax reliefs for any purpose is all the more remarkable.

The distribution of benefits

'For government, a tax expenditure is a loss in revenue; for a taxpayer it is a reduction in tax liability' (OECD, 2010, p. 12): so what is the redistributive impact? There is still very little evidence, and so very limited awareness that with few exceptions fiscal welfare is generally regressive. Stanley Surrey emphasised the 'upside-down effect' (Surrey, 1973, p. 37) of most tax welfare because the marginal rate of tax which would be paid if the relief were not available usually determines the value of a tax benefit to the recipient. For example, a tax allowance of 500 euros or dollars is worth 100 to someone otherwise paying tax at a top rate of 20%, but 150 to the 30% taxpayer and 250 to the 50% taxpayer.

These higher tax rates would otherwise be paid by those with higher incomes. With more income to invest in tax-privileged activities, the better-off are able to draw even greater value from these tax benefits, such as buying their own home or contributing to a pension, since the few ceilings on tax reliefs are usually generous. One independent study in the UK found tax reliefs enabled the top 10% to exploit some 70% of the extra tax relief above the basic personal tax allowance (estimates from Brewer et al., 2008, Table 1). The top tenth of the top 1% had a pre-tax income 31 times the average, but benefited from tax reliefs 86 times the average, enabling those at the very top to 'race away' even further at considerable public cost.

As a result, those on higher incomes, conventionally assumed to be not only in less need but also better able to make a larger contribution in taxes to the common wealth, actually derive greater benefit from fiscal welfare and pay even less in taxes. Meanwhile the rest assume the richer are paying more tax, not less, and are unaware that, as a result, their own taxes are higher and/or public services more limited. The upside-down redistribution of most income tax reliefs in the UK contributes to making the incidence of total taxes proportional, not progressive as widely believed (Barnard et al., 2011, Tables B and C).

In recent years there has been some, but still very limited, recognition of the upside-down effect. OECD acknowledged: 'this incentive pattern might be judged absolutely perverse – giving the most inducement to those who need the inducement least – and yet it is the common practice in at least some countries' (OECD, 2010, p. 28): the World Bank noted that it 'violates' vertical and horizontal equity (World Bank, 2003, p. 2). There is also growing acceptance that this 'reverse targeting' is not inevitable. Instead of regressive exemptions or allowances, tax credits help families and low-paid workers in some countries. The credit is deducted from the tax to be paid rather than deducted or exempted from income before tax. As a result all taxpayers can benefit to the same amount, and the credit be made refundable to those whose incomes are so low that they pay little or no income tax. In hybrid schemes, as in the UK, the tax credit has been developed to provide even more support to those on lower incomes.

The uses of fiscal welfare: recognising and supporting the needs of the family

The ways that fiscal welfare recognizes needs and rewards, and encourages and promotes certain activities, reveal both similarities and differences to public spending programmes. Most tax benefits operate indirectly, encouraging more use of the market. Direct support is mainly directed to the family where needs have long been met in forms comparable to and often more generous than public welfare. In most countries the very first income tax arrangements took family responsibilities into account in assessing the ability to pay tax, usually long before any public benefit was available outside the poor law.

Support for children has been a very common tax relief, sometimes varying with the age and/or number of dependent children. The tax benefit may be more generous, continue longer than social security benefits, and exist even where there is no general family benefit in public welfare, as in the United States. In most European Union (EU) countries tax welfare provides part of child benefit packages with tax credits growing in importance (van Mechelen and Bradshaw, forthcoming).

Special reliefs for marriage are also common, whether or not couples are living together, and some continue into widowhood. Tax allowances have also been extended to single parents and are sometimes equivalent to the married couple's allowance.

Recognition of marriage and family is so institutionalised in many countries that reliefs are part of the benchmark system and so not regarded as tax expenditures. Nevertheless their addition to family income needs to be taken into account in assessing the extent and distribution of fiscal welfare. France 'considers the household as the tax unit: favourable tax treatment of families', including the *quotient familial* and *quotient conjugal*, 'is thus an integral part of the tax system' and not a tax expenditure. Yet its support to children was 'reported to be around 11.5 bn euros in 2007' (Adema, Fron and Ladaique, 2011, p. 112 and n19), much more than any published tax expenditure. With the *quotient conjugal* also costing half as much, the whole range of family-related tax reliefs may exceed total public spending on family benefits. They constitute a very considerable demand on the overall budget and benefit high earners substantially more than other families in both absolute and relative terms (Terra Nova, 2009, pp. 24–6).

In Germany married couples are jointly assessed with income splitting, a particular advantage with only one earner or a great difference in the level of earnings, both common in that country. This is also regarded as part of the basic tax system. No regular data are provided on the considerable cost which may exceed all published tax expenditures.

In one country at least income tax and social security systems have been used to promote differential family policies. In Singapore generous tax incentives are provided to encourage women university graduates to marry and have more children while less educated women are urged to have only two, preferably one, child by a cash grant to their social security savings fund.

Fiscal support for other dependent relatives has been available in many countries, particularly when they are living in the same household. These have included special relief for the cost of a housekeeper or caretaker for a dependent with specific disabilities. Much support to the wider family has been removed, but there have been new schemes. In Hong Kong a tax deduction is available for 'elderly residential care expenses' to the taxpayer when his/her or a spouse's parent or grandparent lives with them or support is provided for them in a care home. Singapore also encourages taxpayers to support parents and grandparents.

The upside-down impact can be considerable but in most countries remains little discussed and analysed alongside public welfare benefits. However, tax credits have recently been deployed to help some, particularly families, on lower incomes provided that they take jobs (OECD, 2010, pp. 34–43). In 1975 the United States introduced an earned income tax credit 'as a minor amendment to a forgettable tax bill' which 'became in the 1980s one of the most popular programs in Washington', and 'by the early 1990s ... the policy equivalent of penicillin' (Howard, 1997, pp. 404 and 405). 'Making work pay' credits for low-paid workers and additional ones for children mean that support through the tax system exceeds means-tested support to poor families and workers.

In countries where 'welfare' carries a stigma, payments through the tax system are seen as more acceptable both to recipients and the wider community as well as reducing public spending totals (only tax paid out is included, not the tax waived). Canada, New Zealand, Australia, and the UK followed the American example to help make work pay, especially for families, but with varying success with the professed aim of reducing poverty.

Some continued to focus tax help on families with at least one earner and adding childcare subsidies, while others made support available for most or all children, irrespective of anyone in the household working. Some also provided it to low-paid workers without children. Canada has since abandoned tax credits to direct help through social security and the UK is planning to do the same.

Providing for retirement

Some countries help older people with higher tax allowances: often phased out at modest levels, these help taxpayers on lower or average incomes. However, in most countries the most generous tax benefits are regressive and related to private pensions. Most commonly, while the pension in regular payment is taxed, no taxes are raised on pension contributions made by employee and employer (often with a maximum level for employee); on investment income from funded arrangements (or tax at a preferential rate); and on any lump sum payable on retirement (but usually tax-free to a certain level only).

The revenue loss has generally been increasing, exceeding 1% of GDP in five countries in the OECD TBSP analysis (although, as indicated above, omitted from their main accounting). In some English-speaking countries net pension tax expenditure has exceeded the cost of means-tested and non-contributory pensions for the poorest old people and rivals the cost of social insurance pensions (Hughes and Sinfield, 2004). In the UK the cost doubled in the decade up to 2008–9 (UK Treasury, 2009, para 2.14). Only in New Zealand, with a minority of workers contributing to non-state pensions, has most tax support been removed.

With the tax benefit usually available at the marginal rate of tax, the inequality is further compounded by the fact that the higher the status and pay, the more likely a taxpayer will be contributing to a non-state pension, and the more s/he will be able to pay in. In most countries women derive less benefit from this fiscal welfare because of their weaker position in the labour force with lower wages, less security and the greater chance of part-time work (Ginn et al., 2001). Without the protection of tax-assisted pensions their greater longevity makes the risk of prolonged poverty all the greater for women.

Distributive analyses have been scarce, but the UK Treasury recently revealed that 'the top 2% of pension savers ... receive around a quarter of all pensions tax relief on contributions' alone, 20 times more per person than basic-rate pension savers (UK Treasury, 2009, para 2.14). Directors and senior executives take particular advantage of the tax reductions, especially in the financial sector.

Amid increasing labour market insecurity, many countries in continental Europe have been planning to encourage greater reliance on non-state pensions with tax reliefs despite experience elsewhere of their large, regressive, and long-term costs. Given heightened concern to reduce budget deficits and gain 'value for money', governments might be expected to cut these subsidies without clear evidence of real public spending savings. But the interests benefiting from these tax benefits are very powerful including top management, the pension industry and the funds benefiting from its investments.

However, there have been some restraints, and these might be increasing. In recent years successive UK governments, for example, attempted to reduce the revenue loss. The initial effort by Labour may have led to greater losses, but later changes by it and a Conservative-Liberal Democrat coalition, more committed to reducing the budget deficit faster, could be more effective.

Other forms of fiscal welfare

The promotion of home ownership is probably the next major area common to most countries, despite much debate over what the main tax expenditure really is – the deductibility of mortgage or loan interest on an owner-occupied home or its imputed rental value. Where a figure is given, it is usually the former, and this is generally among the most expensive tax benefit to governments and the most valuable to recipients. In addition there is often exemption from capital gains taxes on the sale of an owner-occupied home and sometimes full or partial exemption from property taxes or rates.

In the UK the cost of mortgage interest relief became so considerable that a Conservative government decided to phase it out because this subsidy to home-ownership was seen as both contributing to a housing boom that created problems for the economic cycle and diverting more savings into housing at the expense of industry. The fact that this regressive relief cost more than public spending on housing benefits for low-income households apparently weighed little in the decision.

The subsidy of private health services is another important area in some countries including Germany, Canada, and particularly the United States with especially large reliefs for employer contributions to medical insurance premiums and medical care. Education and the work of charities have also been areas to benefit from special tax privileges in many countries.

There are many other ways in which taxpayers and/or their employers can take advantage of the tax system to improve their welfare. Many other employee benefits in kind are not taxed, or not as much as wages, such as company cars, which can also be used privately, personal and concierge services, loans at reduced rates of interest, childcare tax vouchers, and severance payments. The main beneficiaries are those who receive greater occupational welfare (cf. Chapter 4) are those liable to higher tax rates take particular advantage of the tax-reductions. Directors and senior management may receive financial advice tax-free to maximise tax-mitigating opportunities in their fringe benefit packages including further tax saving through tax havens (Kohonen and Mestrum, 2008).

In the mid-1980s New Zealand and Australia sought to reduce the revenue loss by levying 'fringe benefit taxes' on employers providing the benefits. At the time these created much controversy but became accepted within a year. The tax authorities benefited by only having to pursue the much smaller number of employers providing than taxpayers receiving, especially as larger companies were more likely to offer fringe benefits. How the tax charge is shared between employer and worker is unclear.

The political economy of fiscal welfare

Fiscal welfare and tax expenditures have rarely been the specific focus of policy, but the worldwide move towards lower taxes in the mid-1980s was accompanied by measures to broaden the tax base that abolished some and restricted other tax benefits. Lower tax rates also reduced revenue losses, but the long-term impact on fiscal welfare was generally smaller than claimed with most cuts to little-used reliefs.

The development and significance of the politics of fiscal welfare has been particularly well brought out by two major historical studies examining 'the prominent place of tax expenditures in the provision and subsidization of private social benefits' (Hacker, 2002, p. 294) in health and pensions in the United States. In *The Divided Welfare State: The Battle over Public and Private Social Benefits in the United States* Jacob Hacker analysed 'subterranean' politics and policy development, building on Christopher Howard's innovative study, *The Hidden Welfare State: Tax Expenditures and Social Policy in the United States* (1997). The two books complement each other well, with Hacker taking greater account of 'the heavy distributional skew of tax breaks for private benefits [that] must be placed at the heart of any explanation of the distinctive political dynamics that Howard's study identifies' (Hacker, 2002, pp. 39).

Republicans' exploitation of the tax route to welfare was shown by the trends in direct social spending and indirect, largely fiscal, welfare from 1967 to 2006. While Democrats largely developed public welfare, 'Republicans use policy to allocate resources and jurisdiction to private markets'. This resulted in government subsidy 'shifts from more vulnerable to more privileged constituencies', reinforcing inequalities (Faricy, 2011, pp. 77–78). 'More than just the innocuous selection of a policy tool, it is essentially a choice about altering the balance between public and private power in society' (Faricy, 2011, p. 74).

In Australia scrutiny of 'social tax expenditures' (STEs) revealed 'a more expansive, but less equitable, conception of the Australian welfare state' (Stebbing and Spies-Butcher, 2010, p. 586). 'In a context of fiscal austerity, [they] provide a route to extend welfare with low political resistance' and also reduce that 'resistance by reducing public accountability' and 'minimising state bureaucracy' (Stebbing and Spies-Butcher, 2010, pp. 593, 594, and 596). This use of a policy 'back door' supports the privatisation of welfare services (ibid., p. 595). While the conventional welfare state may appeal to the poorer and average workers, 'STEs provide a political framework for uniting the interests of middle- and higher-income earners' (ibid., p. 599).

Developments in Denmark and the UK confirm the subterranean operation of fiscal welfare. Generally change was to individual tax benefits, and their cost rather than their inequity provoked reform by governments both left and right (Kvist and Sinfield, 1996 and 1997). Denmark appears to be the only country that has withdrawn publication of tax expenditure statistics.

In the United States market economists' attacks on the concept of tax expenditures led to increasing scrutiny with the Joint Committee on Taxation proposing a revision into 'tax subsidies' and 'tax-induced structural deviations' (Kleinbard, 2008, p. 9). Tea Party and other groups now advocate scrapping or radically reducing tax expenditures to reduce the budget deficit, some stressing the need to do so alongside cuts in public welfare.

Investigation of fiscal welfare and TBSPs has paid little attention to new market economies or Third World societies although international advisers and consultants often build in standard tax reliefs from their own countries with little, if any, indication of revenue loss or distributive implications. Some international agencies press for tax reliefs to stimulate private pension markets while pushing for more targeted public assistance. In consequence expensive elements of fiscal welfare benefitting the better-off become institutionalised in taxation as universal public welfare is cut back.

Conclusion

Despite the use of tax credits, fiscal welfare remains an alternative and little known welfare state generally providing more support to those with higher incomes. Amid increasing spending cuts, this form of backdoor spending may be becoming generally accepted as part of a new 'realism' of lower taxation, greater privatisation, increased citizen choice and the end of budget deficits without understanding of the longer-term implications.

Higher unemployment and job insecurity increase those who cannot access most forms of fiscal welfare and subsidy, while reduced revenue from these privileges further limits funds for public welfare for these outsiders. The more the limit, the more that stimulation of private welfare via fiscal welfare compounds the problem as it enables those with the resources to make use of tax opportunities to buy more support.

This weakens the support for and so the legitimacy of 'the welfare state', as well as its extent and quality. Those providing for themselves by means of fiscal welfare are little aware of the scale and inequity of the subsidy and are often among the most vocal in attacking welfare dependency and weakening collective support for pooling risks and promoting solidarity. Posing policy alternatives as either universal or selective ignores the selective privileges to some through less visible and less accountable fiscal welfare. In consequence inequalities are widened while universal policies are threatened and often cut back.

Analysis of shifts from more solidaristic and collective systems to more individualistic models with hidden upside-down redistribution through the tax system needs to take account of the power of the various interests involved including the pension fund industry. 'The invisibility of tax expenditures represents both a democratic problem and a problem of political steering' (Ervik and Kuhnle, 1996, p. 93).

'Tax expenditure programs are lobbied for on the *supply side* and "off-budget"' by private providers (Faricy, 2011, p. 82, emphasis in the original). Future research in fiscal welfare should give more attention to identifying not only its full scale and distribution but also the supplier beneficiaries in the market and their lobbying within and across countries and agencies. This could show how welfare debates are being reframed in ways that conceal the scale and distribution of inequitable tax benefits while undermining support for the welfare state. 'Though evaluation of tax expenditures may be difficult, a more serious problem may be the failure to try. ... An out-of-sight, out-of-mind attitude can arise and continue to insulate inefficiencies from scrutiny for periods of years' (OECD, 2010, p. 29) – and, it should be added, inequalities.

In some countries the 'heavy distributional skew' of fiscal welfare (Hacker, 2002, p. 39) is receiving more attention in analysis and even some changes in policymaking, but it is more than half a century since Richard Titmuss drew attention to its inequitable growth. Today welfare states and the majority of their people are suffering the consequences of not paying this warning enough attention.

Note

1 Curiously this work which has been developed for more than a decade receives no mention in OECD, 2010.

References

Alcock, P. et al. (eds) (2001), *Welfare and Wellbeing: Richard Titmuss's Contribution to Social Policy*. Bristol: The Policy Press.

Adema, W., Fron, P., and Ladaique, M. (2011), 'Is the European Welfare State Really More Expensive?: Indicators on Social Spending, 1980–2012; and a Manual to the OECD Social Expenditure Database (SOCX)', *OECD Social, Employment and Migration Working Papers*, no. 124. OECD Publishing. doi: 10.1787/5kg2d2d4pbf0-en.

Anderson, B. (2008), 'Tax Expenditures in OECD Countries', 5th annual meeting of OECD-Asia SBO Bangkok, January 10–11, powerpoint. Online: www.oecd.org/dataoecd/40/6/39944419.pdf (accessed June 2012).

Barnard, A., Howell, S., and Smith, R. (2011), 'The effects of taxes and benefits on household income, 2009/10: Further analysis and methodology', Office for National Statistics. Online: www.ons.gov.uk:80/ons/rel/household-income/the-effects-of-taxes-and-benefits-on-household-income/2009–2010/index.html (accessed June 2012).

Brewer, M., Sibieta, L., and Wren-Lewis, L. (2008), *Racing Away? Income Inequality and the Evolution of High Incomes*. Institute for Fiscal Studies, IFS Briefing Note no. 76. Online: www.ifs.org.uk (accessed June 2012).

Ervik, R. and Kuhnle, S. (1996), 'The Nordic Welfare Model and the European Union', in B. Greve (ed.), *Comparative Welfare Systems: The Scandinavian Model in a Period of Change*. Basingstoke: Macmillan.

Faricy, C. (2011), The Politics of Social Policy in America: The Causes and Effects of Indirect versus Direct Social Spending, *The Journal of Politics*. vol. 73, no. 1, January, pp. 74–83.

Ginn, J., Street, D., and Arber, S. (eds) (2001), *Women, Work and Pensions: International Issues and Prospects*. Buckingham: Open University Press.

Hacker, J. S. (2002), *The Divided Welfare State: The Battle over Public and Private Social Benefits in the United States*. Cambridge: Cambridge University Press.

HR Revenue and Customs (HMRC) (2011), 'Tax expenditures and ready reckoners'. Online: www.hmrc.gov.uk/stats/tax_expenditures/ menu.htm (accessed June 2012).

Howard, C. (1997), *The Hidden Welfare State: Tax Expenditures and Social Policy in the United States*. Princeton, NJ: Princeton University Press.
Hughes, G. and Sinfield, A. (2004), 'Financing Pensions by Stealth', in G. Hughes and J. Stewart (eds), *Reforming Pensions in Europe: Evolution of Pension Financing and Sources of Retirement Income*, pp. 163–92. Cheltenham: Edward Elgar.
Kleinbard, E. D. (2008), *Rethinking Tax Expenditures*, Address to the Chicago-Kent College of Law Federal Tax Institute, 1 May.
Kohonen, M. and Mestrum, F. (2008), *Tax Justice: Putting global inequality on the agenda*. London: Pluto.
Kvist, J. and Sinfield, A. (1996), *Comparing Tax Routes to Welfare in Denmark and the United Kingdom*. Copenhagen: Danish National Institute of Social Research.
——(1997), 'Comparing Tax Welfare States', in M. May, E. Brunsdon and G. Craig (eds), *Social Policy Review 9*, pp. 249–75. London: SPA.
McDaniel, P. R. and Surrey, S. S. (eds) (1985), *International Aspects of Tax Expenditures: A Comparative Study*. Deventer: Kluwer.
Organisation for Economic Co-operation and Development (OECD) (2010), *Tax Expenditures in OECD countries*. Paris: OECD.
Stebbing, A. and Spies-Butcher, B. (2010), Universal Welfare by 'Other Means'? Tax Expenditures and the Australian Welfare State, *Journal of Social Policy*, vol. 39, no. 4, October, pp. 585–606.
Surrey, S. S. (1973), *Pathways to Tax Reform*. Cambridge, MA: Harvard University Press.
Terra Nova (2009), *Politique familiale: d'une stratégie de réparation à une stratégie d'investissement sociale*, Projet 2012, Contribution no. 10. Online: www.tnova.fr (accessed June 2012).
Titmuss, R. M. (1958), *Essays on 'the Welfare State'*. London: Allen and Unwin.
UK Treasury (2009), *Implementing the Restriction of Pensions Tax Relief*. London: HM Treasury.
van Mechelen, N. and Bradshaw, J. (forthcoming), 'Trends in child benefit packages for working families, 1991–2009', in I. Marx and K. Nelson (eds), *The State of Minimum Income Protection in the European Union*. Basingstoke: Palgrave Macmillan.
World Bank (2003), 'Why worry about tax expenditures?', *PREMnotes* Economic Policy, no. 77, January.

4

Occupational welfare

Kevin Farnsworth

Introduction

There is nothing new about occupational welfare – various social benefits provided by employers to employees (Goodin and Rein, 2001). In fact, employers dominated early 'social' provision until the beginning of the twentieth century, providing educational services, housing, and community provision (Hay, 1977, pp. 435–55; Russell, 1991). And workplace provision continued to play a role – a key role for some – in overall receipts of welfare benefits even after the establishment of the modern 'welfare state'. Richard Titmuss (1976) recognised its importance and argued that occupational welfare was one of the key pillars of the welfare state. The role that occupational welfare plays in today's welfare systems varies, however, between welfare states and between categories of worker. Categorising and measuring it is a complex task. As a result, occupational welfare continues to receive pretty scant treatment in social policy analysis today (but see Farnsworth, 2004, pp. 437–55; Greve, 2007; May and Brunsdon, 1994, pp. 146–69; Rein, 1983, pp. 3–22, 1996, pp. 27–43). This chapter deals with three key questions in turn: 1) What constites occupational welfare?; 2) What is the purpose of occupational welfare?; and 3) How much does occupational welfare cost? The chapter then raises some key questions relating to occupational welfare that remain unanswered before concluding with a plea for more research into the area.

What constitutes occupational welfare?

At least one of the reasons for the lack of attention paid to occupational welfare relates to definitional problems. Although few would disagree with the broad definition offered in the first sentence of this chapter, there is disagreement concerning the detail of what constitutes occupational welfare as opposed to general non-wage perks in overall employment provision (and whether this is even an important question). Since Titmuss's (1976) influential examination of occupational social provision as one of the key forms of welfare, definitions of occupational welfare have tended to oscillate between broad and narrow conceptualisations and there has been some debate regarding which approach is most useful to students of the welfare state.

The broadest conceptualisations focus on the full gamut of employee fringe benefits, including goods and services as diverse as sports club membership, subsidised canteens, travel expenses, company cars, uniforms, and clothing allowances. Bryson (1992) includes intangible benefits such as 'contributions to general enjoyment and personal development'. Such broad definitions of occupational welfare could include a whole range of undoubtedly important things related to the work environment, including the ergonomics of office furniture and the relative safety of industrial equipment. In their definition, May and Brunsdon (1994, p. 147; 2007, p. 151) follow Murlis (1974) in defining occupational welfare as non-wage provision that increases the well-being of employees at some cost to the employer. In 2007 May and Brunsdon offered one of the most comprehensive conceptualisations of occupational welfare yet, including all non-wage benefits provided to employees plus some of the various community engagements that are referred to more commonly as corporate social responsibility.

Narrower definitions of occupational welfare seek to distinguish occupational welfare from occupational fringe benefits, perks and other general non-wage benefits. In particular, they seek to investigate the parallels between state social welfare and occupational welfare, where one might substitute for the other. Although Titmuss's definition of occupational welfare was broad, he did make some attempt to distinguish between general non-wage benefits and other forms of provision which, he argued, functioned to meet 'certain dependencies', including old age, sickness, childhood, and widowhood. Most non-wage benefits do not function in this way. The only 'function' that is common to the majority of non-wage benefits is that they increase the value of the total compensation paid to employees in receipt of such benefits (and some do not even achieve this). For this reason, in previous work (Farnsworth, 2004) I have argued that it is important to try to distinguish between occupational 'perks' and work-based social provision. The latter includes statutory social provision (occupational pensions and employer income maintenance schemes that are required to be provided by law) and non-statutory (voluntary) social provision that eliminates or reduces the risks and harms associated with work. The problem with attempting to locate effective means of distinguishing social and non-social occupational provision – for instance by arguing that occupational pensions and above-statutory sickness benefits constitute occupational welfare but gym membership and company cars do not – is, however, tenuous for May and Brunsdon:

> Why, for example, can sports-club membership or company cars not be preventive health measures maintaining fitness in the one instance and alleviating the stress of travelling in the other?
>
> *(May and Brunsdon, 2007)*

May and Brunsdon do have a point. The focus of social policy more generally is, at times, too narrow and without good reason. In fact, there may be a strong argument for extending the focus of occupational welfare beyond non-wage benefits towards general wage levels, wage distribution within the firm, labour regulations, health and safety at work, and employee autonomy. On the other hand, the inclusion of all of these items under the occupational welfare banner risks undermining the distinctiveness of social policy analysis (as opposed to public policy and/or human resource management) and risks undermining the comparability of occupational welfare with other parts of the welfare state.

The reason for examining occupational welfare is to try to understand and compare the relative benefits obtained from work with those obtained from other means, including the state, and the trade-offs and complementarities between them. If a similar approach to state welfare was adopted to that advocated by the broadest approaches to occupational welfare, it would be impossible to distinguish public policy and social policy on the basis that most things that the state does brings some benefits. Approaches to social policy analysis of state welfare programmes tend to be more selective. Certainly, if the intention is to examine the contribution of occupational provision to the welfare state, we have to look for delimiters that allow for meaningful comparisons between occupational and state provision. Here it is relevant to draw again upon the work of Titmuss. Although Titmuss did list a whole range of benefits that he argued come under the 'occupational welfare' umbrella, the spirit of his argument concerning the definition of social policy and the welfare state in fact suggests a more limited approach. In focusing on occupational welfare, Titmuss sought to draw attention to '*collective interventions* to meet *certain* needs' (1976, p. 42). He made it clear that occupational welfare, as a category of the welfare state, was important because it shared with social welfare similar 'functions' and 'aims'. As he put it, '[t]he definition … of what is a "social service" should take its stand on aims; not on the administrative methods and institutional devices employed to achieve them' (ibid.). Thus, the definition of occupational welfare should not be based on its broadest categorisation (for example, all non-wage benefits) but on the aims or functions that such provision shares with social welfare. And a large number of non-wage benefits simply do not share the aims (or functions) of social welfare.

The purpose of occupational welfare

However it is conceptualised, broadly or narrowly, doesn't detract from the fact that occupational welfare has been extremely important throughout the history of industrial societies. And for much of this time, occupational welfare has been at least as important to most workers as state provision. As industrial societies developed, increasingly large employers required workers to be locally available, reasonably housed, and sufficiently skilled. Some employers may also have felt that they had some duty of care for their employees and their families, which went beyond the wage relationship. Thus, some employers built whole villages and small towns around their factories for their workers. And in some advanced industrial societies, employment has been a very central and important source through which welfare, including statutory welfare, is delivered (Greve, 2007).

One of the key functions of occupational welfare has been to shape human capital within the workplace. For instance, training and healthcare packages have been made available to employees to increase productivity (Fitzgerald, 1988) and pensions and other benefits have been provided to increase employee loyalty as well as to ease the shedding of older workers (de Swaan, 1988; Gordon, 1991, pp. 15–207; Jones, 1983, pp. 61–75). The quality of provision often increases with the length of employment and access is often conditional (Papadakis and Taylor, 1987). Some benefits, for instance, have had no-strike clauses written into them (Graebner, 1980; Quadagno, 1984, pp. 632–47). In that it allows employers to provide distinct and cost-effective methods of rewarding staff, occupational welfare also helps informally to tie employees to their current employer. Giving up a job may be easier for employees to contemplate than giving up a company house or a pension plan. In this respect, employers have relied upon occupational welfare to help to retain existing workers, control demands for higher pay, or to try to attract new workers (Papadakis and Taylor-Gooby, 1987, p. 106). Thus, occupational welfare can be used to retain employees that the employer has invested heavily in, or can be used to attract skilled workers to the company (that other employers have invested in). In this respect, occupational welfare can help to prevent freeloader problems, where other companies entice skilled employees, trained at the expense of other companies, with financial and non-financial incentives. Employees that enjoy occupational welfare may be less inclined to move elsewhere.

The attractiveness to employers of occupational welfare is also increased (or decreased) by the tax system. For employers in many states, occupational welfare allows them to pay staff in more tax efficient ways. Many of the benefits that have traditionally been provided to employees – including company cars, health plans, or subsidised housing – have been exempt from, or subject to lower rates of, income taxes. In this respect, some forms of occupational welfare represent a publicly subsidised form of occupational reward (Rein, 1983, p. 5). The benefits to employers of occupational welfare, therefore, can be substantial.

The benefits for workers can also be significant of course. Occupational welfare programmes can considerably boost the value of money wages and can, through collectivised provision, bring benefits that individuals may struggle to obtain alone. Provision can also bring wider unintended or unanticipated benefits. Training provision, if it is good quality, will likely increase productivity to the benefit of employers, but for employees it may also increase the employment prospects of individuals and the wages they are able to command. Employers may then have to provide other rewards in order to retain trained staff in order to avoid freeloader problems (as already discussed).

There is a difference between such general benefits, which may be distributed widely within a company, however, and very selective benefits targeted on one or two workers. Where benefits are very selective, the net result may be that they build resentment amongst workers who are unable to enjoy them. Thus, the unintended consequences of occupational welfare can be negative as well as positive for employers and employees.

There can also be widely variable effects from the very same forms of occupational provision, depending upon the purpose of the provision for the employer. Employer-provided housing, to take one example, may bring real benefits if it is good quality and located in a good area. Better still if employees are free to use housing subsidies in accommodation of their choosing. But if the housing is lower quality and provided only in order to ensure that employees are effectively permanently on-call, the 'diswelfare' effects may far outweigh any benefits. To return to the earlier discussion, the risks of such diswelfare effects increase as we shift the focus away from occupational welfare to general 'perks'. A net effect of a range of perks, from company cars to mobile phones, may only impose greater stress on employees by enabling employers to make more demands upon workers. In this respect, the 'welfare' effects of certain forms of provision may be no greater than the welfare effects that stem from the installation of new machinery in the company.

At its most beneficial, occupational welfare operates to pool various social risks that are associated with the workplace and provides benefits that exceed the effective 'cost' of such provision to the employee. The cost here refers to any reduction in pay that results from occupational provision. Occupational welfare of different forms does not tackle all occupational risks, but it may go some way to ameliorating some of the most important: the risks of older age are reduced by occupational pensions; the risks of sickness are reduced by sickness benefits and/or employer health insurance; the risks associated with family life are reduced through child care facilities; the risks associated with a lack of skills can be combatted through workplace training programmes etc. Some key examples may not even bring any real costs (and can bring real benefits) to employers such as flexible working for families and/or the elderly. What is also important to note here is that occupational welfare also operates to fulfil the needs of employers. A whole range of occupational welfare benefits operate to increase employee productivity, availability, flexibility, and loyalty.

The particular benefits of occupational welfare are likely to be different from employer to employer. This is especially true when it comes to who bears the costs of provision. If the firm operates as a monopoly, it is more likely to be able to push the costs of provision onto consumers. If it operates within a non-unionised sector, it is more likely to be able to push the costs onto employees. If it operates in an area with labour shortages, especially in high-skilled sectors, the company is likely to seek out ways of ensuring that it develops a range of tax-efficient occupational rewards in order to attract and retain workers. This relationship between occupational welfare and firm characteristics is another area that requires further research.

In addition to socialising key risks associated with the workplace, occupational welfare can bring net benefits to workers in various other ways. Employers can often utilise economies of scale to deliver better occupational pensions than could be purchased from individuals from the private sector. In some cases, employers offer more comprehensive forms of cover in certain areas – notably in dental and eye care – that many governments are unwilling or unable to provide.

On the other hand, as already touched upon, occupational welfare is often distributed extremely unevenly, not just between firms, but also often within the same company. And provision tends to favour already privileged workers. In this respect, occupational welfare can have greater divisive effects than other forms of social provision (Mann, 2011, pp. 1–18). In the UK, public sector occupational welfare is more generous and it is more evenly distributed (Farnsworth, 2004). More generally, men tend to obtain greater benefits than women from occupational welfare, especially in the private sector. Thus, occupational welfare inequalities tend to mirror and reinforce wage inequalities (Sinfield, 1978). And just as higher wages for higher paid staff are often afforded out of lower wages for other staff, so are higher occupational benefits for privileged workers often afforded by cutting the benefits of lower paid workers.

While employers and employees play a role in pushing the development (or indeed the demise) of occupational welfare, the state also plays its part. In the UK, for instance, successive governments since the 1980s have sought to place greater emphasis on employers in funding and delivering welfare services that previously the state took responsibility for. During the 1980s and 1990s, Conservative Governments transferred to employers responsibility for first administering and then funding sickness and maternity provision (Dean and Taylor-Gooby, 1990, pp. 47–67; Moss, 1992, pp. 20–31; Taylor-Gooby and Lakeman, 1988, pp. 23–39). In 1997, the Labour Government increased the statutory requirement on employers to make available occupational pensions for employees (Farnsworth and Holden, 2006, pp. 473–94).

This discussion of the variable benefits of occupational welfare provides some clues as to why employers should provide benefits to workers in this way. What is missing so far is any discussion of the role of employees. As might be expected, workers and trade unions have actively pushed for occupational benefits and, in some cases, have themselves established workplace benefit schemes that they operate in partnership with employers (Greve, 2007, p. 64). Moreover, employees and trade unions have lobbied employers hard for provision that provides the widest benefits to workers, especially where state provision is inadequate or non-existent. This is especially true of occupational pension schemes, but it is also true of health schemes in states that rely heavily on private health care. Trade unions are equally likely to oppose non-wage benefits that accrue only to the most privileged within the company. Thus, there tends to be strongest support from employees for occupational welfare where the benefits are more widely distributed and where state provision is low.

There is another problem with occupational welfare as a long-term solution to social risks. The affordability of non-wage benefits is a challenge for companies at certain points in the economic cycle or during certain periods of the corporate 'life-course'. Companies cope with economic challenges, which occur with some regularity, by cutting costs and this often translates into cuts to occupational welfare (see Berkowitz and McQuaid, 1978, pp. 121–22 for a discussion of the impact of the Great Depression on US occupational welfare in the 1930s). Such cuts also have to be made during the most economically difficult times, when claims on provision are likely to be higher.

Measuring occupational welfare

This last section moves on to examine indicators of how comprehensive occupational welfare is within welfare states. Available data are relatively sketchy and are not, for the most part, collected in order to gauge the extent of occupational social provision at all; instead the focus tends to be on trying to establish measures of total employee compensation costs as means of gauging national competitiveness levels. One of the key sources of comparative data is the quadrennial European Labour Costs Survey. This sheds some useful light onto the key forms of occupational welfare within different sectors in different countries.

We begin with an examination of employers' contributions to national insurance contributions (a major statutory form of occupational provision) as a percentage of total labour costs. Table 4.1 illustrates a great deal of variation between countries, but also some consistency over time (between 1997 and 2008). On this measure of statutory occupational welfare, Sweden has amongst the most 'generous' occupational provision with the UK and Denmark having the least generous. Of course, this provision is only part of the equation, we also have to consider the balance between statutory and non-statutory provision, and between tax contributions and direct financial and non-financial benefits delivered through employers.

Figure 4.1 reveals the relative breakdown of different components of total labour costs for the EU15 countries. This reveals the various components that make up the total wage bill in these countries. The final tally doesn't quite equal 100% because of rounding errors. In addition to this, state subsidies effectively reduce the size of the wage bill because they represent income

Table 4.1 Social security paid by employer (% share of total labour costs)

	1997	*1998*	*1999*	*2000*	*2001*	*2002*	2003	*2004*	*2005*	*2006*	*2007*	*2008*
Austria	24.37	24.2	24.15	24.01	23.86	24.18	24.1	24.24	23.98	23.97	23.48	23.32
Czech Republic	25.7	25.6	26	26.6	26.6	26.9	26.9	26.9	26.2	26.1	26.9	:
Denmark	7.14	8.03	7.77	8.13	9.37	9.98	10.61	10.23	10.93	11.59	12.12	:
Estonia	25.95	25.96	25.93	25.5	25.47	25.77	25.42	25.27	25.28	25.08	25.06	25.3
Finland	21.9	21.9	21.8	21.3	21.33	21.12	20.62	20.96	20.85	20.73	20.55	20.26
France	29.15	29.21	29.2	28.85	28.53	28.47	28.6	28.69	28.75	28.55	28.43	28.28
Germany	23.1	23.1	22.8	23.3	23.3	23.3	23.5	23.4	23.1	23.3	22.9	:
Italy	:	:	:	:	29.48	29.51	:	:	:	:	:	:
Latvia	22.57	22.75	22.78	22.43	21.75	21.83	20.75	20.5	20.7	20.6	20.4	20.7
Lithuania	24.7	24.1	24.1	27.6	27.8	27.7	27.8	28.2	28.1	28.2	28.2	:
Luxembrg	14.44	14.73	14.59	13.98	14.03	14.1	14.12	15.37	15.38	15.24	15.22	14.26
Netherlands	20	20.2	20.3	20.4	19.1	20.1	20.6	21.4	21	:	:	:
Poland	16.43	16.52	16.45	16.16	15.99	15.49	:	16.59	16.59	:	:	:
Portugal	20.61	20.12	19.65	19.35	19.8	20.3	20.7	21.2	21.2	21.2	21.2	21.2
Romania	21.66	25.03	28.51	29.88	26.84	25.84	24.8	23.1	24.97	26.12	24.93	:
Slovakia	26.29	26.35	27.61	26.15	26.31	25.39	25.54	25.11	23.74	24.06	24.15	:
Slovenia	17.5	17.8	18.1	14.1	14.5	14.6	14.3	13.01	13.22	13.44	14	:
Spain	24.41	24.42	24.43	24.45	24.62	25.01	24.97	24.89	24.96	24.91	24.97	:
Sweden	29.46	29.46	29.46	29.6	29.6	29.6	29.6	30.56	30.56	30.56	30.56	:
United Kingdom	15.36	15.28	15.4	15.66	15.65	16.13	17.63	18.05	14.92	14.64	14.63	:

Source: Eurostat, 2011. Downloaded 11 Jun 2011 from epp.eurostat.ec.europa.eu/tgm/table.do?tab=table&init=1&plugin=1& language=en&pcode=tps00108.

Compensation and Wage Costs, EU 15															
Wages and Salaries				*Employers' Social Contributions*							*Other non-wage labour costs*				*Total*
Total Wages and Salaries	Direct remuneration	Holiday pay	Other	Total Statutory	Total Voluntary	Voluntary: Sickness	Voluntary: Pensions and Health	Voluntary: Redundancy	Voluntary: Employee savings scheme	Voluntary: Other	**Total Other Non-Wage Costs**	Vocational Training Costs	Other costs (including company cars)	Other Taxes	
75.08	66.99	7.39	0.70	**20.0**	**2.51**	0.98	0.26	0.46	0.62	0.19	**2.15**	0.78	0.75	0.62	99.74

Figure 4.1 Breakdown of wage costs

(which in the EU15 is equal to around 1% of the total wage bill). This reveals that around one fifth of the total wage bill is accounted for by taxation (essentially NI contributions) with a further 10% accounted for by holiday pay plus voluntary social provision (the bulk of occupational welfare). Holiday pay constitutes the single largest cost after statutory social contributions. Sickness is the largest social contribution and the costs of voluntary pensions and health care provision are relatively (and surprisingly) low.

Moving on to individual country provision reveals a great deal of variability in terms of occupational welfare between states. The causes of this variability need to be more fully tested and examined in further studies. There are several possibilities – the strength and demands of trade unions; the sectoral breakdown of the economy (especially between large and small firms and the public and private sectors); the relationship between occupational welfare and pay, etc. One relatively strong determinant of the extent of occupational welfare appears to be the level of statutory provision (Farnsworth, 2004b). The latest evidence from the OECD's Social Expenditure database appears to confirm this. Figure 4.2 plots the relationship between public and private social expenditure. Figure 4.3 reveals more about private expenditure by plotting mandated and voluntary social expenditure. Although the OECD terms this provision 'private' it refers to collective – thus primarily occupational – provision (it excludes, for instance, individually purchased private services). Figure 4.2 suggests that more generous and comprehensive public expenditure results in less generous occupational provision. Figure 4.3 suggests that higher mandated state provision results in lower voluntary provision. As already mentioned, more investigation needs to be carried out, but the strong suggestion from these data is that, for one reason or another, there is a trade-off between occupational and state provision. An increase in one will result in a decrease in the other. Employers will have to bear some responsibility for social provision whether they do so through voluntary means or by statute.

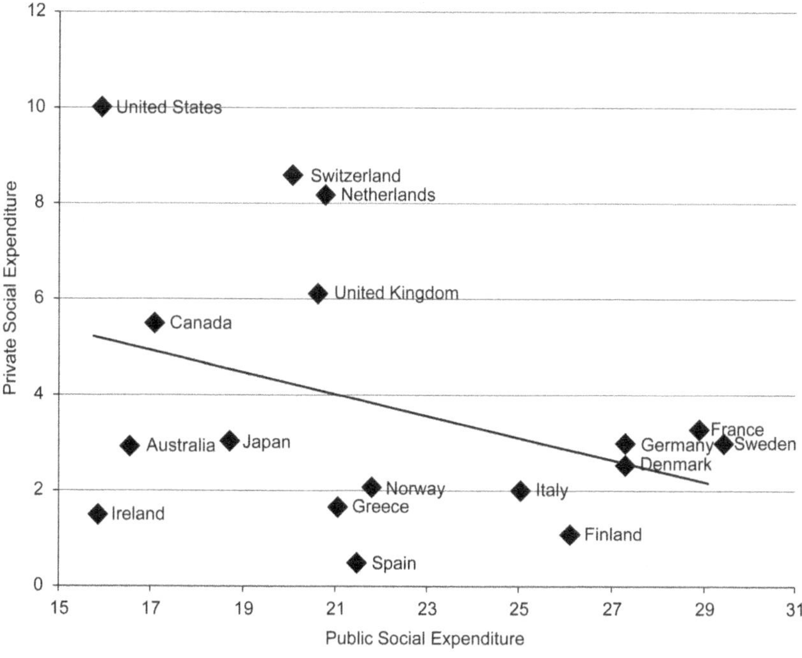

Figure 4.2 Private and public expenditure

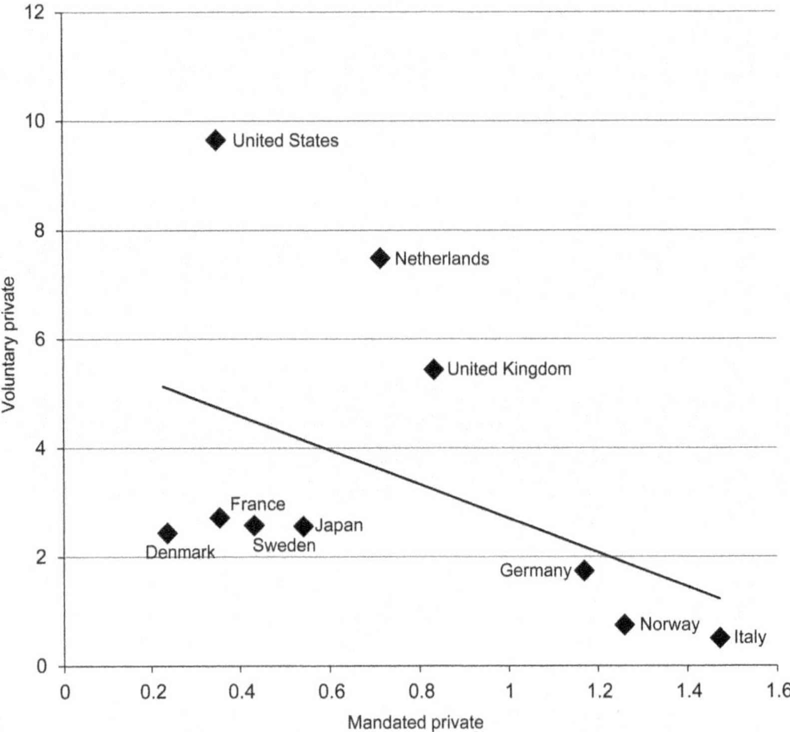

Figure 4.3 Mandated and voluntary occupational provision

Outstanding questions relating to occupational welfare

The above discussion highlights the importance of occupational welfare as a field of study and as an important aspect of the welfare state. However, it also raises a number of important questions.

First of all, although previous work has raised the issue of occupational welfare and equality, what is less clear is what the benefits to the state and for citizens would be of increasing the emphasis on mandated provision. Some governments have attempted to place greater statutory responsibility on employers for occupational pensions (as already noted above) and there is no reason why this could not be extended further. As yet it is unclear whether this would undermine voluntary provision and whether the net benefits would be higher or lower if it did.

A second important question is what is the relationship between occupational welfare and money wages? There is surprisingly little research on the relationship between occupational welfare and pay beyond untested assumptions.

Third, although it is important to distinguish between occupational welfare and other in-work benefits, it is important to investigate the relationship between them. Do certain forms of non-wage benefits divert resources from another?

Fourth, more work is required on the effects of occupational welfare on the productivity and competitiveness of firms.

Fifth, related to this, how does occupational welfare develop in different modes or varieties of capitalism?

Conclusion

Occupational welfare remains an important element of the welfare state. Although it has been a neglected area in social policy, there are signs that it is beginning to come of age as a legitimate and important area of analysis. The discussion above illustrates the complexities that surround it. As austerity moves are put in place by a number of governments in the aftermath of the financial crisis, occupational welfare may yet prove to be more important. But this raises additional questions regarding the total distribution of welfare and whether governments might encourage or shape certain forms of occupational welfare through regulations and/or fiscal incentives. However, if it continues to evolve in the future, students of social policy will need to keep a closer eye on occupational welfare.

Bibliography

de Swaan, A. (1988), *In Care of the State: Health Care, Education and Welfare in Europe and the USA in the Modern Era*. Cambridge: Polity Press.

Hartley, D. and Taylor-Gooby, P. (1990), Statutory Sick Pay and the Control of Sickness Absence, *Journal of Social Policy*, vol. 19, no. 1, pp. 47–67.

Farnsworth, K. (2004), *Corporate Power and Social Policy in Global Context: British Welfare Under the Influence?* Bristol: Policy Press.

——(2004), Welfare through work: An audit of occupational social provision at the turn of the new century. *Social Policy & Administration*, vol. 38, no. 5, pp. 437–55.

Farnsworth, K. and Holden, C. (2006), The business-social policy nexus: Corporate power and corporate inputs into social policy. *Journal of Social Policy*, vol. 35, pp. 473–94.

Fitzgerald, R. (1988), *British Labour Management and Industrial Welfare, 1846–1939*. London: Croom Helm.

Gordon, C. (1991), New Deal, Old Deck: Business and the Origins of Social Security, 1920–1935. *Politics and Society*, vol. 19, no. 2, pp. 15–207.

Graebner, W. (1980), *A History of Retirement: The Meaning and Function of an American Institution*. New York: Yale University Press.

Greve, B. (2007), *Occupational Welfare: Winner and Losers*. Cheltenham: Edward Elgar.

Hay, R. (1977), Employers and Social policy in Britain: The Evolution of welfare legislation, 1905–14. *Social History*, vol. 2, pp. 435–55.

Jones, H. (1983), Employers' Welfare Schemes and Industrial Relations in Inter-War Britain. *Business History*, vol. 25, no. 1, pp. 61–75.

Mann, K. (2011), Remembering and Rethinking the Social Divisions of Welfare: 50 Years On. *Journal of Social Policy*, vol. 38, no. 1, pp. 1–18.

May, M. and Brunsdon, E. (1994), Workplace care in the mixed economy of welfare. *Social Policy Review*, vol. 6, pp. 146–69.

Moss, P. (1992), Employee Child Care – Services for Children, Carers and Employers. *Employee Relations*, vol. 14, no. 6, pp. 20–31.

Papadakis, E. and Taylor-Gooby, P. (1987), *The Private Provision of Public Welfare: State, Market and Community*. Sussex: Wheatsheaf.

Quadagno, J. S. (1984), Welfare Capitalism and the Social Security Act of 1935. *American Sociological Review*, vol. 49, pp. 632–47.

Rein, M. (1983), 'The Social Policy of the Firm'. In *From Policy to Practice*. London: Macmillan Press, pp. 3–22.

——(1996), 'Is America Exceptional? The Role of Occupational Welfare in the United States and the European Community', in M. Shalev (ed.) *The Privatisation of Social Policy*, pp. 27–43. London: Macmillan Press.

Russell, A. (1991), *The Growth of Occupational Welfare in Britain*. Aldershot: Avebury.

Taylor-Gooby, P. and Lakeman, S. (1988), Back to the Future: Statutory Sick Pay, Citizenship and Social Class. *Journal of Social Policy*, vol. 17, no. 1, pp. 23–39.

Titmuss, R. M. (1976), *Essays on the Welfare State*. London: Allan and Unwin.

5
Citizenship

Janet Newman

Introduction

The creation and transformation of Western European welfare states since World War II rests on changing formations of citizenship. This chapter begins by tracing the different welfare 'settlements' that inscribed particular forms and meanings of citizenship. The main body of the chapter traces different ways in which these settlements have been contested. Struggles from 'below' sought to expand citizenship rights and to encompass the claims of feminism and other social movements. But nation states have also attempted to transform citizenship in order to displace or minimise welfare claims and to mitigate patterns of social and cultural exclusion. In addition a series of citizenship struggles – around gendered inscriptions of public and private, around age and generation, and around nationality and migration – continue to disrupt taken for granted meanings and practices of citizenship.

The core concepts that the chapter uses are:

WELFARE SETTLEMENT: The ways in which political, economic, social and organisational lines of contestation were partly and temporarily 'settled' in the formation of welfare states.

CLAIMS AND RIGHTS: The chapter will draw on T. H. Marshall's conception that links citizenship to civil, political, and social rights, but will criticise the evolutionary conception of citizenship which Marshall's conception depends on.

INCLUSION/TRANSFORMATION: The chapter distinguishes between struggles for inclusion into an already established and institutionalised set of rights and struggles for transformations in the meanings and practices of citizenship.

ACTIVE CITIZENSHIP: new discourses and practices emerged as welfare states sought to enhance 'choice', to promote inclusion through work, to foster democratic renewal and to shift responsibility for welfare provision away from the state and onto citizens themselves.

PUBLIC/PRIVATE: One of the most significant struggles for transformation has been that emerging from second-wave feminism. This successfully (in some states) brought issues previously considered to be private and personal – issues of care, sexuality, and domestic violence, for example – into the public domain of citizenship and thus legitimate objects of concern for social welfare.

BORDERS AND BOUNDARIES: Global patterns of migration have served to challenge the integrity of the nation as the territorial basis of citizen claims and rights, generating in turn simultaneous loosening and tightening of national boundaries and opening up new cycles of struggles for inclusion and rights.

The rise of European welfare states is generally associated with the emergence of class settlements between 'labour' and 'capital', in which legitimacy for the economic interests of capital was won by the provision of political rights and welfare resources for working classes. This political-economic settlement was sustained by Keynesian policies that supported the expansion of state welfare, and that enabled the accretion of social rights on top of a foundation of political and civic rights (see Marshall, 1950). But in *The Managerial State* (1997) John Clarke and I argue that welfare states were founded not only on this political-economic settlement but also on a social settlement based on a gendered divisions of labour and care. In Britain and some other nations welfare was predominantly accessed through the rights of the male 'breadwinner', reflecting the historical conception of citizenship as a male preserve. Of course the social settlement based on gendered divisions of labour varied between nation states, with Scandinavian countries offering a more women-friendly conception of welfare, while in many Catholic-dominated nations women were able to access welfare through their rights as mothers, a very partial conception of citizenship. The social settlement was also racialised, with strong assumptions about the equivalence between national citizenship rights and ethnicity – assumptions that were inscribed not only in policies and institutions but also in the everyday norms of service providers (Lewis, 2000). This was particularly marked in nations with strong colonial histories, including the UK: citizenship rights within the nation state, this suggests, is marked by the racialised exclusions of others. This is perhaps why changing patterns of migration have presented both cultural and economic challenges to the legitimacy of welfare states.

These social settlements were significantly challenged by the social movements of the 1970s and beyond: feminism, service user and patient movements, movements of disabled people, migrants and asylum seekers, mental health service users, carers, and others. Some such struggles were for inclusion: struggles for access to the citizenship rights that would enable access to existing welfare provision. Some, however, were also struggles for transformation – both in the meanings of citizenship and in the practices of welfare provision. Some of the transformations that have taken place, including second-wave feminism, both appropriated the language of citizenship to argue for acceptance of women as full economic and political subjects, but also sought to transform its meaning to include issues of sexuality, care, and informal labour. The disability movement has also pursued both kinds of struggle, arguing that disabled people should be regarded as autonomous, rights-bearing citizens rather than as dependent subjects of a benevolent welfare state, whilst also offering ways of re-inflecting 'care' and 'citizenship' with ethical and moral ideals that take it beyond the limitations of legal and political rights. Finally some of the most significant transformations have arisen through the flourishing of participatory forms of democracy: this has not only changed the meaning of the 'political' but has also helped transform professional/service-user relationships around notions of user involvement, the recognition of user expertise, and the 'coproduction' of services.

These transformations mean that citizenship now results in much more than a collection of civic, political, and social rights. It is the basis for multiple claims and offers sources of inclusion, belonging, and identity; a practice of participation and action; a performance of collective and individual political practice; and a discursive resource that enables new claims and identities to be mobilised (Coll, 2010). The work of transformation has been conducted not just by individual citizens but also by policy actors, welfare professionals, care workers, and those in non-governmental organizations (NGOs) and voluntary bodies. It is no longer possible to ignore the ways in which such groups exercise their own citizenship to bring about social and organisational change (Barnes and Prior, 2010).

But as welfare states began to feel pressure, not only from global economic forces but also from demographic change and rising citizen expectations, so change also began to come about from 'above'. That is, governments sought to transform the meanings and practices of citizenship in order to pursue projects of modernisation and reform. Therefore four particular political projects sought to install new meanings and practices of 'active' citizenship. The first concerns the *worker citizen*. Here equality and inclusion are deemed to flow not from state action but from the economic benefits accruing from labour market participation (van Berkel and Valkenburg, 2007). This is both an economic and cultural argument. Economically, work provides income and opportunities for social mobility; moreover it is viewed as a means of breaking cycles of poverty in which those without work (for example, lone mothers) inculcate the habit of worklessness on their children, thus reproducing dependence on welfare and unemployment benefits. Work is also viewed as a cultural and social benefit, inculcating social inclusion, health, well-being, and even happiness. But the discourse of work as the route to citizenship is based on its own exclusions and erasures. Some of these are based on the definition of paid work: unpaid labour (for example informal care) is not included; others (volunteering) are highly valued by governments but do not 'count' as employment. And the discourse of work as a route to social inclusion and the resolution of equality claims, especially of women but also of disabled people, people with learning disabilities, those with long-term sickness and others, erases the processes through which paid work might be the route to greater hardship. That is, the idea that work serves as the principal route to inclusion and equality does not take account of the intensifications of inequality produced by work itself. The consequences of de-regulation, privatization, contracting out to off-shore providers, flexibilisation, and other trends are profound, and further limit the power of trade unions to protect workers. The growth of marginal and peripheral workforces operating in the 'grey economy' maps uneasily onto existing patterns of marginal/peripheral citizenship (for example the use of 'illegal immigrants' in industries of exploitation). This reminds us that the attempt to form a new economic settlement for a global age based around the worker citizen rests on particular images of the nation and the maintenance of its borders (Soysal, 1994).

The second political project concerns the constitution of the *citizen consumer*. As welfare states matured and became subject to neo-liberalising forces so the idea of welfare citizens as clients and dependents of the state became challenged; the citizen consumer emerged as a key figure around which claims from below were accommodated and through which state projects of marketisation could be pursued.

The citizen consumer as an ideal governmental figure emerged most clearly in nations associated with 'neoliberal' formations of welfare, but is also evident in many other nations within Europe. Its attraction for governments is twofold. First, it offers a new form of legitimacy for public services in which power is invested in the citizen rather than in the state professional. The citizen consumer can thus, it is imagined, drive change 'from below'. This can be understood as a response to some of the 'transformational' claims noted above; citizens are offered more rights, enhanced flexibility, and services more tailored to individual needs and preferences by taking on the identity of consumer. The proliferation of new claims and demands can thus be deflected. Second, the citizen consumer helps drive through market-based reforms, whether purchaser provider splits within the public sector or the transfer of services to private sector providers. The citizen consumer is thus detached from the solidaristic and collective foundations on which welfare states were created; they become individuals bearing the right to choose between providers and the entitlement to high-quality services rather than a member of a social body founded on mutuality and membership. There have been many telling critiques of the consumer model of citizenship (Clarke et al., 2007; Needham, 2003), not only drawing attention to these individualising pressures, but also to the failure of consumer-driven services to act in the wider public interest or to address issues of inequality: consumerism assumes equality of access to knowledge (who provides the best service), voice (willingness to push one's own claim), and networks (how can I get access to what I want).

Alongside and somewhat in tension with the consumer citizen is the image of the *participating citizen*, linked to conceptions of democratic renewal, local involvement and co-production (Fung and Wright, 2003; Cornwall and Coehlo, 2004). The participatory imperative varied across European welfare states (see the seven-nation study in Newman and Tonkens, 2011), with different emphases on locality-based and policy-related participation, and with citizens being summoned to greater or lesser degrees as service users, consumers, community members, and members of the public. But across these categories we saw a proliferation of deliberative forums such as citizens' panels, citizens' juries, service user consultations, governance boards, and evaluation projects. Governments also turned to web-based and other technologies to expand opportunities for participation. This turn to collaborative governance has diverse origins, bridging concerns about the health of civil society, the decline of trust between governments and people, the performance of services, and problems of social exclusion.

But the opening up of new spaces of participation outside the domain of formal politics is taking place in parallel to an erasure of space where collective claims making practices take place. Enhancing participation – both of service users and of citizens in local communities – is a central concern of policymakers, but in the process activist notions of citizenship tend to disappear from view (Newman and Tonkens, 2011). And the focus on local participation fosters particular forms of identity and action; local citizenship serves to displace the focus on common membership of a wider public sphere of decision-making and judgement. It can also serve to intensify the exclusion of groups that local residents view as 'outsiders', or as 'not belonging here'. It might be argued that participation exercises tend to be focused more on issues of social inclusion and cohesion than on fostering citizenship and democracy. But at the same time new patterns of global participation – on environmental issues, poverty, and struggles against human rights abuses – stretch the concept of citizenship beyond the national state, the institution within which citizenship claims have traditionally been pursued and rights granted.

The fourth political project of active citizenship is concerned with the constitution of *responsible citizenship*. Responsibility is not a 'new' dimension of citizenship but is already invested in liberal conceptions of the state. But as welfare states seek to reduce expenditure, citizens are increasingly being asked to provide for their own care and welfare, to contribute to their neighbourhoods, to sustain their own health and well-being rather than relying on the state, and to engage in voluntary and philanthropic activity. This invokes a communitarian concept of citizenship which privileges notions of ethical and moral, rather than rights-based, judgements. Notions of reciprocity and social capital are overlaid on liberal (consumerist or rights-based) and republican (participative and democratic) models of citizenship inscribed in welfare provision (see Johansson and Hvinden, 2007, for definitions). We need, however, to take account of important differences between the kinds of responsibility being devolved to citizens in different services, sectors, and countries (economic, consumerist, democratic, and developmental). It is also important to examine the dynamic ways in which responsibility is 'shared' between state and citizen, with the state often taking on additional roles in empowerment, development, and regulation as well as moving towards coercion, conditionality, and/or retreat. Finally critiques of responsibilisation begin from a given set of responsibilities enshrined in welfare states that are now being devolved or shed through neo-liberal or communitarian political projects. They thus fail to address the relational, affective, and ethical forms of responsibility inscribed in feminist-inflected conceptions of citizenship itself.

Citizenship struggles

The four discourses traced in the preceding section are not imposed onto static and settled formations of European citizenship. Rather, they are overlaid onto existing patterns of contestation and struggle over the boundaries to, and meanings of, citizenship. Citizen participation is viewed in many of the countries of Western Europe as a means of overcoming welfare dependency, and of ensuring that older people and other welfare users take an active part in society, thus enhancing their health and well-being. It is also viewed as a means of enhancing local democracy and overcoming social exclusion. But participation cannot be considered solely as a set of governmental discourses: it also denotes a wide range of struggles for inclusion into and for the transformation of the public sphere, whether local, regional, national, or transnational. Such struggles have, in part, been transformed through the rise of new media and web-based technologies, but are usually mediated by a range of professional and governance actors who, of course, each bring their own citizenship to bear (Barnes and Prior, 2009). Many such actors have been very concerned to expand the range of voices that can be heard in policy and service delivery, and thus have taken measures to tolerate a wider range of forms of expression.

One key struggle has been that of gender. Lister (2003) and others have noted the difficulty of reconciling classic notions of citizenship with changing definitions of public and private. Citizenship 'belongs' to and takes place in a public sphere defined through its opposition to the personal and private domains – domains associated with women's agency in home, neighbourhood, and community. The classic forms of participation – through representative democracy – invoke a gender-neutral sense of personhood. However, feminist critiques of the public/private distinction highlight ways in which the public sphere of participation has been one to which women have struggled to gain access. Although women won formal rights to vote, to hold public office, to take their place in the civil service, professions, and business, their citizenship remains more closely tied to the social and personal realms than the economic or political, though this takes different forms in the welfare settlements of different European nations (Siim, 2000; Lister et al., 2007). The concept of responsibility that was outlined earlier remains one that oscillates between women's social and caring responsibilities in the home and community on the one hand, and women's social and caring responsibilities as front-line workers in welfare services on the other. The balance may shift over time, but does not significantly disrupt the gendered associations of responsibility. From a different perspective the proliferation of opportunities to participate in public service provision and public policy suggests a reframing of public and personal, such that new forms of voice and new modes of expression can now be recognised. This acknowledges feminist arguments about recognition and respect (Young, 1990); the voicing of personal experience is now valued by public authorities as a means of assessing the effectiveness of service provision and for enhancing local involvement in decision making. But enhanced voice and enhanced responsibility may sit uneasily with each other. For example Barnes (2011) traces how the development of a carers' movement has resulted in the elaboration of new social policies directed towards supporting and 'empowering' carers, but also suggests that the claims of social movements and the official discourse exist in an uneasy relationship. In particular the relational notions of responsibility in the context of care conflict with the more limited conception of consumer responsibility dominant in current policy.

Issues of age, generation and disability intersect with questions of the boundary between access to the public domain of rights and responsibilities. The recognition of children's rights has opened up research and debates on children's citizenship (Invernizzi and Williams, 2008; Willow et al., 2004). The emergence of strong disability movements has given rise to struggles for recognition and rights made in the name of adult citizenship (rather than dependent status) alongside research and debate on issues of voice, engagement, and participation (Beckett, 2006). Citizenship is also a discourse through which issues of older people's exclusion might be addressed (Craig, 2004). But such debates are increasingly taking place within a context in which access to rights and services can no longer be contained inside the nation state. Ackers and Dwyer (2002) debate citizenship questions raised by increasing post-retirement migration within the European Union (EU), and the problems of access to welfare in nations other than those in which social security contributions were made.

But the citizenship struggles that have been at the forefront of political debate – and that prefigured the rise of populist political movements across Europe – has centred on the contested place of nation and nationality as the basis for citizenship. The Marshallian framework of citizenship was firmly based on the nation state as the source of both recognition and rights. It is national belonging that has formed the basis of citizenship identity, and nationality that has been the basis for citizenship status. But a variety of globalising economic, cultural, and spatial dynamics have disrupted the coherence of nationhood and nationality. Soysel (1994) argued that what was emerging was a 'post-national' conception of citizenship based on personhood and human rights; a conception that 'superseded the dichotomy that opposes the national citizen and the alien ... rights that used to belong solely to nationals, thereby undermining the very basis of national citizenship' (2004, p. 137). However a few years later John Clarke and I traced the contours of what we termed a 're-nationalisation' of citizenship resulting from the attempt by nation states to 'defend' themselves from multiple threats: threats to the sustainability of welfare states in the face of pressures from 'migrant' populations; threats to national cohesion and the solidarities on which welfare states had been built; and threats to security linked, in no small part, to the rise of the category 'Muslim' and its constitution as both 'other' and 'danger' (Newman and Clarke, 2009). Projects of 'securitisation' (Huysmans, 2006) are associated with the intensification of the management of borders, boundaries, and populations; and 'problem populations' have been subject to increased forms of surveillance and regulation. At the same time the moves, through much of the late twentieth century, to recognize 'difference' (for example in notions of multiculturalism) have been challenged by an intensified concern with integration and assimilation. 'Through such changes', we argued, 'citizenship' is being re-nationalized. The citizen is being revived as a figure of nation-building/nation-securing programmes. S/he is being invested with a history, values, and a culture that must be 'shared'. Citizenship is being increasingly viewed as a form of recruitment that is calculative, cultural, and disciplinary (Newman and Clarke, 2009, p. 172).

Conclusion

This chapter has traced the evolution of welfare citizenship from a gradual accretion of political, economic, and social rights to a series of cultural projects concerned with the remaking and governance of populations. It has traced a range of political projects concerned with constituting various forms of 'active' citizen – the worker citizen, the participating citizen, the citizen consumer, the responsible citizen – each of which is integral to current programmes of welfare state retrenchment. The chapter has also traced different axes of struggle and contestation: those of gender, age, and national belonging. It has brought into question the notion of a clearly defined public sphere in which citizenship is exercised, and has challenged the coherence of the nation state as the basis both of rights and responsibilities. Challenges to the nation state produced by global flows of people, resources, and both evoke greater openness and fluidity of citizenship as membership or identity, but have also generated projects of 're-nationalisation' and the closure of borders and boundaries. Citizenship, it seems, is likely to continue to be the focus of struggles for recognition and rights, as well as the site of projects of assimilation and exclusion.

Bibliography

Ackers, L. and Dwyer, P. (2002), *Senior Citizenship? Retirement, Migration and Welfare in the European Union*. Bristol: Policy Press.

Barnes, J. and Prior, D. (eds) (2009), *Subversive Citizens: Power, Agency and Resistance in Public Services*. Bristol: Policy Press.

Barnes, M. (2011), 'Caring Responsibilties: The Making of Citizen Carers', in J. Newman and E. Tonkens (eds), *Participation, Responsibility and Choice: Summoning the Active Citizen in Western European Welfare States*. Amsterdam: University of Amsterdam Press.

Barnes, M., Newman, J., and Sullivan, H. (2007), *Power, Participation and Political Renewal*. Bristol: Policy Press.

Beckett, A. (2006), *Citizenship and Vulnerability: Disability and Issues of Social and Political Engagement*. Basingstoke: Palgrave.

Clarke, J. and Newman, J. (1997), *The Managerial State: Power, Politics and Ideology in the Remaking of Social Welfare*. London: Sage.

Clarke, J., Newman, J., Smith, N., Vidler, E., and Westmarland, L. (2007), *Creating the Citizen Consumer*. London: Sage.

Coll, C. (2010), *Remaking Citizenship*. Stanford, CA: Stanford University Press.

Cornwall, A. and Coehlo, V. (eds) (2004), *Spaces for Change: The Politics of Citizen Participation in New Democratic Arenas*. London: Zed Books.

Craig, G. (2004), Citizenship, Exclusion and Older People. *Journal of Social Policy*, vol. 33, no. 1, pp. 95–114.

Fung, A. and Wright, E. O. (2003), *Deepening Democracy: Institutional Innovations in Empowered Participatory Governance*. London: Verso.

Huysmans, J. (2006), *The Politics of Insecurity: Fear, Migration and Asylum in the EU*. London: Routledge.

Invernizzi, A. and Williams, J. (2008), *Children and Citizenship*. London: Sage.

Johannson, H. and Hvinden, B. (2007), 'What do we mean by active citizenship?', in B. Hvinden and H. Johannson (eds), *Citizenship in Nordic Welfare State: Dynamics of Choice, Duties and Participation in Changing Europe*. London: Routledge.

Lewis, G. (2000), *'Race', Gender and Social Welfare: Encounters in a Post Colonial Society*. Cambridge: Polity.

Lister, R. (2003), *Citizenship: Feminist Perspectives* (2nd edn). Basingstoke: Palgrave Macmillan.

Lister, R., Williams, F., Anttonen, A., Bussemaker, J., Gerhard, U., Heinen, J., Johannson, S., Leira, A., and Siim, B. (2007), *Gendering Citizenship in Western Europe*. Bristol: Policy Press.

Marshall, T. H. (1950), *Citizenship and Social Class*. Cambridge: Cambridge University Press.

Needham, C. (2003), *Citizen-Consumers: New Labour's Market-Place Democracy*. London: Catalyst.

Newman, J. and Clarke, J. (2009), *Publics, Politics and Power: Remaking the Public in Public Services*. London: Sage

Newman, J. and Tonkens, E., (eds) (2011), *Participation, Responsibility and Choice: Summoning the Active Citizen in Western European Welfare States*. Amsterdam: University of Amsterdam Press.

Siim, B. (2000), *Gender and Citizenship: Politics and Agency in France, Britain, and Denmark*. Cambridge: Cambridge University Press.

Soysal, Y. (1994), *Limits of Citizenship: Migrants and Postnational Membership in Europe*. Chicago, IL: Chicago University Press.

van Berkel, R. and Valkenberg, B. (2007), *Making it Personal: Individualising Activation Services in the EU*. Bristol: Policy Press.

Willow, C., Marchant, R., Kirby, P., and Neale, B. (2004), *Young Children's Citizenship: Ideas into Practice*. York: Joseph Rowntree.

Young, I. M. (1990), *Justice and the Politics of Difference*. Princeton, NJ: Princeton University Press.

6

Prevention

The cases of social security and healthcare

Jos Berghman, Annelies Debels, and Ine Van Hoyweghen

In the member states of the European Union (EU) social security and healthcare systems have become important institutions. The welfare state – of which social security and healthcare represent the core and cornerstones – might even be considered to be one of the characteristics of these European states and societies. Yet these systems are not only very important institutions; they are also dynamic ones. During the last decades they have in fact been subject to far-reaching changes, in their practical operation but even more so in the reasoning about them. One of the discoveries has been the possible relevance of prevention and preventive action. But before dealing with the ins and outs of prevention we need some further clarifications on social protection, its major instruments, and logics

Social protection and risk

In social protection traditionally two kinds of instruments are distinguished. Firstly there are replacement income schemes that are intended to secure an income in case primary earnings are interrupted as, for example, in the case of unemployment, sickness, or retirement. Secondly there are adjustment income schemes that are intended to meet exceptional expenditures such as, for example, those connected with children or medical care. Yet these systems are not magnanimous; they transfer income to beneficiaries only because a reason is found to do so (Gilbert et al., 1993). There are in fact two reasons – or bases of allocation, as they are called – that can be distinguished:

- Recognized social contingencies which are crucial for insurance-based schemes; and
- Need, which may open eligibility in assistance-like schemes.

As the core social protection systems are insurance based it is worthwhile to have first a closer look at the characteristics of insurances. The core idea of private insurance is to spread a particular risk over many shoulders on the basis of an equitable actuarial relationship. In this context 'risk' refers to the combined effect of two aspects, the first one being the probability (P) by which a contingency will occur and the second one being the amount of damage (D) that will result when the contingency occurs. The risk (R) can then be calculated as the product of the probability and the damage.

$$R = P \times D$$

In order to guarantee that the damage can be covered adequately when the contingency occurs, actuarial equity requires that the insurance contributions are calculated according to the risk that is covered. Thus the insurance technique aims at guaranteeing that every insured person can be sure of getting the real damage compensated on condition that his or her contributions may be set at a level that corresponds to the risk he or she runs.

In schemes of the social insurance-type, benefits are granted automatically when the envisaged social contingency occurs. With the latter as basis of allocation no test of need has to be applied by way of an income or means test. This characteristic of social insurance schemes explains the overwhelming enthusiasm with which early mutual aid initiatives and, later on, social insurances were welcomed (Rimlinger, 1971; Heclo, 1974).

The second basis of allocation is need. It is used in assistance schemes – originally this referred to private and public practices to grant help to people in need. These practices used to be of a voluntary, facultative, and discretionary character. Nowadays, however, entitlement to social assistance has been operationalized in many countries within the law, and the benefit levels have to some extent been standardized. Yet the benefit amount continues to be dependent upon assessed need, even though in the end it is not *need* as such but *income and means* that are assessed. It goes without saying that schemes of the social assistance type focus on minimum income protection.

An important breakthrough: prevention

On the whole social security policy and thinking have remained highly influenced by traditional social security definitions that begin with an enumeration of social contingencies and go on to describe which programmes and schemes have to be included under that cover (Pieters, 1993). Yet the quite one-dimensional focus on curative policy instruments has been highly criticized (Berghman et al., 2002). Also preventive instruments have to be taken into account.

Reparation and prevention

The central role that preventive action should play in social security has been revealed by Viaene, van Steenberge, and Lahaye by applying damage theory to social protection (Viaene et al., 1993). They argue that social security lies first of all in the prevention, afterwards in the reparation, and finally in the compensation of human damage (see Table 6.1). The core of this logic is their proposition that human damage has to be kept as minimal as possible. Hence the prevention of damage should get absolute priority over the indemnification of it. Only when a

Table 6.1 Human damage theory

Policy	*Reality*	*Policy*
Prevention (1)	Human damage $R=P\times D$	Indemnification reparation (2) compensation (3)

reasonable input of appropriate medical and situational instruments cannot prevent damage from arising should indemnification be pursued. In their reasoning, indemnification refers both to the reparation of damage and the compensation of irreparable damage. Since compensation only represents a palliative, unable to remove the existing damage, reparation should always get priority over compensation. However, when these ideas are confronted with the existing social security systems, policies, and budgets, one finds an illogicality. Instead of making the existing compensatory schemes as redundant as possible, in reality priority is given to the income transfer schemes, to the detriment of reparative and preventive action (Berghman, 1997).

Not only in social security policies but also in social security thinking, the importance of preventive actions has remained highly undervalued. And yet the existing social security schemes do not enhance social security; they only help to mitigate the level of social insecurity that has emerged. Social security consists first of all in making available work opportunities that may guarantee an appropriate income level and of healthy living conditions. Only in the second place should the traditional curative social security and healthcare provisions play a role.

The last decades have made it abundantly clear that labour opportunities are of the utmost importance in this connection. Yet the elaboration of active employment policies is far from easy. Nevertheless, elaborating these kinds of preventive social security policies seems unavoidable in order to safeguard the broader societal function of the social protection system (Berghman et al., 2002).

The basic social policy chain

This function can best be explained by pointing to the logical chain that underpins social policy. This logical chain holds that we educate and train people to secure that they could be adequately inserted into the (paid) labour market. Such an insertion would give them the opportunity to gain a primary income, and this income in turn enables them to have command over resources to guarantee their social participation. Yet when this logical chain is interrupted because of unemployment, incapacity to work, or old age, social protection systems operate to provide replacement income in order not to endanger social participation. Meanwhile restorative actions like healthcare, work mediation, retraining, and even partial reemployment schemes are activated with an aim to secure a quick reinsertion in the labour market, restoring the logical chain. When both these reinsertion devices and the income protection schemes are inadequate, however, the risk of social exclusion – of deficient social participation – materializes (Berghman, 1997).

So, for as far as the core replacement income schemes are concerned, and as is illustrated in Figure 6.1, social security basically operates as a bypass mechanism in those cases where insertion in the labour force is no longer possible or desirable. In such cases its aim is to mend the chain by guaranteeing the availability of (replacement) income in order to safeguard social participation. One may even argue that replacement income schemes all cover the same basic social risk, i.e. incapacity to work. In the case of unemployment the risk materializes because there is no work; in the case of sickness and invalidity because there is no work capacity. Taking

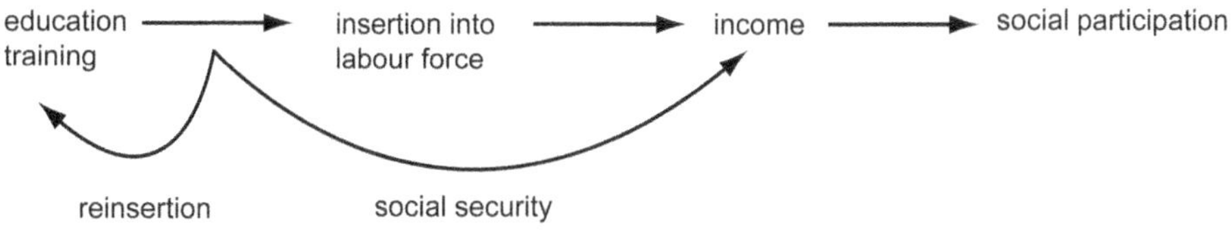

Figure 6.1 Basic social policy chain

into account the way pension schemes were introduced, they must be classified as a particular form of invalidity schemes in which incapacity to work is presumed as soon as the pensionable age is reached and hence any proof of incapacity is no longer used as entitlement condition. Prevention in social protection should then in the first place focus on limiting the prevalence and consequences of 'incapacities to work'.

Prevention in social protection

The most logical and efficient policy approach according to human damage theory would be to aim for prevention first, then for reparation and only finally for compensation. However, in this section a more subtle picture emerges. It is pointed out that prevention can be achieved at not just one, but at three stages in the basic social policy chain (see Figure 6.1). The first stage of prevention coincides with the concept of prevention as in human damage theory and aims at avoiding social contingencies such as unemployment, illness, and disability from happening. In terms of the insurance formula it aims at lowering the probability 'P'. This will henceforth be called primary prevention. The second stage of prevention coincides with the concept of repair in human damage theory: it intervenes after the social contingency has occurred, but aims at restoring the original situation as swiftly as possible, so at limiting the damage 'D' in the insurance formula. It is also prevention as it prevents further damage caused by longer-term exclusion from the labour market. It is therefore called secondary prevention. Third, prevention may also be achieved via the bypass mechanism in the basic social policy chain, by providing compensation for the damage done. This is called tertiary prevention, because it avoids further downward spirals of social exclusion.

Primary prevention policies

The prevention of unemployment and labour market exclusion requires an understanding of the mechanisms causing it. These mechanisms are the subject of debate among economists. For an overview we refer to O'Sullivan and Sheffrin (2003). Generally speaking, three strategies can be discerned: 1) focusing prevention at the supply side, for example by changing the characteristics and skills of labour supply; 2) focusing prevention with respect to the functioning of the labour market, for example by diminishing existing labour market institutions; and 3) focusing prevention at the demand side, for example in a Keynesian sense by boosting job creation.

With respect to the first strategy, there is large consensus that initial education is a decisive factor in the prevention of unemployment at the individual level. The higher educated earn more than the lower educated and also have lower chances of unemployment (Psacharopoulos and Patrinos, 2004; OECD, 2010). However, will investments in initial education also lead to lower unemployment at the aggregate level? The answer to this question is less clear, because general efforts to raise educational skills may result in an inflation of degrees. Still, most agree that a highly educated labour force is a major advantage in knowledge-based societies and in view of the rapid technological changes and restructurings facing current economies (see the discussion on the transitional labour market in Schmid and Gazier, 2002). In particular, initial education provides workers with the skills required to be able to learn new things and to adjust swiftly in later life (de Koning, 2007a).

Another important question in this respect is whether prevention of unemployment through investments in initial education is cost effective. Generally speaking, the rate of return from initial education tends to be high with benefits exceeding costs, both for individuals and for society (OECD, 2010). The benefits arise because unemployment can be avoided, and because education leads to higher earnings and more derived taxes for governments. A further important finding in this literature is that the rate of return to investments in human capital is highest at pre-school age and declines rapidly afterwards. This is because the cognitive abilities of children are more malleable at young ages. Proper early education and high-quality childcare facilities start an upward spiral of cumulating advantages by facilitating later learning (Esping-Andersen, 2009). Moreover, the returns to investments in early education are higher for children with the lowest socio-economic backgrounds (Currie, 2001; Cunha et al., 2006).

Another part of the debate has focused on whether labour market institutions intended to protect workers (e.g. with minimum wages and unemployment benefits), pushing their wages above the market clearing level and thus leading to unemployment. Yet, the idea that plain deregulation is a panacea for unemployment has increasingly been abandoned. For example, Nickell and Layard (1999) have shown that the positive correlation between generous unemployment benefits and the unemployment rate is offset by active labour market policies (ALMPs). Moreover, the unemployment rate seems to be influenced in important ways by product market regulation and fiscal and monetary restrictions (e.g. Krueger and Pischke, 1997). Blau and Kahn (2002) have integrated much of this literature by arguing that it is an interaction between macro-economic demand shocks and labour market institutions that causes unemployment. Prevention policies should hence be adjusted accordingly. In a sense, this is what active labour market policies do, as they embody a wide range of programmes (Kluve et al., 2007): training programs, wage placement or self-employment subsidies, job creation schemes in the public sector, and services and sanctions that support job search efficiency. The ALMPs will be further discussed under secondary prevention, as a lot of these schemes address the already unemployed.

Secondary prevention policies

Although ALMPs have become the new buzz word of the latest decades, and spending on this type of policies has increased substantially, their effectiveness is sometimes debatable (Kluve et al., 2007; OECD, 2007), see also Chapter 12. The major conclusion of ALMP-programme evaluations is that the effectiveness of the programmes depends on the details of the program. First, it depends strongly on the type of programme involved: while job search assistance and monitoring are particularly effective, public job creation schemes are not (de Koning, 2007b). Second, it depends on the way in which the programme has been implemented: it is important to keep the programmes well targeted (and hence small scale), of short duration, and closely monitored (Martin and Grubb, 2001). Third, the effectiveness depends on the characteristics of the participants: they tend to work for women, but not for (out-of-school) youths.

Even if ALMPs are successful and lead to (re)integration on the labour market, there is no guarantee that they also entail genuine social integration. This is because labour market participation does not lock out working poverty nor precarious labour market conditions. There is some evidence that jobs especially created to reduce unemployment run a higher risk of being bad jobs (e.g. Martin and Grubb, 2001). In other words, there is a fundamental problem with the exclusive focus on jobs and labour market integration in primary and secondary prevention policies. A more integrated policy approach is needed that alongside education and employment also includes aspects of child, family, health, housing, care, and wellbeing policy.

Tertiary prevention policies

From the above discussion, it was already clear that primary and secondary prevention do not always work. In fact, societies are usually confronted with a residual group of unemployed who cannot easily be activated (van Berkel and Hornemann, 2004). So, when employment policy and ALMPs fail, there is still need for a compensatory policy. The latter type of policy is usually not considered to be preventive policy, but here we argue why it should be. In particular, social benefits can prevent the start of a downward spiral of social exclusion. Social exclusion is indeed often the result of cumulating and mutually reinforcing economic and social disadvantages (Gallie and Paugam, 2000).

Furthermore, replacement incomes have a preventive effect on longer-term unemployment, because they support individual investments in job search by decreasing the constant worries of daily survival. Yet at the same time high and unconditional benefits – i.e. so-called passive policies – may generate unemployment and productivity traps (de Koning, 2007).

However, the tightening of eligibility conditions raises a number of normative issues. In particular, they cannot be justified when it is not sure whether activated individuals are in a position to respond adequately to such prevention policies (Dubois, 2011). This may not be the case, for example, when a lack of aggregate demand is driving unemployment, when the individuals have to deal with discrimination on the labour market, or when they are faced with problems beyond their own control, such as handicaps or complex situations of social exclusion from which they can not escape under their own initiative.

Prevention in healthcare

Finally, let us see how prevention works out in that other part of social protection – i.e. the adjustment schemes – with healthcare as the main and instructive representative.

Healthcare academics and policy makers increasingly acknowledge that they can no longer rely on treatment-oriented strategies alone, but that new strategies are needed to prevent disease. While traditional preventive interventions such as pure water and food, hygiene, and vaccination have been fully exploited in Western countries, recent programmes in healthcare reflect a preventive approach in the form of more individualized prevention programmes, such as lifestyle interventions and risk factor screening. Many costly and disabling conditions – cardiovascular diseases, cancer, diabetes, and chronic respiratory diseases – are linked by common preventable risk factors, such as smoking, unhealthy nutrition, physical inactivity, and excessive alcohol consumption. Moreover, it has been suggested that preventive interventions targeted at lifestyle-related risk factors have the potential of not only increasing public health but at the same time lowering healthcare expenditures (OECD, 2005) or reducing mortality at a lower cost (Maciosek et al., 2006). With the shift from treatment to prevention, preventive action in healthcare is considered to combine the best of both worlds: sound healthcare spending with a healthier population.

Lifestyles

This emphasis on investing in prevention programmes in healthcare has been accompanied by the development of so-called 'prevention policies' (Dubois, 2011) – i.e. insurance policies constructed to give incentives to investments in prevention or promote desirable behaviour and thereby reduce reliance on insurance. Some health policy academics have suggested for assigning larger responsibility for health to individuals to contain costs through rewarding healthy lifestyles in health insurance. In particular, health insurance premiums are commonly related to smoking and body mass index (BMI) as an indicator of obesity, and private and social healthcare insurers have increasingly turned to policies that rely on coinsurance and deductibles, or various forms of incentive-based healthcare plans and bonus policies (Ter Meulen and Maarse,

2008; Schmidt et al., 2010). Apart from rewarding healthy lifestyles, prevention policies can also be directed to targeting bad lifestyle behaviour in insurance. In the Netherlands, the Healthcare Insurance Board and the Council for Public Health and Care recently introduced the idea of a sharpening of individual responsibilities in healthcare. Those who have a bad lifestyle (i.e. smoking, excessive alcohol consumption, obesity) should pay more insurance premium, it is argued.

Debates and evidence

Yet the elaboration of lifestyle prevention programmes in healthcare and prevention policies is far from self evident. Currently, these preventive initiatives in healthcare are the topic of many debates. For example, it is questionable whether prevention programmes and incentives work at the individual level. Over the years, many studies have shown how prevention programmes could reduce disease burden and mortality; however, there is a great deal of evidence that these policies fail to change people's lifestyles in the long run because unhealthy living habits are strongly predicted by a person's socio-economic position and social circumstances (Marmot, 2010). Also the effectiveness of prevention policies, such as incentives in health insurance, is the topic of current academic and policy debate. Some studies indicate that co-insurance might influence individuals' lifestyle choices. For example, Bhattacharya and Sood (2005) suggested that increased coinsurance may help reduce the prevalence of obesity. Conversely, other studies indicate the scarce and contradictory empirical evidence of the effects of particular prevention policies in promoting healthier lifestyles. Moreover, some sources indicate that prevention programmes may lead to unintended side effects. One of these side effects is that focusing on prevention may actually reinforce existing socio-economic equalities (Schmidt et al., 2010). By offering prevention programmes and incentives, the initial advantage of the well educated and well paid may tend to beget further advantage, and disadvantage those in most need of health improvements, creating widening gaps between haves and have-nots. While these incentives may be voluntary, for those on a lower income they may feel obligatory, if the only way to obtain affordable insurance is to meet the targets of these incentives. 'To them, programmes that are offered as carrots may feel more like sticks' (Schmidt et al., 2010). Prevention policies could also give rise to behavioural responses that are harmful with regard to prevention or lead to generally undesirable consequences (European Commission, 2007).

Cost savings?

The popularity for prevention programmes in healthcare is often based on the argument that these prevention programmes are 'cost-saving'. However, it is debated whether prevention programmes actually 'pay off' treatment costs in healthcare. Evidence on the cost issue has accumulated since the 1970s, when cost-effectiveness analysis (CEA) was first applied to health and medicine. Some reports claim that effective prevention programmes would save the state billions of euros or dollars (Levi et al., 2008; Flack et al., 2007), while others predict the reverse (Kahn et al., 2008; Russell, 2009; Cohen et al., 2008). Most recent cost-effectiveness studies advocate a careful assessment of the costs and savings associated with health prevention. It initially costs more to deliver preventive services; the savings and the resulting health benefits which will incur over time are less clear (Woolf, 2009). Whether any preventive measure saves money depends entirely on the particular intervention and the specific population in question. For example, drugs used to treat high cholesterol yield much greater value for the money if the targeted population is at high risk of coronary heart disease, and the efficiency of cancer screening can depend heavily on both the frequency of the screening and the level of cancer risk in the screened population (Russell, 1993).

In a recent overview article on the economic argument for disease prevention, Woolf (2009) highlighted the role of methodological issues (e.g., in regard to the choice of criteria and incorporation of particular cost categories) in economic evaluations of preventive healthcare interventions. In general, he argued, some factors enhance the economics of prevention, in ways that often elude disease care. For example, addressing a single risk factor (e.g. smoking) can influence outcomes across multiple diseases, from preterm birth to lung disease and cancer. The long time horizon that poses a challenge for prevention is also an opportunity for 'compounding' of health benefits. Addressing obesity in today's children will alter the prevalence of many diseases they will encounter decades later, a return on investment that may be profound.

Another issue is the choice of inclusion criteria, such as unrelated medical costs in life years gained, when asserting the cost-effectiveness of preventive interventions. In a recent study, Rappange et al. (2010) argue that although preventive interventions may reduce illnesses and expenditures related to risk factors, they will increase illnesses and expenditures unrelated to those risk factors primarily in gained life years. However, these unrelated costs are often not included in the cost-effectiveness of prevention studies. Yet, they have been demonstrated to outweigh the savings on related illnesses for the important risk factors. Obesity and smoking, for example, do not only cause morbidity but may also reduce life expectancy. Preventive interventions may thus reduce this risk of premature death and subsequently extend life. During these life years gained, as a consequence of other, unrelated diseases, people may consume additional healthcare. Or, as the former Dutch Minister of Health, Dr Els Borst, said: 'Dementia is something we witness in people of ages normally not reached by smokers and obese'. These additional expenditures due to unrelated diseases in these life years gained may offset savings from avoiding risk factor-related diseases. Therefore, Rappange et al. conclude, effective preventive interventions may increase rather than decrease healthcare costs.

Value for money

However, while the cost-saving argument for prevention intervention may be controversial, the investments themselves may still be worthwhile (Rappange et al., 2010). A related argument that is often claimed in this context is that preventing sickness has value in human terms that econometrics cannot capture (alone). Even if prevention and treatment cost the same per QALY (the quality-adjusted life years measurement[1]), patients prefer the former to avoid the ordeal of illness. Other societal benefits of improved health – e.g., workforce productivity and corporative competitiveness, and the ripple effects these trends bring to households, education, crime, and other societal outcomes – are among the intangibles that typically go unmeasured in cost-effectiveness studies. Prevention, then, like other care, does not have to be cost-saving in order to be attractive (Cohen et al., 1991). Such a requirement would implicitly hold prevention 'to a higher standard of cost-effectiveness than other medical care' (Russell, 1993). In the same vein, Woolf (2009) critically discusses the 'double standard' that is currently applied in discussions on the economics of healthcare. The question that dogs prevention – will it save money? – is rarely posed for an imaging device, a new antibiotic, or a surgical procedure. Therefore, Woolf argues, the economic scrutiny of cost-effectiveness studies applied to prevention should be expanded to disease care programmes as well.

In sum, beyond the controversies having to do with the 'cost of prevention', we can detect a change in perspective from a narrow health economics perspective of 'cost-saving' of prevention to a broader societal perspective of 'value for money'. In this regard, it is increasingly acknowledged that whether prevention 'pays off' treatment is not the right question. Instead, it is argued that healthcare policy makers should rather focus on the question of whether prevention offers value for money. Preventive interventions do not necessarily have to alleviate the financial burden on healthcare systems in order to be eligible for funding, but rather, like other interventions, have to demonstrate good value for money (Cutler et al., 2006). Prevention, then, may be a relatively cost-effective means of improving public health. In this respect, Rappange et al. (2010) for example reiterate the argument that saving money is not the primary aim of healthcare. Rather, he says, the aim is optimally to enhance health with the available resources. Exclusively focusing on the input side of the balance between costs and benefits may be considered a rather restrictive view, 'as it ignores the value of the output of prevention and healthcare and may consequently lead to underinvestment in these areas' (Brouwer et al., 2007). Thus, as Goetzel (2009) succinctly puts it: 'Instead of debating whether prevention or treatment saves money, we should determine the most cost-effective ways to achieve improved population health … ' Prevention, in that respect, should be evaluated within the same framework as other curative interventions, implying a focus on 'value for money'.

Back-to-basic questions

Finally, the introduction of lifestyle prevention programmes in healthcare and prevention policies has triggered debates on its normative implications and fundamental questions on the legitimacy of social security. In this sense, some authors have suggested how these programmes may reflect a more fundamental shift from collective to individual responsibility for health (Ter Meulen and Maarse, 2008; Feiring, 2008). With the shift to preventive medicine, illness has stopped being a fatality or a social contingency and is increasingly considered an individual responsibility – something for which we can, or even must, be responsible in taking preventive actions. This has led to the idea of sharpening of individual rights and responsibilities in healthcare, illustrated in policy initiatives targeting lifestyle behaviour by shifting the financial costs from the state to the individual. Often these prevention policies in health insurance are justified by arguments that individuals have responsibility for their health or lifestyles (Schmidt, 2008). To what extent it is reasonable to expect that individuals can be responsible for their health and change their lifestyles in response to prevention policies raises controversial and substantial normative issues about individual and societal responsibility (Feiring, 2008; Van Hoyweghen et al., 2006). In challenging the 'deservingness criteria' for healthcare, preventive actions and policies bear important questions for the legitimacy of social security systems. The importance of these normative questions suggests that arguments and distinctions drawn from moral and political philosophy should play a more prominent role in the debate on the shift towards an active welfare state and the introduction of prevention policies in social as well as in private insurance. For example, an extensive discussion about which lifestyle choices it is reasonable to hold individuals liable for could enhance the efficiency, and thereby also the legitimacy, of prevention policies in health insurance to the benefit of both the individuals insured and society at large.

Conclusion

If, as the human damage theory holds, social security resides in the first place in making available work opportunities to guarantee an appropriate income level and in healthy living conditions, we cannot limit ourselves to the traditional curative social security instruments of income transfer schemes and healthcare facilities. The insurance logic points to the importance of the probability/prevalence and damage factors. Yet, the basic logical chain has shown where the alternatives can be found: primary and secondary prevention should be activated. After this, tertiary prevention by way of compensatory and curative instruments can play its role. Developments in social policy thinking during the last decades have prepared us for policy shifts whereby a preventive approach became feasible. The EU has very much promoted this through its Lisbon and 2020 strategies (Marlier et al., 2010).

In retrospect, however, a preventive approach is not unproblematic. As with other policy innovations, preventive policies also tend to pose new questions and ask for a well-balanced approach. For as far as guaranteeing income via social protection is concerned, the results are in fact mixed. Labour market institutions and educational policies indeed seem crucial for primary prevention, but questions arise on their cost effectiveness and macro-level results. Secondary prevention by ALMPs raise similar reservations and point to doubts on its contribution to genuine social integration: jobs are not necessarily good and safe jobs.

In healthcare the traditional preventive policies of pure water and food, hygiene, and vaccination are complemented by more individualistically oriented interventions aiming at healthy lifestyles. The promotion of them can be of the 'carrot' style, but may turn out to represent a 'stick' approach. Whether they are cost-saving is unsettled and rather difficult to assess, but in the end the question is whether they are worthwhile in themselves and thus give value for money.

All this leads to a three-part conclusion. Firstly, it was right to enlarge the social policy scope by complementing the traditional curative instruments by preventive and re-integrative actions and services. Yet in doing so it appears that there is a need for shared responsibilities: between compensatory and preventive measures, but also between all instances involved – the individual citizen, employers, services (such as labour mediation offices and schools), and the state.

Secondly, prevention has its limits. It is not the panacea for the problems that are left by the traditional, curative approach, and certainly not a full guarantee for efficacy and cost effectiveness. Its input should rather be conceived and assessed in the much broader policy realm to which it is called to contribute.

Finally, however, to the extent that contingencies can be prevented, the veil of ignorance that inspires insurance, is lost. Social contingencies no longer represent socially accepted fatalities. This poses normative questions on the legitimacy of insurance-based policy schemes and asks for fundamental discussions on private and public responsibilities. Social policy is then in need of inspiration by social philosophy.

Note

1 A QALY gives an idea of how many extra months or years of life of a reasonable quality a person might gain as a result of treatment (particularly important when considering treatments for chronic conditions). Source: www.nice.org.uk

Further reading

Blau, F.D. and Kahn, L. M. (2002), *At Home and Abroad. U.S. Labor-Market Performance in International Perspective*. New York: Russell Sage Foundation.

Glied, S. and Smith P.C. (eds) (2011), *The Oxford Handbook of Health Economics*. Oxford: Oxford University Press.

Viaene, J., et al. (1993), 'Prevention and related policy issues', in J. Berghman and B. Cantillon (eds), *The European Face of Social Security*, pp. 281–311. Hampshire and Vermont: Ashgate Publishing.

References

Berghman, J. (1997), The resurgence of poverty and the struggle against exclusion: a new challenge for social security in Europe? *International Social Security Review*, vol. 50, no. 1, pp. 3–23.

Berghman, J., et al. (2002), *Social Security in Transition*. The Hague, The Netherlands: Kluwer Law International.
Bhattacharya, J., and Sood, N. (2005), *Health Insurance and the Obesity Externality*. (RAND Health Working Paper w11529). Cambridge, MA: National Bureau of Economic Research.
Blau, F. D. and Kahn, L. M. (2002), *At Home and Abroad. U.S. Labor-Market Performance in International Perspective*. New York: Russell Sage Foundation.
Brouwer, W. B. F., van Exel, N. J. A., van Baal, P. H. M. et al. (2007), Economics and public health: engaged to be happily married! *European Journal of Public Health*, vol. 17, pp. 122–23.
Cohen D. R. and Henderson J. B. (1991), *Health, Prevention, and Economics*. New York: Oxford University Press.
Cohen, J. T., Neumann P. J. and Weinstein M. C. (2008), Does preventive care save money? Health economics and the presidential candidates. *New England Journal of Medicine*, Feb, vol. 7, pp. 358, 661–63.
Cunha, F. Heckman, J. J. Lochner, L. and Masterov, D. V. (2006), 'Interpreting the evidence on life cycle skill formation', in E. A. Hanushek, and F. Welch (eds), *Handbook of the Economics of Education, Volume 1*. Amsterdam: North Holland.
Currie, J. (2001), Early Childhood Education Programs. *Journal of Economic Perspectives*, vol. 15, no. 2, pp. 213–38.
Cutler, D. M., Rosen A. B. and Vijan S. (2006), The value of medical spending in the United States, 1960–2000. *New England Journal of Medicine*, vol. 355, pp. 920–27.
Dubois, M. (2011), Insurance and prevention: ethical aspects. *Journal of Primary Prevention*, vol. 32, no. 1, pp. 3–15.
de Koning, J. (2007a), 'Introduction', in J. de Koning (ed.), *The Evaluation of Active Labour Market Policies*, pp. 1–20. Cheltenham and Northampton: Edward Elgar.
——(2007b). 'Is the changing pattern in the use of active labour market policies consistent with what evaluations tell us about their relative performance?', in J. de Koning, (ed.), *The Evaluation of Active Labour Market Policies*, pp. 23–45. Cheltenham and Northampton: Edward Elgar.
Esping-Andersen, G. (2009), *The Incomplete Revolution: Adapting to Women's New Roles*. Cambridge: Polity Press.
European Commission (2007), *Joint Report on Social Protection and Social Inclusion: Social Inclusion, Pensions, Healthcare and Long Term Care*. Luxembourg: Office for Official Publications of the European Communities.
Feiring, E. (2008), Lifestyle, responsibility and justice. *Journal of Medical Ethics*, vol. 34, pp. 33–36.
Flack S. M., Taylor M. J., and Trueman, P. (2007). *Cost-effectiveness of Interventions for Smoking Cessation. Final Report*. National Institute for Health & Clinical Excellence. Online: www.nice.org.uk/nicemedia/pdf/CostEffectivenessModel/%20Aug07SCS.pdf
Gallie, D. and Paugam, S. (eds) (2000), *Welfare Regimes and the Experience of Unemployment in Europe*. Oxford: Oxford University Press.
Gilbert, N., Specht, H., and Terrell, P. (1993), *Dimensions of Social Welfare Policy*. 3rd edn. Englewood Cliffs, NJ: Prentice Hall.
Goetzel, R. Z. (2009), Do prevention or treatment services save money? The wrong debate. *Health Affairs (Millwood)*, Jan–Feb, vol. 28, no. 1, pp. 37–41.
Heclo, H. (1974), *Modern Social Politics in Britain and Sweden – From Relief to Income Maintenance*. New Haven, CT and London: Yale University Press.
Kahn, R., Robertson, R. M., Smith, R., and Eddy, D. (2008), The impact of prevention on reducing the burden of cardiovascular disease. *Diabetes Care*, vol. 31, no. 8, pp. 1686–96.
Kluve, J. et al. (2007), *Active Labor Market Policies in Europe: Performance and Perspectives*. Berlin and Heidelberg: Springer.
Krueger, A. B. and Pischke, J. S. (1997), *Observations and Conjectures on the U.S. Employment Miracle. NBER Working Paper Series. Working Paper 6146*. Cambridge: National Bureau of Economic Research.
Levi J., Segal L. M. and Juliano C. (2008), *Prevention for a Healthier America: Investments in Disease Prevention Yield Significant Savings, Stronger Communities*. Washington, DC: Trust for America's Health. Online: healthyamericans.org/reports/prevention08/Prevention08.pdf. Accessed July 4, 2010.
Maciosek, M. V., Coffield, A. B., Edwards, N. M., Flottemesch, T. J., Goodman, M. J., and Solberg, L. I. (2006), Priorities among effective clinical preventive services: results of a systematic review and analysis. *American Journal of Preventive Medicine*, vol. 31, pp. 52–61.
Marlier, E. and Natali, D. (eds) (2010), *Europe 2020 – Towards a more social Europe?* Brussels, Bern and Berlin: P.I.E. Peter Lang.
Marmot, M. (2010), *Fair Society, Healthy Lives: A Strategic Review of Health Inequalities in England Post-2010*. London: Marmot Review.

Martin, J. P. and Grubb, D. (2001), What works and for whom: a review of OECD countries' experiences with active labour market policies. *Swedish Economic Policy Review*, vol. 8, no. 2, pp. 9–56.

Nickell, S. and Layard, R. (1999), 'Labor Market Institutions and Economic Performance', in: O. Ashenfelter and D. Card (eds), *Handbook of Labor Economics. Volume 3C*, pp. 3029–84. Amsterdam: Elsevier.

Organization for Economic Cooperation and Development (OECD) (2007), *Employment Outlook 2007*. Paris: OECD.

——(2010), *Education at a glance*. OECD Indicators. Paris: OECD.

——(2005), *Health at a Glance*. Paris: OECD.

O'Sullivan, A. and Sheffrin, S. M. (2003), *Economics: Principles in Action*. Upper Saddle River, NJ: Pearson Prentice Hall.

Pieters, D. (1993), *Introduction into the Basic Principles of Social Security*. Deventer, The Netherlands: Kluwer Law and Taxation Publishers.

Psacharopoulos, G. and Patrinos, H. A. (2004), Returns to Investment in Education: A Further Update. *Education Economics*, vol. 12, no. 2, pp. 111–34.

Rappange, D. R., Brouwer, W. B., Rutten, F. F., and van Baal, P. H. (2010), Lifestyle intervention: from cost savings to value for money. *Journal of Public Health*, Sep, vol. 32, no. 3, 440–7.

Rimlinger, G. V. (1971), *Welfare Policy and Industrialization in Europe, America and Russia*. Toronto: John Wiley & Sons, Inc.

Russell, L. B. (1993), The role of prevention in health reform. *New England Journal of Medicine*, vol. 329, pp. 352–4.

——(2009), Preventing chronic disease: an important investment, but don't count on cost savings. *Health Affairs* (Millwood), vol. 28, no. 1, 42–5.

Schmid, G. and Gazier, B. (eds) (2002), *The Dynamics of Full Employment. Social Integration Through Transitional Labour Markets*. Cheltenham and Northampton: Edward Elgar.

Schmidt, H. (2008), Bonuses as incentives and rewards for health responsibility: A good thing? *Journal of Medicine and Philosophy*, vol. 33, pp. 198–220.

Schmidt, H., Voigt, K., and Wikler, D. (2010), Carrots, sticks, and healthcare reform: problems with wellness incentives. *New England Journal of Medicine*, vol. 362, no. 2.

Ter Meulen, R. H. J. and Maarse, H. (2008), Increasing individual responsibility in Dutch healthcare: is solidarity losing ground? *Journal of Medicine and Philosophy*, vol. 33, pp. 262–79.

van Berkel, R. and Hornemann, I. (2004), 'The experience of activation policies', in D. Gallie (ed.), *Resisting Marginalisation – Unemployment Experience and Social Policy in the European Union*. Oxford: Oxford University Press.

van Hoyweghen, I., Horstman, K., and Schepers, R. (2006), Making the normal deviant: the introduction of predictive medicine in private insurance. *Social Science & Medicine*, vol. 63, pp. 1225–35.

Viaene, J., et al. (1993), 'Prevention and related policy issues', in J. Berghman, and B. Cantillon (eds), *The European Face of Social Security*, pp. 281–311. Hampshire and Vermont: Ashgate Publishing.

Woolf, S. H. (2009), A closer look at the economic argument for disease prevention, *Journal of the American Medical Association*, vol. 301, no. 5, pp. 536–38.

7 Poverty

Peter Saunders

Introduction

Poverty is an issue that has attracted the attention of leading academic scholars and has inspired some of the greatest works of fiction. Whether it be Victor Hugo's *Les Miserables* in nineteenth-century France, Dickens's characters living in the squalid slums of Victorian London, or those excluded from today's advanced democratic societies or struggling to survive famine in sub-Saharan Africa, throughout history poverty has motivated the search for understanding and been a rallying call for action. It has attracted the attention of the world's leading social scientists, inspiring the conflicting theories of Adam Smith and Karl Marx, the policies developed by welfare state pioneers Bismarck and Beveridge, and the conceptual and measurement skills of generations of researchers, from Booth and Rowntree to Townsend and Sen. Poverty has featured prominently on the post-war policy agenda, whether it be the 1960s US 'war on poverty', the British government's attack on child poverty in the 1990s, or the United Nations (UN)'s Millennium Development Goals, which include halving extreme poverty by 2015. A central idea that links these diverse developments is the notion that poverty is bad – bad in terms of its immediate effects on those who experience it, bad also because of its longer-term consequences, particularly for children, and bad for those societies whose inaction implicitly condones it.

Yet there is a lack of clarity about what poverty is, how it can be identified, and what needs to be done to address it – both in developing countries who lack the resources for an all-out attack, and in affluent countries where average living standards are higher, but where unmet need still exists, at least in a relative sense. The eradication or alleviation of poverty has been at the forefront of the social policy agenda since the medieval poor laws were first enacted in fourteenth-century England. These laws, expanded under legislation enacted in the 1530s, were generally piecemeal, operating at the local parish level and distinguished between the 'deserving' and 'undeserving' poor – the latter being denied support because their plight was seen as the result of their own idleness or immoral behaviour. It was not until the development of the welfare state that a coherent policy framework for tackling poverty at the national level was assembled, with legislated entitlements replacing the discretionary judgements implicit in the distinction between deserving and undeserving poor. Even so, the moral overtones that characterised these earlier periods still exert an influence on some theories of poverty and an even more powerful impact on the design of some anti-poverty policies.

In order to understand why this is the case, it is necessary to examine how poverty is defined and measured – the two are often confused or conflated – and this is one of the main goals of this chapter. The following section examines how the concept of poverty has evolved over the last three centuries, while the next section reviews measurement issues, distinguishing between poverty line studies and those approaches that locate poverty within a broader living standards framework. This is followed by an examination of the problems associated with measuring the impact of the welfare state on poverty and some summary findings, while the final section summarises the main conclusions canvasses some of the issues that lie at the forefront of contemporary poverty research.

The concept of poverty

Poverty exists when people do not have the resources to obtain the items that are necessary to meet basic needs. In order to make this idea operational so that it can be used to identify who is poor, the terms 'resources' and 'necessary' must be specified more precisely. Much of the attention of poverty researchers has been on identifying the meaning of 'necessary', with many still adopting the approach proposed by Adam Smith (1776) in *The Wealth of Nations*, where he noted that:

> By necessities, I understand not only the commodities which are indispensably necessary for the support of life but *whatever the custom renders it indecent for creditable people, even of the lowest order, to be without.*
>
> *(p. 691; emphasis added)*

Smith gave the example of a linen shirt as being a necessity that even a day-labourer 'would be ashamed to appear in public without' because it would break prevailing social norms. The idea that necessities cannot be identified independently of existing material conditions and social norms was captured two centuries after Smith in what is widely regarded as the classic modern definition of poverty advanced by British sociologist Peter Townsend:

> Individuals, families and groups in the population can be said to be in poverty when they lack the resources to obtain the types of diet, participate in the activities and have the living conditions and amenities *which are customary, or at least widely encouraged or approved, in the societies to which they belong.*
>
> *(Townsend, 1979, p. 31; emphasis added)*

This definition is more explicit about which kinds of things are 'indispensably necessary' in a modern society, including the avoidance of social exclusion amongst these and raising questions about how poverty and exclusion are related (Nolan and Marx, 2009; Saunders, 2011). However, it is the emphasis given to a lack of resources as being the underlying cause that makes this a definition of poverty. It shares this feature with the definition adopted by Seebohm Rowntree (1901) who, in the first attempt to quantify the extent of poverty, defined a family as poor if 'their total earnings are insufficient to obtain the minimum necessities of merely physical efficiency'. Rowntree's approach can be thought of as a subsistence definition of poverty, in contrast with Townsend's more comprehensive participatory approach that is relevant to contemporary living conditions and social circumstances.

Townsend's definition, which forms the basis of the deprivation approach that is described in more detail later, has much in common with that taken by Sen (1985), although Sen defines poverty not in terms of a lack of the commodities that require resources, but in terms of a failure to achieve the freedom provided by a given level of capabilities. These capabilities reflect a person's ability to achieve the various living conditions (or functionings) that he or she has reason to value. In drawing the distinction between commodities and capabilities, Sen notes that from a living standards perspective:

> … commodities are no more than means to other ends. Ultimately, the focus has to be on what life we lead and what we can and cannot do, can or cannot be.
>
> *(Sen, 1987, p. 16)*

He then defines poverty as 'the failure of basic capabilities to reach minimally acceptable levels' and argues that:

> The functionings relevant to this … can vary from such elementary physical ones as being well-nourished, being adequately clothed and sheltered, avoiding preventable morbidity, etc., to more complex social achievements such as taking part in the life of the community, being able to appear in public without shame, and so on.
>
> *(Sen, 1992, p. 39)*

This definition has many similarities with that proposed by Townsend, including the idea that poverty is a multi-faceted problem and requires a multi-dimensional approach to identification and measurement. The main difference is the focus given by Townsend on a lack of resources as the underlying cause, whereas Sen concentrates on the functionings themselves, not all of which are constrained by available resources because other factors (e.g. discrimination, or powerlessness) may also be important – possibly more so.

An important feature that is embodied in all of the above definitions is the idea that poverty is unacceptable. As Ringen (2007, p. 222) has argued: 'The conditions we justly call poverty are not simply unfair or unfortunate, they are *unacceptable*' (emphasis in the original). Although this unacceptability must be related to the living conditions (or functionings) actually experienced, it leaves open the question of who is to decide what constitutes an unacceptable situation. One approach would involve letting experts decide by making the judgements that ultimately determine whether or not someone is identified as poor. This approach has been shown to lack credibility when it generates disagreement among 'the experts', and critics of poverty studies have exploited this by creating the disagreement needed to undermine the research. Another approach, now gaining more support, is to leave it to members of the community to express a view about whether or not a particular situation is unacceptable, and to base the identification and measurement of poverty on those views.

Irrespective of the precise approach taken, this brief review highlights the two key characteristics of any definition of poverty: that it reflects a situation that is unacceptable, and that the cause is a lack of income or access to economic resources more generally. These two features are captured in the definitions used by bodies that have a direct interest in addressing poverty, like the European Commission (2004) and the Irish Combat Poverty Agency (2004). The former has defined poverty to include:

> … persons, families and groups of persons whose resources (material, cultural and social) are so limited as to exclude them from the minimum acceptable way of life in the Member state in which they live.
>
> *(Cited in Nolan and Marx, 2009, p. 316)*

The Irish definition captures the same basic features, specifying that:

> People are living in poverty if their incomes are so inadequate as to preclude them from having an acceptable standard of living.
>
> *(Irish Combat Poverty Agency, 2004, p. 1)*

The two key words in this definition are 'inadequate' and 'acceptable' and this has led to the development of two strands in the poverty literature: poverty line studies that seek to identify whether or not incomes are adequate by comparing them with a poverty line; and living standards studies that examine living standards actually achieved in order to establish whether or not they are acceptable. Exactly how the two approaches go about these tasks is described in detail in the following section.

Before then, it is useful to address some of the conceptual issues that are common to all poverty definitions, the first of which relates to whether poverty is absolute or relative. This distinction has been the source of great controversy, although as Ringen (1987) has pointed out the distinction is artificial because all approaches contain a degree of relativism. Even Rowntree's subsistence budgets included some items that were not necessary to achieve 'merely physical efficiency' but were widely consumed and thus represented an accepted standard or social norm. To exclude these items would have meant that the budgets did not reflect what people actually do, thus severing the link between measurement and experience. However, it is one thing to accept that poverty is relative, but quite another to determine what this implies for how it can be identified and measured. Although poverty should be expressed (and hence measured) relative to prevailing customs, norms, and consumption practices, this still leaves a multitude of potential methods for operationalising this idea. The fact that in *practice* the relative nature of poverty has been captured by using a poverty line expressed relative to a measure of average income (see below) does not mean that this is the only way in which the relative nature of the *concept* of poverty can be expressed.

One criticism that has been levelled at the use of relative income benchmarks to measure poverty is that this confuses poverty with the broader question of income inequality. Proponents of this view have argued that measuring poverty in this way means that improvements in average living standards that benefit everyone equally will have no impact on the poverty rate since the benchmark used to identify poverty will shift upwards to reflect the rise in incomes. Although this is arithmetically correct, it is also true that if the poor do not share equally in the rise in average income, they will indeed become poorer relative to others (even if they experience an increase in real income) and the measured poverty rate should reflect this. Although some will see it as paradoxical that the poverty rate has increased even though the poor are better-off, this is a natural consequence of measuring poverty using a relative income standard. There is no axiomatic relationship between poverty, measured by the proportion of the population with incomes below a relative income threshold and inequality, which captures individual income differences at all points in the income distribution. It may be useful to complement relative poverty rates by measures that capture changes in the real incomes of those below the poverty line or (as some countries now do) estimate poverty rates using both a relative poverty line and a poverty line that is adjusted to reflect only movements in consumer prices. To do so does not, however, imply that the use of a poverty line whose value remains constant in real (absolute) terms reflects acceptance of the (mistaken) view that poverty itself is absolute in a conceptual sense.

Measurement issues

Poverty line studies

Until recently, the vast majority of poverty studies involved comparing incomes with a poverty line. This has proved to be a challenging task, for several reasons. First, there are the problems associated with measuring income. The social surveys that are often used for this purpose have been shown to contain a number of weaknesses that can affect the accuracy or reliability of estimated poverty rates. The incomes reported in surveys by the self-employed, for example, is unreliable because of the difficulty of distinguishing between the 'own' and the 'business' incomes of those who operate their own business. Income also tends to be more generally under-stated in surveys, and this can lead to an over-estimate of the numbers in poverty. These problems are less acute when poverty is estimated from official register of administrative data, although different problems may then arise because of other required data (for example, on household size and composition) may not be available in the degree of detail required. In addition, both survey and register data may provide the incomes of individuals, which must then be aggregated to derive the combined income of the family unit or household. That income is assumed to be shared (or pooled) among unit members so as to equalise the standard of living of each member. The assumption of equal pooling of resources has been criticised by feminists and others on theoretical grounds, and because the evidence suggests that intra-household inequalities (in income and time) are common (Burton, Phipps, and Woolley, 2007).

Further complications arise because households differ in size and composition, making it impossible to compare how well a given level of household income can support a specific standard of living of individuals. This problem is normally overcome by adjusting household income using an equivalence scale, which expresses how relative needs vary with household size and composition. For example, if the equivalence scale value for a couple with two children is equal to 2.1 (which it is under one of the most commonly used scales, the modified Organisation for Economic Co-operation and Development (OECD) scale), this implies that the two-child couple needs 2.1 times the income of a single adult in order to achieve the same standard of living. The scale rises less than in proportion with household size because of economies of scale in common living arrangements (so that the four-person family may need two but not four cars, televisions, or bathrooms), and because larger households tend to contain more children, whose needs are below those of adults. The equivalence scale is used to deflate household income and these deflated (or equivalised) incomes reflect the ability of household income to meet the needs of its members.

The approach described above takes account of differences in household composition only and thus ignores other factors that may affect the ability of a household to meet its needs from a given level of income. One such factor is the stage of the life cycle, which is likely to imply, for example, that the needs of a young married couple may differ from those of a retired pensioner couple so that their susceptibility to (or risk of) poverty will differ even if their incomes are identical. Whereas the younger couple may be purchasing a house and having to service a large debt out of their current income, the pensioner couple are far more likely to own their house free of debt and thus have a substantial capital asset that supplements their income. This example highlights that inadequacy of relying on income alone to estimate poverty because individuals and households vary their savings patterns over the life cycle to smooth their consumption.

Despite these limitations, most studies do use income when estimating poverty (although some argue that consumption expenditure, broadly defined, is superior), and income adjusted using an equivalence scale must then be compared with a poverty line in order to determine whether or not the household is poor, and such households aggregated to provide a measure of the extent of poverty. Both procedures give rise to a number of additional problems, although the following discussion focuses only on the first of them. (The aggregation issue is examined by Atkinson, 1987). There is no agreed method for deriving a poverty line and the different approaches that have been used tend to produce different results (Callan and Nolan, 1991). The original method used by Rowntree involved identifying the specific items required to meet identified needs (housing, nutrition, clothing, health and personal care, an allowance for social participation, and so on) at a specific level and costing these to derive the household budget that would allow the items to be purchased.

A variant of the budget approach is based on the idea, originally captured in Engel's law, that the proportion of the budget spent on food provides a good (inverse) indicator of the standard of living. A poverty line can then be derived by costing a nutritionally adequate food budget and multiplying it by the inverse of the proportion of the budget that is spent on food. This approach forms the basis of the official US poverty line first developed in the 1960s (Ruggles, 1990). Since then, the resulting poverty line has been updated in line with movements in consumer prices, an approach that takes no account of improvements in US living standards, which would have lowered the food budget proportion and thus raised the multiplier used to derive the poverty line.

Other studies have used a poverty line derived from responses to survey questions that ask people to estimate how much they need to make ends meet (Hagenaars, 1986) or that correspond to the prevailing level of social benefits. Both approaches have their limitations – the former because the end result is sensitive to the methods employed, the latter because it produces the paradoxical outcome that poverty can be reduced by cutting benefits. Reflecting these limitations, many poverty line studies now use one of the two international poverty lines that have been developed by international agencies with an interest in poverty. In developing countries, different variants of the 'dollar a day' poverty line proposed by the World Bank (which is based on the food budget multiplier method described above) have been used to estimate poverty and monitor progress in its reduction (Ravallion, Datt and van de Valle, 1991). In rich industrial countries, an explicitly relative poverty line set at one-half of (equivalised) median income is now most commonly used (OECD, 2008). Under this approach, the relative position of the poverty line is maintained as incomes (and hence the median) rise, and it has the added advantage that the results are independent of national currencies, thus facilitating the cross-country comparisons that are one of its main purposes. The use of a benchmark set at half of median income is justified as representing an agreed threshold below which incomes are so low as to prevent an acceptable degree of economic and social participation.

Although both are widely used, the World Bank and OECD poverty lines are essentially arbitrary and suffer from all of the weaknesses of other income-based poverty lines. In both cases, some of those with incomes below the line may have other resources on which to draw without experiencing poverty (for example, older people with substantial private savings), while some of those with incomes above the line (for example, people affected by a disability) may face special needs that force them into poverty. For these reasons, caution must be applied when drawing conclusions from the findings produced by poverty line studies, a point that was highlighted in the distinction between primary poverty (which reflects a lack of resources) and secondary poverty (which is often a consequence of mis-directed or 'wasteful' spending) that Rowntree identified in his original study. If poverty reflects an unacceptable standard of living, then it has to be acknowledged that there are many factors other than income that determine one's standard of living (see Perry, 2002). This implies that poverty is multidimensional and that its measurement should reflect this since, in practice, as Nolan and Marx (2009, p. 319) have noted 'low income may fail in practice to distinguish those experiencing distinctively high levels of deprivation or exclusion'. Poverty line studies are thus best thought of as providing estimates of the *poverty risks* facing different groups rather than as producing definitive estimates of *poverty rates* as such.

Living standard studies

The rationale for adopting a living standards approach reflects the idea that it is better grounded in the actual experience of poverty than the income approach which is indirect because it presumes that low income automatically equates with poverty. It is therefore important, as Ringen (1987, p. 162) has argued, to demonstrate that those identified as poor 'live as if they were poor [and] do so because they do not have the means to avoid it'. Living standard studies of poverty have adopted the concept of deprivation that was developed by Townsend in the study cited earlier. In that study, people were asked if they had a list of items that had been identified as basic necessities, and a deprivation index was derived by summing the number of items that each person said they did not have. Townsend went on to show that the resulting deprivation index increased sharply once income fell below a threshold and argued that this could be regarded as a deprivation-based poverty line. Subsequent studies have chosen not to follow this path, but to improve the methods used to derive the deprivation index and to use that index as an indicator of poverty.

Several refinements have been introduced to address the limitations of Townsend's original approach (see Mack and Lansley, 1985; Pantazis, Gordon and Townsend, 2006). First, the list of items itself has been modified to reflect community views on which items are necessary or essential, rather than being imposed by those conducting the research; second, only those items that are seen as necessary by a majority (i.e. those that are 'widely encouraged or approved') are included; third, people who do not have these items are asked if this is because they cannot afford them or because they do not want them, with only those in the former category defined as deprived; fourthly, different methods have been used to aggregate the separate instances of deprivation into a summary measure by varying the weights that apply to each item (see Willitts, 2006). These refinements have improved the scientific robustness of the approach and produced estimates that are more grounded in community views and thus have greater credibility.

However, a decision still has to be made about how many items people should be deprived of before they are identified as poor. It can be argued that the absence of any single item is indicative of poverty since the failure to be able to afford items that are widely regarded as necessary corresponds to what is generally understood by poverty. Against this, some of those who report not being able to afford items on the list of necessities also possess some of the items that are not identified as necessary, raising doubt over the interpretation of the findings (McKay, 2004). These developments suggest that it is prudent to identify poverty in the sense of deprivation as existing when people are deprived of more than one necessity, although there is no scientific basis for choosing the precise number – any more than there is for setting a poverty line.

The above discussion treats the poverty line and living standards (deprivation) approaches as alternatives, when both have something important to contribute. It thus makes sense to combine the two indicators, as has been done in what has been called the notion of consistent poverty, which exists when income is below the poverty line and where a minimum level of deprivation is experienced (Nolan and Whelan, 1996). Both the level of the poverty line and the number of deprivation items can then be varied in order to assess the sensitivity of the results (Saunders and Naidoo, 2009). The consistent poverty measure is now widely used in poverty research (and by government agencies with an interest in poverty) and has many advantages including that it:

> ... resonates well with the perception that poverty should encompass some idea of the practical effects of low income ... [and is] ... concerned with outcomes rather than processes and in this sense it was believed to reflect the public perceptions of poverty and the feelings of distress felt by those in poverty ... a measure that chimes better with the public understanding of poverty would be able to gain public and political credibility.
>
> *(Department for Work and Pensions, 2003, pp. 20–1)*

The approach recognises not only the limitations of income-based measures, but acknowledges the multidimensional nature of poverty, since deprivation has many dimensions. Combining income and a non-monetary indicator like deprivation into a single measure makes sense because:

> ... the evidence suggest that such non-monetary indicators contain valuable information, and when combined with information on financial constraints, do help in identifying those who are experiencing exclusion due to lack of resources.
>
> *(Nolan and Whelan, 2007, p. 154)*

The living standards approach has revitalised the measurement of poverty in ways that connect better with the experience of poverty and this in turn has given greater credibility to the estimates, making them more relevant to policy and hence more attractive to policy makers.

Poverty and the welfare state

Rowntree showed for the first time that poverty was the result of factors such as low wages or unemployment, challenging the prevailing view that the poor were largely responsible for their own plight. He showed that individuals were more susceptible to poverty in old age and early childhood, and these findings lead to the view that exposure to poverty fluctuated systematically over the life cycle. Despite over a century of major economic and social change, this finding remains relevant in today's world characterised by more fluid and diverse family structures, greatly improved (but cyclical) economic performance, and increased material affluence. The expanded role for social policies that has accompanied the growth of the welfare state has done much to moderate the trends identified by Rowntree (and subsequently by many others) but the idea that the risk of poverty varies over the life cycle has presented policy makers with an enduring set of challenges.

Poverty was one of the 'giant evils' that were the focus of William Beveridge's proposals that led to the development of the British welfare state. The German pension system introduced earlier by Bismarck was also motivated by a desire to protect living standards of German workers after retirement. The post-war period saw the introduction and expansion of social benefits for the unemployed and sole parents, and a network of other family policies that sought to protect children from poverty, and that addressing of life cycle fluctuations in poverty has shaped the development of the welfare state since its inception.

In light of this, it is no surprise that researchers have focused considerable attention on examining the impact of the welfare state on poverty in general, and on children and older people in particular. This has generally involved comparing observed poverty rates (estimated using a poverty line approach) with an estimate of what they would have been in the absence of welfare state policies. Many of these studies have adopted a comparative approach, in which the impact and effectiveness of the policies adopted in different countries are examined and compared. This approach requires information that can be compared cross-nationally and great effort has gone into producing such data, either through cross-national research projects like the Luxembourg Income Study (Atkinson, 2004) or as a result of work undertaken by international agencies like the OECD. The results are of interest, not only because of their policy implications, but also because they provide a fascinating insight into how poverty rates differ in different jurisdictions.

However, while cross-country differences in the poverty rates facing different groups are of great interest, a number of problems make it difficult to draw implications about the impact of different policy regimes or approaches. The most important of these is the 'counterfactual problem', which arises because estimating the impact of policy involves comparing the situation that exists when the policy is in place with a hypothetical situation that is assumed to exist if the policy was different or did not exist. Determining what form this second (counterfactual) situation will take presents analysts with a major challenge, particularly when the policy under review (for example, the pension or family benefits system) has become so deeply ingrained in the existing structure. Most studies compare the situation that actually exists, in which poverty rates are based on each household's disposable income given the existing structure of income transfers and the income taxes that finance them (the post-tax, post-transfer situation), with an estimate of poverty rates based on each household's private or market income (the pre-tax, pre-transfer situation), where the latter is derived by deducting the transfers received and taxes paid by each household and re-calculating the poverty rate.

Considerable caution must be applied when deciding what the results of such an exercise imply about the impact of the welfare state (captured by the tax and transfer system) on poverty. This is because if the thought experiment implied by the calculation were actually to be implemented (i.e. if all existing transfers and taxes were removed), households would adjust their behaviour to reflect this in ways that would affect their private incomes and hence the likelihood that they would be in poverty. If pension systems did not exist, for example, people would have to make their own retirement provisions by saving while they were working and these savings would generate a market income after they retired. Put differently, the reduction in poverty among older people caused by OECD pension systems arises in part because they remove the need for people to save whilst working in order to generate a private income in retirement. Estimating the 'true' impact of public pensions (and the taxes that pay for them) on poverty would require these kinds of behavioural changes to be allowed for in some way, but the pre- and post-comparisons described above assume that no such changes take place, making them of dubious relevance.

Figure 7.1 compares overall poverty rates in OECD countries before and after taking account of cash transfers paid to, and income taxes paid by, households in each country. Countries have been ranked by the pre-transfer, pre-tax poverty rate and the estimates are based on a poverty line set at 50 per cent of each country's median (post-transfer, post-tax) income. (It should be noted that poverty is usually estimated in European Union (EU) countries using a higher poverty line, set at 60 per cent of median income). Wherever the poverty line is set, linking it to a summary measure of overall income like the median does not mean that the poverty rates are comparable because no account is taken of country differences in demographic structure or other factors like the incidence of sole parenthood or the unemployment rate that will affect the national poverty rate.

Despite these reservations, the estimates reveal some interesting patterns. Before taking account of transfers and taxes, the poverty rate varies from around 17 per cent (in Switzerland,

Finland, Spain, and South Korea) to over twice that level (in Poland, Italy, and Germany). After taking account of transfers and taxes, national poverty rates vary from below 6 per cent (in the Czech Republic, Denmark, and Sweden) to over 14 per cent (in Ireland, Japan, Korea, Mexico, Poland, Spain, and the United States). An estimate of the impact of transfers and taxes on poverty is provided by the proportional difference between the pre- and post-transfer and taxes poverty rates, which varies from below 20 per cent (in South Korea, Mexico, and Spain) to over 75 per cent (in the Czech Republic, Denmark, France, Hungary, Luxembourg, Sweden, and the United Kingdom). Although these estimated policy impact estimates are misleading as explained above, they do indicate that countries differ greatly in terms of the impact of the welfare state on poverty. This is an important finding because it illustrates the general point that *policies do matter* and where poverty reduction is given priority by policy makers the experience and evidence shows that this goal can be achieved. Brady (2009, p. 91) has shown that, however it is measured the welfare state exerts a 'powerful impact on poverty' and this is an important and enduring finding.

It is, however, important to note that Figure 7.1 takes no account of the volume of spending in each country and this information is of vital importance in establishing how efficient tax and transfer programs are in reducing poverty. Information on spending levels would need to be combined with the policy impacts implied by Figure 7.1 before any conclusions could be drawn about the relative merits of the policy approaches adopted in different countries. Despite this, it is clear that welfare states (particularly in Europe) have been successful in reducing poverty overall and (although not shown) among older people in particular. Welfare states have also been successful in reducing poverty among families of workforce age (and hence among children, who live in working-age households), with evidence presented by Brady (2009, Figure 4.1), Bradbury and Jäntti (1999, Figure 5.1) and the OECD (2008, Figure 5.13) all showing a clear cross-national relationship between levels of social spending and poverty rates for those of workforce age. There is also evidence that pre-transfer, pre-tax (market income)

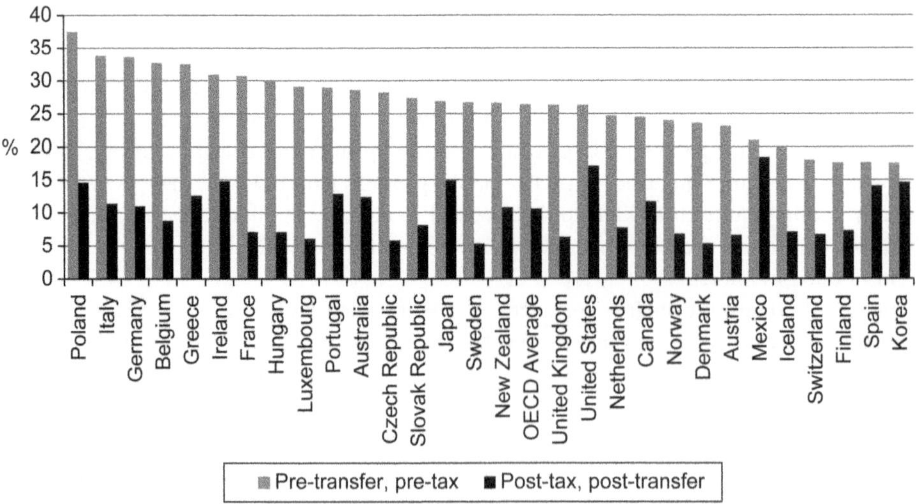

Figure 7.1 Poverty Rates before and after transfers and taxes in OECD countries in the mid-2000s (based on poverty lines set at 50 per cent of median income in each country)

Source: Data © OECD Stats Extracts, available online at stats.oecd.org/Index.aspx?DataSetCode=POVERTY, accessed on 24 August 2011.

poverty has increased over recent decades and that this has been only partly offset by an increase in the poverty-reducing impact of transfers and taxes (OECD, 2008, Figure 5.11). Overall, the evidence indicates that welfare states have been able to reduce the peaks and troughs in the life cycle poverty profile identified by Rowntree, but that this has not been a universal achievement and will require on-going vigilance and effort to ensure that past gains are not eroded or lost.

Conclusion

This chapter has provided an overview of approaches to the conceptualisation and measurement of poverty and has examined some of the evidence on the impact of the welfare state on poverty. Our understanding of the nature and causes of poverty has increased greatly since modern poverty studies began in the 1960s, but the nature of the topic makes it inevitable that many issues remain unresolved. The period has seen a move away from a narrow focus on income and the development of new conceptual advances that have emphasised the multidimensional nature of poverty in terms of both its outcomes (material deprivation or social exclusion) and its relation to choice and freedom as articulated in the capabilities approach. These advances have been accompanied by a rapid expansion in national and international (comparative) empirical studies of poverty that have been made possible by major improvements in data quality and accessibility, and in the sophistication of the analytical techniques that have been used to examine such data. The result has been a greater awareness of the need for empirical studies of poverty to have a sound conceptual basis backed by measurement approaches that are grounded in the actual experience of poverty and its consequences.

One important facet of poverty that has not been discussed relates to its dynamic aspects. This is another rapidly expanding field that is being driven by the interest of policy makers in better understanding the transitions into and out of spells of poverty, so that policies can be better designed and targeted, and facilitated by the growth in longitudinal (panel) data sets that allow the dynamics of poverty to be studied – both within and between countries. Many countries now produce estimates of the persistence of poverty, which Eurostat, for example, defines as the proportion of households who spend more than three consecutive years below the poverty line, as a way of highlighting the fact that many households move into and out of the poverty pool as their circumstances change. These studies have produced a new perspective on the nature of poverty and have identified new challenges for policy formulation and the design of anti-poverty policies (Jenkins and Micklewright, 2007). Comparative research conducted by the OECD (2008, Chapter 6) using panel data is producing a number of important new insights about the length of poverty spells, the (economic) destinations of those who escape, the groups most susceptible to chronic (longer-term) poverty, and the extent of national differences in poverty turnover rates. Together, these developments and those discussed earlier will ensure that poverty will continue to attract the minds of our greatest thinkers as well as the efforts of our best statistical agencies and empirical researchers.

References

Atkinson, A. B. (1987), On the measurement of poverty, *Econometrica*, vol. 55, no. 4, pp. 749–64.

——(2004), The Luxembourg income study (LIS): past, present and future, *Socio-Economic Review*, vol. 2, no. 4, pp. 165–90.

Bradbury, B. and Jäntti, M. (1999), *Child Poverty Across Industrialized Nations*, Innocenti Occasional Paper No. 71, Florence: UNICEF International Child Development Centre.

Brady, D. (2009), *Rich Democracies, Poor People. How Politics Explain Poverty*. New York: Oxford University Press.

Burton, P., Phips, S., and Woolley, F. (2007), 'Inequality within the household', in S. P. Jenkins and J. Micklewright (eds), *Inequality and Poverty Re-examined*, pp. 103–25. Oxford: Oxford University Press.

Callan, T. and Nolan, B. (1991), Concepts of Poverty and the poverty line: a critical survey of approaches to measuring poverty, *Journal of Economic Surveys*, vol. 5, no. 3, pp. 243–62.

Combat Poverty Agency (2004), *What is Poverty?* Dublin: Combat Poverty Agency.

Department for Work and Pensions (2003), *Measuring Child Poverty Consultation. Preliminary Conclusions.* London: Department for Work and Pensions.

European Commission (2004), *Joint Report on Social Inclusion.* Brussels: European Commission.

Gordon, D. (2006), 'The concept and measurement of poverty', in C. Pantazis, D. Gordon, and R. Levitas (eds), *Poverty and Social Exclusion in Britain. The Millennium Survey*, pp. 29–69. Bristol: Policy Press.

Hagenaars, A. (1986), *The Perception of Poverty*. Amsterdam: North Holland.

Jenkins, S. P. and Micklewright, J. (2007), 'New directions in the analysis of inequality and poverty', in S. P. Jenkins and J. Micklewright (eds), *Inequality and Poverty Re-examined*, pp. 3–33. Oxford: Oxford University Press.

Mack, J. and Lansley, S. (1985), *Poor Britain*. London: George Allen and Unwin.

McKay, S. (2004), Poverty or preference: what do 'consensual deprivation indicators' really measure?, *Fiscal Studies*, vol. 25, no. 2, pp. 201–23.

Nolan, B. and Whelan, C. T. (1996), *Resources, Deprivation and Poverty*. Oxford: Clarendon Press.

——(2007), 'Multidimensionality of poverty and social exclusion', in S. P. Jenkins and J. Micklewright (eds), *Inequality and Poverty Re-examined*, pp. 146–65. Oxford: Oxford University Press.

Nolan, B. and Marx, I. (2009), 'Economic inequality, poverty, and social exclusion', in W. Salverda, B. Nolan, and T. M. Smeeding (eds), *The Oxford Handbook of Economic Inequality*, pp. 315–41. Oxford: Oxford University Press.

OECD (2008), *Growing Unequal? Income Distribution and Poverty in OECD Countries*. Paris: OECD.

Pantazis, C., Gordon, D., and Townsend, P. (2006), 'The necessities of life', in C. Pantazis, D. Gordon, and R. Levitas (eds), *Poverty and Social Exclusion in Britain. The Millennium Survey*, pp. 89–122. Bristol: Policy Press.

Perry, B. (2002), The mismatch between income measures and direct outcome measures of poverty, *Social Policy Journal of New Zealand*, issue 19, pp. 101–26.

Ravallion, M., Datt, G., and van de Valle, D. (1991), Quantifying absolute poverty in the developing world, *Review of Income and Wealth*, vol. 37, no. 3, pp. 345–61.

Ringen, S. (1987), *The Possibility of Politics*. Oxford: Clarendon Press.

——(2007) *What Democracy is For. On Freedom and Moral Government.* Princeton, NJ: Princeton University Press.

Rowntree, B. S. (1901), *Poverty. A Study of Town Life*. London: Macmillan.

Ruggles, R. (1990), *Drawing the Line: Alternative Poverty Measures and Their Implications for Public Policy.* Washington, DC: The Urban Institute.

Saunders, P. (2011), *Down and Out: Poverty and Exclusion in Australia*. Bristol: Policy Press.

Saunders, P. and Naidoo, Y. (2009), Poverty, deprivation and consistent poverty, *Economic Record*, vol. 85, no. 271, pp. 417–32.

Sen, A. K. (1985), *Commodities and Capabilities*, Amsterdam: North Holland.

——(1987), *The Standard of Living*. Cambridge: Cambridge University Press.

——(1992), *Inequality Re-examined*. Oxford: Clarendon Press.

Smith [1776] (1976), *An Inquiry into the Nature and Causes of the Wealth of Nations*, R. Campbell, A. Skinner, and W. Todd (eds). Oxford: Clarendon Press.

Townsend, P. (1979), *Poverty in the United Kingdom*. Harmondsworth: Penguin Books.

Willitts, M. (2006), 'Measuring child poverty using material deprivation: possible approaches', *Working Paper No. 28*, London: Department for Work and Pensions.

8
Social exclusion

John Pierson

Introduction

Social exclusion is a multi-dimensional conceptualization of poverty, one that acknowledges both monetary and non-monetary causes. Its first formulation in the mid 1970s was in essence a symbolic phrase that highlighted the fact that certain social groups had comprehensively failed to find their place in post-industrial capitalism and were cut off from the main institutions of society and state. As the concept was explored and refined it reshaped policy development particularly in Britain and the European Union (EU). From the mid 1990s on it has provided a ready construct that both defines social problems and suggests policy responses to those problems.

From the beginning social exclusion has been a contested idea. Some critics have said it diverts attention from the fundamental issue of gross inequality in wealth and income while others have argued that it casts too wide a net embracing more social problems than policy can possibly deal with. Yet the concept has also highlighted new kinds of deprivations and provided a platform for significant research and policy initiatives that address the many linked facets of disadvantage.

This chapter explains the different aspects of social exclusion and familiarizes readers with the debates that have surrounded the concept since its inception. It is in three sections: The first, 'A concept in search of a definition', discusses meanings of social exclusion and its emergence within a centrist discourse on social solidarity. The second section, 'Social exclusion and social policy', examines various policy initiatives in Europe that explicitly tackled the effects of social exclusion from the late 1990s onward and contrasts that approach with major initiatives to tackle disadvantage in the United States which did not explicitly draw on the discourse of social exclusion but shared the sense that poverty has many dimensions. The third section, 'Social exclusion and poverty knowledge' considers some of the areas that exploration of social exclusion has added to our knowledge about poverty. A brief conclusion then examines the place of social exclusion within the extended period of economic crisis, now widely termed the 'great recession', that began in 2008.

A concept in search of a definition

Since the late nineteenth century social investigators have regarded poverty as an objective, quantifiable condition, one that can be measured against a calculated standard: the poverty line. Largely developed within an Anglo-American tradition of empiricism the concept of the poverty line was used to determine eligibility for poor relief and as a prod for social policy to do more. Poverty was no longer regarded as a natural phenomenon about which little could be done but its causes could be explained and the numbers of poor reduced by rational policies (O'Connor, 2001, p. 14). Alongside this approach, however, was a contrary one, intermittently embedded in government policy and in the popular mind, that poverty was a product of dysfunction, deviance or the self-perpetuating 'tangle of pathology' to be found in certain groups. In this account poverty is a product of individual character and behaviour, of psychological and cultural practices that are resistant to participation in the labour market, and are all to willing to take advantage of state provided welfare programmes.

Social exclusion, as a concept, can best be understood as trying to bridge the gap between these two contrary approaches, at once able to shed light on *structural causes* of poverty – low wages, economic disorganization, racial discrimination – and on its *cultural, moral, and behavioural sources*. Elasticity is built into the concept for this very reason; its objective is to define a number of factors both individual and familial as well as social and economic to account for the extent of poverty in a society *and* the psychological disengagement, alienation, that is its by-product. Fundamentally the kinds of policy solutions that emerge have not only to do with income support but seek to change individual behaviour.

In 1974 Rene Lenoir, then in the French government, is widely credited with first using the phrase in his book *Les exclus: un français sur dix* (Lenoir, 1974 and 1989). Lenoir referred to the excluded as not only the poor but also the disabled and learning disabled, young offenders, substance abusers, and '*quatre million d'inadaptés sociaux*' (or social misfits) – in all about 10 per cent of the French population. *Les exclus*, Lenoir argued, lacked the substantial rights of *les citoyens*, either in practice because they were victims of discrimination or because their behaviour cut them off from mainstream society, such as drug addicts, or because they were not citizens of the state in the first place, such as immigrants. Crucially they fell outside the welfare system and did not have access to those powerful institutions that might have helped them gain voice such as the courts to uphold their rights or trade unions to protect their wages.

His formulation was timely. A restructuring economy had begun to substitute relatively well-paid semi-skilled jobs with jobs that demanded higher levels of knowledge and skills. The workforce now had to be suited to a service- and information-based economy creating new pools of structural unemployment and disaffection of those left behind, such as working class young people on public housing estates, that were unable to share in otherwise rising levels of affluence. The fact that those on very low incomes were prevented from participating in society was noted by others at about the same time. Peter Townsend's investigation of relative poverty for example shares considerable overlap with social exclusion. In his classic work Townsend (1979) argued that standards of living are defined within each society; these have to do not only with income but also with levels of health and well-being and access to those goods and services that the particular society considers necessary.

As a concept, however, social exclusion proved difficult to pin down. In part this was due to the different ideological strands that it embraced. In an influential text Ruth Levitas (2005) uncovered three separate, conflicting discourses within discussions on social exclusion:

> The 'redistributionist' discourse concerned with the extreme inequality of wealth which only redistribution of that wealth through taxation, benefits and services, can overcome. The 'underclass' discourse which concentrates on individual delinquency and failure to uphold the norms of society particularly in regards to the work ethic. It pinpoints, for example, the behaviour of absentee fathers who evade child-support responsibilities, young male offenders, and young teenage women who have children outside a stable relationship. Proponents of this discourse argue that the excluded in effect exclude themselves by engaging in certain behaviours such as drug addiction, crime and having children out of wedlock.

> A 'social integrationist' discourse whose primary focus is on paid work and entrance into the labour market as a way of achieving a cohesive society. Levitas argues that this discourse remains uppermost in the policy and practice of the Labour government in the UK that came to power in 1997.
>
> *(Levitas, 2005)*

A weakness lay in the wide range of deprivations that came to be associated with it – food poverty and malnutrition, lack of educational attainment, health inequalities, inadequate housing, financial precariousness, lack of participation in social, cultural and political life, and lack of individual aspiration. As Amartya Sen noted 'the language of exclusion is so versatile and adaptable that there may be a temptation to dress up every deprivation as a case of social exclusion. There is, I fear, some evidence in the vast – and rapidly growing – literature on social exclusion that the language has run well ahead of the creative ideas involved' (Sen, 2000, p. 9).

But as the idea of social exclusion attracted increasing attention within policy circles and among poverty researchers greater efforts were made to define it more precisely. In general, definitions commonly stressed 1 the multi-dimensional nature of exclusion – social, economic, and psychological; 2 the *relational* nature of exclusion and the subjective, felt-experience of those excluded in the form of social distance, humiliation, shame, or rejection, not able to participate; 3 that exclusion was *relative* to the society within which it took place; and 4 the dynamic nature of exclusion – how it is self-reinforcing, tends to perpetuate itself and be resistant to measures to combat it (Atkinson et al., 2002; Silver and Miller, 2002; Burchardt et al., 2002).

One definition of social exclusion

> My own definition at the time sought to bring together several strands that were generally found in academic discussion, in particular emphasizing that it was dynamic and as a concept did not replace but complemented definitions of poverty: Social exclusion is a process over time that deprives individuals and families, groups and neighbourhoods of the resources required for participation in the social, economic and political activity of society as a whole. This process is primarily a consequence of poverty and low income, but other factors such as discrimination, low educational attainment and depleted social capital also underpin it. Through this process people are cut off for a significant period in their lives from institutions and services, social networks and developmental opportunities that the great majority of a society enjoys.
>
> *(Pierson, 2010, p. 12)*

Within the EU, and in particular within the British Labour Party then in opposition social exclusion offered a holistic conceptualization of disadvantage and offered a framework for tackling discrete social problems – homelessness, teen pregnancy, and youth who were neither employed nor in education. The European Commission's 'Towards a Europe of solidarity' described social exclusion as the result of 'mechanisms whereby individuals and groups are excluded from taking part in the social exchanges, from the component practices and rights of social integration and of identity' (European Commission, 1992, p. 7). As Room noted (1995) this marked a significant step because up to that point, the French apart, poverty studies in Europe, developed within Anglo Saxon empirical methodologies, had primarily focused upon *distributional* issues such as the lack of income at the disposal of an individual or a household. In contrast, social exclusion focused primarily on *relational* issues – inadequate social participation, lack of social integration and lack of power (Room, 1995, p. 105).

Official definitions, however, could not supply the hard, measurable conceptualization that programmes to tackle social exclusion needed. From the Lisbon and Nice summits of 2000 member states of the EU were required to put in place national action plans for social inclusion with specific policies left to the discretion of each country. To monitor progress a common set of 'indicators' – measurable data that are in effect proxies for exclusion – were developed across the EU (see Box 8.1 below) without a statement of priorities for member nations to follow.

Box 8.1 European Union indicators of social exclusion

Distribution of income (ratio of share of top 20 per cent to share of bottom 20 per cent)
Share of population below 60 per cent of national median income after social transfers
Distribution of income across the population
Persistence of low income (share of population below the poverty line in at least two of the three previous years)
Persons living in jobless households
Regional disparities through unemployment rates
Proportion of 18–24 year olds who are not in education or training and have only lower secondary education
Long-term unemployment rate
Life expectancy at birth
Self-defined health status – ratio of those in the bottom and top income quintile groups who classify themselves in a bad or very bad state of health

(Adapted from Atkinson et al., 2002)

Social exclusion and social policy

In no country did social exclusion become more prominent as a basis for social policy than in Britain. For a dozen years, from 1997 onwards, the Labour government sought to overcome specific social problems that it linked to policies of the previous Conservative government. That period had led to the fastest rising rate of income inequality *in the developed world* (with the exception of New Zealand) and one of the highest rates of child poverty in Europe except Italy, (Sutherland, 2002). Tackling social exclusion set a fundamental agenda for the major public services following up promises by the newly elected prime minister to cut child poverty in half by 2010 and to promise 'no forgotten people, and no no-hope areas' (quoted in Hills and Stewart, 2005, p. 8). The new government established a cross-departmental Social Exclusion Unit (SEU) at cabinet level to provide 'joined-up solutions for joined up problems'. From the start, government defined social exclusion as a condition in which poverty (low income) was tucked into a series of other characteristics:

> a short-hand label for what can happen when individuals or areas suffer from a combination of linked problems such as unemployment, poor skills, low incomes, poor housing, high crime environments, bad health and family breakdown.
>
> *(DSS, 1999, p. 23)*

Indeed the remit for the SEU specifically excluded the possibility of the redistribution of wealth (the Treasury retained full control over tax and income redistribution); instead it was to report on a number of pressing social problems such as rough sleeping, teen pregnancy, young runaways, ex-prisoners reoffending, anti-social behaviour, and young people not in education, employment or training. The first of the annual government survey on exclusion, *Opportunity for all*, summarised its intentions in tackling 'the complex, multi-dimensional problems' of social exclusion (DSS, 1999, p. 2). It listed the key features of exclusion: lack of opportunities to work, lack of access to education and skills training, childhood deprivation, disrupted families, barriers preventing older people from living active lives, health inequalities, poor housing, disadvantaged neighbourhoods, fear of crime, and discrimination on grounds of age, ethnicity, gender, and disability.

It was an extremely ambitious agenda and the stream of programmes included:

- Sure Start – a comprehensive service for parents and children under five in disadvantaged neighbourhoods
- Connexions service – an advisory and guidance service for young people to assist in their transition to adulthood
- Working tax credits to assist those in work on low wages or caring for children
- New Deal programmes to help specific groups of people – young people aged 18–24, long-term unemployed adults, lone parents – find work
- Neighbourhood renewal aimed at the most disadvantaged neighbourhoods, these including regeneration projects (the New Deal for Communities) and the introduction of neighbourhood management schemes – localised partnerships delivering joined-up services to address local needs.

Subsequent evaluations for each of these programmes indicated some progress in delivering outcomes but not as complete or clear-cut as government might have expected. (See Hills and Stewart, 2005, for a comprehensive analysis of the impact of these programmes, as well as the annual monitoring reports on social exclusion published by the Joseph Rowntree Foundation.) For example the level of child poverty was reduced but missed that target. Drawing on the NPI indicators (see Box 8.2 below) Palmer and colleagues found that the number of children living in low-income households had fallen, but only by half of what was required to meet government's own target while the number living in workless households had fallen by a fifth (Palmer et al., 2008, p. 39; see also Power et al., 2011 for a comprehensive discussion of indicators of children's well-being).

Box 8.2 Indicators for determining the number of socially excluded children in Britain (New Policy Institute)

Number of children living in workless household
Number living in households with below half-average income
Percentage of low birth weight babies
Number of accidental deaths

Low educational attainment
Number of permanent school exclusions
Number of births to girls under age 16
Number in young offender institutions (age 10 to 16).

(New Policy Institute Monitoring Poverty and Social Exclusion *1999, thereafter annual)*

Social exclusion in the United States

In contrast to Britain social exclusion as a concept rarely appears as the focus of research in the United States or provides the basis for federal or state social policy. In part this is because 'exclusion' has overtones of race discrimination and exclusionary actions on the part of clubs or institutions, zoning decisions regarding property, or exclusion from high prestige resources, such as particular neighborhoods or private schools (Silver and Miller, 2002).

It is also generally deemed too difficult to define concisely or measure. In fact the United States has had an official poverty line since the mid 1960s for the War on Poverty under the Johnson administration (Orshansky, 1965). This set different thresholds of income in relation to a minimum diet for families of various sizes and compositions to determine a family's poverty status. It assumes that households above the poverty line are able to afford the basic needs of all members of those households. The official poverty line has thus maintained a focus on income poverty while regarding non-monetary measures of hardship and social exclusion as complementary to income poverty measures which can be useful in illuminating aspects of people's well-being (Iceland, 2005, p. 30).

The US Census Bureau (Short, 2011) has recently published a supplemental poverty measure (SPM) to overcome some of the limitations of the official poverty line which did not take into account expenses necessary to hold a job such as transportation costs and child care, nor the income transfers that a family might receive in the form of tax credits or food stamps. The supplemental measure goes some way to repairing these problems:

- Its thresholds represent a dollar amount spent on a basic set of goods that includes food, clothing, shelter, and utilities.
- It includes the costs of child care and transportation, as well as the rise in costs of housing and healthcare insurance.
- It includes a small additional amount to allow for other needs (for example household supplies, personal care and non-work-related transportation).
- It takes account of income transfers into low income families such as food stamps, housing subsidies, subsidies for child care, tax credits, school breakfast, and lunch subsidies which the earlier measure had also ignored.

The SPM will not supplant the official poverty line – which will continue to define eligibility for programmes and funding distribution. But it brings US poverty measurement more in line with a 'necessities'-orientated definition of relative poverty because it takes into account the costs of the particular features of American society. These include the high cost of healthcare, profound regional differences in family expenditure, and changes in family structure – rising levels of divorce and co-habitation (Iceland, 2005; DeNavas-Walt et al., 2011). (Fuller scales based on a 'necessities' definition of poverty are available from the National Centre for Children in Poverty at Columbia University while measuring well-being and broader capabilities is available from the Gallup-Healthways Well-being Index.)

In addition to redefining poverty many of the components of exclusion have been analysed particularly through investigations of concentrations of poverty in urban neighbourhoods and in the use and misuse of the term 'underclass'. Wacquant and Wilson (1993) argued that the interrelated set of phenomena captured by the term 'underclass' was primarily social and economic in origin, that African American ghettos – and other areas of concentrated poverty – experienced a crisis not because a 'welfare ethos' had taken over residents but because joblessness and economic exclusion had reached dramatic proportions, triggering a process of 'hyperghettoization' (Wilson and Wacquant, 1989, p. 9). Their research highlighted the enormous penalties that beset African American urban neighbourhoods through deindustrialisation and the loss of secure manufacturing jobs for the semi-skilled inner city working class. Not only did this take away the means for regular income for sustaining a family, but it removed whole neigbourhoods from connections to society's main source of significance, discipline, and organization for daily life.

Two very different solutions have been underway in the United States for fully twenty years attempting to deal with the consequences of this extreme spatial concentration of exclusion: relocating residents from disadvantaged neighbourhoods in inner cities and comprehensive community initiatives.

Relocation

The Gautreux programme is a court-ordered housing programme under which the Chicago Housing Authority was required to provide rental subsidies and tenant counselling to help low-income families – virtually all African American and many female-headed – to move from public housing projects in high-poverty, high-crime neighbourhoods to low-crime, mostly white suburban areas with high levels of employment some 20 or 30 miles away. From 1976 to 1998, the housing authority moved nearly 25,000 poor African Americans from crumbling public housing to subsidized housing in suburbs where no more than 30 per cent of the population was African American.

In doing so it provided a ready-made source of experimental data that compared with similar families who stayed in Chicago, indicated those who moved had greater stability of housing and showed much higher rates of children going to college, of youth employment as well as greater life satisfaction for adults. Not all families adjusted well to the significant change of neighbourhood but a majority did and the programme is generally regarded as a unique demonstration of what a sustained shift in neighbourhood quality can provide for disadvantaged families (Deluca and Rosenbaum, 2004).

Principles of relocation have subsequently been adopted by hundreds of high-cost housing markets in the United States that have developed inclusionary zoning policies. The zoning policy of Montgomery County, Maryland, for example, aims not just to build entry-level homes, but allows the local authority to purchase one-third of these homes within each sub-division and to operate them as federally subsidized public housing, allowing households typically earning below the poverty line to live in affluent neighbourhoods and send their children to schools where the vast majority of students come from families that do not live in poverty. Fundamentally the schemes provide access to improved levels of social capital. The outcomes are greater stability for family structure, better access to services such as libraries and health clinics, increased skilled employment opportunities for parents close to home and association with pro-social attitudes and behaviours with less exposure to peers and adults engaged in anti-social activities or drug use (Schwartz, 2010).

Comprehensive community initiatives

Comprehensive community initiatives (CCIs), largely sponsored by major foundations such as Ford, Annie Casey, and Rockefeller, have over a thirty-year period addressed the multi-dimensional roots of poverty and low-income neighbourhoods. CCIs shore up social capital in disadvantaged neighbourhoods by providing capacity building for residents and coax new neighbourhood organizations into being, to engage in local revitalization (Fulbright-Anderson and Auspos, 2006).

The Annie Casey Foundation's 'Making Connections' is one such effort. It runs across multiple disadvantaged urban neighbourhoods in cities such as Denver, Indianapolis, and Louisville. Beginning in 1999 it adopted a 'two-generation' approach, developing local programmes to both enhance parents' earning capacity and to get children ready for success at school. The programme also recognized the multi-prong nature of effective responses to disadvantage and built up working partnerships in each city – offices of economic development, community colleges, job training and employment agencies, housing partnerships, and community organizing collaboratives among others. The indicators the Foundation developed for evaluating this work to some degree overlap with the EU indicators for social exclusion. They track the number of:

- households with children that report earned income and one or more adults in work
- households with employer-provided family health benefits
- households with children who have accumulated savings
- children in preschool programmes
- children assessed as ready for school
- children's attendance in the early grades
- children reading at or above proficiency level in third or fourth grade.

(Annie Casey Foundation, 2011)

Social exclusion and poverty knowledge

Explorations of social exclusion have taught us a great deal about the effects of poverty that result from inequality in developed countries: exclusion 'from the lives, the understanding and the caring of others' (Dorling, 2011, p. 91). As Dorling argues, exclusion results now not from living in abject poverty but as the consequence of a new range of social assumptions based on the extraordinary disparity in incomes in the developed world – particularly in the United States and Britain. That the incomes of the affluent are so much higher than the lower sixth has produced, among policy elites, the general assumption that poverty should no longer exist: that because the worst of twentieth-century poverty has been dealt with, the poor have not done enough themselves to avoid being poor (ibid., p. 92).

But research into social exclusion has shown there are different ways in which people are rendered poor. In their research Bradshaw and Finch (2003) used three different measures of poverty to determine the number of poor households in Britain. They looked at the percentage of households that 1) cannot afford basic necessities; 2) subjectively considered themselves poor, and; 3) live on an income below the poverty threshold (two-thirds of the median wage in Britain). Thus it is possible that some households can have an income above the poverty line but not be able to afford things seen as essential by most people. From this they found that 5.6 per cent of British households were poor by all three standards and 16.3 per cent poor by two of the standards, while households found to be poor across all the three standards approached 30 per cent. It is likely, as Dorling concludes, that families that fall into two of these categories are excluded from the norms of society, a differentiated social class that cannot escape taking on debt, debt that they are unable to repay (Dorling, 2011).

Research has also paid considerable attention to the functions and attributes of social networks with the intent to determine in what ways they can empower excluded individuals and families. Briggs (1997) has discussed the difference between networks for 'getting by' – the close, supportive networks embedded in everyday relationships of friends, family, and neighbours – and networks for 'getting ahead' – those that provide crucial information for individuals and families on jobs, education pathways, training, and other options for advancing individual human capital. The excluded are bereft of both but particularly the second, those networks that lie outside the immediate neighbourhood, that are occasional and episodic in nature and more tenuous than a close personal relationship. It is now well understood that networks based on 'the strength of weak ties' (Granovetter, 1973) facilitate connections between people and employment and cultural opportunities to be found outside their usual range of experience lacking in disadvantaged neighbourhoods. But network analysis has also become finer grained. Both Wenger (1997) and Scharf et al. (2005) have, for example, explored the different kinds of networks that sustain older people in both rural and urban areas of Britain, while Morrow (2004) examined the social networks of children age 12–15 in disadvantaged neighbourhoods.

The fact that social exclusion is spatially concentrated has prompted research on the dynamics of excluded neighbourhoods – how high levels of unemployment, poor health, and high crime reinforce each other in ways that affect the behaviour and choices of all residents living there. A formidable amount of research on such 'neighbourhood effects' now exists. For example, child and adolescent outcomes such as infant mortality, low birth weight, teen child bearing, school exclusions, and anti-social behaviour can all be linked to neighbourhood (Pierson, 2007, p. 13). Beyond these specific effects Lupton and Power (2002) have well described the cycle by which entire neighbourhoods are excluded in a process that once underway is difficult to break (see Figure 8.1). Their research established how evidence of anti-social behaviour and less social

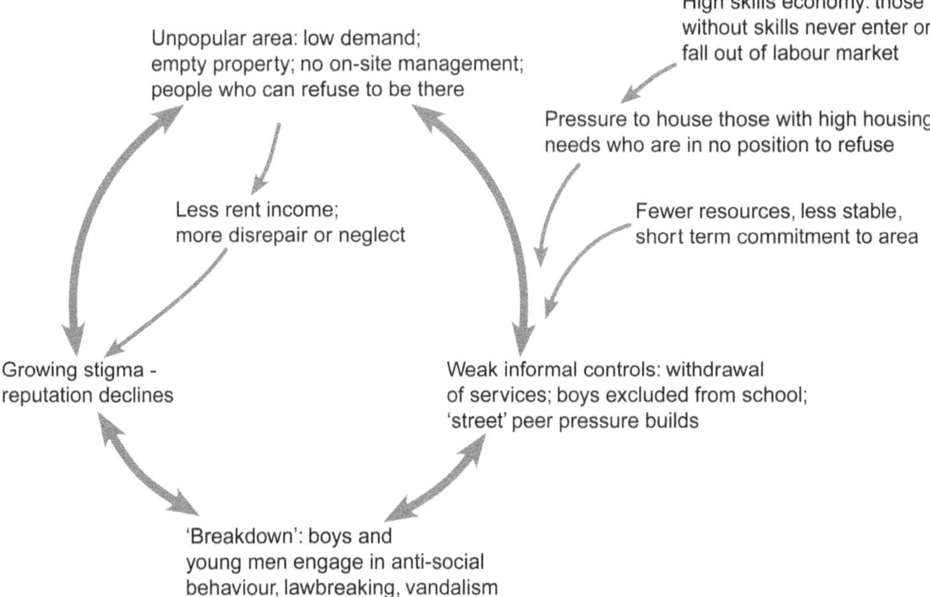

Figure 8.1 Cycle and decline in some disadvantaged neighbourhoods
Source: Adapted from Lupton and Powell (2002).

control leads to less social contact and informal supervision of pro-social norms which in turn changes public attitudes toward the estate as its reputation declines and those who can leave do so. A tipping point can then be quickly reached as the neighbourhood becomes more unpopular: properties are empty, there is less rent income and more disrepair and neglect, families with little housing choice available to them are moved in, more problems emerge with fewer resources to fix them. Social capital – trust in neighbours, social contact – is depleted and the estate finds itself estranged from the wider urban context.

Conclusion

Social exclusion and austerity

The 'great recession' – as the severe economic downturn that began in 2008 is widely named – has completely changed the context within which efforts to reduce social exclusion take place (see Box 8.3). The very phrase 'social exclusion' implies that programmes need to be constructed to reverse it. Not only has the great recession seen sharply rising inequality across the developed world and greater numbers thrown into poverty but the severe cutbacks in public expenditure across Europe and the United States make further programmatic efforts to reduce exclusion unlikely.

Box 8.3 Impact of the great recession

- In the United States a recent Census Bureau report highlighted that the median wealth of Hispanic households fell by 66 per cent from 2005 to 2009. By contrast, the median wealth of whites fell by just 16 per cent over the same period. African Americans saw their wealth drop by 53 per cent. Asians also saw a big decline, with household wealth dropping 54 per cent (DeNavas-Walt et al., 2011).
- The numbers of children in poverty have also increased. In the United States in 2009, 21 per cent of all children ages 0–17 (15.5 million) lived in poverty. This is up from the low of 16 per cent in 2000 and 2001. In the state of Montana 44 per cent of children now live in low-income families – defined as income below twice the federal poverty level. Despite 86 per cent of these children having at least one parent who is employed, many of their families struggle to make ends meet on earnings alone. While in work supports are available, they are withdrawn sharply as wage levels decrease leaving families facing a 'benefits cliff' (Chau, 2011). Native American, African American, and Hispanic children are disproportionately poor (Wright et al., 2011).
- In the UK two very different patterns were apparent among children in low-income households. The number of children in low-income, *working* households ('in-work poverty') has never been higher – some 2.1 million in 2008 and 2009. By contrast the number of children in *workless* families, that is those families whose income was derived wholly from child benefit, child tax credit, and other supports, actually dropped to the lowest level since 1984, to 1.6 million children (Parekh et al., 2010). Such data from Montana and Britain indicate the weakness of welfare systems that rely wholly on work-linked conditionality: wages so low that jobs fail to provide routes away from poverty (Sheldrick et al., 2010).

The prospect of an extended period of austerity raises profound questions over the direction of social policy and in particular over those policies that tackle social exclusion. In brief, what happens to redistributive policies – using public expenditure and income transfers to minimize exclusion – when the economy sours? It is likely that the multi-dimensional nature of social exclusion is too broad and too closely associated with large-scale programmes for conservative governments committed to austerity. Centre-right policies seek to narrow the band of the defined poor, not broaden it. Welfare measures are targeted and means tested for 'the poorest, the most vulnerable, those in the greatest need' – a smaller group than the socially excluded. In a period of sharp cutbacks in public expenditure it is likely that governments of all kinds will tend to focus on changing attitudes in relation to work, parenting, and informal social control as a means to tackling disadvantage and exclusion.

It is probable that while EU policy will continue to rely formally on multi-dimensional conceptualisations of poverty, considerable variants will exist from country to country. 'Social Europe' has not yet developed a single policy on income protection or work conditions and several countries are drastically restructuring their welfare systems, whether by ideological design or in attempt to reduce debt levels.

Britain offers a good example of both. In restructuring the welfare state the Coalition government elected in 2010 has re-established a principle that was at the heart of the nineteenth-century Poor Law: that state benefits for able-bodied adults should not be higher in value than the lowest wage. While careful to avoid overt reference to traditional elements of an 'underclass', policy has tied benefits to rigorous investigation of individual incapacity and efforts to find work. The Coalition has also argued that earlier targets under Labour, based on relative household income, were a poor indicator for achieving the eradication of child poverty. An independent review, commissioned by the government, has shown how a multi-dimensional approach to poverty can virtually ignore income support if it so chooses. The review called for a new index of children's 'life chance' measurements and its author, the Labour MP Frank Field, noted that poverty is a 'much more subtle enemy than purely lack of money' (Field, 2010, p. 12). He argued that funding be concentrated on services for children under five, as opposed to income support, so that children's centres 'identify, reach and provide targeted help to the most disadvantaged families' yet remain welcoming, inclusive, socially mixed, and non-stigmatising (ibid., p. 7). The Coalition seeks behavioural change, using individual caseworkers to sort out the problems – addiction, debt, worklessness, poor parenting, truancy, anti-social behaviour – of the hundred thousand families that it views as a prominent source of social problems (Department for Education and Department for Work and Pensions, 2011). Much of this picks up on programmes developed by the previous Labour government but linked now to substantial cuts in income support.

Two issues, however, will continue to exert pressure on governments across the developed world to address social exclusion. One is the lack of social mobility for those growing up in poor households. The appeal to aspiration and the capacity for individuals to leave behind disadvantaged circumstances in order to improve their lives cuts across the political spectrum and is taken up by all parties in the United Kingdom. Even in the United States, where contrary to expectation social mobility is less than in many countries of Europe and particularly problematic for children in the bottom quintile of income (DeLeire and Lopoo, 2010), right of centre voices have argued that social mobility must be accelerated. Thus in the age of austerity we can expect policy to focus not just on the attitudes and culture of 'hard-to-reach' families but on the barriers and lack of resources that prevent whole layers of society from obtaining a reasonable standard of living. Linked to this is a second structural issue – the shuttle between unemployment and low paid employment. Simply put, casualised labour markets do not provide sufficient remuneration to lift individuals and families out of poverty, however it is defined. For welfare regimes geared primarily to requiring individual claimants to find work, both issues present a challenge with no easy answers.

References

Atkinson, A., Marlier, E., and Nolan, B. (2004), Indicators and targets for social Inclusion in the European Union. *Journal of Common Market Studies*, vol. 42, no. 1, pp. 47–75.

Atkinson, A. and Davoudi, S. (2000), The concept of social exclusion in the European Union: context, development and possibilities. *Journal of Common Market Studies*, vol. 38, no. 3, pp. 427–48.

Atkinson, A., Cantillon, B. Marlier, E., and Nolan, B. (2002), *Social Indicators: The EU and Social Inclusion*. Oxford: Oxford University Press.

Bradshaw, J. and Finch, N. (2003), Overlaps in Dimensions of Poverty. *International Social Policy*, vol. 32, no. 4, pp. 513–25.

Briggs, X. (1997), *Social Capital and the Cities: Advice to Change Agents*. Bellagio, Italy: International Workshop on Community Building.

Burchardt, T., Le Grand, J. and Piachaud, D. (1999), Social Exclusion in Britain 1991–95. *Social Policy and Administration*, vol. 33, no. 3, pp. 227–44.

Annie Casey Foundation (2011), 'Making Connections.' Online: www.aecf.org/majorinitiatives/making connections.aspx. Retrieved 6 July 2011.

Chau, M. (2011), *Making Work Pay in Montana*. New York: National Center for Children in Poverty, Columbia University.

DeLeire, T. and Lopoo, L. (2010), *Family Structure and the Economic Mobility of Children*. Washington, DC: The Pew Charitable Trusts.

Deluca, S. and Rosenbaum, J. (2003), If low income blacks are given a chance to live in white neighborhoods, will they stay? Examining mobility patterns with quasi-experimental data. *Housing Policy Debate*, vol. 14, no, 3, pp. 305–45.

DeNavas-Walt, C., Proctor, B., and Smith, J. (2011), Poverty and Health Insurance Coverage in the United States: 2010. *US Census Bureau*. Washington, DC: Department of Commerce.

Department of Social Security (1999), *Opportunity for All: Tackling Poverty and Social Exclusion*. Cmnd 4445. London: The Stationery Office.

——(1999), *Opportunity for all*. London: HM Government.

Field, F. (2010), *The Foundation Years: Preventing Poor Children Becoming Poor Adults*. London: HM Government.

Fulbright-Anderson, K. and Auspos, P. (2004), *Community Change: Theories, Practice and Evidence*. Washington, DC: The Aspen Institute.

Gordon, D. et al. (2000), *Poverty and Social Exclusion in Britain*. York: Joseph Rowntree Foundation.

Granovetter, M. (1973), The Strength of Weak Ties Hypothesis. *American Journal of Sociology*, vol. 78, no. 8, pp. 1360–80.

Hanley, T. (2011), *The Implications of Globalisation for Poverty and Communities in the UK*. York: Joseph Rowntree Foundation.

Hills, J. and Stewart, K. (eds) (2005), *A More Equal Society? New Labour, Poverty, Inequality and Exclusion*. Bristol: Policy Press.

Iceland, J. (2005), *Measuring Poverty: A New Approach Experimental Poverty Measures*. Washington, DC: National Research Council.

——(2006), *Poverty in America: A Handbook*. 2nd edn. Berkeley: University of California Press.

Kubisch, A., Auspos, P., Brown, P., and Dewar, T. (2010), *Voices from the Field III*. Washington, DC: The Aspen Institute.

Lenoir, R. (1974 and 1989), *Les exclus, un français sur dix*. Paris: Seuil.

Levitas, R. (2006), 'The concept and measurement of social exclusion', in C. Pantazis, D. Gordon, and R. Levitas (eds), *Poverty and Social Exclusion in Britain: The Millennium Survey*. Bristol, Policy Press.

——(2005), *The Inclusive Society? Social Exclusion and New Labour*. Basingstoke: Macmillan.

Lupton, R. and Power, A. (2002), 'Social Exclusion and Neighbourhoods', in Hills et al. (eds), *Understanding Social Exclusion*. Oxford: Oxford University Press.

Morrow, V. (2004), 'Networks and Neighbourhoods: Children's Accounts of Friendship, Family and Place', in Phillipson et al. (eds), *Social Networks and Social Exclusion Sociological and Policy Perspectives*. Aldershot: Ashgate.

National Centre for Social Research (2011), *British Attitudes Survey 2011.* London.
O'Connor, A. (2001), *Poverty Knowledge Social Science, Social Policy, and the Poor in Twentieth-Century U.S. History.* Princeton, NJ: Princeton University Press.
Orshansky, M. (1965), Counting the Poor: Another Look at the Poverty Profile. *Social Security Bulletin* 28, 1, pp. 3–29
Palmer, G., MacInnes, T., and Kenway, P. (2008), *Monitoring Poverty and Social Exclusion 2008.* York: New Policy Institute/Joseph Rowntree Foundation.
Parekh, A., MaxInnes, T., and Kenway, P. (2010), *Monitoring Poverty and Social Exclusion 2010.* York, New Policy Institute/Joseph Rowntree Foundation.
Phillipson, C., Allan, G. and Morgan, D. (2004), *Social Networks and Social Exclusion: Sociological and Policy Perspectives.* Aldershot: Ashgate Publishing Limited.
Piachaud, D. and Sutherland, H. (2002), *Changing Poverty Post 1997.* London: Centre for Analysis of Social Exclusion. CASE Paper 63.
Pierson, J. (2010), *Tackling Social Exclusion*, 2nd edn. Abingdon: Routledge.
——(2007), *Going Local: Working in Communities and Neighbourhoods.* Abingdon: Routledge.
Power, A., Serle, N., and Willmot, H. (2011), *Obstacles and Opportunities: Today's Children, Tomorrow's Families.* London: Centre for Analysis of Social Exclusion, London School of Economics. CASE Report 66.
Rahman, M., Palmer, G., Kenway, P. and Howarth, C. (2000), *Monitoring Poverty and Social Exclusion 2000.* York: New Policy Institute/Joseph Rowntree Foundation.
Room, G. (1995), Poverty in Europe: competing paradigms of analysis. *Policy and Politics*, vol. 23, no. 2, pp. 103–13.
Scharf, T., Phillipson, C. and Smith, E. (2005), *Multiple Exclusion and Quality of Life amongst Excluded Older People in Disadvantaged Neighbourhoods.* London: Office of the Deputy Prime Minister.
Schwartz, H. (2010), *Housing Policy is School Policy: Economically integrative housing promotes academic success in Montgomery County Maryland.* New York: Century Foundation.
Sen, A. (2000), Social Exclusion: Concept, Application, and Scrutiny. *Social Development Papers No. 1.* Manila, Office of Environment and Social Development, Asian Development Bank.
Sheldrick, T., MacDonald, R., Webster, C., and Garthwaite, K. (2010), *The Low-pay, No-pay Cycle: Understanding Recurrent Poverty.* York: Joseph Rowntree Foundation.
Short, K. (2011), *The Research Supplemental Poverty Measure 2010.* US Census Bureau.
Silver, H. and Miller, S. (2002), Social Exclusion: The European Approach to Social Disadvantage. *Indicators*, vol. 2, no. 2, pp. 5–21.
Tavernise, S. (2011), Soaring Poverty Casts Spotlight on 'Lost Decade'. *New York Times*, September 13.
Tunstall, R., Lupton, R., Kneale, D., and Jenkins, A. (2011), 'Growing Up in Social Housing in the New Millennium: Housing, Neighbourhoods, and Early Outcomes for Children Born in 2000'. *CASE/143.* London: Centre for Analysis of Social Exclusion, London School of Economics.
Wacquant, L. and Wilson, W. (1993) 'The Cost of Racial and Class Exclusion in the Inner City', in W. Wilson (ed.), *The Ghetto Underclass Social Science Perspectives.* London: Sage Publications.
Wenger, C. (1997), Social Networks and the Prediction of Elderly People at Risk. *Ageing and Mental Health*, issue 1, pp. 311–20.
Wight, V., Chau, M., and Aratani, Y. (2011), *Why Are America's Children Poor?* New York: National Center for Children in Poverty, Columbia University.

9
Benefits in kind and in cash

Manos Matsaganis

Introduction

Social benefits can be provided either in cash or in kind. Cash benefits are *income transfers*, such as retirement pensions, unemployment benefits, and social assistance. Benefits in kind can be defined as commodities (i.e. goods or services) directly transferred to recipients at zero or below-market prices (Glennerster, 2009; Barr, 2012).

This chapter describes the characteristics of benefits in kind and cash benefits, reviews the main arguments for and against in-kind provision, and discusses the implications of choosing one type of benefit over the other in terms of distributional effects, incentives to participate in the labour market, and administrative ease.

Core concepts

Benefits in cash and in kind may be found in all areas of social policy, for example, old age (see Chapter 34), health (Chapter 33), unemployment (Chapter 12), disability (Chapter 35), family (Chapter 36), housing (Chapter 32), etc.

Retirement pensions, unemployment benefits, disability allowances, child benefits, housing allowances, and income support to poor households are all examples of social benefits provided in cash.

Long-term care for the elderly, retraining courses for the unemployed, residential services for the mentally ill, kindergarten-type care for pre-school children, the allocation of social housing to eligible households, and the direct provision of food to the poor are all cases of social benefits in kind.

Benefits in kind: goods vs. services

In Europe, benefits in kind are usually *services*, such as education (see Chapter 40), healthcare and child care. For example, hospital care in most countries is provided either free of charge or at near-zero prices (at the point of use). User fees are even rarer in the case of education: enrolment is compulsory up to a certain age (e.g., 15), while tuition is provided free of charge to all children attending state schools, irrespective of family income. Moreover, child care is often heavily subsidised (Matsaganis and Verbist, 2009); kindergartens are run by the state or (more commonly) local government, while user fees, where applicable, are usually income-related (in the sense that higher-income families pay higher fees, while lower-income ones pay less or are fully exempted). Furthermore, social care (e.g., for the elderly) may also be available on similar terms; besides, several countries such as Germany have developed long-term care insurance schemes to cater for the future needs of an ageing population (Rothgang, 2010).

Benefits in kind in the form of *goods* rather than services are rather uncommon in Europe. Even though food parcels may be handed out by charities, and soup kitchens may be organised by municipalities, these are sporadic or are limited to emergencies, or cater for the needs of marginal groups such as the homeless. Moreover, in some countries council flats are allocated at subsidised rents (or free of charge) to eligible families, but in many countries rent subsidies and the direct provision of social housing are being phased out in favour of means-tested housing allowances (in cash). Finally, in most countries emergency accommodation is also available for selected groups in acute need (i.e. the homeless, refugees, victims of family abuse, and so on).

The direct provision of food to the poor as a matter of course (i.e. not only in the case of famine relief and other emergencies) is still quite common in Latin America (see Chapter 23) and the USA (Chapter 21). For instance, under the Food Support Programme (*Programa Apoyo Alimentario*, PAL) in Mexico, families living in rural poor communities receive a monthly food basket. In the USA, welfare recipients are issued with Food Stamps – vouchers exchangeable for food at supermarkets – usually in the context of Temporary Assistance for Needy Families (TANF) or, before 1996, Aid to Families with Dependent Children (AFDC).

Conditional cash transfers

Finally, in some countries, cash benefits may be actually tied to in-kind provision. For example, under the popular *Bolsa Família* programme in Brazil, low-income families receive a monthly cash allowance on condition that their children attend school and regularly visit healthcare facilities. Similarly, the *Progresa* programme in Mexico distributes nutritional supplements as well as cash on the same conditions (school attendance and regular health checkups). Similar programmes exist in other Latin American countries but also in Asia and elsewhere. The general intention is to link cash assistance with an investment in children's human capital (World Bank, 2009).

In Europe, conditional cash transfers can be said to exist in the form of the 'new generation' of guaranteed minimum income schemes, for example the French *Revenu minimum d'insertion* (*Revenu de solidarité active* since 2009). These schemes provide cash assistance in cases of extreme financial hardship, but beneficiaries are required to participate in 'social reintegration' activities. The same principle applies in Britain in the case of Education Maintenance Allowance, a means-tested programme that subsidizes children to remain in school for up to two years beyond the statutory age (Dearden et al., 2011), or 'Welfare to Work' programmes like the New Deal for the Unemployed, where the receipt of cash benefits is conditioned on participation in active labour market policies (see Chapter 12).

Relative weight of benefits in kind versus cash

On balance, most social benefits are in cash – at least in Europe. In 2008, the 27 member states of the European Union (EU) as a whole spent 16.5% of gross domestic product (GDP) on cash benefits and another 8.8% of GDP on benefits in kind. In other words, approximately 65% of all social expenditure was associated with cash benefits, with the remaining 35% corresponded to benefits in kind (Eurostat, 2010).

The share of in-kind benefits in total social spending was highest in Sweden, Ireland, Britain, and Denmark (between 42% and 45%), near average in Spain (36%), France (35%), and Germany (33%), and lowest in Poland and Cyprus (around 22% to 23%).

Healthcare accounts for three quarters of all expenditure on benefits in kind in the EU (6.6% of GDP in 2008). Education, which is not included in European social expenditure statistics, is the next largest item. In the Organisation for Economic Co-operation and Development (OECD) area, education and healthcare (at 4.3% and 5.8% of GDP respectively) make up the bulk of benefits in kind, while child care, services to the elderly and social housing account between them for another 2.2% of GDP (Verbist et al., 2011).

Means testing

Social benefits, whether in cash or in kind, may be means tested or not (Atkinson, 1995). With means testing, benefits are restricted to the poor; alternatively, eligibility thresholds could be set at higher levels, designed merely to exclude the rich ('affluence testing'). Administrators may assess applicants' incomes plus other assets such as bank deposits and housing wealth (in which case the term 'means test' applies), or their incomes alone (in which case the term 'income test' is used). Means tested benefits are almost always non-contributory, i.e. funded out of general taxation (see Chapter 38).

Non-means tested benefits can be either contributory or not. Social insurance benefits are contributory: a specific contributory record (i.e. a minimum number of insurance days or years) is among the eligibility conditions that recipients must meet. The required contributory record is rather long in the case of old-age pensions (e.g., 35 or 40 years), but is typically much shorter in the case of unemployment insurance (e.g., 2 or 3 years). On the other hand, child benefits or child care services are almost always non-contributory, whether income-related or not.

Non-means tested benefits are considerably more common: in 2008, means-testing accounted for a mere 11% of all social expenditure in Europe (Eurostat, 2010). Benefits in kind were somewhat more likely to be means tested than cash benefits (15% vs. 9% of all expenditure in the relevant category). The share of means-tested benefits was comparatively high in Ireland (25%) and in the United Kingdom (16%). At the other extreme, it was around 3% in Denmark and Sweden, and even less than that in the Czech Republic and the Baltic countries.

Arguments for benefits in cash versus kind

Even though redistribution of income from rich to poor through cash benefits (and, as shown in Chapter 4, the tax system) seems to be the standard case, the very substantial presence of in-kind benefits in actual systems of social protection around the world (as seen in the previous section) begs the question of why and when the latter are preferred over the former.

The case for benefits in cash

The main argument in favour of cash provision is personal autonomy – or, translated in the language of economists, 'consumer sovereignty'. Recipients of an income transfer can spend the money involved as they like, rather than being constrained to consume a particular quantity (and quality) of a particular good provided in kind. Similarly, using the tools of economic theory, it can be shown that a consumer will reach a higher level of utility if paid a benefit in cash than if given a benefit in kind, and that the former will be less costly than the latter.

Furthermore, cash benefits are superior to in-kind provision on the grounds of administrative costs as well: paying recipients a transfer of €100 in cash will be cheaper than providing them with a food basket worth €100.

The case for benefits in kind

A common justification for in-kind provision is paternalism and inter-dependent preferences (Currie and Gahvari, 2008). Under inter-dependent preferences, if the rich care for the condition of the poor, a transfer from the former to the latter will leave both better off. The transfer may be funded out of taxation, but could also be purely voluntary.

However, the rich generally are concerned neither with the welfare (as such) nor with the level of income of the poor: their most specific concern is with poor families' consumption – and, more specifically, with 'good' rather than 'bad' consumption (both as defined by the rich). In particular, the welfare of the rich increases as the poor consume certain items (e.g. children's clothing or food), but it declines as they consume other items (e.g. cigarettes or alcohol).

Therefore, from the point of view of tax payers, the provision of an income transfer will be inferior to the provision to eligible recipients of particular goods and services, either directly (e.g. healthcare and education) or indirectly (e.g. through vouchers such as food stamps).

Paternalism is intimately related to the idea of merit goods and merit wants. Society may be concerned that certain goods should be available to all its members – or even that all its members should be forced to consume certain goods. Therefore, school attendance up to a certain age is compulsory, rather than left to the individual preferences of children or their parents.

A related idea is the notion of 'specific egalitarianism'. For instance, it has been argued that while many people have no problem with income inequality *per se*, they would like to see that all individuals receive adequate food, medical services, or housing (Tobin, 1970). It follows that, even where political preferences are generally pitched against large-scale redistribution via social security and the tax system, there remains a strong argument in favour of public provision in kind of essential goods and services.

Another argument concerns price effects. Benefits in cash increase (as intended) the purchasing power of recipients, and hence push up their demand for several goods and services. Depending on supply conditions, some of the increase in demand may be translated in higher prices rather than increased consumption alone. Conversely, the price effect of benefits in kind will be difficult to predict *a priori*. When benefits in kind increase the overall supply of the commodity in question, prices will be lower than with cash benefits. For instance, the availability of social housing may help keep market rents affordable. However, when the public provision of a good or service simply displaces private provision, or creates its own demand, prices may remain as high as would have been without the benefit in kind. This is especially the case with medical care, where private practitioners are likely to maintain high prices in spite of competition from public providers by engaging in 'supplier-induced demand' (as discussed in Chapter 33).

The case for benefits in kind is also supported by the 'Samaritan's dilemma' (Buchanan, 1975). When recipients are entitled to benefits as long as they are poor, this provides them with an incentive to remain poor. As a result of this, the very existence of social assistance may in fact induce a demand for social assistance, generating an increase in the numbers of persons in need. Abstracting from the more controversial aspects of libertarian political economy and the perverse incentives of targeted benefits, the 'Samaritan's dilemma' provides a distinct justification for benefits in kind, along the lines of the Chinese proverb that it is better to teach someone how to fish than simply give them a fish. Indeed, whether or not one accepts the thesis that cash benefits breed dependency, there can be little doubt that healthcare and education constitute investments in human capital, and therefore help individuals escape poverty in the future.

Feasibility of in-kind provision

Even when desirable, in-kind provision may not always be possible. In some cases, recipients may subvert the preferences of social planners or tax payers. For example, this will happen if the benefit in kind is 'tradeable' – that is, when recipients can sell the good and use the money to buy a different consumption bundle. As seen below, the risk of this happening will be smaller when in-kind provision is 'inframarginal' – i.e., when the quantity of the good or service transferred is lower than what was consumed prior to the intervention (Moffitt, 1989).

The same problem will arise if the good provided in kind is 'fungible' – that is when, following the receipt of a food parcel, an individual can spend freely the money he or she would have otherwise spent on food (including the 'bad' consumption mentioned above – alcohol, etc.).

Market failure

While paternalism and merit goods can go some way to explaining why governments provide health and education directly (rather than paying recipients cash benefits to enable them to buy as much healthcare and education as they like), in certain cases a more powerful explanation of in-kind provision involves market failure. Since doctors have more knowledge about the type and quantity of healthcare their patients need, this information asymmetry would create insurmountable problems in the context of the free market. The ensuing market failures (such as moral hazard, adverse selection, and so on) will result in both high costs overall as well as coverage gaps among the most needy (e.g. the poor, the old, the chronically sick, etc.). In view of that, not only do most societies entrust doctors with the relevant decisions, but actually do so in the context of publicly funded healthcare (Chapter 33). Similar arguments apply in the case of education.

In other words, the choice between benefits in cash and benefits in kind to achieve some *equity* objective is constrained by considerations of *efficiency*. In general, when market allocation is efficient, equity objectives can be pursued via benefits in cash, enabling recipients to buy what they need at market prices. In contrast, when markets fail (for example, because of asymmetric information) cash benefits cannot be the solution: economic theory suggests that in such cases equity objectives ought to be pursued through benefits in kind, such as publicly funded healthcare and school education (Barr, 2012).

Implications of provision in cash versus in kind

This section will review the implications of provision in cash or in kind for household resources, redistribution, labour supply, and benefit administration.

Household resources

International comparisons of household incomes and the distributional role of social transfers, such as those routinely produced by Eurostat – currently drawing on the European Union Survey of Income and Living Conditions (EU-SILC) database – include cash benefits but exclude benefits in kind. This can be misleading. The experience of an average-income family living in a country where, for example, healthcare is publicly provided at no cost to users will be radically different from that of another family, also at average income, but living in a country where healthcare is only available privately at a substantial cost to individuals.

For this reason, the Commission on the Measurement of Economic Performance and Social Progress (Stiglitz, Sen, and Fitoussi, 2009) recommended in its final report that household income should include in-kind services (such as healthcare, education, child care, etc.) provided by the government. Verbist et al. (2011) did just that, and found that it made a difference: if the value of all publicly provided social services is imputed in disposable cash income, the resources of European households increase by an average of around 30% (over 40% in Sweden).

Redistribution

Social benefits may redistribute resources horizontally (across the life cycle) and vertically (between individuals belonging to different income classes), reflecting the two aspects of the welfare state as a 'piggy bank' and 'Robin Hood' respectively (Barr, 2001). It has been estimated that, if measured on a lifetime basis, about two thirds of all redistribution in Britain is horizontal (Hills, 2004).

Benefits in kind are generally considered to be less redistributive than benefits in cash. In particular, their contribution in reducing poverty and inequality has been questioned, for instance by Le Grand (1982), who suggested that 'almost all public expenditure on the social services benefits the better off to a greater extent than the poor'.

Part of the difficulty in assessing whether and to what extent this is true lies in the fact that social services actually affect the 'primary' distribution of incomes (i.e. before taxes and benefits) in a variety of ways, often subtle. For instance, child care and elderly care arguably promote equality through their effect on female employment – both by freeing up women from family responsibilities so as to pursue careers, and by providing women with job opportunities in the social services sector (Esping-Andersen and Myles, 2009).

Empirical work on the redistributive role of benefits in kind has proliferated since the pioneering work of Smeeding (1977). Some years later, Smeeding et al. (1993) examined the distributional impact of health, education, and housing in seven European countries, whereas Evandrou et al. (1993) analysed the role of services in the British welfare state, and their effect on the distribution of incomes. More recently, Harding et al. (2006) compared the redistributive effect of cash and non-cash benefits in Australia and the UK, while Marical et al. (2006) provided estimates of the distributional impact of a range of publicly provided services in all OECD countries. Also, Paulus et al. (2010) estimated the size and incidence of education, healthcare, and public housing subsidies in Belgium, Germany, Greece, Italy, and the UK.

What these studies seem to suggest is that, on the whole, benefits in kind reduce poverty and inequality, even though less redistributive than benefits in cash. The redistributive effect of benefits in kind is strongest in Nordic welfare states (where their role is greatest), in particular if one focuses on services other than health and education (Esping-Andersen and Myles, 2009).

In this sense, it is unfortunate that child care tends to be relatively neglected in comparative analysis. Among the studies that are available, Matsaganis and Verbist (2009) estimated the distributional effects of subsidies to publicly funded child care in Belgium, Finland, Germany, Greece, and Sweden, and found that treating child care benefits in kind as additions to monetary income reduced poverty (especially child poverty) and made the income distribution less unequal.

Institutional design may be crucial in determining distributional impact. As van Lancker and Ghysels (2011) showed in their study of child care in Sweden and Flanders, the distributional impact of benefits in kind may be influenced by a number of factors. The study found that in terms of equity the Swedish system of child care outperformed the Flemish one. In Flanders, greater use of child care by higher-income groups and the generosity of tax deductions (also benefiting higher incomes) offset the pro-poor design of the tariff (parental fees) structure in public child care centres.

Furthermore, the question of redistributive effect is made complex by the fact that benefits in kind are typically provided in response to greater need associated with the onset of some life event (from child birth to illness and frailty in old age). Controlling for need – which is not straightforward – will generally reduce the 'gross' distributional impact of services. For instance, a comprehensive analysis of Norwegian local public services (Aaberge et al., 2010) concluded that even though the inclusion of non-cash income reduced inequality by about 15 per cent and poverty by almost one third, adjusting for differences in need offset a significant part of that impact.

In the most comprehensive analysis available to date, Verbist et al. (2011) concluded that benefits in kind reduce income inequality quite substantially: by between one fifth (on the basis of the Gini coefficient) and one third (on the basis of the S80/S20 quintile share ratio). Moreover, benefits in kind significantly reduce poverty rates, by between 40% (using a 'floating' poverty line) and 80% (using a 'fixed' poverty line), as well as the poverty gap (by 80% on average), compared to a counterfactual situation in which publicly funded social services had not existed.

Labour supply

A large literature addresses the issue of the implications of social benefits in general (Moffitt, 2002), and of in-kind provision in particular (Currie and Gahvari, 2008), for one crucial aspect of economic efficiency: incentives to work. The combination of low wages when working with (relatively) generous benefits when not working can create situations in which 'work doesn't pay'. As explained elsewhere (Chapter 12), an early concern with the adverse effects of social benefits on labour supply has led to a policy shift towards 'activation'. Of course, the goal of making work pay can be achieved through very different policies: to put crudely, either by reducing benefits when not working, or by increasing wages when working; both have similar effects on employment rates, but very different implications in terms of poverty and inequality.

The design of benefits may also determine work incentives. When means tested benefits are withdrawn *pari passu* (i.e. euro per euro), or nearly, as recipients' incomes rise, beneficiaries are no better off taking a job than simply relying on benefits. In fact, if the costs of working – whether explicit (such as travel costs) or implicit (such as the cost of child care when the mother is out working) – are taken into consideration, not taking a (low-paid) job actually makes better sense. In this way, while on the one hand social benefits protect recipients against extreme poverty, on the other hand their design prevents them from escaping poverty altogether. This phenomenon is known as the 'poverty trap' (Atkinson, 1995).

The proportion of income earned that is lost again through a combination of reduced benefits, income taxes, and social contributions is the 'marginal effective tax rate'. Reducing that rate (and, therefore, improving incentives to work) is possible. With universal benefits, the amount of benefit is entirely independent of earned income, and therefore the question does not arise. With in-work benefits, such as the Working Tax Credits in Britain or the Earned Income Tax Credits in the USA, benefit is withdrawn more slowly as income rises, and therefore continues to be paid at higher levels of income, than is the case with ordinary means tested benefits. With both universal and in-work benefits, reductions in marginal effective tax rates for benefit recipients come at the cost of increases in fiscal costs, and hence in average tax rates for other tax payers (Barr, 2012).

The theoretical literature distinguishes between the work incentives ofbenefits in kind and of cash benefits, and predicts positive labour supply effects of in-kind provision of goods that are complementary to labour: 'The labour supply effects of in-kind transfers differ from those of cash transfers because they subsidize a good which may be a complement or substitute for leisure, and because the in-kind transfers typically provide minimum or fixed quantities of the good in question and hence have the potential to constrain the consumption choices of the family' (Moffitt, 2002). Nevertheless, the empirical evidence remains rather inconclusive (Currie and Gahvari, 2008). On the whole, the choice of benefits in kind versus cash benefits from the point of view of work incentives may be secondary to the choice of the marginal effective tax rate to prevent poverty traps.

Administration

As discussed above, the cost of administering benefits in-kind is higher (often considerably so) than that of provision of cash benefits. We also know that means-tested benefits are associated with higher administrative costs than either universal or contributory benefits. In turn, the fact that the latter involve no stigma and require less proof of eligibility results in far fewer targeting errors than is the case with means tested benefits (Atkinson, 1995).

Targeting errors involve both the non-payment of benefit to legitimate recipients ('non-take up') and/or the payment of benefit to illegitimate recipients ('leakage' or 'overpayment'). The problem is quite extensive: recent surveys have found that in many European countries the non-take up of social assistance typically spans a range of 20 to 60 per cent (Hernanz et al., 2004; Matsaganis et al., 2008), while the extent of non-take up is similar (if not greater) in North America (Currie, 2004). On the whole, non-take up is likely to be higher where the claiming process is less automatic, where expected benefits are lower, and where transaction costs and/or stigma are greater.

As a recent review of benefits in kind points out, 'there is a great deal of evidence that potential recipients of in-kind transfers are sensitive to application costs' (Currie and Gahvari, 2008). However, the extent of non-take up is likely to be determined by benefit characteristics and the nature of the claiming process, rather than by the choice of benefits in kind versus cash benefits as such.

Conclusion

Benefits in kind and cash benefits are both significant components of European welfare states. In-kind provision is the preferred option where market provision is prone to failure, and where the emphasis is placed on the consumption by recipients of specific goods and services (rather than on their income or 'welfare'). In the USA and elsewhere, a presumption against large-scale government intervention, a preference for means tested provision, and a greater dose of paternalism often result in public assistance being provided to the poor in kind. In Europe, income support is typically complementary to a range of publicly funded (and, often, publicly provided) services in health, education, child care, and care for the elderly while, with the exception of social housing, direct provision of goods is far more limited. On the whole, benefits in cash reduce poverty and inequality more than benefits in kind, even though the latter may be more redistributive in the long run, once their role in increasing female employment is taken into consideration.

References

Aaberge, R., Bhuller, M., Langørgen, A., and Mogstad, M. (2010), The distributional impact of public services when needs differ. *Journal of Public Economics*, vol. 94, pp. 549–62.

Atkinson, A. B. (1995), *Incomes and the Welfare State: Essays on Britain and Europe*. Cambridge: Cambridge University Press.

Barr, N. (2001), *The Welfare State as Piggy Bank: Information, Risk, Uncertainty and the Role of the State*. Oxford: Oxford University Press.

——(2012), *Economics of the Welfare State*, 5th edn. Oxford: Oxford University Press.

Buchanan, J. M. (1975), 'The Samaritan's dilemma', in E. Phelps (ed.), *Morality and Economic Theory*. New York: Russell Sage.

Currie, J. (2004), The take up of social benefits. *Working Paper 10488*. Cambridge MA: National Bureau of Economic Research.

Currie, J. and Gahvari, F. (2008), Transfers in cash and in-kind: theory meets the data. *Journal of Economic Literature*, vol. 46, no. 2, pp. 333–83.

Dearden L., Emmerson C., Frayne C., and Meghir C. (2011), Conditional cash transfers and school dropout rates. *IFS WP05/11*. London: The Institute for Fiscal Studies.

Esping-Andersen, G. and Myles, J. (2009), 'Economic inequality and the welfare state', in W. Salverda, B. Nolan and T. Smeeding (eds), *Oxford Handbook of Economic Inequality*. Oxford: Oxford University Press.

Eurostat (2010), Social protection expenditure: tables by functions, aggregated benefits and grouped schemes – in % of the GDP (spr_exp_gdp). Last update: 06-12-2010, Online: http://epp.eurostat.ec.europa.eu/portal/page/portal/social_protection/data/database.

Evandrou, M., Falkingham, J., Hills, J., and Le Grand, J. (1993), Welfare benefits in kind and income distribution. *Fiscal Studies*, vol. 14, no. 1, pp. 57–76.

Glennerster, H. (2009), *Understanding the Finance of Welfare*, 3rd edn. Bristol: Policy Press.

Harding, A., Warren, N., and Lloyd, B. (2006), Moving beyond the traditional cash measures of economic well-being. *Working Paper 61*. Canberra: National Centere for Economic and Social Modelling.

Hernanz, V., Malherbet, F., and Pellizzari, M. (2004), Take-up of welfare benefits in OECD countries: a review of the evidence. *Social, Employment & Migration Working Paper 17*. Paris: Organisation of Economic Co-operation and Development.

Hills, J. (2004), *Inequality and the State*. Oxford: Oxford University Press.

Le Grand, J. (1982), *The Strategy for Equality: Redistribution and the Social Services*. London: George Allen & Unwin.

Marical, F., d'Ercole, M., Vaalavuo, M., and Verbist G. (2006), Publicly provided services and the distribution of resources. *Social, Employment & Migration Working Paper 45*. Paris: Organisation of Economic Co-operation and Development.

Matsaganis, M., Paulus, A., and Sutherland, H. (2008), The take up of social benefits. *Social Situation Observatory Research Note 5&2008*. Brussels: European Commission.

Matsaganis, M. and Verbist, G. (2009), 'Distributional effects of publicly funded childcare', in T. Ward, O. Lelkes and H. Sutherland (eds), *European Inequalities: Social Inclusion and Income Distribution in the European Union*. Budapest: TÁRKI.

Moffitt, R. (1989), Estimating the value of an in-kind transfer: the case of Food Stamps. *Econometrica*, vol. 57, no. 2, pp. 385–409.

——(2002), 'Welfare programs and labor supply', in A. J. Auerbach and M. Feldstein (eds), *Handbook of Public Economics*, pp. 2393–2430. Amsterdam: Elsevier.

Paulus, A., Sutherland, H., and Tsakloglou, P. (2010), The distributional impact of in-kind public benefits in European countries. *Journal of Policy Analysis & Management*, vol. 29, no. 2, pp. 243–66.

Rothgang, H. (2010), Social insurance for long-term care: an evaluation of the German model. *Social Policy & Administration*, vol. 44, no. 4, pp. 436–60.

Smeeding, T. (1977), The antipoverty effectiveness of in-kind transfers. *Journal of Human Resources*, vol. 12, pp. 360–78.

Smeeding, T. M., Saunders, P., Coder, J., Jenkins, S., Fritzell, J., Hagenaars, A. J. M., Hauser, R., and Wolfson, M. (1993), Poverty, inequality, and family living standards impacts across seven nations: the effect of noncash subsidies for health, education and housing. *The Review of Income and Wealth*, vol. 39, pp. 229–56.

Stiglitz, J., Sen, A., and Fitoussi, J. P. (2009), Report by the Commission on the Measurement of Economic Performance and Social Progress. Online: www.stiglitz-sen-fitoussi.fr.

Tobin, J. (1970), On limiting the domain of inequality. *Journal of Law and Economics*, vol. 13, no. 2, pp. 263–77.

van Lancker, W. and Ghysels, J. (2011), Who reaps the benefits? The social distribution of public childcare in Sweden and Flanders. *GINI Discussion Paper 10*. Amsterdam: Amsterdam Institute for Advanced Labour Studies.

Verbist, G., Förster, M., and Vaalavuo, M. (2011), The impact of publicly provided services on the distribution of resources: a review of new results and methods. *Social, Employment & Migration Working Paper* (forthcoming). Paris: Organisation of Economic Co-operation and Development.
World Bank (2009), Conditional cash transfers: reducing present and future poverty. *Policy Research Report.* Washington, DC: The World Bank.

10
Gender issues in welfare states

Sheila Shaver

Introduction

> Gender is a primary feature of the institutions that make up welfare states, the politics that shape them and the policy outcomes that result. It is central to contemporary transformation of advanced economies from the industrial societies of the post-war period to the post-industrial ones of the future. Its empirical importance is obvious in labour market shifts towards a substantially female service sector, demographic changes in family structure and fertility, and the increased salience of gender issues in politics and community affairs. Theoretically, questions about gender have driven productive engagement between mainstream theory of politics and the state and feminist theorising of gender, power and agency. Comparative study of welfare state development has been a particularly effective area of this intersection
>
> *(Orloff, 2009)*

This chapter discusses the part welfare state institutions play in forming and maintaining gender relations. Welfare institutions bridge the public sphere of economic and political life and the private sphere of family, parenthood, and personal life. The key ideas informing the analysis of gender and social policy derive from this interaction between the public and the private. The chapter introduces these ideas and their application to the welfare states of nations with advanced economies, primarily in Europe, North America, and Australasia. It then examines the way gender has been institutionalised in the social policy frameworks of advanced welfare states, and the way policy institutions are changing in response to the new social risks posed by post-industrial transformation.

Gender and gender equality

Gender

Gender is a social concept that applies to both women and men. It is useful to distinguish between sex and gender, with sex referring to the biological dimensions of male and female and gender to the socially constructed identities of men and women. At its most basic level, gender refers to men's and women's ways of seeing themselves and the world, roles, and life course patterns, resources and capacities. Although not reducible to biology, gender is closely intertwined with male and female bodies and bodily capacities. These include sexuality and sexual orientation, fertility and reproduction, and bodily changes over the life course. As a social construction, gender has its foundations in time, place, and culture, so that societies vary in expectations about social identities of masculinity and femininity and the social behaviour of men and women.

Being social, gender is relational with male and female, masculine and feminine, understood in relation to one another. Gender inheres not only in the social identities of individuals but also in the social fabric that connects them as members of society. These relations are patterned in both personal lives and collective social arrangements. Gender thus forms a primary dimension of social structure shaping relations between men and women, and, just as importantly, relations among women and among men.

The social structuring of gender relations has multiple dimensions, most importantly the division of labour in paid and unpaid work, the hierarchy of power and authority in public and private life, the discursive framing of social relations, and the structuring of emotion in social and sexual bonding (Connell, 1987; Orloff, 2009). These dimensions are interwoven in the institutions of daily life, in families, workplaces, schools, sports and leisure activities, political organisation, and media and entertainment. In families parents earn income, care for children, shop and clean: how these roles are shared matters for their autonomy as individuals and their attachment to their children and each other. Gender is a central feature of paid work, in the jobs people do, the pay and authority attached to them, and the personal identities realised through them. It also shapes citizenship, democratic government, and the identities and expectations of the citizens themselves.

Gender is deeply embedded in the material forms and ideological discourses of social policy and the welfare state. There are obvious gender interests in forms of social provision such as pensions, sickness and unemployment compensation, sole parent support, and child and elder care. Perhaps less obviously, social policies form part of the social scaffolding on which men and women live their lives, and in this way play a part in constituting gender identities and gender relations. Early feminist writing observed that at the same time that welfare states assisted women with vital needs they also institutionalised women's roles as wives and mothers dependent on breadwinner husbands. It was argued that the welfare state fostered gender inequality by reinforcing patterns of male dominance and female dependence in economic and family life (McIntosh, 1978; Wilson, 1977). In the three decades since, feminist analysis has established the centrality of gender in the forces motivating welfare state development, the forms and functions of welfare institutions, and the outcomes of these for men and women. This literature has pointed to significant variation in the gendering of national policy frameworks and charted ongoing changes in the frameworks themselves (Hernes, 1987; Bock and Thane, 1991; O'Connor et al., 1999). These developments and their implications for gender will be discussed below.

Gender equality

Gender is a complex dimension of social inequality entailing both material inequalities and unequally valued social identities. Welfare states are implicated in both dimensions, in the kinds of social protection they offer and the ideological frames that surround them.

Gender is a primary axis of social stratification, with women generally occupying lower positions than men in hierarchies of social status, economic power, and political authority. Women's disadvantage is most evident in their economic vulnerability. In all Organisation for Economic Co-operation and Development (OECD) countries they face a greater risk of poverty than men, with this difference widening significantly in old age (see Chapter 7). Although wage gaps have been decreasing in most OECD countries, women continue to earn less than men; in the mid-2000s the average wage gap was 18 per cent, with gaps in individual countries varying from less than 10 to more than 30 per cent. More women are in paid work than in the past, although employment rates vary considerably among countries. These rates are generally low for mothers of young children. Women spend more time, in most countries more than twice as much, as men on unpaid care work for children or another adult (OECD 2010). They are underrepresented in national legislatures and government cabinets. It is nevertheless important to recognise that not all women are vulnerable, poor, or disadvantaged relative to men. In many countries professional women especially earn incomes comparable with those of equivalently qualified men. Gender inequalities interact with inequalities of class, race, ethnicity, and bodily abilities and disabilities, and there are substantial inequalities among men and among women.

Many feminists challenge concepts of gender inequality based on conventional economic measures such as income and employment, arguing that such comparisons are blind to the realities of many women's, and some men's, lives. Women's economic vulnerability and political marginality are closely linked to responsibility for children and family. Feminists have been critical of mainstream social theorising for its blindness to the social division between public and private spheres of social life encoded in the separation of state and civil society. Such theorising privileges the public worlds of economy and politics while obscuring their interdependence with the private worlds of personal and domestic life. The effect has been to valorise an apparently autonomous individual unencumbered by responsibility for the care of others, while denying full personhood to those supplying the kinship, nurturance, and household provisioning underlying the appearance of independence. Much of mainstream welfare state theory has been similarly gender blind, according central place to capital, labour, church, and class interest as developmental forces of the capitalist welfare state. These arguments focused most squarely on social provision for risks faced by employed workers, such as pensions, disability benefits, and unemployment and sickness compensation. In effect these theories portrayed welfare state citizenship as implicitly masculine, framed by beneficiaries' status as wage-earners and breadwinners (Pateman, 1989; Lister, 2003).

Feminists argue for understanding the welfare state in terms not simply of state and market, but of state, market, and family. This brings into the theoretical frame the largely unpaid work of social reproduction such as domestic labour, child care, and the provisioning of the household. It also opens analysis to the social values of mutual concern that reflect the interdependence of the human condition.

Concepts of interdependence, care, and family models

These arguments have given starting points for important feminist theoretical innovation with concepts such as *care, interdependence, male breadwinner, dual-earner* and *dual-earner dual-carer family models*, and *defamilization.*

Care refers to the socially necessary work that men and mainly women do outside the paid labour force to meet the needs of dependent others. More specifically, it concerns the care of dependent children, spouses, and others such as elderly parents and persons with disabilities by members of the nuclear or extended family. Care is a form of labour, requiring the commitment of time, the application of skills, and the maintenance of responsibility, but because it is usually embedded in close familial relationships it often has an emotional character that distinguishes it from work for pay in the public sphere. Ideologically, care has been seen as a natural expression of women's concern with home and family. As work, its demands of time and schedules framed by the needs of others weaken the positions of carers in paid labour markets, while its affective dimension imbues it with distinctive rewards, power relations and ethical significances.

Welfare states have long been recognised as supporting and regulating paid employment. Feminist argument has shown that they also support and regulate the social organisation of care, through the direct provision of services and indirect measures facilitating care within the household. This shows the individual wage earner is not the independent actor of labour market exchange, but part of a larger social relation of work and care. The normal human condition is thus not independence but *interdependence* (Daly and Lewis, 2000; Jenson, 1997; Lister, 2003).

Welfare states play an important part in shaping the contours of such interdependence. Social policy arrangements contain a variety of family models reflecting different expectations about marital partnership and family life, of which two are most salient (Lewis, 1992; Sainsbury, 1996). The *male breadwinner model* builds on societal norms of the traditional family of the post-war period. Under this model, policy is framed on the expectation of the husband having primary responsibility for the economic support of the household through full-time, paid employment, and the wife having the main responsibility for the work of the household and the care of its dependent members. The welfare states of most advanced industrial countries first took shape around this model, and at least remnants of it remain in most. It has commonly been rewritten in gender-neutral terms allowing either of husband and wife to be the breadwinner, and more importantly modified to enable the partner with domestic responsibility to also be a secondary earner. Increasingly, policy frameworks concentrate support for a partner engaged in full-time care in the life course period when children are young and facilitate increasing paid labour as they mature. Contrasting with these is the *dual earner family model* predicated on the expectation that both partners are employed, usually on a full-time basis. The same development is also referred to as the *adult worker model*, the term signalling individualization of status and entitlements. This model is most commonly found in Nordic countries. Increasingly welfare arrangements based on this model have been incorporating policy measures aimed at inducing male partners to take greater part in the care of children. In a further variant aiming at still greater gender equality, a *dual earner-dual carer model* facilitates part-time work enabling both parents to share fully in the care of children. This model is most commonly associated with the Netherlands welfare state.

To the role of welfare states in shielding workers from the most abject dependence on the labour market, feminists add that of protecting citizens, and especially those responsible for children, from unchosen dependence on the support of a partner. Orloff (1993) terms this 'capacity to form an autonomous household', by which she refers to support enabling an individual to survive without being forced into marriage or other family relationships. The poverty rates of sole parents are generally high, and most welfare states provide some form of income support, usually subject to conditions such as means testing and limited time periods. Other forms of assistance include housing, child care, and the enforcement of the child support obligations of non-custodial parents. Hobson (1990) has argued that the conditions faced by lone mothers are a measure of this capacity to form an autonomous household, since they give married mothers an indication of their 'exit options' from marriage. For this reason, Hobson argues that strong support for sole parents also empowers women within marriage.

Defamilization (Lister, 2003) is a similar idea. It refers to the degree to which individual adults can maintain an adequate standard of living independently of family relationships. Coined originally to refer to the way that welfare provision may underpin women's economic independence, it has also come to be used in the more general sense of the extent to which welfare states contribute to the work of care and in so doing facilitate women's paid employment. The latter usage avoids any reference to gender inequalities.

Gender and social policy regimes

Comparative analysis of welfare state formation and change has helped to identify the important elements of gender in the social policy frameworks of nation states. Marking key points of connection between state, market, and family, these show characteristic patterns of gender logic extending across multiple institutional and policy domains. There are three principal dimensions of gender in the social rights of citizenship in such countries.

The first is the social division of paid work and unpaid care, and the assumptions about gender and family that underpin it. Expectations about how men and women will share the rewards and burdens of paid and unpaid work are encoded across the social policy spectrum. These expectations inform labour market regulation and the terms under which men and women have access to paid jobs and services facilitating labour market participation. The same is true of policies mitigating the social risks attending rising rates of maternal employment. Gender ideologies permeate income support systems, in rules of eligibility and provisions for workers and dependents in retirement and disability pensions, unemployment and sickness benefits, the taxation of income, and access to social services such as child and elder care.

A second dimension lies within social bonding in emotional and reproductive relationships and associated capacities and vulnerabilities. It concerns the meaning of individual personhood and gender-specific expectations about sexuality and sexual expression, fertility and reproduction, bodily integrity, and personal safety at home and on the street. In policy terms, it shapes the contours of access to services supporting reproductive rights and fertility management, the privileging of heterosexual over same-sex relationships in the definition of family entitlements, and the kinds of services provided to the victims of rape, incest, and domestic assault. There are closely related concerns in policy areas such as health, law and policing, such as the control of sexual and domestic violence, drug and alcohol policies, and the treatment of prostitution.

Legal rights form a third gender dimension in social policy frameworks. These include political rights as well as basic human rights such as equal protection under the law, access to courts and legal services, and freedom of speech and assembly. Most countries have legislation regulating hours and conditions of employment, and many also prohibit discrimination in hiring and pay on the basis of gender. Laws governing marriage specify the rights of husbands and wives as partners and as parents, as well as their rights of one another in separation, divorce, and child custody and support.

Most debate about the gender structures of social policy regimes has focused on women's employment and policy stances toward the gender division of labour between earning and caring in the family household. These have significant consequences for income, employment, and economic security over the life course. There has been less systematic comparative discussion of differences in the way welfare states support social bonding and individual legal rights.

The gender logics of social policy regimes reflect the gendered politics of their formation and development, including national history and ideology, economic development, and political contestation. Relevant political forces have included political parties and trade unions, religious bodies, military and veterans' organizations, and social reform groups, all of whose programmes have had gender subtexts. In some periods feminist movements have been influential. Early visions were explicitly maternalist, seeking to imbue society with a feminine ethos of care, while second-wave feminist movements envisioned a welfare state oriented to equal opportunity in employment and shared care in the home (Bock and Thane, 1991; Fraser, 1997). In some countries women's policy units within government have represented women's interests within the machinery of the state (Stetson and Mazur, 1995; Eisenstein, 1996). Contemporary welfare reform ideologies envision gender equity in the more limited terms of a universal obligation to paid employment in which the social identities of men and women are constituted as the same (Orloff, 2009).

Gender is central in the new social risks associated with the transformation to the post-industrial economy. The shift in employment from manufacturing to services has changed gender balances in labour markets, weakening the position of unskilled men and strengthening demand for occupations in which women are most commonly employed. The accompanying shift from Fordist to flexible employment patterns has compounded these effects, increasing the share of non-standard and precarious employment. Families are less stable and more diverse in form than in the past, with two-earner households increasingly the norm but sole parent households also more common and especially disadvantaged. Welfare states are adapting to these new risks in different ways, but with common concerns for labour market activation, including for sole parents, and family policies to alleviate conflicts between employment and care (Taylor-Gooby, 2004; Yerkes, 2011).

The last two decades of comparative welfare state discussion have been dominated by Esping-Andersen's (1990) typology in which he identified three types of social policy regime: 'liberal', 'corporatist', and 'social democratic' (see Chapter 14). Derived from 1980s data, the typology has become dated by three decades of continuous policy evolution, but its use continues as a set of ideal types illustrating policy choices and trade-offs. The original three regime types, and others identified in subsequent argument, show systematic differences in the characteristic gender logics shaping the nexus of state, market, and family across multiple policy domains. These differences have important consequences for the gendering of social rights and gender equality. Gender went unacknowledged in the typology's original formulation but is now recognised as central to the way different policy regimes work. In particular, family models of breadwinner and dependent spouse or dual-earner partnership impart distinctive gender logics across a broad range of policy areas. The extent of defamilization – social provision relieving households of care work – is most salient from a gender perspective, but policy effects on employment and social stratification also matter.

Liberal welfare regimes are found in those countries where the liberal political tradition has been dominant, most clearly the United Kingdom, the United States, Canada, Australia, and New Zealand. Their social policy frameworks are marked, though to varying degrees, by traditions of liberal individualism and ideological privileging of the market, with welfare playing a residual role when market and family fail. There is a traditional presumption against public authority intruding in the private relations of household and family, though feminism and new social risks have put this presumption under challenge. The central gender logic of liberal regimes is largely neutral with respect to male breadwinner or dual-earner family models, which are regarded as matters of choice for the individuals concerned, but the family unit is expected to play a strong safety-net role for its members. Because of women's generally lower earnings capacities, market solutions to needs such as retirement income and social care often have gendered outcomes.

In actuality liberal welfare regimes differ considerably from country to country. O'Connor et al., (1999) found both broad similarities and significant variations in the liberal welfare regimes of Australia, Canada, Great Britain, and the United States. Dual-earner households are increasingly the norm, but it is more usual for mothers to be employed full-time in the United States and Canada than in Australia and Great Britain. Gender wage gaps are around the OECD average, but lower in Australia than in the other three countries. These countries have largely residual welfare systems with low levels of social provision geared primarily to the alleviation of poverty. Poverty rates are higher than in comparable European countries, with sole mother poverty especially high. UK and Australian governments provide significant support to families, mainly as cash allowances. The United States and Canada offer only low levels of support, in Canada primarily as cash allowances and in the United States as tax breaks. In all four countries there is little public support given to defamilization and care needs, such as in paid parental leave and early childhood education and care (OECD, 2010; LIS, 2011). Especially in the United States, there are wide economic disparities among women, with professional women especially able to purchase services supporting their full-time employment. Activation has taken the form of welfare reform, sharpening economic incentives to paid work, tightening rule compliance and conditionality, and in the United States instituting lifetime limitations on eligibility for assistance. In all countries it has reduced sole-parent access to forms of support enabling them to be full-time mothers or fathers.

Corporatist welfare regimes have developed in countries with political histories of conservative and religious party rule and policy traditions of concertation between organised interests/social partners. Found mainly in continental Europe, corporatist regimes have generous welfare states designed to foster stability and social integration. Reflecting religious party influences, their gender logic has policy biases towards traditional gender roles with low levels of female labour force participation, male authority, and the principle of subsidiarity, by which the state avoids taking on roles that would supplant that of the family. In the result, women's social protection is often provided through their husbands rather than in their own right. Services defamilizing care responsibilities are often little developed.

There is considerable variation in the particular forms that corporatist social policy frameworks take. Increasing labour force participation of married women with children has brought pressures for adaptation, especially of family models assuming a family of male breadwinner and dependent wife. In Germany, France, and Netherlands it is now more common than not for women with children to work for pay; in France most mothers work full-time, while in Germany and especially the Netherlands they generally work part-time. All three countries support motherhood with long periods of paid maternity leave and extended periods of further unpaid parental leave. Support to families is especially generous in France and Germany, with France providing much of such assistance in the form of child care and other services. While poverty rates are generally low, those for sole mothers with children are high, especially in Germany. Activation policies have aimed at increasing women's labour force participation, combining social investment measures such as training with liberal elements such as sharpening work incentives and individualised case management. Policies to reconcile conflicts between work and family have featured strongly in all three countries, including improved access to child care and extended parental leave. In a discourse of concern about poverty, sole parents, previously supported as primarily mothers, have been a particular focus of activation (OECD, 2010; LIS, 2011; Weishaupt, 2010; Knijn, Martin, and Millar, 2007).

In southern Europe policy regimes predicated on the traditional male breadwinner families have also been coming under pressure from women's growing labour force participation. In countries such as Italy, Greece, and Spain women's employment rates remain low compared to other OECD countries, and pay gaps are large. Portugal is an exception. A majority of households have both parents employed full-time. These welfare states are small, and family services and child care little developed. Low fertility is one expression of the unresolved tensions between employment and family. In Portugal, where fertility has declined particularly sharply, parental leave reform includes incentives for fathers to share in leave (OECD, 2010).

The social policy frameworks of the Nordic countries of Denmark, Norway, Sweden, and Finland provide a sharp contrast. Evolved in long histories of social democratic government, these regimes put the state at the centre of relations between state, market, and family. These are large welfare states with generous provision through both transfers and services. With entitlements predicated on employment, their policy frameworks have long incorporated activation approaches. Their gender logic aims to combine high labour force participation by women over the life course with equality between men and women. Generous parental leave, subsidised child care, and the treatment of partners as individuals in the tax and benefit systems underpin a family model of dual-earner couples. The occupational structures are highly segmented by gender, with much of women's employment in public sector service positions. Extensive service provision and female public sector employment act together create a virtual circle sustaining both full female employment and welfare state generosity. The Nordic countries have low levels of poverty, including among sole mothers.

There are fewer policy variations among countries in this group. All have faced pressures to reduce public spending and achieve public sector efficiencies by introducing market mechanisms into public service provision. At the same time, several have introduced dedicated parental leave for fathers on a 'use it or lose it' basis.

There have been common policy shifts toward dual-earner family arrangements and measures to reconcile tensions between work and family across most Western welfare states. There is debate about the new policy paradigms into which these developments are being incorporated. Some analysts see a paradigm shift from the passive, protective welfare state of the twentieth century to a pro-active post-industrial welfare state concerned with social investment and the development of human capital. This view sees promoting female labour force participation with measures such as parental leave and early childhood education and care as part of a larger policy agenda also including life-long learning, employability, and the social inclusion of marginalised groups (Esping-Andersen et al., 2002; Jenson, 2009). Others see social policy responding to economic demands for labour market flexibility with reforms addressing the new social risks of post-industrial employment and facilitating transitions between work and care. Still a third paradigm envisages a radical shift from collective to individualised social provision enabling individuals to use private savings schemes to move between employment, care, education, and other choices (Knijn and Smit, 2009). Importantly, in all three of these paradigms concerns for economic competitiveness in the knowledge-based economy have displaced earlier policy concerns with gender equality. In actuality, as Daly (2009) shows, in some countries at least welfare reform continues to frame policy in family rather than individual terms. She sees contemporary European policy as tending, for different reasons in its conservative neo-familialist and liberal 'third way' variants, towards a dual earner, gender specialized family model of one full-time and one part-time worker. In both cases, the objectives of the model put a higher value on economic competitiveness than gender equality and equalising the distribution of care work.

Current developments in welfare and work

In 2002–7 the OECD conducted a comprehensive review of policies concerned with tensions between work and family in 13 member countries. With the dual-earner household now the norm across most of the OECD, it found good cause for governments to assist families in achieving their desired balance between employment and family life. Arguing for social investment benefiting economic growth, demographic balance, poverty alleviation, and child development, its final report *Babies and Bosses* (OECD, 2007) cautiously advanced a policy agenda for reconciliation of work and family life. Its founding proposition was systemic support for families, from support to parents at home with young children, assured child care, pre-school education and out-of-hours care for school children. Such care will, it is argued, give families the necessary confidence to have the number of children they desire and employers the confidence to manage their labour forces. A minority of countries, notably the Nordic countries, Hungary, and to a lesser extent France and the Canadian province of Quebec achieve this. The high level of spending requires others to focus on particular policy areas or target groups. The agenda called for tax/benefit policies strengthening work incentives, especially for sole parents; paid parental leave of moderate duration and with measures encouraging fathers to take leave; affordable, good quality child care and out-of-hours care; and family-friendly employment practices such as part-time work, flexible workplaces, and leave to care for sick children.

Underlying the *Babies and Bosses* agenda is a gender-neutral, dual-earner family model with cautious aspirations towards the sharing of earner and carer roles. It endorses gender equity as a desirable policy goal likely to be in the national interest, defining equity in terms of women's increasing parity with men in matters such as income and opportunity. The report argues that women's increasing labour force participation, especially in full-time or near full-time work, challenges employer discrimination and opens career trajectories to them. It advocates measures encouraging fathers to take parental leave including provision on terms in which fathers must 'use it or lose it'. The *Babies and Bosses* agenda does not give any support to maternalist arguments for gender equity based on claims to support for sole parents to be full-time mothers. Contrarily, it advocates policies giving sole parents strong incentives to undertake substantial employment. *Babies and Bosses* notes that for most welfare states gender equity is only an incidental policy objective. Only in the Nordic countries and Portugal is it given primacy. It also observes that even after several decades of women's movement into paid work gender equity remains far off. Women remain responsible for the main work of caring while they miss out on jobs with future prospects, pay parity and career opportunities.

A further consequence of the movement of women into the paid labour force has been increased outsourcing of domestic work including that of care for children and the elderly. In a number of countries migrants, usually women from poorer countries, are taking up this work. The phenomenon reflects a feminisation of migration, with women making up some 51 per cent of international migrants and more than in the past migrating on their own account rather than as part of a family group. Many of these women have left their own children behind to be cared for by others. The remittances they send back are important sources of income, and migration often opens a path to wider opportunities. As employees their circumstances make them vulnerable, especially if their migration has been illegal or their employment conditions are irregular. Feminist writers have characterised these relations as 'global care chains' enmeshing women across social boundaries of class, race and nation (Hochschild, 2002). Gender concerns relations among women as well as with men, and global care chains entail condensed relations of power and interest between women.

The phenomenon is not wholly new, but globalisation has given it new impetus. Its growth may be facilitated by social policy developments supporting the reconciliation of tensions between work and family in some countries. This is particularly the case for policy strategies emphasising individual choice and market-based arrangements for the care of children and the elderly, where measures such as tax allowances and cash payments facilitate private solutions to care needs.

Conclusion

The last decade has seen convergences in some areas of gender and social policy. The dual-earner household is increasingly the norm in OECD countries, even among families with dependent children, so that the daily lives of women and men, mothers and fathers, are becoming more similar. There is some evidence that the increase in women's paid work is inducing men to do more unpaid work, though the extent of this change and the nature of the work are disputed.

The gender logic of social policy institutions has been changing in concert, with family models reframed in gender-neutral terms supportive of parental employment. Measures such as maternal and parental leave and childcare commonly facilitate a pattern in which women withdraw from employment when their children are very young but return by the time they reach school age. The general tendency is toward policy frameworks assuming a parental division of labour in which although both are in paid employment one remains a primary and the other a secondary earner. To some extent also, policy agendas driven by globalization are tempering the contrasting gender logics of liberal, corporatist and social democratic social policy regimes. Countries with liberal regimes are doing more to support and regulate early childhood education and care. Corporatist and southern European countries are also moving to accommodate dual-earner households. Nordic countries are seeing the public provision of care services and the associated large public sector challenged by neoliberal pressures to reduce taxes and increase service sector competition. Substantial policy differences nevertheless remain. Gender continues to be an important constituent factor, with class, race, and others, in the old and new social risks with which welfare states are concerned, including low pay, precarious employment, fragile families, the personal cost of unpaid work, and the vulnerabilities of sole parenthood and old age.

Policies concerned with work-life balance and social investment in children and education, such as the OECD's *Babies and Bosses*, stress the contribution of present social expenditure to future economic growth. Importantly, gender equality is not an objective of these policies, which are concerned rather with raising fertility rates and improving economic competitiveness. Gender equality has thus moved both into the mainstream of social policy and out of focus as an objective in its own right.

Further reading

Daly, M. (2011), What adult worker model? A critical look at recent social policy reform in Europe from a gender and family perspective, *Social Politics*, vol. 18, no. 1, pp. 1–23.
Lister, R. (2003), *Citizenship, Feminist Perspectives*, 2nd edn. New York: New York University Press.
Mahon, R. (2009), The OECD's Discourse on the Reconciliation of Work and Family Life, *Global Social Policy*, vol. 9, no. 2, pp. 183–204.
Orloff, A. S. (2009), Tendering the comparative analysis of welfare states: An unfinished agenda, *Sociological Theory*, vol. 27, no. 3, pp. 317–43.

References

Bock, G. and Thane, P. (eds) (1991), *Maternity and Gender Policies, Women and the rise of the European welfare states, 1880s–1950s*. London: Routledge.
Connell, R. W. (1987), *Gender and Power*. Sydney: Allen & Unwin.
Daly, M. (2011), What adult worker model? A critical look at recent social policy reform in Europe from a gender and family perspective, *Social Politics*, vol. 18, no. 1, pp. 1–23.
Daly, M. and Lewis, J. (2000), The concept of social care and the analysis of contemporary welfare states, *British Journal of Sociology*, 51(2): 281–98.
Eisenstein, H. (1996), *Australian Femocrats and the State*. Sydney: Allen and Unwin.
Esping-Andersen, G. (1990), *The Three Worlds of Welfare Capitalism*. Cambridge: Polity.
Esping-Andersen, G., D. Gallie, A. Hemerijck and J. Myles (eds) (2002), *Why We Need a New Welfare State*. Oxford: Oxford University Press.
Fraser, N. (1997), 'After the family wage: a postindustrial thought experiment', in *Justus Interruptus, Critical reflections on the 'postsocialist' condition*. New York: Routledge.
Hernes, H. (1987), *Welfare States and Woman Power*. Oslo: Norwegian University Press.
Hobson, B. (1990), No exit, no voice: Women's economic dependency and the welfare state, *Acta Sociologica*, 33, pp. 235–50.
Hochschild, A. (2002), The nanny chain. *The American Prospect*, Nov. 30.

Jenson, J. (1997), Who cares? Gender and welfare regimes. *Social Politics*, 4(2), pp. 182–87.

——(2009), Lost in translation: The social investment perspective and gender equality. *Social Politics*, 16(4): 446–83.

Knijn, T., C. Martin and J. Millar (2007), Activation as a common framework for social policies towards lone parents. *Social Policy & Administration*, 41(6), pp. 638–52.

Knijn, T. and A. Smit (2009), Investing, facilitating, or individualizing the reconciliation of work and family life: Three paradigms and ambivalent policies. *Social Politics*, 16(4), pp. 484–518.

Lewis, J. (1992), Gender and the development of welfare regimes. *Journal of European Social Policy*, 2(3), pp. 159–73.

Lister, R. (2003), *Citizenship, Feminist perspectives*, 2nd edn. New York: New York University Press.

Luxembourg Income Study (LIS) (2011), *Gender Key Figures*. www.lisproject.org/php/gkf/main (accessed 24 April 2011).

McIntosh, M. (1978), 'The state and the oppression of women', in A. Kuhn and A.-M. Wolpe (eds), *Feminism and Materialism*, pp. 254–89. London: Routledge and Kegan Paul.

O'Connor, J. S., A. S. Orloff and S. Shaver (1999), *States, Markets, Families: Gender, Liberalism and Social Policy in Australia, Canada, Great Britain and the United States*. Cambridge: Cambridge University Press.

Organisation for Economic Co-operation and Development (OECD) (2007) *Babies and Bosses, Reconciling work and family life, A synthesis of findings for OECD Countries*. OECD ilibrary, Paris: OECD.

——(2010), *Gender Brief*. www.oecd.org/els/social (version March 2010).

Orloff, A. S. (1993), Gender and the social rights of citizenship: State policies and gender relations in comparative perspective. *American Sociological Review*, 58(3), pp. 303–28.

——(2006), 'From maternalism to "employment for all": state policies to promote women's employment across the affluent democracies', in J. Levy (ed.), *The State After Statism: New state activities in the era of globalization and liberalization*, pp. 230–68. Cambridge, MA: Harvard University Press.

——(2009), Tendering the comparative analysis of welfare states: An unfinished agenda. *Sociological Theory*, 27(3), pp. 317–43.

Pateman, C. (1989), *The Disorder of Women*. Cambridge: Polity Press.

Sainsbury, D. (1996), *Gender, Equality and Welfare States*. Cambridge: Cambridge University Press.

Stetson, D. McBride and A. G. Mazur (eds) (1995), *Comparative State Feminism*. Thousand Oaks, CA: Sage Publications.

Taylor-Gooby, P. (ed.) (2004), *New Risks, New Welfare, The Transformation of the European Welfare State*, Oxford: Oxford University Press.

Weishaupt, J. T. (2010), Germany after a decade of Social Democrats in government: The end of the continental model? *German Politics* 19(2), pp. 105–22.

Wilson, E. (1977), *Women and the Welfare State*. London: Tavistock.

Yerkes, M. (2011), *The Transformation of the Dutch Welfare State, Social Risks and Corporatist Reform*, Bristol: The Policy Press.

11

Welfare states and the life course

Mara A. Yerkes, Bram Peper, and Janeen Baxter

Introduction

In recent years there has been an increased interest in understanding the welfare state from a life course approach. On the one hand, the welfare state through its laws, policies, and institutions, shapes and structures the life course. The welfare state influences both the timing of life course events, such as the age at which people marry or have children or the age at which people retire, as well as the duration of life course events, such as education and training. On the other hand, individual needs in relation to the welfare state change across the life course. During certain stages of the life course an individual may have more need for help or assistance from the welfare state than at other times. These needs can, in turn, give rise to new welfare state arrangements, as welfare states adjust policies to address changing social risks in society (Yerkes, 2011). In other words, individual life courses and the welfare state are inextricably linked (see Mayer and Schoepflin, 1989). In this chapter we take a closer look at this relationship, introducing the concept of the life course and examining how it has changed in recent years.

We begin by defining the life course, as well as introducing a number of other core concepts. In the sections that follow, we look at how the life course has become increasingly dynamic and diversified as a result of the social and economic process of post-industrialisation, as well as differences in the gender order, and other demographic changes. In post-industrial societies, welfare states are increasingly faced with pressures associated with changing and emerging social risks – risks which are no longer absorbed by the family or the labour market (Esping-Andersen, 2002). These risks pose significant challenges to welfare states and we discuss this in sections two and three. In the next section, using examples from Western welfare states we show how the welfare state structures the life course and how macro-level processes affect welfare states (and therefore impact the life course). The final section provides a brief conclusion.

Core concepts

The welfare state and the life course are inextricably linked. To understand this relationship, we must first consider a number of core concepts, including the definition of the term life course, transitions and trajectories within the life course, and, lastly, the concept of post-industrialisation. The most important concept in this chapter is the *life course*. The term life *course* differs from the term life *cycle*, which reflects a rather biological approach to individuals. The life cycle refers to the various stages of individual life from birth through death. 'In simple terms, the "life-cycle" can be reduced to a developmental model or models which outline the social and psychological change encountered as a person passes through the major "stages" of life: childhood, adolescence, mid-life, old age, and eventually death' (Hunt, 2010, p. 171). Key to understanding the concept of the life *course* is recognizing that a life course approach is broader than a life cycle approach and is more sociological in its perspective, viewing individual life stages as embedded in social, cultural, and historical contexts (Hunt, 2010). The life course is necessarily a social construction, and, as such, the boundaries of each life stage are shifting and dynamic, and will depend upon the social and cultural context in which individuals live.

The life course is marked by *trajectories* and *transitions*. 'Trajectories are life course dynamics that take place over an extended period of time' (Macmillan, 2005, p. 5); they are marked by a beginning and an end. Traditionally, trajectories include education, employment, marriage, parenthood, and retirement. The beginning and end of trajectories are conceptualized as transitions, which are shorter in duration than trajectories. Transitions 'index changes as people move from one role to another, begin or cease a course of activity, experience a particular state, or stop doing so. Importantly, transitions are always embedded in trajectories that give them discrete form and meaning' (Macmillan, 2005, p. 5). Transitions and trajectories across the life course are not necessarily sequential, for example transitioning from an educational trajectory into an employment trajectory. It is plausible that individuals will experience transitions and trajectories at different times, such as returning to education at a later stage in the life course, even after a period of employment. In addition, it is possible to experience multiple trajectories at one time during the life course. In fact, life course transitions and trajectories have become increasingly complex due to changing socio-economic contexts. In this sense, we can imagine individuals negotiating multiple transitions, such as the start or end of a marriage, parenthood, education, or employment. Even retirement has become increasingly fluid, as people continue to work longer or combine retirement with other trajectories.

The duration and timing of life course events, and trajectories and transitions differs across countries due to variation in educational systems, labour markets and industrial relations structures, family structures, and the welfare state (Blossfeld, 2009). As discussed in earlier chapters, the welfare state defines individuals' access and rights to minimum levels of income, education, housing, and health. The welfare state is there to protect individuals across the whole of the life course – in essence, from the cradle to the grave. In addition, the welfare state plays a key role in regulating many aspects of life course trajectories and transitions, including transitions into and out of employment, decisions about how couples should divide paid and unpaid work, the gender division of labour within households, and decisions about who should be the main carers of young children. Through its definition and regulation of social rights and norms, the welfare state helps construct notions of life course trajectories and transitions as well as their timing and duration. Social rights, and hence entitlements to welfare state policies, do not come without obligations, however. The most notable of these obligations in modern welfare states is employment. For a significant proportion of the individual life course individuals are obliged to participate in paid employment to have access to welfare state arrangements. The expectation that both men and women will participate in paid employment increases the likelihood of multiple trajectories across the life course, as individuals seek to combine employment trajectories with trajectories of parenthood, education, and care, for example.

Thinking about the structure of welfare state policies and regulations in relation to the life course, it is important to note that this relationship is not static but is in a constant state of flux. During industrial times, social, economic, and political institutions were structured around a male-bread-winner model, meaning that men were the primary wage earners and women were homemakers and mothers. These structures created life course norms, influencing the timing and duration of life course events and leaving little room for diversity in the timing and sequencing of transitions. Educational trajectories were relatively short with the transition into working life taking place at an early age, anywhere between 16 and 18 years old. Men and women married relatively early in life and women generally gave birth to their first child before the age of 25. While women would work for a short period of time, they would leave the workforce after getting married or giving birth. Men, in contrast, were expected to work until the age of 65, at which point they could retire. The welfare state of the industrial age supported these life course trajectories and transitions. It provided limited educational support for post-secondary schooling and protected the family wage earned by men, through the creation of unemployment, disability, and sickness policies and pensions. Each of these policies attempts to provide financial protection for the primary breadwinner to ensure a minimum standard of living and prevent poverty should they be unable to work due to job loss, sickness, incapacity, or old age. Policies to support the employment of women or a combination of work and care were non-existent. At the time, most welfare states encouraged the care of children to take place within the home, and in many countries laws were in place that prevented women from working after marriage or having children. The welfare state also supported families after retirement through pensions and widowers' pensions, and in some cases encouraging early retirement for men.

During the 1960s and 1970s, however, significant changes occurred marking a shift from industrial to post-industrial societies. *Post-industrialism* is the term used to describe a marked decline in industrial and manufacturing jobs and an increase in service sector employment. In addition, female labour market participation increased dramatically. At the same time, international competition increased and we witnessed a rise in part-time and temporary work forms and an increase in structural unemployment. Changes were not limited to employment structures, however. Family structures became increasingly complex, with an increase in divorce rates, an increase in lone parenthood and the emergence and welfare state recognition of various family formations, such as same-sex relationships and co-habitation. Social structures changed as women increasingly took part in education and the labour market, often remaining in employment following marriage or having children. In sum, the broad socio-economic process of post-industrialisation led to significant changes in employment, family, and social structures, which had significant consequences for both welfare states and welfare state arrangements. The impact of these changes on welfare states has varied, however, due to differences in welfare state configurations. Post-industrialisation, as discussed above, has also had a significant impact on individuals, the shaping of individual biographies, and individual needs across the life course by producing significant changes in the constellation of social risks (Esping-Andersen, 2002; Hacker, 2004). This, in turn, creates pressures for welfare states to adapt existing policies or create new policies to deal with these risks. We now move on to look at some examples of these variations in welfare states.

Presentation and analysis

Welfare states differ in the way in which social rights and protection are provided. While no two welfare states are exactly alike, they share similarities in how social rights are defined, allowing for a categorization of welfare states into welfare regimes. The most often-used categorization is the one created by Esping-Andersen (1990, 1999), discussed in several chapters, which considers three types of welfare regimes: social democratic, conservative corporatist, and liberal. It can be useful to look at the relationship between the welfare state and the life course within these different regime types.

In social democratic welfare regimes, like Sweden and Denmark, social rights tend to be universal and generous with high levels of de-commodification and de-familialisation. In this manner, the social democratic welfare regime attempts to aid individual action and planning across the life course, making it easier for men and women to combine multiple trajectories such as employment and parenthood and to transition between trajectories. Greater freedom of choice in life course transitions is also likely in social democratic countries with generous welfare state provisions. For example, research has shown that state transfers reduce the risk of poverty for single mothers and divorced women thus allowing greater choice for women to live independently of men, if not the state (Sainsbury, 1996). In addition, social democratic welfare regimes have, to varying degrees, been successful in adjusting existing policies or introducing new policies in response to changes in individual life courses and the social risks experienced by individuals. The early timing of post-industrialisation in most social democratic welfare states made it financially feasible (Bonoli, 2005) to create generous child care and leave policies, for example, as discussed below. These policies ease the adoption of multiple roles across the life course.

Welfare states classified as conservative corporatist regimes, such as Germany, are historically centred around a single (male) breadwinner and the protection of the family wage. De-commodification levels are high but de-familialisation levels are low. The focus on labour market insiders and emphasis on family responsibility affects the timing and duration of individual life course transitions and trajectories differently than welfare states that emphasise universal, generous welfare state provisions for all individuals. Multiple trajectories can be difficult to maintain, particularly for women. These welfare states often lack adequate policies aimed at combining work and care, for example. Transitions from education into employment can be difficult due to the protection of labour market insiders, disadvantaging young people, older workers, migrant workers, and women entering the labour market. For example, in many conservative welfare regimes, active labour market policies developed during the 1980s and 1990s were focused less on removing barriers to employment, which would be beneficial to labour market outsiders, and focused more on helping labour market insiders by keeping them busy during a period of unemployment, through job creation or work experience programmes (Bonoli, 2010).

Southern European countries, not originally addressed in Esping-Andersen's typology but later recognized by welfare state scholars as similar to conservative corporatist welfare regimes but distinct in their own right, often only provide mixed coverage, meaning de-commodification levels are not high and individuals must rely heavily on family throughout the life course, again making it difficult to maintain multiple trajectories, particularly for women. Here, as in conservative welfare states, work and care policies are inadequate or non-existent. In addition, the structure of southern European welfare states means transitions into adulthood, marriage, and parenthood are delayed.

Lastly, liberal welfare regimes have the narrowest definition of social rights, emphasising individual responsibility and have limited state involvement. The absence of welfare state involvement does not mean an absence of influence on the individual life course. Rather, the absence of welfare state policies or regulations can exacerbate class, race, gender, and age differences across the life course. For example, individuals with a higher socio-economic status will have more choice in constructing their individual biographies, whereas impoverished individuals will face significant constraints. This influence of inequalities will affect many trajectories (education, employment, retirement) as well as transitions into and out of these trajectories. In addition, while spending on social policy differs across liberal welfare regimes, in those countries where welfare state spending on the working age population is low, such as the USA, individuals face greater risks of inequality and poverty across the life course (Castles, 2009).

Given these differences across welfare regimes, it is not surprising that broader political, social, and economic processes, such as post-industrialisation, affect welfare states differently. In turn, the way in which individual life courses are affected by these processes is filtered through this variation in welfare state institutions as well as stratifications in gender, age, class, and race. The life course perspective offers a means by which to understand the interdependencies of these three areas and life course theory centres on understanding the relationship between individual life courses, welfare state institutions and broader social and economic structures. Heinz and colleagues (2009) refer to these three interrelated areas as 'historical time', referring to social and economic processes; 'institutional time', or welfare state institutions and provisions; and 'individual time', referring to individual actions and biographies. The relationship between these 'times' is not necessarily linear, but rather one of structure shaping and being shaped by individual action. In relation to the welfare state, then, the life course approach places equal emphasis on both structure (the welfare state) and agency (individuals giving shape to their own life course through purposeful action) as well as the interplay of these two (e.g. changes in risks faced by individuals leading to changes in welfare state policies (for an example, see Yerkes, 2011)). Stated differently, while welfare states shape the choices individuals make across the life course, individuals are linked to welfare state institutions 'by exercising agency, both through cognitive and emotional transformation of self-identity through role-taking and through decision-making in various changing social arenas' (Heinz et al., 2009, p. 24).

The relationship between welfare states and the life course has changed and continues to change as a result of post-industrialisation, or an alteration in 'historical time'. At the individual level, individual action and biographies are evolving: the life course is less orderly and more heterogeneity is evident. Macmillan (2005) outlines four dimensions of change: a general decompression of markers of adulthood (increased time between transitions); the occurrence of multiple social roles; the increased reversibility and instability of roles; and a decoupling of social roles, which is a consequence of some roles being delayed, while other roles are in decline (for example, getting married). As a result, individual needs across the life course have changed and individuals face different constellations of social risks across the life course. As a result of post-industrialisation, welfare state structures are being adjusted to accommodate transformations in employment, family, and social structures and to adapt to the change in risk constellations faced by individuals. For example, in many welfare states, various types of active labour market policies have been created to encourage employment in a post-industrial economy where full-employment is no longer the norm (Bonoli, 2010). In addition, the intensified link between education and employment has led to a growing emphasis on lengthy educational trajectories (Elchardus et al., 2003). And in many welfare states, new policies have been developed in response to the changed set of risks individuals face as a result of these post-industrial transformations in employment, family, and social structures. The latter is the focus of our first example on how welfare states shape the life course: looking at different welfare states and work–family balance policy. We then move on to our second example, which takes a closer look at the various ways in which the welfare state shapes and responds to the individual life course within a single country.

Example 1: Work–family balance policy

A clear example of the changes outlined above and the effect on the life course is the increased attention within welfare states for work–life balance. In the post-industrial society the combination of work and care highlights the intersections of family, state and (labour) market. This differs from industrial society, where the transition to parenthood had almost no effect on the breadwinner, at least not in the work domain. For the non-breadwinner of the couple, predominantly women, the effect was huge. Women usually left the labour market, or heavily reduced their working hours after the birth of a child. In essence, in industrial society, work and care were two separate domains – domains which were heavily gendered.

Post-industrial welfare states increasingly demand employment of both men and women, resulting in an increase in dual-earner couples, which challenges the gendered separation of work and home. Men and women increasingly have to deal with the combination of work and care tasks, or take on multiple social roles (Macmillan, 2005). The different work and care patterns of working parents can be understood as a result of historical circumstances, attitudes, and preferences of working parents, and the availability of policies which enable or constrain the combination of work and care at the level of the organisation and the welfare state.

While there has been a rise in dual-earner families in Western welfare states, many of these same countries have also witnessed a decline in fertility rates. This is particularly true in countries with fewer public support measures for working parents (Künzler, 2002), and countries with a declining economy and growing insecurity in the labour market. This decline is most notable in Eastern Europe, indicative of a decompression of markers of adulthood (Macmillan, 2005), whereby women increasingly postpone motherhood, have fewer children or remain childless. While individual preferences surrounding motherhood cannot be discounted, the lack of work–family balance policies in many welfare states profoundly affects decisions of motherhood. With the possible exception of the social democratic welfare regime, the conservative and liberal welfare regimes '[…] seem to be lagging behind the trends in family life, their changing employment patterns and their need for affordable provisions and support' (den Dulk et al., 2005, p. 36). As it is generally accepted that the sustainability and affordability of modern welfare states require a higher labour force participation rate than most countries have been able to achieve, the combination of work and family life is not only a main research theme in most countries, but it is also high on political and policy agendas (Abendroth and den Dulk, 2011).

Work–family or work–life policies are developed to support the combination of paid work and care tasks. They can exist as statutory provisions, be included in collective agreements, or be formally or informally arranged within organisations. Different examples of work–family policies are flexible work arrangements, such as part-time work; flexible start and finishing hours; leave arrangements, such as parental, paternity, and emergency leave; care arrangements like financial support or referral services; and supportive arrangements such as training and counselling programs (den Dulk, 2001). In other words, there are work–life policies that enable employees to take on care tasks themselves, such as flexible working hours, and there are policies that enable employees to buy or outsource care, such as child care (Appelbaum et al., 2005).

The availability of these work–family policies, particularly the public provision of these policies through welfare states, varies significantly across welfare regimes. In accordance with the Esping-Andersen typology discussed above (1990, 1999), the work–life balance of working parents across the life course depends on the degree of de-commodification and de-familialization evident in welfare state policy and regulation (Abendroth and den Dulk, 2011). To maintain a comfortable work–life balance, working parents in liberal welfare regimes like the UK, USA, and Australia often have to rely on work–life policies offered by organisations and companies, as welfare state policy in this area is often lacking. Research shows these countries offer a wide range of different policies, but with little regulation. Therefore, individuals in these welfare states are heavily dependent upon the market (den Dulk, 2001). For instance, working parents in the UK are entitled to three months of parental leave but this is unpaid and child care costs upwards of one quarter of net family income (den Dulk and van Doorne-Huiskes, 2007). While rapid developments in child care are taking place throughout Europe, availability and affordability remain problematic in some welfare states, such as the UK. The result is a great deal of uncertainty and insecurity across the life course. This is particularly true for lone parents, for example, where the decoupling of social roles (Macmillan, 2005), such as parenthood and marriage, in combination with a lack of welfare state policy, puts pressure upon lone parents' time and finances.

In conservative regime types, in countries like Germany, and in conservative Southern regimes, such as Italy and Portugal, individuals are highly dependent upon the support of family in balancing work and private lives, including care responsibilities. Welfare state and company policies are still very biased towards male breadwinners. For example, while many southern European countries offer paid leave for mothers, most fathers are only entitled to very brief periods of (un)paid leave or no leave (Organisation for Economic Co-operation and Development (OECD), 2011). And when both parents are working, most care tasks become the 'second shift' for women (Hochschild and Machung, 1989). The social democratic welfare regime, e.g. Sweden and Finland, offer the most de-commodified and de-familialized work life policies. In this regime, transitions in the life course of working parents are secured by statutory regulations and welfare state policies. For instance, child care is publicly provided and social democratic welfare states offer the most generous forms (both in pay and duration) of parental leave for both mothers and fathers, in an attempt to create more egalitarian work–family balance choices across the individual life course. For example, Swedish working parents are entitled to eighteen months of paid parental leave and child care costs are minimal, generally taking up 7 per cent of net family income (den Dulk and van Doorne-Huiskes, 2007).

Example 2: The Australian welfare state

We will now take a closer look at specific welfare state policies and laws in one country. In the Australian welfare state, policies and regulations have contributed to gendered differences in employment and have affected family formation. The pattern of state regulation about how to manage life course transitions in Australia is similar to countries such as the UK, Canada, and the USA, and falls broadly within a liberal welfare regime. Where Australia differs from other countries is in terms of the specific forms of policy interventions in personal relationships and the ways in which these policies manifest in their effects on the organisation of private lives. For example, although a gender gap in wages is evident in many Western countries, the historical development of this gender gap is distinctive to each country. One of the defining moments in the history of the gender wage gap in Australia was the setting of the first basic wage in 1907 by Justice Higgins of the High Court of Australia. The wage was intended to provide for a man, his wife, and two or three children in frugal comfort (Bryson, 1992), typifying a male breadwinner model. Higgins claimed that whereas the normal needs of a man included domestic life and a legal obligation to support a family if he had one, the same was not usually true of women. He concluded that women were not therefore entitled to equal pay, but merely to a wage that would enable a single woman without dependants to find her own food, clothing and shelter. It was only in industries where women competed for male jobs that women should be paid the male rate in order to prevent men from being pushed out of those jobs. This legislation effectively enshrined in law the view that women are dependants and that a family should consist of a full-time male breadwinner and a stay-at-home wife. Despite the abolition of the family wage and successive 'equal wage for equal work' policies from the end of the 1960s onward in Australia, a gender wage gap remains with women earning somewhere in the range of 10 to 27 per cent less than men, depending on the quartile and labour force sector under examination (Bryson, 1992).

As in many other Western countries, there has been considerable change in women's access to public institutions in Australia. For example between 1986 and 2005 Australian women's labour force participation rate rose from 48 to 58 per cent and the proportion of women with a Bachelor's degree rose from 5 to 25 per cent. However, most of the growth in women's labour force participation during this period was in part-time employment, particularly casual employment (Campbell et al., 2009), and it was during this period, in 1996, that a conservative federal government was elected with a range of policies broadly supportive of male breadwinner families. Australia ranks second only to the Netherlands in the percentage of employees in part-time employment at 24.1 per cent of all Australian employees, and well above the OECD average of 15.3 per cent (OECD, 2009). But like other countries, there are marked gender disparities in the distribution of part-time employment with the rate for women at 38.5 per cent, compared to 12.4 per cent for men (OECD, 2009). Compared to some other welfare states then, the male breadwinner model has proved remarkably resilient in Australia (Campbell et al., 2009). The welfare state has played a key role in shaping men and women's labour force involvement, not just by directly regulating women's access to the labour market, but also by directly regulating couples' decisions about who is responsible for providing economic support for families and who should withdraw from the labour market to care for children.

There is also evidence of the shaping role of the welfare state on the organization and timing of other life course transitions. One of the major changes in patterns of family formation in Australia has been the rise of unmarried cohabitation as an increasingly standard and acceptable pathway into legal marriage. Cohabitation has become the preferred route into marriage for the majority and most people will live in a cohabiting relationship at some stage in their lives (Bumpass, 2000), another example of the decompression of markers of adulthood through increased time between leaving the family home and transitioning into marriage (Macmillan, 2005). Like many other Western nations, Australia has seen an enormous growth in the percentage of marriages preceded by a period of *de facto* cohabitation, sometimes referred to as 'indirect marriages'. Sixteen per cent of Australian couples cohabited prior to marriage in 1975 compared to over three quarters in 2006 (Australian Bureau of Statistics, various years). At the same time, the percentage of couples in Australia who are cohabiting at any one point in time has more than doubled between 1986 and 2006 from just below 6 per cent to almost 15 per cent, with about 40 per cent of these proceeding to marriage (Australian Bureau of Statistics, various years). This is similar to several other countries including the USA, Canada, Britain, and other parts of Europe such as Germany or the Netherlands (Kiernan, 2004). Comparative research shows that Australia has lower cohabitation rates than the Scandinavian countries where more than 70 per cent of co-residential couples aged 25–34 cohabit (Kiernan, 2004) but has higher rates than Southern Europe where less than 40 per cent of similarly aged couples cohabit. Thus as the state has increasingly moved to recognize unmarried cohabitation as a legitimate form of partnering, a new life course stage has emerged. Variations across countries highlight the importance of investigating the specific historical features of the timing and degree of institutionalisation of this life course stage, but within welfare state regimes we see broad similarities.

Conclusion

This chapter focused on the ways in which the welfare state shapes the life course. The life course – stages of individual lives structured by social, cultural and historical contexts – can be studied in terms of trajectories (education, parenthood, marriage, employment, and retirement) and transitions into and out of these trajectories. As a result of post-industrialisation, demographic changes, and shifts in the gender order, the life course has become less orderly and more diverse. Individuals increasingly take up multiple trajectories, and transitions into and out of these trajectories are delayed or put off altogether. Welfare states shape the life course through policies and regulations as well as an absence of policy and legislation, or in other words, the way in which they address the risks individuals face across the life course. Examples of the way in which this occurs is evident when we compare life course trajectories and transitions across, as well as within, welfare states. Our chapter has highlighted some examples of these processes in relation to variations in work–family balance policies across countries, women's access to employment and gender equity within the labour market, and the emergence of cohabitation within a single country. We have also noted that the way in which the welfare state structures the life course varies across historical periods. The relationships are thus dynamic. The tasks for social researchers are to identify the similarities and differences in the effect of welfare states on the life course and to understand the outcomes for social inequality.

Further reading

Elder, G. H. and Giele, J. Z. (2009), *The Craft of Life Course Research.* New York and London: The Guildford Press.

Heinz, W. R., Huinink, J. Weymann, A. and Swader, C. (2009), *The Life Course Reader: Individuals and Societies Across Time.* Frankfurt: Campus Verlag.

Hunt, S. (2005), *The Life Course. A Sociological Introduction.* New York: Palgrave Macmillan.

Macmillan, R. (2005), The Structure of the Life Course: Classic Issues and Current Controversies. *Advances in Life Course Research* 9, pp. 3–24.

Mayer, K. H. and Schoepflin, U. (1989), The State and the Life Course. *Annual Review of Sociology,* 15, pp. 187–209.

References

Abendroth, A.-K. and Den Dulk, L. (2011), Support for the work-life balance in Europe: the impact of state, workplace and family support on work-life balance satisfaction. *Work, Employment & Society,* 25, pp. 234–56.

Appelbaum, E., Bailey, T., Berg, P. and Kalleberg, A. (2005), 'Organizations and the intersection of work and family', in S. Ackroyd, R. Batt, P. Thompson, and P. S. Tolbert (eds), *The Oxford Handbook of Work and Organization.* Oxford: Oxford University Press.

Australian Bureau of Statistics (various years) 'Marriages'. Australia: Canberra.

Blossfeld, H.-P. (2009), 'Comparative Life Course Research. A Cross-national longitudinal perspective', in G. H. Elder and J. Z. Giele (eds), *The Craft of Life Course Research.* New York and London: The Guildford Press.

Bonoli, G. (2005), The Politics of the New Social Policies: Providing Coverage against New Social Risks in Mature Welfare States. *Policy and Politics,* 33, pp. 431–449.

——(2010), *The Political Economy of Active Labour Market Policy.* Edinburgh: RECWOWE.

Bryson, L. (1992), *Welfare and the State.* London: Macmillan.

Bumpass, L. A. H.-H. L. (2000), Trends in Cohabitation and Implications for Children's Family Contexts. *Population Studies,* 54, pp. 29–41.

Campbell, I., Whitehouse, G. and Baxter, J. (2009), 'Australia. Casual Employment, Part-Time Employment and the Resilience of the Male-Breadwinner Model', in L. F. Vosko, M. Macdonald and I. Campbell (eds), *Gender and the Contours of Precarious Employment.* Abingdon: Routledge.

Castles, F. G. (2009), What Welfare States Do: A Disaggregated Expenditure Approach. *Journal of Social Policy,* 38, pp. 45–62.

Den Dulk, L. (2001), 'Work-family Arrangements in Organizations', in *A Cross-national study in the Netherlands, Italy, the United Kingdom and Sweden.* Amsterdam: Rozenburg Publishers.

Den Dulk, L., Peper, A. and van doorne-huiskes, A. (2005), 'Work and Family Life in Europe: Employment Patterns of Working Parents Across Welfare States', in A. Peper, A. Van Doorne-Huiskes and L. Den Dulk (eds), *Flexible Working, Organizational Change and the Integration of Work and Personal life.* Cheltenham: Edward Elgar.

Den Dulk, L. and Van Doorne-Huiskes, A. (2007), 'Social Policy in Europe: its Impact on Families and Work', in R. Crompton, C. Lyonette and S. Lewis (eds), *Women, Men, Work and Family in Europe*. Basingstoke: Palgrave Macmillan.

Elchardus, M., Marx, I. and Pelleriaux, K. (2003), 'De nieuwe sociale kwestie: begripsverduidelijking en hypothesevorming', in B. Cantillon (ed.), *De nieuwe sociale kwesties*. Antwerp: Garant.

Esping-Andersen, G. (1990), *The Three Worlds of Welfare Capitalism*, Cambridge: Polity Press.

——(1999), *Social Foundations of Postindustrial Economies*, Oxford: Oxford University Press.

——(2002), *Why we need a new welfare state*, New York: Oxford University Press.

Hacker, J. S. (2004), Privatizing Risk without Privatizing the Welfare State: The Hidden Politics of Social Policy Retrenchment in the United States. *American Political Science Review*, 98, pp. 243–260.

Heinz, W. R., Huinink, J., Weymann, A. and Swader, C. (2009), *The Life Course Reader: Individuals and Societies across Time*, Frankfurt: Campus Verlag.

Hochschild, A. R. and Machung, A. (1989), *The Second Shift: Working Parents and the Revolution at Home*, New York: Viking.

Hunt, S. (2010), 'Life-Cycle or Life-Course?', in A. Giddens (ed.), *Sociology: Introductory Readings*. Cambridge and Malden, MA: Polity Press.

Kiernan, K. (2004), 'Cohabitation and divorce across nations and generations', in P. L. Chase-Lansdale, K. Kiernan and R. J. Friedman (eds), *Human Development across Lives and Generations*. Cambridge: Cambridge University Press.

Künzler, J. (2002), 'Paths towards a modernization of gender relations, policies, and family building', in F. X. Kaufmann, A. Kuijsten, H. J. Schulze and K. P. Strohmeier (eds), *Family Life and Family Policies in Europe. Problems and Issues in Comparative Perspective*. Oxford: Oxford University Press.

Macmillan, R. (2005), The Structure of the Life Course: Classic Issues and Current Controversies. *Advances in Life Course Research*, 9, pp. 3–24.

Mayer, K. U. and Schoepflin, U. (1989), The State and the Life Course. *Annual Review of Sociology*, 15, pp. 187–209.

Organisation for Economic Co-operation and Development (OECD) (2009), *Society at a Glance 2009 – OECD Social Indicators*. Paris: OECD.

——(2011), Key characteristics of parental leave systems. *OECD Family database*. Paris: OECD.

Yerkes, M. (2011), *Transforming the Dutch Welfare State: Social Risks and Corporatist Reform*, Bristol: The Policy Press.

12
Active labour market policies

Madelene Nordlund

This chapter deals primarily with Active Labour Market Policies (ALMPs) which mainly consist of educational and employment incentives offered to the unemployed. ALMPs aim at relieving or preventing the negative effects that spells of unemployment often bring about for the individual as well as for the labour market as a whole. The subject that researchers continually investigate is whether or not participation in ALMPs is fruitful. This chapter shows that it is difficult to make universal statements about this because the success of ALMPs seems to vary as a consequence of how they are designed, individual heterogeneity among participants, and methodological issues. Nevertheless, despite the difficulty in drawing conclusions, some general tendencies as regards the supply of ALMPs and subsequent micro level effects of ALMPs will be highlighted in this chapter.

Unemployment scarring

In what way do unemployment spells affect the unemployed? The unemployed are definitely exposed to a temporary risk of economic misfortune but they also risk suffering long-term scarring effects even after the spells of unemployment have ended. Common scarring effects include labour market exclusion and/or future negative wage trajectories and the longer the unemployment period, the greater the risk of long-term negative effects. In this sense, unemployment should not be viewed as a temporary problem that lasts as long as the jobless period. Instead it should be seen as a process that starts soon after entering unemployment and, in many cases, continues even after the person has returned to the labour market. First of all, unemployed people start losing human capital, i.e. skills and experience, fairly quickly after the beginning of the unemployment spell (see, for instance, Becker, 1993, as regards the Human Capital theory). Then after some time, potential employers often hesitate to employ people who have been unemployed, particularly those with longer unemployment spells, because the unemployed are thought to be less reliable and productive than others. As time passes and their job applications continue to be rejected, the unemployed also tend to lower the intensity of their job searching and eventually stop looking for new jobs. Under such circumstances there is a rapid increase in the risk of individual negative effects such as labour market exclusion or a negative wage development if there is any return to the labour market at all. To avoid such negative scarring effects, the unemployed should return to the labour market as soon as possible since the length of the unemployment spell influences how much damage the unemployed may experience. (See Layte et al., 2000, regarding unemployment as a cumulative disadvantage on the labour market.)

The unemployment insurance

Unemployment insurance systems regulate the conditions for the eligibility of the unemployment benefit. The unemployment insurance system is by tradition called a passive measure and is used to alleviate the risk of direct economic misfortune but can also reduce the more long-term negative consequences the unemployed are exposed to. This chapter focuses on active measures (ALMPs), but before that the passive measure of unemployment insurance deserves some attention.

The way unemployment insurance is formed to fit in with a certain welfare state depends on the type of welfare state in question. In a social democratic type of welfare state (for instance, Sweden or Denmark), the idea is to redistribute resources with the aim of reducing inequalities between social groups. Basically, this gives rise to rather generous unemployment benefit which covers a relatively large proportion of the unemployed. In more conservative welfare states (Germany for instance), unemployment insurance is based on the unemployed person's previous achievement on the labour market. In this case, unemployment benefit is generous for those who have contributed most on the labour market but much more limited for those who have contributed less. In a liberal welfare state (for instance, the UK and the USA), the unemployment insurance system is designed only for the poorest, those who would have difficulties surviving without it. In liberal welfare states, unemployment benefit is therefore limited both in coverage and duration. Thus, in general, the conditions of different unemployment insurance systems vary in terms of the level and duration of compensation for the eligible recipients and they also vary in terms of how much individuals must contribute on the labour market before receiving any benefit. (See Esping-Andersen, 1990, as regards welfare state typologies.)

There is a constantly ongoing debate regarding the most appropriate design of unemployment insurance. Generally speaking, and as pointed out earlier in this chapter, it is important for the unemployed to return to the labour market as soon as possible to avoid the risk of long-lasting negative scarring, and when seen from this perspective, generous unemployment benefit may delay a return to the labour market. In this context, the Search Theory has had an influence on the choices made by countries when designing their unemployment insurance systems. The Search Theory suggests that generous compensation makes the unemployed less inclined to search for jobs and more selective before accepting job offers. According to the Search Theory, this behaviour by the unemployed will lengthen the unemployment spell. In contrast, less generous compensation is expected to shorten unemployment spells because a less favourable economic situation will make the unemployed more active in job search activities and they will be less selective when accepting job offers. (See, for instance, Mortensen 1977; 1990, regarding Search Theory.) Seen from the perspective of the Search Theory, unemployment insurance systems should mainly provide for the poorest and only for a limited time. However, while such a link between level and length of unemployment compensation and job probabilities has been empirically confirmed by some researchers (see, for instance, Katz and Meyer, 1990; Meyer, 1990; Layard et al., 1991; Roed and Zhang, 2004), others have not been able to confirm this (Carling et al., 1996; Bennemarker et al., 2005; Nordlund and Strandh, 2008).

Although the Search Theory contributes important knowledge with regards to the search behaviour of the unemployed, it needs to be balanced by other aspects of the effects of unemployment benefit on the unemployed. In fact, it has been found that unemployment benefit can function as a human capital preserver, since a generous compensation facilitates for the unemployed to search for suitable jobs that match their skills and experience, rather than having to take the first available job. This has been found to have positive effects on post-unemployment incomes (Nordlund and Strandh, 2008). Seen from this perspective, the system should perhaps provide economic compensation over a relatively long period.

In this context it should also be mentioned that other incentives, apart from the economic one, seem to have an impact on the job search behaviour and job probabilities of the unemployed. Such incentives are related to psychosocial and psychological needs (Strandh, 2000) as well as to other characteristics related to human capital, demography, and of course local labour demands (Korpi, 2001; Åberg, 2001; Hjerm, 2002; the Swedish Integration Board, 2003; Adison, 2004; Caliendo et al., 2010). Thus, economic incentives usually underlie the design of unemployment insurance in order to maximise the outflow from unemployment to employment. However, economic incentives do not explain all. Other incentives and individual characteristics must also be taken into account when explaining why some unemployed people have shorter unemployment spells than others.

A common trend in most welfare states today is the downscaling of the unemployment insurance system. During the past twenty years, reductions have been made either in the level or duration of benefits or in both. Furthermore, several welfare states have also tightened up the work requirements, which make the unemployed eligible for benefit. (For a detailed comparison of specific countries, see the MISSOC database run by the EU). The recession in Europe at the beginning of the 1990s resulted in many major reforms with cuts in the unemployment insurance system but even after improved labour market conditions in the latter part of the 1990s, many countries have faced further reforms with reductions in the unemployment insurance system. Such later reforms have in several cases been referred to as a tendency of structural changes where welfare regimes have moved from the idea of welfare to the concept of workfare. Workfare emphasizes that individuals must work for welfare to a larger extent, which has in turn resulted in enforced work requirements for individuals. In exchange for active job searching, participation in short-term work preparation courses etc., the job-seeker receives coaching and, if eligible, unemployment benefit (see, for instance Kildal, 2001). With this shift from welfare to workfare, the passive measure of unemployment insurance has become more closely linked to traditional active measures, since the workfare model is actually based on some of the active measures.

To sum up, we find that the overall purpose of reductions in the unemployment insurance system is to hasten benefit recipients back onto the labour market. The design of the unemployment insurance system does to some extent have an impact on the outflow from unemployment to employment but that is not the only determinant of how well a country manages to include working age persons on its labour market. Psychosocial and psychological incentives, the overall labour demand, as well as individual characteristics also play decisive roles for inclusion. This brief discussion of the passive measure will now be followed by a more extensive review of the active measures (ALMPs), which are another means of including the unemployed on the labour market.

Active Labour Market Policies (ALMP)

A retrospective overview

The history of ALMPs derives from the economic and labour market depression that hit most of the Western world in the 1930s. The common belief prior to this was that self-regulating components without any public interventions would solve many of the problems that market economies were exposed to. This belief changed to some extent during the depression because it was understood that unemployment followed by a depression could not automatically be eliminated and, along with the increase in wealth in many Western countries, the ambition to invest in ALMPs to regulate the unemployment level grew (Keynes, 1936; Axelsson, 1985). As early as in the 1930s, 'Public relief work' was introduced in Sweden. These jobs were specially created for the unemployed in order to hold down the unemployment level and a specific feature of these interventions was that the workers received a wage equal to market wages.

In the 1940s, two Swedish economists, Gösta Rehn and Rudolf Meidner, came up with an economic model, known as the Rhen-Meidner model. In general, it was believed that low inflation led to high unemployment and vice versa but Rhen and Meidner argued that it should be possible to create an economic model that brought about both low inflation and lowered unemployment rates. An important part of this model (together with other features not mentioned here) was that it contained a wage policy that promoted equal pay for equal work. This policy aimed to reduce wage spans and increase wages for the most exposed groups on the labour market. Equal wages would be set regardless of businesses' ability to pay and consequently, the policy accelerated the closure of businesses or industries with poor profitability. This was a rational way to start the modernisation of Swedish society in the post-war era, the focus being on upcoming lines of industry rather than giving support to weak sectors. The risk was that inflation would increase as a result of the economic goals but that was to be prevented through a subdued demand policy. The combination of a subdued demand policy and the solidarity wage policy increased the risk of structural unemployment, since workers were pushed into unemployment when businesses closed. To prevent the negative effects of structural unemployment, it became necessary to enable efficient movement of workers between lines of business and ALMPs were created in this context in order to direct the unemployed back onto the labour market. ALMPs would educate and train the unemployed so as to match expanding industries with a growing labour demand and they would also prevent bottlenecks during booms. Another purpose of ALMPs was to facilitate efficient matching between employers and employees through unemployment services. (For more details about the Rhen-Meidner model, see, for instance, Erixon, 2008.)

At first ALMPs appeared in economic policy mainly in the Scandinavian countries but in the 1990s, an increasing number of labour market strategies including ALMPs were developed in other European countries and the USA. This was a result of the sharp rises in unemployment Organisation for Economic Co-operation and Development (OECD) countries had experienced over several decades. Along with increasing unemployment rates, long-term unemployment spells also increased and therefore it became urgent to improve the employment prospects of the unemployed and hence ALMPs were developed (see, for instance, Kluve et al., 2007).

Today many countries are having to cope with an ageing population and in order to limit the ensuing consequences of a smaller workforce, broader actions have been taken to involve a larger number of people in work. Therefore, the ALMPs have changed from being an active measure to cut unemployment levels to becoming elements of the 'making-work-pay' policy together with the unemployment insurance system. As pointed out earlier in this chapter, unemployment benefit has likewise changed from being welfare to workfare, with the aim of improving the employability of unemployed and other working-age persons, and making them more active in their job search process. To facilitate the 'making-work-pay' policy, more priority has been given to the efficiency and administration of ALMPs. (See, for instance, OECD, 2006; Kluve et al., 2007.)

Types of ALMPs

ALMPs are used to counteract labour shortage and to mobilise the workforce by holding down the overall unemployment level. At the same time, on an individual level, the unemployed get help to maintain or increase their human capital and thereby improve their future labour market prospects. These aims can be facilitated by organizing different types of activities for the unemployed and also by promoting an active matching between vacancies on the labour market and the unemployed.

The types of measures applied differ across countries, which makes it difficult to be precise in the description of ALMPs from a cross-national perspective. However, a study of different countries' expenditure on ALMPs gives an indication of how ALMPs have been prioritised as an important part of labour market policy. For instance, in 2009, Belgium, Denmark, the Netherlands, and Sweden were the countries putting most money into ALMPs (from 1.1 % to 1.6% of gross domestic product (GDP)) while most Anglo-Saxon countries were spending much less on ALMPs (the UK, USA, and Australia, for example, spent from 0.1 to 0.2% of GDP) (OECD, 2011).

In order for ALMPs to be successful, they need to be constantly adjusted in order to fit the overall labour market situation in a country. It is therefore not possible, or even relevant, to mention particular programmes since these vary both across countries and over time within countries. Furthermore, a closer study shows that when measures are compared at different points in time, in the mid 2000s, ALMP measures were split and renamed (Grubb and Puymoyen, 2008). For the purpose of this text, it is sufficient to identify the main types of ALMPs that serve rather different purposes on the labour market.

One type of ALMP aims at promoting an efficient exchange of information between employers and employees/unemployed. It is called *Public employment services and administration*, and its aim is to increase the matching process by offering coaching and different types of job search activities to the unemployed. However, another task is to administrate unemployment benefit sanctions in the event that the job search behaviour of the unemployed is deemed insufficient.

Another type of ALMP is *training activities* through classroom education, training at workplaces, and special support for apprenticeships. The focus of this type of programme is on the actual skill development of the participant. Through education and skill development, the unemployed enhance their human capital, which in turn often improves their employability and productivity. Human capital enhancement should in turn lead to better labour market prospects. The activities are often directed at skills that are expected to be in future demand on the labour market.

Apart from human capital increasing activities, there are also programmes directed more towards *employment incentives*. The aim of this type is to give subsidies to regular employment on the regular labour market, to support direct job creations within the public sector and to give support to unemployed people who decide to set up their own business. This type of programme mainly helps the unemployed to stay active and to establish networks on the labour market. The focus is more about creating and maintaining abilities and social competences during the unemployment spell, rather than building up human capital. The challenge with this type of programme is to provide the unemployed with tasks that do not push aside the regularly employed.

In addition to or alongside the types of ALMPs mentioned here, there are also *supported employment and rehabilitation* measures directed at youth and people with disabilities, since they are particularly exposed and at risk of labour market marginalisation.

ALMPs from macro- and micro-level perspectives

Economists have contributed important knowledge about effects from a macro-level perspective: what policies are effective with regards to making the labour market more efficient, and what policies can be used to address structural problems or to reduce short-term or long-term unemployment. Others focus more on the micro-level outcomes of ALMPs: to what extent ALMPs manage to increase the human capital and employability of the unemployed and to what extent ALMPs help to prevent misplacements in future job situations on the labour market.

Additionally, some micro-level researchers look at the ALMPs from yet another dimension, arguing that ALMPs can have an important purpose even if ALMP participation does not increase job probability. Training activities, for instance, improve the skills and competences of the unemployed, giving people the opportunity to make choices in life that they would not be able to do without such training. Training can lead to important qualities that the individual needs in order to interact in society, such as being able to read, to be healthy, or politically active – skills which have been found to increase with education (Ross and Wu, 1995; Ross and Mirowsky, 2010). Such qualities can of course be an achievement in themselves but they may also be crucial for individual opportunities in the process of directing/redirecting life plans (Robeyns, 2005). For a more detailed account of how ALMPs can be viewed from a capability approach see, for instance, Sen (2002) or Nordlund (2010).

The examples above show how the benefits of ALMPs can be viewed from different perspectives. Macro- and micro-level goals often overlap but they may also be conflicting. For instance, in order to reduce the number of long-term unemployed, unemployed people should return to the labour market as soon as possible. A speedy return to the labour market means the unemployed should accept the first available job offer. However, seen from a micro perspective a swift return to the labour market may at times come in conflict with the aim of reducing the risk of individual misplacement on the labour market. The risk of labour market misplacement increases when the unemployed are pushed to take the first available job, instead of accepting the first suitable job. A suitable job is a job where previous human capital comes to use, which in turn reduces the risk of downward social mobility (the transition of people from a higher economic group or social class to a lower) and thus increases the chance of returning to a job with an income similar to the pre-unemployment income.

ALMP outcomes are usually studied and discussed from a macro perspective. In order to present a more balanced picture, the following section focuses on the micro-level outcomes of ALMPs rather than macro-level effects.

Effects of ALMPs

Evaluating the impact of ALMP participation is clearly important because the supply of programmes for the unemployed is economically demanding for a country. Moreover, participation in ALMPs may also cause negative lock-in effects for the participants since they then miss out on the opportunity to search for vacancies on the regular labour market. With the awareness of possible lock-in effects, it is particularly important to evaluate programmes in order to reduce the risk that unemployed people are placed in activities that waste their time or even ruin their job prospects on the regular labour market. Innumerable evaluations have been carried out in order to measure the effects of ALMPs and researchers have contributed with some important knowledge on this matter. Nevertheless the results appear to be diverse and it is difficult to identify clear cross-national patterns. A very brief summary of ALMP micro-level effects is presented below and for a more detailed overview of country-level summaries as regards design and outcomes of ALMPs, I refer to Kluve et al., 2007 and Kluve, 2010.

As will be shown in the following section, ALMPs can lead to an increase in human capital and higher employment probabilities among the unemployed. However, in this context it should be mentioned that there are no truly reliable methods to capture what is called the 'counter-factual state', i.e. what the effect would have been if the unemployed person had not participated in the ALMP in question. While research may be able to show that a particular ALMP generated positive outcomes for the individual, it cannot be said for sure that the positive effect is a consequence isolated to the effect of the programme. The participants may possess certain characteristics which in themselves could have an impact on the outcome. Some participants would perhaps have found jobs even without participating in ALMPs. In such circumstances, programmes result in a deadweight loss, which is of course undesirable since ALMPs are costly and other priorities should perhaps have been considered instead.

Training – employment incentives

Several studies have shown that *employment incentives* produce rather positive outcomes, both in terms of employment probability and post-unemployment incomes (see, for instance, Gerfin et al., 2002; O'Connell, 2002; Sianesi, 2002; Strandh and Nordlund, 2008; Kluve, 2010). One main factor for success seems to be the extent to which these are linked to a country's regular labour market. To transfer from unemployment to employment, the unemployed need good networks and contacts and in several cases employment incentives seem to be able to provide this. However, the risk here is that successful programmes are too closely linked to the regular labour market. If so, the design of the programme in question may push aside the regularly employed (displacement effects) and this is of course neither the intention nor a desirable outcome of ALMP activities.

For ALMP *training measures*, the main factor for success would be the quality of the training/education the participants receive, together with countries' possibilities to match the supply of training/education with future needs for competence. Evaluations show mixed results where some indicate rather modest effects in terms of employment probabilities while others are much better. See Kluve (2010) for an overview in this respect. This inconclusiveness would seem to be because the content of particular programmes has an impact on their effectiveness. For instance, while some programmes are short, others extend over a much longer period and this diversity seems to give different effects, where longer programmes produce better outcomes on employment probability than shorter programmes do (OECD, 1996; Strandh and Nordlund, 2008). Furthermore, not only is the actual human capital investment (the content of the training and the duration of training) important for the outcome, it must also be matched with the demand for labour. This effectiveness certainly differs from region to region and time to time. Other reasons for inconclusive results may be linked to at what point in a business cycle the ALMP activity took place and how long the time span was from activity to evaluation.

The impact of different business cycles

It has been reported that many of the programme participants in the 1980s and early 2000s (boom periods) experienced different types of positive effects while those who participated in the 1990s (recession period) experienced no positive – or even negative – effects. Some argue here that programme participation is useful when there are few jobs to search for on the labour market, while participation during boom periods – when there are plenty of jobs available – may hinder the unemployed from searching for and accepting jobs (Ackum Agell, 1996; Regnér and Wadensjö, 1999). However, Nordlund (2011a) studied how the effects varied depending on when in a business cycle participation in ALMPs took place and found that regardless of the state of the market, ALMPs functioned to protect the Swedish unemployed from negative effects. An important finding here was that *training incentives* had a bridging effect during economic downturns meaning that the investment in training activities during a recession paid off long after the end of a programme.

Heterogeneity in outcomes

ALMP participation is not equally effective for all. Even if the same ALMP investment is made in all unemployed persons, the participants will respond differently to the investment. For instance, the labour market is segregated in such a way that male and female workers are tied to rather different labour market sectors. The labour market sector that women, men, the young, the old, the less or more educated etc. belong to may contribute to the explanation of the heterogeneity of ALMP outcomes. Some unemployed people may actually waste their time in ALMPs while others are more fortunate and increase their labour market prospects after ALMP activities. Age and educational background are examples of individual characteristics that have been shown to be an important factor for ALMP outcomes. (Hammer, 1997; Gregg, 2001; Nordlund, 2011b). Furthermore, those already marginalized on the labour market may gain from some types of ALMPs while people unemployed on structural bases may gain from other types of ALMPs. These are examples, and in order to fully explain the heterogeneous nature of ALMP outcomes, more research is needed.

Long-term effects

Most programmes are evaluated relatively soon (from a few months up to a couple of years) after the end of programme participation while, so far, only a few studies have measured the long-term impact (up to ten years). In the OECD report from 1996, Reutersward argued that, on the one hand, *employment incentive programmes* produce rather immediate effects and can therefore be evaluated soon after the end of programme participation. On the other hand, it can be argued that evaluations regarding the outcomes of *training programmes* should be done much later since this type of investment is meant to be a human capital investment, which is a long-term investment. Similarly, Strandh and Nordlund (2008) argued that the impact of training activities should to a larger extent be evaluated after a relatively long time, the reason being twofold. Firstly, if a training programme is completed when the unemployment rate is high, there are very few jobs to search for, but as soon as the condition of the labour market improves, the participants stand ready with new improved skills that are needed on the labour market. Secondly, some people who enter training programmes continue to further studies within the regular educational system after finishing the training programme, and the effects cannot therefore be correctly measured until they finish their studies, four, five, or even six years later. The findings of Calmfors et al., (2002) mean that more time should pass from ALMP participation until evaluation, especially in times when demand for labour is low. Thus, the effects of such a chain of events demand a long-term approach. This may well be one reason why the outcome of *training incentives* fairly often points to rather mediocre results. The real effects are quite simply not yet apparent, if the time span from training activity to evaluation is short.

Conclusion

This chapter began with a short account of the unemployment process, the risk of long-lasting negative scarring effects, and unemployment benefit insurance systems that aim at alleviating more direct negative economic effects. To avoid more long-term negative effects, the unemployed need to return to the labour market as soon as possible since open unemployment has a negative impact on future labour market chances. This, as such, is sometimes used as an argument against generous unemployment benefit since unemployment benefit is thought to lengthen the spell in unemployment. Active measures, ALMPs, can also delay labour market entrance for the unemployed because ALMPs last for quite some time and while participating in an ALMP, the unemployed have very little time to search for jobs on the regular labour market. However, when ALMPs fulfil their purposes – when training programmes are of a high quality and the skill training is directed to match future labour demands, or when employment incentives are closely linked to the labour market – research indicates that the programmes often have positive individual effects. Thus, ALMPs may possibly delay labour market entry to some extent, but it has been shown that ALMPs have the power to maintain or increase the human capital of the unemployed during a period of unemployment, which is certainly a vital factor for labour market inclusion.

References

Åberg, R. (2001), Equilibrium unemployment, search behaviour and unemployment persistency. *Cambridge Journal of Economics*, 25, pp. 131–47.

Ackum Agell, S. (1996), Arbetslösas sökaktivitet. [Search Activity Among Unemployed] *SOU 1996:34. Aktiv arbetsmarknadspolitik [active labour market policy]. Bilaga till arbetsmarknadspolitiska kommitténs betänkande.* Stockholm: Fritzes.

Addison, J. T., Centeno, M., Portugal, P. (2004), *Reservation Wages, Search Duration, and Accepted Wages in Europe.* IZA Discussion Paper no 1252.

Axelsson, R., Löfgren, K.-G., Nilsson, L.-G., (1985), *Den svenska arbetsmarknadspolitiken under 1900-talet.* Stockholm: Bokförlaget prisma.

Becker, G. S. (1993), *Human Capital: A Theoretical and Empirical Analysis with Special Reference to Education.* 3rd edn. Chicago, IL: The University of Chicago Press.

Bennemarker, H., Carling, K. and Holmlund, B. (2005), *Leder höjd A-kassa till längre arbetslöshetstider?* En studie av de svenska förändringarna 2001–2. Rapport 2005:16 Institutet för arbetsmarknadspolitisk utvärdering.

Caliendo, M., Cobb-Clark, D. and Uhlendorff, A. (2010), *Locus of Control and Job Search Strategies.* IZA Discussion Paper No. 4750.

Calmfors, L., Forslund, A. and Hemström, M. (2002), Vad vet vi om den svenska arbetsmarknadspolitikens sysselsättningseffekter? *Institutet för arbetsmarknadspolitisk utvärdering.* Rapport 2002:8.

Carling, K., Edin, P.-A., Harkman, A., Holmlund, B. (1996), Unemployment duration, unemployment, unemployment benefits, and labour market programs in Sweden. *Journal of Public Economics*, 59, pp. 313–34.

Erixon, L. (2008), The Rehn-Meidner model in Sweden: its rise, challenges and survival. Department of economy, University of Stockholm. Online: www.ne.su.se/paper/wp08_02.pdf

Esping-Andersen, G. (1990), *The Three Worlds of Welfare Capitalism.* Cambridge: Polity Press.

European Commission (MISSOC) (2011), ec.europa.eu/social/main.jsp?catId=815&langId=sv.

Gerfin, M., Lechner, M., Stieger, H. (2002), Does subsidised temporary employment get the unemployed back to work? An econometric analysis of two different schemes. *Labour Economics 12*, pp. 807–35.

Groot, L. F. M., Schippers, J. J., Siegers, J. J. (1990), The effect of unemployment, temporary withdrawals and part time work on workers wage rates. *European Sociological Review* 6(3), pp. 257–73.

Grubb, D. and Puymoyen, A. (2008), Long time series for public expenditure on labour market programmes. *OECD Social, Employment and Migration Working Papers*, No. 73, OECD Publishing. dx.doi.org/10.1787/230128514343.

Hammer, T. (1997), History Dependence in Youth Unemployment. *European Sociological Review 13*(1), pp. 17–33.

Hipple, S. (1999), Worker displacement in the 1990s. *Monthly Labor Review 122*, 15–32.

Hjerm, M. (2002), 'Sysselsättning' in J. Vogel, M. Hjerm and S.-E. Johansson (eds), *Integration till svensk välfärd?* Stockholm: SCB, Rapport 96.

Katz, L. F, Meyer, B. D. (1990), The impact of the potential duration of unemployment benefits on the duration of unemployment. *Journal of Public Economics*, 41, pp. 1, 45–72.

Keynes, J. M., (1936), *The General Theory of Employment, Interests, and Money*. London.

Kildal, N., (2001), Workfare Tendencies in Scandinavian Welfare Policies. *Working Paper*, International Labour Office, Geneva, Switzerland.

Kluve, J., (2010), The effectiveness of European active labor market programs. *Labour Economics*, 17, pp. 904–18.

Kluve, J., Card, D., Fertig, M., Góra M., Jacobi, L., Jensen, P., Leetmaa, R., Nima L., Patacchini, E., Schaffner, S, Schmidt, C., van der Klaauw, B., Weber, A., (2007), *Active Labor Market Policies in Europe. Performance and Perspectives*. Berlin and Heidelberg; Springer-Verlag.

Korpi, T. (2001a), Good Friends in Bad Times? Social networks and job search among the unemployed in Sweden. *Acta Sociologica*, 44, pp. 2, 157–70.

Layard, R., Nickell, S., Jackman, R. (1991), *Unemployment. Macroeconomic performance and the Labour Market*. Oxford: Oxford University Press.

Layte, R., Levin, H., Hendrickx, J., Bison, I. (2000), 'Unemployment and Cumulative Disadvantage in the Labour Market', in D. Gallie and S. Paugam (eds), *Welfare Regimes and the Experience of Unemployment in Europe*. Oxford: Oxford University Press.

Meyer, B. D. (1990), Unemployment insurance and unemployment spells. *Econometrica*, 58, pp. 757–82.

Mortensen, D. T. (1977), Unemployment insurance and job search decisions. *Industrial and Labor Relations Review*, 30, pp. 4, 505–17

——(1990), 'A Structural Model of Unemployment Insurance Benefit Effects on the Incidence and Duration of Unemployment', in Y. Weiss and G. Fishelson (eds), *Advances in the Theory and Measurement of Unemployment*, Basingstoke: Macmillan.

Nordlund, M., (2010), *Long-term Unemployment Scarring and the Role of Labour Market Policies*. The case of Sweden in the 1990s. Doctoral Thesis at the Department of Sociology, No 97, Umeå. Sweden.

——(2011a), What works best when? – A study of how ALMPs can play different roles depending on when in a business cycle participation takes place. *International Journal of Social Welfare*, Vol. 20:1, pp. 43–54.

——(2011b), Who are the lucky ones? Heterogeneity in the outcomes of ALMPs. *International Journal of Social Welfare*. Vol. 20:2, pp. 144–155.

Nordlund, M., Strandh, M., (2008), Göra illa för att hjälpa eller hjälpa till att göra illa? Arbetslösas reservationslöner, jobbchanser och återanställningsinkomster. *Sociologisk forskning*, 3.

Organisation for Economic Co-operation and Development (OECD) (1996), *Enhancing the Effectiveness of Active Labour Market Policies: Evidence from Programme Evaluations in OECD Countries*. OECD.

——(2011), Public expenditure on active labour market policy. Online: www.oecd-ilibrary.org/employment/public-expenditure-on-active-labour-market-policies_20752342-table9

Regnér, H. and Wadensjö, E. (1999), *Arbetsmarknadens funktionssätt i Sverige [The functioning of the Swedish labour market]. En beskrivning baserad på nya intervjudata*. Sofi, Stockholms universitet.

Robeyns, I., (2005), The Capability Approach: a theoretical survey. *Journal of Human Development*, 6(1), pp. 94–111.

Roed, K. and Zhang, T. (2004), Unemployment duration and economic incentives – a quasi random-assignment approach. *European Economic Review*, 49: 1, 799–1825.

Ross, C. E. and Wu, C. (1995), The links between education and health. *American Sociological Review* 60, pp. 719–45.

Ross, C. E. and Mirowsky, J. (2010), Gender and the Health Benefits of Education. *Sociological Quarterly*, 51:1–19.

Sen, A. (2001), *Development as Freedom*. New York: Alfred A. Knopf Inc.

Strandh, M. (2000), *Varying Unemployment Experiences? The economy and mental well-being*, Doctoral Thesis at the Department of Sociology, No. 11, Umeå: Department of Sociology.

Strandh, M., Nordlund, M. (2008), Active Labour Market Policy and Unemployment Scarring: A Ten-year Swedish Panel Study. *International Journal of Social Policy*, 37:3, 357–82.

Swedish Integration Board (2003), *Report integration 2002*. Norrköping: Integrationsverket.

13

Flexicurity

Concepts, practices, and outcomes

Frank Tros and Ton Wilthagen

Introduction

The origins of the concept of flexicurity, which emerged in the mid 1990s, have to be seen in a historical context of labour market and welfare state developments. In many Western welfare states, the job and social security systems were developed after the Second World War, reaching a stage of 'completion' in the late 1960s and 1970s. The 1980s, however, can be typified as an era where deregulation and privatization appeared as the dominant political responses to economic and state budget crises. In the early 1990s, policy scientists started to notice that the 'deregulation versus regulation' or 'flexibility versus security' debates might be positioned and conceptualized too narrowly. Certain settings and forms of (re)regulation were considered conducive to economic performance (Streeck, 1992). Social policy was increasingly seen as a 'production factor' and social institutions were either perceived as 'harmless' with regard to economic growth, or thought to matter in a positive sense (Auer, 2001). Besides this regulation–deregulation nexus, the scientific debate observed a flexibility–security nexus (Wilthagen and Rogowski, 2002).

The quest for a new (dynamic) equilibrium, facilitating and enhancing the adaptability and capacity to deal with change of both individuals and companies has come to be labelled 'flexicurity'. Flexicurity is defined as 'a policy strategy to enhance, at the same time and in a deliberate way, the flexibility of labour markets, the work organization and employment relations on the one hand, and security–employment security and social security – notably for weaker groups in and outside the labour market – on the other hand' (Wilthagen and Tros, 2004). From a theoretical point of view this concept can be considered as a post-deregulation strategy (Keller and Seifert, 2000, p. 293) and can be characterized as a form of integration and synchronization of economic and social policy (Wynn, 2000, p. 501). The concept further has some common characteristics with the approach of 'transitional labour markets', as it is strongly connected to promoting and analysing transitions in the labour market and between the labour market and non-paid life domains (Schmid and Gazier, 2002).

European politics quickly picked up 'flexicurity' as a normative concept within the European Employment Strategy (EES) to strive for both economic adaptability and social cohesion (Bekker, 2011). Policy makers were inspired by the good economic performances – especially the high employment participation – in the 1990s of countries that were presented as 'flexicurity-countries', notably Denmark and the Netherlands. Besides acclaim, the concept has also met with criticism (see below). Nevertheless, the European Union (EU) has adopted 'flexicurity' as a key policy concept within the European Employment Strategy, as documented by the adaptation of 'Common Principles on Flexicurity' by the European Council on 6 December 2007; the report and resolutions on flexicurity from the European Parliament on 29 November; the joint labour market and flexicurity analysis presented by the European social partners on 18 October 2007; the Communication on flexicurity by the European Commission dated 27 June 2007; and the much debated Green Paper on the Modernization of Labour Law issued 22 November 2006. The concept has become a European flagship policy that has been re-confirmed within the EU's 2020 strategy and, most recently, the Euro Plus Pact.

The European Commission has mapped out 'flexicurity pathways' that can be designed and implemented across the following four policy components:

- Flexible and reliable contractual arrangements
- Efficient active labour market policies to strengthen transition security
- Systematic and responsive lifelong learning
- Modern social security provisions that also contribute to good mobility in the labour market.

The first pathway addresses the issue of flexibility at the margin of the labour market. It suggests reducing asymmetries between standard and non-standard work by promoting upward transitions in the labour market and by integrating non-standard contracts fully into labour law, collective agreements, social security, and lifelong learning systems.

The second pathway emphasizes safe and productive job-to-job transitions either within the company (especially to enhance the employability and skills of workers) or outside the company once the necessity arises.

The third pathway recommends the access to learning and good transitions for all, notably groups in the labour market that risk exclusion. It recommends strengthening investments in skills and research and development to enhance productivity and employment.

The fourth pathway starts from the urgent need to increase the employment opportunities of persons who are on social security benefits or working in the informal sector. Active labour market policies and social security should offer sufficient opportunities and incentives to return to work and to facilitate this transition. Long-term welfare dependence could thus be prevented. By formalizing informal economic activities, increased financial resources can be raised for building up a more comprehensive social security system. For a clear understanding, it has to be stressed here that these policy concepts are principles and not necessarily practices in Europe (see also Chapter 12 about ALMPs).

The EU respects the autonomy of each Member State regarding labour market and social policies – and differences in country traditions and conditions – and therefore does not promote a 'one-size-fits-all' approach.

Defining flexicurity and analytical frameworks

Since the launch of the term there has been a boost of literature about flexicurity. It has become a buzzword. Among academics and politicians and social partners there is often confusion and controversy on how to define and measure flexicurity (Chung, 2011, Viebrock and Clasen, 2009).

In literature and debates the following three definitions and frameworks of 'flexicurity' can be observed in terms of: 1) policy efforts; 2) institutional configuration; and 3) 'outcomes' in the labour market.

In the first section of this chapter, we have already given the definition in which flexicurity is seen as a policy concept. This definition of enhancing both flexibility and security in a coordinated way is broadly cited in the literature. The element of 'synchronization' in the definition is an important condition in the concept. It distinguishes it from policies that are reactive, usually with significant delay, and are designed to repair excess flexibility or security. Traditionally, policies to enhance flexibility are reactions to adjust arrangements or institutions that are considered 'too tight', and policies to promote security are reactive on the observation that the insecurity for groups of workers is too high. The assumption underlying the concept is that flexibility and security can be complementary and mutually supportive, so an integrative and broad approach of flexibility issues in combination with security issues is needed at negotiation tables.

Additionally, flexicurity can be seen as 'state of affairs'. Here a distinction can be made by an institutional state and a labour market state. Referring to the first, flexicurity can be defined as a configuration of institutions that enhance flexibility as well as security for workers (active or inactive) and companies, and in labour markets. The (re)presentation of the Danish flexicurity model (or 'golden triangle') is particularly framed by an institutional approach (although it is, to support or illustrate the functioning of the institutions, combined with labour market data) (see Madsen, 2004). The first pillar of this Danish system concerns the low set of regulations on hiring and firing, generating a flexible labour market. The second pillar consists of generous income protection in case of unemployment, providing a safety net. The third pillar of the Danish system is an activating, tripartite organized labour market approach, aimed at re-integrating redundant workers into other companies. So, the combination of these three institutional pillars of the Danish system guarantees and facilitates high degrees of flexibility (external-numerical) *and* security (of income and re-employment) in the welfare state and labour market. This institutional constellation is the result of a long historical development with 'struggles' in industrial relations (see also Madsen, 2004). Inspired by this institutional approach, researchers have tried to measure the EU countries by institutional indicators that guarantee and facilitate forms of flexibility and security.

A third analytical framework for flexicurity concerns the *outcomes* in the labour markets and welfare states. Are flexicurity policies or balanced configurations of institutions also leading to flexibility and security results in practice? One of the problems of merely assessing policies or regulations by desk-research is the complexity in which formal rules are working in the legal and employment relations practices, as is showed by Bertola et al. (2000) in their critique of the Employment Protection Legislation indicator (EPL) used by the Organisation for Economic Co-operation and Development (OECD). Another trap pertains to phenomena that develop outside the scope of traditional institutions (to stay with the same EPL-example: flexible contracts that emerge in the shadow of the 'normal' employment contracts). Because flexicurity refers to transitions during life courses of citizens, it is important to make longitudinal analyses in which individual workers are followed in their income and working careers. Existing data sets only partly allow for this kind of analysis.

The complexity regarding the concept of flexicurity is increased further by the fact that policies can be developed at different levels and the outcomes can vary at these different levels. Therefore a multi-level approach is needed in the analyses of strategies, regulations, and outcomes. European, national, sectoral, regional, local, firm, and individual workers' level can be distinguished. The firm level should not be neglected because here the flexicurity opportunities (or barriers) – and therefore negotiations – often come together. Furthermore, company policies can develop rather autonomously by transforming firm-external institutions for their own profits (Teubner, 1994).

Moreover, both flexibility and security are multi-dimensional concepts, which take various forms. Inspired by Atkinson (1985) four forms of flexibility can be distinguished: external-numerical,

Table 13.1 Trade-offs and interconnections between types of flexibility and types of security

	Job security	*Employment security*	*Income security*	*Combination security*
Flexibility:				
External- numerical				
Internal- numerical				
Functional				
Wages/variable pay				

internal-numerical, functional and wage flexibility. Wilthagen (Wilthagen and Rogowski, 2002; Wilthagen and Tros, 2004) has linked these with four forms of security: job, employment, income, and combination security (see Table 13.1). Where job security is defined as the security to stay in the same job with the same employer, employment security refers to the possibility for workers to remain employed, not necessarily in the same job or with the same employer, and the possibility for the unemployed to make the transition to paid work. Income security regards the security of income replacement in the case the job is lost. Combination security is the security of a worker being able to combine his or her work and the private domain of life. As already indicated, an important assumption in the flexicurity concept is that forms of flexibility and forms of security can be complementary and mutually supportive.

Another fundamental idea is that flexibility is not just profit for capital and security not only profit for labour. Also an employer wants to be sure about a committed and qualified workforce and an employee needs flexibility in order to combine work and private life.

These underlying ideas become more clear if concrete forms of flexibility and security are combined. Both external-numerical flexibility and employment security can be enhanced by productive and sustainable job-to-job transitions. The same goes with the combination of internal-numerical flexibility and job security by varying working hours and at the same time maintaining stability in the number of employed staff. Functional flexibility through investments in the workers' employability of work (by means of training and education or task/job rotation) can enhance job as well as employment security. Likewise more complementary configurations of flexibility and security are possible and can be observed in employment practices.

The four forms of security and the four forms of flexibility can be put in a flexicurity matrix and serve as an analytical and heuristic framework at various levels, including companies' HR practices.

Practices of flexicurity policy

In this section we briefly present national examples of flexicurity according to the policy definition.

The Netherlands

The Flexibility and Security Act (1999) is the most illustrative example of flexicurity policy in the Netherlands because several longer existing policy dossiers on dismissal legislation, atypical workers and (activating) social security were integrated in the discussion that led to it. Another important characteristic of this flexicurity case is that this reform could not have been launched and implemented without the early active involvement of the social partners. With this Act several measures have been introduced. Dismissal procedures for regular employees were fastened, the permit system for temporary work agencies was abolished, the legal position of temporary work agency workers was strengthened (such as sickness benefits and building up rights to more secure employment contracts), on-call employees were given rights to a minimum number of paid hours and the number and total duration of consecutive fixed term contracts was set at a maximum of three contracts (previously two) within three years. In collective bargaining deviations from the latter provision were made possible. The relationship between the worker and the temporary work agency is in principle considered as a standard employment contract, the agency being the legal employer, in which the workers built up rights after some time. As part of the whole flexibility and security package deal the employers and trade unions in the temporary work agency agreed on new regulations in their collective labour agreements. Several evaluation studies of the Flexibility and Security Act have been conducted in better and in worse economic conditions. It is clear that the Act has contributed to a political and juridical acceptation of atypical contracts and has increased flexibility options for employers. Especially the use of fixed-term contracts has grown significantly. There is much discussion on the question of whether the Act has indeed increased the security for flexible workforces. Houwing (2010) studied the implementation of the Act and concludes that the more the implementation is done at the local level (which is the aim of the flexible multi-level regulation system), the less security for flexible workers seems to be guaranteed. In recent years the Dutch trade unions increased their criticism on the unbalanced effects of the law. Also longitudinal research in the Netherlands shows relatively low levels of transitions into open-ended employment contracts, lower investments in education and training, and higher feelings of insecurity.

Sweden

In Sweden the employers' organizations and trade unions play an important role in designing 'employment security agreements' and 'transition agreements'. The first agreement dates from 1974 when there was massive job loss of white collar workers in Sweden. Over the last decades the social partners have created more frameworks for how restructuring should take place in their labour market segments. Some agreements aim at avoiding dismissal and facilitate voluntary job mobility, while others aim at compensation and 'transition support' in terms of outplacement and education facilities or, in fewer cases, severance payment to redundant workers (Borghouts-van de Pas, 2012; Bergstrom, 2009; Sebardt, 2006). In relation to these collective agreements, the social partners established bipartite 'employment security councils' or transition agencies at the sector level, financed by employers' fees based on 0.3% of the labour costs. The system operates as a form of insurance system, distributing the risk and costs of economic dismissals among the companies in the branches. The councils provide consultation in early stages of restructuring along with outplacement services for redundant workers, and finance temporarily salary gaps in case of outplacement to lower-paid jobs. Sometimes these councils employ job coaches/trainers, sometimes these services are outsourced to private providers.

There are extra incentives for employers to bargain with trade unions if they want to deviate from legal standards in the seniority rules that are set by law. It is a common practice in larger companies that legal standards are put aside by offering prolonged dismissal period (to have more time to look for other jobs) and extra 'transition packages' to the benefit of redundant employees. Similar developments – 'change security funds', tripartite 'Flexicurity Committees' at the sector level – can be witnessed in Finland.

Sweden is one of the countries that has been hit hard by the recent financial crisis, but many redundant workers have found new jobs. At the same time, however, youth unemployment has increased substantially, leading to increased discussion about the inequality between 'insiders' and 'outsiders' in the Swedish labour market (see Bergstrom, 2009).

Belgium

In 2009 the Federal government in Belgium introduced the Economic Recovery Law, in which outplacement rights and obligations for redundant workers were strengthened and all private employers in restructuring were obliged to install 're-employment cells' to promote fast replacement of their dismissed workers to other paid work. This legislation is a follow-up of the Belgian approach to promote longer working careers of older workers by giving workers aged 45 and above rights to 60 hours of outplacement support in case they are collectively or individually dismissed (Generation Pact, 2005; national CLA 82bis, 2007). In addition, since 2009 redundant workers over the age of 45 have entitlements to outplacement support – 30 hours during three months – and not only companies that concluded pre-pension arrangements, but all restructuring companies have to organize and finance outplacement support.

The implementation of these legislative measures is tested in the juridical procedure with the regional governments for getting permission for the effectuation of the restructuring. If bipartite social plans or companies' restructuring programmes are not 'activating' enough, the company is not allowed to do the restructuring. Before effectuating the first dismissal, the employer has to install a re-employment cell, boarded by the public employment service (chair), trade union(s), the sector/local education fund, and the employer. Already in their notice periods the redundant workers have to enrol in this 'cell' and to participate in the outplacement programme that is organized and that is respecting the quantitative and qualitative standards in legislation and the applicable national collective labour agreements. In case of insufficient efforts by the employee in this reintegration phase in looking for another job or to following a re-training or re-education programme, the public employment service can sanction the employee by lower unemployment benefits.

This Belgian case is an example of a structural and encompassing policy of enforcing 'activating restructuring'. All workers aged 45 and above, as well as those who lose their jobs by individual dismissal, have outplacement rights and obligations, including standards of length and timing. Although the access to outplacement support is increased significantly by this policy, the effective re-placement rates for employees aged 50 are rather low, far lower than for younger workers. Overall, in the period 2007–10, 35–54% of the redundant employees found other paid employ- ment within six months after registration due to this system. For the workers aged 50+, the figure lies between 11 and 24% (Tros, forthcoming). Further, it is evident that the replacement rates are significantly lower among the low-educated employees. Not only do the age and level of education play a significant role in the chance to find a new job, but also the entitlement for pre-pension arrangements. 50+ workers in firms with pre-pension schemes make less than half of the job-to-job transitions compared to those in firms that do not arrange such schedules. Therefore it can be concluded that the policy on supporting re-placement of dismissed workers is not integrated with an activating approach in social security arrangements The majority in pre-pension arrangements are dispensed from the obligation to apply for new jobs and the threshold for pre-pension in Belgium can be still set on the age of 50 (although this might change quickly due to the austerity measures the recently appointed government is considering). There are also shortcomings in low education and training investments. Further criticism can be formulated with respect to the missed opportunities to negotiate these unilateral legislative measures synchronically with measures to enhance job security and investments in the employability of the older workers and more flexibility in the procedures on collective dismissals and restructuring (see Tros, forthcoming).

France

The actors in the French industrial relations system do not tend to use the word flexicurity or *flexicurité* so much, but discuss similar subjects under the flag of *sécurisation des parcours professionnels* (making professional career pathways more secure), including work-life careers for vulnerable citizens and workers (see Meda, 2011).

In 2004 France introduced workers' rights to individual learning accounts (*Droit Individuel à la Formation*, DIF). These saving accounts (*comptes individuelles*) are open for all employees with open-ended employment contracts after one year of seniority. Rights for part-time workers are calculated *prorata tempori* of the contractual hours. Every year 20 hours are capitalized in the individual account and remain available for six years. Although this number of hours could be considered modest, this law is conceptually interesting because of the idea of the portability of the rights that are saved in the account, in case the workers make a transition to a different employer or in case of unemployment.

The introduction of the transferability of rights was part of a broader national agreement in 2008 in which more measures in flexibility and security subjects were taken to modernize French labour market institutions (Grimault, 2009). The DIF is also interesting because of the idea that individual training and education rights are explicitly linked to the professional career development of the worker, for example, it is used for IDEM *Validation des acquis de l'expérience* (recognitions of obtained competences). Other experiments in individual learning accounts in Europe are less oriented to the work environment or career development. In France it is discussed if these accounts just reflect a responsibility for the individual worker for his/her own employability or if the DIF will be organized further in a more collective way (Gautié and Perez, 2010).

Germany

The unemployment figures of Germany in the last years have amazed academics and politicians, and some speak about the 'German labour market miracle'. Where the other EU countries and the United States showed far rising unemployment in 2008–10, Germany showed stability in employment participation, notwithstanding the sharp drop of German gross domestic product (GDP). Although many reasons are given in the literature (such as the strict employment protection and the relative low numbers of workers that were employed by German firms before the crisis), there is less controversy on the statement that the German working time accounts and complementary short-time work allowances (Kurzarbeit) have played an important role to support labour hoarding in the economic downturn (for example, Eichhorst et al., 2010; Boeri and Brueckner, 2011).

Working time accounts in Germany facilitate flexibility in the number of hours (internal-numerical flexibility) by day, by week or over the year and are widely regulated in collective agreements and company arrangements in German workplaces. In 2009 it was estimated that in total 30% of German companies made use of working time accounts, either in the form of a reduction of hours that are saved in individual accounts or in the form of working time credits which will have to be worked in the future when business recovers (Dribbusch, 2009). In some months in 2009 there were in total 1.4 million persons in Germany in short-time work.

In reaction to the financial crisis several countries introduced new arrangements or expanded the scope of existing short-time work arrangements. These schemes are publicly sponsored facilities to prevent too much loss in human capital or bankruptcy caused too fast by temporary downturns in the economy. They function as a buffer to external-numerical flexibility by facilitating internal, working hours flexibility. Sometimes these schemes are an integral part of the unemployment insurance system. In practice firms make regular contributions to a pool or a fund and then draw money from these funds to compensate workers for the reduction in the hours worked during downturns. In some countries like Italy, Japan, and Germany between 2.5 and 5% of the workforce participated in such schemes in the high recession periods.

In other countries, such as the UK, no formal schemes exist, but a reduction of working hours is accepted by workers on a voluntary basis, by, for example, taking leave or holidays.

Flexicurity outcomes

Because the concept of flexicurity is intrinsically dynamic and focuses on transitions during people's life courses and on institutions that affect these behavioral patterns during the various stages of life, it is important to construct indicators within a dynamic and life course framework. An important dynamic indicator regarding the first flexicurity pathway is the mobility rate from temporary jobs into permanent jobs. This represents the so-called stepping-stone mechanism. Dynamic indicators for the second and third pathways include the transition of trainees moving into a better-paid job or into a permanent job after training or the number of people re-entering employment after some time in training. A dynamic indicator for the fourth pathway is the re-entry rate into employment within six or twelve months. Another dynamic indicator for social security is the degree the working or the non-working poor can escape from poverty minus the ones who jump towards poverty (see further Muffels et al., 2010).

Using dynamic outcome indicators (many more than illustrated above) with the European Union Statistics on Income and Living Conditions for the years 2003–08 we can observe substantial differences among the various country clusters (or 'regimes') within Europe. The Nordic countries but also the UK appear to attain fairly high levels of dynamic employment and income security, notwithstanding the significant differences in industrial relations and labour market governance systems (Muffels et al., 2010; European Commission, 2010). In the UK the risks to income drops for those outside the labour market are relatively high. Additional social security could be developed to guarantee a better balance between flexibility and security. The findings on the Eastern and Southern countries reflect strongly the relative meagre outcomes of these segmented labour markets with respect to displaying low levels of mobility in terms of job, contract, and wage mobility and simultaneously low levels of income and employment security. The continental countries form a mixed picture. The Netherlands, Austria, and Germany might have relatively low rates of job mobility but manage to keep unemployment levels rather low, thereby relying on a growing shell of flexible employment. Here a risk of growing labour market segmentation exists. France and Belgium also have low mobility but offer a decent level of income protection to people that are not working. Whether these countries can continue to pay for this, given the impact of the crisis on public budgets, remains to be seen.

Dynamic indicators too have pitfalls when not combined with institutional indicators or when not evaluated in a qualitative institutional framework. To give some concrete examples: high job-to-job mobility (even when it is upwards) can reflect a bad allocation on the labour market. Or high rates of movement out of poverty or out of poor jobs can still mean that a country has lots of working poor or poor citizens. This remark also implies that not only does transition and duration matter, but so does the standard of quality of institutions in the labour market and welfare states. Institutional indicators are particularly important with regards to the security and flexibility of workers. Given the unequal power and dependency relations between labour and capital, labour law and collective agreements not only serve to enhance economic efficiency but also to promote equity and protection of the workers and citizens.

Furthermore, for a multifaceted concept as flexicurity, it is important – for the input side (institutions) as well as for the output side – to combine quantitative with qualitative research methods (see also Bertozzi and Bonoli, 2009).

A last remark we would like to make here is that over-aggregated figures at the national level (see European Commission 2010; RWI, 2011) can hide unequal distributions of flexibility and security. It is important to follow (in longer-time perspectives) specific weaker groups in the labour market such as low-educated workers, younger workers, older workers, and those in segments of low-quality working conditions.

Conclusion

Some commentators have criticized the concept as 'old wine in new bottles'. Although it is true that a search for flexibility and security in labour markets is not new, it can be considered new that this nexus is now more systematically conceptualized in the European context of consolidating economic policies with social policies. The concept of flexicurity has without a doubt given inputs to the European social dialogue and the European Employment Strategy. 'Flexicurity' has even become a European flagship policy and will remain so within the EU's 2020 strategy. Policy responses on the financial and economic crisis have shown that the concept is also still alive in – at least some – EU member states.

The recent emergence of new flexicurity policies, or elaborations on strategies established earlier, support the statement that the concept holds not only in favourable business cycle conditions. However, the (first) victims of the crisis have clearly been the workers with flexible employment contracts, while national policy practices were mostly restricted to the workers with open-ended employment contracts. European countries seem to be more active on the second flexicurity pathway (securing job-to-job transitions) and less to the first and fourth pathway (preventing segmentation and long term social exclusion). Flexible workforces still have limited access to training facilities and other forms of social protection (Alphametrics, 2009). This situation risks further segmentation in labour markets in which flexibility and security is very unequally distributed in societies. Persistent youth unemployment risks negative effects in the following living and working stages of this young generation (so-called scarring effects). Another limitation has been seen in European countries since the Dutch case of 1999 (Flexibility and Security Act) less integrated bargaining of several forms and combinations of flexibility and security has been done, although good practices are available (Eurofound, forthcoming).

How to progress further? It is clear that the concept is not an easy 'policy tool' that can be implemented by technocrats or 'policy engineers' by simply pushing the right buttons. It needs tripartite and bipartite bargaining, social dialogue, and political initiatives. Burroni and Keune (2011) have argued that the concept is vague and cannot overcome the traditional views and positions between the social partners at the European level. It is even argued that flexicurity reflects a friendly package that just contains the message of individualization and deregulation (Keune and Serrano, forthcoming; see also Meda, 2011). We have argued in this chapter that flexicurity is a (re-)regulation approach that has come in to rebalance the one-sided and narrow-focused liberal political debates of the 1980s. The way the concept is often used in the discussions in the last decade has shown that the concept comes easily in the territory of mere flexibility and employers interests while securities and flexibilities that work for workers are still underdeveloped. If further policy responses to the crisis are dominated by liberalization and cost-cutting in public budgets for social policy, then the concept of flexicurity will be further eroded. It will undermine the most important condition for developing flexicurity strategies: mutual trust and working on better perspectives for decent jobs and (working) lives. In our view, national and local governments as 'third actors' can play a role in bridging the positions of labour and capital and need to provide long-term perspectives for groups of vulnerable workers in society. However, too much polarization or fragmentation between the positions of employers and trade unions can also mean that governments will take unilateral measures that will lead to unbalanced policy outcomes. Moreover, new networks, such as associations of self-employed people, will and should also come into play, as the traditional social partners can not be the only carriers of flexicurity.

Maybe the picture is not so bleak. In some countries the social partners share a more common view on the concept and a majority of trade unions in the EU member states in 2011 (even in the crisis) still believe that flexicurity has the potential to provide win-win situations (Voss and Dornelas, 2011, p. 70). There is a hunger to learn from flexicurity practices in other countries. But concrete initiatives have to be taken, preferably with broad views to combine (several forms of) flexibility and security over the life course. We agree with Schmid (2006) and the European Expert Group on Flexicurity (2007) that for this to happen new forms of solidarity and risk-sharing are needed to achieve a joint risk management by encouraging people to take more risks – and for this to happen not less, but *more* security is needed. A collective version of social investments and career management is needed to give work-life perspectives, especially to the weaker groups in the labour market.

The question is whether a real alternative to flexicurity exists. The hybrid, multi-sided approach of the concept at least guarantees the interest of both employers and workers and their representatives. Alternative concepts, that merely focus on one dimension, can probably not achieve this. Flexicurity is well in line with Europe's overall ambition to maintain and further develop a competitive social market economy with full employment and high levels of protection, as formulated in the Lisbon Treaty.

At the end of the day it is an empirical matter: can welfare and well-being be ensured during the life courses of the citizens under rapidly changing economic conditions?

Further reading

Bekker, S. (2011), *Flexicurity. Explaining the Development of a European Concept.* Nijmegen: Iskamp Drukkers.

Ester, P., Muffels, R. J. A., Schippers, J. and Wilthagen, A.C.J.M. (2008), *Innovating Labour Markets in Europe. Dynamics and Perspectives.* Cheltenham: Edward Elgar.

Jørgensen, H. and P. K. Madsen (eds) (2007), *Flexicurity and Beyond. Finding a New Agenda for the European Social Model.* Copenhagen: DJØF Publishing.

Muffels, R. J. A. (ed.) (2008), *Flexibility and Employment Security in Europe. Labour Markets in Transition.* Cheltenham: Edward Elgar.

Viebrock, E. and J. Clasen (2009), Flexicurity and welfare reform: a review, *Socio-Economic Review* 7 (2), pp. 305–31.

References

Alphametrics (2009), *Flexicurity: Indicators on the Coverage of Certain Social Protection Benefits for Persons in Flexible Employment in the European Union*, VC/2007/0870.

Atkinson, J. (1985), *Flexibility. Planning for an Uncertain Future. Manpower Policy And Practice*, 1.

Auer, P. (2001), *Changing Labour Markets in Europe. The Role of Institutions and Policies.* Geneva: ILO.

Bekker, S. (2011), *Flexicurity. Explaining the Development of a European Concept.* Nijmegen: Iskamp Drukkers.

Bergstrom, O. (2009), National Background Paper Sweden in '27 National Seminars Anticipating and Managing Restructuring, A.R.E.N.A.S., VC/2008/0667, November 2009, International Training Centre, ILO.

Bertola, G., Boeri T. and Cazes, S. (2000), 'Employment protection in industrialized countries: the case for new indicators'. *International Labour review*, 139 (1).

Bertozzi, F. and Bonoli, G. (2009), *Measuring Flexicurity at the Macro Level. Conceptual and Data Availability Challenges*, REC-WP 10/2009.

Boeri, T. and Bruecker, H. (2011), *Short-time Work Benefits Revisited. Some Lessons from the Great Recession*, Discussion paper no. 5635, IZA.

Borghouts-van de Pas, I.W.C.M. (2012), *Securing job-to-job Transitions in the Labour Market: A Comparative Study of Employment Security Systems in European Countries.* Nijmegen: Wolf Legal Publishers.

Burroni, L. and Keune, M. (2011), Flexicurity. A conceptual critique, *European Journal of Industrial Relations*, 17(1), pp. 75–91.

Chung, H. (2011), 'Measuring flexicurity: precautionaly notes, a new framework, and an empirical example', Springerlink.com.

Dribbusch, H. (2009), *Working Time Account and Short-time Work used to Maintain Employment*. WSI: EIRO online.

Eichhorst, W., Feil, M. and Marx, P. (2010), *Crisis, What Crisis? Patterns of Adaptation in European Labour Markets*. Discussion Paper no. 5045, IZA.

Eurofound (forthcoming 2012), *The Second Phase of Flexicurity: An Analysis of Practices and Policies in the Member States*. Dublin.

European Commission/JRC-IPSC (2010), *Towards a set of Composite Indicators on Flexicurity: a Comprehensive Approach*. Luxembourg: Publication Office of the European Union (JRC Scientific and Technical Reports).

European Expert Group on Flexicurity (Wilthagen, T. et al.) (2007), *Flexicurity Pathways: Turning Hurdles into Stepping-Stones*. Brussels: Expert Report for European Commission.

Gautié, J. and Perez, C. (2010), *Les comptes individuels de formation: fondements et enseignements*, in XXXèmes Journées de l'Association d'Economie Sociale, Charleroi.

Grimault (2009), *France: Flexicurity and Industrial Relations*. IRES, European Industrial Relations Observatory online.

Houwing, H. (2010), A Dutch approach to flexicurity? *Negotiated Change in the Organization of Temporary Work*. dissertation Universiteit van Amsterdam.

Keller, B. and Seifert, H. (2000), Flexicurity. Das Konzept für mehr soziale sicherheit flexibler beschaftigung, *WSI Mitteilungen*, 53 (5), pp. 291–300.

Keune, M. and Serrano, A. (forthcoming), 'The power to name and struggles over meaning: the concept of flexicurity', in. M. Keune and A. Serrano Pascual (eds), *Deconstructing flexicurity and constructing alternative perspectives*, London: Routledge.

Madsen, P. K. (2004), The Danish model of 'flexicurity'. *Transfer*, 10 (2), pp. 187–216.

Méda, D. (2011), 'Post-face: La flexibilité peut-elle encore constituer une ambition pour l'Europe'. *Formation emploi*, no. 113, pp. 97–109.

Muffels, R., Wilthagen, T. and Chung, H. (2010), *The State of Affairs of Flexicurity: A Dynamic Perspective*. paper delivered to DG Employment of the European Commission.

RWI (2011), *Paper on the Identification of the Flexicurity Profile of Member States using Micro-economic Data*. Research Project for the European Commission. Essen: RWI.

Schmid, G. (2006), Social risk management through transitional labour markets, in *Socio-Economic Review*, 4, pp. 1–33.

Schmid, G. and Gazier, B. (eds), (2002), *The Dynamics of Full Employment: Social Integration through Transitional Labour Markets*. Cheltenham: Edward Elgar.

Streeck, W. (1992), *Social Institutions and Economic Performance*. London: Sage.

Sebardt, G. (2006), *Redundancy and the Swedish Model in International Context*. Deventer: Kluwer Law International.

Teubner, G. (1994), 'Company interest: the public interest of the enterprise in itself', in R. Rogowski and T. Wilthagen (eds), *Reflexive Labour Law*. Deventer: Kluwer.

Tros (forthcoming), *Securing Outplacement for Dismissed Workers in Belgium. Ambitions, regulations and outcomes*. Tilburg: Reflect Research Paper series.

Viebrock, E. and Clasen, J. (2009), 'Flexicurity and welfare reform: a review', *Socio-Economic Review* 7 (2), pp. 305–31.

Voss, E. and Dornelas, A. (2011), 'Social partners and flexicurity in contemporary labour markets'. Synthesis report, Brussels.

Wilthagen, T. and Rogowski, R. (2002), 'Legal regulation of transitional labour markets', in G. Schmid and B. Gazier (eds), *The Dynamics of Full Employment: Social Integration through Transitional Labour Markets*. Cheltenham: Edward Elgar.

Wilthagen, T. and Tros, F. (2004), The concept of 'flexicurity'. A new approach to regulating employment and labour markets, in *Transfer* 10 (2), pp. 166–86.

Wynn, M. (2000), 'European social dialogue. Harmonisation or new diversity?', in H. Collins et al. (eds), *Legal Regulation of the Employment Relation*, pp. 491–511. London: Kluwer Law International.

Part II
Typologies and methods

14

What are welfare state typologies and how are they useful, if at all?[1]

Kees van Kersbergen

Introduction

This chapter examines the need and utility of typologies for the comparative analysis of welfare capitalism. There exist various typologies, such as Castles's (1993) classification of different 'families of nations' that was developed to capture and express similarities between countries' public policies, based on common cultural, historical, and geographical features. The best-known and most prolific classification of types of capitalism (rather than welfare) is Hall and Soskice's (2001) distinction between different production regimes, labelled the 'Varieties of Capitalism' approach. However, the field of comparative welfare state research is dominated by, and greatly indebted to, the work of Gøsta Esping-Andersen, whose landmark study *The Three World of Welfare Capitalism* (1990) completely revolutionized the way social scientists look at the welfare state. Two innovations were particularly powerful. First, he introduced the concept of a welfare *regime* that allowed a much broader and better understanding of how the major institutions of society (state, market, and family) interacted to produce work and welfare. In this way he not only helped to remove the field's exclusive and theoretically unsatisfying preoccupation with the state and social spending, but also opened up a whole new area for innovative research. Second, he not only introduced, documented, and explained the qualitative variation in welfare regimes (as the dependent variable), but also showed how these regimes (as the independent variable) were systematically related to differences in social outcomes that really matter, particularly in terms of the differential structuring of post-industrial employment trajectories.

Much intellectual effort has been invested in further developing, testing, adjusting, expanding, criticizing, and, in various ways, applying the regime typology as a classificatory and heuristic research tool. Arts and Gelissen (2010, p. 569) recently argued that the regime typology has become a paradigmatic one. On the basis of their review of empirical studies that use Esping-Andersen's regime typology they conclude ' … in spite of all kinds of conceptual, operationalization, and data problems that must be solved – that his typology is promising enough for work to continue on welfare state models' (p. 581). They add, however, that further progress will very much hinge on the ability to devise a firmer theoretical foundation of contemporary and future welfare state models as explanatory categories. This resonates well with Powell and Barrientos's (2011) thesis that welfare state research has not focused enough on further theorizing. I agree with these positions, although the contours of better theorizing have not yet been outlined. Also,

I am somewhat concerned about the confusion between empirical typologies and ideal-types (see Chapter 29) that continues to exist and that may stand in the way of the desired theoretical progress. This chapter aims to explain the intellectual background of the regime typology, discusses the criteria for good typologies, critically re-examines and evaluates the operationalization of the three-worlds typology, and discusses how to distinguish between relevant and not-so-relevant criticisms of typologies.

Intellectual roots of the regime approach

Welfare states have been analysed and discussed using empirical typologies practically since systematic welfare state research became a major branch of comparative social policy analysis (see Chapter 27). Wilensky and Lebeaux's (1965 [1958]) functionalist study of how industrialization affected social welfare in the United States, for instance, already early on introduced the highly influential distinction between two types of welfare. The first kind they characterized as a *residual* version, where 'social welfare institutions should come into play only when the normal structures of supply, the family and the market break down' (p. 138). The second model they called the *institutional* variety because it assumes 'welfare services as the normal first line function of industrial society' (p. 138).

Titmuss (1968, p. 113, 128) initially used a similar two-fold typology that distinguished between universal (later labelled universalist) and selective models of social services and redistribution. In his later work, Titmuss (1974) came to promote a classification of welfare states as existing in three forms: 1) a residual type that only intervenes in cases of serious market and family failure; 2) an industrial-achievement-performance model where a person's performance on the labour market is decisive for his or her social entitlements; and 3) an institutional redistributive variety that is encompassing and egalitarian. As Esping-Andersen (1999, p. 74, n. 1) himself indicated, his and Titmuss's typologies have a close affinity.

The intellectual roots of the regime approach that Esping-Andersen developed can be traced back to a double critique. First, there had been long-standing dissatisfaction with the functionalist literature for its failure to explain the huge differences in social expenditure between similarly advanced and industrialized capitalist countries. Second, the view that democratization explained the expansion of the welfare state did not fare much better because neither could it account for the variation in social spending among equally democratic nations.

The basic political economy model for how democracy leads to income redistribution was presented early on by Meltzer and Richard (1981). Their argument was that when income inequality increases, the demand for income redistribution among voters also increases. Typically, the income distribution is right-skewed and the income of the median voter is below the average income. The median voter, then, has a preference for income redistribution towards the average income. The more unequal the distribution is, the louder the demand for income redistribution is. And the more poor people vote, the higher the degree of redistribution is. So, democracy leads to redistribution via the welfare state.

This theory has two major shortcomings. First, equally democratic countries tended to have widely diverging levels of welfare effort. Second, the most unequal societies did not redistribute the most. In fact, countries that already had relatively modest wage differentials were also redistributive leaders (say, Sweden), while highly unequal countries were welfare state laggards (say, the US). The power resources (Korpi, 1983) critique stressed that the working class could only influence public policy via democracy if it mobilized both socially in labour unions and politically in a socialist or social democratic party. The 'power of numbers' (membership and votes) was a necessary condition for bringing about income redistribution through democratic means.

However, since social democracy nowhere was able to win parliamentary majorities, political coalitions decided the kind and extent of redistributive policies. A large number of studies corroborated the thesis that the stronger politically organized labour (social democracy and labour unions) was, the more redistributive the welfare state tended to be.

However, the social democratic impact on redistribution could be questioned too because universalism and generosity did not necessarily imply redistribution from the rich to the poor, but were very much favourable for the middle classes. One major source of inspiration for the formulation of the regime typology was tapped when researchers started to hunt the social democratic effect not so much in welfare *effort* and the *level* of redistribution (quantity – how much welfare states spend and redistribute), but increasingly in the variation in the properties of welfare arrangements (quality – how well workers are protected against the market; how well social service programmes serve their clientele). Social democrats typically promoted universalism, state-guaranteed social rights and high protection against the whims of the market (de-commodification: the extent of independence from market forces), full employment, and lenient conditionality).

Esping-Andersen re-specified the welfare state concept with reference to qualitative features and it was this aspect that radically changed the field's orientation. Starting from the judgement that 'expenditures are epiphenomenal to the theoretical substance of welfare states' (1990, p. 19) and the reflection that 'it is difficult to imagine that anyone struggled for spending *per se*' (ibid., p. 21, italics in original), he suggested that the study of welfare states had much to gain by looking at three dimensions that typify a welfare state regime. First, the quality of social rights is important. How good are welfare states actually at shielding people from the uncertainty of markets and against social risks associated with the life course? Second, the typical patterns of stratification that social policies foster mattered. Do social policies distinguish between classes of people and do all have equal social rights? Do social policies overcome or reproduce status and other relevant social differences? Third, it is not just the state that produces welfare, but the market and the family are always inextricably involved as well. How do these major public and private institutions of society interact to form a welfare regime that shapes a nation's work and welfare?

By empirically mapping various indicators that capture these three dimensions, Esping-Andersen was able to distinguish three types of welfare state regimes: a social democratic, a liberal, and a corporatist or conservative regime. The regimes differed with respect to the major institutions guaranteeing social security (the state, the market, or the family); the kind of stratification systems upheld by the institutional mix of these institutions (the extent of status and class differentiation, segmentation, and inequality typically implied in social security systems); and the degree of de-commodification, i.e. 'the degree to which individuals, or families, can uphold a socially acceptable standard of living independently of market participation' (Esping-Andersen, 1990, p. 37).

The three-worlds typology

To explain the three-worlds typology well and to be able to evaluate its many criticisms, it is necessary to start the exposé with a short discussion of the analytical status of typologies. A typology, unlike the theoretical device of ideal types, is an empirical classificatory tool that reduces observed complexity by cataloguing existing cases as meaningful representatives (types) of some concept of interest. This is done by using relatively arbitrarily chosen values of theoretically relevant features as criteria for placement in the cells of the classification scheme, i.e. the typology. Cases that have similar or nearly identical scores on the variables are classified as belonging to the same type.

Although a typology is necessarily constructed on the basis of some implicit or explicit (proto-)theory, it is at heart simply a classificatory device that helps to arrange the observable empirical 'mess' of phenomena in a more ordered, transparent, and therefore comprehensible manner. A good typology, in addition to being efficient and reliable in reducing complexity, should be exhaustive and mutually exclusive. That a typology should be exhaustive implies two things: 1) all theoretically relevant dimensions should be included in the construction of the types; and 2) it should be possible to assign all existing cases to one of the types. That a typology should be mutually exclusive means that an empirical case can be assigned to one type only. In sum, a typology is first and foremost designed for conceptual and descriptive purposes.

Applied to the welfare state regime typology, this implies that first of all the theoretically relevant dimensions of variation must be identified. Esping-Andersen (1990, p. 21) defined the core idea of the welfare state as social citizenship, embodied in the granting of de-commodifying social rights (first typological dimension) and the extent to which stratification is upheld or modified by such rights (second typological dimension). In addition, the third dimension of variation relevant for the construction of the typology concerned the extent to which the state's welfare activities are interconnected with the market's and the family's contribution to social welfare. On each of these dimensions, Esping-Andersen compared the existing worlds of welfare and found that welfare states were systematically clustering around specific values of the identified dimensions.

To operationalize the de-commodification potential of social rights (pensions, sickness insurance and unemployment benefits), Esping-Andersen looked at: 1) the rules of access to benefits (eligibility and restrictions on entitlements, such as contribution record and needs test); 2) the level of income replacement offered; and 3) the range of entitlements. The decision how to draw a line between high, medium, and low levels of de-commodification was not theoretically justified but technically solved on the basis of one standard deviation below (low) or above (high) the mean (medium) (Esping-Andersen, 1990, p. 54, Appendix). However, the final ranking of countries in the three types was based 'roughly on how nations cluster around the mean' (Esping-Andersen, 1990, p. 51).

Stratification, the second dimension of the typology, was specified by arguing that one needs to look at how social policies affect the social structure. A welfare state 'may cultivate hierarchy and status', writes Esping-Andersen (1990, p. 58), as is done in conservative social policy, 'another dualisms', as is characteristic for the liberal type, 'and a third universalism', which is the distinctive feature of the social democratic variety. The conservative stratification dimension of the typology was operationalized by looking at the differentiation of social insurances (corporatism) and the privileges of civil servants (etatism). Liberalism was measured by looking at the importance of means testing, the level of individual contributions, and the strength of the private sector. And universalism was the main feature of socialism (Esping-Andersen, 1990, p. 69). The empirical result (Esping-Andersen, 1990, p. 75, Table 3.3) was again roughly based on the mean scores and standard deviations of the cumulated index scores and showed that three clusters came to the fore.

The third dimension of the typology was theoretically meant to capture a nation's specific mix of state, market, and family in the provision of social welfare, but Esping-Andersen empirically exclusively looked at the public-private mix in pension policies. Pensions were argued to be the logical choice, because they were the largest and most important part of social transfers. Esping-Andersen distinguished public pensions, civil-service pensions and private pensions and measured the public-private mix. Again, three pension regimes emerged from the classification (Esping-Andersen, 1990, pp. 85–7).

This short overview shows that the typology is above all a classificatory device that reduces the empirically existing complexity of the many worlds of welfare to three. It also seems clear that the boundaries between the three types occasionally are drawn in a theoretically relatively arbitrary way, but cases end up in one of the types because of similar scores on the various variables. The worlds of welfare come in three regime types.

The liberal regime of countries such as the US, the UK, Australia, and New Zealand, relies on low and flat rate benefits for which very strict eligibility or access criteria are formulated and applied. Benefits are means tested, low, primarily meant to prevent or alleviate poverty, and for the most part tax-financed. If citizens wish more than basic protection, for instance life insurance or a private pension scheme, they need to purchase that on the market or acquire it via the employer. Such arrangements are often stimulated through tax exemptions and allowances. Public social spending is comparatively low. The regime has limited collective provisions and is service-lean. The welfare state solely targets the poor, the extremely vulnerable and the neediest. It reinforces social differences, particularly between welfare recipients, the middle classes and the privileged, and between the well-paid professionals and the underpaid underclass of the working poor. In short, this is a tightfisted welfare state that offers little protection and does not interfere much with the inequalities generated by the market.

The social democratic regime as found in the Scandinavian countries is also tax-financed, but much more lenient in its eligibility rules (no means testing) and generous in the provision of benefits and services; it works with compulsory social insurance with earnings-related benefits. It aims to offer a high level of social protection through benefits and services as a matter of rights to all citizens. It is an expensive welfare type and public social spending and tax levels are high. As a result, maximum labour market participation of all groups is highly valued, not just as a commendable goal in itself, but also as necessary for upholding the universal and expensive welfare state. This regime excels in the provision of public social services (social care, health, labour market, and education). The role of the market is downplayed. The social democratic welfare state itself is a big employer, where women in particular find jobs. Because of its universal features, the regime greatly diminishes social distinctions.

The conservative regime stresses that social rights are earned on the basis of one's economic contribution to society (employment) or one's social function in the family (primarily parenting). Hence, social benefits are financed through payroll contributions and those who have no job, especially women in their role as mothers, are entitled to benefits via their relationship with an employed person (husband, father, or other family members). Eligibility is strict to the extent that actuarial principles link performance (such as contribution period and employment) to entitlements. Unlike the other regimes, the conservative welfare regime discourages female employment and the employment of the elderly and disabled. The level of social benefits depends on former income and contributions to the insurance funds. There are usually many different collective schemes, with special treatment of civil servants. Also in this regime, the market plays a relatively limited role. The particularist features of the regime tend to reproduce existing social stratification, reinforcing differences between occupational status groups, men and women, and types of families. This regime is a minimal service provider (for example, underdeveloped child care) and primarily relies on cash transfers through a myriad of occupationally distinct schemes.

The quality of the typology and the confusion of types and ideal types

What is the quality of the typology? That is, to what extent does it conform to the criteria of a good typology specified above? Esping-Andersen's typology is arguably exhaustive, first, because de-commodification, stratification and the public-private mix are the relevant dimensions that needed to be included, and, second, because roughly all 18 cases (for which data were available) could be classified in one of the types. The single biggest missing aspect in the classification exercise concerns the role of the family in the public-private mix of social provision.

The typology cannot unambiguously be qualified as mutually exclusive, however, because there emerged several marginal borderline cases of which it was not clear to which type they should be assigned. For instance, as Esping-Andersen (1990, p. 51) honestly reports, Belgium, the Netherlands, and Austria have high levels of de-commodification and are put together with the social democratic countries. However, the distance between Austria (the lowest of the high scores) and Denmark (the lowest of the social democratic countries) is exactly the same as the distance between Austria and Italy (the lowest in the conservative group). So, should Austria be placed in the conservative or in the social democratic group?

We encounter comparable classification difficulties with respect to the other dimensions of the typology, such as the problem of the high degree of universalism of benefits in the liberal countries Canada and Switzerland and the high degree of social democratic regime attributes in the Netherlands. In all cases, Esping-Andersen points to the problematic issues and cases, although he does not always justify well the choices he had to make to ensure that all cases could be assigned to one of the three types, and to one type only.

In any case, Esping-Andersen clearly struggled with the placement of some of the cases in an attempt to meet the 'mutually exclusive' criterion. In fact, in his re-examination of the three-worlds typology, he (1999: 73ff) explicitly inculcates that his was first and foremost a classification device and exercise. He furthermore explains that typologies are useful because they allow for parsimony, may highlight underlying patterns and causalities, and help to generate hypotheses that can be tested. He also defends the typological approach against various criticisms.

In trying to answer the question whether the typology had remained robust and valid, Esping-Andersen (1999, p. 86) confusingly argued that since typologies 'are, in a sense, ideal types, there are bound to be ambiguous cases' and he mentioned the Dutch case as an example. In the context of the typology method, however, it is not possible and therefore incorrect to label cases as ambiguous. The only thing that might be ambiguous is the way the researcher classifies a case as of a certain type. If it is difficult to categorize a specific case, for instance because the scores on the relevant dimensions allow for assignment to more than one type, the typology clearly has the problem that it is not mutually exclusive. It is the typology that is ambiguous, not the case.

The problem is that Esping-Andersen is confusing both his typological method with the ideal type approach, and cases with types (see Chapter 29), a misunderstanding subsequently and uncritically reproduced in the literature (Arts and Gelissen, 2010, pp. 572ff; Aspalter, 2011; Powell and Barrientos, 2011). An ideal type is a theoretical construct that has no empirical cases that fit any of the types, whereas a typology is a classification device in which all empirical cases must find a place as belonging to one of the types and to one type only. In a typology, an empirical case either belongs to a type or does not. In ideal-typical analysis, the question concerns not whether an empirical case fits the theoretical ideal, but the extent or degree to which it does. The question of 'goodness of fit' only makes sense when working with ideal types.

The distinction between a typology and an ideal type is important, because it helps to distinguish between constructive and to-the-point criticisms of the original regime typology and not very useful (because ill-conceived) attacks on the three worlds as ideal types. For example, a valid criticism would be that the regime typology is not exhaustive because it did not include all the theoretically relevant features of welfare states into the toolbox of classification, including the institution of the family or household and social services (Esping-Andersen, 1999, p. 73), as a result of which it does not capture well the important differences and similarities between the regimes.

Potentially equally valid is the criticism that the chosen dimensions for the construction of the typology make it impossible to classify all the existing cases of welfare states in the correct categories. Castles and Mitchell (1993) proposed to broaden the three-way typology by including the so-called wage-earner type that guarantees income through another dimension, namely the wage arbitration system. As a result of the focus on public policies, the three-worlds typology underestimated the extent to which the welfare regimes of Australia and New Zealand guaranteed income. They were more de-commodifying and less liberal than Esping-Andersen classification suggested. Esping-Andersen (1999, p. 89) admitted this, but argued that, in fact, since the 1990s, this model was effectively dismantled by large-scale market liberalization, turning these welfare regimes into fully fledged cases of the liberal regime.

Some argued that it would be useful to add a Mediterranean type (Leibfried, 1992; Ferrer, a 1996) because Southern welfare states are special in one dimension: they only have residual social assistance programmes. This point did not convince Esping-Andersen. Unless the regimes of such countries as Spain and Italy could be shown to have some specific features that the three-worlds classification did not yet pick up, there was no reason to sacrifice parsimony. But the fact that the underdevelopment of social assistance seemed to be an expression of the strong familialism of these countries might be a reason to introduce a fourth world. Ultimately, however, this option was rejected for empirical reasons, because the distinction between the conservative and Mediterranean model was too small to be considered germane.

Others have taken up the task of developing and expanding the regime typology beyond the world of advanced welfare capitalism by exploring to which extent distinct patterns can be discerned among welfare states outside Europe, North America and the Antipodes. There is a lively debate on the characteristics of an emerging Asian or Confucian regime (for example, in Japan, South Korea, and Taiwan) (see Peng and Wong, 2010), on the distinct trajectory of Latin American public policies and their similarity to the conservative and Mediterranean regime (see Huber and Bogliaccini, 2010), and on the possible emergence of a distinct post-communist regime in Eastern Europe and Russia (see Cook, 2010). If anything, these debates underscore the heuristic prolificacy of the regime typology.

An ill-conceived criticism of the three-worlds typology concerns the argument that the worlds of welfare are far too complicated and have changed too much to be captured by any typology. This is, for instance, the position taken by Schubert et al. (2009), who argue that we need to take a step back to a pre-comparative stage so as to be able to document the real complexities of social and welfare policies. As a result, studying the diverse European Union systems of welfare necessarily means studying 27 individual countries on as many variables as possible. That is obviously a step back analytically and after 27 single country chapters, Bazant and Schubert (2009) unsurprisingly conclude that there is no such thing as the welfare state and that there is no systematic patterned variation in the key dimensions of spending, financing, actors, and 'Leitmotifs' (guiding principles). The main conclusion of the exercise: 'it is neither possible to ratify any of the existing groupings we know from the relevant literature […] nor to identify clear-cut new clusters' (p. 533).

This type of criticism of typological work misses the whole point of what a typology is about: a meaningful reduction of complexity for analytical and comparative purposes. It also misses the point that every typology that reduces complexity does so by necessarily simplifying reality. That is not a disadvantage, but it is what typologies are *meant* to do. Therefore, to criticize a typology that it does not do justice to the full complexity of empirical reality is entirely beside the point. What we end up with the Schubert et al. approach is a complete loss of analytical power without real gains in terms of empirical accuracy.

Conclusion

Esping-Andersen's welfare regime typology has been by far the most influential and fruitful classification and it has been successfully orienting research to the present day. The original typology was designed with the help of data of around 1980 and made a pretty strong case that there are three worlds of welfare capitalism. There have been many attempts to test the adequacy of the empirical typology with different techniques, the results of which have been mixed and sometimes indicated the likely utility of additional types.

Do the three regimes still exist? The robustness of the typology has been questioned but also partly corroborated by Scruggs and Allan (2006) using data from around 2000. They found that several countries were misplaced originally and that the coherence within the clusters of countries was less strong than Esping-Andersen proposed. They also concluded that there was limited empirical support for the continuing relevance of the regime classification. This, however, was a surprising inference in the light of the evidence Scruggs and Allan themselves present. Looking at the data for the late 1990s, it is striking how strong the clustering of countries by regime type comes to the fore.

In conclusion, it made perfect sense then as it still does now to reduce the complexity of the very varied worlds of welfare by grouping countries into distinct regimes. Various empirical analyses that make use of a wide range of techniques not only confirm the correct assignment of countries to one of the three types, but also corroborate the robustness over time of the regime clustering. It seems sensible to discuss the usefulness of adding types to the classification scheme or accept the existence of cases that are difficult to classify. Moreover, decades of social policy reforms may necessitate the development of a new typology. However, it is important to remember that a typological classification has the function of effectively grouping together empirically the many worlds of welfare capitalism and rearranging them into distinct types so as to reduce complexity for analytical and comparative purposes. Nothing more, nothing less.

Note

1 This chapter makes use of Van Kersbergen and Vis (forthcoming), Chapter 3.

References

Arts, W. A. and Gelissen, J. (2010), 'Models of the Welfare State', in F. G. Castles, S. Leibfried, J. Lewis, H. Obinger and C. Pierson (eds), *The Oxford Handbook of the Welfare State*, pp. 569–83. Oxford: Oxford University Press.

Aspalter, C. (2011), The Development of Ideal-Typical Welfare Regime Theory. *International Social Work*, 54, 6, pp. 735–50.

Bazant, U. and Schubert, K. (2009), 'European Welfare Systems: Diversity beyond Existing Categories', in K. Schubert, S. Hegelich and U. Bazant (eds), *The Handbook of European Welfare Systems*, pp. 513–34. Abingdon: Routledge.

Castles, F. G. (ed.) (1993), *Families of Nations: Patterns of Public Policy in Western Democracies*. Aldershot: Dartmouth.

Castles, F. G. and Mitchell, D. (1993), The Three Worlds of Welfare Capitalism or Four? *Discussion paper 21*. The Australian National University.

Cook, L. J. (2010), 'Eastern Europe and Russia', in F. G. Castles, S. Leibfried, J. Lewis, H. Obinger, and C. Pierson (eds), *The Oxford Handbook of the Welfare State*, pp. 671–86. Oxford: Oxford University Press.

Esping-Andersen, G. (1990), *The Three Worlds of Welfare Capitalism*. Cambridge: Polity Press.

——(1999), *Social Foundations of Postindustrial Economies*. Oxford: Oxford University Press.

Ferrera, M. (1996), The 'Southern' Model of Welfare in Social Europe. *Journal of European Social Policy*, 6, 1, pp. 17–37.

Hall, P. A. and Soskice, D. (eds) (2001), *Varieties of Capitalism: The Institutional Foundations of Comparative Advantage*. Oxford: Oxford University Press.

Huber, E. and Bogliaccini, J. (2010), 'Latin America', in F. G. Castles, S. Leibfried, J. Lewis, H. Obinger, and C. Pierson (eds), *The Oxford Handbook of the Welfare State*, pp. 644–55. Oxford: Oxford University Press.

Leibfried, S. (1992), 'Towards a European Welfare State? On Integrating Poverty Regimes into the European Community', in Z. Ferge and J. E. Kolberg (eds), *Social Policy in a Changing Europe*, pp. 245–79. Frankfurt am Main: Campus.

Meltzer, A. H. and Richard, S. E. (1981), A Rational Theory of the Size of Government. *Journal of Political Economy*, 89, 5, pp. 914–27.

Peng, I. and Wong, J. (2010), 'East Asia', in F. G. Castles, S. Leibfried, J. Lewis, H. Obinger, and C. Pierson (eds), *The Oxford Handbook of the Welfare State*, pp. 656–70. Oxford: Oxford University Press.

Powell, M. and Barrientos, A. (2011), An Audit of the Welfare Modelling Business. *Social Policy & Administration*, 45, 1, pp. 69–84.

Schubert, K., Hegelich, S. and Bazant, U. (2009), 'European Welfare Systems: Current State of Research and Some Theoretical Considerations', in idem (eds), *The Handbook of European Welfare Systems*, pp. 3–28. Abingdon: Routledge.

Scruggs, L. and Allan, J. P. (2006), Welfare-State Decommodification in 18 OECD Countries: A Replication and Revision. *Journal of European Social Policy*, 16, 1, pp. 55–72.

Titmuss, R. M. (1968), *Commitment to Welfare*. London: Allen and Unwin.

——(1974), *Social Policy: An Introduction*. London: Allen and Unwin.

——(1958), Review of Wilensky and Lebeaux 1958. *British Journal of Sociology*, 9, 3, pp. 293–95.

Van Kersbergen, K. and Vis, B. (forthcoming) *Comparative Welfare State Politics: Development, Opportunities and Reform*.

Wilensky, H. L. and Lebeaux, C. N. (1965 [1958]), *Industrial Society and Social Welfare: The Impact of Industrialization on the Supply and Organization of Social Welfare Services in the United States*. New York: The Free Press.

15

Nordic welfare states

Olli Kangas and Jon Kvist

Introduction

Utopia or dystopia?

The Nordic countries are world-known for their comprehensive welfare states and their low levels of inequality. Some people think that such a welfare state is a dystopia to be avoided at all costs. Others believe the Nordic welfare state is a paradise on earth. Both critics and supporters agree that the Nordic countries share a number of features that in a catch-all term can be said to be 'the Nordic welfare model' with a distinct set of goals, policies, and outcomes.

The goal of equality, most notably between rich and poor and between men and women, constitutes a beacon of hope for egalitarian thinking in many countries. At the same time other observers see the same phenomena, equality, as at odds with efficiency. The big trade-off between equality and efficiency, as aptly labelled by neo-classical economist Arthur Okun (1975) nearly 40 years ago. Okun believed that providing generous benefits to people will result in economic inefficiencies as compared to a situation without such benefits. The other perspective is that benefits nurture the economy, most notably through social investments, by mitigating the detrimental effects of economic downturns and by stimulating productive but risk-based economic behaviour (Myrdal, 1960; Kuusi, 1964).

In this chapter we focus on the principles, policies, and outcomes in the Nordic welfare state. In the next section we introduce the goals of the Nordic model in terms of key principles like universality and inequality and describe how these principles were first instigated in policies and what challenges they are said to confront in the 2010s. In the following section we analyse policy outcomes in a number of central areas from a comparative perspective. In the concluding section we assess these policy developments and welfare outcomes in view of current challenges in a discussion of the future for the Nordic welfare model in the Nordic countries and in other countries.

The Nordic welfare model key concepts: Inequality and mobility through universal, generous and high quality benefits

In this section we present the goals of the Nordic welfare model and the policies used to try to achieve these goals. We focus on key concepts of inequality and social mobility on the side of goals and outcomes, and we focus on concepts like universalism and generosity when setting out the policy side. We briefly look into the roots and development of these concepts.

The Nordic welfare model is known under many names. The 'Social Democratic welfare regime' pertains to the alleged political forces behind the model (Esping-Andersen, 1990). The 'institutional model' pertains to the characteristics of the model that is seen as having institutionalised a lot of tasks in the social sphere *vis-à-vis* the market and the family. The 'institutional model' stands in contrast to the 'residual model' where the state is the provider of welfare of the last resort (Titmuss, 1974; Alber, 1981).

If we place the Nordic countries in a wider international perspective they look very much the same: long common history, shared cultural values, blurred boundaries between the state and civil society, strong state bureaucracy that is capable of implementing various social policy measures and effectively collecting taxes, heavy bias on public social services and transfers with high coverage among the populace, and consequently small income differences and low poverty rates (Kangas and Palme, 2005).

However, if we compare the Nordic countries with each other they look rather different and the verdict of intra-Nordic comparisons is condensed in the telling adage by Christiansen et al. (2005): one model with five variations. Although the Nordic countries are not identical they do share a high degree of family resemblance when compared to the situation in other countries. For this reason we find it justified to speak of a Nordic welfare model as an adequate label for the Nordic welfare states.

Poor laws and municipal poor help were the first forms of official social policy also in Scandinavia. Municipalities became gradually responsible for expanding welfare obligations and even now, social services are delivered by local authorities that have their own political decision-making arenas and right to collect taxes to finance services they are providing. Within certain limits the municipalities can decide on their own welfare activities and municipal tax rates to finance those activities (Kangas and Palme, 2005). This combination of centralized stateness and local democratic decision-making had important ramifications for the subsequent development of the Nordic societies. The distance between the state/public sector and civil society came to be close and blurred, and often it is hard say where the civil society ends and the public sector begins. One indication of this is that in Scandinavia 'state' is often used synonymously with 'society' (Allardt, 1986; Alestalo and Kuhnle, 1987).

The Nordic countries differ in the timing of their first social policy programmes. Usually Denmark and Sweden paved the way and Norway and Finland trot along a decade or so behind. For example, Denmark was one of the first countries in the world to implement a pension law (1891) followed by Sweden (1913), whereas Norway (1936) and Finland (1937) were late-comers. In some cases, for example in work accident insurance, the order was reversed: Norway introduced the first scheme in 1894, followed by Finland a year later, while Denmark and Sweden implemented the law in 1916. In child and family policy and in social services it was typically Sweden that led the way, although the traditional laggard Finland was the first to introduce care allowances as an alternative to institutionalised care. However, if one inspects the development in these countries diachronically, there are lots of similarities. The countries follow a similar path but the chronological timing is different in their moves. Today, they are all modern comprehensive welfare states and changes in their social policies take place more or less simultaneously.

Goals and policies in the Nordic welfare model

The goals of the modern Nordic welfare model reach further than the goal of alleviating poverty for the deserving needy as dominant in the Anglo-Saxon Model and the goal of securing income maintenance for labour market insiders as in the Continental European model. The Nordic countries do try to tackle poverty and guarantee insurance against income loss, but also to address a wider range of social inequalities. The goal is not only to provide people with an amount of money they can live on but also provide people with skills and abilities that enable them to become full members of the society they are living in through their own efforts, primarily in the labour market. The vision is to help people to maximize their human potential in a belief that this is good for both individuals and the society. For example women should therefore have the same possibilities to participate in the labour market as men, and children from less privileged backgrounds should be enabled to take education on a par with children from privileged backgrounds. To obtain these goals, the Nordic welfare model has provided encompassing benefits in cash and in kind. The income maintenance system has combined basic security with earnings-related benefits to prevent poverty and safeguard the achieved standard of living. Social, education, and health services aim to give individuals possibilities to conduct a decent life independent of their socioeconomic background and capacity to pay.

The central policy features of the Nordic model usually refer to generous and universal social policy that is effective in combating poverty, reducing inequality, and promoting social mobility. Universalism is about coverage of the national relevant population. Generosity deals with the adequacy of cash benefits and the quality of social, education, and health services. Inequality and poverty refer to those factors in society that prevent persons from realising their human potential and in particular to raise the levels for less privileged groups.

One of the most important trademarks of the Nordic welfare state is its universalism. In principle, social benefits are for all – they are targeted neither at specific vulnerable groups nor are they exclusive benefits for privileged occupational groups. Thus, in the ideal Nordic model, all population categories are covered by the same programmes – which is seen to be a solid guarantee for high popular support for the welfare state (Korpi and Palme, 1998). Ideally, since everybody contributes and everybody benefits there is no wedge between the well-off payers and the worse-off beneficiaries; there is no room for 'welfare backlash' (Korpi, 1980; Svallfors, 1989). It has also been shown that good income-related benefits have guaranteed rather a high level of basic security as in basic pensions, social assistance etc. (Nelson, 2003).

The Scandinavian inclination towards universalism is evident in the construction of the post-World War II welfare state – see Figure 15.1.[1] In the 1950s and 1960s, national pension reforms guaranteed basic pension to everyone and the coverage of the other forms of social insurance expanded. The introduction of employment-related pensions and other income maintenance schemes, for their part, improved the income loss. The Nordic welfare states are not always the most generous, especially benefits in Central and Southern Europe may be higher (see Ferrera, 2010). The Scandinavian model is unique by combining generosity with universality. In Central Europe benefits might be more generous but not that universal and in the liberal or Anglo-American model they neither are universal nor generous (Kvist, 2007).

As can be seen in Figure 15.1 the Nordic model had its heyday in the late 1980s and early 1990s (the dotted lines in the separate panels pertain to the mean generosity and universalism rates in 1990). Sweden, Norway, Denmark, and Finland formed a group with a high degree of universalism and generous benefits. Reforms since then mean the Nordic countries remain the most universal, but lost some of their distinctiveness in generosity. With the exception of Norway, benefit levels are cut and generosity is moving towards the Organisation for Economic Co-operation and Development (OECD) mean, while some countries are passing by and other countries moving closer to the Nordic cluster.

Because of the generosity of social insurance, Nordic social assistance is expected to provide high benefit for a small group of claimants. Indeed, the level of social assistance in the North used to be high in comparison to those in other countries. However, during the past decade the replacement levels have been cut by about 10 per cent. The cuts are mirrored in the efficacy of

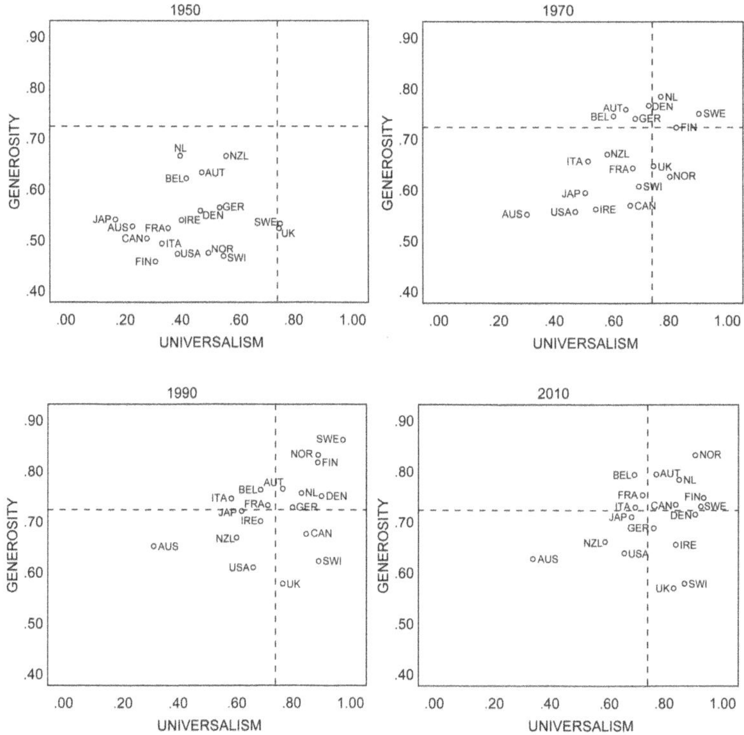

Figure 15.1 Generosity and universalism of social insurance in 18 OECD countries 1950, 1970, 1990 and 2010

social assistance, and, consequently, poverty rates among the social assistance recipients have increased markedly – from 30 per cent in the early 1990s to 40 per cent in the late 2000s (Kuivalainen and Nelson, 2012). The interaction of increasing unemployment and the decreasing adequacy of social assistance may result in increasing poverty rates – if this trajectory materializes, the Nordic model, prized for its low poverty, could be a thing of the past.

Increasing conditions to get access to benefits or to remain entitled to benefits is a new trend that has already transformed the Nordic welfare model. So far we have examined universalism and generosity, however, this is too narrow a picture. In Scandinavia, as elsewhere, entitlements to benefits are more and more targeted by various forms of condition. Taking this conditionality into account we expand from a two- to a three-dimensional perspective as illustrated in Figure 15.2. First, we can see that the replacement levels (generosity) are higher in Germany and France than in any other country but the coverage among the labour force (universalism) is the highest in the Nordic hemisphere. With the exception of Norway, the Nordic countries are not significantly less conditional than France, Germany, or the UK.

Among the OECD countries there is a trend of increasing conditionality. In the case of unemployment the crucial condition is the contribution period, i.e. the time the unemployed must have been employed or a member of the unemployment insurance system before getting right to benefit. While up to early 1990s the reference period in the Nordic countries was on average 19 weeks, the number is now 30 weeks. A similar trend is visible in Continental Europe where the reference period has been lengthened from 37 to 42 weeks (SCIP). In this process the Nordic cluster has become more similar, while there is growing diversification

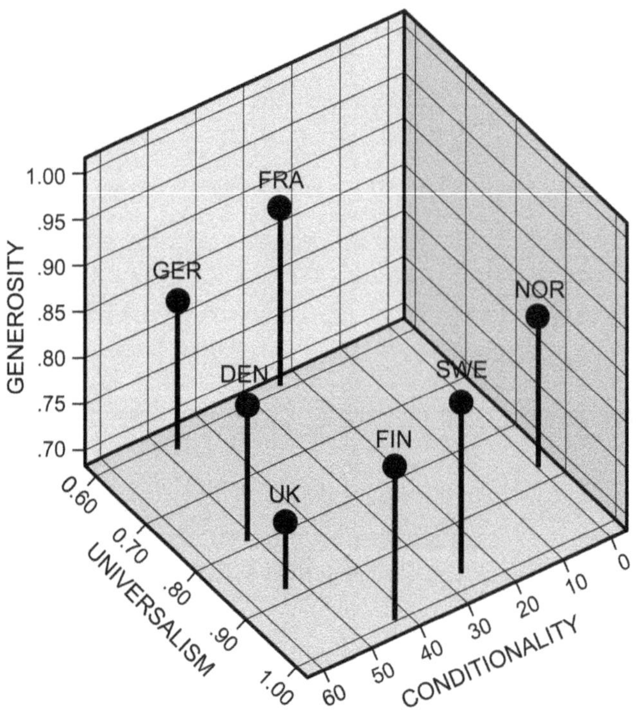

Figure 15.2 Generosity, universalism and conditionality in unemployment insurance in some countries, 2010

among the Continental cluster. Today the Nordic welfare model can thus be characterized as less universal, less generous, and more conditional than one to two decades ago.

Inequality, poverty, and deprivation

International comparisons (Fritzell, Bäckman and Ritakallio, 2012) show that there are no major differences in factor income inequalities between developed countries, whereas there are substantial differences in inequalities of disposable income. The Gini-index for factor income in the Nordic countries is about the same as in the US (Wang and Caminada, 2011, p. 13). However, due to the equalizing effects of taxes and income transfers the countries are placed at opposite ends of the continuum of disposable income inequalities.

The same pattern is visible in poverty levels. The poverty alleviation effect in the Nordic countries is 75 per cent, i.e. social transfers lift 75 per cent of the pre-transfer poor out of poverty. The numbers for the Central European states are about the same, while the corresponding percentage for the US is less than 30 per cent (Smeeding, 2005, Table 4). The story is much the same when it comes to child poverty (see Gornick and Jäntti, 2009).

Social policy models thus differ in their capacity to decrease income inequalities and alleviate poverty. Although the Nordic welfare model has done well, the rise of poverty rates and inequality are faster in the Nordic countries that in countries with other welfare models (OECD, 2008). However, the poverty gap, i.e. the distance from average income of the poor to the national mean, is still narrowest in the Netherlands and Nordic countries (OECD, 2011a, p. 52).

Monetary poverty is one measure to evaluate if people have insufficient means to participate in society. The measure is linked to income distribution: those countries with low income disparities display low poverty figures. For example, Hungary has the same low relative poverty levels as the Nordic countries but the poverty threshold in Scandinavia (about €11,000) is twice that as in Hungary (about €5,000). This means that the standard of living for the poor in Scandinavia is more than twice that in Hungary, or the other post-socialist countries showing low relative poverty levels.

To overcome this problem included in relative income-based poverty measures, more absolute kinds of deprivation indicators have been taken into use. Material deprivation is one of them. This measure expresses individuals' inability to afford basic necessities for adequate life. The picture given by the deprivation index[2] is quite different to an income-poverty picture. The relationship (correlation coefficient r = .34) between the two poverty measures is given in Figure 15.3 (data from Bradshaw and Mayhew, 2010).

The two-way scatter-plot shows how some of the post-socialist countries have low income poverty but high levels of material deprivation. The Nordic countries together with the Netherlands and Austria form a group with low levels of both monetary and deprivation poverty.

In the Anglo-American political discourse the working-poor phenomenon has been at the fore. Due to holes in the safety network, many people do not have adequate social security. Even worse, in some cases getting employment does not help to escape poverty. European level comparisons show that in-work poverty is lowest in the Nordic countries (less than 5 per cent, lowest in Norway at 2.7 per cent) closely followed by the Central European (about 5 per cent) and Liberal countries (about 7 per cent), whereas more than 10 per cent of the working population is above the poverty threshold in Southern Europe (Hussain, Kangas, and Kvist, 2012, p. 130).

The Nordic countries – Denmark and Sweden, in particular – are renowned for their investment in activation and active labour market policies. On average, the Nordic cluster is investing more than the other welfare models in active labour market measures and, consequently, long-term unemployment rates tend to be lower in Scandinavia than elsewhere, although there are no substantial differences in the overall unemployment rate in comparison to the other regimes (OECD, 2011d).

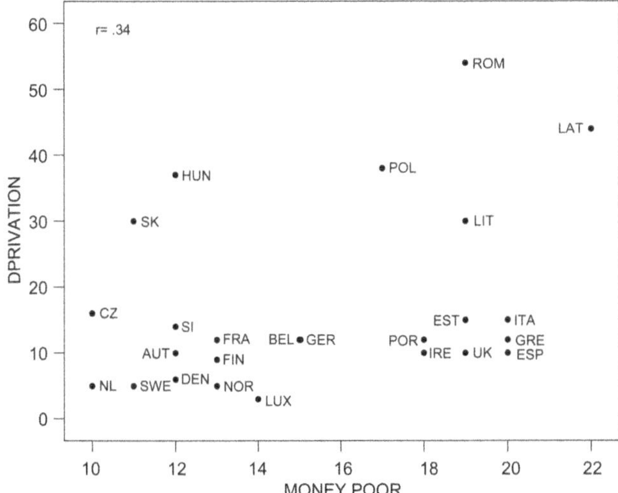

Figure 15.3 Monetary poverty (poverty threshold = 60% of median) and material deprivation in Europe around 2010

To conclude the inequality discussion, we can say that despite growing inequality, the Nordic countries are still equal societies, but less so than two decades ago.

Income mobility

In addition to the incidence of poverty it is important also to consider the *persistence* of poverty, or, more broadly, income mobility. According to John Rawls's (1971, 1996) influential concept of justice even a high level of inequality is acceptable if it is based on openness of society. Thus high degrees of cross-sectional inequality and poverty could be forgiven if there are high degrees of income mobility and high exit-rates out of poverty.

Long-term poverty is a derivate of income mobility and poverty exit rates. The longitudinal European Community Household Panel (ECHP) data prove that the annual exit rate is 60 per cent for Denmark (there are no data for the other Nordic countries), 48 per cent for the Central European cluster of nations (Belgium, Germany, France, Luxembourg, and the Netherlands), 45 per cent for the liberal regime (UK, Ireland, the US, and Canada), and 42 per cent for the Southern European regime (Greece, Italy, Portugal, and Spain) (OECD, 2011b). Due to these marked differences in poverty exit rates, there also are differences between welfare regimes in the incidence of long-term poverty. Countries with low cross-sectional poverty also display low levels of long-term poverty.

One important indicator of the Rawlsian openness is the correlation of incomes between children and their parents. The lower the association the more open the society is. The Nordic countries are not as open societies as they perhaps would like to be. But they may be less closed that some other countries. The intergenerational income correlation is highest in the UK (.50) and in the US (.47), while it is lowest in Denmark (.15), Norway (.17), Finland (.18), and Canada (.19). Sweden is somewhat lagging behind its Nordic neighbours (r = .27) but displaying clearly lower coefficients than the continental France (.41) and Germany (.32) (Jäntti et al., 2006; Corak, 2006).

The educational system is crucial when explaining how strongly the parental background is inherited (Esping-Andersen, 2009). According to the educational achievements results from Program for International Student Assessment (PISA), the family background explains 11 per cent of the pupils' achievements in the Nordic countries, 16 per cent in Central Europe, 14 per cent in the Liberal cluster, and 14 per cent in the Southern and post-socialist countries, but the means conceal a substantial intra-regime variation, e.g. the numbers are low for Finland and Norway (7–8 per cent) but comparatively high for Denmark and Sweden (13–14 per cent). Maintaining educational equality is a challenging task given the important role of private schools in Denmark and the expansion of private elite education in Sweden. The private school system plays a minor role in Finland and Norway. In all countries we can detach effects of intra-generational transmission of educational attainment and in that sense no country fulfils the Rawlsian principle but some countries are more open than others.

To combat the detrimental effects of poor childhood conditions it is important to invest in children early (Esping-Andersen, 2009; OECD, 2001b and 2006). Kindergartens, pre-schools and primary education are investments in future. The idea is not new. Already in the 1930 a Swedish social democratic politician Alva Myrdal demanded that child care was arranged collectively (Hirdman, 1989). Collective, public day care was seen to fulfil objectives of equality: children with different backgrounds were given equal chances. Child care provision accessible to everybody should provide a means of compensation for children with scarce resources at home. On the United Nations Children's Fund (UNICEF) child welfare index the Nordic countries, the Netherlands, and Switzerland are the six best performers (UNICEF, 2007).

The inspection of poverty and income mobility – be it short or long term – gives a relatively good testimony of the Nordic countries. In fact, the Nordic welfare state has been well-suited to meet the 'old social risks' but it is perhaps not that distinctively good to combat 'new risks' of single parenthood, one person households, youth poverty, etc. (Fritzell, Bäckman, and Ritakallio, 2011). There are also problems in integrating immigrants into the labour markets and in that respect the liberal countries are doing better (Esping-Andersen, 2009, p. 129). There are also signs that educational attainments and educational skills among immigrant children are substantially lagging behind of those of natives. Thus, in the years to come, the Nordic countries may need to invest more on the integration of certain groups of immigrant children in kindergartens, preschools, and schools if emerging inequalities are not to expand.

Social services and employment

Universal, tax-financed social services are from many points of view a cornerstone of the Nordic model. First, high quality child care and school services provide equal possibilities for all children. Second, universal access to healthcare is essential for population health and well-being. Third, home service helps the elderly to live longer in their own homes and, if needed, institutional care is given in service homes. Fourth, public services are important from the employment and gender equality perspectives. Child care gives possibilities for both genders to equally participate in paid labour and parenthood. In the Nordic countries the universal child care is most important facilitator for this goal (Datta Gupta, Smith and Verner, 2006).

However, when it comes to the utilization of public day care, the Nordic countries display different trajectories (Meager and Szebehely, 2012). Whereas child care take-up rates among small children is about 90 per cent in Denmark, Norway, and Sweden, it is 45 per cent in Finland. The explanation is home care allowance that is paid to those parents who either take care of their children themselves or use private providers (Hiilamo and Kangas, 2009). Most families choose the home care option and, consequently, the labour force participation of Finnish mothers with small children is as low as the Southern European levels at around 50 per cent. In the other Nordic countries the maternal labour force participation rates are close to those of fathers. The Nordic picture becomes more homogenous if we look at mothers who have school-aged or older children. Now the Finnish female labour force participation rates are the highest in the OECD hemisphere (81 per cent). Thus, the overall employment activity is high in all Nordic countries (including Finland): 73 per cent for women and 78 per cent for men. The corresponding numbers for Central Europe are 62 per cent and 74 per cent; for the Liberal regimes 63 per cent and 78 per cent; and for the Southern European countries 56 per cent and 77 per cent (Hussain, Kangas, and Kvist, 2012, p. 125).

All in all gender equality in employment rates is a smaller problem in the Nordic countries than elsewhere (OECD, 2011a) but nevertheless the 'revolution' still is incomplete (see Esping-Andersen, 2009) and the welfare state plays a central role in contribution and inhibiting gender equality. The example of home care allowance indicates that policies can make a huge behavioural difference: home care allowance may be good from some points of view but there are clear class- and culture-related patterns in the utilization of care allowance. Working-class and immigrant mothers are more prone to use the possibility, which in turn may jeopardize the equalizing efforts the educational system has as its overarching goal. There also are numerous problems related to the 'glass ceiling' that prevents women gaining the highest position in society, and in that respect the Nordic countries are not always doing any better than other countries (Datta Gupta, Oaxaca, and Smith, 2006).

In all the Nordic countries there is a trend towards marketization and privatization of public services. With the motivation of choice, quality, and efficiency, private kindergartens and schools, private hospitals, and elderly care institutions are gaining ground (Kautto, 2010; Kvist and

Greve, 2011). The development may nullify the Nordic ethos of equal treatment regardless of the thickness of the wallet. For-profit providers may offer good 'products' for the 'good' customers who can pay. The task is finding the delicate balance between economic profit and good care. There are some warning examples of how firms maximizing profits to their investment capital owners on Cayman Islands may neglect the principle of good care in Stockholm.

Trust and subjective welfare

Fukuyama (1995, p. 7) argues that ' ... a nation's well-being, as well as its ability to compete, is conditioned by a single, pervasive cultural characteristic: the level of trust inherent in society'. Fukuyama indicates that social trust may have important ramifications for economic performance as well as for individual well-being. The Nordic countries are high-trust societies and despite their strong welfare states and heavy tax burdens – often said to be poison to competitiveness – are doing well in economic terms: they are prosperous, have labourious populations, balanced budgets, low public debts and according to the global competitiveness indices (World Economic Forum, 2011) they occupy top positions in the list of competitive countries (in 2011 Sweden occupies the third position, Finland is number 4, Denmark, 8, and Norway, 16).

In the international debate on welfare there is a shift from money-based measures towards more subjective indicators of well-being, for example EU-SILC and European Social Survey offer lots of material on subjective well-being. For space considerations we discuss only one dimension of them that is often regarded as the most important welfare indicator: general life satisfaction. According to the European Social Survey, the mean for the Nordic cluster is 8.0 which is the highest regime mean (the scale goes 0 = extremely dissatisfied to 10 = extremely satisfied). Furthermore, the within regime variation is the smallest one ($\delta = 1.6$). The corresponding life-satisfaction scores for the other welfare clusters are 7.1 ($\delta = 2.1$) for the Liberal, 7.2 for the Continental European ($\delta = 2.1$), 6.9 ($\delta = 2.2$) for the Southern European, and as low as 5.8 ($\delta = 2.5$) for the East European cluster (Fridberg and Kangas, 2008).

Not only is the general life satisfaction high among people from the Nordic countries, but also when it comes to the various aspects of trust the story is very much the same. The Nordic countries display high degrees of trust in all dimensions (trust in their national institutions and in their country wo/men). There seems to be a 'good circle' between the Nordic welfare model, social trust and various subjective measures of welfare.[3]

Conclusion

By way of conclusion we discuss if challenges make the Nordic welfare model unsustainable or obsolete. The premise is that if the Nordic countries cannot maintain a Nordic-style welfare model it seems unlikely that the model is sustainable elsewhere. Indeed, the days of the Nordic welfare model have been numbered ever since it was first talked of. However, the diagnosis of the malaise has changed (Esping-Andersen, 1996; Jæger and Kvist, 2003). For the 2010s the list of challenges include not least demographic change and its spill-over effects on economic sustainability and political dynamics.

Demographic changes are perhaps the biggest challenge to the Nordic welfare model. Because the Nordic welfare model is heavy on services and has a wide range of universal cash benefits the need for everybody in work is pertinent. With ageing populations the need increases for more social and health services at the same time as there are fewer persons in their working active age who can staff and finance those services. Already now municipalities who are largely responsible for the social services witness their elderly care workers retire and their tax base diminish. This is due to not only to the economic crisis but is also a result of demographic developments with relatively fewer of working age.

Ethnicity issues make up another set of demographic challenges, i.e. integration of persons from other countries, migration flows, and levels of solidarity in national populations. Because of generally lower labour market participation rates among persons from third-world countries, especially women, much of the active labour market policies in recent years have been on integration such groups into the labour market. There have also been national debates in the Nordic countries of whether the universal, generous benefits would attract people from other countries interested in such benefits at the same time as making insiders in the Nordic labour market move abroad to avoid high(er) taxes to finance the social benefits. Primarily Denmark has led such fears, resulting in lower minimum income benefits (although these were raised again after a change of government in 2011). This indicates that politics still matters and it remains to be seen what kind of impact the diminishing support for social democratic parties in the Nordic countries has on the welfare state model. At least, it will be less 'social democratic'.

Is the support for universal welfare only possible in small and homogenous populations where benefits are for 'us'? Does cultural and ethnic heterogeneity hollow out universalism? While empirical results show that Americans in particular are sensitive to in-group 'us' and out-group 'them' distinction, the Nordic attitudes are not that much affected by the dyadic division, therefore, the increasing ethnic diversity does not directly constitute a threat to the Nordic welfare state (Finseraas, 2012: 39). However, the impact may be indirect. Given the high level of unemployment among immigrants the in-group and out-group distinction may begin to play its role (Albrekt Larsen, 2012). In fact, populist parties using anti-immigration banderols take a substantial share of votes in the Nordic countries: about 20 per cent in Denmark, Finland and Norway and about 5 per cent in Sweden.

Is the special Nordic passion for equality (Graubard, 1986) on the wane? Recent research (Jæger, 2012) shows that the love of the Nordic people to their welfare state is as passionate or as luke-warm as elsewhere. General support for social policy in Scandinavia is high – not necessarily stronger than in Continental European countries, but stronger than in the Liberal countries.

Our results indicate that it still is possible to talk about a welfare model consisting of the Nordic countries. The Nordic welfare model today is less universal, less generous, and more conditional than it was twenty years ago. Furthermore, many countries have caught up the Nordic countries and consequently differences between welfare regimes are melting away. However, the Nordic welfare model is still distinct in many respects and fares well in comparison with other welfare state models on most dimensions of welfare. Poverty and inequality rates are low, gender equality is rather high, income mobility – be it short-term or inter-generational – is high, all this combined with high level of subjective welfare. This is very much in line with the basic Nordic ideas how the state should work: it should provide individuals with resources to master their own lives. Whether the Nordic welfare model can continue to do so seems to be as much a question of political decisions over the harsh economic or social realities.

Notes

1 Indicators used in the figure pertain to mean values of old-age pensions, sickness, work accident, and unemployment insurance programmes. Universality is a mean for coverage of those schemes (insured/total population in pensions (per cent), and insurance/total labour force for other insurance programmes (per cent)). Pensions weigh 2, work accident 0.5, and sickness and unemployment insurance 1 each. Generosity is mean replacement level for the four schemes expressed as a ratio between net benefit and net wage at the average income level. These numbers are weighted as explained above. The

interpretation of the indices is straightforward: in universality 0 per cent indicates that nobody is insured under any programme and 100 per cent tells that the total population in risk in covered. Consequently, 0 per cent in generosity refers to a situation where there are no benefits at all available in any of the four schemes, while the maximum value of 100 per cent pertains to full compensations in all the schemes (net benefit = net income). Data for the indicators are derived from the SCIP data based housed at the Swedish Institute for Social Research, University of Stockholm (see e.g. Korpi and Palme, 1998). Data for 2010 are provisional.

2 Deprivation measure consists of indicators of economic strain (cannot afford to face unexpected expenses, a one-week annual holiday away from home, to pay for arrears, a meal with meat, chicken or fish every second day, to keep the home adequately warm), involuntary lack of durables (a washing machine, a colour TV, a telephone, a personal car) and problems with housing (leaking roof, damp walls/floors/foundations or rot in the window frames, accommodation that is too dark, no bath or shower, no indoor flushing toilet, lack of space and spending more than 40 per cent of income on housing). The material deprivation index pertains to those who are lacking three or more items in the lists given above.

3 Health is one welfare component where the Nordic model is not doing that well. See Clare Bambra's contribution in this volume.

References

Alber, J. (1981), *Vom Armenhaus zum Wohlfahrsstaat*. Frankfurt a.M.: Campus.

Albrekt Larsen, C. (2012), Ethnic heterogeneity and public support for welfare: Is the US experience replicated in Britain, Sweden, and Denmark? *A paper presented at the 9th annual ESPAnet conference*, Valencia, 8–10 September.

Alestalo, M. and Kuhnle, S. (1987), 'The Scandinavian Route: Economic, Social, and Political Developments in Denmark, Finland, Norway and Sweden', in R. Erikson, E.J. Hansen, S. Ringen and H. Uusitalo (eds), *The Scandinavian Model. Welfare States and Welfare Research*, pp. 3–38. New York: M.E. Sharpe.

Allardt, E. (1986), 'The civic conception of the welfare state in Scandinavia', in R. Rose and R. Shriatori (eds), *The Welfare State. East and West*, pp. 107–25. New York: Oxford University Press.

Bradshaw, J. and Mayhew, E. (2010), Understanding Extreme Poverty in the European Union. *European Journal of Homelessness*, 4, December, pp. 171–86.

Christiansen, N.F., Petersen, K., Edling, N. and Haave, P. (2005), *The Nordic Model of Welfare*. Copenhagen: Museum Tusculanum Press.

Corak, M. (2006), Do Poor Children Become Poor Adults? Lessons from a Cross Country Comparison of Generational Earnings Mobility. *Research on Economic Inequality*, 13 no. 1, pp. 143–88.

Datta Gupta, N., Oaxaca, R. and Smith, N. (2006), Swimming Upstream, Floating Downstream: Comparing Women's Relative Wage Progress in the United States and Denmark. *Industrial and Labour Relations*, 59 (2), pp. 243–66.

Datta Gupta, N., Smith, N. and Verner, M. (2006), Child Care and Parental Leave in the Nordic Countries: A Model to Aspire to? *Discussion Paper 2014. Institute for the Study of Labour*: Bonn, Germany.

Esping-Andersen, G. (1990), *Three Worlds of Welfare Capitalism*. London: Polity Press.

——(2009), *The Incomplete Revolution. Adapting to women's new roles*. Cambridge: Polity Press.

Ferrera, M. (2010), 'The South European Countries', in F. Castles, S. Leibfried, J. Lewis, H. Obinger and C. Pierson (eds), *The Oxford Handbook of the Welfare State*, pp. 616–29. Oxford: Oxford University Press.

Finseraas, H. (2012), 'Anti-immigration attitudes, support for redistribution and party choice in Europe', in J. Kvist, J. Fritzell, B. Hvinden and O. Kangas (eds), *Changing Social Equality: The Nordic Welfare Model in the 21st Century*, pp. 23–43. Bristol: Policy Press.

Flora, P. (1986), *Growth to Limits: The Western European welfare states since World War II*. Berlin: De Gruyter.

Fridberg, T. and Kangas, O. (2008), 'Social capital', in H. Ervasti, T. Fridberg, M. Hjerm and K. Ringdal (eds), *Nordic Attitudes in a European Perspective*, pp. 65–85. Cheltenham: Edward Elgar.

Fritzell, J., Bäckman, O. and Ritakallio, V.-M. (2012), 'Income inequality and poverty: do the Nordic countries still constitute a family of their own?', in J. Kvist, J. Fritzell, B. Hvinden and O. Kangas (eds), *Changing Social Equality: The Nordic Welfare Model in the 21st Century*, pp. 165–85. Bristol: Policy Press.

Fukuyama, F. (1995): *Trust: The Social Virtues and the Creation of Prosperity*. London: Penguin Books.

Gornick, J. and Jäntti, M. (2009), Child Poverty in Upper-Income Countries: Lessons from the Luxembourg Income Study. *LIS working papers series* – No. 509. Luxembourg: Luxembourg Income Study (LIS).

Graubard, S. (ed.) (1986) *Norden – Passion for Equality*. Oslo: Norwegian University Press.
Hiilamo, H. and Kangas, O. (2009), Trap for women or freedom to choose: Struggle of cash for child-care schemes in Finland and Sweden. *Journal of Social Policy*, 38 (3), pp. 457–75. gcr.weforum.org/gcr2011 (retrieved 20. Nov. 2011).
Hirdman, Y. (1989) *Att lägga livet till rätta – studier i svensk folkhemspolitik* Stockholm: Carlssons.
Hussain, A. M., Kangas, O. and Kvist, J. (2012), 'Welfare state institutions, unemployment and poverty', in J. Kvist, J. Fritzell, B. Hvinden and O. Kangas (eds), *Changing Social Equality: The Nordic Welfare Model in the 21st Century*, pp. 119–42. Bristol: Policy Press.
Jæger, M.M. (2012), 'Do we all (dis)like the same welfare state? Configurations of public support for the welfare state in comparative perspective', in J. Kvist, J. Fritzell, B. Hvinden and O. Kangas (eds), *Changing Social Equality: The Nordic Welfare Model in the 21st Century*, pp. 45–68. Bristol: Policy Press.
Jæger, M. M. and Kvist, J. (2003), Pressures on State Welfare in Post-industrial Societies: Is More or Less Better? *Social Policy & Administration*, 37(6), pp. 555–72.
Jäntti, M., Bratsberg, B., Røed, K., Raaum, O., Naylor, R., Österbacka, E., Björklund, A. and Eriksson, T. (2006), American Exceptionalism in a New Light: A Comparison of Intergenerational Earnings Mobility in the Nordic Countries, the United Kingdom and the United States. *Discussion Paper 1938. Institute for the Study of Labour*: Bonn, Germany.
Jäntti, M. and Danziger, S. (2000), 'Income poverty in advanced countries', in A.B. Atkinson and F. Bourguignon (eds), *Handbook of Income Distribution*, pp. 309–78. Amsterdam: Elsevier.
Kangas, O., Lundberg, U. and Ploug, N. (2010), Three Roads to Pension Reform: Politics and institutions in Reforming Pensions in Denmark, Finland and Sweden. *Social Policy and Administration*, Vol. 44: 3, pp. 265–84.
Kangas, O. and Palme, J. (eds), (2005), *Social Policy and Economic Development in the Nordic Countries*. Houndsmills: Palgrave MacMillan.
Kautto, M. (2010), 'The Nordic Countries', in F. Castles, S. Leibfried, J. Lewis, H. Obinger and C. Pierson (eds), *The Oxford Handbook of the Welfare State*, pp. 586–600. Oxford: Oxford University Press.
Korpi, W. (1980), Social Policy and Distributional Conflict in the Capitalist Democracies, *West European Politics*, 3, pp. 294–316.
Korpi, W. and Palme, J. (1998), The Paradox of Redistribution and Strategies of Equality: Welfare State Institutions, Inequality and Poverty in the Western Countries, *American Sociological Review*. 63, pp. 661–87.
Kuivalainen, S. and Nelson, K. (2012), 'Eroding minimum income protection in the Nordic countries', in J. Kvist, J. Fritzell, B. Hvinden and O. Kangas (eds), *Changing Social Equality: The Nordic Welfare Model in the 21st Century*, pp. 69–87. Bristol: Policy Press.
Kuusi, P. (1964), *Social policy for the sixties*. Helsinki: Finnish Social Policy Association.
Kvist, J. (2002), 'Changing rights and obligations in unemployment insurance', in R. Sigg and C. Behrendt (eds), *Social Security in the Global Village*, pp. 227–45. Brunswick: Transaction Publishers.
——(2007), Fuzzy set ideal type analysis. *Journal of Business Research*, 60(5), pp. 474–81.
Meager. G. and Szebehely, M. (2012), 'Equality in the social service state: Nordic child care models in comparative perspective', in J. Kvist, J. Fritzell, B. Hvinden and O. Kangas (eds), *Changing Social Equality: The Nordic Welfare Model in the 21st Century*, pp. 89–117. Bristol: Policy Press.
Myrdal, G. (1960), Beyond the Welfare State: Economic Planning and its International Implications. London: Duckworth.
Nelson, K. (2003), Fighting Poverty: Comparative Studies on Social Insurance, Means-tested Benefits and Income Redistribution. Stockholm: *Dissertation Series No. 60. Swedish Institute for Social Research.*
Organisation for Economic Co-operation and Development (OECD) (2001a), *Employment Outlook*. Paris: OECD.
——(2001b), *Starting Strong: Early Childhood Education and Care*. Paris: OECD.
——(2006), *Starting Strong II: Early Childhood Education and Care*. Paris: OECD.
——(2008), *Growing Unequal? Income Distribution and Poverty in OECD Countries*. Paris: OECD.
——(2011a), *How's life. Measuring well-being*. Paris: OECD.
——(2011b), www.oecd.org/dataoecd/29/55/2079296.pdf (retrieved 10 November 2011).
——(2011c), Social Expenditure. stats.oecd.org/Index.aspx?datasetcode=SOCX_AGG (retrieved 10 November 2011).
——(2011d), Labour Force Statistics. stats.oecd.org/index.aspx?queryid=251 (retrieved 7 December 2011).
Okun, A. (1975), *Equality and Efficiency: The Big Trade Off*. Washington, DC: Brookings.
Rawls, J. (1971), *A theory of social justice*. Cambridge, MA: Harvard University Press.

——(1996), *Political liberalism*. New York: Columbia University Press.

SCIP (nd), *Social Citizenship Indicator Program*, housed at Swedish Institute for Social Research, Stockholm University.

Smeeding, T. (2005), Government Programs and Social Outcomes: The United States in Comparative Perspective. *LIS working papers series* – No. 426. Luxembourg: Luxembourg Income Study (LIS).

Svallfors, S. (1989), *Vem älskar välfärdsstaten?: attityder, organiserade intressen och svensk välfärdspolitik*. Lund: Arkiv.

Titmuss, R. (1974), *Social Policy: An Introduction*. London: Allen & Unwin.

United Nations Children's Fund (UNICEF) (2007), *The State of the World's Children 2007*. New York: UNICEF.

Wang, C. and Caminada, K. (2011), Disentangling Income Inequality and the Redistributive Effect of Social Transfers and Taxes in 36 LIS Countries. *LIS Working Paper Series* – No. 567. Luxembourg: Luxembourg Income Study (LIS).

World Economic Forum (2011), *The Global Competitiveness Report 2011–2012*. Online: gcr.weforum.org/gcr 2011).

16

Central European welfare states

Daniel Clegg

Introduction

The social protection systems of Western and Central European countries have their origins in the social reforms of Otto von Bismarck in Imperial Germany in the 1880s. For that reason this distinctive model of social provision is sometimes referred to as the *Bismarckian* model (Palier, 2010a) as well as, for reasons discussed below, the *conservative-corporatist* (Esping-Andersen, 1990), *Christian Democratic* (van Kersbergen, 1992) or *industrial achievement-performance* model (Titmuss, 1974). Nations whose welfare systems are of this characteristic variety include France, Germany, and the Benelux countries, as well as Austria, and, following a period of comparatively late welfare expansion in the 1970s and 1980s, Switzerland. Due to some shared institutional characteristics Eastern and especially Southern European countries are sometimes also considered to have Bismarckian systems of social protection, though their specific developmental features justify seeing the welfare models of these regions as distinctive (see Chapters 17 and 18 in this volume).

As shown in Figure 16.1, by 2008 all larger countries with Bismarckian social protection systems devoted a higher share of their national wealth to social protection than is, on average, the case elsewhere in Europe. This is true even in comparison to the Nordic countries, long considered the 'gold standard' for welfare state generosity (see Chapter 15). While levels of social expenditure have fallen back considerably from their historic highs of the mid-1990s in most Nordic countries, in Western and Central Europe these have remained much more stable going into the twenty-first century. Though this is a reflection of a very solidly institutionalised commitment to using collective mechanisms to protect citizens against social risks, the Bismarckian model of social protection is, however, not without its critics. Despite the now larger sums generally devoted to social policy than elsewhere, at-risk-of-poverty rates remain markedly higher in many of these countries than they are in Nordic Europe. And although their employment performance has improved since the mid-1990s (Hemerijck and Eichhorst, 2010), levels of employment remain structurally lower in many countries of Western and Central Europe than elsewhere in the continent. To an extent, indeed, it might be said that the high levels of expenditure that characterise these social protection systems are partly a reflection of some socio-economic problems that these systems themselves engender.

This chapter discusses the forces behind the historical development of these large social protection systems, the particular aims and objectives of this type of social policy, and how these are promoted through the common institutional features of Bismarckian social protection systems.

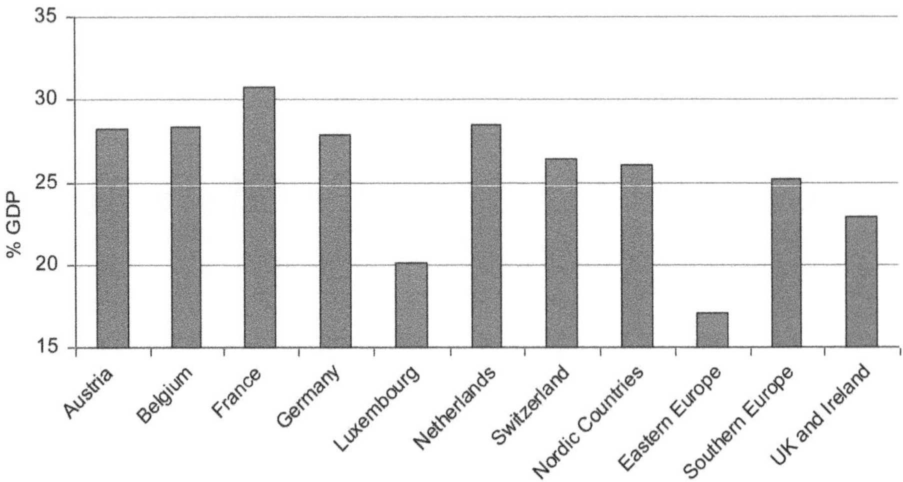

Figure 16.1 Social protection expendition for 25% of GDP
Source: Eurostad.

It then explores how in the last quarter-century these design features have made social protection reform simultaneously particularly pressing and unusually difficult. The chapter concludes by assessing the future prospects for this social model in the light of the reforms that have been accomplished in recent years.

The development and core features of welfare systems in Western and Central Europe

Alongside the typical functional drivers of economic and social change (see Chapter 28), the development of welfare systems in Western and Central European countries has been shaped as much by *conservative* and *religious* forces as by the class-based mobilisation of workers and the success of the political left. Bismarck, whose social reforms in the 1880s laid the foundations for this model, was a 'revolutionary conservative', and by introducing compulsory sickness, work accident, and old age insurance programmes, he intended to secure the *pacification and political allegiance of the working class* to the Empire in the face of a growing and increasingly restive labour movement (Hennock, 2007). The years following the Second World War, when as elsewhere in the developed world the welfare systems of Western and Central European countries enjoyed their period of fastest expansion, was furthermore a period when *Christian Democratic* forces of the centre-right dominated the politics of most continental West European countries, with the notable exception of France (van Kersbergen, 1995).

The imprint of these social and political forces helps to understand the particular aims and objectives of social provision in Western and Central Europe. Though they are generous in expenditure terms, these are systems focused on *security* and *stability* rather than equality or emancipation. Occupational and status differentials in the labour market are largely mirrored in the level of social protection citizens receive in the event of major life-course events such as sickness, unemployment, or retirement. At least explicitly, the systems favour *horizontal redistribution*, across the life course, rather than vertical redistribution, across income groups. As *status maintenance* in the social protection system rewards labour market performance, these systems have often been understood as 'handmaidens' of the industrial economy (Titmuss, 1974). Individual social rights are traditionally derived – directly or through a family member – from employment status, and the regulation of compulsory welfare provision is often articulated in complex ways with free collective bargaining between trade unions and employers – the *social partners* – at firm, sectoral and national levels. One result of this is that in areas such as sickness and pensions there are often separate compulsory social insurance schemes in different companies or economic sectors, resulting in these systems being characterised by considerable internal *fragmentation and diversity*.

With the partial exception of Belgium and France, these social protection systems have also traditionally upheld conventional *familialist* conceptions of the gender division of labour, privileging the income protection of the main (usually male) breadwinner, but providing only limited social services to facilitate the reconciliation of (female) labour market participation and household care provision (Morel, 2007). A number of the aims of this model of social provision can be related to the importance of *subsidiarity*, a principle that is particularly central to Catholic social doctrine and holds that direct state intervention is only appropriate when the self-protective capacities of lower level social organs – the family, voluntary organisations, and professional and vocational communities in the labour market – cannot be effectively supported through public subsidies (van Kersbergen, 1995, p. 188). It is for this reason that the state often plays a rather arms-length role in the regulation and delivery of welfare provisions, to the extent that the concept of 'welfare state' should be applied to these systems only with caution (Palier, 2010a, p. 24).

Despite the social protection systems of Western and Central European countries seeking to provide increasingly universalistic cover in the post-World War II decades, *social insurance* remained – and still remains – the dominant form of welfare provision in this welfare model. Individuals are protected against the risk of temporary or permanent inability to earn income in the labour market by the specific contributions that they (and their employers, if they are salaried employees) pay when they are in work, making these systems strongly *contributory* in both their entitlement logic and financing systems. Even transfers designed to supplement additional costs, such as family benefits, often operate on an insurance-like basis, and are to a large extent financed out of employer- and employee-contributions. Cash transfers are the main form of welfare provision that individuals receive, including for many basic medical services, which are reimbursed by sickness insurance funds rather than being directly collectively financed and free at the point of receipt. It was intended that through the development of comprehensive social insurance systems to cover all major social risks resulting from family and market failures, the direct provision of extensive social or labour market support services would be unnecessary and the role of tax-financed welfare payments, such as social assistance, could be reduced to an absolute minimum. Indeed, a number of these countries had no general tax-financed minimum income scheme until the 1970s (Belgium) or 1980s (France).

The ability of this social insurance-based model to protect the vast majority of the population was strongly dependent on full (male) employment and stable family structures. More perhaps than elsewhere in Europe, deindustrialization and the return of mass unemployment in the 1970s seriously undermined the basic logic of social protection in Western and Central European countries. Moreover, the institutional structures of the Bismarckian social protection system encouraged a series of short-term, defensive responses to the changed economic environment within which welfare states have found themselves since the last decades of the twentieth century. Through policies of *labour shedding* governments responded to mass unemployment by using the social protection system to provide less productive workers with more-or-less permanent access to income outside work, through prolonged unemployment or disability benefits or the expansion of early retirement pensions. As well as leading to the rapid development of highly *unfavourable dependency ratios*, the unintended consequence of these measures, however, has been to further impede job creation, particularly in low-skill sectors of the economy. As a result Western and Central European countries came in the 1980s and 1990s to face *low employment, structural unemployment* and growing concerns about problems of *social exclusion* among sections of their populations.

The apparent inability of governments in Western and Central European countries to adapt their structures of social protection to new social and economic risks and problems led some in the 1990s to argue that these were *frozen welfare systems* (Esping-Andersen, 1996). While the institutional structures of Bismarckian welfare systems have indeed militated against sudden and radical structural reforms, it is today evident that substantial changes have taken place in recent years (Palier and Martin, 2008). Though these reforms have to an extent succeeded in making both labour markets and welfare systems more inclusive in Western and Central European countries, some argue that this has been at the price of institutionalising a form of *dualism* in the social protection treatment of stable-employed 'insiders', on the one hand, and 'outsiders' with precarious attachment to the labour market, on the other (Palier, 2010b). Simultaneously, however, there are also some indications of an as yet tentative shift towards a more proactive and service-centred approach to welfare provision than has typically characterised this model.

Bismarckian welfare institutions and the challenge of adaptation

To understand fully the recent development and current contours of welfare systems in these countries, it is useful to look in closer detail at the common institutional characteristics of welfare systems of this type. Following Palier (2010a), Bismarckian social protection systems have similar entitlement principles, benefit structures, financing mechanisms, and governance arrangements. These institutional parameters reflect the various objectives underlying this model of social protection, but also help to explain the particular ways these systems have responded to the ongoing challenge of adapting to social and economic change.

- *Entitlements based on work and contributions*: In Bismarckian welfare systems, social rights are traditionally derived from contributions paid in employment. Beneficiaries are not all citizens or all the needy, but instead workers and their families who are facing life-course events. In social insurance schemes for risks such as old-age and unemployment, the individual's work and contribution record is often used to calculate the level and/or duration of entitlement to benefit, according to what in Germany is known as the 'equivalence principle', whereby the financial benefit any individual receives is a reflection of the financial contributions they have made. Having a compulsory benefit system in which individuals 'earn' their level of social protection through their work intensity and effort is one of the main ways that these welfare systems have helped to support and stabilise the standard employment relationship that was central to industrial production.
- *Wage-related benefits*: The benefits individuals receive in the event of inability to earn income from work are not flat-rate, but related to and expressed as a percentage of their previous salary. Levels of wage replacement have been historically somewhat lower for the unemployed, but were often around 70 per cent in pension and sickness insurance schemes in the heyday of these systems. Though benefit ceilings exist they are generally higher than in similar schemes in Nordic countries. This is central to the status-maintaining aims of Bismarckian social protection and the preference for promoting security over redistribution and equality. According to one influential, if controversial, account of social policy development, generous wage-replacing benefits in the event of unemployment also served the economic function of

encouraging individuals to make otherwise risky investments in the specific and non-transferable skills that industrial employers required (Häusermann, 2010, p. 18).

- *Contribution financing*: Like in Southern and Eastern European countries, the welfare systems found in West and Central Europe are heavily financed through employer and employee contributions, or what are sometimes known as payroll taxes. In 1990, the share of social contributions in all social protection revenues ranged from 60 per cent in the Netherlands to 80 per cent in France. By comparison, social contributions at the same time represented under half of all revenues in the UK and Ireland, and only a third, on average, in Nordic countries. In continental Europe, furthermore, social contributions are explicitly not considered as a tax, and are generally not directly collected and controlled by the national finance ministry. Instead, contributions are held in specific managerially autonomous social insurance funds.
- *Social partner governance*: These funds are not part of the central or local state administration, but rather non-profit entities whose governance or management is partly delegated to the social partners, trade unions, and employer associations. This is the 'corporatist' element of this welfare model that was identified by Esping-Andersen (1990). The involvement and regulatory autonomy of the social partners in Bismarckian social insurance varies across countries and, within countries, between social insurance branches (Ebbinghaus, 2010), but nowhere in Western and Central Europe has the state traditionally been free to manage social insurance alone. This is partly a historical legacy of the first compulsory systems having been grafted onto pre-existing occupational or mutual trade funds, and the reluctant acceptance of reformers such as Bismarck to grant self-administration rights to the very organized workers whose power resources he was trying to undercut. But it is also congruent with, and has been reinforced by, the subsidiarity principle and its emphasis on 'self-government' by lower level social organs rather than direct control by the state (van Kersbergen, 1995: 188). In this view self-government is in turn intimately related to self-sufficiency, and for this reason contribution financing (financing by workers and their employers) and governance by the social partners (management by the *representatives of* workers and their employers) have always been mutually sustaining features of Bismarckian welfare systems.

Since the late 1970s, the welfare systems of Continental European countries have faced similar challenges to welfare states across the developed world, related to lower aggregate growth rates, intensified international competition and changing demographic profiles. The significant consequences of their shared institutional characteristics for the electoral and non-electoral politics of welfare reform in Bismarckain social protection systems help explain why these countries, despite their widely varying political situations and economic capacities, have followed a broadly similar trajectory of adaptation (Palier, 2010b).

If overhauling established welfare systems is generally an electorally risky undertaking for governments, key features of their inherited *modus operandi* has made it particularly so for governments in Western and Central Europe. Because these systems provide guarantees of generous earnings replacement far up the wage distribution, they are relevant to and strongly supported by a large share of the electorate, including the politically engaged middle classes (Esping-Andersen, 1996). Furthermore, as entitlements are widely perceived as having been earned through the payment of contributions while in work, they benefit from some of the strong legitimacy attached to property rights in market economies. As the specific social contributions largely used to finance benefits are not traditionally understood as taxes, the systems are simultaneously less vulnerable to tax backlash. In this context, adjusting revenue sources to meet rising demands is likely to be considerably less electorally unpopular than adjusting entitlements to contain costs.

In addition to their strong electoral support, the welfare systems of these countries are also especially open to the influence of powerful organised interest groups. This is a direct result of the governance role of the social partners, which gives trade unions and employers associations an institutionalised role in decision-making processes that they can use to block changes they oppose and to inflect reforms in line with the interests of their members (Ebbinghaus, 2010). This diminishes the capacity of elected governments to implement their programmatic commitments, and gives preponderant influence over social policy development to the constituencies represented by unions and employers associations. As these actors owe their role in the management of the welfare system and the power and status it affords them to a web of interlocking features of these systems – such as their insurance character and their financing through contributions paid by employers and employees – they also have interests vested in the institutional *status quo*, and often oppose reforms that challenge the institutional order even if they have little direct impact on the immediate redistribution of the burdens and benefits of welfare provision.

These institutionally mediated political dynamics help to understand why continued system expansion was the first reaction of governments in these countries to the increasing demands that the combination of economic change and slower-moving processes such as population ageing placed on these systems from the mid-1970s onwards. Faced with the mounting cost of providing generous pensions, healthcare and unemployment benefits, alongside declining contribution revenues due notably to fast-rising unemployment, governments across Western and Central Europe did not attempt to reign in their existing social welfare commitments, as happened elsewhere, but instead increased contribution rates or simply allowed large deficits to build up in the social insurance funds. New entitlement programmes were also created, and/or eligibility conditions for existing ones relaxed, to provide passive income support to the victims of deindustralisation. In Belgium, France and – particularly after reunification in 1990 – Germany, early retirement programmes were for this reason sharply expanded, while the Netherlands saw massive increases in claimants of disability benefits in the 1980s and early 1990s.

As Palier (2010b) has pointed out, it is wrong to reduce this policy response to simple inertia, as the 'frozen welfare state' argument commonly made about Bismarckian social protection systems seems to imply. It is true, however, that the adaptive changes initially adopted allowed the systems to continue functioning according to their traditional logics even under radically changed economic conditions, and in this sense the pattern of adaptation was defensive or conservative. In the context of the Bismarckian welfare state legacy, however, continued expansion best fitted the immediate interests of political and social actors. Governments could raise social insurance revenues without fear of the electoral punishment that would follow increases in more visible forms of taxation, and by so doing avoid explicit retrenchment measures that would have been enormously unpopular and take some measures to palliate the effects of structural economic change. For the large industrial employers that dominated peak employer associations in most countries, these new or expanded social programmes offering good 'exit routes' out of the labour market were an opportunity to externalise some of the cost of internal restructuring and layoffs, while reducing the threat of bitter industrial disputes. For unions, finally, labour shedding through the welfare system helped to reduce competitive pressures on the remaining employed workforce, in principle improving both their job security and bargaining power. Reductions in labour supply thus reinforced the effects of highly restrictive rules on compulsory redundancies, which are another inherited institutional feature of many economies of Western and Central Europe.

This strategy had important second-order effects, however. In part as a result of the extremely high non-wage labour costs that employers in Western and Central European countries came to face, as well as still relatively restrictive hiring-and-firing legislation in many cases, employment growth in these economies remained comparatively sluggish even in periods of aggregate growth, with employers preferring to adopt new technology and to squeeze further productivity increases from their existing employees rather than taking on new workers, particularly in lower-skill sectors of the economy where the 'tax wedge' represented by social contributions was proportionally highest. Albeit in a somewhat less extreme form than in Southern Europe (see Chapter 18), low employment rates among young people (especially in Belgium and France) and over-55s (everywhere except Switzerland) had become defining features of the economies of Continental European countries by the 1990s. With the exception of Switzerland, in these countries female activity rates also lagged far behind those found in Denmark and Sweden and, to a lesser extent, the UK. By maintaining a large section of the population outside the labour market, policy in these countries aggravated dependency ratio problems that were already worsening as a result of demographic developments and diverted resources away from more active measures – such as childcare, employer subsidies, or training programmes – that might have been deployed to support labour force expansion. The adaptation path also posed increasing challenges for social cohesion. Unemployment rates declined much more slowly and less significantly in West and Central European countries after the recession of the early 1990s than they did in Northern Europe, and in the mid-1990s somewhere between 40 and 60 per cent of unemployed people had been out of work for more than a year in most of these countries, compared to only a quarter in Denmark or Sweden. High long-term unemployment led in turn to many people exhausting their right to insurance-based support, and to growing concerns about resulting problems of social exclusion.

Policy actors have not been blind or indifferent to these problems. Governments have faced quite immediate pressures to address structural unemployment and the problems of social cohesion that follow from it, while employers have grown increasingly critical of the burden of high labour costs, even if some have exploited the possibilities for easier plant-level restructuring that availability of generous social programmes has afforded. Furthermore, in the early 1990s the signature of the Maastricht Treaty imposed new fiscal austerity constraints on the majority of these countries, future members of the Eurozone. For all these reasons, both labour market reform and cost containment in the welfare system have become progressively more prominent in reform agendas in many Western and Central European countries.

However, many of the second-generation adaptive measures implemented have been characterised by an apparent unwillingness to restructure welfare or labour market institutions in ways that would threaten the protections enjoyed by the majority of stably employed workers. With respect to the labour market, most of these countries have thus introduced the flexibility believed necessary to encourage improved job creation through a highly selective form of deregulation, which has expanded employers' possibilities to recruit workers on fixed-term or otherwise atypical contracts while leaving the protections attached to regular employment contracts largely untouched. With respect to classic welfare entitlements, meanwhile, reforms have often tightened the application of the classic Bismarckian principle of benefits reflecting prior contributions made in employment, meaning cost containment efforts have often fallen on those with the weakest attachments to the labour market. Thus, in most countries contribution requirements for a full pension have been substantially tightened and access to unemployment insurance benefits made more difficult for those with limited or broken records of previous employment. To compensate partially the social insurance systems becoming less 'social' in this way (Palier, 2010b), many countries have, however, simultaneously introduced or expanded minimum pensions and/or general minimum income guarantees, tax-financed and paying means-tested benefits, and for working-age claimants often entailing activation requirements (Clegg, 2008).

This second generation of reforms bears the imprint of basic electoral calculation, as for governments it is considerably less risky to reform welfare and labour market institutions at the margins than it would be to attack frontally the entitlements of the majority of salaried employees. However, they also display some political dynamics that are more specific to Bismarckian welfare states. The considerable influence of the social partners in the politics of social protection reform in these countries is still visible, insofar as many changes have protected unions' core constituency of stable employed workers while simultaneously preserving some exit routes out of work for those more senior employees that would be, for employers, most costly to lay off. For the social partners together, moreover, transferring the cost of protecting certain groups away from the social insurance system altogether has helped to recast the mutually supporting Bismarckian principles of self-sufficiency and self-responsibility, preserving the contributory 'purity' of the main welfare system on which the historic governance role of the social partners depends. Likewise, reinforcing the 'equivalence principle' of a close link between benefits and contributions has offered actors keen to drive through cuts a way of doing so while simultaneously celebrating the basic logic on which the strong legitimacy of this type of welfare system rests. Here too, then, the particular patterns of reform adopted in these welfare systems has been strongly influenced by their inherited institutional characteristics.

Judging by their more impressive employment performance in the first decade of the 2000s, these reforms have had some success in partially reversing the 'welfare without work' spiral that Western and Central European countries faced in the 1980s and 1990s. Furthermore, the introduction or strengthening of basic safety nets has helped to palliate a weakness of the traditional Bismarckian model. However, alongside the fact that partial reforms can by definition only partially address the sustainability challenges that these welfare systems are facing, criticisms have also mounted as to the distributive implications of these marginal adaptations of the Bismarckian model. In many of these countries much recent employment growth has come through the expansion of the newly liberalised atypical jobs, creating an increasingly segmented labour market in which some workers enjoy stable, permanent employment while others cycle between successive temporary contracts interspersed with periods out of work. Given the continuing and even strengthened role of the contribution principle in the reformed social insurance schemes, it is, however, ever-more difficult for the latter group to build up entitlement to insurance-based protection for their temporary periods of work absence, or indeed to make the contributions they will need for a full pension in the future. In this way, recent reforms to the welfare systems of Western and Central European countries may be argued to reinforce and institutionalise a sort of social and economic dualism, between stable employed workers with good status-maintaining social protection guarantees (as well as better access to supplementary non-state provision) and precarious workers who will be forced to fall back on minimum income protection to support them in the event of life-course risks and in old age (Palier, 2010b).

While such dualistic tendencies are clearly visible in the recent transformations of social protection in Western and Central European countries, it would, however, be a mistake to reduce all contemporary reforms to this trend. There are also some recent developments that push against the traditional political and institutional dynamics of Bismarckian social protection reform and point to a more fundamental change in the basic objectives of these welfare systems. Particularly in Belgium and France, the share of general tax sources in all social protection revenues thus increased between 1990 and 2008 considerably more than could be explained by the growth of social assistance schemes alone, as governments have sought to move the funding of social insurance to a more diversified and 'employment-friendly' mix. In many countries governments have also moved to increase their control of social protection reform by significantly limiting the policy-making autonomy of the social partners in this field and, in the case of the Netherlands, excluding them from their traditional co-governance role altogether.

Partly for this reason, perhaps, securely employed 'insiders' have in reality also been less insulated from cuts than the dualisation account suggests. For example, reforms to unemployment insurance have in many countries reduced the generosity and duration of benefits for 'good contributors' and extended activation requirements to them, while recent pension changes across Western and Central Europe mean that even if current workers have complete employment biographies they will receive considerably less generous levels of income replacement on retirement than in the past. Alongside the gradual universalisation of health care, some efforts have also been made to extend other forms of basic social insurance to those with non-standard employment biographies, most notably but not uniquely in the Netherlands. Finally, many countries have invested sharply increased resources in family policies such as child care and parental leaves, which aim to facilitate female employment and in so doing challenge the male-breadwinner basis of Bismarckian welfare systems, as well as active labour market policies, thereby abandoning the traditionally compensatory approach to labour market policy. Hermerijck and Eichhorst (2010, p. 323) go so far as to argue that these welfare systems 'are in the midst of a general paradigmatic shift away from systems geared to income and status maintenance and towards more universal, but activating and employment-friendly as well as gender-neutral welfare systems'. Suggesting an alignment on Nordic approaches to social protection that would arguably question the continuing existence of distinctive welfare models (see Chapter 14), this would be less the dualisation of Bismarckian welfare than what Bleses and Seeleib-Kaiser (2004) have called its 'dual transformation', whereby the aim of protecting achieved living standards is progressively abandoned in favour of supporting individuals and families through improved service provision. At present, the somewhat contradictory developmental dynamics of the welfare systems of Western and Central European countries make it difficult to assess which of these alternative welfare futures is most probable.

Conclusion

As with an institutional model, the welfare system of Western and Central European countries has proved remarkably resilient, largely outliving the political and religious forces that supported the objectives it was designed to realise. It has helped to cement a solid collective commitment to extremely generous welfare provision in countries that are often larger and less socially and culturally homogenous than in Nordic Europe. In recent decades, however, its very resilience has come to appear problematic, as a commitment to institutional preservation in a context of social and economic change has driven reforms in directions that have been problematic both for economic performance and for social solidarity and cohesion in countries with this welfare model. While there are indications that some current reform trends are leading to the partial convergence of Bismarckian welfare systems on the less narrowly protective but more universalistic and proactive approach to social policy that has long characterised Nordic Europe, it remains to be seen whether the unpicking of the Bismarckian institutional model that these reforms require will prove compatible with the maintenance of a strong commitment to generous social protection. The welfare model of Western and Central Europe is currently at a crossroad, and the direction it takes in coming years will tell us much about the more general prospects for generous social protection in the new economic and social environment that all developed welfare states today confront.

References

Bleses, P. and Seeleib-Kaiser, M. (2004), *The Dual Transformation of the German Welfare State*. Basingstoke: Palgrave Macmillan.

Clegg, D. (2008), 'Continental drift: On unemployment policy change in Bismarckian welfare states', in B. Palier, and C. Martin (eds), *Reforming the Bismarckian Welfare Systems*. Oxford: Blackwell.

Ebbinghaus, B. (2010), 'Reforming Bismarckian corporatism: The changing role of social partnership in continental Europe', in B. Palier (ed.), *A Long Goodbye to Bismarck: The Politics of Welfare Reform in Continental Europe*. Amsterdam: Amsterdam University Press.

Esping-Andersen, G. (1990), *The Three Worlds of Welfare Capitalism*. Cambridge: Polity Press.

——(1996), 'Welfare states without work: the impasse of labor shedding and familialism in Continental European social policy', in G. Esping-Andersen (ed.), *Welfare States in Transition: National Adaptations in Global Economies*. London: Sage.

Häusermann, S. (2010), *The Politics of Welfare State Reform in Continental Europe: Modernization in Hard Times*. Cambridge: Cambridge University Press.

Hemerijck, A. and Eichhorst, W. (2010), 'Whatever happened to the Bismarckian welfare state? From labor-shedding to employment-friendly reforms', in B. Palier, (ed.), *A Long Goodbye to Bismarck: The Politics of Welfare Reform in Continental Europe*. Amsterdam: Amsterdam University Press.

Hennock, E. P. (2007), *The Origins of the Welfare State in England and Germany, 1850–1914*. Cambridge: Cambridge University Press.

Morel, N. (2007), 'From subsidiarity to "free choice": Child- and elder-care policy reform in France, Belgium, Germany and the Netherlands', in B. Palier, and C. Martin (eds), *Reforming the Bismarckian Welfare Systems*. Oxford: Blackwell.

Palier, B. (2010a), 'Ordering change: Understanding the Bismarckian reform trajectory', in B. Palier (ed.), *A Long Goodbye to Bismarck: The Politics of Welfare Reform in Continental Europe*. Amsterdam: Amsterdam University Press.

——(2010b), 'The long conservative corporatist road to welfare reform', in B. Palier (ed.), *A Long Goodbye to Bismarck: The Politics of Welfare Reform in Continental Europe*. Amsterdam: Amsterdam University Press.

Palier, B. and Martin, C. (eds) (2008), *Reforming the Bismarckian Welfare Systems*. Oxford: Blackwell.

Titmuss, R. (1974), *Social Policy: An Introduction*. London: Allen & Unwin.

van Kersbergen, K. (1995), *Social Capitalism: A Study of Christian Democracy and the Welfare State*. London: Routledge.

17

Eastern Europe[1]

Steven Saxonberg

Introduction

When the communist regimes fell a variety of hybrid types of policies developed. Not only do policies differ between countries, but also the types of policies differ within single countries, as some social policy areas might have, for example, more liberal-residualist characteristics, while other policy areas in the same country might have more conservative-Bismarckian aspects. For example, in the area of childcare, most of the post-communist countries provide nearly universal daycare coverage for children three to five years old, while implementing three-year parental leave along the conservative model, which encourages mothers to leave the labour market for long periods. The development of post-communist social policies has been influenced mainly by a combination of path dependency (often with universalist and conservative elements), a discourse dominated by market-liberal hegemonic tendencies, and the desire of large portions of the population to have relatively generous welfare policies. The one area where international organizations seem to have played a major role is pension reforms.

Path dependency makes its impact from two stages. First there are the developments from the pre-communist era, which include the policy legacies as well as the actual institutional arrangements. In most cases the pre-communist policies, especially in countries of the former Austro-Hungarian Empire, had a strong Bismarckian influence, although policy areas that were not highly prioritized were more residualist. In addition, countries with weaker state capacities also had less generous welfare policies than their neighbours. Even countries that had not been part of the Austro-Hungarian Empire, such as Romania and Bulgaria, still looked to the Bismarckian model for inspiration.

When the communists came to power in Central and Eastern Europe in 1948, they generally introduced more universalistic policies in the beginning. However, they did not simply copy the Soviet Union, as they had to build upon pre-existing institutions. In addition, their universalism differed in many ways from the Scandinavian social democratic welfare states. For example, even if most policies did not have means testing based on incomes, policies often gave discretionary powers to local Party and state officials, who could use political criteria in making decisions. Some Bismarckian traditions also continued, such as the idea of giving different benefits based on one's profession, although the professions that were given priority changed somewhat under communist rule. Another conservative policy common among the communist-led regimes was the introduction of flat-rate benefits. Even though such policies do not correspond to the Bismarckian notion of insurance-based benefits tied to different professional groups, they are 'conservative' in the sense of leading to moderate rates of decommodification – they pay more than residualist, liberal, means tested programmes, but much less than the social democratic types of generous, decommodifying, insurance-based benefits that replace most of one's former income. They are also conservative in the sense that when flat-rate policies are applied to the carrying sector (parental leave, caring for the sick and elderly), flat-rate benefits encourage women to do the caring rather than men, since given the fact that men most often have higher incomes than the woman in the family, men are likely to avoid missing work to care for family on the grounds that the loss of family income would be too high.

During the 1960s the communist regimes generally started to modify their policies once they gave up their ideas of radically transforming society. Their reforms from this era onward tended to go in a more conservative direction, although sometimes also in a liberal-residualist direction (by introducing more means-tested programmes). In general the communist regimes also backed down from their original goals of emancipating women and instead started to perceive women more as mothers and less as workers, thus shaping policies in a manner that gave them greater responsibility for caring for family members (including longer maternity leave, measures to induce them to take care of sick children, parents, and spouses, etc.). The policies that they chose were often influenced by policy legacies dating back to pre-communist times.

When the communist regimes lost power, the new governments had to focus first on establishing a safety net and getting the labour market to function. These policies were formulated rather quickly and given top priority. Policy makers were highly influenced by the market-liberal discourse that was become rather hegemonic in the West, but the policies were generally much more pragmatic than traditional market-liberal policies and to some extent based on the idea of 'divide and pacify' (Vanhuysse, 2006), in which the weaker social groups were divided by policies so that they would not be able to unite around their interests and protest against market reforms. In the areas with longer social policy traditions, the post-communist regimes were bound by higher degrees of path dependency as there were greater entrenched interests as well as stronger policy legacies. The main exception eventually was pension reform, as international organizations had great influence there in promoting the three-level model. Even though many of the policies developed in the early post-communist period were much more generous than traditional residualist policies, benefit levels often were not indexed to keep up with inflation. This brought about a trend toward 'liberalism by decay' (Saxonberg and Sirovátka, 2009b).

This chapter now proceeds by examining the pre-communist, the communist, and the post-communist developments of social policy in Eastern Europe.

Pre-communist policies: Bismarckian with liberal elements

The Eastern European countries were highly influenced by the Bismarckian model of social welfare policies, especially those countries that had been a part of the Austro-Hungarian Empire. These policies included heavy reliance on profession-based social insurance schemes. In addition, the male-breadwinner model was very strong, as women were expected to be full-time carers. The basis for this in the Austro-Hungarian Empire was the General Civic Law (in Czech: Obecný občanský zákoníkč. 946/1811) from the year 1811, which stated that 'above all, the father is obliged to care for livelihood of children until they are able to care for themselves. The mother shall attend to her children's physical condition and health' (Havelková, 2009, p. 185).

Already during the late 1800s, what later became the Czech Republic, Hungary, and Slovakia introduced sickness insurances. The Czech Republic introduced insurances for injuries in 1887, while Slovakia and Hungary did so in 1907. Poland, as a partitioned country, did not introduce such reforms until shortly after the country was united (sickness in 1920 and injuries in 1924) (Szikra and Tomka 2009, p. 19). As is usual in Bismarckian systems, some groups were favoured over others. Thus, since 1889 miners and civil servants received their own separate mandatory social protection programmes. Salaried employees also had additional supplementary pension plans (Inglot 2008, p. 63). During the First Republic, when the Czech lands and Slovakia united to form Czechoslovakia, this Bismarckian tradition continued. According to Inglot (2008, p. 67), 'white collar employees and select industrial workers maintained and in some cases even increased their privileged positions'. Miners and steelworkers managed to keep their special separate pensions even when the government tried to unite them all under the General Pension Institute in Prague. Meanwhile, a growing number of salaried employees also succeeded in getting their funds to continue to be managed separately.

Neighbouring Poland also basically followed the Bismarckian model, but it was a less generous version. The country had 'meagre resources' (Inglot, 2008, p. 82) during the interwar period which made it more difficult to build up welfare institutions. Only some select professions were covered by the social insurances and the benefit levels remained comparatively low even during communist rule (Inglot, 2008, p. 83).

Similar to Czechoslovakia, Hungary has Bismarckian roots for its social policies going back to the Austro-Hungarian Empire. Since it had greater political autonomy than the other territories of the empire, it could shape its social policies more according to the wishes of the national elite. In 1891 it introduced the law on Mandatory Sickness Insurance for Workers, in 1907 the law on Work Injury Insurance, and in 1912 law on Pensions and Family Benefits for Civil Servants. These social insurances were originally based on self-governing territorial funds based on the German model, as well as on unions, companies, the miners' guild, and other units (Inglot, 2008, p. 97).

Even the Baltic states, which had gained independence during the interwar years, basically followed Bismarckian policies of occupationally based social insurances (Aidukaite, 2009, pp. 99–100). One might imagine that the poorer and less industrialized countries, such as Romania and Bulgaria would follow different types of social policies, since the Bismarckian model was originally developed to coopt the working-class so that it would not support socialist movements. Given the lack of workers, this threat was not anywhere as great in Romania and Bulgaria. However, a strong urban-agricultural divide still existed, even if the urban elite did not include many people from the working class. The most powerful urban political and economic elites pushed for Bismarckian insurance principles (Cerami and Stanescu, 2009, p. 114). Thus, both countries introduced Bismarckian types of social insurance programs. In Romania the first old-age benefits were established in 1912, while in Bulgaria they were established in 1924 (Cerami and Stanescu, 2009, p. 112). Health and sickness insurance also followed Bismarckian principles (being established in Romania in 1912 and in Bulgaria in 1918).

Despite these clear Bismarckian trends, as most of the countries were newly formed they did not have the time or resources to develop social insurances for all areas of social support. For example, in Czechoslovakia no economic support was available for those who had to take care of sick or elderly family members. If family members were not available and the sick and elderly were able to claim that they had a 'non-functioning family' then they could only turn to stigmatizing 'poor care', which was means tested and included being forced to live in poor asylums, infirmary asylums, or homes for seniors. This is an example of liberal, residual types of means testing policies that existed in social-policy areas that were not well developed. Regardless of whether policies were more liberal or more conservative, they clearly favoured the male-breadwinner model and gave women the prime responsibility for caring (Kotous et al., 2003; Matoušek, 2007).

Communist rule

When communist parties came to power throughout Eastern and Central Eastern Europe they proclaimed themselves to be revolutionaries who wanted to make a sharp break with the past. Even though it is true that they did make important changes in social policies, such as sharply increasing support to daycare and making social benefits more universally available, they still did not completely break from the Bismarckian model. Moreover, in Central Eastern Europe, in the post-Stalinist thaw, the regimes often took steps back in a more conservative, Bismarckian direction. As Cook (2007, p. 9) observes, 'The old communist welfare state combined a dominant universalism (i.e. broad social security coverage and access to basic social services) with stratified provision that better fits the conservative model'. Writing about the first communist-ruled regime, the Soviet Union, Cook (2007, p. 38) adds that the communist welfare system

> had strong conservative features. Most social goods and services were distributed through restricted-access networks that were vertically subdivided (i.e. closed stores and tiers of privilege). There was a great deal of administrative discretion in the awarding of benefits. Production managers, for example, systematically manipulated access to divide and stratify workers. The system privileged political, state, security, and military elites as well as some categories of industrial workers.

Similarly, for Central Eastern Europe Inglot (2008, p. 28) observes that the Stalinist model 'reinforced the preexisting hierarchical structure of social insurance benefits, conferring substantial privileges on certain categories of employees while keeping payments to other groups (women, for example) very low or denying social insurance to some occupations altogether (for example, to private farmers, the self-employed, clergy, political "enemies of the state," etc.)'.

Thus, for example, in Czechoslovakia, the regime established three different pension levels depending on one's profession, with miners getting the highest pensions, followed by workers in chemistry and heavy industry, with the remaining workers receiving the lowest pensions (Matějček, 1973). In Poland in 1954 two occupational categories were created, with most workers in heavy industry belonging to the privileged group (including miners), as did state officials, military, and the police. Much lower benefits were offered to those outside of manufacturing, such as trade, transport, and services (Inglot, 2008, p. 153).

Another type of conservative benefit which the communist regimes often used was the flat-rate benefit. On the one hand this could be seen as universal and social democratic, since everyone receives it, on the other hand such policies are commonly used by the conservative, continental West European welfare states as a type of paternalist policy that gives a moderate level of decommodification (Esping-Andersen, 1990), but pays much lower levels of benefits than the more generous Nordic social democratic welfare states, based upon the income-replacement principle. In addition, in the area of caring, flat-rate benefits re-enforce separate gender roles as only women are likely to utilize these benefits, given the fact that in most families the men have higher incomes than women and thus have more to lose economically by leaving paid work for these benefits.

In Czechoslovakia the communist regime introduced several types of flat-rate benefits in the 1960s. One was the 'helplessness pension' in 1964, which paid a lump-sum benefit (ÚRO, 1989, p. 12; Rendlová, 1982). Another example was the extended maternity leave, which the regime introduced to induce mothers to stay at home for longer periods after their initial maternity leave ended. Hungary also introduced a flat-rate extended maternity leave in the 1960s and in both countries these benefits were eventually paid for up to three years (Saxonberg and

Sirovátka, 2006). In 1985, however, the Hungarian regime also introduced a more generous two-year leave based on the income replacement principle (paying 75 per cent of the previous salary) (Haney, 2002, p. 178). Yet, even this policy had a conservative bent, because in contrast to the Nordic parental leave that tries to induce fathers to share in the parenting, this leave was not open for men until after the communists lost power.

To some extent the communist rulers in the 1960s consciously decided to go back to pre-communist, interwar policy legacies in order to move away from the Stalinist model. Inglot (2009, p. 84) notes for Poland that the Polish welfare doctrine that emerged had its roots in the Great Depression and favored 'a paternalistic welfare state, built on the imperial Bismarckian foundations'. The communists tried in the 1960s to 'reinvent their own national welfare doctrine' by bringing about a 'partial return to a conservative Bismarckian model' and then in the 1970s that tried to develop more universalistic elements. 'Still, the basic tenets of the conservative model of social protection survived almost intact' (2009, p. 85). The Polish reform communists still kept social privileges and bonuses for the groups such as miners, steelworkers, and security apparatus that were favoured under communism and private farmers who are favored now.

In fact, in the original Stalinist model no room existed for social policy as a special field, as the command economy was to solve all the social problems. Thus, the communists eliminated the ministries of social welfare or social caring. As Ferge (1979, p. 62) put it:

> This vision was based on a simplified Marxist interpretation of historical evolution, which held that social development inevitably followed change in economic relations, and which saw only one element of economic relations: property. Hence economic policy and planning did not need to be complemented by societal policy or social planning.

In Czechoslovakia, the government dissolved the Ministry of Social Care in 1951 (Schiller, 1971). In Poland, the communist regime tried to eliminate the central social insurance institution in the mid-1950s, but the communist-controlled unions demanded their reinstatement since they could guarantee stability in benefit payments (Inglot, 2009, p. 85). However, as part of the later restorationist policies, all countries reintroduced ministries of welfare, but they were usually reconstructed as part of the Ministry of Labour. For example, in 1968 the Czechoslovak government introduced a Federal Ministry of Labour and Social Affairs with two branch ministries in Prague and Bratislava. Each republic-level ministry had vice ministers in charge of pensions and family policy respectively (Inglot, 2008, p. 142).

For the Romanian and Bulgarian cases, Cerami and Stanescu (2009, p. 115) note that pension, healthcare, and sickness insurances were not extended to the rural populations until the late 1960s and even then at a lower level of quality. 'Benefits continued to be granted according to the occupational status of citizens, but since the entire population was employed in the central planned economy and wage differences were practically non-existent, the Bismarck system of social insurance still in place succeeded in achieving universal aspirations'.

The post-communist (non)-transformation

Many authors have claimed that the collapse of the communist regimes in Central Eastern Europe in 1989 (and 1991 in the Soviet Union) represented a 'critical juncture' in which governments could introduce new policies that led to path departure (i.e. Vanhuysse, 2009, p. 55). The former Polish Finance Minister Balcerowicz (1995) called the collapse of communism a 'window of opportunity' for carrying out 'extraordinary politics'. While such assessments might have been true for some times of economic policies, such as privatization and price liberalization, it did not turn out to be so true for most social policies.

Offe (1994) notes that during the first stage of post-communist social policy development, the new democratic governments had to concentrate on the 'early stage of emergency measures', in which policy makers had to quickly introduce measures creating some kind of social safety net and unemployment insurances, as many people would surely lose their jobs, while other weak groups (such as pensioners) would have trouble getting by on their incomes. In this area, governments were free to develop policies as they had no institutional legacies to build upon. In other areas, such as pensions, healthcare, and family care, the governments were much more bounded by previously chosen paths, although in the case of pensions, eventually internal organizations were able to pressure governments into making reforms.

Thus, in most areas, Cerami (2009, p. 46) is more correct in claiming that incremental transformative change took place after 1989 rather than path divergence at a critic juncture. In his words, 'The institutional incoherence that resulted from central planning opened up space to the cultivation of a new market-oriented social policy logic in which dormant latent institutions and policies have been both rediscovered and reactivated. This reactivation concerned the re-enforcement of Bismarckian characteristics already present during communism'. Besides the usual problems of path divergence, such as the entrenched interests of bureaucracies and increased costs associated with going against these bureaucracies, other problems existed such as the lack of public support for radical welfare reforms and the lack of knowledge of how to reshape social policies. As Inglot (2008, p. 31) observes:

> the new political elites lacked necessary knowledge and expertise in social policy, which made them less prone to experimentation and more dependent on the older cohort of experts and bureaucrats. In addition, government experts quickly realized that a radical overhaul of the welfare state was impossible not only due to institutional legacies, but also because of the deeply engrained and enduring patterns of policy making. These 'policy legacies' offered workable and well-tested solutions to lingering social policy problems.

When it comes to welfare attitudes, even if citizens often voted for right-wing parties because they saw it as a guarantee to prevent the communists from coming back to power (including reformed post-communist parties that were now wearing social democratic clothing), they were still used to having the state being responsible for the welfare of its citizens. Thus, support for generous welfare policies remained high in the post-communist countries (Renwick and Tóka, 1998; Saxonberg 2005; 2007). Support for welfare policies was so high that Andreß and Thorsten (2001) hypothesized a fourth world of welfare was arising in the post-communist countries. In the Czech Republic, even supporters of the market-liberal Thatcherist Prime Minister Václav Klaus and his Civic Democratic Party, were generally more supportive of generous welfare policies than the average Swede, despite the fact that Sweden is generally considered to have one of the most generous welfare policies in the world (Saxonberg, 2003). So even though the post-communist political elite was swept away from the neo-liberal hegemonic discourse that had been encouraging West European countries to privatize and cut back on welfare spending, citizens of the post-communist countries did not support welfare retrenchment.

Even if no strong relationship existed between welfare attitudes and voting (Saxonberg, 2005; 2007), Vanhuysse (2006) argues that the post-communist governments were afraid that radical cut-backs in social programmes could lead to waves of protests, which could threaten the stability of the new democracies. Consequently, they devised a policy of 'divide and pacify', in which they pacified the weakest groups by dividing them and giving some of them relatively generous benefits. This strategy of protest avoidance (Vanhuysse 2009, p. 55) might not win votes, but it at least prevents protests from threatening the stability of the new democratic regimes.

Vanhuysse (2006, p. 53) writes: 'Divide and pacify policies split up a fairly homogenous population of workers into three different groups with a distinct work-welfare status. In addition to the two prior work-welfare categories, working workers and normal pensioner, two new ones are created: unemployed workers, and early pensioners.' By dividing the groups they became weaker and by giving some of them relatively good benefits they also become pacified. For example, the unemployed tend to leave their unions as do the retired, which makes the unions weaker (Vanhuysse, 2006, p. 55).

In addition to encouraging early retirement, the post-communist governments also made it easier to receive disability pensions. Thus, from 1989 to 1996 the number of disability pensioners increased by 11 per cent in the Czech Republic, 22 per cent in Poland and 49 per cent in Hungary (Vanhuysse, 2006, p. 88). Cerami and Stanescu (2009, p. 118) note that the number of people retiring early in Romania grew from 316,800 in 1989 to over 3 million in 1995 and also grew 'rapidly' in Bulgaria. Benefit levels also favoured pensioners over the unemployed, thus creating a generation gap between the privileged elderly and the less privileged younger workers, who were too young to go into early retirement. In addition, early retirement schemes and increases in disability pensions meant that the younger working generation had to pay more for older generations, as fewer working people were supporting more retired people.

However, not all countries followed this strategy. In the Czech Republic, despite his market-liberal ideology, Klaus generally tried to keep unemployment levels low by preventing insolvent firms from going bankrupt rather than by inducing people to leave the labour market (Saxonberg, 2003; Sirovátka and Rákoczyová, 2009; Vanhuysse, 2006). He did so by hesitating to privatize the banks, so that state-owned banks could keep on subsidizing inefficient firms rather than allowing them to go bankrupt. When the banks were eventually privatized and legislation was passed that made bankruptcies easier, the once low Czech unemployment rates increased to the average level of the region. Sirovátka and Rákoczyová (2009, p. 206) thus conclude that the country avoided unemployment through its anti-bankruptcy policy rather than active labour market policies. During 2004–6 active labour market policies amounted to only 0.12–0.14 per cent of gross domestic product (GDP) compared to 0.89 per cent in Finland, 1.36 per cent in Sweden, and 0.28 per cent in post-communist Hungary.

Despite the dominance of market-liberal ideology during the 1990s, governments still hesitated to make any radical liberal welfare reforms. For example, in Hungary, when the post-communist Socialist Party decided to make the parental leave means tested, widespread protests broke out, as women cried 'we are still mothers' (Haney, 1997). Even though the Socialists did not back down, they lost the next elections, the new conservative government re-installed parental leave based on the income replacement principle (but lowered it from 75 per cent to 70 per cent) and later Socialist governments did not dare tamper with it again (Saxonberg and Sirovátka, 2006).

Rather than directly assault the welfare state, post-communist governments have tended to follow a strategy of 'neo-liberalism by decay' (Saxonberg and Sirovátka, 2009b). This entails letting once generous policies gradually become more residualist by such methods as not indexing benefits to keep up with inflation or by progressively lowering benefit levels. Vanhuysse (2006, p. 74ff) shows that between December 1991 and December 1995, in Hungary the coverage rate for unemployment benefits decreased from 80 to 40 per cent of the unemployed, in Poland from 75 to 55 per cent of the unemployed and in the Czech Republic from 72 to 48 per cent. The percentage that one receives during the first three months of unemployment decreased in this period from 75 to 58 per cent in Hungary, from 70 to 45 per cent in Poland and 65 to 60 per cent in the Czech Republic. Although the decrease was rather small in the Czech Republic, for those unemployed between three months and one year, the coverage rate decreased from 58 to 30 per cent.

Eventually, economic pressures forced the post-communist regimes to abandon somewhat their divide and pacify strategy, as it became increasingly untenable to increase pension payments while decreasing the labour force that was paying for the pensions. Thus, in this area the East and Central European governments gave in to international pressure and introduced reforms to the pension system. As Orenstein (2009, p. 130) points out, the pension reforms came about shortly after the World Bank published *Averting the Old-Age Crisis* in 1994, which recommended introducing a three-tier pension system with a state pension, a mandatory private pension (where employees can choose among competing funds) and a voluntary supplementary pension. The World Bank actively pushed for this reform by making loans to countries that carried out this reform. The World Bank made 93 loans to 25 countries in Europe and Central Asia between 1984 and 2004 for $1.6 billion that had a 'pension component' Orenstein (2009, p. 135). He further notes that 'Transnational actors have normally formed coalitions with at least one major domestic partner in each country, usually a Minister of Labour or Minister of Finance' Orenstein (2009, p. 138).

When it comes to family policies, to a large extent the post-communist countries continued the policies from the communist era. The Czech Republic, Slovakia, Hungary, and Poland all basically have the same kinds of parental leave schemes as under communist rule, based on a combination of an insurance-based maternity leave and a less generous parental leave, although some changes were made in child allowances, so for example, they became means tested in the Czech Republic (Saxonberg and Sirovátka, 2006).

Poland has a more residualist system with a shorter maternity leave of four months and means tested parental leave benefits for the remaining period until a child reaches the age of three. In Slovakia, the country continues to have a six-month maternity leave followed by a flat-rate benefit until the child reaches three. As already noted, Hungary has also continued to have an insurance-based parental leave (but it has been slightly lowered). This leave continues to be for two years, but a three-year flat-rate leave has also continued to exist since the 1960s. The Czech Republic is a slight exception in that it added a fourth year of possible parental leave and then later introduced a three-track system that pays more per month if one takes a two-year leave than a three year leave, and the least per month if one takes a four-year leave (but the total payment is about the same; Saxonberg and Sirovátka 2009a). However, all four countries succumbed to European Union (EU) pressure and opened up the leave benefits for fathers.

In the area of childcare, access to kindergartens for pre-school children over three remains also around the same as under the communist era at nearly 90 per cent for the Czech Republic, Hungary, and Slovakia, while Polish rates continue to be only around half that amount (Saxonberg and Sirovátka 2006). The one really important change is that most of the nurseries for children under three have been closed down in the Czech Republic, Poland, and Slovakia, although Hungary has managed to keep attendance rates only a few percentage points lower than in 1989. This has made it much more difficult for women to balance work and family life, as they are pressured into leaving the labour force for three years when they have a child, given the lack of affordable childcare and the fact that that the parental leave schemes do not encourage fathers to share in the parental leave time.

Nevertheless, despite these changes that reinforce traditional gender roles in which women are the sole carers, it should be emphasized that the trend toward 'refamilialization' (Hantrais, 2004) started already in the 1960s, when the communist regimes introduced an extended maternity leave and thereby gave the family greater responsibility for raising children. This trend toward refamilialization took place in other spheres as well. For example, the Czechoslovak government introduced legislation in 1975 that paid flat-rate benefits for people who take care of close family members (such as parents, children, grandparents, parent-in-laws, or siblings) (Act No. 121/1975 and Decree of the Federal Ministry of Labour and Social Affairs No. 128/1975 Coll.). Unlike the extended maternity leaves, these caring leaves were open to men as well, but the flat-rate benefit was too low to encourage men to utilize this possibility.

Russia provides an interesting exception, to some extent, to the other cases, as the first post-commuist government was not as restricted by institutional restraints as in other countries. Cook (2007, p. 55) observes that after winning the June 1991 presidential election, Boris Yelstin 'was granted extensive decree powers by the holdover legislature, the Supreme Soviet'. The legislature did not have democratic legitimacy and except for Communist Party members, few had clear partisan affiliations (Cook, 2007, p. 58). During this period Yelstin tried to go further in introducing residualist policies than in the other post-communist countries.

However, this 'window of opportunity' soon faded once Russia had its first democratic elections to the Duma in 1993. After these elections, an anti-reformist majority emerged in parliament that now had democratic legitimacy Cook (2007, p. 100).

In addition to hardline opposition of liberal reforms coming from communists, xenophobic radical rightist parties, etc., Cook (2007, p. 121ff) notes that a group of moderate reformers also emerged comprising of the women's party and Yabloko. The women's party cooperated with women from all the other parties and had a strong sense of accountability that the pro-government parties did not have, as they were directly tied to their voters. After the December 1995 election, anti-reformist leftist parties dominated the Duma, as the communists became the single largest party. Meanwhile, the women's party failed to return to parliament (Cook, 2007, p. 122).

Unable to directly implement market liberal reforms, Yelstin resorted to a neo-liberalism-by-decay strategy similar to those in Central Eastern Europe. Thus, 'Retrenchment without restructuring meant that entitlements, institutions, and social-sector salaries were progressively defunded' (Cook, 2007, p. 136). Thus, from 1993 to 1999 the minimum wage declined from 39 per cent of the subsistence level to 10 per cent, while the monthly benefit per child fell from 19 to 7 per cent, the minimum old age pension fell from 63 to 42 per cent and the maximum from 138 to 70 per cent (Cook, 2007, p. 137). When Putin came to power and succeeded in establishing a more authoritarian regime, he was able to implement much more far-reaching market-liberal reforms, as anti-reform parties no longer had much influence over the Duma.

Interestingly, during the period in which Yelstin was able to rule by degree and generally pursued a market-liberal agenda, his team of reformers never seriously contemplated introducing an American-style private healthcare system. Gaidar, who was in charge of the economic reforms, wanted to accelerate laws on medical insurance to help finance healthcare, but he 'favoured maintaining the public health system' (Cook, 2007, p. 62). Instead, the government opted for the creation of Compulsory Medical Insurance Funds and Health Insurance Organizations. The funds would collect and manage payroll-based employer contributions for those with jobs and from municipal budgets for those without jobs. The Funds would contract with insurers, who would purchase medical services (Cook, 2007, p. 77ff). Even though the reforms eventually failed due to opposition from the municipalities, it is interesting that they tried to introduce a system that had much more in common with Germany's conservative model than American free-market liberalism. In fact, this basically holds true of all the post-communist governments. Even the Thatcherist Klaus introduced a healthcare reform in the Czech Republic that comes close to the German model with mandatory health insurance, a dominating public fund, the possibility of choosing private alternative insurance funds and a continued dominance of public hospitals over private ones (Saxonberg and Sirovátka, 2009b).

The Baltic countries are the most market-liberal in the region. As Aidukaite (2009, p. 96) notes, the Baltic countries have had the highest growth rates in the region, but they still spend much less on social protection compared with either the West EU countries or the other post-communist countries. They also have the highest relative poverty rates, with Lithuania being the highest at 29 per cent. It is also more difficult for them to raise taxes, as their largest shadow economies are among the greatest in Europe. It amounts to 39 per cent of GDP in Latvia, 38 per cent in Estonia and 30 per cent in Lithuania. Only Romania is higher, at 51 per cent. Nevertheless, they still have a mixed system that combines a mixture of basic (flat-rate benefits based on contributions or citizenship) and corporatist (with eligibility based on labour force participation and earnings-related benefits) security (Aidukaite, 2009: 100). The health sector is also more market-liberal than in neighbouring countries, but still has a large public component, making it a mixture of liberal and conservative, as citizens can either use public healthcare services financed through the sickness fund (based on obligatory healthcare insurance) or visit private healthcare clinics or hospitals that have no agreements with the sickness funds. In the latter case patients must pay the full amount (Aidukaite, 2009, p. 100ff).

These examples show that although the exact welfare mix differs from place to place, the post-communist countries all seem to have developed hybrid models that combine conservative-Bismarckian legacies from the pre-communist era with communist-era policies (which combined certain aspects of conservatism, liberalism, and universalism) and tendencies toward neo-liberal residualist reforms. Despite great differences in some policy areas, all the countries discussed here have adopted healthcare policies that come closer to the German healthcare model than the American liberal one; they have also maintained family policies that largely encourage separate gender roles (although the Hungarian model gives greater encouragement for fathers to share in the parental leave, since they are insurance-based); and they have all allowed benefit levels to decay and become more residualist over time.

Conclusion

Even though the welfare mixes have moved in an increasingly residualist direction, the differences are still too great among countries to expect some kind of convergence, except in some selected areas, such as pensions, as most countries have basically followed the World Bank strategy for pension reform. To a large extent, path dependency is still rather strong and the differences that existed between the countries during communist rule remain today. It is questionable, however, how sustainable these welfare mixes are. For example, in the area of family policy, even normally market-liberal international organizations, such as the World Bank, are starting to criticize the post-communist countries for not investing more in human capital by making childcare more readily available for children under three. These policies have made it increasingly difficult for women to balance work and life responsibilities and have consequently led to rapid declines in fertility rates. These low fertility rates in turn threaten the pension system and other welfare areas, such as healthcare, as the ageing population means that a decreasing number of young workers has to support an increasing number of elderly, who have greater healthcare needs the older they become.

In general the lack of support for the public sector is causing grave problems, so the lack of support for child care is no exception. For example, it is becoming increasingly common for doctors to go on strike throughout the region as salaries for doctors have continued to deteriorate or stagnate, leading many doctors to quit their jobs or search for jobs in Western Europe. Meanwhile, hospitals also suffer from a lack of investment in facilities. Thus, it is likely that the healthcare sector will soon face a crisis if governments in the region do not reverse their free-market, anti-public sector trend and instead start to invest more in public services such as healthcare and education.

Note

1 The research for this article was financed by a grant from the Czech Grant Agency (GAP404/10/1586).

References

Aidukaite, J. (2009), 'The Transformation of Welfare Systems in the Baltic States: Estonia, Latvia and Lithuania,' in A. Cerami and P. Vanhuysee (eds), *Post-Communist Welfare Pathways: Theorizing Social Policy Transformations in Central and Eastern Europe*, pp. 96–111. Basingstoke: Palgrave.

Andreß, H.-J. and Heien, T. (2001), Four Worlds of Welfare State Atttitudes? A Comparison of Germany, Norway, and the United States. *European Sociological Review*, Vol. 17, no. 4, pp. 337–56.

Balcerowicz, L. (1995), *Socialism, Capitalism, Transformation*. Budapest: CEU Press.

Cerami, A. (2009), 'Mechanisms of Institutional Change in Central and Eastern European Welfare State Restructuring,' in A. Cerami and P. Vanhuysee (eds), *Post-Communist Welfare Pathways: Theorizing Social Policy Transformations in Central and Eastern Europe*, pp. 35–52. Basingstoke: Palgrave.

Cerami, A. and Stanescu, S. (2009), 'Welfare State Transformations in Bulgaria and Romania,' in A. Cerami and P. Vanhuysee (eds), *Post-Communist Welfare Pathways: Theorizing Social Policy Transformations in Central and Eastern Europe*, pp. 112–28. Basingstoke: Palgrave.

Cook, L. J. (2007), *Postcommunist Welfare States: Reform Politics in Russia and Eastern Europe*. Ithaca, NY: Cornell University Press.

Esping-Andersen, G. (1990), *The Three Worlds of Welfare Capitalism*. Oxford: Oxford University Press.

Ferge, Z. (1979), *A Society in the Making: Hungarian Social and Societal Policy 1945–75*. White Plains: M.E. Sharpe.

Haney, L. (1997), But We Are Still Mothers: Gender and the Construction of Need in Post-Socialist Hungary. *Social Politics*, vol. 4, no. 2, pp. 208–44.

Hantrais, L. (2004), *Family Policy Matters*. Bristol: Policy Press.

Havelková, B. (2009), 'Genderová rovnost v období socialismu', in M. Bobek, P. Molek, V. Šimíček, (eds), *Komunistické právo v Československu. Kapitoly z dějin bezpráví*. Brno: Mezinárodní politologický ústav, Masarykova univerzita.

Inglot, T. (2008), *Welfare States in East Central Europe, 1919–2004*. Cambridge: Cambridge University Press.

——(2009), 'Czech Republic, Hungary, Poland and Slovakia: Adaptation and Reform of the Post-Communist "Emergency Welfare States"', in A. Cerami and P. Vanhuysee (eds), *Post-Communist Welfare Pathways: Theorizing Social Policy Transformations in Central and Eastern Europe*, pp. 73–95. Basingstoke: Palgrave.

Kotous, J., Munková, G. and Peřina, P. (2003), *Úvod do sociální politiky*. Praha: PF UK – nakladatelství Vodnář.

Matějček, J. (1973), *Sociální zabezpečení v ČSSR*. Praha: Orbis.

Matoušek, O. (2007), *Sociální služby*. Praha: Portál.

Offe, C. (1994), *Der Tunnel am Ende des Lichts: Erkundungen der politischen Transformation im Neuen Osten*. Frankfukrt: Campus Verlag.

Orenstein, M. A. (2009), 'Transnational Actors in Central and East European Pension Reforms,' in A. Cerami and P. Vanhuysee (eds), *Post-Communist Welfare Pathways: Theorizing Social Policy Transformations in Central and Eastern Europe*, pp. 129–47. Basingstoke: Palgrave.

Renwick, A. and Tóka, G. (1998), 'East Meets West,' in R. Jowell et al. (eds), *International Social Attitudes: The 15th British Social Attitudes Report*, pp. 149–71. Aldershot: Dartmouth.

Saxonberg, S. (2003). *The Czech Republic before the New Millennium: Politics, Parties and Gender*. New York, Boulder, CO: Columbia University Press, East European Monographs.

——(2005), 'Transition Matters: Bringing Welfare Attitudes into the Debate,' *European Societies*, vol 7. no. 2, 2005, pp. 287–319.

——(2007), 'Post-Communist Welfare Attitudes: Was Czech Exceptionalism a Myth?' *East European Quarterly*, vol. 41, no. 1, 2007, pp. 81–115.

Saxonberg, S. and Sirovátka, T. (2006), 'Failing Family Policy in Post-Communist Central Europe'. *Journal of Comparative Policy Analysis*, Vol. 8 (2), pp. 185–202.

——(2009a), 'Czech Family Policy: Refamilialization in the Face of Contradictory Public Attitudes' *Journal of Societal and Social Policy*, vol. 7, no. 3, pp. 95–106.

——(2009b), Neo-Liberalism by Decay? The Evolution of the Czech Welfare State. *Social Policy & Administration* vol. 43, no. 2, pp. 186–203.

Saxonberg, S. and Szelewa, D. (2007), The Continuing Legacy of the Communist Legacy. *Social Politics: International Studies in Gender, State & Society* 14 (3), pp. 351–79.

Schiller, M. et al. (1971), *Péče o děti v ČSSR*. Prague: Státní pedagogické nakladatelství.

Sirovátka, T. and Rákoczyová, M. (2009), 'The Impact of the EU Social Inclusion Strategy: the Czech Case,' in A. Cerami and P. Vanhuysee (eds), *Post-Communist Welfare Pathways: Theorizing Social Policy Transformations in Central and Eastern Europe*, pp. 199–216. Basingstoke: Palgrave.

Streeck, W. and Thelen, K. (eds) (2005), *Beyond Continuity: Institutional Change in Advanced Political Economies*. Oxford: Oxford University Press.

Szikra, D. and Béla, T. (2009), 'Social Policy in East Central Europe: Major Trends in the Twentieth Century,' in A. Cerami and P. Vanhuysee (eds), *Post-Communist Welfare Pathways: Theorizing Social Policy Transformations in Central and Eastern Europe*, pp. 17–34. Basingstoke: Palgrave.

Vanhuysse, P. (2006), *Divide and Pacify*. Budapest: Central European University Press.

——(2009), 'Power Order, and the Politics of Social Policy in Central and Eastern Europe', in A. Cerami and P. Vanhuysee (eds), *Post-Communist Welfare Pathways: Theorizing Social Policy Transformations in Central and Eastern Europe*, pp. 53–72. Basingstoke: Palgrave.

18

Southern Europe

Maria Petmesidou

Introduction

Late industrialization, a record of authoritarian regimes (and/or political instability) until late in the post-war period, and a configuration of rent-seeking statist-clientelistic practices (of varying prevalence across the region) are among the main features of South European (SE) countries that, to one degree or another, account for their being laggards in welfare state formation. An upward trend of social expenditure is manifest since the early 1980s through to the turn of the century, accompanied by landmark reforms (e.g. establishment of national health systems, devolution of healthcare, and social welfare functions to regional entities in the case of Spain and Italy). Hence SE welfare states can no more be considered rudimentary.

In light of the three welfare state regimes put forward by Esping-Andersen (1990), SE welfare arrangements starkly manifest a hybrid form. First, there is a core element concerning income transfers (primarily pensions) developed on an occupational basis according to the Bismarckian model. Traditionally highly fragmented, social insurance systems have undergone significant changes in the direction of levelling out benefits and introducing occupational pensions and private insurance. Secondly, in the late 1970s to the early 1980s, a social-democratic element was introduced in healthcare indicating a significant path shift that was accomplished with varying success in each country. Thirdly, social care services and social assistance remain a less-developed element of social protection. Meagre provision, funded mostly through taxation, has traditionally been based on means testing, indicating a liberal orientation. In parallel, a strong variation as to the role of non-governmental organizations (NGOs) (including religious organizations) is observed. A denser network of such welfare providers is prominent in the Latin Rim countries (Italy, Spain and Portugal) with the Catholic Church playing a crucial role, while this is not the case in the Balkan area where the values of Eastern Orthodoxy and its historical limitations of social activism did not provide fertile ground for institutionalized voluntary action.

Most importantly, SE welfare states started expanding at a time of welfare state restructuring in North-West Europe in the face of growing fiscal problems and the ascendancy of neo-liberal forces (particularly in the Anglo-Saxon world) seeking to roll back the welfare state. Soon fiscal constraints in SE countries became highly pressing, particularly during the task of joining the European Monetary Union (EMU). Even before the eruption of the current economic crisis, SE welfare states were confronted with extensive unmet need, serious inequalities and imbalances in social welfare, and significant functional and administrative inefficiencies. The crisis severely hit all four countries. Ensuing structural adjustment (more or less directly enforced by supranational institutions – EC, ECB, IMF, rating agencies) embraces sweeping austerity measures exerting strong pressures on social spending.

In the second section we briefly review the academic analysis on the SE social protection model and highlight major similarities and differences in the region. The third section discusses the reforms over the last two decades and traces the impact of the economic crisis. In light of drastic changes underway, the conclusion raises the question of whether harsh austerity measures may deal a serious blow to SE welfare states.

The Southern European model and main explanatory perspectives

Early attempts at locating SE countries within the main classificatory schemes of the comparative literature stressed welfare residualism (manifesting a liberal ideology), as well as the central role of the Catholic Church and of the traditional family in welfare delivery (Leibfried, 1992; Castles, 1995). These approaches, however, ignored the south-east of Southern Europe, namely the Balkan Peninsula, influenced by the socio-cultural values of the Orthodox tradition and statist features (Petmesidou and Polyzoidis, 2012).

It is particularly the Bismarckian orientation of welfare state development that gathered much attention. Katrougalos (1996) considered southern welfare states a less-developed version of the conservative model. More recently, Jessoula (2007) emphasized the persistent significance of the Bismarckian design in the institutional make-up of the Italian welfare state.

Ferrera (1996) brought the southern model into sharper focus. He considers welfare configurations in SE as reflecting the male-breadwinner/family care model. Gradually income maintenance and particularly pensions emerged as the most important element of the system, traditionally organized along the lines of occupationally fragmented social security funds (managed by the state and social partners), while other elements (e.g. social services and social assistance) remained undeveloped. Moreover, wide inequalities in the level of benefits offered by social security funds deepened gaps between generously and weakly protected beneficiaries. A double polarization thus emerged: 1 between workers enjoying a stable career in the formal sector and those unable to secure such conditions because of high spells of unemployment or persistent informal activity; and 2 between peaks of generosity characterizing certain social insurance funds and inadequate protection provided by others. Weak administrative capacity in benefit distribution constitutes another serious predicament. A departure from the Bismarckian logic emerged through the establishment of national health services, though with great variation among the four countries as to the reform roadmap, organizational aspects, and scope of universalism.

In light of a number of concurrent change factors transforming the social-risk profile in SE countries (rapid demographic ageing; a shift towards postfordism seriously diminishing opportunities for stable work careers; changing family patterns and gender roles; eroding national policy autonomy due to globalization challenges and EU integration), Ferrera and Hemerijck (2003) stressed the urgent need for 'retuning' the southern model. Both authors strongly criticized the pension bias of SE welfare states 'crowding out' resources for other social programmes (family, housing, and social assistance benefits), and argued in favour of policy 'recalibration' so as to transfer resources from 'grandfathers' to social investment in families, children and the young unemployed, to introduce/improve social safety nets, and to promote active employment measures.

Some critical issues can be raised here. First, traditionally social protection in SE embraced a weak variation of the male-breadwinner model. Thus the average male worker's earnings and social wage were not sufficient to cater for family welfare needs. Striking evidence concerns the persistently high poverty rates in SE countries. Notably the family (and kin) traditionally played a crucial role in pooling resources (derived from the formal and informal job market, social benefits, 'protected' employment in the public sector, and other sources) and distributing them to its members. This pattern is accentuated towards the south-east of SE (Greece and south Italy). It is strongly linked with statist-clientelistic practices that allow families to take advantage of 'soft budgets' (Petmesidou, 1996, 2006). That is, an institutional configuration is developed in which budget imbalances for individuals, households, and enterprises are transferred to the state through strategies of income appropriation by political means. Arguably, over the last decade, intensified conflicts and deadlocks of this institutional constellation disclosed serious dysfunctions of the southern model, critically compounded by adverse demographics and job market conditions, and a weakening ability of the family to function as a welfare clearinghouse.

Second, the insider/outsider divide (in labour market terms) is meaningful particularly in countries where Fordist patterns developed more intensively in some regions (offering stable jobs) in contrast to others (e.g. the north/south divide in Italy). Greece experienced a rapid shift from agrarian structures to a service-oriented economy well before industrialization had deepened. Among its distinctive features are the protracted dominance of statist-paternalistic forms of social organization and an extensive informal economy. Strikingly, in this context the insider/outsider divide has persistently been nurtured by political criteria of differential access by groups and individuals to the rent-yielding state apparatus, hence the wide differences in the generosity of social benefits among socio-occupational groups. Getting resources through rent-seeking statist-clientelistic practices functioned for a long time as a substitute of a welfare state, albeit with perverse distributional effects. Under these conditions, crossing the formal/informal divide constitutes part of an array of family strategies to pool resources, and thus 'informality' does not absolutely reflect a rigid insider/outsider divide in labour market terms. It is mostly in respect of the steadily increasing new forms of atypical work (i.e. short-term contracts) in SE, and the influx of immigrants lacking the capacity to benefit from family, kin support (and clientelistic ties) that the insider/outsider divide became more pronounced in labour market terms, requiring new policy measures. Particularly in Spain and Italy, a strongly marked insider/outsider labour market divide is due to a deeper and more extensive industrialization process over the 1960s and 1970s, followed by a shift to increasingly flexible employment arrangements (in Spain, since the early 1980s temporary contracts have been widely used).

Third, the argument that pensions should be curbed so as to secure resources for other welfare functions does not seem to be strongly supported by the empirical evidence, although tackling inequalities in the level and scope of benefits, and addressing rapid demographic ageing and issues of pension sustainability have persistently been key reform challenges. Evidently, at

Table 18.1 Social expenditure

	Social expenditure as per cent of GDP, 2008	*Per capita social expenditure (in PPS, EU-15 = 100)*		*GDP per capita (in PPS, EU-15 = 100)*
		2000	*2008*	*2000/2008*
Italy	27.8%	93	94	101/88
Greece	26.0%	64	81	73/87
Spain	22.7%	64	78	84/93
Portugal	24.3%	55	64	68/66
EU-15	*27.1%*	*100*	*100*	*100/100*
EU-27	*26.4%*	*85*	*88*	*87/90*

Source: created from Eurostat data, to be found at epp.eurostat.ec.europa.eu/portal/page/portal/social_protection/data/database (Column 1; Columns 2 and 3 calculated on the basis of data accessed at the above website). Column 4 calculated on the basis of data accessed at epp.eurostat.ec.europa.eu/portal/page/portal/eurostat/home/

the time of the eruption of the economic crisis, SE countries (with the exception of Italy) lagged behind the EU-15 average in terms of social expenditure as per cent of gross domestic product (GDP) (Table 18.1). Most importantly, particularly in Spain, Portugal, and Greece, per capita social spending did not improve as fast as their per capita GDP (measured against the respective EU-15 average). This indicates that, in terms of their wealth, SE countries underspent in social protection. Adequacy of pensions is highly questionable too, given the persistently high risk of poverty and social exclusion among elderly people (Table 18.2). It is also worth mentioning a condition reinforced by the current crisis: that pension income contributes to pooling resources within the family – often in exchange for care services – particularly as unemployment among the young dramatically increases (nearing 50% in Spain and Greece in late 2011).

Striking a balance between reasonably equitable and economically viable reform solutions constitutes a major challenge. In this respect the EU social policy agenda has significantly influenced debate on a transition from a corrective and passive welfare state to a more proactive social investment strategy, with much greater attention paid to prevention, activation, and social servicing. Nevertheless, 'recalibration' along these lines runs the risk of overemphasizing an 'individualized market-centred model' to the detriment of collectivist values supporting redistribution and equity criteria. All the more so in SE countries, as universalist principles and public trust in welfare state institutions were never particularly strong. Furthermore, entering a phase of drastic austerity in the late 2000s made a gloomy scenario of increasing flexibility, without much security, all the more probable.

Welfare reform dynamics

Following the restoration of democracy in Spain, Portugal, and Greece, constrained social pressures around unmet needs led to fast-increasing social expenditure in the late 1970s and most of the 1980s. Italy experienced a more protracted period of welfare state consolidation since the end of World War II, yet it was still a welfare laggard in the late 1970s. Over much of the 1980s a concern about the impact of rapidly rising social expenditure on public finances was not a major issue of political concern. Particularly in Italy and Greece, public deficits and indebtedness began to soar dramatically during this time partly because of a significant expansion of earnings-related schemes (proliferation of new funds, early retirement, disability pensions). Due to some distinctive socio-political features in these two countries (such as the

Table 18.2 Poverty and severe deprivation, 2009 (based on 2008 incomes)

	Population at-risk-of-poverty and social exclusion %*	*Older people at-risk-of poverty and social exclusion (65+/75+)*%*
Italy	24.7	22.8/24.5
Greece	27.6	26.8/29.0
Spain	23.4	26.1/28.5
Portugal	24/9	26.0/32.2
EU-15	21.1	19.5/21.9
EU-27	23.1	21.7/24.1

*=Measured by Eurostat on the basis of a composite deprivation indicator.
Source: Eurostat, epp.eurostat.ec.europa.eu/portal/page/portal/employment_social_policy_equality/omc_social_inclusion_and_social_protection/social_inclusion_strand.

polarized pluralist party system in Italy for much of the post-war period, and the strong populist current in Greece over the 1980s), welfare policies came to be a crucial instrument in clientelistic-particularistic exchanges. It is largely the intense political crisis, in the early 1990s, sweeping the existing party structure in Italy, as well as the challenges of joining the Economic and Monetary Union (EMU), which gave an impetus to social reform and provided propitious conditions for social concertation around wide-ranging changes in social protection, industrial relations, and labour market policies (Ferrera and Gualmini, 2004). Contrarily, policy stalemates and reform impasses characterized Greece, which persistently lacked any focal actors (think-tanks or policy communities) for driving policy debate.

Since the early 1980s Spain has embarked upon a piecemeal but steady process of rationalization and modernization of social protection. Transition to democracy through elite pacts highly influenced a reform trajectory based on negotiating compromises setting the rules of the game for policy making (the Toledo Pact of 1995 on pensions epitomizes such a negotiated, steady route to reform). In Portugal, transition to democracy occurred under large-scale revolutionary mobilizations, but soon the prospect of accession to the EU and, later on, the challenge of joining the EMU prompted a shift in policy-making towards more consensual forms (through social pacts) of interconnected reforms in incomes, labour market, social security, and welfare policies.

Notwithstanding differences in reform momentum, all four SE welfare states faced similar challenges over the last two decades. The economic recession in the first half of the 1990s and serious fiscal pressures in the run up to joining the euro brought imbalances at centre-stage. Tackling great gaps and inequalities in social protection, while at the same time experimenting with new diversified welfare mixes, mostly influenced by the policy visions and options promoted by the EU (for example, the Lisbon Agenda), oriented reform (Guillén and Petmesidou, 2008). Yet, after entrance into the EMU, social pacting faltered in Italy (as well as in Portugal) and reform dynamism subsided. Interestingly, Spain continued on a steady route of (more-or-less) negotiated piecemeal reform. Among the four countries, Greece ostensibly failed to deal with wide inequities and sustainability problems in social protection, a condition seriously aggravated by the current severe sovereign debt crisis.

The 1990s and 2000s

Austerity challenges and the need for fiscal rectitude in social insurance, in the face of dismal demographics, were brought to the fore with the Maastricht Treaty. Historically social insurance relied on a public, first-pillar, earnings-related system, embracing a large number of socio-professional funds with wide inequalities in the scope and level of benefits. Social pensions on a means tested basis for elderly people without a contributions record were varyingly introduced in all four countries in the post-war period.

In Italy, in the 1990s, an array of internal and external factors (i.e. the changing political opportunities following the corruption revelations in the beginning of the decade that swept away traditional parties, in parallel with the intensification of international competition and the fiscal pressures for joining the EMU) set in motion a rigorous reform dynamic. Between the early and mid-1990s successive technocratic governments, by putting forward the 'fairness goal' in social protection, gathered support by social partners for drastically reducing fragmentation in social insurance. Also, a shift to a multi-pillar social insurance system was enacted (a first pillar operating as a notional defined contributions scheme, to which supplementary-second and third-funded pillars are added). However, a particularly prolonged phasing-in period accompanied the reform, setting a long-term horizon for system rationalisation.

In Spain early reforms drastically reduced the number of social insurance funds (from over 100, in the mid-1970s, to fewer than ten), stipulated convergence of the few 'special regimes' to the conditions characterizing the 'general regime' for all salaried and wage workers, and clearly distinguished between funding sources for contributory and non-contributory benefits (the latter, together with health and social care services were to be funded out of the state budget rather than social contributions, and managed by the autonomous regions). However, by far the most important landmark is the signing of the Toledo Pact (in 1995) that endorsed the above funding split and launched a steady context of negotiated policy making. Reforms have been predominantly parametric – that is, increasing pensionable age, reducing early retirement, extending minimum contribution periods and adjusting pension formulae so as to accommodate ageing and sustainability pressures. Importantly, minimum pensions and (social assistance) top-ups significantly increased with a positive effect on redistribution. Due to early measures of system rationalisation, accompanied by a sharp increase of employment from the mid-1990s until the bursting of the 'construction bubble' in 2008, the Spanish social security system recorded substantial surpluses, a condition put in jeopardy by dramatically increasing unemployment under the current crisis (23 per cent in December 2011). Private schemes were introduced in 1988 but accessibility remains limited.

Fragmentation of social security has been lowest in Portugal. Legislation in 2007 defined the main provider of public (contributory) pensions (the Social Security System) as the institution that eventually absorbed all remaining special schemes. As in Spain, the mandatory earnings-related contributory system underwent several parametric changes over the last decades. Enactment of legislation in 2002 and 2007 expanded pensionable earnings so as to cover the whole work career and tightened accrual rates for pension calculation. In 2008, a sustainability factor was introduced too – a pension discount factor taking account of changes in life expectancy. Funded (occupational and private) schemes cover only a tiny section of the labour force. Social pensions are fully funded by state transfers, and old-aged people are also eligible for benefit under the RMI (minimum income scheme) launched in 1996, on means testing criteria.

High fragmentation, polarization and great gaps in coverage characterized Greece's pension system until recently. In the early 1990s the right-wing party in power used the fiscal crisis and the Maastricht requirements to leverage in some parametric changes (among others, increasing the pensionable age and the rate of contributions, lowering the replacement rates for new entrants, and discontinuation of pension indexation to wages). No major concertation platform emerged. In 2000, a reform plan for dealing with the system's fiscal and organizational problems was met with strong opposition of the unions and was aborted. The next major reform act just before the onset of the current crisis intended to considerably tidy up the system through large-scale amalgamations of funds, a considerable levelling out of regulations and benefits, measures discouraging early retirement and promoting active ageing, as well as supporting gender equality (in terms of early exit pathways and parental leave provisions). Implementation of organizational changes has been deficient though and serious sustainability issues came forcefully to the fore amidst the deep sovereign debt crisis faced by the country.

EU influence either through 'soft policies' (the guidelines of the EU employment and social OMC), or 'hard measures' (EU directives and ECJ rulings – e.g. on equal treatment of men and women in social insurance) is more or less evident in all four countries. Major EU policy options (system modernization, adaptability, sustainability, etc.) to one degree or another have been infiltrated into national policy making. All four countries proceeded to the liberalization of employment services and, if not successfully in practice, at least in principle, they embraced the idea of promoting a more diversified mix of passive and active employment policies. Labour market rigidity (strict rules for dismissals, high reservation wages, and strict work demarcations) and varieties of dualism (e.g. through a large informal economy in the case of Greece and South Italy, or deep segmentation between a 'fringe' of weakly protected temporary contract workers and a 'core' of protected permanent workers characterizing Spain), have persistently been considered major disadvantages of SE countries. Ideas and policy options entering the national debate over the last two decades shifted attention towards 'relaxing' labour market rules, and introducing social protection of atypical employment and interrupted work careers. In this respect reforms signpost an attempt at broadening the concept of social protection rights by weakening the link with regular employment. This is reflected in the expansion of social assistance and of integrated measures for social inclusion and family–work balance, on the basis of citizenship and need (indicating a 'selective universalism'; Jessoula 2007). The introduction of the RMI scheme in Portugal, in the mid-1990s, embraces such an integrated policy. Also, in Spain, minimum income schemes have been implemented by the autonomous regions since the late 1980s. Social assistance policy reform has been erratic in Italy, with great inequalities among regions; while in Greece this is still an undeveloped field.

Transition from health insurance to a national health system (NHS) (from the late 1970s to the early 1980s) took place at a different pacing and level of coverage and effectiveness among the four countries (Petmesidou and Guillén, 2008). In Greece, private health expenditure remains comparatively high (over 40 per cent of total health expenditure, consisting mostly in out-of-pocket payments), and a mixed funding system of the persists, through both state revenues and social health insurance contributions, with wide inequalities in the NHS range and scope of benefits among the, up until lately, large number of health funds. Distinctively in Spain and Italy reform presented a double aspect, as a deep transformation from a centralized to a regionalised system accompanied the introduction of the NHS. Universalist principles are more salient in the Spanish NHS, in parallel with a complete devolution of health powers to the regions by the early 2000s. In Italy, regionalization of the NHS started earlier but took longer, due mostly to a less marked trajectory of political devolution, compared to Spain. However, since the turn of the century recognition of regional powers in health, social care and social assistance (as well as social insurance, through legislation allowing the establishment of region-specific supplementary pension funds enacted in the early 2000s; see Ferrera, 2003) was strengthened.

Soon after launching changes in the health system's architecture, all four SE countries faced serious problems of cost escalation. Innovative solutions promoting 'managerialist models' in healthcare organization (managed competition, regulation) and various forms of private–public mixes (e.g. contracting out various healthcare and ancillary services by the NHS) were embraced in national health policies. User charges and co-payments were also introduced (though varyingly among the four countries), in parallel with changes in the pricing system of pharmaceuticals and the promotion of generics. Changes in the contours of the private–public mix (strengthening the role of private provision) were more pronounced in Italy. In Spain the private sector remains persistently complementary to public health activity. There are no co-payments on visits or diagnostic tests and a gate-keeping system is in place. In Greece and Portugal primary healthcare has been deficient so far. An ineffective referral system in Portugal, and lack of a gate-keeping mechanism in Greece, account for overuse of expensive specialist services.

Rapid demographic ageing indicates increasing long-term care need (forecasts by the EC Economic Policy Committee set the old-age dependency ratio at 55 to 60 per cent in the four countries by 2060). Policies in this field, however, remain extremely fragmented (particularly in Greece and Italy). Public provision is limited and inefficient, consisting mostly of cash benefits. Thus families largely undertake care provision, in the context of an expanding informal privatization of long-term care, with immigrant helpers providing the services.

A significant policy innovation is recorded in Spain and Portugal. The enactment of the law on dependency (2006) in Spain introduced universal coverage of long-term care through a mixed funding by the central state, the autonomous regions, and co-payments by users, proportional to their incomes. Yet, the launch has been beset by serious problems, such as wide regional disparities, inefficient coordination with healthcare, and too much reliance on cash benefits rather than services. Similarly, in Portugal, a national network for integrated care was established in the mid-2000s, with the aim to cover big gaps in long-term care. It embraces a wide array of (public and private) units providing post-acute rehabilitation and long-term care. It operates under common standards of service provision, along the lines of the purchaser-provider split management model and is subsidised by the state. However, the severe economic crisis puts strains on funding these newly established schemes.

The impact of the economic crisis

With the exception of Spain where the international crisis aggravated an economic slowdown already underway because of the building market crash, SE countries were hit by the global credit crunch with some delay and experienced primarily a serious sovereign debt crisis that soon led their economies into deep recession. In Greece and Portugal the debt crisis undermined their fiscal credibility causing borrowing costs to escalate. Bailout loan packages were agreed for Greece and Portugal by the EC-IMF-ECB under the terms of sweeping austerity measures and structural reforms, including drastic lowering of incomes; cuts to health, education, and social security budgets; a reduction in the public sector wage bill; severe curtailment of public sector recruitment and extensive privatizations; hikes in VAT rates and excise duties on specific commodities, in parallel with tax increases; and labour market reforms increasing flexibility, albeit, under conditions of diminishing security. Successive austerity packages were also introduced by the governments of Spain and Italy in order to rein in the public deficit and ease fears of a worsening debt crisis.

In Greece, under structural adjustment, pensions have been the 'flagship' of reform moving away from a highly fragmented, Bismarckian social insurance system (based primarily on the first pillar), to a unified, multi-tier system that distinguishes between a basic (quasi-universal) non-contributory and a contributory pension. In parallel with significant cuts in salaries and current pension benefits, replacement rates for future retirees are drastically reduced; pensionable income is redefined on the basis of total career earnings; stricter conditions are introduced for early retirement; measures are taken for equalising men's and women's retirement conditions in the public sector (in a phased-in way); and provisions are made for linking longevity to retirement age (from 2021 onwards). Securing long-term viability and eliminating accumulated privileges in a system long nurtured by clientelistic criteria, are key aims. Nevertheless, fairness problems remain, while harsh cuts in current and future pensions impact negatively on benefit adequacy. Furthermore soaring unemployment adds extra pressure on social insurance due to drastic drops in contributions in all four countries.

The memorandum that Portugal signed with its international donors embraces nominal cuts in pensions over the time span of the bailout programme, stricter targeting criteria for social benefits, increase of pensionable age, and incentives for supplementary funded retirement schemes. In Spain, along the lines of the Toledo Pact agreement, one more parametric reform was decided, in early 2011, that, among other provisions, increased retirement age as well as the years taken as a reference base for pensionable income (from the current 15 to 25 years) were to be considered. Additionally, long-term system sustainability will be supported by periodically reviewing contributions and benefits (from 2027 onwards) with respect to longevity. Similarly in Italy an upward adjustment of pensionable age to longevity every three years was decided, in parallel with a periodic revision of the coefficient for converting notional accounts into annuities. Most recently, the 'Save Italy' decree by the technocratic government under Mario Monti, formed in November 2011, amidst a deepening economic crisis, sped up implementation of the notionally defined contributions scheme for pensions (to be in force from 2012 for all the working population), increased minimum pensionable age for both men and women, and froze pensions that are over twice the statutory minimum.

In Spain, the expansionary trend in healthcare followed in the previous decades came to an abrupt end. Accumulated debt for medical supplies and pharmaceuticals in some Spanish regions reached a record high, threatening the very survival of the system. In Greece the bailout agreement embraced a drastic overhaul of public healthcare (measures include the merging of health funds, closing down/merging of hospitals, and significant reduction in the scope of diagnostic tests and drugs covered by social insurance, as well as a drastic decline in the number of and remuneration levels of contracted medical doctors in primary health care). Increasing privatization of the NHS ('ticket-payment' for all regular outpatient services, fees charged to outpatients in the afternoon visits to specialists in public hospitals), and diminishing scope and quality of care plague the system at a time when demand for public provision steeply increased due to the crisis.

Overall, sustainability concerns override equity and adequacy criteria. The 'White Paper on Welfare' issued by the Italian Labour Ministry in mid-2009 clearly resonates the retrenchment of public provision by stressing that 'the current balance between state, market, and family should be shifted in favour of more market, more family, and less state'. Such a policy orientation starkly indicates that any trends of widening the scope of institutionalised social rights in SE (e.g. in social assistance and social care), evident in the previous decades, feel heavily the pressure of the crisis. In Spain the newly introduced policy of universal long-term care services is at risk of being seriously under-resourced, while in Italy and Greece the crisis leaves little room for reform that could relieve the family (and particularly women) from the burden of care, even though the family's ability to provide protection is eroding.

Conclusion

In the 1950s and 1960s social spending was limited and a familialist model of social protection prevailed in South Europe. Compared to North-West Europe, welfare state expansion proceeded with a considerable time lag and embraced primarily social insurance and healthcare, while social assistance and social services developed sluggishly. Moreover, the expansion of social rights and social programmes (e.g. NHS schemes) took place in a rather short time period amidst a turbulent economic environment (after the early 1980s). Soon SE welfare states came under strong pressure by economic and financial constraints, rapidly changing demographics, new risks, and the need to rationalize and reform institutions in the context of European integration. SE countries more or less differ in respect to the reform roadmap they followed over the last two decades. Yet under the grip of a serious economic crisis over last few years, convergence on harsh austerity measures and receding social protection is evident.

In Spain, an early-starting, steady reform, tackling serious predicaments of the pension system, and a carefully designed and executed transition to a devolved NHS, account for the very low support that issues of private provision garner in public debate. However, in the face of soaring unemployment and rapid population ageing, pressures for a change in the system's architecture are seriously mounting. In Italy the reforms over the 1990s prioritized pension sustainability, which left benefit adequacy alarmingly at stake. Greece embarked upon reforms for dealing with major predicaments of its social protection system rather belatedly under the strong pressure of a severe fiscal crisis, which puts at risk its 'feeble' welfare state.

It is difficult to forecast the duration and social-structural effects of the crisis. Yet protracted fiscal austerity and structural adjustment 'recipes' (of international organizations), with a strong neo-liberal orientation, for years ahead, will squeeze social spending and progressively dismantle social and labour rights, with irreversible effects on social protection. Such a gloomy scenario of rapidly deepening socio-economic divides in the EU periphery (looking more like a 'Latin American' future) is likely, as long as deeper economic and political union in Europe is not forthcoming. Instead, substantial leaps forward in European integration and a reinvigoration of the EU social model could rekindle optimism about a way out of the crisis that puts redistributive solidarity at the focus of socio-economic reform.

References

Castles, F. (1995), Welfare state development in Southern Europe. *West European Politics*, 18(2), pp. 291–313.

Esping-Andersen, G. (1990), *The Three Worlds of Welfare Capitalism*. Oxford: Polity Press.

Ferrera, M. (1996), The 'Southern Model' of welfare in Social Europe. *Journal of European Social Policy*, 6(1), pp. 17–37.

——(2003), European integration and national social citizenship. Changing boundaries, new structuring. *Comparative Political Studies*, 36(6), pp. 611–52.

Ferrera, M. and Hemerijck, A. (2003), 'Recalibrating Europe's welfare regimes', in J. Zeitlin and D.M. Trubek (eds), *Governing Work and Welfare in the New Economy. European and American Experiments*, pp. 88–128. Oxford: OUP.

Ferrera, M. and Gualmini, E. (2004), *Rescued by Europe?* Amsterdam: Amsterdam University Press.

Guillén, A. and Petmesidou, M. (2008), 'The public-private mix in Southern Europe. What changed in the last decade?', in M. Seeleib-Kaiser (ed.) *Welfare State Transformations*, pp. 56–78. Basingstoke: Palgrave.

Jessoula, M. (2007), *Italy. An Uncompleted Departure from Bismarck*. Working Paper 4. Milan: University of Milan.

Katrougalos, G. (1996), The South European welfare model: the Greek welfare state, in search of an identity. *Journal of European Social Policy*, 6(1), pp. 39–60.

Leibfried, S. (1992), 'Towards a European Welfare State? On Integrating Poverty Regimes into the European Community', in Z. Ferge and J. E. Kolberg (eds), *Social Policy in a Changing Europe*, pp. 245–79. Frankfurt: Campus.

Petmesidou, M. (1996), Social protection in Southern Europe: trends and prospects. *Journal of Area Studies*, 9, pp. 95–125.

——(2006), 'Tracking social protection: origins, path peculiarity, impasses and prospects', in M. Petmesidou and E. Mossialos (eds), *Social Policy Developments in Greece*, pp. 25–54. Aldershot: Ashgate.

Petmesidou, M. and Guillén, A. (2008), 'Southern-style' National Health Services? Recent reforms and trends in Spain and Greece. *Social Policy & Administration*, 42(2), pp. 106–24.

Petmesidou, M. and Polyzoidis, P. (2012), 'Religion und Wohlfahrtsstaat in Griechenland', in K. Gabriel and H.-R. Reuter (eds), *Religion und Wohlfahrsstaatlichkeit in Europa*. Tübingen: Mohr Siebeck.

19

Liberal welfare states

Paul Spicker

Introduction

The description of values as 'liberal' means many different things. In academic writing, 'liberal' thought is principally associated with an individualist, *laissez-faire* approach. A 'liberal' education is one that promotes independence and opportunity. The 'liberal professions' are professions that are independent – motivated by moral codes and responsibility rather than financial incentives. 'Liberal democracy' is based in the rights of individual citizens, and the protection of minorities. 'Liberal' provision is open and generous: in the United States, 'liberal' politics is left wing, and associated with a commitment to extensive social responsibility.

The different uses of the term are linked through a family resemblance – a constellation of inter-connected ideas. Liberal individualism developed as a critique of traditional views of status and duty, usually characterised in terms of 'feudalism'. Politically, individualism was used to emphasise political and civil rights, the equality of persons and the case for social mobility – the 'career open to the talents'. Economically, liberalism was associated with individual choice, property rights, and the economics of the market. Those values were initially a challenge to the established order, but they have also come over time to represent a conservative defence of property interests. In the process, liberalism has come to represent not a uniform doctrine, but a complex and sometimes contradictory cluster of concepts.

Liberal values

Individualism. Liberal individualism is in the first place a set of values, asserting the moral status of each person as an individual. In mediaeval societies, people were born into a particular status and set of roles. Individualism denied the validity of ascribed status, holding that each person should be able to determine his or her own position and course of action. Liberal individualism was, and is, radically egalitarian. Because the ideas are now so widely accepted, it can be difficult to see how radical they were; but it should be understood that for much of the world's history it would not have been accepted that people of different races, women, people with disabilities, or members of lower classes or castes were of equal value to others. As a way of thinking, liberalism is still centrally important to arguments for equality, including feminism (which opposes the status traditionally assigned to women) and anti-racism (which denies the ascription of characteristics, status, or roles by 'race').

Rights. The individualist position is expressed in liberalism through the medium of rights. Rights are rules governing social relationships, but they are rules that are located in the individual, rather than the structure of social obligation. Locke's (1690) defence of life, liberty, and estates, or the US constitution's alternative formulation of life, liberty or the 'pursuit of happiness', are cornerstones of liberal values.

The most characteristic liberal right is freedom, or liberty; it is represented in ideas like freedom of speech, freedom of assembly, and freedom of religion. The implications of personal freedom are interpreted differently by different writers: for example, Hayek (1960) confines his discussion of freedom to the absence of coercion, and puts particular emphasis on coercion by the state; Sen (1999) emphasises the critical role of capabilities, linking freedom with capacity, entitlement and economic development.

Pluralism. Freedom of thought and action implies diversity – differences in thought, behaviour and the exercise of choice – rather than homogeneity (e.g. see Raz, 1986). Pluralism is often accused of being a conservative doctrine, unable to accommodate conflict. The opposite is true: pluralism depends fundamentally on a defence of the rights of minorities. In a pluralist system, conflict is continual, but because relationships are shifting and unstable, no single faction is capable of consistently dominating the process. In terms of values and culture, pluralism means that there may be differences, but that there needs to be a degree of tolerance – multi-culturalism is the child of liberal values. In political terms, the conflicts implied by diversity have to be managed by rules of engagement – the 'checks and balances' of the American constitution. Madison argued that there should be no consistent majority: on different issues, people would form different factions and alliances.

> If a majority be united by a common interest, the rights of the minority will be insecure. There are but two methods of providing against this evil: the one by creating a will in the community independent of the majority – that is, of the society itself; the other, by comprehending in the society so many separate descriptions of citizens as will render an unjust combination of a majority on the whole very improbable, if not impracticable.
>
> *(The Federalist Paper, 1789–88, p.311)*

The root of the democratic convention for majority rule was not, then, that the majority of the population has priority over the minority, but rather that policies could only be determined by shifting coalitions of interests; a majority is constituted from diverse minorities.

Economic liberalism. The values of diversity, independence, and freedom are often expressed, in liberal thought, in terms of the economic market. For Hayek (1960) and Friedman (Friedman and Friedmand, 1981), the market is both an expression of freedom and the outcome of it. If people interact and exchange freely, a market will arise. Markets facilitate choice, which is the expression of freedom; suppression of the market is a suppression of freedom at a basic, personal level. And economic freedom enhances welfare, because it makes it possible for people to maximise their own utility.

These are strong arguments. It is true, as a general proposition, that exercising choice is basic to freedom; it is probably true that markets express choice; it is difficult to deny that the growth of democracy and individual rights has been strongly associated with economic prosperity and the development of market-based economies. At the same time, it is not true that the market advances or expresses personal freedom in every case. Markets do not necessarily deliver desired outcomes; the operation of the market can deny people entitlements and access to essential services; and the freedoms of some people can limit the freedoms of others. Liberal values do not imply an unqualified support for every kind of market. Markets have to be regulated; transactions which suppress choice or liberty (for example, the action of cartels) are not sanctioned; and because poverty denies choice, the distribution of resources has to be considered.

Liberal opposition to welfare

Many of the criticisms of the welfare state associated with liberalism predate most conceptions of the modern welfare state. The work of Herbert Spencer (1851, 1884) from the nineteenth century contains many ideas that today are attributed to liberals like Hayek and Friedman: individualism, reliance on economic markets, the defence of property rights, and opposition to state intervention. This pattern of thought is usually referred to as 'neoliberalism', though it is hardly new; it rests on a fundamentally conservative acceptance of the legitimacy of the existing pattern of property rights and the political status quo.

Individualism. The neoliberal critique begins with a particular form of individualism. Individualism is not only a set of values; it is also a way of looking at the world. 'Methodological individualism' – thinking of people as individuals, rather than as households, tribes, communities, or nations – was central to the development of micro-economics. Individual well-being, or utility, is constructed in terms that reflect the choice made by a theoretically representative, rational individual, or 'homo economicus'. Individual utilities are satisfied by individual choices; indeed, they can only be satisfied by individual choices. Kaplow and Shavell (2001) argue, for example, that 'any non-individualistic social welfare function violates the Pareto principle'. That means that only an individualistic approach can ever achieve optimal use of resources in satisfying individual utility. (Pareto optimality is one of a series of questionable concepts widely referred to in welfare economics: it is blind to distributive justice, and Ryan comments that at times its outcomes are 'repulsive' (Ryan, 1988, p.47).) Preferences are considered in aggregate, rather than social, terms. There is no such thing as society. For Jeremy Bentham:

> The community is a fictitious body, composed of the individual persons who are considered as constituting as it were its members. The interest of the community is, then, what? – the sum of the interests of the several members who compose it.
>
> *(Bentham, 1962[1789], p. 35)*

That rationale informed utilitarianism, and it has been carried forward into analytical welfare economics. Arrow's famous 'impossibility theorem' purports to show, by combining a version of the Pareto principle with the preposterous assumption of 'unrestricted domain', that no social welfare function can exist unless it is imposed by a dictatorship (Arrow, 1951). So much for socialisation, culture, shared values, political negotiation, or common sense.

The denial of the validity of social preferences has a profound effect on the way that economic principles are translated into practice. So, for example, economic textbooks argue that the main reason why individual utility is not satisfied is 'market failure' (Connolly and Munro, 2006, Ch. 9), where the market is not able to function in terms of a conventional competitive equilibrium. Examples include public goods, externalities, and uncertain information. The UK Treasury's guidance on public policy suggests that market failure is the primary justification for the establishment of public services (HM Treasury, 2003). But there are many other reasons why public services might be established, which are not based in the maximisation of individual utility, and are not necessarily evidence of market failure: they include the development of economic infrastructure, the promotion of social capital, minimum standards and human rights. If liberalism is a doctrine which values and protects the rights of the individual, there is no incompatibility with such approaches. The problem rests in the narrow construction of methodological individualism, and its definition in terms of utility, rather than in terms of the value of each individual.

Economic markets. The most prominent advocates of free market economics – Spencer, Hayek, Friedman – argue not only that markets are legitimate, but that collective provision is not. Markets are both an expression of free choice and as the mechanism through which choice can be exercised. The uncoordinated actions and transactions of individuals are expressed, cumulatively, in the actions of the economic market. Collective provision, by contrast, is taken to represent an imposition of authority on the actions of individuals, typically through paternalism, social control, or simply through a presumptive arrogance that the state knows best. Equally, the pro-market liberals believe that markets work, and collective provision fails to deliver. Markets are seen as encouraging economic development and prosperity. State intervention is associated with tales of incompetence, waste, producer capture, the abuse of patronage and the denial of choice. The market, Seldon argues, is a set of signals guiding judgements, an educator that teaches people about choice, and a spur to efficient production (Seldom, 1977).

These arguments are obviously partisan, but more than that they are often misdirected. The implicit assumption that is being made is that collective provision arises through a different process from the operation of the market. In much of continental Europe, collective provision arose not through state action, but in the same way as market mechanisms: through spontaneous, independent action. The idea of 'solidarity' refers to mutual responsibility, the voluntary actions of people working together, and the process of exchange (Baldwin, 1990). Mutual insurance is redistributive, but it is voluntarily redistributive: individuals pool their resources in order to protect themselves against risk.

Property rights. Liberal ideas were formed as a critique of established interests, often represented in terms of a relationship to landholding. As individualist views gained the ascendancy, however, liberalism shifted from being a radical critique of established interests to a defence of property rights. An illustration might be Robert Nozick's arguments against redistribution. For Nozick (1974), the only defensible rights are those established through legitimate accession and succession. Once those are accepted no other principle – such as social justice, equality or fairness – can legitimately alter the distribution of resources. Taxation, in Nozick's view, is theft. One objection to this principle is that rights of succession and accession are rarely sufficient to account for the rights that people hold; the ownership of property is as much as a legacy of inequality, injustice, and arbitrary misfortune as it is of labour, merit, or desert. Nozick himself recognises this when he suggests that reparations may have to be made for groups, like native Americans, who have been dispossessed. Another, more fundamental, objection is that property rights are conventional; the wages that people receive reflect not intrinsic value, but a series of circumstances and conditions, including the liability for taxation.

Opposition to state intervention. In much of the material written in English from a liberal or neoliberal perspective, there is a view that action taken by the state is illegitimate. The primary function of the state is the maintenance of order (Nozick, 1974); the state proceeds by coercion;[19] collective action generally means state action; even if state action is undertaken with good intentions, it finds itself on the path to restricting people's liberty (Hayek, 1960); the most legitimate state is a minimal state. If redistribution is incompatible with people's rights, it is hard to justify even the most limited provision.

It is certainly questionable whether the primary function of the state is security. That may or may not be true, but there is no good reason to start from that point. Government, as Edmund Burke (1790) once said, is a contrivance of human wisdom to provide for human wants. A clutch of new states have been founded in the course of the last twenty-five years, and what most of them have in common is not a primary concern with security, but with prosperity. In the course of the last fifteen years, more than sixty developing countries have produced Poverty Reduction Strategy Papers: strategies and plans for governance and economic development, mainly based on the establishment of sound economies, property rights and partnership working with non-governmental organisations – just the sort of role, one might have thought, that an open-minded liberal theorist would approve of.

It is no less questionable whether the provision of welfare can be seen as coercive. Redistribution happens, in many cases, not because the state is taking money away from people, but because people voluntarily pool risks. That, not state action, is the source of many of the mechanisms for social protection in continental Europe. In much of Europe, the state came to welfare late in the day (de Swaan, 1988; Spicker, 2000). The welfare systems of several countries – most notably in Scandinavia, which still has voluntary unemployment insurance (Clasen and Viebrock, 2008) – developed outwith the state. The main effect of state intervention to impose compulsion has been to extend coverage to those who might otherwise be excluded from the choices that are open to the rest of the population. It is not clear why an action which is legitimate when it is done by a small group of people in cooperation should not be legitimate for a larger group; nor why an action which is legitimate when done in the private sector should cease to be legitimate at the point where it is taken on by government.

Residualism. Given the strength of neoliberal opposition to government intervention, it follows that any provision of welfare should be held to the minimum. The residual model of welfare is based on the idea that people should be seeking to manage, as far as possible, from their own resources, or from the assistance of those who are prepared to help them; the role of the state is to act only in the last resort, as a safety net, when other options are not available. Residual welfare is not necessarily minimal, but minimal provision, like the Victorian Poor Law, is likely to be residual; in the context of opposition to all residual government provision it has come to be strongly associated with a view of welfare as a 'public burden' (Titmuss, 1968, p. 129). A 'liberal welfare state' seems to many to be a euphemism for residual, market-based services, marked not by their liberalism, but by the relative meanness of their provision, the perception of welfare as a public burden, and the disengagement of the state. However, none of this necessarily follows from the principles of liberal welfare states. A welfare state which respects individual rights, supports diversity and asserts the value of the individual may well be actively engaged in welfare provision.

The liberal welfare state

Ruggie's initial formulation of the idea of a liberal welfare state was one in which 'the proper sphere of state behavior is circumscribed by the functioning of market forces' (cited in Quadagno, 1987). When Esping-Andersen adapted this idea to a cluster of 'liberal welfare regimes', he intended the classification to refer primarily to market-oriented states with a limited commitment to welfare.

> Means-tested assistance, modest universal transfers, or modest social-insurance plans predominate … entitlement rules are strict and often associated with stigma; benefits are typically modest … the state encourages the market.
>
> *(Esping-Andersen, 1990, p. 26)*

The classification is consequently based on two key factors. The first is commodification, or the extent to which the delivery of welfare services depends on the market. Support in kind, like the provision of healthcare or education, is decommodified; support in cash allows people to benefit from market distribution. That implies that pro-market liberals tend to favour income maintenance – giving people financial support – rather than giving them a service. The second factor is the extent of collective provision. Liberal welfare states are characterised as those with limited state provision. This is associated with some of other features of *laissez-faire*, including residual welfare, punitive attitudes to the poor, and a sense that welfare is a public burden. If liberalism is associated with opposition to welfare, with market mechanisms, and with the private sector, it is debatable whether the pattern of provision can be said to represent a 'welfare state' at all.

This narrow focus misses important dimensions in the liberal position. The first is the extent to which welfare is conceived in terms of individual rights, rather than social responsibility. Part of the argument for individual rights is egalitarian, in the sense of a belief of equality of persons. Esping-Andersen notes that liberal regimes may lean, without inconsistency, to universalism: universal provision can help to offer a 'level playing field' for the operation of market provisions (Esping-Andersen, 1990, p. 44). It would be a mistake, however, to expect a homogenous pattern of provision. Equal rights are not necessarily rights to equal things. Rights in many welfare systems are particular, rather than general: they are based on contractual relationships, family relationships and occupational circumstances. Pensions provision, for example, is much more likely to depend on work record than on a structure of citizenship rights. The diverse, multi-faceted character of provision in the US or UK is not inconsistent with the liberal model.

It does not follow, because rights are individualised, that they offer lower levels of protection. In a revealing comparison, Sheila Shaver considers the rights of women to obtain an abortion. The countries which resist abortion more tend to be those which take a social view of rights and responsibilities. The effect of considering the issue from a social perspective is that many parties are considered to have an interest in the decision, and the more people who need to be involved, the more complex and difficult the decision becomes. In the United States, by contrast, a series of decisions have implied that the question of abortion is fundamentally a matter of the rights of the woman involved. It follows, then, that some countries which have a greater commitment to welfare and more generous welfare services may also be more restrictive when it comes to abortion (Shaver, 1993/1994).

Second, there is voluntarism. Individualists and neoliberals may have reservations about collective action, but nothing in the liberal model is directly opposed to cooperative or mutualist action. If it is legitimate for an individual to enter a contractual arrangement, it is legitimate for many individuals to do so; and that is the basis of many mutualist arrangements (including the welfare systems of several countries which developed, not through state direction, but through solidaristic social networks and mutual agencies entered on a voluntary basis). This is not simply equivalent to marketisation, and it can be argued, I think, that there is sometimes a tension between the market regulation and signals favoured by some neoliberals and the development of civil society on mutualist or voluntaristic lines.

Third, there is the extent of pluralism. Virtually all welfare systems are pluralistic to some degree. Rein and van Gunsteren (1984) once argued that there was a 'dialectic' of public and private – that in no system had attempts to create a uniform, homogenised approach ever succeeded. That is, indeed, one of the objections to Esping-Andersen's classification of welfare provision: the devil is in the detail (Ditch, 1999). Liberalism, however, values diversity, and if there is anything in the idea of a 'liberal welfare state', it can be taken to imply that even if there are general rules, there will not be a principal dominant provider of services, or a single pattern of service delivery.

Fourth, there is localism. The issue is hardly considered in English-speaking varieties of liberalism, but it is a key element of liberal thought in continental Europe. Benjamin Constant (1815) argued that just as there were issues that were private for an individual, there must be issues that are private to a couple, to a family, to a community, to a region, or to a country. This is, basically, the argument for self-determination, and it links liberal individualism with individual choice, localism and ultimately with nationalism. However, uniform systems – such as national systems of education, pensions, or healthcare – are difficult to reconcile with liberalism in this sense. It is easier to see the local diversity in systems like Belgium or the

Netherlands as part of a liberal welfare state than the Australian pensions system or the UK's National Health Service.

Are there any liberal welfare states?

Reality rarely conforms to an idealised pattern, and none of the categories used by Esping-Andersen closely reflect the characteristics of particular regimes within the broad classification. Principles and approaches which are true of one service do not necessarily apply to another; there is no evident reason why the same principles should be expected to apply to pensions, education systems, employment policy, or healthcare (Mabbett and Bolderson, 1999). Even if liberal values have a widespread influence, it would not necessarily follow that any state could be said to be wholly, or even largely, liberal in its conception or practices.

It can legitimately be argued, however, that some states conform more to the liberal model than to either social-democratic or conservative models. Esping-Andersen offers several prime candidates, including the USA, Australia, and the UK (Esping-Andersen, 1990). Of these three, the US is probably the best fit. The United States is often described in terms of individualism, *laissez-faire*, residualism, and a punitive view of poverty. These issues often seem to dominate US debates on welfare: examples are the introduction of 'workfare', the exclusion of long-term benefit dependents, and the criticism of the 'underclass'. The USA does not, however, have a unified welfare system. Federalism has meant that many important functions are held by the States, including public assistance, social care, and various health schemes (Hawaii has had mandatory health insurance and a state-funded health system since the 1970s); the current reforms of healthcare will reinforce that diversity. By comparison with other developed countries, central government has had a limited role in social welfare provision: the main developments of federal provision were during the Roosevelt administration of the 1930s, which laid the foundations for the social security system, and the 'War on Poverty' of the 1960s, which provided some important benefits (notably healthcare for people on low incomes) and engaged the federal government in a wide variety of projects and activities at local level.

In practice, the USA is pluralistic. There are significant departures from the residual model – state schooling, social insurance, services for military personnel, veterans, and their families – which provides for more than 60 million people. In addition to federal and state activity, there are extensive private, mutualist, and corporate interests in welfare provision. The USA has a strong tradition of mutual and voluntary effort, strengthened by a tax system that gives substantial relief to voluntary donation. The resulting systems are complex (and expensive): the guiding principle is less one of consistent individualism than what Klass (1985) has called 'decentralised social altruism'.

Australia is classified by Esping-Andersen as a liberal welfare state on the basis that services are highly commodified. That classification was hotly disputed when Esping-Andersen published it. Castles (1994) objected that what mattered was the extent of coverage, not the reliance on means tested benefits. Bettina Cass and John Freeland (1994) argued that Australia was 'radically redistributive'. I have argued that there is no inconsistency between classification as a liberal welfare state and extensive provision and redistribution. If those were the only criteria, the characterisation of Australia as liberal would be defensible. It is potentially more of an issue whether the Australian system could be said to be liberal in other terms – if it is pluralistic, localised, and rights-based. The Australian constitution is federalist, and Castles and Uhr (2007) have argued that federalism has had a significant impact on welfare. The impact, however, has not so much been to promote diversity as to multiply the number of veto points. The Commonwealth has had substantial powers over finance and legislation, and the development of social policy has to be understood principally in terms of a centralised, unitary government.

The question of voluntarism is also problematic. In a climate of retrenchment, the Australian governments have increasingly turned to private and voluntary providers. Oppenheimer (2005) argues that the scope and importance of voluntary action has been underplayed, and that it has always played a substantial part in the delivery of services. At the same time, the very way that the argument is stated suggests its limitations: that social welfare has been principally conceived in terms of the actions of central government. All welfare states have diverse elements, and the plea suggests that the arguments being made are about the direction of movement towards a more liberal model, rather than being evidence of the *existence* of such a model.

The UK is difficult to classify, for similar reasons. The elements of marketisation and decommodification in the UK are consistent with some of the features of the liberal model; there have also been substantial moves in recent years towards measures depending on individual rather than collective rights, including, for example, the individualisation of pensions, significant reforms in access to litigation (the adoption of the US model of contingency fees), and the growth of litigation on human rights. The confusing diversity of provision in pensions is also consistent with liberalism. At the same time, however, the UK is also characterised by centralised, unitary government. The model of the UK welfare state is based not only on universality, but also on uniform standards; local variations are routinely condemned by politicians and media. There have been recent moves to devolution in Scotland, Wales, and Northern Ireland, but these hardly compensate for a considerable reduction in the role and scope of local government, which since 1945 has substantially lost responsibility for the administration of health, social security, housing, policing, water, gas, buses, electricity and telecommunications, not to mention financial powers. Taylor-Gooby and Larsen (2004, p. 55) call the UK a 'centralised liberal welfare state'. That is an oxymoron, and the authors go on to suggest that the system is more a hybrid, 'Janus-faced', 'genuinely liberal, genuine welfare state' (ibid., p. 73).

Identifying liberal welfare states

Esping-Andersen's categorisation of 'liberal welfare regimes' has been influential, not least because it seems to offer an appropriate terminology for an identifiable pattern of services. However, the simplistic association of liberalism and market provision with residualism and a reluctance to spend is potentially misleading. In methodological terms, it has led to an emphasis in comparison on levels of provision. The problem with this is that low spending is liable to be confused with systematic differences in approach, and 'systems differ, not when the frequency of particular characteristics differ, but when the patterns of the relationships among variables differ' (Przeworski and Teune, 1970, p. 45). In conceptual terms, the characteristics of liberal approaches are not just about markets, residualism, and parsimonious provision: the emphasis on the market and commodification is certainly part of the mix, but it is debatable whether residualism or parsimoniousness have much directly to do with the conceptual structure of liberalism. Besides being market-orientated, a liberal welfare state is one that is based in individual rights, pluralistic and localised. Failing to consider those elements runs the risk of confusing liberal provision in developed economies with a pattern of provision in other countries which is only limited because it is not yet fully formed.

References

Arrow, K. (1951), *Social Choice and Individual Values*. New York: Wiley.
Baldwin, P. (1990), *The Politics of Social Solidarity*. Cambridge: Cambridge University Press.
Bentham, J. (1789) 'An introduction to the principles of morals and legislation', in M. Warnock (ed.), *Utilitarianism*, Glasgow: Collins.

Burke, E. (1790), *Reflections on the Revolution in France*. New York: Holt, Rinehart and Winston.
Castles, F. (1994), Comparing the Australian and Scandinavian Welfare States. *Scandinavian Political Studies*. 17(1), pp. 31–46.
Castles, F. and Uhr, J. (2007), The Australian welfare state: has federalism made a difference? *Australian Journal of Politics and History* 53(10), pp. 96–117.
Cass, B. and Freeland, J. (1994), 'Social Security and Full Employment in Australia', in J. Hills, J. Ditch and H. Glennerster (eds), *Beveridge and Social Security*. Oxford: Clarendon Press.
Clasen, J. and Viebrock, E. (2008), Voluntary unemployment insurance and trade union membership, *Journal of Social Policy* 37(3), pp. 433–52.
Connolly, S. and Munro, A. (2006), *Economics of the Public Sector*. Hemel Hempstead: Pearson, Ch 9.
Constant, B. (1957 [1815]) 'Principes de politique', in B. Constant (ed.), *Oeuvres*, Paris: Editions Gallimard.
Ditch, J. (1999), 'Full circle: a second coming for social assistance?', in J. Clasen (ed), *Comparative Social Policy*. Oxford: Blackwell.
Esping-Andersen, G. (1990), *The Three Worlds of Welfare Capitalism*. Brighton: Polity.
The Federalist Papers (1787–88[1961]), New American Library, New York.
Friedman, M. and Friedman, R. (1981), *Free to Choose*. Harmondsworth: Penguin.
Locke, J. (1965 [1690]), *Two Treatises of Civil Government*, ed. P. Laslett. New York: Mentor.
Hayek, F. (1944), *The Road to Serfdom*. London: Routledge and Kegan Paul.
——(1960), *The Constitution of Liberty*. London: Routledge and Kegan Paul.
HM Treasury (2003), *The Green Book*, www.hm-treasury.gov.uk/media/785/27/Green_Book_ 03.pdf.
Kaplow, L. and Shavell, S. (2001), Any non-welfarist method of policy assessment violates the Pareto Principle. *Journal of Political Economy*, 109(2), pp. 281–87.
Klass, G. (1985), Explaining America and the welfare state. *British Journal of Political Science*. 15, pp. 427–50.
Mabbett, D. and Bolderson, H. (1999), 'Theories and methods in comparative social policy', in J. Clasen (ed.), *Comparative Social Policy: Concepts, Theories and Methods*. Oxford: Blackwell.
Nozick, R. (1974), *Anarchy, State and Utopia*. Oxford: Blackwell.
Oppenheimer, M. (2005), Voluntary action and welfare in post 1945 Australia, *History Australia* 2(3), pp. 82.1–82.6.
Przeworski, A. and Teune, H. (1970), *The Logic of Comparative Social Inquiry*. New York: Wiley.
Quadagno, J. (1987), Theories of the welfare state. *Annual Review of Sociology* 13, pp. 109–28.
Raz, J. (1986), *The Morality of Freedom*. Oxford: Clarendon Press.
Rein, M. and van Gunsteren, H. (1984), The dialectic of public and private pensions. *Journal of Social Policy*. 14(2), pp. 129–50.
Ryan, A. (1989), 'Value judgements and welfare', in D. Helm (ed.), *The Economic Borders of the State*. Oxford: Oxford University Press.
Shaver, S. (1993/94), Body rights. social rights and the liberal welfare state. *Critical social policy* 39, pp. 66–93.
Seldon, A. (1977), *Charge!* London: Temple Smith.
Sen, A. (1999), *Development as Freedom*. Oxford: Oxford University Press.
Spencer, H. (1851), *Social Statics*, obtained at files.libertyfund.org/files/273/Spencer_0331_EBk_v5.pdf;
——(1884), *The Man Versus the State*, files.libertyfund.org/files/330/Spencer_0020_EBk_v5.pdf.
de Swaan, A. (2000 [1988]), *In the Care of the State*. Cambridge: Polity.
Spicker, P. (2000), *The Welfare State: A General Theory*. London: Sage.
Taylor Gooby, P. and Larsen T. (2004), 'The UK – a test case for the liberal welfare state?', in P. Taylor Gooby (ed.), *New Risks, New Welfare*. Oxford: Oxford University Press.
Titmuss, R. (1968), *Commitment to Welfare*. London: Allen and Unwin.

20
Third Way

Martin Powell

Introduction

This chapter examines the 'Third Way' in social policy. The term is generally associated with the British academic, Anthony Giddens, and the New Labour government in Britain from 1997 to 2010, especially with Labour Prime Minister between 1997 and 2007, Tony Blair. For Blair, the label of 'modernisation' pre-dated the Third Way, but their themes remained broadly similar (2008, p. 4). The Third Way label featured highly in the 1997 Labour Election manifesto and the government's early policy documents – Blair (1998) wrote a pamphlet entitled 'The Third Way' (see Powell, 1999). However, the main point of reference is generally taken as Giddens's (1998) text, *The Third Way*. Giddens (1998, p. vii) claims that the term 'Third Way' is of no particular significance in and of itself. Similar terms such as 'progressive governance', 'modernizing social democracy', and the 'modernising left' have been used. For example, 'Progressive Governance' conferences have been held since 1998 (www.policy-network.net; Giddens, 2007, xii). Powell (2004, p. 3) suggests 'Tonyism' – after Blair and Giddens. While the term was ubiquitous, at least in Britain, around the turn of the century, it has become less used in Britain, and was always less common elsewhere. Blair (2001) attempted to launch 'Third Way, phase two' (see Giddens 2002), but the term declined in use, especially with Gordon Brown replacing Blair as Prime Minister in 2007, and the replacement of New Labour with a Conservative–Liberal Democrat Coalition government in 2010.

Many commentators regard the Third Way as an Anglo-Saxon construction, based on Clinton's New Democrats in the USA and Blair's New Labour in the UK. For example, according to Pierson (2001, p. 129) the politics of the Third Way has a peculiarly Anglophone provenance. However, Giddens (1998, p. viii) writes that some policies such as active labour markets draw inspiration more from Scandinavia than from the USA. Moreover, Blair's break with Old Labour was similar to those made by virtually all Continental social democratic parties, in what has been termed doing a 'Bad Godesberg' (where the German Social Democratic party renounced Marxist socialism). Indeed, 'in many respects the debate in the UK needs to catch up with the more advanced sectors of Continental social democracy'. It has been noted that former Dutch Prime Minister Wim Kok is sometimes seen as the first real leader of the Third Way, and that some themes can be seen in the Australian Labour Party under Bob Hawke and Paul Keating in 1980s and 1990s (Pierson, 2001).

According to Giddens (2002, pp. 3–4) the third way debate is a worldwide phenomenon, and almost all centre-left parties have restructured their doctrines in respect to it. He cites Merkel's

(2001) observation that 'the debate about the third way has become the most important reform discourse in the European party landscape'. Merkel (2001) distinguishes four third ways among EU social democratic parties: the New Labour model, the 'polder model' in the Netherlands, the 'reformed welfare state path' in Sweden and the 'statist path' of the French socialists. Centre-left parties in other EU countries tend to approximate in their policies to one or other of these positions.

However, very few social democratic parties explicitly associate with the third way label (briefly Germany, Belgium and Italy) and even then it was favoured more by liberals than social democrats (Bonoli and Powell, 2004). Nevertheless, third way themes were found in countries such as the Netherlands, Belgium, France, Germany, Austria, Sweden, Portugal (Bonoli and Powell, 2004). Put another way, although labels may vary, contents – albeit spoken with different accents – are similar in a number of countries. In this sense, rather than the third way, there are third ways (Giddens, 1998; Bonoli and Powell, 2004). In its various guises (e.g. new social democracy; Die Neue Mitte, etc.), the Third Way was part of the 'magical return of social democracy' (Cuperus and Kandel, 1998) that broadly aimed to combine social solidarity with a dynamic economy. However, the magic began to wear off (Powell, 2004), with only Britain being governed by a centre/left party for much of the first decade of the twenty first century.

Core concepts

There remains much uncertainty about the precise nature of the 'Third Way'. In historical terms, the phrase has been associated with movements as different as Swedish social democracy and Italian fascism. As Pierson (2001, p. 130) puts it, it has been hotly contested but consistently under-specified. For some it is a 'middle way' between market and state. For others, it transcends or goes beyond these terms. While many critics portray it as tending towards neo-liberalism or Christian Democracy (Powell, 2004, p. 4), its supporters such as Blair (1998), Blair and Schroder (1999), and Giddens (1998) regard it as a left of centre position, concerned with the renewal of social democracy.

A number of tables indicating the main characteristics of the Third Way have been produced, which broadly compare the Old Left, New Right, and Third Way (e.g. Giddens, 1998, p. 18; Powell, 1999; 2004). Similarly, new social democracy has been characterised by: rights and responsibilities; equity and efficiency; market and state failure; inclusion; positive welfare; minimum opportunities; employability; conditionality; civil society/market/state finance and delivery partnerships; flexicurity; networks; pragmatic tax to invest; high services and low benefits; high asset redistribution; pragmatic mix of universalism and electivity; national minimum Wage; and tax credits (Powell, 2004). However, it is important to differentiate discourse, values, policy goals, and policy means or mechanisms (see Powell, 2004).

The Third Way generated a new discourse or a new political language. For example, Clinton and Blair shared a number of key slogans or mantras such as being 'tough on crime; tough on the causes of crime'; 'a hand up, not a hand out'; 'hard working families that play by the rules'; and 'work is the best route out of poverty'. The Third Way was a political discourse built out of elements from other political discourses to form, in Blair's term, political 'cross-dressing'. The language of the Third Way was a rhetoric of reconciliation, such as 'economic dynamism as well as social justice', or 'enterprise as well as fairness'. The Third Way was not deemed antagonistic: while neo-liberals pursued the former, and traditional social democrats pursued the latter, the third way claimed to deliver both.

Some commentators suggested a number of core values for the Third Way. Blair (1998, p. 3) writes that four values are essential to a just society: equal worth, opportunity for all, responsibility, and community. These included CORA (community, opportunity, responsibility, and accountability) (Le Grand, 1998) and RIO (responsibility, inclusion, and opportunity) (Lister, 2001). However, the values of the Third Way remained problematic. This was mainly for two reasons. First, adequate understanding of values required more than one-word treatments. Terms such as 'equality' are essentially contestable concepts, meaning different things to different people (see below). Second, and linked, it is not clear whether the Third Way was concerned with 'old' values, 'new' values, or redefined meanings of 'old' or 'new' values.

Blair claimed that policies flow from values. In this sense, goals or objectives may be seen as a more specific operationalisation of values. For example, 'equality' may result in very different policy objectives such as equality of opportunity or equality of outcomes. New Labour probably set itself more targets than any previous British government. Critics who argue that *all* of New Labour's *aims* are less radical than Old Labour were wide of the mark. Old Labour would be proud of the introduction of the national minimum wage, and of the child poverty and health inequality targets. However, the health inequality targets were not met, as inequalities increased rather than fell (Toynbee and Walker, 2010, p. 49). The commitment was to end child poverty by 2020, but there are significant doubts about whether it will be achieved.

It was claimed that traditional values and goals must be achieved by new means. In some ways this had parallels with 'Croslandite revisionism'. 'Third Wayers' such as Blair and Giddens claimed that the 'new times' of the 1990s called for new policies, arguing that the world had changed and so the welfare state also had to change. New Labour insisted that the enduring values of 1945 were to be applied to the very different world of today, and that the policies of 1997 cannot be those of 1947 or 1967, but values remained the same. In his introduction to the 1997 manifesto, Tony Blair claimed that 'In each area of policy a new and distinctive approach has been mapped out, one that differs from the Old Left and the Conservative right' (in Powell, 1999, pp. 7, 13).

Table 20.1 Third Way in terms of moves in rethoric and policy

Dimension	*Old Left*	*Third Way*	*New Right*	*Move of Rhetoric*	*Move of Policies*
Approach	Leveller	Investor	Deregulator	NR?	NR?
Citizenship	Rights	Both rights and responsibilities	Responsibilities	TW	TW?
Outcome	Equality	Inclusion	Inequality	TW	NR?
Mixed Economy of Welfare	State	Public/private; civil society	Private	NR	NR
Mode	Command and control	Cooperation/ partnership	Competition	NR	NR
Expenditure	High	Pragmatic	Low	TW	OL
Benefits	High	Low?	Low	TW	TW
Accountability	Central state/ upwards	Both?	Market/ downwards	NR	NR
Politics	Left	Left of centre/ post-ideological	Right	TW	NR

Adapts the table presented in Powell (1999), adding two columns that seek to update the 'blueprint' of the Third Way in terms of moves in rhetoric and policy.
Source: Data from Eurostat webpage on income and living conditions (epp.eurostat.ec.europa.eu/portal/page/portal/income_social_inclusion_living_conditions/data/database)

Analysis

This section focuses on the British Labour Government (1997–2010), examining the content and evolution of Third Way social policy. It focuses on changes in rhetoric and policy content over time.

Approach

New Labour emerged during the long period of opposition to the Conservative government of 1979–97. The Labour leader of the time, John Smith, set up the Commission on Social Justice (CSJ, 1994) which flagged up many elements of the Third Way. It rejected the approaches to social and economic policy of the 'Levellers' (the old left) and the 'Deregulators' (the New Right) and advocated the 'middle way' of 'Investor's Britain'. This approach featured much of the discourse which became central to New Labour: 'economic efficiency and social justice are different sides of the same coin'; 'redistributing opportunities rather than just redistributing income'; 'transforming the welfare state from a safety net in times of trouble to a springboard for economic opportunity'; 'welfare should offer a hand up not a hand out'; 'an active, preventive welfare state'; 'paid work for a fair wage is the most secure and sustainable way out of poverty'; and 'the balancing of rights and responsibilities'.

This has parallels with Giddens's (1998, p. 117) view of the Third Way as being based on investment in human capital, resulting in a 'social investment state' operating in the context of a positive welfare society (see also Dobrowolsky and Lister, 2008). The key concerns of an investor's welfare state may be seen in four areas: an active, preventive welfare state; the centrality of work; the distribution of opportunities rather than income (see below); and the balancing of rights and responsibilities (see below).

The issue of prevention differentiates an active from a passive welfare state, and has clear similarities with Giddens's (1998) discussion of positive as opposed to negative welfare. Many early documents stressed the importance of prevention (Powell, 1999, pp. 15–16). Perhaps the clearest expression can be found in the notion of 'employability' rather than the old Keynesian notion of 'full employment'. As globalisation meant that the old world of working for the same company for a working life had disappeared, the government's role was to ensure that individuals had the education, skills, and training to compete for new jobs.

Paid work was central to Third Way approaches to welfare. Key policy goals were seen in the slogans of 'work for those who can; security for those who cannot' and 'making work pay'. The Third Way stressed 'full employment', but this was to be achieved in terms of 'employability' through the 'supply side' rather than by 'old'-style Keynesian demand management. Paid work was more 'flexible', with an increase in part-time and temporary employment. The third way's work-centred social policy had a mix of carrots and sticks. On the one hand, it may have emphasised carrots in the form of giving information about job opportunities, preparing CVs and job interviews. The slogan of 'making work pay' included a national minimum wage, in-work benefits of tax credits (or fiscal welfare) and increasing the availability of high-quality affordable child care. On the other hand, critics argue that there was an element of US policy that tended to 'starve the poor back into work' through low or time-limited benefits. However, the aim of rebuilding the welfare state around work was only partially successful. Although many public and private sector jobs were created during the period of the New Labour government, an estimated 80 per cent of these jobs were taken up by immigrants (Butler, 2009). This illustrates the impossibility of delivering Brown's slogan of 'British jobs for British workers' within the EU, with around 1 million NEETs (not employed or in education or training) aged between 16 and 24.

Citizenship

It was argued that Old Labour stressed rights while the New Right stressed responsibilities. Blair insisted that 'The rights we receive should reflect the duties we owe' (in Dwyer, 2008, p. 199). According to Giddens (1998, p. 65, italics in original) 'One might suggest as a prime motto for the new politics, *no rights without responsibilities*'. The most obvious domain concerns the obligation to look actively for work. However, in principle, unemployment benefits were always underpinned by job search obligations. The rhetoric of conditionality was not new, but the Third Way involved more active enforcement, and a changing balance of carrots and sticks for different groups. However, some recent critics have argued that the rhetoric of the obligations and sanctions associated with seeking employment may be tougher than its application in practice. For example, recent research has suggested that Jobseekers Allowance (JSA) claimants spend as little as eight minutes a day searching for work, and that research commissioned by the government Department of Work and Pensions found that a large portion of claimants were happy to live a life on benefits. Other research has shown that while sanctions are notionally applied when conditionality requirements are not adhered to, these sanctions can be so small that claimants sometimes do not realise that they have been sanctioned. Overall, the bark of the current sanctions regime is a lot worse than its bite. Moreover, significant proportions of the British public report in opinion polls that they consider that sanctions should be tougher (see Oakley and Saunders, 2011).

Dwyer (2008, p. 200) writes that 'New Labour has been keen to extend its rights and responsibilities agenda into other policy areas, including housing, education, health, pensions, and the management of anti-social behaviour and problem families'. However, New Labour appears not to have followed Giddens's (1998, pp. 65–6) argument that 'no rights without responsibilities' must apply not only to welfare recipients but to everyone, as many bankers and top public sector leaders appear to be rewarded for failure.

Outcome

The Third Way aims for inclusion rather than the old equality of outcome of the Old Left or inequality of the New Right. Blair stated that he aimed for 'a diverse but inclusive society', while Labour MP Tony Wright claimed that 'liberal socialism' will be 'egalitarian enough to be socially inclusive' (in Powell, 2002, p. 26). According to Giddens (1998, pp. 102–3), the new politics defines equality as inclusion and inequality as exclusion. He is concerned about exclusion at the bottom and voluntary exclusion ('the revolt of the elites') at the top. While Giddens is concerned about levels of inequality of income and wealth, he seems to stress 'civic liberalism' or inclusion within the public realm (see Powell, 2002).

However, New Labour was 'relaxed' about people being 'filthy rich'. It appeared to be dazzled like a rabbit in the headlights at wealth (whether deserved or successful), and seemed to subscribe to the idea that poor people need poverty as an incentive but rich people need 'filthy' levels of wealth to spur them on. Income inequality (as measured by the Gini coefficient) rose during New Labour's term (Toynbee and Walker, 2010, p. 199).

Rather than stressing greater equality of outcome, New Labour stresses equality of opportunity, but a 'radical' or 'maximalist' version of equality of opportunity (Giddens, 1998; Powell, 2002) Blair was concerned about life chances, meritocracy and social mobility (Powell, 2002, pp. 23–4). However, New Labour's health inequalities targets were missed, as inequalities rose rather than fell (Toynbee and Walker, 2010, p. 199). Similarly, a report by former New Labour Cabinet Minister Alan Milburn in 2009 showed that top professions such as medicine and law are increasingly being closed off to all but the most affluent families, and that the professions have become more and not less exclusive over time.

Mixed economy of welfare

It is claimed that Old Labour favoured state, while the New Right favoured the private and voluntary sectors. Giddens (1998, p. 99) writes that Third Way politics advocates a 'new mixed economy', which looks for a synergy between public and private sectors, utilizing the dynamism of markets but with the public interest in mind. He supports movement from a welfare state to a welfare society where expenditure on welfare will be generated and distributed not wholly through the state, but by the state working in combination with other agencies – third-sector agencies should play a greater part in providing welfare services, and top-down dispensation of benefits should cede place to more localized distribution systems (pp. 127, 117–18).

New Labour's first sign of a changed view of the private sector came in its 1997 manifesto. Only a few years previously, the Conservatives' 'Private Finance Initiative' (PFI, where facilities are built and operated by the private sector and leased to the public sector, typically for 25 to 35 years) had been termed 'totally unacceptable' and 'the thin end of the wedge of privatisation' (Shaw, 2007). New Labour relied heavily on such 'Public Private Partnerships' to deliver improvements in public infrastructure such as the 'largest hospital building programme in the history of the NHS'. New Labour later stressed the importance of promoting greater plurality or diversity in supply, and promoted a concordat with private providers; 'Independent Sector Treatment Centres' (ISTC) and new autonomous organisations ('Foundation Trusts') (see Shaw 2007, Chapter 5). Drakeford (2008) argues that New Labour entailed the onward march of marketisation and privatisation across the whole welfare frontier. There were some mixed signals under Brown's period as Prime Minister, with the NHS being seen as the 'preferred provider' of NHS services but the overall direction of travel was clearly towards more private provision of public services. There was also broad encouragement of provision by the voluntary sector and by 'social enterprise' as part of stimulating 'civil society'.

Mode

Early New Labour rhetoric stressed the importance of collaboration (cooperation, partnership, and networks) rather than command-and-control or competition (see Glendinning et al., 2002). However, while there was always a mixture of approaches, there is little doubt in practice Labour relied heavily on command-and-control (performance management, 'targets and terror') which has now given way to increased competition over time (Le Grand, 2007). To use Le Grand's terms, while the 'knavish' 'engines' or 'motors' of competition or command were fairly clear, the 'knightly' motor of trust and altruism associated with collaboration appeared to be more problematic. Having initially attempted to abolish markets in sectors such as healthcare, New Labour re-introduced and extended choice and competition, stressing the importance of individual choice in sectors such as healthcare, social care, and education.

Expenditure

New Labour aimed to be 'wise spenders' not 'big spenders'. This appears to have two main elements. First, 'investment' in facilities or human capital or benefit for the non-working population is 'good', but 'relief' for the working population is 'bad', termed 'the bills of economic and social failure'. Second, services should be judged by outputs and outcomes rather than cash inputs (Powell, 1999, pp. 21–2). New Labour rejected in 1997 Old Labour 'tax and spend', and promised to stick to planned Conservative spending limits. There would be 'prudence for a purpose'. However, Labour later increased public spending, resulting in a rise of over 50 per cent since 1997 which was termed 'return to spender' or a 'return to Old Labour' by the right (Butler, 2009, but see Toynbee and Walker, 2010).

It is far from clear what impact this expenditure had. Toynbee and Walker (2010, pp. 298, 297) claim that 'public services measurably improved', and that Labour 'bequeathed a public realm that shone', building new schools and hospitals, and reducing 'public squalor'. However, much of this will result in expensive PFI 'mortgages' for many years to come (see above). On the other hand, Butler (2009, p. 149) claims that the huge rise in public spending has not brought a huge improvement in public services, with much of the extra money dissipated in higher salaries and pensions. There have been some very sharp increases for the best-paid public managers, meaning that there are a large number paid more than the Prime Minister. Labour presided over a number of projects that spiralled out of financial control and have yet to deliver proportionate benefits (such as the NHS IT strategy).

With the financial crisis of 2007, it was clear that (to use the words of Tony Crosland about the 1970s Labour Government) 'the party's over'. Brown gave huge sums of money to prop up the banks, *de facto* achieving an Old Labour dream of nationalising some banks. Unfortunately, this *de facto* nationalisation does not appear to have brought any measure of control as it is 'business as usual' in terms of bankers' bonuses. Putting all these diverse arguments together, it might be fair to say that Labour's spending achieved some positive results, but probably not as much as would have been hoped for. In short, contrary to the claim, Labour tended to be big rather than wise spenders.

Benefits

The New Labour view of individual benefits is less clear than its view of overall spending (above). However, there are a number of reasons to suspect benefits were to be less generous than Old Labour. While the balance between carrots and sticks might vary between groups, 'making work pay' must imply some degree of 'less eligibility' to use the term of the New Poor Law. Even for non-working groups, New Labour did not restore the 'earnings link' that it criticised the Conservatives for breaking, and left pensions to rise by prices rather than earnings. Rather than raising benefits across the board, New Labour tended to favour selectivity rather than universalism, which was pursued through greater means testing and a complex system of in-work tax credits, which were later extended to pensions and child care. Labour also stressed asset-based welfare (such as Child Trust Funds). In short, Labour appeared to favour 'investment' over 'spending', resulting in prioritising collective provision (such as schools and hospitals) over individual benefits.

Accountability

While Old Labour favoured state/upwards accountability and the New Right favoured market/downwards accountability, New Labour stressed both. In practice, this resulted in a complex and confused web of accountability. At times, New Labour talked 'localism' but carried out centralisation through central performance management. Labour claimed to square the accountability circle through 'earned autonomy' which was defined as 'intervention in inverse proportion to success', but this essentially meant 'the power to do what we tell you'. New Labour also favoured 'arms length' regulators. Organisations such as the 'National Institute for Clinical

Excellence' (rationing treatments in healthcare) are broadly considered a success, but some others such as the Financial Services Authority and the Care Quality Commission have seen some regulatory failure as vital warning signs were missed. Over time, the market/downwards accountability has increased as individual choice has been the dominant policy element in a number of sectors. Similarly, New Labour increasingly tended to stress the 'state failure' discourse of the New Right rather than the 'market failure' discourse of the Old Left.

Politics

As discussed above, while New Labour stressed that the Third Way was a centre-left project, a number of critics considered that it had more in common with neo-liberalism. These different readings are ultimately influenced by ideology (see below), but it is hard to resist the argument that both in discourse and policy New Labour moved more to the right over time (but see Giddens, 2010). Another strand of Third Way politics stresses a pragmatic rather than ideological nature. Instead of old dogmas, it is claimed that 'what counts is what works' and 'evidence-based policy' is emphasised.

The Third Way legacy

There are a number of ways of examining the Third Way legacy. In terms of politics, Tony Blair was the longest serving British Labour Prime Minster, and his three election victories led to the longest Labour government in British history. Just as New Labour embraced 'post-Thatcherite' politics, having to take certain elements of Conservative politics as 'given', it is possible that the Conservative–Liberal Democrat government has embraced 'post-Third Way' politics. As seen earlier, the period around the turn of the century briefly saw 'Third Way' governments in power across much of Europe, but only the British Labour Party held power continuously for a significant period of time.

In terms of social policy, there are three ways of examining the Third Way legacy, from the perspectives of the Old Left, New Right and middle way. An Old Left perspective might point to changed values, diluted policy goals, timid delivery and the embracing of former enemies such as private medicine. A New Right perspective (such as Butler, 2009, subtitled 'how Gordon Brown lost a fortune and cost a fortune') suggests an economy steered onto the rocks; a bloated public sector; a public pensions scandal; and a record of failure.

A middle way perspective focuses on 'intrinsic evaluation', examining the achievements of the third way in its own terms (Powell, 2008). Blair's resignation in 2007 and later New Labour's electoral defeat in 2010 saw a range of judgements so different that it was difficult to believe that commentators were examining the same events. Jordan (2010, p. 1) writes that the Iraq War and economic crash left almost all Blair's grandiose moral slogans in ruins. On the domestic front, improvements in poverty, youth unemployment, workless households, and educational opportunity had all been reversed, and New Labour's reforming energies exhausted. According to Toynbee and Walker (2010), the great expectations in 1997 were almost bound to bring disappointment. They conclude that the good Labour did and the bad they avoided make an impressive list (p. 298). However, it wasted the extraordinary opportunity of ten years of economic prosperity and secure parliamentary majorities under a leader of great political talent, facing only weak opposition (p. 303). They sum up a performance of, say, six out of ten, which was not good enough (p. 304). Rawnsley (2010, p. xi) points to the move from triumph to disaster, highlighting the 'hyperbolic rhetoric' (p. 9) and that 'education, education, education' was a slogan not a strategy and '24 hours to save the NHS' was a sound-bite not a plan (p. 10). He concludes that 'things did get better' and there was a 'creditable range of achievements'. Britain became a more social democratic country. Britain became a more tolerant, more diverse, more socially just, more outward-facing and, despite the recession, more prosperous nation than in the Tory eighties and nineties. It also became a more indebted, more authoritarian, more statist, and more cynical country (pp. 739–40). On the other hand, Diamond (2010) claims that the public realm in Britain is now stronger, safer, and more sustainable than in the previous decade. On inequality, Labour's record was rather more contentious, with the gap between rich and poor widening during this period. While admitting its record is 'distinctly patchy', Giddens (2010) writes that it is possible to mount a robust defence of Labour's core policies, and that it would be hard to deny that it had far more impact than did any of the other roughly contemporary centre-left administrations of Clinton, Jospin, or Schroder.

According to Blair's resignation speech: 'only one government since 1945 [...] can say all of the following: more jobs, fewer unemployed, better health and education results, lower crime and economic growth in every quarter' (Powell, 2008, p. 259). Some of this changed with the brief and unhappy period of Gordon Brown premiership (2007–10) which saw the scandal of MPs' expenses, a banking crisis, an economic crisis, and the need to sharply reduce public expenditure and the national debt. In short, boom turned to bust, and Brown was – in cricket terms – playing on the back foot. Brown's mistaken claim that he had 'saved the world' (not saved the banks – by a vast injection of public money) did not save his job as PM. Blair (2010, p. 679) believes that Labour lost the 2010 Election because it stopped being New Labour.

It is difficult to sum up all these diverse strands, but the Third Way probably saw few paradigmatic changes for three reasons. First, many of New Labour's themes built on earlier Conservative reforms (especially the later rather than the earlier years of New Labour). As former Conservative Prime Minister John Major put it in 1999: 'I did not appreciate at the time the extent to which Blair would appropriate Conservative language and steal their policies. The attractive candidate was to turn out to be a political kleptomaniac' (in Powell, 2008, p. 267). Second, it is difficult to specify the 'counterfactual': what the Conservatives would have done if they had been re-elected in 1997. Third, there was no clear linear policy development over time, as policy changed in a series of phases with some U-turns. There were many changes over time. If we had 'New Labour' and the 'Third Way' in 1997, perhaps we had in later years 'New New Labour', 'Even Newer Labour', or the 'Fourth Way'.

From a wider international perspective, Ryner (2010) writes that whilst European social democrats looked to New Labour, New Labour was in turn taking inspiration from Bill Clinton's New Democrats in the United States and their pursuit of welfare objectives through markets. Keman (2010) points out that in some countries – most notably Australia, Flemish Belgium, Finland, Germany, Great Britain, Italy, the Netherlands, and Sweden – not only is there a move towards the 'radical centre', but also this is accompanied by more emphasis on Third Ways ideas and less on maintaining the traditional welfare state.

Conclusion

The British Third Way was a remarkable electoral success, but its influence in terms of lasting impact on the British welfare state, influencing subsequent governments, and governments in other countries, remains far from clear. The British Labour Government appeared to adopt more neoliberal characteristics, and it eventually ran out of steam, ideas, and money as boom turned to bust in the financial crisis. In terms of policy impact, it can claim some positive results but it fell short of own grand aims. New Labour promises of 'welfare reform', 'world-class public services', and a 'modern welfare state' have only been partially delivered, resulting in an incomplete New Labour legacy. There was a sense of 'implementation failure' as a large increase in inputs resulted in a less significant increase in outcomes. Blair's legacy is probably less far reaching than Attlee (1945) or Thatcher (1979), in the sense that their governments made it almost impossible to return to previous policies.

Nevertheless, it can be argued that some of the key features of the Third Way live on both in ideas such as the 'Big Society' and Philip Blond's 'Red Tory' which can be seen in the British Conservative–Liberal Democrat Coalition government, and in international terms in policies in other countries and influences on agencies such as the World Bank. There is clearly some shared ground between New Labour and the Coalition. It is likely that elements such as 'active' and 'positive' welfare, consumerism, obligations, and a more pluralist welfare state are here to stay, and it is very doubtful that there will be a return to the traditional social democratic welfare state. According to Diamond (2010), no party can win an election in Britain any longer on an avowedly right-wing policy agenda. This is the ultimate triumph of New Labour, redefining the centre-ground of British politics. According to Jordan (2010, p. 9) the political dominance of the Third Way in the UK, and the new regime at the World Bank from 1997 onwards, meant that it continued to be deployed, modified, and tested, and to influence centrist and liberal left politics worldwide during all the years from 1992 to 2010.

Further reading

Bonoli, G. and Powell, M. (eds) (2004), *Social Democratic Party Policies in Contemporary Europe*. London: Routledge. (This collection places the Third Way in the broader context of the policies of European Social Democratic parties.)

Giddens, A. (1998), *The Third Way*. Cambridge: Polity Press. (The influential original source written by the leading academic proponent of the Third Way. A second edition was published in late 2011.)

Powell, M. (ed.) (2008), *Modernising the Welfare State The Blair Legacy*. Bristol: Policy Press. (This examines the successes and failures of the British New Labour government from a range of perspectives.)

www.policy-network.net (Provides details of the international 'Progressive Governance' network.)`

References

Blair, T. (1998), *The Third Way*. London: Fabian Society.

——(2001), Third way, phase two. *Prospect*, March, pp. 10–13.

——(2010), *A Journey*, London: Hutchinson.

Bonoli, G. and Powell, M. (eds) (2004), *Social Democratic Party Policies in Contemporary Europe*. London: Routledge.

Butler, E. (2009), *The Rotten State of Britain*, London: Gibson Square.

Commission on Social Justice (1994) *Social Justice: Strategies for National Renewal*. London: Vintage.

Cuperus, R. and Kandel, J. (eds) (1998), *European Social Democracy*. Freudenberg/Amsterdam: Friedrich Ebert Siftung/Wiardi Beckman Stiching.

Diamond, P. (2010), *The British Labour Party: New Labour out of Power*, IPG 4.

Dobrowolsky, A. and Lister, R. (2008), Social investment: the discourse and the dimensions of change, in M. Powell (ed.), *Modernising the Welfare State. The Blair Legacy*. Bristol: Policy Press, pp. 125–142.

Driver, S. and Martell, L. (2006), *New Labour*, 2nd edn, Cambridge: Polity Press.

Dwyer, P. (2008), 'The conditional welfare state', in M. Powell (ed.), *Modernising the Welfare State. The Blair Legacy*, pp. 199–218, Bristol: Policy Press.

Giddens, A. (1998), *The Third Way*. Cambridge: Polity Press.

——(2002), *Where Now for New Labour?* Cambridge: Polity Press.

——(2007), *Over to you, Mr Brown*. Cambridge: Polity Press.

——(2010), The rise and fall of New Labour, *New Statesman*, 17 May, pp. 25–27.

Jordan, B. (2010), *Why the Third Way Failed. Economics, Morality and the Origins of the 'Big Society'*. Bristol: Policy Press.

Keman, H. (2010), Third ways and social democracy: the right way to go? *British Journal of Political Science*, pp. 1–10.
Le Grand, J. (1998), The Third Way Begins with CORA, *New Statesman*, 6 March, pp. 6–7.
——(2007), *The Other Invisible Hand*. Princeton, NJ: Princeton University Press.
Lister, R. (2000), To RIO via the Third Way, *Renewal*, 8(4), pp. 9–20.
Merkel, W. (2001), 'The third ways of social democracy', in A. Giddens (ed.), *The Global Third Way Debate*. Cambridge: Polity Press.
Oakley, M. and Saunders, P. (2011), *No Rights without Responsibility. Rebalancing the Welfare State*. London: Policy Exchange.
Pierson, C. (2001), *Hard Choices. Social Democracy in the Twenty First Century*. Cambridge: Polity.
Powell, M. (ed.) (1999), *New Labour, New Welfare State?* Bristol: Policy Press.
——(2002), 'New Labour and social justice', in M. Powell (ed.), *Evaluating New Labour's Welfare Reforms*. Bristol: Policy Press.
——(2004), 'Social democracy in Europe: renewal or retreat?', in G. Bonoli and M. Powell (eds), *Social Democratic Party Policies in Contemporary Europe*. London: Routledge.
——(ed.) (2008), *Modernising the Welfare State The Blair Legacy*. Bristol: Policy Press.
——(2012), 'Modernisation and the Third Way', in P. Alcock et al. (eds), *The Student's Companion to Social Policy*. Oxford: Blackwells
Rawnsley, A. (2010), *The End of the Party The Rise and Fall of New Labour*. London: Penguin.
Ryner, M. (2010), An obituary for the Third Way, *Political Quarterly*, 81(4), pp. 554–63.
Shaw, E. (2007), *Losing Labour's Soul*. London: Routledge.
Toynbee, P. and Walker, D. (2010), *The Verdict. Did Labour Change Britain?* London: Granta.

21

Welfare states in North America

Social citizenship in the United States, Canada, and Mexico

Robert Henry Cox

Introduction

The scope of a country's welfare state is often measured in one of two ways. One way is to calculate the amount of money a country commits to social welfare. Another is to examine the scope of social rights the country's welfare state guarantees to its citizens. By either measure, the welfare states of North America are less generous than most European welfare states. In terms of social spending, the United States spent 16.2 per cent of its gross domestic product (GDP) on social welfare in 2007. Canada spent slightly more, 16.9 per cent (OECD, 2011a). All of the wealthier countries of Western Europe during that year spent more than 20 per cent of their GDPs on social welfare. This pattern has been consistent over time, and marks these two countries as among the least generous welfare states. This status as laggard also applies when North American welfare states are compared in terms of social rights. Canada and the United States are often classified among the 'liberal' welfare states, those that outline a limited scope for state responsibility in providing for the welfare of their citizens. This classification stands in sharp contrast to the wealthier European countries, most of which are classified as 'social democratic' or 'occupational' welfare states.

When we speak of social rights, we speak of the normative principles that legitimate a welfare state. The notion of social rights was best first articulated by T. H. Marshall, who coined the term to describe the types of rights that allow citizens to share in the material and cultural heritage of their countries (Marshall, 1981). For the purpose of examining the welfare states of North America, we focus on the liberal type of welfare state (see also Chapter 17). Here the defining characteristics are a commitment on the part of state to provide a minimal level of social support to all citizens because they are of the national community. Social rights are called universal, because they are rights held by all citizens. In addition, social rights are categorical, meaning establishing a right requires that the state take steps to guarantee that its citizens can enjoy those rights. However, beyond the minimum, citizens are expected to take care of their own welfare needs.

Mexico, the third country in North America, occupies a special place. For most of the period since World War II, Mexico has been a developing country and consequently social policy was not a priority for public funds. During the last twenty years this has begun to change, but

Mexico does not yet have a welfare state that easily compares with more developed countries. For example, in 2007, social spending in Mexico was only 7.2 per cent of GDP (OECD, 2011a). Likewise, a conception of social rights is also only beginning to emerge.

The objective in this chapter is to outline the basic characteristics of the welfare states of these three countries and to compare them with one another and with the more expansive European models. This comparison is conducted through the prism of social rights. For each country, we examine the historical debates about social rights, and the efforts to expand them. Then, especially for the cases of Canada and the United States, we examine the efforts during the past two decades to retrench welfare states and limit the scope of social rights. The basic lesson of this comparison is that each of the three countries reached a golden age for the establishment of social rights. This came in the 1970s for the United States and Canada, but only recently for Mexico. Since the golden age, however, efforts to retrench welfare systems have circumscribed the expression of social rights. A desire to contain the rising costs of the welfare state has been an important driver of change, but more importantly, these reforms have been justified with new conceptions of social rights. Instead of categorical rights that all citizens can claim, social rights in these countries are conditional on the quality of one's conduct as a citizen.

From social rights to conditional welfare in the United States

The origins of the welfare state in the United States is often traced to the Social Security Act (1935), one of the central pieces of legislation enacted by President Franklin D. Roosevelt to respond to the economic challenges posed by the Great Depression. Two major programmes resulted from this legislation. The first was to create a universal programme of public assistance called Aid to Dependent Children that provided income support for mothers with young children. The second major component of the law created a universal pension system that provided income assistance to the unemployed, the elderly, widows, and orphans. These programmes were modifications on a typical income insurance scheme. The premiums for the insurance programmes were collected from working individuals in the form of payroll taxes, but the benefits were awarded all those who met the standard of need, regardless of their history of premium payments. This provision was introduced because the Great Depression had destroyed the personal savings of millions of citizens, at a time when records of employment histories were not easy to reproduce. Thus, to respond to the need, Roosevelt devised the programme to provide assistance and called it an insurance scheme to avoid the stigma that was then associated with charity assistance.

These programmes are often cited as the beginning of the American welfare state because prior to this time, social programmes were based either on the organizing ability of certain groups in society to press for assistance (such as war veterans), or on charity assistance whereby those who received assistance usually depended on the discretion and generosity of programme officers. The Social Security Act was important for the expansive responsibility it assigned to the state, but it did not establish universal social rights. Women were only eligible for assistance if they had children to support, and men were not eligible at all unless they qualified for unemployment, disability or retirement assistance (Katz, 1996).

Over the years, the US federal government expanded the criteria to provide income assistance for more individuals, such as the parents of dependent children and some disabled adults in the household. However, individual states, which were responsible for administering the programme, were also allowed a great deal of latitude in setting criteria for eligibility. As a result, the programme provided assistance for poor individuals, but did not meet the condition of universality that is part of the definition of a social right. Depending on where in the United States one lived, the level of assistance, and even whether one received assistance, varied dramatically.

Moreover, in 1996, this programme of assistance was replaced by legislation, introduced by President Bill Clinton, called Temporary Assistance for Needy Families (TANF). The major change introduced by TANF was to place a five-year life-time limit for receiving assistance. For many years prior to the passage of this legislation, a vigorous public discussion took place that claimed public assistance created a culture of dependency. The lifetime limits were designed to address this concern by creating firm incentives for able-bodied, working-age people to find jobs and get off public assistance. This change, more than any other in the United States, dramatically altered the notion of social rights. By placing lifetime limits on assistance, this programme dispensed with the notion of public assistance as a categorical claim one could make. Instead, the right to assistance became conditional on one's efforts to find work and keep a job. This reform also gained international attention, and similar programmes were adopted in many other countries (Wincott, 2011).

In contrast to public assistance, the system of social insurance expanded dramatically in the United States, and each expansion solidified the notion of entitlement that was the foundation of the programme. This is because unlike public assistance, social insurance was based on the notion that citizens earned their benefits by making contributions. The irony of this perception is that successive expansions of the programmes increased the benefits to levels far greater than one would receive based on their contribution histories alone. The programme has always been funded on a pay-as-you-go basis, meaning that current benefits are funded with the taxes collected from current contributors. Nonetheless, the public perception that people earn their social security has made this programme immune from major cutbacks. Indeed, during the 1960s and 1970s, most of the amendments to the programme made the criteria for eligibility and the levels of benefits more generous, allowing for early retirement options and introducing cost-of-living adjustments. This is not to say the benefits were generous. Consistent with the idea of a liberal welfare state, the pensions provided by social security were intended to provide a basic income to keep elderly citizens out of poverty. Those who desired to live comfortably in retirement needed to secure other pension incomes, either from their own savings or through programmes sponsored by their employers. Unlike many European countries, such programmes that provide income beyond the basic social security have never been mandatory for employees.

Beginning in the 1980s, the rising cost of social security led to concerns about its long-term viability. As a result, the levels of contributions have been increased, and the retirement age has been extended for 65 to 67 years. Early retirement options, which offer a reduced pension for those who retire younger than the normal retirement age, have been made less generous to encourage people to stay in the work force longer. These changes have done much to ensure the long-term solvency of the programme, but social security is still a modest income support. The amount of support provided to an elderly couple is about ninety per cent of the US federal poverty level.

Healthcare in the United States has had a troubled history. The first public programmes for healthcare were introduced in 1965 as part of President Lyndon Johnson's 'Great Society.' Like the Social Security Act, this programme consisted of two parts, a programme to provide medical care for the elderly (Medicare), and a programme to provide medical care for people without an income (Medicaid). It should be noted that these programmes did not provide healthcare as a universal right, but rather they identified target populations to support. All citizens who were not yet 65 years of age, and who had incomes beyond a minimum threshold were responsible for securing their own healthcare needs. As a result, a complex system of private and non-profit insurance has developed to provide numerous health insurance options to the working population. The right to healthcare in the United States is a 'residual' right, meaning that a public commitment to meeting health needs only applies to people of limited incomes or the elderly. Other people with incomes might obtain healthcare in the private market, either by purchasing insurance or by paying fees directly to healthcare providers. In case of emergency, hospitals in the United States are prohibited from denying care to any in need, citizens who do not qualify for either Medicare or Medicaid are responsible for the cost of that care.

This healthcare system has always provided sub-optimal results. Private insurers have been able to restrict access to their programmes by imposing conditions, such as 'pre-existing condition' clauses, that allow them to deny coverage to people with substantial healthcare needs. The result has been that fully twenty-five per cent of the population lack any type of healthcare coverage, and this group largely comprises children and the 'working poor,' meaning people with low wage jobs.

Another problem with healthcare in the United States is that it is expensive for the level of coverage. The US spends fifty per cent more per person on healthcare than any other country. According to the Organisation for Economic Co-operation and Development (OECD, 2011b), the US spent $7,960 per person in 2009, while second-place Norway spent $5,352 per person. In recent years, rising costs of healthcare in the United States have been addressed by increasing the amount paid by individuals, with the result that people on limited incomes find it difficult to afford coverage. One notable exception was the Medicare Modernization Act, passed in 2003 by President George W. Bush. This law was the first major reform of the Medicare programme – the healthcare programme for elderly citizens. Its most notable change was to expand prescription drug benefit at a projected cost of $400 billion in its first ten years (Congressional Budget Office, 2005). Thus, one of the major challenges for healthcare spending in the United States is to reduce cost, but efforts to expand coverage prove to be extremely expensive.

Reforms introduced by President Barack Obama in 2009 sought to address the inadequacy of healthcare coverage in the United States and rein in costs by dramatically altering the fundamental structure of the system. The legislation would have required all citizens to carry health insurance, and would have provided public funds to pay the enrollment fees for citizens who lacked an adequate income. To do this, it would have placed restrictions on the abilities of insurance carriers to limit coverage. The programme was extremely contentious and before it was passed in 2010, its scope was reduced substantially during legislative debates. Nonetheless, it will go far in broadening healthcare coverage. The legislation will place substantial limits on the ability of insurance carriers to deny coverage, and it will allow uninsured citizens to elect health insurance among a number of public, as well as private schemes. The strongest effect of the Affordable Care Act, as it is called, will be to reduce the rapid increase in the cost of healthcare, though most of its more contentious provisions will not go into effect until 2014, and there is a chance that future reforms might stop these provisions from ever taking effect.

Thus, when measured against the metric of social rights, the American welfare state has never had a complete system of social rights. During the 1960s and 1970s, efforts were made to expand the various programmes by creating a guaranteed floor of income support. However, healthcare was never considered to be a basic part of the set of entitlements enjoyed by citizens of the United States. Then, as the era of austerity prompted reforms in the 1990s and 2000s, the effect has been to transform categorical rights into conditional rights, where the condition for receiving assistance is participation in the work force. Citizens unable to maintain a consistent employment history will have a basic claim to either income or health assistance.

A social liberal welfare state in Canada

Among the advanced industrial societies, Canada was relatively late in establishing comprehensive welfare programmes. Prior to World War II, social programmes in Canada were largely handled by the provinces, and most were based on the same principles as private charity, providing assistance to the 'worthy poor,' or those individuals who were deemed by public officials to have lived morally proper lives. Beginning in Manitoba in 1916, and quickly copied by other provinces within the next five years, programmes of mothers' aid were established that were the forerunners of today's poverty assistance programme. Yet public pressure continued to mount for a system of social security and in 1927 the first programme to fund public pensions were adopted. These early programmes comprised block grants awarded to provinces by the federal government for the purpose of creating pension schemes. However, they were administered like the mothers' aid programmes – pensions were given to 'the worthy poor', and only based on a means test.

The Great Depression of the 1930s had an enormously devastating effect on the Canadian economy, but it did not lead to the kinds of sweeping reforms that were adopted in the United States at the same time. In 1935, Prime Minister Richard B. Bennett introduced a 'New Deal' that was similar to the package of support President Roosevelt created the same year in the United States. Bennett's plan created a federal responsibility for unemployment, social insurance and a minimum wage. However, because the legislation was passed without the approval of the provinces, it was declared unconstitutional. The reason for this was that the British North America Act (BNAA), the agreement with the British crown that served as the Canadian constitution, awarded responsibility for health and social welfare issues to the provinces.

Instead, it was World War II that proved to be the watershed for the expansion of the Canadian welfare state. During the war the provinces agreed to transfer responsibility for unemployment insurance to the federal level, and the BNAA was revised to allow this. Also, Canadian officials were inspired by the ideas circulating among allied countries that laid the groundwork for post-war expansion of welfare states in a number of European countries. The British Beveridge report, which inspired many countries to create plans for expanding social policy, found its Canadian equivalent in the Marsh report of 1943. Also, in 1944 Canada adopted its first universal programme for income support: a child allowance. This programme awarded a universal benefit to all families with children under the age of 16. To avoid conflict with the BNAA, the programme required that eligible citizens apply for the benefit, rather than awarding it directly. This innovation was repeated for other federal income assistance programmes (Béland, 2005).

The foundation for universal assistance laid during the war was expanded substantially in the post-war years. This was made possible in part due to a dramatic growth in the Canadian economy in the decades after the war. Another important factor, however, was the expansion of the ideas of federal universal assistance to more areas of support. Legislation that gave organized labour a stronger voice led to an increase in the size of the unionized work force, and they became a strong proponent of expanded social insurance. This is not to say the programmes were always warmly accepted. Though popular among the public, the expansion of a federal role was resisted by conservatives on ideological grounds, and by French-speaking *Québécois* on national grounds (Béland and Lecours, 2008).

After World War II, however, social policy in Canada began to expand. The hated old age scheme was replaced in 1951 with an old age pension (Old Age Security – OAS), that provided a universal benefit to all Canadians aged 70 years or older, who had lived in the country for at least ten years. Benefits vary depending on how long one has lived in the country. A full benefit requires 40 years of residency. Initially, the programme also provided a means tested benefit for those aged 65 to 69 years, but this was ended in the 1960s and now the full universal benefit is provided beginning at the age of 65. In addition to OAS, pensioners with limited resources are eligible for a means tested Guaranteed Income Supplement (GIS). Both OAS and GIS represent a basic, universal pension. In contrast to the social security programme in the United States, the Canadian programme did not require a work history for a full benefit. However, these programmes are subject to taxation, with the effect that pensioners who have other sources of income find their pension benefit washed-out by their tax obligation (Marier, 2008).

In addition to the basic pension, Canada goes farther than the United States in having a mandatory, earnings-related pension for the people in the work force. The Canada Pension Plan (CPP) was adopted in 1966, as was a separate but coordinated programme in Quebec (RRQ). These are like 'second-tier' pension schemes in other European countries, and do not have an equivalent in the United States. CPP/RRQ pensions are contributory, and are designed to replace up to 25 per cent of the average wage. Unlike European second-tier programmes, and more consistent with the objectives of a liberal conception of social rights, the income replacement rates are modest. As a result, Canadian pensioners rely heavily on private pension insurance. Moreover, taken together the Canadian pension plans do not go far in protecting the elderly from poverty. As late as 1982, nearly 30 per cent of the elderly were living on pensions below the Low-Income Cut-Off, a poverty level among the elderly that placed Canada near the bottom among OECD countries (Mahon, 2008).

The CPP/RRQ underwent a major reform in 1997 intended to respond to growing concerns about the long-term solvency of the programme. Contribution rates were increased substantially. The result was that the programme continues to provide the targeted 25 per cent replacement income, but introduced a significant intergenerational inequity, as current workers were paying higher contributions to fund the pensions of current retirees.

Healthcare is one area where Canada has gone far beyond the United States in establishing a social right. All provinces in Canada provide universal, publicly funded healthcare for those services which are considered 'medically necessary.' The Medical Care Insurance Act, adopted in 1966, systematized what had until that point been a piecemeal system of provincial healthcare. It established the principle of the state as a single payer, universality of entitlement, and portability of services across provincial lines. The programme provides a list of medical services that are covered. Individuals are allowed to purchase private insurance for services not on the list. But, Canada is alone among single-payer healthcare systems for banning people from purchasing private insurance for services that are already covered by the public plan. This was designed to prevent the creation of a two-tier programme whereby wealthier citizens could pay for private care, leaving poorer citizens in the public schemes. To a degree, however, wealthy citizens already were able to this, as they only needed to cross the border into the United States to pay for an unlimited array of services.

The Canadian healthcare system has been chronically underfunded, with the federal government providing only 50 per cent of the actual costs incurred by provincial authorities. This has produced a rationing of care by default that has engendered complaints about long delays for necessary services. As a result, the Supreme Court of Canada ruled in 2005 that the ban on private care could be unconstitutional if it caused unreasonable delays for patients.

Thus, the Canadian welfare state conforms to the liberal conception of social rights. The state holds a responsibility for the providing for the basic welfare needs of the population. The programmes are universal, but they are minimal and leave a large space for private welfare services to fill in the gap between a minimum and a more generous level of support. In comparison with the classically liberal United States, Canadian programmes are quite generous, a difference we can best describe as a social liberal conception of entitlement. Social liberalism is a political philosophy that stresses the positive role states can perform in guaranteeing the rights of citizens by establishing the conditions to help citizens better enjoy those rights, such as providing for basic needs of health, income, and housing.

Mexico's emerging welfare state

During the last half of the twentieth century, Mexico made tremendous progress as a developing country. One measure of this progress has been the emergence of a welfare state. In recent years, austerity has led the state to cut back on the generosity of these systems of support, but these retrenchments have been supplemented with programmes that target assistance directly towards citizens in situations of extreme poverty. This system of support is beginning to look like a liberal welfare state, though the scope of coverage is still far below that of its northern neighbours, the United States and Canada. However, this welfare state is still in formation and the best description of it is a system designed to do little more than address the situations of citizens in extreme poverty.

Mexico did not participate in the first wave of welfare adoption that took place in Europe, the United States and Canada during the first half of the twentieth century. Priorities during this period were placed on nation-building. In the postwar period some small programmes were created that reflected the clientilistic nature of the Mexican state. They provided benefits for groups deemed essential to shore up the legitimacy of the Mexican state, and to build support for its strategies of economic development. Pension and disability programmes for the military and civil servants, for example, were extremely generous. Beginning in 1940, to build support for the state's programme of import-substitution industrialization (ISI), generous insurance schemes were created for workers in key economic sectors. The two major programmes established at this time were the *Instituto Mexicano del Seguro Social* (IMSS), created in 1943 for industrial workers, and the *Instituto de Seguridad y Servicios Sociales para los Trabajadores del Estado* (ISSSTE), created in 1960. These two programmes provided old age and disability pensions, as well as healthcare benefits. However, they covered less than half the working population, and their coverage was concentrated in the cities, not rural areas.

In 1973 a programme was created to address the plight of the rural poor. The National Programme for Depressed Areas and Marginal Groups created income and healthcare support based on one's place of residence. However, the programme suffered from chronic underfunding and by all measures failed to alleviate the grinding poverty in many rural areas. Moreover, the programme was not based on a right to assistance. Rather, the grants were given to local governments to establish workfare programmes.

In the 1980s came a shift in economic thinking in Mexico. A shift in oil prices caused Mexico to default on its debt, leading to a recessionary 'lost decade.' When circumstances began to improve in the 1990s, import-substitution industrialization was replaced with neo-liberal thinking. This meant that Mexico never experienced the type of Keynesian thinking that had given rise to expansive social policies in many European countries. Neo-liberalism sought to promote economic growth through trade, and did so by loosening the regulations on industry and promoting trade relations, notably through the North American Free Trade Agreement (NAFTA) with the United States and Canada. Neo-liberalism brought change to the pension system. The main thrust of this has been a privatization of pensions. This will lead to lower income replacement rates and more unequal incomes across pensioners, as actual pension income depends more and more on the private investment strategies of individuals.

A series of reforms to the rural assistance programme have slowly moved it from a patronage to a more effective programme of poverty relief. In 1988, President Carlos Salinas created the National Solidarity Programme (PRONASOL) which changed the block grant assistance for rural communities into targeted benefits for the rural poor. The programme was harshly criticized for being politically manipulated, so in 1997 President Ernesto Zedillo established a new programme called PROGRESA (National Programme for Education, Health and Nutrition).

By 1999, PROGRESA covered 40 per cent of all rural families and was praised for its efficiency and transparency. In 2000, President Vicente Fox renamed the programme *Oportunidades* and expanded it to cover the urban poor (Dion, 2008). The programme now covers virtually the entire poor population. Its benefits are means tested, but the rights are conditional, as recipients must meet some conditions. For example, children must maintain good school attendance and mothers must attend health and nutrition workshops. In 2006, *Oportunidades* covered 5 million families, nearly one quarter of the population, 70 per cent of whom lived in rural areas (Bayón, 2009, p. 306).

Healthcare in Mexico is another area where legislative goals have moved faster than the resources needed to meet those goals. In 1984, a universal right to healthcare was written into the constitution but these rights were granted without any infrastructural investment to make them effective in practice. Some healthcare services had been made available to the poor through *Oportunidades* and its predecessor programmes. However, these focused assistance on the poor, and were not well resourced. In 2001, the creation of People's Health Insurance (*Seguro Popular*) was a major reform to create a public, voluntary insurance scheme, targeted at low-income families who have no entitlement to social security benefits. The programme was enacted over the stiff opposition of private insurance companies. As a result, Mexico now has healthcare for the poor, a public, voluntary health insurance programme for low-income workers and their families, and an extensive system of private health insurance. One could say that the guarantee of health insurance to low-income workers is an expansion of the Mexican welfare state that is only now being introduced in the welfare state in the United States.

The net effect of recent reforms in Mexico can best be summarized as the creation of a floor for universal social rights, but an erosion of the benefits that once were enjoyed by well-placed workers. Moreover, a persistent problem for the Mexican welfare state is the scope of coverage. Despite the improvements, the system suffers from a low rate of take-up, meaning that eligible people fail to enroll in the programmes. By 2006 less than half of the urban, employed population was covered by pensions and health coverage. The scope of coverage in rural areas was higher, but not complete (Moreno-Brid, Pardinas Caprpizo, and Ros Bosch, 2009).

Conclusion

Thus, the three countries of North America bear a striking similarity in one respect. All have welfare states that are rather limited in their scope. Compared to European countries, they spend less per capita, and less as a percentage of their GDP. In terms of social rights, they identify a relatively limited responsibility for the state in providing for the needs of the population. Cultural values, and in the case of Mexico sheer limited resources, have led these three countries to devote less to the care of their citizens. Instead, in each country, citizens rely more on the market, or on private (especially family) networks, to provide their welfare needs. In these respects, they bear a strong similarity to the liberal, or residual models of welfare found in the United Kingdom, Ireland, Australia, or New Zealand. The heavy reliance on neighbourhood and family networks found especially in Mexico and the United States bear some similarity to the Mediterranean model of welfare where a weaker role of the state is taken up by a stronger family network. The North American examples stand in sharpest contrast to the 'social democratic' models of welfare found in Scandinavian countries where more extensive mandates to carry health insurance or to enrol in pension schemes, spread the costs of social welfare among the wider population.

Further reading

Béland, D. (2005), *Social Security: History and Politics from the New Deal to the Privatization Debate*. Lawrence, KS: University Press of Kansas.

Dion, M. (2008), Retrenchment, Expansion and the Transformation of Mexican Social Protection Policies, *Social Policy and Administration*, 42(4), pp. 434–50.
Katz, M. B. (1996), *In the Shadow of the Poorhouse: A Social History of Welfare in the United States*, 2nd edn. New York: Basic Books.
Lightman, E. (2003), *Social Policy in Canada.* New York: Oxford University Press.
Mahon, R. (2008), Varieties of Liberalism: Canadian Social Policy From the 'Golden Age' to the Present. *Social Policy and Administration*, 42(4), pp. 342–61.

Bibliography

Bayón, M. C. (2009), Persistence of an Exclusionary Model: Inequality and Segmentation in Mexican Society, *International Labour Review*, 148(3), pp. 301–15.
Béland, D. and Lecours, A. (2008), *Nationalism and Social Policy: The Politics of Territorial Solidarity.* Cambridge: Cambridge University Press.
Béland, D. (2005), *Social Security: History and Politics from the New Deal to the Privatization Debate.* Lawrence, KS: University Press of Kansas.
Congressional Budget Office (2005), Projection of Spending for the Medicare Part D Benefit. www.cbo.gov/doc.cfm?index=6113&zzz=28917. Download date 12 Sept 2011.
Dion, M. (2008), Retrenchment, Expansion and the Transformation of Mexican Social Protection Policies. *Social Policy and Administration*, 42(4), pp. 434–50.
Katz, M. B. (1996), *In the Shadow of the Poorhouse: A Social History of Welfare in the United States.* New York: Basic Books, 2nd edition.
Mahon, R. (2008), Varieties of Liberalism: Canadian Social Policy From the 'Golden Age' to the Present. *Social Policy and Administration*, 42(4), pp. 342–61.
Marier, P. (2008), The Changing Conception of Pension Rights in Canada, Mexico and the United States. *Social Policy and Administration*, 42(4), pp. 418–33.
Marshall, T. H. (1981), 'The Right to Welfare' and 'Afterthought on the Right to Welfare,' in *The Right to Welfare and Other Essays*, pp. 83–103. London: Heinemann Publishing.
Moreno-Brid, J. C., Pardinas Carpizo, J. E. and Ros Bosch, J. (2009), Economic Development and Social Policies in Mexico. *Economy and Society*, 38(1), pp. 154–76.
Organisation for Economic Co-operation and Development (OECD) (2011a), 'Social Expenditure—Aggregated Data.' stats.oecd.org/Index.aspx?DataSetCode=SOCX_AGG. Download date 12 Sept 2011.
——(2011b), 'OECD Health Data 2011 – Frequently Requested Data.' www.oecd.org/document/16/0,3343,en_2649&34631_2085200_1_1_1_ 1,00.html. Download date 12 Sept 2011.
Wincott, D. (2011), 'Ideas, Policy Change and the Welfare State,' in D. Béland and R. H. Cox (eds), *Ideas and Politics in Social Science Research*, pp. 143–66. New York and Oxford: Oxford University Press.

22 Welfare state changes in China since 1949

Bingqin Li

This chapter gives a brief overview of the changes in welfare policies of China since 1949 when the Communist Party came into power. It shows that the welfare policies in China are centred on two themes: facilitating economic growth and maintaining the political authority of the Communist Party.[1] Despite that, China has moved from a command economy pursuing Communist ideology to a market economy following 'Socialism with Chinese Characters', the approaches the state has responded to changing welfare needs have not really drifted away from the two themes. What has changed is the understanding of what types of policies and institutions can help to fulfil greater economic growth and legitimising control by the Communist Party.

There are many ways to define the stages of reform in China. To show how pursuing economic growth and political authority has led to welfare changes, this chapter presents the welfare history in a chronological order: 1) pre-1978, the period of Central Planning; 2) 1978–2003, the period in which economic growth played a dominant role; and 3) post-2003, the period that many scholars claim to be the 'spring' of social policy.

Central planning and the setting up of the welfare state (pre-1978)

In the early 1950s, China set up a state welfare system that was modelled against the Soviet Union. In the post-war period, the Communist government was challenged both economically and politically. The country was in dire poverty. The Communists were concerned about international hostilities and the return of National Government in exile. It was understood that to make the country strong and prosperous, it was necessary to develop heavy industries and build up national defence power. As a result, heavy industries became a national priority for the coming years.

Several conditions needed to be satisfied for the strategy to work: Labour costs in heavy industries should be kept low, workers should devote their lives to their jobs, and heavy industries should be guaranteed of good labour supply. The welfare state in the early stage of the Communist China was intended to help in meeting these conditions (Lin, Cai, and Z. Li, 1996).

The welfare state was intended to take care of a worker's basic welfare needs so that he/she would not worry about earning a low income. First, the state at the same time minimised the overall spending on a worker by providing services at a large scale, while the welfare level remained stringent. Second, the welfare entitlement was tied to a person's Household Registration (Hukou), and a person was discouraged to move to other jobs or to other parts of the country

(Lin, Cai, and Z. Li, 1996). To facilitate labour control, urban welfare had two parts: employer-based welfare and government welfare. Employers (work units, *Danwei*, including enterprises), government agencies, and the attached institutions, played different roles in the system (Dixon, 1981). Employers provided a number of welfare items, including housing, healthcare and health checks, nursery, dining halls, subsidies for transport and heating, hardship funds, pensions, childcare, and funeral expenses. Apart from the formalised welfare, depending on the work unit, workers could receive various in-kind benefits such as labour protection products (including gloves, masks, etc., depending on the industry concerned), summer cooling products, and life products (including food and sometimes family appliances) during festivals, etc. The state took up poverty relief for people who could not receive support from their employers and extended families. The two-tier system guaranteed that workers would find it difficult to change jobs, as their welfare entitlement was tied to employment.

During this period, rural welfare system was a collaborative system in which members of the communes received five guarantees: food, clothes, heating, children's education, and funeral for the dead (Cheng, 2008). With the help of the dual Hukou system, it was very hard for peasants to migrate to cities (Li and Piachaud, 2006).

On the whole, the urban welfare system during the Central Planning era followed three principles: guaranteed employment (iron rice bowl), egalitarianism, and cradle-to-grave welfare coverage (Ngok, 2010). To maintain such a system, the national income had to grow steadily in order to cover the growing population. The economy indeed grew. However, Mao's leadership was challenged politically. To stay in power, he started waves of political campaigns aiming to secure his political authority and the focus on economic growth was distracted (Weatherley, 2006). It is difficult to tell these days if had there been no political campaigns, the economy would have grown smoothly. Theoretically, the national strategy to prioritise heavy industry suffered from several problems. First, the closed economy and public ownership cultivated disincentives to improve productivity and encouraged welfare dependency (Leung, 1994). Second, the egalitarian ideal when put into practice turned out to be in favour of party members, and people in more senior positions in terms of welfare entitlements (Bian and Logan, 1996). Also, the long-lasting rural/urban divide cultivated a strong sense of privilege among urban residents. The impact of the Hukou system is so profound that, even to this day, many urban residents take it for granted that the welfare coverage they enjoy should not be offered to rural-urban migrant workers in cities, and not to farmers.

After Mao's death, the political and economic situations were unstable. Reform to leave the Central Planning System gained wide support despite that Mao had appointed a loyal supporter, who was soon sidelined politically. Reformers were able to push for radical changes in the welfare regime.

Increasing economic efficiency, political freedom, and the reconstruction of welfare state (1978–2003)

The post-Mao leadership, particularly Deng and his followers, believed that the free market could improve economic efficiency and ultimately lead to economic prosperity. The previous welfare system was considered to be a burden for economic efficiency. It had been reformed to free the enterprises from providing many welfare services.

Politically, the Communist Party and the government, though reluctant to make radical changes in the political system, had gone through some transformations. For example, after Deng's retirement, a new rule was introduced that members of the Standing Committee for the Political Bureau could only be in power for no more than two terms. Though this is not democracy, the fixed terms made it impossible for a leader to be able to become the next Mao. The recent history shows that when a new leader came into power, he tried to establish that he did not follow his predecessor sheepishly during his term of office. He would come up with a new theme that would become his own guiding theory. This practice left room for making major shifts in the foci of the 'reform', at least every other two political terms. However, the shift is not without limit. Sticking to Communist Party's leadership has always been in the Constitution. This means that despite dramatic changes, great efforts were devoted to maintaining the 'socialist' skin. At the same time, it reassured the people that the social welfare they enjoyed in the past would not be taken away from them immediately. This was a particularly important promise at the early stage of the reform. Therefore, years into the reform, many people still had 'a sure sense of their entitlement to social security and services and an equally sure sense of the governments' matching obligation to supply these' (Croll, 1999).

This period has two stages: 1978–1989 (Huaguo Feng, replaced by Deng Xiaoping who was followed by Hu Yaobang) and 1989–2003 (Jiang Zemin).

The defining feature of the period between 1978 and 1989 is the great effort to break the institutional barriers that prevented the economy from being liberalised. Various economic reforms were unleashed, such as the rural household responsibility system, the manager responsibility system in urban enterprises, price reform, and labour contract reform. All these changes in the economic system were intended to give the economy greater flexibility and push individuals to become more independent.

Immediately after 1978, unemployment became a serious problem. Fast population growth encouraged by Mao generated great difficulty in arranging jobs for young people in the 1960s and 1970s. In the planning era, unemployment had long been taught as the fatal weakness of capitalism. To avoid social tension, many young people were sent to the countryside to support the development of the remote areas. When the Cultural Revolution ended, tens of millions of people returned to their hometowns. Many of them could not find jobs and often turned to alcoholism and violence (Li, 2008). Social stability was seriously threatened.

To solve the problem, a number of policies were introduced. First, economically the state started to promote entrepreneurship. The initial success of some self-employed people motivated many others. Some people with formal jobs quitted to enter the private sector. However, they soon learnt to appreciate the value of the work unit welfare they used to enjoy – their higher cash income might not be enough to cover the loss of benefits. The work unit welfare became the bottleneck of economic liberalisation (Wu and Xie, 2003). Second, it was believed that unemployment was ultimately an oversupply of labourers. Therefore, the 'One Child Policy' was introduced to reverse the population trend set by Mao. This policy also had profound implications for welfare provisions in the coming years. Third, a social security system was set up. The intention was to reduce the welfare burden of work units (employers), and the state and individuals were expected to share the costs. A social pension system was also set up to help establish social pooling of pension funds. Finally, enterprises were required to gradually withdraw from providing social services. Some social services were taken care of at the community level.

In rural areas the collective social protection system also stopped, as rural collectives were replaced by household responsibility. At the same time, to cope with rural poverty, organised development programmes (Ngok, 2010).

However, the marketisation process was not smooth. Economically, there were several rounds of inflation, which caused panic responses from the public. As a result, reforms in the housing, pricing and the labour contract systems were put on hold for several times. They were only resumed when the economy improved. In the same period, the determined shift towards economic liberalisation also reassured that there would be no return to the Mao-style government, and the pursuit of political freedom surfaced. Several waves of political movements in the 1980s, especially the one in 1989, made the top politicians realise that the threat to challenge party authority was real. For several years after the crackdown in Tiananmen Square in 1989, reformers became hesitant. Until 1992, a speech given by Deng reignited the marketisation reform.

The ten years between 1992 and 2002 witnessed radical changes in the state's role in providing welfare. Deng's speech defined the spirit of the reform in this period: the country would focus on removing the institutional constraints for a prosperous market economy. In this period, political reform was brushed aside. Politicians championing market liberalisation were put in top positions to make sure that the direction of economic reform would not be reversed and radical political reforms would be avoided (Perry, 1993).

The central theme of the reform in this period was to improve the productivity of existing state and collective enterprises and encourage business investment from other sources. However, as more private and foreign enterprises were set up, the pressure to free competition caused major concerns in the Chinese business and academic circles. Some scholars argued that despite the growing private sector, state and collective enterprises were still the largest employers in China. After the long-lasting state planning and control, Chinese enterprises and businessmen were not yet used to the challenge of market competition. Newly emerged industries would need a transitional period so that they could grow before they could become fully fledged competitors with foreign companies which had far more resources and better management skills (Leung, 2003). Also, without setting up a social security system, Chinese enterprises bearing all the welfare burdens would find it difficult to compete in the market. What is more, the successful example of the four Tigers in the Pacific (South Korea, Taiwan, Hong Kong, and Singapore) also supported this line of argument. These countries/regions were known for their states' active promotion of export-oriented industries. Many industries such as car manufacturing in South Korea were heavily subsidised and supported by the state (Unger and Chan, 1995). A large country like China would need to have 'brand names' created locally.

To fulfil the dream of making domestic businesses competitive, in the early 1990s there were some moves in the establishment of a social security system. The first was the guideline to establish a multi-tiered social protection system in 1994 which included social insurance, social relief, social welfare, special care, and mutual help and individual savings accumulation (Ngok, 2010). A housing provident fund was set up in 1991 to help people to save money and pool funds to build up the capacity to buy houses in the private market. At the same time, the cost of public rental was increased in order to push people out of the rental sector (Li, 2005). On the whole, in early 1990s, there were louder voices for reform but progress continued to be cautious.

However, state protection did not generate expected economic outputs and many state enterprises continued to run inefficiently. Hesitation of the reformers portrayed as a success of 'incremental reform' generated the public expectation that the Chinese reform would be less painful than the reforms in East Europe. However, increasingly, it was realised that the heavily subsidised sector consumed scarce resources that were crucial for new businesses. The overall costs for the reform might not be lower than the 'Big Shock' (Fan, 1994). In the late 1990s, signs of dissatisfaction reappeared. Falungong emerged as a direct challenge to the Communist Party's authority. Although it was soon suppressed as a cult, some of the social problems raised by the movement such as unaffordable healthcare and its popularity reminded the reformers that without taking decisive measures to improve social protection, the legitimacy of the Communist government would be challenged.

Economically, the East Asian economic crises and the radical reforms that South Korea had to go through in the late 1990s under the International Monetary Fund (IMF) woke up the Chinese reformers. At the same time, China was pressured to open the economy further during the negotiations at the General Agreement of Tariffs and Trade (GATT) and World Trade Organization (WTO). To level the playing ground, state enterprises had to operate like private enterprises. To achieve this, Chinese enterprises were reformed.

The first was the removal of guaranteed life-time employment. Unemployment, still a politically sensitive term then, was expressed in the form of 'Xia-Gang', in which workers were laid-off, but continued to receive welfare benefits from ex-employers. To help people cope with the shock of Xia-Gang, a social safety net with three protection mechanisms were adopted: a social insurance against unemployment; living allowances offered by the previous employers or the reemployment centres; and a minimum income guarantee system.

The second was pension reform. In 1997, a basic pension insurance system that requires contribution by both employers and employees was set up. It included a social pooling account and an individual account. With some further changes in 2000, the system is still used today.

The third was the reform in funding healthcare. In 1998, a basic health insurance scheme was introduced. Similar to a pension, employer and employee contributions were also required. 30 percent of all contributions were put in the individual account and the rest were put in the social pooling account. At the same time, hospitals began to operate like private businesses. The idea was that competition would motivate hospitals to improve productivity.

The fourth was housing reform. In 1998, employer housing provision was officially abandoned. New employees were expected to use the money they have accumulated in the housing provident funds or get bank loans to buy houses in the private market (Li and Gong, 2003).

These moves seemed to be logical. However, as commented by Ngok (2010), the entitlement then was based on status rather on needs, e.g. more senior carders were able to enjoy more subsidies to larger housing and better healthcare coverage. Another problem was each social insurance item had its own account. Adding all the accounts together, the total contribution rate became high. The result was inactive participation and the coverage rate was low.

During this period, other areas of welfare state were also reformed. For example, rural education was reshaped to improve education efficiency. Schools were merged and more concentrated. However, it affected poorer students in remote rural areas (Li and Piachaud, 2004).

On the whole, welfare reform in this period (1992–2002) was serving the purpose of improving economic efficiency. The economy started to take off and foreign direct investment flew into China. The government of this period enjoyed its success. The President Zemin Jiang suggested that the Communist Party should represent 'advanced productivity' and local government officials were measured by their gross domestic product (GDP) contribution.

These changes can be observed through the changing spending pattern by the government. As shown in Table 22.1, the total government expenditure had dropped from about 30 per cent of GDP to 11.7 per cent in 1997. The trend began to reverse from 1998 when the then Prime Minister Rongji Zhu was determined to start radical enterprise reforms. The amount spent on unemployment benefits increased faster in the following years. This was because more workers became Xia-Gang. Government expenditure on education increased and its importance as a proportion of total expenditure began to drop after 1998 as a result of the policy to consolidate rural education and improve efficiency. As Li and Piachaud (2006) argued, the reduced expenditure hurt rural areas the most. At the same time, the importance of state spending on health care also dropped in this period. This matched progress in enterprise reform. However, it is important to note that the overall spending on the poor was marginal in comparison to other spending, showing the minimalistic approach to prevent welfare dependency.

Table 22.1 Social expenditure and % of total government expenditure

	Education		*Unemployment Benefits*		*Health*		*Total Government Expenditure (TGE)*		*GDP*
	100 Million yuan	*% of TGE*	*100 Million yuan*	*% of TGE*	*100 Million uan*	*% of TGE*	*100 Million yuan*	*% of GDP*	*100 Million yuan*
1978					35.4	3.2	1122	30.8	3645
1979					40.6	3.2	1282	31.6	4063
1980					51.9	4.2	1229	27.0	4546
1981					59.7	5.2	1138	23.3	4892
1982					69.0	5.6	1230	23.1	5323
1983					77.6	5.5	1410	23.6	5963
1984					89.5	5.3	1701	23.6	7208
1985					107.7	5.4	2004	22.2	9016
1986					122.2	5.5	2205	21.5	10275
1987					127.3	5.6	2262	18.8	12059
1988					145.4	5.8	2491	16.6	15043
1989					167.9	5.9	2824	16.6	16992
1990					187.3	6.1	3084	16.5	18668
1991					204.1	6.0	3387	15.5	21781
1992	728.8	19.5			228.6	6.1	3742	13.9	26923
1993	867.8	18.7			272.1	5.9	4642	13.1	35334
1994	1174.7	20.3	5.1	0.1	342.3	5.9	5793	12.0	48198
1995	1411.5	20.7	8.2	0.1	387.3	5.7	6824	11.2	60794
1996	1671.7	21.1	13.9	0.2	461.6	5.8	7938	11.2	71177
1997	1862.5	20.2	18.7	0.2	523.6	5.7	9234	11.7	78973
1998	2032.5	18.8	20.4	0.2	590.1	5.5	10798	12.8	84402
1999	2287.2	17.3	31.9	0.2	641.0	4.9	13188	14.7	89677
2000	2562.6	16.1	56.2	0.4	709.5	4.5	15887	16.0	99215
2001	3057.0	16.2	83.3	0.4	800.6	4.2	18903	17.2	109655
2002	3491.4	15.8	116.8	0.5	908.5	4.1	22053	18.3	120333
2003	3850.6	15.6	133.4	0.5	1116.9	4.5	24650	18.1	135823
2004	4465.9	15.7	137.5	0.5	1293.6	4.5	28487	17.8	159878
2005	5161.1	15.2	132.4	0.4	1552.5	4.6	33930	18.3	184937
2006	6348.4	15.7	125.8	0.3	1778.9	4.4	40423	18.7	216314
2007	8280.2	16.6	129.4	0.3	2581.6	5.2	49781	18.7	265810
2008	10449.6	16.7	139.5	0.2	3593.9	5.7	62593	19.9	314045
2009	10437.5	13.7	145.8	0.2	3994.2	5.2	76300	22.4	340507

Source: Data from China Statistical Bureau, *China Statistical Yearbook*, various issues.

From pro-growth to social harmony (2002–now)

In contrast to the earlier period in which efficiency was the only priority, starting from 2002, the national development strategy was changed to 'prioritising efficiency and giving consideration to fairness'. This change was influenced by several economic and political factors.

First, after joining the WTO, China was soon turned into the workshop of the world. One reason behind the transition was its rich supply of cheap labour. However, for many years in the past, rural workers were not officially allowed to work in cities. They suffered from various discriminations and could be evicted to countryside or even arrested when they were caught working 'illegally' in cities. This policy became increasingly unpopular. Apart from the concerns of human rights and social rights, preventing rural workers to enter cities forced employers to hire workers in the black market. It increased the risks and labour costs of enterprises. It affected the competitiveness of enterprises that relied on cheap labour supply the most.

Second, the wealth accumulated by the lucky ones did not trickle down. On the contrary, income inequality increased. The Gini coefficient increased to 4.5 in 2005. Both rural-urban and urban income gaps increased over time. Dissatisfaction became visible. Wang (2010) found that between 1988 and 2006, when income inequality increased, there were clearly more criminal offences. There were also numerous protests which were either suppressed or appeased. However, some public concerns such as unaffordable healthcare, urban poverty traps, and increased social inequality reminded the reformers that economic growth needed to be accompanied by social development. In 2003, the SARS crisis shocked the urban Chinese population. As the disease spread fast, the urban middle class who used to be reluctant to help the poor in their healthcare costs began to understand the negative externalities of unaffordable healthcare.

Third, several long-term and structural problems demand for a more balanced approach to achieve economic development. As summarised by Zhang, Xu and Midgley (2007, pp. 16–22):

- The increased social needs of an ageing society were the direct outcome of the 'One Child Policy' introduced in the 1980s.
- When rural labourers moved to cities, only the elderly and young children were left in rural areas. The need for care increased dramatically.
- Cities suffer from a range of illnesses, including over-crowded housing, congested public transportation, high employment pressure, environment pollution, greater social division and inequality, emergence of ghettos, shortage of water and energy, and higher crime rates.
- To cope with these pressures, social development was put on a higher agenda than before. A further elaboration was made in 2005 to bring forward a development strategy to maintain social harmony.

The first major move in this period was to encourage urbanisation. Not only would urbanisation increase labour supply for industries, but also rural workers being able to send money back to their home had contributed greatly to rural poverty reduction (Ravallion and S. Chen, 2007). The initial idea was to unify rural and urban labour market and make it easier for migrant workers to take up jobs in cities. As shown in Figure 22.1, from 2000 onward the proportion of

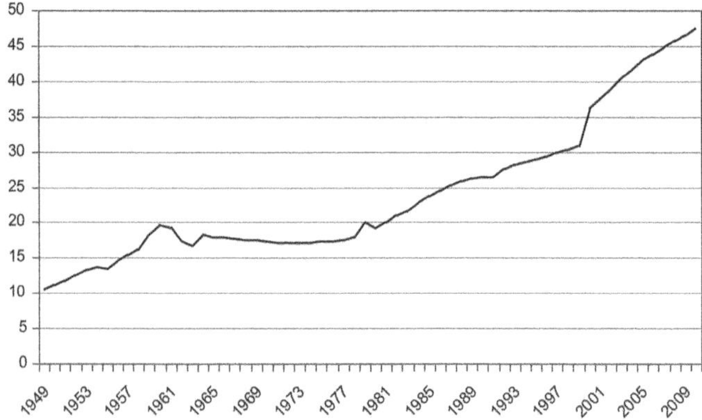

Figure 22.1 Urbanisation rate (% of urban population)

urban population increased due to reduced labour mobility control. As time moves on, it was understood that to push further for urban industrial growth and increase service sector development, it is necessary to make it possible for migrant workers to have a sense of belonging in cities and have their basic needs met. In the last few years some social security coverage was extended to migrant workers.

The second area was the policies that helped to reduce rural poverty. In 2006, agriculture tax was abolished completely. Starting from 2009, a series of rural social protection schemes was introduced, including pension, supporting single-elderly who do not have support from extended families, and support for those below a rural minimum living standard.

The third area was the healthcare system reform. This reform is still in progress and has to face up to many challenges. Health insurance systems that demand individual and state contributions are set up in cities. A rural health insurance system is going to cover the whole country in the next a couple of years. In terms of healthcare delivery, the foci are healthcare cost control and the somewhat hostile relationship between doctors and patients. These demand more fundamental changes in the hospital systems and improve the monitoring of service suppliers. However, hospitals have long been operating like profit-making businesses.

The fourth main area was housing reform. The 1998 reform had successfully pushed people to buy homes and increased the home-ownership rate dramatically (Huang, 2011). However, urban housing has become increasingly less affordable for ordinary wage earners. Young people, lower income groups, and migrant workers find it difficult to afford houses in cities. They end up living in rented accommodations in urban villages and peri-urban farm houses. A housing security system has been developed since 1994. It has three elements: subsidised home ownership; housing provident funds that people can borrow against at more favourable terms; and low-rent public housing for the poor and half-market-rental housing for new-comers in the local labour market.

Urbanisation and abolition of rural agricultural tax helped to reduce rural poverty and narrow the rural-urban income gap. However, as more poor people moved into cities, some rural poverty was urbanised and urban income gaps grew as a result (Ravallion, Chen, and Sangraula, 2007). The crime rates and numbers of collective protests and riots (regarding land acquisition and labour rights) increased by more than ten-fold between 1993 and 2007 (Chen, 2009). To calm down protesters, one-off cash payments and administrative powers were used. For example, powerful actions were used to make sure that construction companies pay the workers on time. Pension increase was paid to retired teachers in various cities.

The 2007 financial crises put strain on China's export businesses. Millions of migrant workers lost their jobs. To avoid a major recession, it was considered necessary to restructure the economy to reduce dependency on export and boost domestic demand. To achieve this, a whole range of policies that are economically driven but bearing social implications were introduced. The areas of investment include: affordable housing and slum clearance; rural basic infrastructures and poverty reduction; transport network and urban power supply; healthcare, education, and cultural facilities in rural areas; infrastructure for environmental improvement; technology advancement and service sector development; disaster relief; income growth; tax reform; and financial support to economic growth. It is not difficult to see the intention to maintain economic growth and at the same time strengthen the 'weakest link' in the social front.

However, the massive increase in public spending turned out to be inflationary. Housing and food prices grew rapidly. The increased monetary supply pushed local governments to look for opportunities to support real estate development which caused land speculation and land-grabbing from farmers (Tang et al. 2010). These activities and the anticipation of further inflation became destabilising again. To quieten down the public resentment, in 2010 the government introduced serious control of housing market speculation and decided to spend a large sum of money to build subsidised houses for ownership and rental, and resume government supply of public housing. These policies have so far helped to curb the housing price increase and the house price in many large cities dropped significantly. The policy, though welcomed by the general public, had caused strong protests from private housing developers. At the time this paper was written, the government had not succumbed to the appeal of developers.

Conclusion

This chapter shows that since the Communist Party came into power in China, social welfare has been actively used by the state to boost economic growth and maintain Communist Party authority. In different periods, there are different priorities. Sometimes economic growth dominated and sometimes political concerns were brought to the front. These changes also showed a pragmatic approach and changing perception of the relationship between growth/ party authority and social development by the Chinese policy makers. In this sense, welfare spending was mostly part of a bigger strategy – either an economic or a political one.

So far, the social support system in China has evolved to include a residual state welfare and a social insurance system. The state plays a growing role in legislating, administrating and delivering some basic welfare and social services (e.g. minimum income guarantee and disaster relief) to the lowest income groups in both urban and rural communities. Social insurance schemes jointly contributed by employers and employees are in place to cover pension, some healthcare, childbirth, unemployment, and industrial accidents. A similar forced savings scheme is also used to support first-time home buyers. On the whole, the state is reluctant to take on more responsibility to the disadvantaged, unless they pose a threat to the stability of the society.

Prioritising economic growth and political stability may have some advantages in the sense that it requires the government to be responsive to immediate threats. In a way, even without democracy, the social groups that are more ready to put pressure on the economy or destabilise the country, ad hoc welfare benefits may be more likely to go in their direction.

However, this approach also suffers from some serious problems. The already fragmented welfare benefits became even more difficult to disentangle, making it difficult to trace the net benefit a person might have received.

The pragmatic and incremental reform leads to frequent policy changes and, sometimes, U-turns. It also tends to blur the division of responsibilities between central and local government. As a result, it is often difficult for policy enforcers and causes confusion and even frustration among the people.

Note

1 Some people also mention the importance of social stability. Since the Communist Party regards social instability as a direct challenge or even a threat to the leadership of the Party and the government, it is therefore often politicised.

References

Bian, Y. and Logan, J. R. (1996), Market transition and the persistence of power: the changing stratification system in urban China. *American Sociological Review*, 61, 5: 739–58.

Chen, C. J. (2009), 'Rising social discontents and popular protests', in G. Wu and H. Lansdowne (eds), *Socialist China, Capitalist China: Social Tension and Political Adaptation under Economic Globalization*. London: Taylor & Francis.

Cheng, H. (2008), A Historical Investigation of the Social Welfare System in China During the Planned Economy Period. *Contemporary China History Studies (dangdai zhongguoshi yanjiu)*, 5, 6, pp. 48–56.
Croll, E. J. (1999), Social welfare reform: trends and tensions. *The China Quarterly*, (159), pp. 684–99.
Dixon, J. (1981), *The Chinese Welfare System, 1949–1979*. Westport, CT: Praeger.
Fan, G. (1994), Incremental Changes and Dual-Track Transition: Understanding the Case of China. *Economic Policy*, 9(19), pp. 100–122. Blackwell Publishing on behalf of the Centre for Economic Policy Research, Center for Economic Studies, and the Maison des Sciences de l'Homme. Retrieved from www.jstor.org/stable/1344602.
Huang, Y. (2011), Second Home Ownership in Transitional Urban China. *Housing Studies*, 26(3), forthcoming.
Leung, J. C. B. (2003), Social security reforms in China: issues and prospects. *International Journal of Social Welfare*, 12(2), pp. 73–85.
——(1994), Dismantling the Iron Rice Bowl? Welfare Reforms in the People's Republic of China. *Journal of Social Policy*, 23, 03, pp. 341–361.
Li, B. (2005), 'Urban Housing Privatisation: Redefining the Responsibilities of the State, Employers and Individuals', in S. Green and G. S. Liu (eds), *Exit the gradon? Privatisation and state ownership in China*, (1st edn) pp. 145–168. London: Chatham House and Blackwell Publishing.
Li, B., and Gong, S. (2003), *Urban Social Inequalities and Wage, Housing and Pension Reforms in China*. Asian Program Working Series. London: Royal Institute of International Affairs at Chatham House.
Li, B., and Piachaud, D. (2006), Urbanization and social policy in China. Development, 13(1), pp. 1–26.
Li, W. (2008), Reasons behind the Continued Growth of Crime since the Reform and Opening Up of China (gage kaifang yilai woguo fanzui chixu zengzhang de yuanyin fenxi), *Legal System And Society* (fazhi yushehui), No. 21.
Lin, J. Y., Cai, F., and Li, Z. (2003), *The China Miracle: Development Strategy and Economic Reform*. Chinese University Press, p. XXXV, 330.
——(1996), The Lessons of China's Transition to a Market Economy. *Cato*, 16(2), pp. 201–231.
Ngok, K. (2010), The changing role of the state in welfare provision: Sixty years of social policy developments in China. *Chinese Public Policy Review (zhongguo gonggong zhengce pinglun)*, 4, pp. 39–69.
Perry, E. J. (1993), China in 1992: An Experiment in Neo-Authoritarianism. *Asian Survey*, 33(1), pp. 12–21. doi: 10.1525/as.1993.33.1.00p0232n.
Piachaud, D. (2004), Poverty and Inequality and Social Policy in China. CASE Papers (Vol. 87). London: Centre for Analysis of Social Exclusion, LSE. Retrieved from sticerd.lse.ac.uk/dps/case/cp/CASEpaper87.pdf.
Ravallion, M., and Chen, S. (2007), China's (uneven) progress against poverty. *Journal of Development Economics*, 82(1), pp. 1–42. doi: 10.1016/j.jdeveco.2005.07.003.
Ravallion, M., Chen, S., and Sangraula, P. (2007), New evidence on the urbanization of global poverty. Population and Development Review, 33(4), pp. 667–701. Wiley Online Library. Retrieved July 2, 2011, from onlinelibrary.wiley.com/doi/10.1111/j.1728-4457.2007.00193.x/abstract.
Tang, H. Wang, P. and Tang, J. (2010), *The Multiplier Effect of Investment and the Anti-inflationary Measures*, 4, pp. 68–75.
Unger, J., and Chan, A. (1995), China, corporatism, and the East Asian model. *The Australian Journal of Chinese Affairs*, 33(33), 29–53. doi: 10.&2307/2950087.
Weatherley, R. (2006), *Politics in China since 1949: Legitimizing Authoritarian Rule Politics in China since 1949: Legitimizing Authoritarian Rule*. Abingdon: Routledge, pp. 150-177.
Wu, X. and Xie, Y. (2003), Does the market pay off? Earnings returns to education in urban China. *American Sociological Review*, 68, 3, pp. 425-442.
Zhang, X., Xu, Y., and Midgley, J. (2007), *Issues on Development Social Policy in China*, 1st edn. Beijing: China Labour and Social Security Press.

23

Inequality and social policy in Latin America

A new analytical framework

Peter Lloyd-Sherlock

Introduction

Across Latin America, overall state spending on social policies compares favourably to countries with similar levels of wealth located in other regions. A recent survey reported that social spending in Latin America accounted for 13 per cent of gross domestic product (GDP) in 2004, compared to 9 per cent in the Middle East/North Africa and 8 per cent in the emerging Asian economies (Clements et al., 2007). Despite Latin America's general adherence to neo-liberal policy frameworks, official data show social spending as a share of GDP increased significantly over the past 15 years (ECLAC, 2007a). This large and resilient social expenditure reflects Latin America's historical legacy as a region with high levels of state intervention in social welfare, roughly in accordance with Esping-Andersen's social democratic welfare regime. It also reflects the relative strength of civil society organisations, particularly trade unions, in the region, which have been able to resist some aspects of neo-liberal restructuring.

It might be expected that comparatively high levels of social spending would foster social equality in Latin America. In the case of Cuba, there is clear evidence that this has happened (Mesa-Lago, 2005). Elsewhere, the picture is different: as a region, Latin America remains characterised by extreme patterns of inequality of wealth, power and access to resources. A World Bank report observed that the Latin American country with least income inequality (Uruguay) was still more unequal than any Organisation for Economic Co-operation and Development (OECD) or Eastern European country (World Bank, 2003).[1] There is evidence that inequality has deep historical roots in the region, dating back to colonial times. In much of the region, large-scale state welfare interventions have been in place for at least half a century, a substantial period of time in which to address established inequalities (Abel and Lewis, 2002). This chapter will argue that, rather than reduce socio-economic disparities, many welfare interventions have actually contributed to them. It shows that, historically, social policies have privileged richer groups, distributing resources away from the poor. The chapter also assesses whether recent developments in social policy, including the emergence of new cash transfer programmes, have led to more progressive social policy regimes.

Resourcing	*Entitlements*	*Capacity to mobilise entitlements*
Overall resourcing	Universal	Discriminatory rationing and other informal practices
Intra-sectoral resource allocation	Targeted/conditional	Opportunity costs
	Social insurance Marketised	Differential service quality

Figure 23.1 Analytical framework for the distributional effects of social policy

In order to assess the distributive effects of different areas of social policy, the chapter applies a simple analytical framework, assessing three separate issues (Figure 23.1). The first of these are patterns of resource allocation, which include both overall resourcing for each social sector and more disaggregated allocation. This can significantly affect equity outcomes in a number of ways. In the health sector, for example, allocation between specialist interventions and more basic services can have significant distributional outcomes.

A second issue is how entitlements to social policies are structured and distributed. Some services may be provided on a largely universal basis as a right of citizenship. Alternatively, services may be provided to a specific group (usually one considered as disadvantaged in some way) on the basis of means testing and targeting. Conditional cash transfer programmes represent a new variant of targeted intervention, whereby the recipient is required to behave in specified ways. A third form of entitlement is through some form of social insurance contract. As in developed countries, this requires that an individual makes financial contributions deducted from their salaries to an insurance fund. These contributions are usually matched with payments from employers and, sometimes, the state. Social insurance can be an equitable and inclusive strategy in countries where the great majority of the labour force is employed in salaried, formal-sector activities. In countries with a large informal sector, however, this model inevitably excludes large sectors of the population who are already economically marginalised. Finally, entitlements to welfare services may be marketised, through private payments for private provision. As will be seen, private welfare schemes can capture government resources and can influence mainstream social policies in a number of important ways.

The third key issue is the extent to which people are able to take full advantage of their welfare entitlements. Research from developed countries suggests that poor and socially excluded groups can face particular barriers in accessing social benefits (Currie, 2004). In regions like Latin America these potential barriers are especially severe, contributing to significant welfare disparities across different socio-economic groups. Whilst many developing countries have notionally universal welfare services, their capacity to deliver them is often limited. Where welfare programmes lack the resources to meet their full set of commitments some form of rationing will inevitably occur. If this rationing is not transparent and carefully supervised, it may discriminate against particular groups. Also, the direct and indirect costs of accessing welfare services (for example, transport from remote rural areas or opportunity costs of lost earnings) may create significant access barriers for poorer groups. Women, ethnic minorities and other socially excluded groups may face particular barriers to mobilising their welfare entitlements (Gacitúa and Davis, 2001). As part of this, it is important to assess the quality of services offered different groups. If the poor are only offered downgraded welfare services, apparently universal welfare programmes may still promote societal inequality.

The remaining sections of the chapter will apply this analytical framework to two different areas of social policy, health and social security, which account for the great majority of social spending in Latin America.[2] Before doing so, it is necessary to consider the general quality of social spending data for the region.

Data quality and reporting

Does Latin America really devote 13 per cent of its GDP to social policies, as is widely claimed and accepted by international agencies? Data on social spending in many Latin American countries are often incomplete and of doubtful quality. Since the 1980s, the financing of social policies in most Latin American countries has become increasingly decentralised and hence fragmented. This poses formidable challenges for reliable and comparable data capture, especially as local governments tend to have less rigorous reporting mechanisms than central ones. The Economic Commission for Latin America and the Caribbean (ECLAC) is the United Nations (UN) agency with lead responsibility for collecting social spending data for the region and an influential reference point for academics and policy makers. ECLAC takes an inconsistent approach to compiling data for different countries and points in time, in some cases including local government spending and in some cases excluding it. Despite this, social spending data are usually presented and discussed in a comparative format as is the case in Table 23.1 (Clements et al., 2007; ECLAC, 2007a). This can be highly misleading. For example, government social spending in Mexico appears to be half Brazil's, whilst Colombia appears to experience a very abrupt step-change in social spending over time. In both these cases, the variations mainly result from the inclusion or exclusion of local government data. The apparent overall rise in social spending over the past 15 years is partly due to the inclusion of local government spending for a larger number of countries, such as Colombia. If ECLAC were able to capture local spending for the entire region, it is likely that the regional average would be considerably higher than 13 per cent of GDP. As such, the region's failure to achieve more equitable development becomes even more notable.

Given the inconsistency of data capture, any comparative analysis across the region must be approached with caution. Table 23.2 provides a breakdown of spending across the main social sectors for selected countries. The main feature of Table 23.2 is the high proportion of government social spending devoted to social security programmes; in some cases accounting for half or more of the social budget. As will be seen, the prominence of social security is a major cause of the inequitable effects of social policy.

Table 23.1 Government spending on social policies*, selected Latin American countries, 1980–2005 (% GDP)

	1980–81	*1990–91*	*2004–5*
Argentina	16.7	19.3	19.4
Brazil	9.7	18.1	22.0
Colombia	7.8**	6.6**	13.4
Costa Rica	15.2	15.6	17.5
Mexico	8.6**	6.5**	10.2**

* These refer to spending on education, health, nutrition, social security, social assistance, housing, water and sanitation
** Excludes local government spending
Source: Adapted from ECLAC (2007a); ECLAC (1994).

Table 23.2 Sectoral allocation of government social spending for selected Latin American countries, 2002/3 (% of total social spending)

	Education	*Health*	*Social security*	*Housing, water and sanitation*
Argentina	22	23	50	6
Brazil	19	15	66	1
Colombia	36	25	29	11
Costa Rica	31	31	30	10
Mexico	39	23	24	14
Latin America	27	21	44	8

Source: Adapted from ECLAC (2007a).

Healthcare

Analysis of spending and equity in the health sector is complex, since state health financing and service provision responsibilities are often divided across separate institutions, catering for different population groups (Abel and Lloyd-Sherlock, 2000). Typically, ministries of health are responsible for a set of universal services, mainly provided through public hospitals. In recent years both financing and provision have become increasingly decentralised to local government and individual hospitals, adding to the sector's complexity and posing major challenges for data capture (Hómedes and Ugalde, 2006). A parallel set of higher quality services are funded through social security ministries, with service provision usually contracted out to private clinics and hospitals. Here, entitlements are structured on a contributory social insurance basis. Thirdly, a substantial and growing privately financed sector exists, with the emergence of large private health insurance funds. This private sector is offered a wide range of tax breaks such as VAT exemptions and income tax deductibility for contributions. The ECLAC data on health spending in Table 23.1 do not include social security or transfers to the private sector and so significantly understate state resourcing.

In most Latin American countries, limited access to formal sector employment restricts the coverage of contributory social health insurance programmes to a minority (Lloyd-Sherlock, 2006). The inclusion of poorer groups, who are less likely to have secure formal sector jobs, is particularly low. For example, Mexico's two main social health insurance funds covered 40 per cent of the population in 2003, but only 10 per cent of the poorest income quintile (Frenk et al., 2005). Despite this, spending on social health insurance is substantially higher than the budget allocated to health ministries for universal services. Most social health insurance programmes receive large direct and indirect transfers from governments which top up income received by workers' and employers' contributions. For example, Mexico's main health insurance fund receives a third of its annual budget directly from government (Gómez-Dantés et al., 2004). In the absence of analytical data specific to health insurance, it may be assumed that these programmes exert a strong regressive effect. Over recent years, some countries in the region have sought to extend social health insurance to informal sector workers and poorer groups through a range of different initiatives. In particular, Mexico's Popular Health Insurance Programme has been identified as highly successful and a potential model for Latin America and beyond (Frenk et al., 2005). Although these schemes have had positive impacts on poorer groups, the funding devoted to them remains a fraction of the resources provided to formal sector ones, and the range of services they offer is quite limited. As such, their impact on the inequity of social spending is marginal.

Table 23.3 Distribution of government social spending across income quintiles, 1997–2004 (% of total government social spend)

	Quintile 1 (poorest)	*Quintile 2*	*Quintile 3*	*Quintile 4*	*Quintile 5 (richest)*
Education	7.4	6.5	6.3	5.9	5.8
Health care	5.1	4.7	4.2	4.0	3.7
Social security	2.0	2.8	4.3	6.3	16.5
Targeted cash transfers	3.3	2.1	1.6	1.3	1.1
Housing	0.8	0.9	1.1	1.4	0.9
Total	18.6	17.0	17.5	18.9	28.0

Theoretically, social health insurance schemes should enable health ministries to focus their efforts on uninsured groups, who will be disproportionately poor. In practice, this rarely happens and large numbers of Latin Americans with social health insurance also make use of universal services. Table 23.3 shows that nearly as many health ministry resources are devoted to rich income groups as to poorer ones. There are several reasons for this. First, poorer groups face particular barriers in mobilising their entitlements to public healthcare. In several countries notionally universal entitlements have been progressively undermined by the introduction of user fees. The overall extent of charging patients for access to these services is unclear, as fees are often levied on an 'unofficial' basis and much is left to the discretion of individual hospitals (Castro, 2008). In some cases, patients have been denied access to care before up-front payments or have been detained in hospitals until they have paid their fees. Where patients are from rural areas, the combined impact of user fees, transport to hospitals and the opportunity costs for accompanying family members can be a formidable access barrier. Across the region health service infrastructure is heavily concentrated in richer regions and urban areas, creating significant geographical access barriers for the rural poor. In Mexico, for example, there were on average 96 doctors per 100,000 people nationally, but only 14 per 100,000 in rural areas with large concentrations of indigenous people (PAHO, 2007).

Second, the mix of services offered by the health sector as a whole, including public healthcare providers, is strongly skewed towards expensive curative interventions rather than more cost-effective primary healthcare (Homedes, 2006). A high proportion of health ministry budgets go to prestigious hospitals offering state of the art services, which are often superior to those available through social health insurance programmes. This creates an incentive for richer, insured groups to access these services, crowding out care for the poor. In most countries, basic healthcare interventions of particular relevance to the poor are under-funded, leading to shortages and quality problems. For example, many public clinics struggle to maintain a regular supply of essential drugs for common conditions, such as diabetes and hypertension (Hómedes et al., 2005). This bias towards complex interventions is both inegalitarian and inefficient. For example, at around 30 per cent of all deliveries, Latin America has by far the highest rate of caesarean section births in the world, which is highly wasteful and potentially harmful (Althabe and Belizán, 2006). Despite this, a study of nine countries found that less than half of poor women were able to give birth in hospitals (Belizán et al., 2007).[3] As a result, only 2 per cent of maternal deaths occur among the richest 20 per cent of the population, and the region as a whole is making little progress in reducing maternal mortality (Alleyne et al., 2002).

In most countries, the private health sector is weakly regulated and so reliable data on financing, coverage, and service provision are not available. There are, however, clear indications that this sector is substantial and continues to grow (Domínguez Ugá and Soares Santos, 2007). Estimates of private insurance financing range from 0.3 per cent of total health spend in Costa Rica to 19.4 per cent in Brazil (Drechsler and Jütting, 2007). Predictably, poorer groups have very little access to private health insurance, and tax exemptions offered to this sector are highly inequitable. A survey of 22 countries in the region reported that out-of-pocket payments (paying for public and private health services at the point of use) accounted for 36 per cent of total health spending in Latin America and the Caribbean, compared to 20 per cent in OECD countries (Drechsler and Jütting, 2007). This represents a substantial access barrier for services for the poor.

Social security

Table 23.2 shows that social security accounted for the largest share of government social spending in the selected countries. Social security is itself an umbrella term that may include a variety of different public interventions, including for retirement pensions, unemployment insurance, invalidity benefits, health insurance, hospital management, home loans and funeral costs (ILO, 2008a). As such, the allocation of resources within social security programmes is a key consideration. Table 23.4 shows that, in the case of Chile and Mexico in 1996, old age and widows' pensions were the largest budget items, followed by health insurance. By contrast, spending on unemployment benefit accounted for only a negligible amount of Chile's social security budget and none at all in Mexico.

The relative importance of pensions and the insignificance of unemployment relief contrasts sharply with social security systems in the developed world. Latin America's low spend on unemployment does not reflect a strong labour market. According to official estimates, urban unemployment for the region was 8 per cent in 2007, and this did not include a substantial part of the labour force that is underemployed or engaged in casual informal sector work (ECLAC, 2007b). Conversely, the high spend on pensions does not reflect a particularly aged population structure. Although population ageing has accelerated in Latin America in recent decades, the share of population aged 65 and over in 2005 (9.6 per cent) is rather lower than that of Western Europe (16.0 per cent) (United Nations Population Division, 2002). At first sight, the data suggest that older people in Latin America may represent a form of 'welfare aristocracy', holding a privileged status within the social security system when compared to younger, jobless adults. In fact, there are high levels of inequality *within* older populations. In most countries, very early retirement ages for civil servants mean that a large amount of pension spending is devoted to the middle-aged. For example, until recently public sector teachers in Brazil were required to retire after only 25 years of service. Despite the high levels of pension spending substantial sections of the older populations in several countries are not provided with benefits. In Mexico around half of the population aged 65 and over are still excluded from the pension system and

Table 23.4 Allocation of social security budget, Chile and Mexico, 1996 (%)

	Chile	*Mexico*
Health and sickness insurance	20.0	15.9
Old age and survivors' benefits	45.6	40.0
Invalidity benefits	5.3	9.0
Unemployment benefits	0.2	0.0
Other benefits	29.1	35.1

Source: Adapted from ILO (2008b).

Table 23.5 Coverage of social insurance pension programmes for selected Latin American countries (%)

	Coverage of economically active population	*Coverage of poorest income quintile*
Argentina (2006)	39	8
Brazil (2002)	42	21
Chile (2003)	59	40
Mexico (2004)	36	7
Peru (2003)	15	2

Source: Adapted from Rofman and Lucchetti (2006).

income poverty among older people is around 70 per cent higher than for the population as a whole (Scott, 2008).

For most services offered by social security systems, entitlements are structured on a contributory social insurance basis. Table 23.5 shows that the proportion of the workforce protected by social insurance pension programmes varies widely across the region, although in most cases it is less than half. Social insurance coverage for the poorest 20 per cent of the population also varies, but in most cases the large majority are excluded. In several countries, a combination of neo-liberal adjustment and an indifferent economic performance has led to a reduction in the supply of formal sector jobs and hence a contraction in social insurance coverage. This has particularly affected poorer groups. In Argentina, for example, social insurance coverage of the poorest quintile fell from 39 to 8 per cent between 1992 and 2006 (Rofman and Lucchetti, 2006). As with social health insurance, contributory pension funds capture substantial state transfers in a variety of ways. For example, in 2001 Mexican pension deficits equivalent to 3.5 per cent of GDP were paid directly by the government (Arza, 2008).

Most social security spending in Latin America is therefore reserved for relatively privileged groups, excluding poorer and more vulnerable social sectors. Even within groups protected by social insurance, there are often substantial redistributions of wealth towards richer groups. Traditionally, people employed in the most highly paid and politically powerful occupations have been provided with substantially more generous benefits and services than those offered to rank and file workers (Mesa-Lago, 1989). A recent survey of pension values in Mexico found that the top 10 per cent of benefits were worth on average 287 times those in the bottom 10 per cent (Scott, 2008). Several countries in the region have seen shifts from state pension funds to privately managed individual accounts in recent years. In theory, this could reduce the extent of benefit disparities between different groups of workers. However, pension privatisations have obliged governments to continue subsidising their old social security funds, since the loss of contributors to private funds has depleted their resources to meet ongoing pension liabilities.

Targeted cash transfer programmes, including assistance pensions and conditional schemes are usually included as part of wider social security budgets. A decade ago, these programmes did not account for a significant amount of government spending in the region (World Bank, 1997; Golbert, 1992). Historically, targeted anti-poverty programmes in Latin America tended to be highly clientelistic and corrupt, which reduced their capacity to reach the poorest (Graham, 1994). In recent years, large programmes have been established in most countries, including Oportunidades in Mexico and Bolsa Familia in Brazil. It is claimed that the new cash transfer schemes have been able to overcome these problems (Rawlings and Rubio, 2005). Table 23.3 shows that these programmes have disproportionately benefited poorer groups, although the leakage to rich income categories demonstrates the difficulties of developing an effective targeting strategy.

While the emergence of these new programmes is an important and welcome development, the huge international interest they have generated may exaggerate their overall significance within the wider portfolio of social policy. According to the United Nations estimates, they accounted for 9 per cent of social spending in the region between 1997 and 2004, less than a quarter of the total devoted to social security (ECLAC, 2007a). For example, at 0.3 per cent of GDP, the budget of Oportunidades is still only around a tenth that of Mexico's two main social security institutes. As a result, the strongly progressive effect of these schemes is dwarfed by the inequality generated by the social security system as a whole, in which over half of the budget goes to the richest income quintile (Table 23.3).

Conclusion

This chapter demonstrates how high levels of social spending in Latin America contribute to social inequalities, rather than reduce them. To understand these effects, it is helpful to examine patterns of resource allocation, distributions of entitlements and the variable capacity of different social groups to mobilise these entitlements. In each of the social sectors studied here, these three elements combine differently to produce inequitable outcomes. In the health sector, key factors included the exclusion of poorer groups from social health insurance funds, which commanded the bulk of resources. Also a healthcare service mix skewed towards expensive, curative services crowded out services of more relevance to the poor. The social security sector accounted for the largest share of social spending and was also the most inequitable component. Here the primary driver of inequality was the predominance of contributory social insurance entitlements. The recent expansion of targeted programmes has done something to reduce the overall inequality of social spending, but its effects have been limited by relatively small budget shares and the leakage of targeted benefits to the non-poor. The ongoing global economic crisis has not led to significant changes in this pattern of social spending and inequality. Between 2005 and 2008 average rates of social spending rose in per capita terms (ECLAC, 2010). However, spending on the region's vaunted cash transfer schemes (0.4 per cent of GDP) represented just 5 per cent of the total social security budget, which remained largely devoted to social insurance schemes for the non-poor.

ECLAC data show that the combined impact of social spending on income distribution in Latin America is inequitable, with the poorest quintile receiving 18.6 per cent, compared to 28 per cent for the richest (Table 23.3). Were state transfers and subsidies for private welfare agencies included, the overall effect would be even more regressive. As such, the persistence of inequality in the region despite high levels of social spending is not a paradox. Nevertheless, poorer groups are not entirely excluded from social provision in the region, and benefit significantly from cash transfer programmes. Table 23.6 shows that poorer households in the region obtain more

Table 23.6 Proportion of income derived from social spending and from primary income sources by income quintile, 1997–2004 (% of total income for each quintile)

	Quintile 1 (poorest)	*Quintile 2*	*Quintile 3*	*Quintile 4*	*Quintile 5*
Primary income	49	70	78	84	91
Social spending	51	30	22	16	9

Source: ECLAC (2007a).

resources through social spending than through primary income (earnings and rents). While this may reflect the low earnings of poorer households as much as the generosity of social policies, their dependence on state support is undeniable. In other words, Table 23.6 shows that social spending in Latin America offers the poor an important safety net even though it redistributes national resources towards richer groups (Table 23.3). This may help explain the political sustainability of policies that are deeply socially unjust.

Notes

1 Cuba does not provide comparable income distribution data and is therefore excluded from the World Bank's analysis.
2 As will be seen, the available data on other aspects of social spending, including housing, social care and basic service provision are too poor to enable a meaningful analysis.
3 Unlike some developed countries, home birth is widely viewed as a strategy of last resort than a potentially preferable option to hospital deliveries.

References

Abel, C. and Lewis, C. (2002), 'Exclusion and engagement: a diagnosis of social policy in Latin America in the long run', in C. Abel and C. Lewis (eds), *Exclusion and Engagement. Social Policy in Latin America.* London: Institute of Latin American Studies.

Abel, C. and Lloyd-Sherlock, P. (2000), 'Health policy in Latin America: themes, trends and challenges' in P. Lloyd-Sherlock (ed.), *Healthcare Reform and Poverty in Latin America,* London, Institute of Latin American Studies.

Alleyne, G., Castillo-Salgado, C., Schnieder, M., Loyla, E. and Vidaurre, M. (2002), Overview of social inequalities in health in the region of the Americas, using various methodological approaches. *Revista Panamericana de Salud Pública* 12, 6, pp. 388–97.

Althabe, F. and Belizán, J. (2006), Caesarian section: the paradox. *The Lancet* 368, 9546, pp. 1472–73.

Arza, C. (2008), 'Pension reform in Latin America: distributional principles, inequalities and alternative policy options'. *Journal of Latin American Studies* 40, 1, pp. 1–28.

Barrera-Osorio, F., Linden, L. and Urquiola, M. (2007), 'The effect of user fee reductions on enrolment. Evidence from a quasi-experiment', www.columbia.edu/~ll2240/Gratuidad%20Draft%202007-01.pdf

Belizán, J., Cafferata, M., Belizán, M. and Althabe, F. (2007), Health inequality in Latin America. *The Lancet* 370,9599, pp. 1599–1600.

Castro, A. (2008), 'In and out: user fees and other unfortunate events during hospital admission and discharge'. *Cadernos de Saúde Pública* 24, 5, pp. 1174–78.

Clarín, (2008), (no title). 29 August, Buenos Aires. www.clarin.com

Clements, B., Faircloth, C. and Verhoeven, M. (2007), 'Public expenditure in Latin America: trends and key policy issues'. IMF Working Paper 07/21, Washington, DC, paper.ssrn.com/sol3/chapters.cfm?abstract_id=961751#PaperDownload

Currie, J. (2004), 'The take-up of social benefits', Discussion Paper 1103, Institute for the Study of Labor, Bonn.

Domínguez Ugá, M. and Soares Santos, I. (2007), An analysis of equity in Brazilian health system financing. *Health Affairs* 26, 4, pp. 1017–28.

Drechsler, D. and Jütting, J. (2007), 'Different countries, different needs: the role of private health insurance in developing countries'. *Journal of Health Politics, Policy and Law* 32, 3, pp. 497–534.

Economic Commission of Latin America and the Caribbean (ECLAC) (1994), *Social panorama of Latin America 1994.* Santiago de Chile: ECLAC.

——(2005), *Social panorama of Latin America 2005.* Santiago de Chile: ECLAC.

——(2007a), *Social panorama of Latin America 2007.* Santiago de Chile: ECLAC.

——(2007b), *Statistical yearbook for Latin America 2007.* Santiago de Chile: ECLAC.

——(2010), *Social panorama of Latin America 2010.* Santiago de Chile: ECLAC.

Frenk, J., Knaul, F., González-Pier, E. and Barranza-Lloréns, M. (2005), Poverty health and social protection. *Paper given at International Conference on Social Health Insurance in Developing Countries*, Berlin, 6 December.

Gacitúa, E. and Davis, S. (2001), 'Introduction: Poverty and Social Exclusion in Latin America and the Caribbean', in E. Gacitúa, S. Davis and S. Davis (eds), *Social Exclusion and Poverty Reduction in Latin America and the Caribbean*. Washington, DC: World Bank.
Gómez-Dantés, O., Gómez-Jáuregui, J. and Inclán, C. (2004), La equidad y la impacialidad en la reforma del sistema mexicano de salud. *Salud Pública de México* 46, 5, pp. 399–416.
Graham, C. (1994), *Safety Nets, Politics and the Poor. Transitions to Market Economies*. Washington, DC: Brookings Institutions.
Hómedes, N. (2006), 'Universal access to health in Latin America. The role of health reform'. *UNCTAD Expert Group Meeting, Geneva*, www.unctad.org/sections/wcmu/docs/c1em30p021_en.pdf.
Hómedes, N., López Linares, R. and Ugalde, A. (2005), 'Generic drug policies in Latin America', *World Bank, Health, Nutrition and Population Discussion Paper*, Washington DC.
Hómedes, N. and Ugalde, A. (2006), *Decentralizing Health Services in Mexico, a Case Study of State Reform*. Center for US-Mexican Studies, San Diego, University of California,
Instituto Nacional de Estadística y Geografía (INEGI) (2008), 'Sistema Nacional de Informacíon Estadística y Geográfica', online: www.inegi.gob.mx/inegi/default.aspx?s=est
International Labour Office (ILO) (2008a), 'Setting social security standards in a global society'. *Social Security Policy Briefings, Chapter 2*, online: www.ilo.org/public/english/protection/secsoc/downloads/policy/policy2e.pdf.
——(2008b), 'Social security expenditure database' online: www.ilo.org/dyn/sesame/ifpses.socialdbexp
Lloyd-Sherlock, P. (2006), 'When social health insurance goes wrong: lessons from Argentina and Mexico'. *Social Policy and Administration* 40, 4, pp. 353–68.
Mesa-Lago, C. (1989), *Ascent to Bankruptcy: Financing Social Security in Latin America*. Pittsburgh, PA: University of Pittsburgh Press.
——(2005), Social and economic problems in Cuba during the crisis and subsequent recovery *CEPAL Review* 86, 2, pp. 177–99.
Pan American Health Organisation (PAHO) (2007), *Health in the Americas, 2007*. New York: PAHO.
Rawlings, L. and Rubio, G. (2005), Evaluating the impact of conditional cash transfer programs *World Bank Economic Observer*, 20, 1, pp. 29–55.
Rofman, R. and Lucchetti, L. (2006), 'Pension systems in Latin America: concepts and measurements of coverage'. World Bank, online: siteresources.worldbank.org/EXTGDLNREGIONLAC/Resources/PensionCoverage_LAC-Rofman-Lucchetti&_Final.pdf, go.worldbank.org/F1RS12MNP0
Scott, J. (2008), 'Social security and inequality in Mexico: from polarization to universality'. *Well-being and Social Policy* 1,1: 55–76.
United Nations Population Division (2002), *World Population Ageing, 1950–2050*. New York: United Nations.
World Bank (1997), 'Evolución del gasto público en America Latina: 1980–95'. Washington, DC: World Bank LCHSD Working Paper.
——(2003), *Inequality in Latin America and the Caribbean: breaking with history*. Washington, DC: World Bank.

24
The Middle East

John Gal and Rana Jawad

Introduction

Social policy has a distinctive capacity to offer a new and insightful narrative about the political dynamics of the region of the Middle East. Indeed, a social policy perspective can highlight the existence of social welfare action, broadly defined, in the public sphere which is bringing about positive change in Middle Eastern societies and yet has so far remained under-represented in the mainstream social policy and development studies literatures. While there is common rhetorical consensus both in academia and policy circles that the main goal of social policy is general social welfare, the history of social policy shows that this field of action is much more concerned with how social welfare is defined, achieved, and measured. We argue that political cleavages underpin the trajectory of welfare state development and it is these debates which we hope to highlight in this chapter on social policy in the Middle East. Indeed, aspects of these debates already resonate in the recent Arab uprisings.

The 'Arab Spring', that has swept through the region starting late 2010, and the 2011 Israeli tent protests, have refocused attention not only on the need for political reform and civil rights in many countries in this region, but also on the underlying social causes that gave momentum to these upheavals and to the policies required to deal with them. Clearly, the spiraling cost of living, unemployment and the unequal distribution of wealth in these nations along with widespread poverty have all played a major role in creating the conditions for public unrest and demands for system change in Middle Eastern nations.

From a social policy perspective, the immediate question is whether the political mobilization that emerged in the region in the second decade of the new millennium may eventually lead to new forms of more adequate welfare provision as can be found in Western countries or if it will lead to another distinctive Middle Eastern form of this. More concerned academic attention on social policy in the Middle East may help push social policy concerns more centre stage and promote a better understanding of them. Thus, a critical overview of this region and its diverse national social policy settings will be the subject of this chapter.

For clarification, the Middle East includes countries in a geographic region which, according to Henry and Springborg (2001) extend 'from Morocco to Turkey along the southern and eastern shores of the Mediterranean and as far east as Iran and south to Sudan, Saudi Arabia, and Yemen'. The region has a population of half a billion, which is Muslim in the majority, but as the seat of the world's three largest monotheistic religions, it is also home to long-standing Christian and Jewish populations.

The Middle East is historically, culturally, and politically diverse. Parts of it like Iran and Turkey were never colonized by Europe, while other nations were greatly influenced by colonial rule; it is not all Arab or Arabic-speaking; some countries have been ruled under dictatorships or Islamic theocracies like Iraq, Libya, or Saudi Arabia whilst others have operated more as liberal democracies such as Turkey and Israel; its outer and inner geographical boundaries remain disputed – the Palestinian Territories are seeking to gain independent status and Cyprus skirts closely the boundaries of the Middle East and the Mediterranean. The Middle East is, of course, also in the throes of one of the world's longest political-religious conflicts (the Arab-Israeli conflict) which casts a long shadow on both the history and prospects of social policy there.

However, regardless of the Arab Spring and the turbulent politics of the region, this chapter asserts that the study of social policy and social welfare action is an academically viable and politically urgent endeavour for the Middle East. Hardly any discussion of social policy in the Middle East, either as a region or of the countries in it as separate nation-states, exists in the social policy literature. The seminal work by Gough and Wood et al. (2004), which sought to explore the welfare regime approach in the extent of non-OECD (Organisation for Economic Co-operation and Development) countries, did not include the Middle East. It is mainly Israel and Turkey that have tended to be mentioned in the literature due perhaps to the availability of reliable data and their closer ties with Europe and the United States. The neglect of the study of social policy in the Middle East, and in the Arab countries in particular, helps to perpetuate misconceptions about the populations of the region as backward or disorganized, and averts critical discussion of social welfare action that is already taking place on the ground. We take a 'strengths/assets-based' approach in this chapter which combines salient analytical trends in social development policy to consider what type of social welfare action is already taking place on the ground in Middle Eastern countries and how this might form the basis of more structured thinking about the situation of social policy and social welfare there.

Given the economic, political, social and cultural diversity across nations in the Middle East, efforts to develop overarching conclusions regarding developments in their social policies or to identify significant commonalities between these nations are clearly premature. Nevertheless a number of issues that require greater attention in all of these countries can be identified. In particular, these include the role of religion in the formulation and provision of social welfare, the crucial importance of civil society in the field of social welfare, and the need to take into account the unique demographic structure of the nations in this region. In this chapter, we consider the following arguments: in the first section, a historical overview of the key forces that have shaped social policy in the region is offered; in the second section we look at the existing theoretical approaches to the study of social policy or rather public policy in the region; in section three, we look at the role of religion and its influence on social policy in both state and none-state forms; in the fourth section we discuss Esping-Andersen's welfare regime classifications and how this approach may be used for analysing social policy in the Middle East; in section five we offer a synthesis of this discussion by proposing possible classifications of social policy in the countries of the region. The concluding section summaries the main arguments of the chapter.

Historical development: the lost opportunities of independence

Social policy in the Middle East has been greatly influenced by international intervention, for example, opening up to the European-dominated economy since the seventeenth century through colonization and mandate rule, which set particular political and economic structures in motion and, since the 1980s, economic reform under the pressure of globalization and structural adjustment programmes led mainly by international development agencies such as the

International Monetary Fund (IMF) and the World Bank. In many cases, the groups that have taken control of state social policy have tended to be local elites made up of tribal, religious, or ethnic leaders and wealthy merchants whose privileged status during mandate rule and afterwards marginalized the interest of a primarily rural agricultural population.

The increasing market-orientation of Middle Eastern economies and the privatization programmes they underwent under the present influence of globalization and international development actors has further retrenched the role of the state as principle provider of social services and employer in the public sector. Karshenas and Moghadam et al. (2006), El-Ghonemy (1998), Henry and Springborg (2003), and Clark (2004) describe how most states in the Middle East, especially the Arab ones, have failed or are failing to develop effective democratic institutions that can ensure representative government and political participation for all citizens. As a result, the impact of citizens and social groups upon the social policy formulation process and the distribution of resources has tended to be minimal and achieved at great price. Whether over-sized and coercive (such as Egypt and Saudi Arabia) or weak and dysfunctional (such as Sudan and Lebanon), these states have been rife with corruption and the embezzlement of public funds.

Basic issues such as access to jobs and adequate incomes have plagued many Middle Eastern countries for many years now (Arab Human Development Report, 2009). State social provisioning is especially hard hit because of several factors such as: the misallocation of resources and the prioritization of military spending over key social sectors such as health and education; the narrow economic focus of public policy, which hinges social progress on economic prosperity; the dominance of minority factions in Middle Eastern countries dating back to the colonial era; political insecurity and military conflict, with the protraction of the Arab–Israeli conflict; high levels of state indebtedness, which have diverted funds from social welfare services; and the introduction of structural adjustment programmes and the increasing privatization programmes, which have reduced the role of the state further as provider of social services and public sector jobs, and have often placed a high financial burden on individuals and families seeking to satisfy basic social needs such as housing, health, and education for themselves or their children. The resulting social ills of unemployment, wealth polarization, and even undernourishment would, therefore, need to be addressed through the reform of public policy and state legislation.

The 1940s and 1950s in the Middle East saw high secular and socialist fervour, the vestiges of which can still be found in countries like Egypt and Syria. Until the 1980s, the Middle East experienced immense social and economic changes, due almost singlehandedly to oil windfall. This was used to establish and fund state social services such as: guaranteed government employment for graduates; new labour legislation (typically favouring workers in large public enterprises) such as health insurance, retirement pay, maternity pay; free education; free hospital care; and basic consumer subsidies, the most important of which were food and housing. Urbanization and economic development were accompanied by significant attainments in education and enhanced female labour participation (Karshenas and Moghadam, 2006).

But, this was a short honeymoon. The easy access to capital that resulted from oil revenues led to the concentration of wealth amongst the urban elites, and left the majority of the populations poorly skilled and ruled primarily via patrimonial and tribal structures. This reliance on natural resource rents for social spending has typically earned the welfare regimes of the Middle East the label of 'rentier' (Beblawi, 1990). Even in countries like Turkey, which is not an oil-producing country and underwent a staunch modernizing agenda after independence, large segments of the population became disenfranchised which led to major rural–urban migration and the emergence of the urban shanty dwellings known as 'geçecondo', especially around Istanbul.

Another major factor hampering social policy is the politicization of welfare and the instrumental use of social policy by the state to gain power and political legitimacy. Some authors argue that even apparently progressive social policy initiatives, such as the introduction of categorical social benefits to workers and employment guarantees to university graduates in Iran and Egypt in the 1950s and 1960s, were in fact motivated by the need to win the support of the working classes in the postcolonial states, and were not based on a civic discourse of social citizenship. Today, social benefits are often channelled through clientelist networks, which link ruling governments to their supporters. Thus, social policy today in the Middle East, particularly in the Arab countries, lacks a sense of its own legitimacy and expectations are high that the Arab Spring may change this. Heartening though this might be, it is important not to lose sight of the history and contemporary challenges for social policy that have been discussed in this section.

Theoretical perspectives: rentierism, corporatism and residualism

Empirical knowledge and more sophisticated theoretical models concerning social policy in the Middle East are limited in the existing literature. While the higher income and more industrialized nations in this region, particularly Turkey, Israel, Iran, and Lebanon, have been the subject of some interest in recent years (Aybars and Tsarouhas, 2010; Buĝra and Keyder, 2006; Doron and Kramer, 1992; Doron, 2001; Harris, 2010; Jawad, 2009), this has clearly not been the case for much of this region. Indeed, in the case of most Middle Eastern nations, discussions pertaining to state policies concerning social welfare issues tended to adopt the rather constricting rentier state paradigm for the Arab and oil-producing countries in the region, particularly the Gulf states and Iran (Beblawi, 1990). Analytical literature examining social policies and outcomes in Middle Eastern nations, and based on a firm empirical foundation and a theoretical basis, have generally been extremely limited in number and scope (although see, for example, the edited collections by Dixon, 1987; Karshenas and Moghadam, 2006; and Gal and Greve, 2010).

Research conducted by the authors of this chapter as well as the other pieces of research cited above indicates that state social policy in Middle Eastern countries is generally residual in character and is primarily focused on the provision of social safety nets and the reintegration of marginalized groups into society. The most comprehensive employment-based insurance goes to urban public sector workers, particularly those who are unionized, with the best protection going to the army and security forces. At the heart of this residual social policy are key conceptual blockages, namely the overly economic focus of public policy and a corresponding lack of importance accorded to the social. A significant example of this residual or piecemeal approach to social policy is highlighted by the Egypt case study in Karshenas and Moghadam (2006) where since the 1990s the state has not been able to cut back on key consumer subsidies, as it has wished, due to the outbreak of violent public protest.

Related to this is the characterization of Middle Eastern states as 'rentier', meaning that their primary source of revenue is from natural resources such as oil and natural gas. This is particularly the case for the oil-rich countries in the Gulf, as well as for Iran, Iraq, and Algeria. The over-reliance on oil revenues has meant that some states were able to provide social welfare and social insurance services to citizens during the oil boom era of the 1960s to 1980s without having to tax citizens on the basis of their civic membership of the nation. The easy access to capital and the sudden overnight affluence brought about by the oil windfall in the region is depicted as a curse by El-Ghonemy (1998) since it has directly undermined the structures of social citizenship and the need to develop the productive capacity of the local population, due to the over-reliance on foreign labour.

For some authors writing about the region, the major challenges for social welfare provisioning in the Arab countries are less about the long-term structures of democratic participation and a share in decision-making by society, and more about the urgent measures of wealth redistribution, income transfers, provision of basic needs, and ensuring the basic support systems of survival. When measures of human well-being are discussed by some authors it is in the developmental/survival terms of child morality, female literacy, sanitation, and housing. At the heart of social policy, then, are key challenges of basic economic and social development. This gives the desired purpose and definition of social policy in much of the existing literature a focus on economic productivity, inherent in female labour participation, creating more employment opportunities, reducing indebtedness, reforming property rights and the Islamic laws that dominate inheritance and family planning. This is not to say that social policies in the past did not bring about improvements in society in the Middle East. In the immediate post-independence era in the 1940s and subsequently the oil-boom era, which lasted until the 1980s, there was rapid social transformation of the region with enormous improvements in education and health, as well as rapid urban transformation. But these gains were rapidly lost, as states became more authoritarian in character and failed to develop adequate economic policies.

This has led to a sense of breakdown in state and society relations in the Middle East – which we are now seeing in the wave of political mobilization as mass populations seek to reclaim a voice – often, this is being expressed in sectarian terms for instance, the Sunnis majority population rising against the Alawite regime in Syria and the Shi'a majority in Bahrain rising against the Sunni regime. The sense of social unrest is exacerbated further by the notion within society that the state should take more responsibility for the welfare of citizens and that the latter have the rights and entitlement to be provided with social services. A main area of contention is basic consumer subsidies, particularly food, where the local population has mounted riots to protest against their withdrawal, for example in Egypt. Competition between state and societal groups over the public sphere is most acutely expressed in the rise of Islamic groups in the Middle East, which are providing vital public and social services to excluded groups in society, and are thus challenging the state not only as a provider of welfare but as a modern secular institution of government. Some of these groups are well-known political groups such as the Muslim Brotherhood (Egypt) and Hamas (Palestinian Territories) but others are more local and less political, such as the Islah Charitable Society in Yemen or the Mustafa Mahmood Health Clinic in Egypt (Clark, 2004).

Religion and social policy

The role of religion in social policy is common to all the nations in the Middle East even though this takes diverse forms (Jawad and Yakut-Cakar, 2010). Islam, Judaism, and Christianity are an important cultural influence on inheritance laws as well as family planning, and exercise a major influence of definitions of poverty and approaches to charity and social action in the Middle East (Jawad, 2009). Islam is, of course, the dominant religion in most countries in the Middle East and its impact upon the provision of social welfare the greatest. In terms of Islam, some authors argue that religion can perpetuate wealth and gender inequalities, although authors differ arguing that women do have rights to property and to work, or do have a say in family planning. Islam is also discussed in terms of its welfare institutions such as *waqf* (religious endowments) and *zakat* (an obligatory 2.5 per cent tax levied on assets). *Zakat* has acted as a hugely important source of poverty alleviation for the poor and *waqf* played a key role in the socio-economic development of the Middle East in the last few centuries prior to colonization –

not least in the urban and political development of Istanbul in Turkey (Heyneman, 2004; Richardson, 2004).

Islamic principles can also inform public policy areas such as health, finance and economy, and human rights legislation. Here, it is argued that Islamic economics remains underdeveloped, but in the health sector, for example, some countries such as Iran, have been able to make substantial improvements to primary care thanks to the influence of Islamic principles in Iran after the revolution (Underwood, 2004). Islamic values are also important as an activating force for social groups and movements in society to engage in public and social service provisioning. In Egypt, Yemen, and Jordan for example, Islamic movements or Islamic charity organizations use social welfare to challenge the basis of the secular modern state, and/or to protect the political status of the professional classes through the provision of employment opportunities and social networks.

In the case of political Islamic groups, contributions in the book edited by Wiktorowicz (2004) depict organizations such as Hamas in Palestine as social movements that have developed locally and are now supported by a comprehensive institutional basis of which the provision of social welfare and public services is a vital component. In these cases, Islam is depicted as the only remaining platform for political contestation and struggle for social justice in the Middle East. To an extent, this is now being tested out in the countries that are undergoing regime change, most notably the case of Egypt where the world is watching how the role of the Muslim Brotherhood will pan out and what shape Islam will take in the emerging political identity of Egypt.

Regime classifications and the production of social welfare

In order to discuss the classification of welfare regimes in Middle Eastern countries, it is apt that we begin with some notion of how social welfare is produced. There are two overarching accounts of the evolution of welfare states, one focusing on the role of industrialisation and the social needs it generates, particularly unemployment and poverty which make the provision of state welfare inevitable, the other focusing on the role of political competition. This latter perspective highlights how new political groups such as industrial workers, feminists, or ethnic minorities emerge and seek to have their interests represented in government and thus their needs met through the welfare state. It is the industrialisation thesis which has tended to dominate accounts of social policy.

This split in perspective parallels two opposing approaches in the study of social policy, both of which rest upon the tension between state and market in the provision of social welfare services: the first approach considers social policy as subsidiary to capitalist development, a tool for serving the needs of the capitalist market and for alleviating the social problems which market forces cause. At the opposite end is a view of social policy as a central pillar of progressive social change, actively employed to achieve a more equitable and just society. In practice, whichever stance is adopted, the key dynamics underpinning the nature and scope of social policy in any particular national setting are affected by the interplay between the main institutions of society: the state, the market, and the family/community.

For this reason, it is more appropriate to speak of the 'mixed economy of welfare' or the 'welfare mix' which refers to the varying configurations of state, market and family/community in the provision of social protection. This means that different elements (of welfare) are delivered in different measure by different means. The Middle East social welfare mix is dominated by a strong role for nuclear and extended family; tribal, sectarian, and religious communities; market-based social welfare such as private medical insurance and paid for domestic help to assist with social care needs; and basic state provision in health and education.

The underlying philosophy behind the welfare regime approach as developed by Esping-Andersen (1990) is to avoid normative statements about the 'best' kind of welfare arrangement and to include a political analysis of welfare systems. In particular, Esping-Andersen followed a long tradition in Western social policy analysis which linked the political strength of labour movements to the development of the welfare state, against a relatively uniform level of economic growth in Western countries. A key feature of the welfare regime approach is to compare states that have generous welfare provision with those that do not. This consists of two key elements which distinguish between different types of welfare state. These are de-commodification and stratification. Based on these two key features, Esping-Andersen identified three types, or 'regimes', of 'welfare capitalism' which focused on the welfare conditions of male wage workers.

Esping-Andersen's model has raised criticism on a number of counts: this has ranged from its lack of gender-sensitiveness, to its assumption of the homogeneity and internal coherency of policy regimes, to questioning of the accuracy of the clusters of nations. Where developing country contexts are concerned, criticisms have been raised regarding the transferability of the model (Kabeer, 2000). Research led by Gough and Wood et al. (2004) on the transferability of the welfare regime model to the non-Western world omits from its analysis the region of the Middle East (including North Africa) entirely. There is discussion of informal security regimes in Africa but this primarily focuses on the high risk of war and violence in agrarian peasant societies there, a situation which does not characterize the more urban societies of the Middle East. Discussion of the segmented public/private provision of welfare in Latin America in the Gough and Wood et al. (2004) volume does, however, bear relevance for the Middle East where the labour market and family are core providers of welfare.

Esping-Andersen's welfare regime approach has also been criticized for its assumption of the internal coherency of social policy formulation since this assumes a false level of stability in the era of globalization and structural adjustment programmes. Other critics note that the concept fails to highlight the importance of health, education, and housing programmes which play a more important role in poor countries than do income-maintenance schemes. This latter argument is quite relevant for the Middle East. Criticisms have also been raised about welfare outcomes in the approach. Needs satisfaction and self-sufficiency, it is argued, are more important in lower-income settings whereas Esping-Andersen's typology is built on de-commodification. Furthermore, it is argued that stratification outcomes over-emphasise class-based social structures at the expense of gender, religious, ethnic, and clientelistic outcomes which are more relevant to social settings in developing countries. Esping-Andersen's typology is also criticized for not devoting enough attention to the critical role of international development institutions without which policy analysis of social welfare in low-income settings would be very lacking. Finally, it is pointed out that there is a problem of terminology inherent in the concept of welfare which in certain country contexts such as the Far East denotes charity and is contrasted with development which implies more long-term notions of social investment. This latter argument also bears relevance for Middle Eastern countries where development is the focus of government policy.

Towards a welfare regime classification of the Middle East

How then can we apply the welfare regime approach to assess social policy in the Middle East region? The simple answer is that the welfare regime offers both opportunities and challenges for the task at hand because it is possible to apply only some aspects of it, and to a certain extent. Moreover, the argument works the other way, in that the particular construction of the welfare regime approach may not capture the entire dynamics of social policy in the Middle

East. This is because the welfare regime approach is underpinned by particular assumptions and values about social welfare which have been described above and which highlight the debate surrounding the transferability of the welfare regime approach to developing countries. Thus, by employing a process of elimination, it becomes clear what elements of the welfare regime classification we can use for the Middle East region. This also begins to draw a picture of the configuration of social policy in the region. For example, we do not have adequate comparable data on social welfare expenditure (the welfare effort) save for Turkey and Israel; labour movements have not had the same importance in the political life in Middle Eastern countries as they did in the West; social security schemes are partial and still in their infancy in most Middle Eastern countries and are confined in the large part to health and pension schemes with more marginal benefits for unemployment and maternity when these exist. As a result of incomplete data availability and problems of definition of social security packages, it is difficult to measure accurately benefit levels and to be confident that rules of entitlement are being correctly applied.

Thus, in order to move this argument toward classification of the welfare regimes of the Middle East forward, we propose four types of countries as a way of categorizing the social contexts and social policies of the region:

> *The oil-rich Gulf countries*, namely Qatar, Bahrain, Oman, Kuwait, United Arab Emirates, and Saudi Arabia which are primarily concerned with reaping and accelerating the benefits of economic prosperity and oil wealth, and integrating their economies into the global market. These countries tend to be much less concerned with problems of social inequalities and deprivation in their respective countries (with the possible exception of Saudi Arabia).
>
> *(Post) Conflict countries*, namely Lebanon, Iraq, Sudan, Palestinian Territories (and, to some extent, Yemen) which are struggling to cope with major issues of debt, weak economic development, unemployment and rising costs of living leading to significant flows of out-migration and brain drain. These countries demonstrate residual welfare regimes whereby family and market-based social welfare supersede state provision.
>
> *Non-oil countries* (also known as diversified economies) with traditionally strong state control over social and economic policy such as Egypt, Syria, and Jordan. These are countries which deal with stark regional imbalances (such as between rural and urban areas) and the challenges of administrative reform. These countries have strong statist tendencies and as in the case of Egypt previously, provided subsidies for essential commodities which have been an essential pillar of the in-kind social assistance welfare regimes of the region
>
> *(Bayat, 2006)*

Mediterranean Welfare States, including Turkey, Israel, and Cyprus. Sharing commonalities with other high-income, industrialized, liberal democracies in the Mediterranean regime, these nations have a common modern history of late industrialization, authoritarian or colonial rule, and weak, ineffective states that have contributed to similarities in the structuring of their welfare states and in their ability to achieve acceptable welfare outcomes. While these countries have relatively extensive welfare and social security systems and their social expenditure is higher than that in most other Middle Eastern nations, spending levels generally remain lower than those in social-democratic and corporatist welfare states though higher than that in liberal welfare states. Poverty levels and the degree of inequality in the Mediterranean welfare states are lower than in other Middle Eastern countries, but nevertheless remain high in comparison to most European welfare states, and equal or higher to

> those in liberal welfare states. This apparently reflects an inability on the part of these welfare states to successfully overcome social gaps through redistribution
>
> *(Gal, 2010)*

Conclusion

The role of social policy in achieving greater social well-being and economic prosperity has been gaining increasing attention amongst national and international policy makers in the Middle East region in recent years. The impending deadline for the Millennium Development Goals has also played a part in this new wave of interest. The recent wave of social protest has brought social policy more into the mainstream of policy discourse and debate. But in order to create effective social policy, there is a need to articulate a coherent vision for how social policy operates and what it is meant to achieve. This requires clear understanding of what social policy means, how it differs to social development, and how it complements it. It is an endeavour that would represent an important step for the Middle East region, where social policy has never really played a central role in public policy or in national development planning more specifically.

This chapter argues that a social policy perspective helps to understand the shortcomings of the traditional 'growth first' approach in development policy, whereby social concerns are relegated to a secondary role or treated as residual outcomes of economic production. Middle Eastern countries hover between corporatist and residual models of welfare regime provision. We have suggested a way forward in terms of classifying the welfare regimes of this region that takes into account their distinctive geo-political profiles. More specifically, we have distinguished between four types of welfare regime in the Middle East: The oil-rich Gulf countries; (Post-)Conflict countries; Non-oil countries; and Mediterranean welfare states. Future research will be needed to study more deeply the way in which political and institutional forces have shaped the development of social policy in the Middle East and how the present social mobilization might present an opportunity for better engagement with social policy there.

References

Aybars, A.I. and Tsarouhas, D. (2010), Straddling Two Continents: Social Policy and Welfare Politics in Turkey. *Social Policy and Administration* 44(6), pp. 746–763.

Beblawi, H. (1990), 'The Rentier State in the Arab World', in G. Luciani (ed.), *The Arab State*. London: Routledge.

Bayat, A. (2006), 'The Political Economy of Social Policy in Egypt', in M. Karshenas and V. Moghadam (eds), *Social Policy in the Middle East,* UNRISD Social Policy in a Development Context Series, pp. 135–55. New York: Palgrave Macmillan.

Benthall, J. and Bellion-Jourdan, J. (2003), *The Charitable Crescent*. London: I.B. Tauris.

Buğra, A. and Keyder, C. (2006), 'The Turkish Welfare Regime in Transformation', *Journal of European Social Policy* 16(3), pp. 211–28.

Clark, J. A. (2004), *Islam, Charity and Activism: Middle Class Networks and Social Welfare in Egypt, Jordan and Yemen*. Bloomington and Indianapolis: Indiana University Press.

Clarke, G. and Jennings, M. (2008), 'Introduction', in G. Clarke, and M. Jennings (eds), *Development, Civil Society and Faith-Based Organizations – Bridging the Sacred and the Secular*. Hampshire: Palgrave Macmillan.

Clarke, J. (2004), *Changing Welfare, Changing State – New Directions in Social Policy*. London: Sage Publications

Deanoeux, G. (1993), *Urban Unrest in the Middle East – A Comparative Study of Informal Networks in Egypt, Iran and Lebanon*: Albany: State University of New York Press.

Dixon, J. (ed.) (1987), *Social Welfare in the Middle East*. Beckenham: Croome Helm.

Doron, A. (2001), 'Social Welfare Policy in Israel: Developments in the 1980s and 1990s', in D. Nachmias and G. Menachem (eds), *Public Policy In Israel.* London: Frank Cass.
Doron, A. and Kramer, R. M. (1992), *The Welfare State in Israel.* Boulder, CO: Westview.
El-Ghonemy, R. (1998) *Affluence and Poverty in the Middle East.* London: Routledge.
Esping-Andersen, G. (1990), *The Three Worlds of Welfare Capitalism.* Cambridge: Polity.
Gal, J. (2010), Is there an extended family of Mediterranean welfare states? *Journal of European Social Policy*, 20(4), pp. 283–300.
Gal, J. and Greve, B. (2010), Regional Issue: The Middle East. *Social Policy and Administration*, 44:6.
Gough, I. and Wood, G. et al. (eds) (2004), *Insecurity and Welfare Regimes in Asia, Africa and Latin America: Social Policy in a Development Context.* Cambridge: Cambridge University Press.
Hall, A. and Midgley, J. (2004), *Social Policy for Development.* London: Sage.
Harik, J. (1994), *The Public and Social Services of the Lebanese Militias*: Papers on Lebanon no.14: Oxford: Centre for Lebanese Studies.
Harris, K. (2010), Lineages of the Iranian welfare state: Dual institutionalism and social policy in the Islamic Republic of Iran, *Social Policy and Administration*, 44:6, pp. 727–45.
Henry, C. M. and Springborg, R. (2001), *Globalization and the Politics of Development in the Middle East.* Cambridge: Cambridge University Press.
Heyneman, S. (2004), 'Introduction', in S. P. Heyneman (ed.), *Islam and Social Policy.* Nashville, TN: Vanderbilt University Press.
Jawad, R. (2009), *Social Welfare and Religion in the Middle East: A Lebanese Perspective.* Bristol: The Policy Press.
Jawad, R. and Yakut-Cakar, B. (2010), Religion and social policy in the Middle East: The (Re)Constitution of an Old-New Partnership, *Social Policy and Administration*, 44(6), pp. 658–72.
Kabeer, W. and Cooks, S. (2000), Editorial Introduction: Re-visioning Social Policy in the South: Challenges and Concepts, IDS Bulletin, Vol, 31 no. 4, Institute of Development Studies.
Karshenas, M. and Moghadam, V. (2009), Bringing social policy back in: A look at the Middle East and North Africa, *International Journal of Social Welfare*, 18, pp. S52–S61.
——(eds) (2006), *Social Policy in the Middle East*, UNRISD Social Policy in a Development Context Series. New York: Palgrave Macmillan.
Kiliç, A. (2010), 'Gender, Family and Children at the Crossroads of Social Policy Reform in Turkey: Alternating between Familism and Individualism', in M. Ajzenstadt and J. Gal (eds), *Children, Gender and Families in Mediterranean Welfare States.* Dordrecht: Springer.
Richardson, G. (2004), 'Islamic Law and Zakat: Waqf Resources in Pakistan', in S. P. Heyneman (ed), *Islam and Social Policy*, pp. 156–80. Nashville, TN: Vanderbilt University Press.
Underwood, C. (2004), 'Islam and Health Policy: A Study of the Islamic Republic of Iran' in S. P Heyneman (ed.), *Islam and Social Policy*, pp. 181–206. Nashville, TN: Vanderbilt University Press.
United Nations Development Programme (2009), *Arab Human Development Report – Challenges to Human Security in the Arab Countries*, accessed on 23 January 2012 at www.arab-hdr.org/publications/other/ahdr/ahdr2009e.pdf.
Wiktorowicz, Q. (ed.) (2004), *Islamic Activism – A Social Movement Theory Approach*, Bloomington: Indiana University Press.

25
Africa

Alfio Cerami and Aïchetou Wagué

Introduction

This chapter addresses the issue of social protection and welfare in Africa. Africa is a highly diversified continent characterized by different socio-economic performances. It comprises the more developed countries of North Africa[1] as well as the less developed sub-region of sub-Saharan Africa.[2] Despite the existence of several problems and challenges, this part of the world remains a poorly researched area in comparative welfare state research. The problems that the populations of Africa face range from the lack of access to basic social protection and services (including inefficient labour markets), as existent in more advanced Western economies, to chronic malnutrition, persistent exposure to environmental challenges (such as drought, famine, and other environmental hazards) and to systemic internal conflicts and wars. These socio-economic and human development challenges have often led to riots and massive migrations, as the Arab Spring or the humanitarian crisis of the Horn of Africa in 2011 have powerfully shown.

Although Africa is characterized by the presence of several significant national specificities, some common characteristics in the approach to social protection exist. These involve: 1) a residual, confessional and clientelistic approach to social protection in the case of North Africa; and 2) a *permanent emergency* orientation of measures in the case of sub-Saharan Africa. More specifically, the former refers to the institutional design of social protection itself which remains, in the North African case, characterized by a limited reach and coverage for the total population. Beyond these structural features, the latter concerns – in the case of sub-Saharan Africa – the type of measures implemented. These, introduced as temporary creations to address urgent problems have, subsequently, become permanent structures over time.

Due to the presence of more extensive challenges, a more comprehensive approach to social protection in Africa is necessary. In fact, as correctly emphasized by Mkandawire (2011), while in advanced capitalist economies health, education, pensions, protection against unemployment, and family policies represent the core of the systems of social protection, this is not the case of sub-Saharan Africa. Besides the classical interventions of the social policy domain, other not less important areas usually ascribed to infrastructural measures (such as water sanitation and malnutrition) must also be considered. This chapter aims to cover this theoretical and empirical gap. It provides a brief overview of the state-of-the-art of social protection and welfare in the continent, shedding light on the associated problems and future challenges. The areas we focus on include poverty, education, health, malnutrition, and access to safe water, as these represent the domains in which a special attention of the international community and of national policy-makers is urgently required. In addressing these sectors of social protection, we also pay a special attention to issues related to discrimination and to the equal access to resources and services.

In order to address these issues, the chapter is structured as follows. The first section provides a brief overview of the current theoretical debate in comparative welfare state research. The goal is to highlight the strengths and the shortcomings of its applicability to the African context. The second section focuses, more in particular, on regime characteristics in North Africa and in sub-Saharan Africa. A special attention of the third section is given, instead, to key human development problems and challenges. The conclusion summarizes the results.

Contemporary theoretical debate in comparative welfare state research

In this first section, we examine Esping-Andersen's (1990) famous welfare regime typology, briefly discussing its limits and prospects. We argue in favour of an explanatory model that carefully takes into account not only the formal institutional foundations of welfare regimes in transition and developing countries, but also the informal set of welfare institutions and practices implemented. These can take the form of religiously sponsored forms of social protection, as in the case of faith-based organizations in North Africa (see Karshenas and Moghadam, 2006; Jawad, 2009; Cammet and MacLean, 2011) or community-based forms of social solidarity as in the case of sub-Saharan Africa (Bevan, 2004; Gough et al., 2004; MacLean, 2010). A better understanding of the regime characteristics with associated forms of social solidarity, we argue, is central to improve the performance of welfare institutions, as these elements greatly influence the life chances of the populations involved.

As several other chapters in this handbook also highlight (see in particular the Introduction by Bent Greve and the chapters in Part II *Typologies and Methods*), the contemporary international welfare state debate has largely been dominated by Esping-Andersen's (1990) regime classification, even though questions about its applicability to developing countries must be raised. In the *Three Worlds of Welfare Capitalism*, Esping-Andersen (1990) has identified three distinct welfare regimes with key characteristics that nicely fit post-industrial welfare economies, that with only a lot of difficulties can be applied to the still under-developed and highly informal welfare economies of Africa. In fact, while questions regarding de-commodification and social stratification measures remain relevant conceptual tools, their direct transfer to the African context is highly problematic. The issues at stake concern, in this context, are not simply the ways which markets are organized (e.g., their formal and informal institutions), but also the structure of welfare benefits, the entitlement criteria, the financing mechanisms, and the administration of social protection.

To summarise, Esping-Andersen (1990) has described the *liberal welfare regime* present in the United States, Canada, Australia, and Great Britain as reliant on means tested benefits, with social rights and entitlements that are conditional upon demonstrable and object needs, and usually associated to social stigma. In this group of countries, the systems of social protection are financed by private or social insurance institutions, while the administration of welfare benefits is highly decentralized and left to the forces of the market. These systems of social protection are dominated by a liberal work ethic, with the market that remains the main provider of welfare benefits and services. In the *conservative-corporatist regime* of France, Germany, and Italy, the systems of social protection aim at the preservation of status differentials through income replacements benefits. In this welfare regime typology, rights and welfare entitlements are the output of class status, whose main source of financing consists of social insurance contributions paid by the employees. The management of these system of social protection is highly decentralized and depend on para-public administrative structures, which often involve different set of social partners in the management of the social insurance funds (often referred to as 'Kassen', 'caisses', and 'cassa' …) (Palier, 2010). In the *social-democratic welfare regime* of Denmark, Norway, and Sweden, welfare institutions do not play a residual or subsidiary role, as it happens in the first two cases, waiting until the market or the family capacity to promote social equality is exhausted, but are strongly committed to the preservation of social rights defined upon citizenship, rather than upon class status. In this group of countries, benefits tend to be flat-rate and granted on a universal basis. Financing the system of social protection is more centralized, being usually funded through general taxation, and administered by state or state-like institutions.

During the years, other welfare regime typologies have been added to this initial classification. These have involved the Southern European countries of Italy, Spain, and Portugal (Ferrera, 1996; see also Petmesidou, this volume), the new democracies of Central and Eastern Europe (Bulgaria, Czech Republic, Estonia, Hungary, Latvia, Lithuania, Poland, Romania, Slovakia, and Slovenia) (Cerami, 2006; Aidukaite, 2010; see also Saxonberg, this volume), and Latin American as well as the South-East Asian models (Aspalter, 2006; Haggard and Kaufman, 2008; see also contribution by Li, in this volume). Slight variations, adaptations, and hybridizations of the main institutional variables have in all these cases been identified, though the key welfare regimes' variables with their impact on social stratification and de-commodification performances have remained almost unaltered. A question that, at this point, should be raised is whether this Western-centric approach to analysing welfare regime performance and functions can also be applied to the case of Africa and, if not, what are the distinct features that characterize this part of the globe.

Welfare regime typologies: residual orientation and permanent emergency welfare regimes

North Africa

As part of North Africa, Algeria, Egypt, Libya, Morocco, and Tunisia have established systems of social protection constituted by a variety of welfare arrangements that correspond to country-specific institutional set-ups with associated path-dependencies and institutional legacies. These systems of social protection can be described as *confessional resource dependent welfare regimes* (Cerami, 2012a), whose key characteristics lie in 1) the *captured nature of resources* by the political elites; 2) the *confessional* orientation of the system of social protection and in its particularistic way of redistributing welfare benefits and social services; and 3) the severe economic vulnerabilities and *dependence* that these countries have to exogenous economic shocks. These systems of social protection do not seem to fit in any of the classifications currently available. As mentioned, Esping-Andersen's (1990) *The Three Worlds of Welfare Capitalism* was primarily concerned with the establishment of welfare institutions in advanced Western capitalist societies and almost no attention has been devoted to religious factors and actors (van Kersbergen and Manow, 2009) or to the captured nature of resources by elites. In this part of the African continent, these are instead important features in the administration and delivery of social protection (Heyneman, 2004; Karshenas and Moghadam, 2006; Jawad, 2009; Cammet and MacLean, 2011). By devolving some of the tasks to decentralized religious non-state actors (or clans and tribes as in the case of Libya), the pressures caused by the state inefficiencies in public administration have, in this way, been reduced, whilst the religious attachment of the population increased (Cerami, 2012a).

To discuss a bit more in detail the welfare organization, the countries in North Africa have established systems of social protection that are based on social insurance and, hence, provide access to welfare benefits and social services after the payment of social insurance contributions.

In this group of countries, coverage tends to include all citizens employed under labour contracts, with some sporadic extensions for household workers, the self-employed, and farmers. Special provisions exist for particular professional categories (ISSA, 2008–9). Welfare benefits and services are often administered and redistributed by religious non-state actors (e.g., charity organizations, such as the Human Relief Agency in Egypt or the national Red Crescent Societies in Algeria, Morocco and Tunisia), which become, in this way, the real welfare providers. As far as the pension system is concerned, as the North African region has a young population, pension schemes continue to be based on a 'pay-as-you-go' system with low retirement ages associated with substantial reductions for some privileged categories of workers (usually civil servants, the police, the military, etc.) (Robalino, 2005). With respect to healthcare, while impressive efforts and progress have been made since the 1970s to protect citizens from several health hazards (see contributions in Karshenas and Moghadam, 2006), improving the often obsolete healthcare infrastructures and extending coverage to a large section of the poor population have remained urgent priorities. Similarly, unemployment benefits also follow the social insurance principle, even though they are extremely poorly developed. A clear system of unemployment insurance exists in Egypt and Tunisia, while in the other countries no formal system of protection against unemployment is available to date (Angel-Urdinola and Kuddo, 2010). As these *confessional resource dependent welfare regimes* are based on a traditional vision of women as mothers and household workers rather than as full-time employees, the system of maternal leave and family benefits does not allow women to be fully integrated in the labour market and in the society. Feminization of poverty is here the most obvious result (World Bank, 2010; Cerami, 2012a).

Sub-Saharan Africa

In contrast to the systems of social protection in North Africa, the welfare regimes in sub-Saharan Africa can be described in terms of *permanent emergency welfare regimes* (Cerami, 2012b), whose main characteristics lie in: a low impact of the state in welfare promotion due to poor budget capacity; political and bureaucratic clientelism in order to obtain access to benefits and services; high production of vertical and horizontal inequalities; vital importance of family, local and religious communities in social protection; strong reliance of informal economy and informal networks in welfare production; decisive involvement of donor countries and external agencies in the transformation of the institutional design of national welfare systems; welfare goals aimed at providing primarily 'basic services and provisions' in order to address permanent emergency situations; increasing importance of migration and related workers' remittances for survival and internal welfare production; and, finally, *survival-oriented skill production regime* characterized by low human capital formation (Cerami, 2012b).

This emergency-oriented approach to social protection was not implemented from one day to another, but it emerged slowly over time. It was dictated by two interrelated reasons. On the one hand, the implementation of *permanent emergency* measures depended on the necessity to address urgent social needs (such as high maternal and children mortality ratio, HIV/AIDS pandemics, etc.). On the other, as it was in line with the dominant economic and social policy doctrine of the 1980s, it aimed to promote and to reinforce in this part of the continent a smooth transition to free market principles. The objective of the new economic doctrine to development promoted by the International Monetary Fund (IMF) and World Bank was, in fact, to limit the involvement of the state in the market; to increase the privatization of the economy; to reduce the high external debt of most of the countries; to shift responsibility from the state to the individual; and to address the most urgent problems creating a priority of economic and social interventions (for a review, see Gough et al., 2004; Adésínà, 2007; Bangura, 2007; Mkwandire, 2011).

Despite good intentions, some negative occurrences materialized (Stiglitz, 2002). These involved not only an increasing reliance on external aid due to the limited regional economic integration capacity (Collier, 2007), but it also produced a precariousness of social protection, a residualization in responsibility and an individualization in social risk management.

Human development challenges

In terms of human development, the countries of North Africa and sub-Saharan Africa continue to face important challenges related to the welfare and social protection of their population. This can be immediately perceived by the low progress that some countries have made in achieving the priorities of the Millennium Development Goals (MDGs). In fact, while North Africa has obtained a remarkable success over the years greatly increasing the health and education level of its population, this has not prevented the sub-region to fall into poverty traps (UNDP, 2009). Even more complex is, in this case, the situation concerning sub-Saharan Africa. Despite some initial positive results, the Commission for Africa (2010, p. 15) has highlighted, for instance, that 'the [sub-Saharan African] region is still not on track to meet any of the MDGs by 2015'. What this means for the populations involved is easy to imagine – slow progress in meeting the MDGs has important implications not only for the daily survival of citizens, but it also implies for single countries lower chances to catch up with more developed nations in the Northern hemisphere of the globe, relegating this part of the African continent to a situation of permanent under-development.

Persistent poverty remains a still unresolved issue both in North Africa and sub-Saharan Africa. In 2005, the UNDP (2009, p. 11) regional report estimated that about 20 per cent of the Arab population in North Africa was living below the two-dollars-a-day international poverty line. Poverty rates were also substantially higher in the cases of women and young people, who represent the most vulnerable groups in the region. Worst is the situation south of the Sahara. Poverty rates in sub-Saharan Africa continue to be among the highest in the world and estimated to 51 per cent of total population living on less than $1.25 a day for 2005 (latest figures available for the whole region) and 38 percent by 2015 (Commission for Africa 2010, pp. 16, 18). Similarly, the Food and Agriculture Organization (FAO) estimates that there are 239 million people in sub-Saharan Africa suffering from hunger, out of 925 million people in the world (FAO, 2010). This means, in other words, that although sub-Saharan Africa counts for only 16 per cent of the world population, 25 cent of those who are hungry in the world are in this region.

In spite of the substantial progress made during the last three decades both in North Africa and in sub-Saharan Africa in the sector of education, with a significant increase in school enrolment for primary level, the quality of education, and its gender neutrality still remain highly problematic (UN, 2011). In North Africa, we are in front of a highly educated population, but with few real chances of getting ahead in the society. In our group of countries, in 2005 the combined gross enrolment ratio for primary, secondary, and tertiary education ranged from 94 per cent in Libya to 76 per cent in Tunisia, 74 per cent in Algeria, 77 per cent in Egypt, and 58 per cent in Morocco (UNDP, 2009, p. 229, Table 1). Brain drain remains, in this context, a major problem that governments in the region still need to address, so as to avoid a deleterious de-pauperization of human resources. Significant progress in the sector of education has been made also in sub-Saharan Africa, even though the results, especially in terms of gender equality, are significantly lower. In sub-Saharan Africa, for instance, according to (UNDP, 2010, p. 20) for every 100 boys, only 91 girls succeed to attend school in 2007/2008. This means not simply that the region missed the target for gender equality in primary education set for 2005, but also implies that it will miss targets for other levels of education – secondary and university level – with clear repercussions for the future levels of employability of women.

Despite urgent needs and substantial achievements made during the last decades, health targets remain of particular concern, especially when the repercussions on the success of societies is considered (Hall and Lamont, 2009). While in North Africa the situation of health is now less dramatic thanks to immense investments made since the 1970s, in sub-Saharan Africa the health condition of the population is significantly different. In particular, when maternal mortality and child mortality are carefully considered, it becomes immediately evident that the reduction in mortality rates was less significant than expected or even decreased in many sub-Saharan countries (UN, 2010, p. 28). Here, what is important to remember is that given the important role played by women in the family in African countries, high maternal mortality produces an additional negative impact on the welfare, well-being and social protection of children and other family members. Large prevalence of malaria and HIV/AIDS are, in the sub-Saharan African context, among the most important factors to explain high under-five and maternal mortality rates (UN, 2011, p. 42), with women and young that continue to represent the most vulnerable group to the pandemic.

With regard to the access to safe drinking water and sanitation facilities, whilst in the North African region this problem seems, at least temporarily, to have been sufficiently addressed by years of infrastructural interventions, with between 80 and 90 per cent of the population usually having access to improved water sources (UNDP, 2009, p. 234, Table 6), the condition of the populations in sub-Saharan Africa continues to be particularly dramatic. In 2008, for example, approximately 330 million people still did not have access to clean water, while 565 million continued to have no access to improved sanitation facilities. This corresponded to approximately 31 per cent of the population in sub-Saharan Africa as in 2005 (Commission for Africa, 2010, p. 16). Interestingly, differences in access to safe drinking water and sanitation facilities are not only characterized by regional disparities, but also by income disparities. It can, in fact, come as a surprise to discover that in several countries in sub-Saharan Africa people from lower social strata have not simply a lower access to safe drinking water and sanitation facilities due to infrastructural deficiencies in poorer areas, but also that they are forced to pay more for the services compared to wealthy people living in richer, better-equipped neighbourhoods.

Conclusion

Unfortunately, poor social protection and welfare remain key characteristics in Africa, affecting the life and living conditions of several million people. As highlighted in the course of the chapter, the causes for the poor performance in social protection and welfare are multifold. They depend, on the one hand, on structural deficiencies (such as those caused by a lack of infrastructures, limited economic growth, or the organization of the welfare architecture) while, on the other, on the residual or permanent emergency understanding of the functions that a welfare state should play. Often by necessity but sometimes also by choice, the existent welfare systems in Africa have been established with the aim of playing a subsidiary role, helping to address only the most urgent social needs emerging in still highly informalized and under-developed labour markets. Compared to other welfare regime models present in more advanced industrial economies, *informality* caused by a devolution of responsibilities to religious non-state actors, or to local communities, represents important constituent elements of these *confessional, resource-dependent, or permanent emergency welfare regimes* in transition.

As a result, we have argued in favour of an explanatory model that explicitly considers the formal institutional foundations of welfare regimes, as well as the set of informal welfare institutions and practices. As briefly discussed in the course of the chapter, these take the form of religiously – or community-based sponsored forms of social protection and of social solidarity that aim to replace the residual and permanent emergency orientation of the systems of social protection established in North Africa and sub-Saharan Africa. Future research and policy interventions more specifically tailored to the African context should not simply have a special focus on institutions seen as crucial elements in institutional change, but they should also take into consideration the cultural peculiarities and historical legacies that can foster or hinder policy and institutional innovation. In short, we argue that the key for success of future policies lies not outside but inside Africa. However, in order to achieve full human development objectives a different understanding and more comprehensive approach to social protection is urgently required.

Notes

1 Algeria, Egypt, Libya, Morocco, Tunisia and Western Sahara.
2 Angola, Benin, Botswana, Burkina Faso, Burundi, Cameroon, Cape Verde, the Central African Republic, Chad, Comoros, Côte d'Ivoire, Democratic Republic of the Congo, Djibouti, Equatorial Guinea, Eritrea, Ethiopia, Gabon, The Gambia, Ghana, Guinea, Guinea-Bissau, Kenya, Lesotho, Liberia, Madagascar, Malawi, Mali, Mauritania, Mauritius, Mozambique, Namibia, Niger, Nigeria, Republic of Congo, Rwanda, São Tomé and Príncipe, Senegal, Seychelles, Sierra Leone, Somalia, South Africa, South Sudan, Sudan, Swaziland, Tanzania, Togo, Uganda, Zaire, Zambia, and Zimbabwe.

References

Adésínà, J. O. (ed.) (2007), *Social Policy in Sub-Saharan Context. In Search of Inclusive Development.* Basingstoke: Palgrave Macmillan.

Aidukaite, J. (2010), Welfare Reforms in Centran and Eastern Europe: A New Type of Welfare Regime? *Ekonomika*, 89, pp. 7–24.

Angel-Urdinola, D. F. and Kuddo, A. (2010), Key Characteristics of Employment Regulation in the Middle East and North Africa. *SP Discussion Paper July 2010 NO. 1006.* Washington, DC: World Bank.

Aspalter, C. (2006), The East Asian welfare model. *International Journal of Social Welfare*, 15, pp. 290–301.

Bangura, Y. (ed.) (2007), *Democracy and Social Policy.* Basingstoke: Palgrave Macmillan.

Bevan, P. (2004), 'The Dynamics of Africa's In/security Regimes', in I. Gough, G. Wood, A. Barrientos, P. Bevan, P. Davis and G. Room (eds), *Insecurity and Welfare Regimes in Asia, Africa and Latin America.* Cambridge: Cambridge University Press.

Cammett, M. C. and MacLean, L. M. (2011), Introduction: The Political Consequences of Non-state Social Welfare in the Global South. *Studies in Comparative International Development (SCID)*, 1, pp. 1–21.

Cerami, A. (2006), *Social Policy in Central and Eastern Europe: The Emergence of a New European Welfare Regime.* Berlin: LIT Verlag.

——(2012a), *Social Protection, Public Administration Reforms and Democratization in the Middle East and North Africa.* Unpublished manuscript.

——(2012b), *Permanent Emergency Welfare Regimes in Sub-Saharan Africa.* Basingstoke: Palgrave Macmillan.

Collier, P. (2007), *The Bottom Billion: Why the Poorest Countries Are Failing and What Can Be Done About It.* Oxford: Oxford University Press.

Commission for Africa (2010), *Still Our Common Interest.* London: UN Commission for Africa.

Esping-Andersen, G. (1990), *The Three Worlds of Welfare Capitalism.* Cambridge: Polity Press.

FAO (2010), *The State of Food Insecurity in the World – Addressing Food Insecurity in Protracted Crises.* Rome: FAO.

Gough, I., Wood, G., Barrientos, A., Bevan, P., Davis, P. and Room, G. (eds) (2004), *Insecurity and Welfare Regimes in Asia, Africa and Latin America.* Cambridge: Cambridge University Press.

Haggard, S. and Kaufman, R. R. (2008), *Development, Democracy, and Welfare States.* Princeton, NJ: Princeton University Press.

Hall, P. A. and Lamont, M. (2009), *Successful Societies: How Institutions and Culture Matter for Health*. Cambridge: Cambrdige University Press.

Heyneman, S. P. (ed.) (2004), *Islam and Social Policy*. Nashville, TN: Vanderbilt University Press.

International Social Security Association (ISSA) (2008–9), *Social Security Programs Throughout the World: Middle East and Africa*. Geneva: International Social Security Association.

Jawad, R. (2009), *Social Welfare and Religion in the Middle East. A Lebanese perspective*. Bristol: The Policy Press.

Karshenas, M. and Moghadam, V. M. (eds) (2006), *Social Policy in the Middle East*. Basingstoke: Palgrave Macmillan.

Kersbergen, K. V. and Manow, P. (eds) (2009), *Religion, Class Coalitions, and Welfare States*. Cambridge: Cambridge University Press.

MacLean, L. M. (2010), *Informal Institutions and Citizenship in Rural Africa: Risk and Reciprocity in Ghana and Cote d'Ivoire*. Cambridge: Cambridge University Press.

Mkandawire, T. (2011), 'Welfare Regimes and Economic Development: Bridging the Conceptual Gap', in V. Fitzgerald and R. Thorp (eds), *Overcoming the Persistence of Inequality and Poverty*. Basingstoke: Palgrave Macmillan.

Palier, B. (ed.) (2010), *A Long-Good Bye to Bismarck? The Politics of Welfare Reforms in Continental Europe*. Amsterdam: Amsterdam University Press.

Robalino, D. A. (2005), *Pensions in the Middle East and North Africa Time for Change*. Washington, DC: World Bank.

Stiglitz, J. E. (2002), *Globalization and its Discontents*. London: Penguin Books.

UNDP (2009), *Arab Human Development Report. Challenges to Human Security in the Arab Countries*. New York: UNDP Regional Bureau for Arab States.

United Nations (UN) (2010), *The Millennium Development Goals Report 2010*. New York: United Nations.

——(2011), *The Millennium Development Goals Report 2011*. New York: United Nations.

World Bank (2010), *Bridging the Gap. Improving Capabilities and Expanding Opportunities for Women in the Middle East and North Africa Region*. Washington, DC: World Bank.

26

States of health

Welfare regimes, health, and healthcare

Clare Bambra

Introduction

This chapter discusses how health research has influenced the development of welfare state regime typologies, and how these typologies have themselves influenced health research. Three key developments are examined: firstly, the integration of healthcare services into the welfare state typologies literature; secondly, the importance of decommodification in regards to health and healthcare; and thirdly, how welfare state regimes have been used by comparative social epidemiologists to examine and explain international differences in population health and health inequalities. The chapter starts with a definition of key terms. It concludes by reflecting on the implications of health research for the further development of welfare state regime typologies and comparative social policy.

Various key concepts are used within this chapter: decommodification, social epidemiology, population health, health inequalities, and the social determinants of health. The key underlying concept in Esping-Andersen's *Three Worlds* typology (1990) was decommodification. Decommodification is 'the extent to which individuals and families can maintain a normal and socially acceptable standard of living regardless of their market performance' (Esping-Andersen, 1987, p. 86). The welfare state decommodified labour because certain services and a certain standard of living became a right of citizenship and reliance on the market for survival decreased (Esping-Andersen, 1990, p. 22). Health can itself be regarded as something which is variously commodified and decommodified (Bambra et al., 2005). Social epidemiology is about the social causes of disease distribution within and between societies, it is 'about why different societies – and within societies, why different societal groups – have better or worse health than others' (Kriegar, 2011, p. vii). Population health refers to the health status of populations as opposed to individuals: the 'extant and changing population distributions of health, disease, and death' (ibid.). Health inequality is a term used to describe systematic differences in health status between different social or demographic groups (such as inequalities by gender or ethnicity). Most usually it is used to refer to socio-economic class inequalities in health (measured by education, income, or occupational class): inequalities in health are 'systematic differences in health between different socio-economic groups within a society. As they are socially produced, they are potentially avoidable and widely considered unacceptable in a civilised society' (Whitehead, 2007, p. 473).

Health inequality is measured in absolute or relative terms (for more detail see Bambra, 2011a). In developed countries, welfare states are important macro-level determinants of health as they mediate the health impact of socio-economic position and the exposure of different population groups to the social determinants of health: access to essential goods and services (specifically water and sanitation, and food); housing and the living environment; transport; unemployment and social security; working conditions; and access to healthcare (Bambra, 2011a).

Healthcare and welfare state regimes

Healthcare is an important social determinant of health and a significant component of a country's welfare state. However, healthcare was long overlooked by regime typologists. For example, Esping-Andersen's influential *Three Worlds of Welfare Capitalism* (1990) typology was devised by focusing almost exclusively on the decommodification of cash transfers and the role of welfare services (such as education, social care, and healthcare) were largely ignored. This was also the case with the rival typologies that were developed in the 'welfare state regimes debate' which followed the publication of the *Three Worlds* (Bambra, 2005a). For example, the typologies of Castles and Mitchell (1993), Ferrera (1996), or Korpi and Palme (1998) all ignored the role of welfare services including healthcare (see Table 26.1). Indeed, what was most remarkable about the 'welfare state regimes debate' was that whilst there were numerous critiques about Esping-Andersen's range, his methodology, and the absence of gender in his typology (for overviews of the critiques see Bambra, 2005b or 2006a), a core procedure attracted less attention: the analytical focus on cash benefits (Bambra, 2005a; 2005b) and the creation of regimes that generalised all forms of social policy provision from this base (Kasza, 2002). Welfare state regime theory had ignored the fact that welfare states are also about the actual delivery of services, such as healthcare, education, or social care, and that, far from being internally consistent, countries vary in terms of the relative emphasis that they place upon cash benefits and/or welfare state services. Indeed, welfare services may well account for the greatest differences both between and within countries' welfare state arrangements (Castles, 1998; Bambra, 2005b). Healthcare is by far the largest area of welfare state service delivery, accounting as it does for an average of around 6.5 per cent of gross domestic product (GDP) in the European Union (EU) member states and it is a strong example of internal welfare state inconsistency in the provision of cash benefits and welfare services.

This was examined via the development of a healthcare decommodification index and a resulting healthcare typology (Bambra, 2005). Healthcare decommodification is 'the extent to which an individual's access to healthcare is dependent upon their market position and the extent to which a country's provision of healthcare is independent from the market' (Bambra, 2005a). This was measured using private health expenditure as a percentage of GDP, private hospital beds as a percentage of total bed stock, and the percentage of the population covered by the healthcare system. For comparability purposes, the resulting healthcare typology was constructed using Esping-Andersen's methodology (despite its noted limitations see Bambra, 2006a) and using only the same 18 Organisation for Economic Co-operation and Development (OECD) countries. A three-fold typology of low, medium, and high healthcare decommodification resulted (Table 26.1). There were notable differences with the cash-transfer based typologies particularly in regards to the positioning of Canada, New Zealand, and the UK which were low in terms of labour market decommodification but highly decommodifying in terms of healthcare. Healthcare provision in the Liberal welfare states of Canada, New Zealand, and the UK is based on principles (universalism), provision processes (public sector) and funding mechanisms (general taxation) that are in stark contrast with the rest of their market-orientated welfare state package.

Table 26.1 Main welfare state typologies used in health research

Author	Measures	Welfare state regimes				
Esping-Andersen (1990)	*18 countries* *Decommodification *Social stratification *Private-public mix	**Liberal** Australia Canada Ireland New Zealand UK USA	**Conservative** Finland France Germany Japan Italy Switzerland	**Social Democratic** Austria Belgium Netherlands Denmark Norway Sweden		
Castles and Mitchell (1993)	***14 countries*** *Aggregate welfare expenditure *Benefit equality	**Liberal** Ireland Japan Switzerland USA	**Conservative** Germany Italy Netherlands	**Non-Right Hegemony** Belgium Denmark Norway Sweden		**Radical** Australia New Zealand UK
Ferrera (1996)	***15 countries*** *Coverage *Replacement rates *Poverty rates	**Anglo-Saxon** Ireland UK	**Bismarck** Austria Belgium France Germany Luxembourg Netherlands Switzerland	**Scandinavian** Denmark Finland Norway Sweden	**Southern** Greece Italy Portugal Spain	
Korpi and Palme (1998)	***18 countries*** *Social expenditure as a % GDP *Luxembourg income study *Institutional characteristics	**Basic Security** Canada Denmark Ireland Netherlands New Zealand Switzerland UK USA	**Corporatist** Austria Belgium France Germany Italy Japan	**Encompassing** Finland Norway Sweden		**Targeted** Australia

Table 26.1 (continued)

Author	Measures	Welfare state regimes				
Navarro and Shi (2001)	***18 countries*** *Political tradition	**Liberal-Anglo Saxon** Canada Ireland UK USA	**Christian Democrat** Belgium Netherlands Germany France Italy Switzerland	**Social Democratic** Sweden Norway Denmark Finland Austria	Ex-Fascist Spain Greece Portugal	
Bambra (2005a)	***18 countries*** *health care decommodification	**Low** Australia US	**Medium** Austria Belgium France Germany Ireland Italy Japan Netherlands Switzerland	**High** Canada Denmark Finland New Zealand Norway Sweden UK		
Bambra (2005b)	***18 countries*** *health care and labour market decommodification	**Liberal** Australia Japan USA	**Conservative** Austria Belgium Canada Denmark France Italy	**Social Democratic** Finland Norway Sweden	**Conservative sub-group** Germany Switzerland Netherlands	**Liberal sub-group** Ireland UK New Zealand

Source: Adapted from Bambra 2007

This analysis was further refined by comparing the relative role of healthcare decommodification and labour market (cash transfers) decommodification (Bambra, 2005b). This work produced a five-fold classification (Table 26.1). Most notably, the composition of the high-scoring group confirmed the existence of a distinctive Scandinavian regime that provides consistently high levels of provision (Esping-Andersen, 1990). A group of key Conservative countries was also identified reflecting comments that the Conservative regime countries tend to place more emphasis upon cash benefits in their welfare mix (Castles, 1998). Finally, the division of the Liberal regime countries into two distinctive groups, one that is consistently low in decommodification and one that is more service-orientated, gives credence to claims about a fourth – radical – world of welfare that is a sub-type of the Liberal regime (Castles and Mitchell, 1993).

However, since these pieces of work were completed, healthcare systems – particularly in the UK and New Zealand – have been subject to extensive reform and marketisation (Leys and Player, 2011). The healthcare typologies, as with all welfare state typologies (Bambra, 2006a), cannot therefore be treated as static entities.

Welfare state regimes, health and health inequalities

In addition to extending welfare state regimes research by including the decommodification of healthcare, health researchers have applied the welfare state regimes concept to the study of international variations in the distribution of disease. Welfare states, through their decommodifying effects, mediate the extent, and impact, of market-derived class and income inequalities within a country (Bambra, 2006b). Therefore, the decommodification provided by welfare states can be expected to have an indirect relationship with health status (Raphael and Bryant, 2004). Countries with a highly decommodifying welfare state package will have less stark class and income inequalities (Esping-Andersen, 1990, 1999) and therefore better national health outcomes (Wilkinson and Pickett, 2009) than those countries that operate a less decommodifying system (Coburn, 2004; Bambra, 2006b).

Welfare states and population health[1]

International research on the social determinants of health has increasingly started to integrate a welfare state regime perspective. These comparative studies have utilised different welfare state typologies – e.g. Bambra (2006b) and Coburn (2004) utilised Esping-Andersen's *Three Worlds,* Navarro et al. (2003, 2006) utilised the Navarro and Shi political traditions typology (2001), whilst Eikemo et al. used Ferrera's (1996) typology (Table 26.1). Most of the studies to date have examined infant mortality rates (IMR) or closely related indicators such as low birth weight. Although Navarro and colleagues (2006) and Karim and colleagues (2010) examined life expectancy, and Eikemo and colleagues (2008a) examined international differences in morbidity. The studies have invariably concluded that population health is enhanced by the relatively generous and universal welfare provision of the Social Democratic Scandinavian countries, especially in contrast to the Liberal welfare states.

Studies have consistently shown that IMR vary significantly by welfare regime type, with rates lowest in the Social Democratic countries and highest in the Liberal and Southern regimes. In a longitudinal cross-national study of income inequalities and welfare provision between countries, Coburn (2004) concluded those countries which were the least neo-liberal in their economic and social policy orientation (i.e. the Scandinavian welfare states) had significantly lower IMR, lower overall mortality rates and less mortality at younger ages. This study also suggested that welfare state regime might be the link between GDP/capita and mortality.

Conley and Springer (2001) examined IMR in Esping-Andersen's three welfare regimes from 1960 to 1992. They found significant differences by regime type, but that these differences decreased over time with a certain degree of convergence in terms of IMR. Their analysis also identified that public expenditure on healthcare had an important association with IMR, particularly in the Conservative welfare state regimes. Similarly, my analysis (Bambra, 2006b) found significant differences in IMR between the three worlds of welfare: weighted IMR for the Liberal, Conservative and Social Democratic regimes were 6.7, 4.5 and 4.0 respectively. This study also found a moderate correlation between decommodification levels (1998 data) and IMR ($r = -0.585$, $p = 0.018$).

Navarro et al. (2003; 2006) examined differences between four different welfare state regimes (the Navarro and Shi, 2001 typology), they found that those countries which have had long periods of government by redistributive political parties (most notably the Scandinavian countries) have experienced lower IMR and, to a lesser extent, increased life expectancy at birth. These findings were reinforced by Chung and Muntaneer's (2006) multilevel longitudinal analysis of welfare state regimes in which they found that around 20% of the difference in infant mortality rate among countries, and 10 per cent for low birth weight, could be explained by the type of welfare state. Social Democratic countries had significantly lower IMR and low birth weight rates, compared to all other welfare state regimes. A wider sample study by Karim et al. (2010) examined differences in IMR and life expectancy in 30 welfare states including those in Eastern European and East Asia (Table 26.2). The analysis found that only life expectancy ($R^2 = 0.58$, adjusted $R^2 = 0.47$, $p < 0.05$) differed significantly by welfare state regime. The study found that 47 per cent of the variation was explained by welfare state regime type. The Social Democratic welfare states had the lowest IMR but not the highest life expectancy (Table 26.2).

Eikemo and colleagues' (2008a) multi-level study utilised Ferrera's typology (Table 26.1) to examine self-reported health in Europe. It also found that the Scandinavian welfare regime fared better with lower rates of limiting long-term illness and poor self-reported health. In addition, the study found that after controlling for individual (socio-economic status, demographics) and regional characteristics, around 10 per cent of cross-national differences in self-reported health were due to type of welfare state regime. However, in contrast to the mortality studies, this study also found that the Anglo-Saxon regime faired comparatively better than the Bismarckian or Southern welfare states. This may be due to the comparatively high healthcare decommodification in the UK and Ireland.

Mechanisms to better population health[2]

The studies thus almost universally suggest that the Social Democratic countries have the best population health outcomes. Commentators have chosen to privilege particular explanations. For example, Coburn (2004) and Bambra (2006) have both suggested that the key characteristics of the Scandinavian welfare state package (universalism, generous replacement rates, extensive welfare services) result in narrower income inequalities and higher levels of decommodification, both of which are associated with better population health (Wilkinson and Pickett, 2009). Coburn (2004), along with Navarro and colleagues (2003; 2006), have also highlighted the importance of the accumulative positive effect on income inequalities of governance by pro-redistribution political parties in the Scandinavian countries. Other commentators have also suggested that increased gender equality and defamilisation within the Scandinavian countries may be another incremental factor behind their better health outcomes (Stanistreet et al., 2005; Bambra et al., 2009). Furthermore, proponents of the social capital approach have highlighted the high levels of social cohesion and integration within Scandinavian societies, something which has also been associated with better population health (Kawachi et al., 1997).

Table 26.2 Infant mortality rates and life expectancy at birth for 30 countries and six welfare state regimes (2003)

Welfare state regime and country	*Infant mortality rate (deaths per 1,000 live births)*	*Life expectancy at birth (in years)*
Scandinavian	3.98	78.52
Denmark	4.90	77.10
Finland	3.73	77.92
Norway	3.87	79.09
Sweden	3.42	79.97
Liberal	5.53	78.49
Australia	4.83	80.13
Canada	4.88	79.83
Ireland	5.34	77.35
New Zealand	6.07	78.32
United Kingdom	5.28	78.16
United States	6.75	77.14
Conservative	4.40	78.65
Austria	4.33	78.17
Belgium	4.57	78.29
France	4.37	79.28
Germany	4.23	78.42
Luxembourg	4.65	77.66
Netherlands	4.26	78.74
Switzerland	4.36	79.99
Southern	5.65	78.47
Greece	6.12	78.89
Italy	6.19	79.40
Portugal	5.73	76.35
Spain	4.54	79.23
Eastern	6.83	74.19
Hungary	8.58	72.17
Czech Republic	5.37	75.18
Poland	8.95	73.91
Slovenia	4.42	75.51
East Asian	5.29	78.70
Japan	3.30	80.93
Korea	7.31	75.36
Hong Kong	5.63	79.93
Singapore	3.57	80.42
Taiwan	6.65	76.87

Source: Karim et al. (2010), reproduced with permission from Elsevier.

An innovative study by Lundberg and colleagues (2008) has provided some of the best empirical explanation of the mechanisms behind better population health in the Social Democratic welfare states. They examined the influence of two key Social Democratic welfare state policies – support for dual-earners (1970–2000) and generous basic pensions (1950–2000) – on IMR and old-age excess mortality in 18 developed countries. They found that every 1 per cent increase in support for the dual earner family model decreased IMR by 0.04 per 1000 births. This was not the case for expenditure in support of the traditional male breadwinner family model (associated particularly with the Conservative regime). Similarly, for every 1 per cent increase in the generosity of basic old age pensions, there was a decrease in old age excess mortality by 0.02 for both men and women. Generosity in earnings-related pensions (a defining characteristic of the Conservative regime) did not decrease mortality.

Similarly, differences in population exposure to the social determinants of health by welfare state could be an important mechanism behind the health premium attached to Social Democracy. By way of example, studies of the psychosocial work environment have shown a lower prevalence of work-related stress in countries with more comprehensive welfare states (where the psychosocial work environment is more regulated such as Sweden or Norway), and that the effects on health of adverse psychosocial work environments are also lessened in these countries (Dragano et al., 2010; Sekine et al., 2009). Another example is that the health burden of unemployment is also reduced in countries with more generous social security systems (Bartley et al., 2006; Bambra and Eikemo, 2009). Further, and as demonstrated in the previous section, there is universal access to healthcare services – another important social determinant (Geleronimo et al., 2011).

Welfare state regimes and health inequalities

Until the late 1990s, the few comparative studies that had been conducted into socio-economic inequalities in health had also concluded that the Social Democratic Scandinavian welfare states (particularly Norway and Sweden) had the smallest socio-economic health inequalities (Black et al., 1980). This was in keeping with the fact that the Social Democratic countries performed better in terms of overall health, and also that from a theoretical perspective, it would be expected that labour market-generated socio-economic class inequalities in health would be smaller in the more highly decommodifying and egalitarian Social Democratic Scandinavian countries. However, the findings of more recent studies have been less homogeneous (Dahl et al., 2006; Bambra, 2011a; 2011b). For example, Mackenbach and colleagues (1997) large-scale comparative study of health inequalities in Europe found that in the 1980s, relative educational, income and occupational class inequalities in morbidity (self-reported health) were present in all the European countries studied (Mackenbach et al., 1997). The Scandinavian countries did not have smaller relative educational inequalities in self-reported health than the other European countries, but they did have smaller relative income inequalities in self-reported health for men (but not women). Mortality was lower for non-manual occupations in all the countries studied but there were little differences in the sizes of relative inequalities by country (Mackenbach et al., 1997). However, the Social Democratic Scandinavian countries did exhibit smaller absolute differences in mortality by occupational class. These findings were confirmed by a follow-up European-wide study of relative health inequalities conducted in the 2000s (Mackenbach et al., 2008).[3]

A number of comparative studies have used welfare state regimes to examine cross-national differences in the magnitude of socio-economic inequalities in morbidity (Bambra, 2011c). Overall, they have all found that socio-economic inequalities in health are present in all types of welfare state. However, the comparative performance of different types of welfare state regime varies by the measure of inequality used. This is demonstrated in Table 26.3 which contains data from Eikemo and colleagues' studies of educational and income inequalities in morbidity (2008b; 2008c). Both studies used data from the European Social Survey and utilized the Ferrera (1996) typology. In terms of educational inequalities, they found that the magnitude of both relative and absolute educational inequalities in self-reported health and limiting long-term illness were largest within the Southern welfare state regime and smallest within the Bismarckian regime. The Scandinavian regime was less favourably placed than the Anglo-Saxon regime.

Table 26.3 Two studies of socio-economic inequalities in self-reported health (bad/poor compared to fair/good/very good) by welfare state regime

Study	*Measure of inequality*	*Typology*	*Summary of results**				
				Men Absolute Prevalence Rate Difference	Relative Prevalence OR (95% CI)	Women Absolute Prevalence Rate Difference	Relative Prevalence OR (95% CI)
Eikemo et al. (2008b)	Education – average education versus one sd below average	Ferrera (1996)	Bismarckian	**6.4**	**1.19** (1.14–1.24)	**5.7**	**1.25** (1.20–1.30)
			Anglo-Saxon	**9.6**	**1.35** (1.23–1.48)	**8.2**	**1.29** (1.18–1.41)
			Scandinavian	**10.5**	**1.44** (1.35–1.53)	**12.1**	**1.54** (1.44–1.64)
			Southern	**14.8**	**1.57** (1.47–1.69)	**17.3**	**1.69** (1.58–1.81)
Eikemo et al. (2008c)	Income – top versus bottom income tertiles	Ferrera (1996)	Bismarckian	**9.8**	**1.68** (1.50–1.89)	**11.6**	**1.81** (1.62–2.03)
			Southern	**10.9**	**1.79** (1.46–2.19)	**14.8**	**2.14** (1.77–2.57)
			Scandinavian	**13.0**	**1.97** (1.70–2.27)	**15.8**	**2.14** (1.84–2.49)
			Anglo-Saxon	**17.4**	**2.86** (2.12–3.70)	**17.4**	**2.73** (2.17–3.44)

* Age standardised differences between the top and bottom socio-economic groups in each analysis.
Source: Adapted from Bambra, 2011b.

However, in contrast, the study of income-related inequalities in self-reported health and limiting long-term illness (Eikemo et al., 2008c) found that the Anglo-Saxon regime had the largest inequalities, the Bismarckian the smallest whilst the Social Democratic and Southern regimes held an intermediate position (Table 26.3).

Findings on health inequalities also vary by population sub-group with comparative studies of the most vulnerable social groups – the old (Avendano et al., 2009), the sick (van der Wel et al., 2010), and children (Zambon et al., 2006) – finding that there are much smaller socio-economic inequalities in the Social Democratic Scandinavian welfare states – particularly Norway and Sweden. Further, the use of relative or absolute measures of health has caused controversy as whilst relative inequalities might not be the smallest in the Social Democratic welfare states, in absolute terms everyone does better: absolute mortality levels among disadvantaged groups are lower in welfare states with more generous, universal, social protection systems (Lundberg and Lahelma, 2001).

Debating comparative health inequalities

In contrast to their comparatively strong performance in terms of overall health, data from most – but not all – of the recent comparative studies of health inequalities in the general population suggest that the Scandinavian welfare states do not have the smallest health inequalities. Given the higher levels of social expenditure in the Scandinavian welfare states, the smaller income inequalities, and the commitment to equality underpinning the Social Democratic welfare model in Scandinavia, it is something of a 'puzzle' as to why the Scandinavian countries do not have the smallest health inequalities (Bambra, 2011b). Attempted explanations for the puzzle are varied, focusing on different issues within the broader debates about the causes of health inequalities – behaviouralism, materialism, and so forth (ibid.). However, most notably, issues of measurement have been flagged up, and this is where the use of welfare state regimes as a methodological device has been heavily criticised.

The existence of the 'public health puzzle' – of why health inequalities are not the smallest in the Scandinavian countries – has been challenged on the basis that it is merely the result of the data and methods used. Certainly, the application of different indicators of social inequality (e.g. income, occupation and education) and the use of different datasets has produced divergent results (see Table 26.3). Different cross-national patterns also emerge in terms of the different ways in which specific indicators of inequality are calculated. For example, studies of educational inequalities can compare those with average years of education to those with one standard deviation below the national average, or the difference between those with no education or only primary education compared to those with tertiary education (Bambra, 2011b). There are also more general issues in terms of making cross-national comparisons of health inequalities as it is not clear whether the bottom groups are the same in each country and whether their composition changes over time. The use of relative or absolute measures of health inequalities is also an important issue as it has been shown that relative measures of inequalities are negatively associated with total population health: countries with lower overall mortality tend to experience larger inequalities in mortality (Eikemo et al., 2009). Further, there have been relatively few studies conducted to date and only two of inequalities in mortality (Mackenbach et al., 1997; 2008).

The other crucial measurement problem is the use of 'welfare state regimes', a concept which assumes a homogenous approach to welfare provision within and between the countries of any particular regime type. This has long been a criticism of the 'welfare modelling business' (Abrahamson, 1999). Kasza (2002) argued that the concept of welfare regimes incorporated two flawed assumptions: firstly, that most of the key social policy areas, such as income maintenance, education, health, or housing, within a welfare regime will reflect a similar, across-the-board approach to welfare provision, particularly in respect of the role of the state; and secondly, that each regime type itself reflects 'a set of principles or values that establishes a coherence in each country's welfare package' (Kasza, 2002, p. 272). Kasza asserted that instead of an internal policy homogeneity or cohesion, welfare states and welfare regimes exhibit significant variation across different areas of social provision. The incremental, piecemeal, and cumulative nature of welfare policy making; the diverse histories of different policy areas within a country's welfare framework; the variation of policy actors across different fields; differences in the policy making process; and the influence on policy of external/foreign welfare models; all undermine the likelihood of cohesion and coherence within a welfare state or, indeed, within a welfare state regime. The regime concept therefore 'does not capture the complex motives that inform each country's welfare programs' and, in pursuit of consistency, it ignores the fact that different areas of welfare state provision – such as healthcare – exhibit different cross-national variations (Kasza, 2002, p. 283). One example of how the welfare state regimes concept obscures important policy differences between welfare states is the labour market approaches in the Social Democratic countries with the flexicurity of Denmark placed together with the protectionism of Sweden or Norway. The broad brush welfare state regimes approach may not be nuanced enough to capture these differences. Indeed, it could be stated that the very purpose of the welfare state regimes concept is to look for what is most similar and whilst this has value when examining the broad political and social macro-level inputs, in terms of outputs, such as health inequalities, slight differences in welfare state policies between countries of broadly similar principles and institutions can – over time – have potentially big impacts. The analysis of specific social policies has therefore been advocated as an alternative way of conducting comparative research (Lundberg et al., 2008; Kasza, 2002).

Conclusion

Application of the welfare state regimes concept into health research has had both positive and negative impacts. Positively, it has resulted in the integration of healthcare decommodification into welfare state regime construction, and the regimes concept has been a productive way of exploring and to some extent explaining international variations in the population health of developed countries. However, on the negative side, the healthcare decommodification index has challenged the internal consistency of welfare state regimes, showing that there are differing service and transfer mixes. Similarly, the use of welfare state regimes to compare and explain differences in the magnitude of health inequalities between developed countries has also resulted in a questioning of the validity of the welfare state regimes approach to comparative research. The implications for typologies are thus three-fold: Firstly, to maintain value within comparative research, the welfare state regimes concept needs to be able to integrate all aspects of welfare provision. Secondly, the limitations of the concept need to be acknowledged by those using it to construct complicated explanations of population outcomes. Finally, the welfare state regimes concept, by identifying broad similarities between countries makes possible more precise natural policy experiments between most similar cases. This will ultimately help advance our understanding of the interaction between welfare policies and health outcomes.

Notes

1 This section is reproduced from Bambra 2011a with permission from Polity Press.
2 This section is reproduced from Bambra 2011a with permission from Polity Press.

3 It should be noted that although Mackenbach et al.'s studies (1998; 2008) did not explicitly use welfare state regimes, the geographic areas which they did use broadly matched Ferrera's 1996 welfare regimes typology.

Further reading

Bambra, C. (2011), *Work, Worklessness and the Political Economy of Health*. Oxford: Oxford University Press.

——(2011), Health inequalities and welfare state regimes: Theoretical insights on a public health 'puzzle'. *Journal of Epidemiology and Community Health*, doi: 10.1136/jech.2011.136333

——(2005), Cash versus services: 'worlds of welfare' and the decommodification of cash benefits and healthcare services. *Journal of Social Policy* 34, pp. 195–213.

References

Abrahamson, P. (1999), The welfare modelling business. *Social Policy & Administration*, 33, pp. 394–415.

Avendano, M., Jürges, H. and Mackenbach, J.P. (2009), Educational level and changes in health across Europe: longitudinal results from SHARE. *Journal of European Social Policy*, 19, pp. 301–16.

Bambra, C. (2005a), Worlds of welfare and the healthcare discrepancy, *Social Policy and Society*, 4, pp. 31–41.

——(2005b), Cash versus services: 'worlds of welfare' and the decommodification of cash benefits and healthcare services. *Journal of Social Policy* 34, pp. 195–213.

——(2006a), Decommodification and the worlds of welfare revisited, *Journal of European Social Policy* 16, pp. 73–80.

——(2006b), Health status and the worlds of welfare, *Social Policy and Society* 5, pp. 53–62.

——(2007), Going Beyond the Three Worlds: Regime Theory and Public Health Research. *Journal of Epidemiology and Community Health*, 61, pp. 1098–1102

——(2011a), 'Social inequalities in health: Interrogating the Nordic welfare state 'puzzle'', in J. Kvist, J. Fritzell, B. Hvinden, and O. Kangas (eds), *Changing Equality: The Nordic Welfare Model in the 21st Century*. Bristol: Policy Press.

——(2011b), Health inequalities and welfare state regimes: Theoretical insights on a public health 'puzzle'. *Journal of Epidemiology and Community Health*, doi: 10.1136/jech.2011.136333

——(2011c), *Work, worklessness and the political economy of health*. Oxford: Oxford University Press.

Bambra, C. and Eikemo, T. (2009), Welfare state regimes, unemployment and health: A comparative study of the relationship between unemployment and self-reported health in 23 European countries. *Journal of Epidemiology & Community Health*, 63, pp. 92–98.

Bambra, C., Fox, D. and Scott-Samuel, A. (2005), Towards a politics of health. *Health Promotion International*. 20, pp. 187–93

Bambra, C., Pope, D., Swami, V., Stanistreet, D., Roskam, A. Kunst, A. and Scott-Samuel, A. (2009), Gender, health inequality and welfare state regimes: a cross-national study of thirteen European countries. *Journal of Epidemiology & Community Health*, 63, pp. 38–44.

Castles, F. G. (1998), *Comparative Public Policy: Patterns of Post-war Transformation*. Cheltenham: Edward Elgar.

Castles, F. G. and Mitchell, D. (1993), 'Worlds of welfare and families of nations', in F. G. Castles (ed.), *Families of Nations: Patterns of Public Policy in Western Democracies*. Aldershot: Dartmouth.

Chung, H. and Muntaner, C. (2006), Political and welfare state determinants of infant and child health indicators: an analysis of wealthy countries. *Social Science & Medicine*, 63, pp. 829–42

Coburn, D. (2004), Beyond the income inequality hypothesis: class, neo-liberalism, and health inequalities. *Social Science and Medicine*, 58, pp. 41–56.

Conley, D. and Springer, K. (2001), 'Welfare state and infant mortality'. *American Journal of Sociology*, 107:3, pp. 768–807.

Dahl, E., Fritzell, J., Lahelma, E., Martikainen, P., Kunst, A.E. and Mackenbach, J.P. (2006), 'Welfare state regimes and health inequalities', in J. Siegrist and M. Marmot (ed.), *Social Inequalities in Health*, pp. 193–222. Oxford: Oxford University Press.

Dragano, N., Siegrist, J. and Wahrendorf, M. (2010), Welfare regimes, labour policies and workers' health: A comparative study with 9917 older employees from 12 European countries. *Journal of Epidemiology and Community Health*, doi:10.1136/jech.2009.098541

Eikemo, T.A., Bambra, C., Judge, K. and Ringdal, K. (2008), Welfare State Regimes and Differences in Self-Perceived Health in Europe: A Multi-Level Analysis. *Social Science & Medicine*, 66, pp. 2281–95.

Eikemo, T.A., Huisman, M., Bambra, C. and Kunst, A. (2008), Health inequalities according to educational level under different welfare regimes: a comparison of 23 European countries. *Sociology of Health and Illness*, 30, pp. 565–82.

Eikemo, T., Bambra, C., Joyce, K. and Dahl, E. (2008), Welfare state regimes and income related health inequalities: a comparison of 23 European countries. *European Journal of Public Health*, 18, pp. 593–99.

Eikemo, T., Skalicka, V. and Avendano, M. (2009), Variations in relative health inequalities: are they a mathematical artefact? *International Journal of Health Equity*, 8, p. 32.

Esping-Andersen, G. (1987), 'Citizenship and Socialism: Decommodification and Solidarity in the Welfare State', in G. Esping-Andersen and L. Rainwater (ed.), *Stagnation and Renewal in Social Policy: The Rise and Fall of Policy Regimes*. London: Sharpe.

——(1990), *The Three Worlds of Welfare Capitalism*. London: Polity.

Ferrera, M. (1996), The southern model of welfare in social Europe. *Journal of European Social Policy*, 6, pp. 17–37.

Gelormino, E., Bambra, C., Spadea, T. et al. (2011), The effects of healthcare reforms on health inequalities: a review and analysis of the European evidence base. *International Journal of Health Services*, 41, pp. 209–30.

Karim, S.A., Eikemo, T.A. and and Bambra, C. (2010), Welfare state regimes and population health: integrating the East Asian welfare states. *Health Policy*, 94, pp. 45–53.

Kasza, G. (2002), The Illusion of Welfare Regimes. *Journal of Social Policy*, 31, pp. 271–87.

Kawachi, I., Kennedy, B.P., Lochner, K. and Prothrow-Stith, D. (1997), Social Capital, Income Inequality, and Mortality. *American Journal of Public Health*, 87, pp. 1491–98.

Korpi, W. and Palme, J. (1998), The paradox of redistribution and the strategy of equality: welfare state institutions, inequality and poverty in the Western countries. *American Sociological Review*, 63, pp. 662–87.

Krieger, N, (2011) *Epidemiology and the People's Health: Theory and Context*. New York: Oxford University Press.

Leys, C. and Player, S. (2011), *The Plot Against the NHS*. Pontypool, Wales: Merlin.

Lundberg, O. and Lahelma, E. (2001), 'Nordic health inequalities in the European context', in M. Kautto, J. Fritzell, B. Hvinden, J. Kvist and H. Uusitalo (eds), *Nordic Welfare States in the European Context*, pp. 42–65,

Lundberg, O., Yngwe, M., Kölegård Stjärne, M., Elstad, J., Ferrarini, T., Kangas, O. et al. (2008), The role of welfare state principles and generosity in social policy programmes for public health: an international comparative study. *Lancet*, 372, pp. 1633–40.

Mackenbach, J., Kunst, A., Cavelaars, A., Groenhof, F. and Geurts, J. (1997), Socioeconomic inequalities in morbidity and mortality in Western Europe. *Lancet*, 349, pp. 1655–59.

Mackenbach, J., Stirbu, I., Roskam, A., Schaap, M., Menvielle, G., Leinsalu, M. et al. (2008), Socioeconomic Inequalities in Health in 22 European Countries. *New England Journal of Medicine*, 358, pp. 2468–81.

Navarro, V. and Shi, L. (2001), The political context of social inequalities and health. *International Journal of Health Services Research*, 31, pp. 1–21.

Navarro, V., Borrell, C., Benach, J., et al. (2003), 'The importance of the political and the social in explaining mortality differentials among the countries of the OECD, 1950–98'. *International Journal of Health Services Research*, 33:3, pp. 419–94.

Navarro, V., Muntaner, C., Borrell, C. and Benach, J. (2006), Politics and Health Outcomes. *Lancet*, 368, pp. 1033–37.

Raphael, D. and Bryant, T. (2004), 'The welfare state as a determinant of women's health: support for women's quality of life in Canada and four comparison nations'. *Health Policy*, 68 (1), pp. 63–79.

Sekine M., Chandola T., Martikainen P., Marmot M. and Kagamimori S. (2009), Socioeconomic inequalities in physical and mental functioning of British, Finnish, and Japanese civil servants: Role of job demand, control, and work hours. *Social Science & Medicine*, 69, pp. 1417–25.

Stanistreet, D., Bambra, C. and Scott-Samuel, A. (2005), Is patriarchy the source of male mortality? *Journal of Epidemiology and Community Health* 59, pp. 873–76.

van der Wel K., Thielens, K. and Dahl E. (2010), Health inequalities and work in a comparative perspective: a multilevel analysis of EU SILC. *13th Biennial Congress of the European Society for Health and Medical Sociology*, 26–28 August 2010 Ghent, Belgium.

Whitehead, M. (2007), A typology of actions to tackle social inequalities in health. *Journal of Epidemiology and Community Health*, 61, pp. 473–78.

Wilkinson, R. G. (1996), *Unhealthy Societies: The Afflictions of Inequality*. London: Routledge.

Wilkinson, R. and Pickett, K. (2009), *The Spirit Level: Why more Equal Societies Almost Always do Better.* London: Penguin.

Zambon, A., Boyce, W., Cois, E. et al. (2006), Do welfare regimes mediate the effect of socioeconomic position on health in adolescence? A cross-national comparison in Europe, North America, and Israel. *International Journal of Health Services*, 36, pp. 309–29.

27

How to analyse welfare states and their development

Barbara Vis

Introduction

To describe and understand the development of welfare states, it is necessary to know how to analyse this development. This chapter describes some of the main quantitative and qualitative approaches. Rather than describing in detail how to conduct the different kinds of analyses (for this, see Chapter 29), this chapter focuses on the available approaches.

In this chapter, I discuss three broad categories of approaches: quantitative, comparative qualitative, and single case studies, focusing on the most important methods available and illustrating each with one or two examples. This overview indicates that which approach is 'best' depends on the researcher's research question and goal.

The dependent variable and data

Before turning to the different approaches, it is necessary to first address two issues that all welfare state researchers have to deal with: 1) which dependent variable to employ, and 2) which data to use. The first issue entails what is known as the *dependent variable problem* (see Clasen and Siegel, 2007). The dependent variable problem concerns how to conceptualize, for instance, the generosity of welfare states theoretically, how to operationalize it empirically and, finally, how to measure it. Since different authors adopt different definitions, their operationalizations differ and, consequently, their findings do too.

In the 1980s and early 1990s, the typical study of welfare state development – at that time focusing mostly on the welfare state's expansion – used aggregate expenditure data to assess this development. Such data were the only ones available for a range of countries and time periods at the time, which explains their widespread use. In his *Three Worlds of Welfare Capitalism*, Gøsta Esping-Andersen (1990) argued that this focus was problematic. Because 'it is difficult to imagine [that] anyone struggled for spending *per se*' (p. 21), Esping-Andersen considered expenditures epiphenomenal for assessing welfare state development. Scholars should rather examine to what extent welfare states allow citizens to maintain a livelihood independent from the market, i.e. to what extent welfare state programmes decommodify citizens. The decommodification index Esping-Andersen developed has subsequently been employed by many other scholars – even though the use of expenditure data did not disappear entirely – indicating that these scholars apparently agreed with him (but see Siegel, 2007, pp. 50–54 for the pros of expenditure analysis). A drawback of the decommodification index was that it was based on data from around 1980 only, and thus did not allow for analyses over time, in addition to getting outdated at some point. With the publication of Scruggs's (2004) *Welfare State Entitlement Dataset* and Korpi and Palme's (2007) *Social Citizenship Indicator Programme*, time-series data from around 1970 to 2000 are available nowadays.

The publication of these two datasets did not put an end to data problems, though. For one, as indicated, there are sometimes good theoretical reasons to focus on expenditures, such as when a researcher is interested in cost containment. Moreover, thus far the generosity data (as Scruggs calls them) and citizenship indicators (as Korpi and Palme label them) are available only for 18 advanced developed democracies. This means that research into, for instance, the development of the welfare states of the new member states of the European Union (EU) or in Asia still needs to turn to expenditure data if it wants to compare a large(r) set of countries or programmes. Unfortunately, as De Deken and Kittel (2007) show, expenditure data in general may be riddled with problems. A major problem is the comparability of the data, which results from the difficulty of having a consistent accounting edifice that is systematically applied to all countries (p. 73). Although the Organisation for Economic Co-operation and Development (OECD) and the EU have been working hard to systematize data across countries, De Deken and Kittel show that essentially the same expenditures, like those on mandatory private pensions, are still sometimes placed under different categories in different countries. This hinders the comparability of the data. Another, related, problem is that missing data for disaggregated measures of social expenditure, such as spending on active labour market policies, lead – if uncorrected – to aggregate social expenditure data which are not comparable across countries or over time (see Siegel, 2007, pp. 62–3). Excluding expenditures on active labour market policies altogether from the aggregate social expenditure measure to circumvent this 'patchy data' problem, like for example Castles (2004) does, is no panacea either. The risen importance of such policies in, among other things, the discourse of the OECD, the EU and governments alike make active labour market policies too relevant to exclude.

Quantitative analyses

Ever since the development of welfare states became a research topic for scholars, quantitative analyses have been conducted. The sophistication of these analyses increased substantially over time. In the first decades, quantitative analyses were typically *cross-sectional*, focusing on the variation across countries and/or programmes in one point in time. The seminal work by Flora and Heideheimer (1981) is an excellent example hereof. In the 1990s and early 2000s, the field turned en masse to conducting their quantitative analyses by means of *pooled time-series cross-sectional analysis*. Garrett and Mitchell's (2001) often cited and re-analysed study is characteristic for this approach, which combines analysing the variation across cases (typically countries) and the variation over time. A third quantitative approach in the study of welfare state development is *typology-building and re-analysing existing typologies*, an approach that sprung an extensive body of research especially after the publication of Esping-Andersen's *The Three Worlds*.

Cross-sectional analysis

In the early days, a lot of (quantitative) comparative welfare state research was mainly cross-sectional in that it examined the differences and similarities of welfare states at one point in time, whereby the findings of different cross-sectional analyses were sometimes compared. In

Flora and Heideheimer's (1981) edited volume that studies the development of the welfare state in Europe and the US, for example, the contributors compare social insurance systems such as unemployment insurance (Chapters 2 and 5), the expenditures on programmes like health services (Chapter 3), political macro-characteristics at the time of Bismarck's social insurance legislation in Germany in the 1880s (Chapter 4), and the introduction of income tax systems (Chapter 6). They also compare the sociopolitical paths of the adoption of social insurance legislation across time periods (Chapter 2), hence contrasting different cross-sections. In terms of dependent variable, the contributions in Flora and Heideheimer focus mostly on the introduction of different programmes and on how much was spent on them, which is in line with their research questions and goals.

A more recent cross-sectional analysis is Castles's (2004) study that puts crisis, myths and measurement at its centre. Specifically, Castles investigates whether processes of globalization, population ageing and declining birth rates that allegedly endanger the welfare state 'will lead to social policy disaster or whether they too will turn out to be mythical in character' (p. 2). Because these globalization and demographic crises hypotheses can be formulated more or less explicitly in terms of expenditure implications, it makes sense that Castles uses measures of social expenditure as his dependent variables to test comparatively these hypotheses. The complexity of his measures increase as the book evolves and shows that, in spite of their problems (see above), the disaggregated data in the social expenditures dataset of the OECD have much to offer to this end. Specifically, Castles first shows that a 'race to the bottom' simply does not materialize in aggregate social expenditure (Chapter 2) and subsequently constructs an expenditure-shares typology based on disaggregated spending data that reveals that the structure of social provision and the priorities of the welfare types barely converge (Chapter 3). Although Castles's cross-sectional analysis enables him to debunk the globalization and population hypotheses for most countries by examining the changes in the expenditure patterns between 1980 and 1998, it cannot remedy the aforementioned problem of the comparability of the expenditure data.

Pooled time-series cross-sectional analysis

Since the mid-1990s, many welfare state scholars, as well as political scientists more generally, turned *en masse* to pooled time-series cross-sectional analysis as their preferred quantitative approach. This technique has two main advantages that explain this. The first is that pooling cross-section and time-series data reduces the so-called small-*n* problem. This problem, which often emerges in comparative welfare state research, pertains to the problem of having too small a number of observations to make all relevant inferences, i.e. test all relevant hypotheses. The rule is that one observable implication can only give independent information about one other fact, i.e. each observation allows for one inference at most. If the observations are not independent, as often is the case in comparative welfare state research, we need (many) more than *n* observations to make *n* inferences. This small-*n* problem of more inferences than observations is often present in qualitative case studies, but also in cross-national research that studies for instance 18 OECD countries. Including both cross-sectional and time series data reduces this problem by increasing the number of observations. For example, adding time series data for 10 years to the 18 OECD countries example increases the number of observations from 18 to 180 (i.e. 18×10). This allows more fully specified models to be estimated and thus for more inferences to be drawn. A second advantage is that pooling allows for the control of exogenous shocks that all units of observation share such as an oil crisis (by controlling for time effects), and limits omitted variable bias (by controlling for unit effects).

Unfortunately, pooling data introduces a wide range of (new) problems too. Specifically, the potential problems of the time-series dimension, such as autocorrelation (i.e. error terms that are not independent from one time period to another) and non-stationarity (i.e. the persistency of variables over time), as well as of the cross-sectional dimension like heteroskedasticity (i.e. the variance of the error terms varies across units) are often present and regularly reinforce one another. Because of the way these problems are (not) handled, the results of pooled time-series cross-sectional analyses are regularly not very reliable (Kittel and Winner, 2005; Plümper et al. 2005). Wilson and Butler's (2007) review of 195 published articles in political science illustrates the problems involved well. Wilson and Butler show that crucial specification issues are usually not discussed or considered and that sensitivity analyses are even rarer. This conclusion relates to the observation of Beck – who in 1995 with Katz told the political science community 'what to do (and not to do) with time series cross-section data' (Beck and Katz, 1995) – that '[…] many analysts thought that the P in PCSE [Panel-Corrected Standard Errors] stood for Panacea and not Panel […]' (Beck 2007, p. 97). Technically, it is possible to test for all potential problems in time-series cross-sectional data and to remedy the occurring ones in order to arrive at an econometrically sound model. However, because fixing problems usually means that the model is re-specified, the regression model to be estimated changes too. A result may be that the findings of the estimated model do not provide an answer to the research question posed.

The advantages as well as the potential problems of pooled time-series cross-sectional analysis are visible in the well-known study of Garrett and Mitchell (2001) on the effect of globalization on welfare state effort (measured by government spending, government consumption and social security transfers) and taxation. By adding a time dimension of 33 years to the data on 18 developed democracies, they have a maximum of around 600 observations in their regressions. This allows Garrett and Mitchell to estimate more complex models, i.e. to include more explanatory variables, than would have been the case if they had conducted cross-sectional analyses. Moreover, the inclusion of a lagged dependent variable allows them to assess the stickiness of government spending over time, another theoretical expectation. However, the re-analyses by Kittel and Winner (2005) and Plümper and colleagues (2005) of Garrett and Mitchell's study show that the latter suffers from many of the potential problems of pooled time-series cross-sectional analysis identified above. Such conclusions have led to a somewhat less enthusiastic stance towards this approach within the field and have been, at least partly, responsible for the rise of the use of other approaches like configurational comparative analysis (see below). They have also resulted in new, more sophisticated ways to address (especially) the statistical problems involved. Overall, however, pooled time-series cross-sectional analysis remains a main quantitative approach for studying welfare state development. Despite these drawbacks, it remains a useful approach when a researcher is interested in the variation in welfare state development across countries and over time and can employ relatively straightforward dependent variables, such as social expenditures or generosity data.

Typology-building and re-analysing existing typologies

A third and final quantitative approach to analysing welfare state development is building typologies and re-analysing existing typologies. This approach uses the fact that individual welfare states vary a great deal but that some are more similar than others; similarities (and differences) that are rather persistent over time. Specifically, welfare states group together in 'worlds', 'regimes' or 'families' and a typology can capture how they group together. Typologies are useful empirical and heuristic devices because they enable comparative analysis by grouping separate entities into simpler categories, thereby reducing the existing complexity and offering a first step towards explaining the cross-national variation. Building on the work of Titmuss (1958), Esping-Andersen (1990) developed his well-known typology of three welfare state regimes: a social democratic regime, a conservative or continental regime, and a liberal regime (see also Chapter 26). For building the typology, Esping-Andersen focused particularly on the degree of decommodification, i.e. the situation 'when a person can maintain a livelihood without reliance on the market' (p. 22), the degree of stratification, and the primary location of welfare production (the state, the market or the family).

Especially since the late 1990s, typology-building and especially re-analysing the empirical value of existing typologies have become a growth industry in welfare state research – although this industry seems to be getting somewhat out of vogue as of late. Regarding the latter, a large body of literature has assessed the empirical value of welfare state regimes (for an overview, see Arts and Gelissen, 2010, pp. 574–77), usually by means of cluster analysis or principal component analysis and, less often, by factor analysis and qualitative comparative analysis. Often, the research question in such re-analyses is how well cases 'fit' the typology, a question that is actually irrelevant in relation to a typology such as Esping-Andersen's. The reason is that a typological approach differs from an ideal type approach (see Van Kersbergen and Vis, 2012). An ideal type is a theoretical construct to which empirical cases may or may not correspond. A typology, conversely, is a classification device in which all empirical cases are located as belonging to one, and only one, of the types. In a typology, a country belongs thus to either the social democratic regime *or* the conservative regime *or* the liberal regime. In ideal-typical analysis, conversely, the question is *to what extent* an empirical case belongs to the ideal type. A country can, for example, have the closest fit to say the social democratic ideal type but also have features of the liberal regime type. The goodness of fit question thus matters only when a researcher works with ideal types.

Comparative qualitative analyses

There are numerous comparative qualitative studies on welfare state development. Such studies are often inspired by empirical puzzles, such as why welfare state retrenchment happened in country A but not in country B. Here, I focus on a 'traditional' medium-*n* or small-*n* case study by Green-Pedersen (2002), and a study applying configurational comparative approaches by Vis (2010). While this selection is admittedly arbitrary, these two studies exemplify two different kinds of ways of conducting a comparative qualitative analysis.

*'Traditional' small-*n *comparative case studies*

A popular way of assessing welfare state development is by conducting a small-*n* comparative analysis of a small number of cases – typically two to four – sometimes alongside a quantitative analysis of a larger set of cases. Which cases to select for a small-*n* comparison is an important question; the case selection should offer the best possible test of the study's theoretical and/or empirical argument. In general, small-*n* welfare state scholars employ either Mills's most similar systems design (MSSD) or, somewhat less often, his most different systems design (MDSD). The former means that the researcher selects two (or more) cases that have all variables in common, i.e. which are most similar, except for the outcome and the one or two variables of key theoretical interest. An MSSD hereby mimics experimental designs in which similar groups are compared that vary only in whether they receive the treatment or not. An MDSD, conversely, implies the selection of cases that differ on all variables, i.e. which are most different, except for the outcome and the one or two variables of key theoretical interest. The idea is that if a similar factor (like leftist partisanship) produces a particular outcome (such as welfare state development) in cases that differ in all other ways that might affect the outcome, the finding is likely true across cases that are more similar as well. What is often considered a drawback of a MDSD is that there is no variation on the dependent variable, hence causing selection bias. A problem when employing a MSSD is finding cases that are sufficiently similar.

An example of a small-*n* comparative analysis that applies a MSSD is Green-Pedersen's (2002) study of the role of party competition in welfare state retrenchment in which he compares retrenchment in old-age pensions, unemployment benefits and disability pensions/early retirement benefits in Denmark and the Netherlands between the early 1980s and the late 1990s. Green-Pedersen argues that two factors are crucial for explaining the variation in retrenchment across these two countries: 1) the type of political party, and 2) the type of party competition. Denmark and the Netherlands, which are argued to be similar in many other respects, differ particularly in terms of party competition. Green-Pedersen argues that when party competition allows for a consensus among parties, implementing unpopular retrenchment initiatives (and getting away with it at the polls) is easier. In so-called bloc systems in which a left- and a right-wing bloc alternate in office, like in Denmark, consensus emerges only if leftist parties reign. In such a system, vote-seeking and office-seeking coincides. In pivot systems like the Netherlands, conversely, a centre party – usually a Christian democratic one – is pivotal in that it dominates both government formation and legislation. The pivot party can focus on vote-seeking (because it automatically will be in office). The major party of the left, however, faces a dilemma between vote-seeking and office-seeking. This produces consensus when the centre party opts for retrenchment, because the left-wing party then has to accommodate the centre party if it wants to gain office. Green-Pedersen's comparative analysis of retrenchment supports this argument.

Green-Pedersen's study is also interesting because of his dependent variable. He defines retrenchment as 'a change in the [social security] scheme making it less attractive to the (potential) claimants' (2002, p. 58). The quality of benefits and the eligibility criteria determine the attractiveness of a scheme, which Green-Pedersen measures by focusing on the reform's budgetary implications. This narrow conceptualization and operationalization of retrenchment fits well with Green-Pedersen's interest in how the electorate responds to retrenchment. If there are no budgetary implications, it is unlikely that the electorate cares a great deal because it does not hurt their own (financial) position.

Configurational comparative approaches

A second (mostly) qualitative approach to study welfare state development is a family of approaches known together as configurational comparative approaches. These techniques have been introduced to the social sciences by Ragin in 1987, are developed since (for example Ragin, 2008) and have become increasingly popular in welfare state research since the late 2000s. Nowadays, three variants exist: Qualitative Comparative Analysis in its original crisp-set variant (csQCA), in a fuzzy-set variant (fsQCA) and in a multi-value variant (mvQCA) (see Rihoux and Ragin, 2009). Configurational comparative approaches can formalize case-oriented analysis and thereby offer tools to improve comparative research. The approaches are particularly apt for identifying the minimally necessary and/or minimally sufficient (combinations of) conditions that bring about an outcome, like welfare state development in Germany or Finland. Moreover, they are especially suited for studies with an intermediate number of cases, i.e. between 5 and 50. Configurational comparative approaches are useful for studying welfare state development because of both their suitability for intermediate-*n* research – which comparative welfare state research typically is because of the limited number of existing welfare states – and their focus on how combination(s) of conditions bring about an outcome.

An example of a fsQCA analysis is Vis's (2010) study of the combinations of conditions that are necessary and/or sufficient for governments' pursuit of different types of welfare state reform. She examines over 20 British, Danish, Dutch, and German governments between the late 1970s and mid-2000s. With this design, Vis combines a MDSD and a MSSD design (see above). The four countries differ with respect to a number of characteristics that possibly influence governments' pursuit of reform, such the type of welfare state, the party competition, and the electoral system. In this sense, the countries are most different and focusing on them helps reveal the robustness of the findings by controlling for the influence of contextual factors. The comparison of different governments within a country, conversely, is the most similar part. In terms of the dependent variable, or outcome in the terminology of configurational comparative approaches, Vis focuses on two measures of so-called unpopular reform: a broad, more qualitative measure and benefit cutbacks. Her analysis shows that governments accept the risk of electoral punishment involved in unpopular welfare state reform only when they find themselves confronted with losses (necessary condition) in the form of a deteriorating socio-economic situation and/or a deteriorating political position. Only then are they prepared to confront the risk of losing votes involved in unpopular reform in, so to speak, a final attempt to try to recoup (some of) the losses incurred. A deteriorating socio-economic situation is only sufficient for triggering reform when combined with one or two other conditions: a worsening political position or a rightist government composition. Testing Vis' theoretical argument by means of a 'traditional' quantitative approach like pooled time-series cross-sectional analysis or a 'traditional' case study approach would have been more difficult, to say the least.

Single case studies

A final body of literature analyses welfare state development by means of single case studies. The studies typically ask questions such as how to explain why a particular reform was successfully implemented in country X, possibly against all odds. Or why did a particular reform fail to come about in that country? What is the detailed process, including the actors involved, their positions and ideas, behind this? Single case studies generally define and operationalize their dependent variable specific and encompassing, tailored to the country they focus on and the specific research question.

Still, many studies in welfare state research that focus on one country and that labelled single case studies are actually comparative, because they examine the development within this country over time, for instance by comparing different reforms (or the absence thereof) or across welfare state programmes. Stiller's (2010) study of welfare state reform in Germany is no exception here. She examines four so-called structural reforms that took place in the 1990s and 2000s: two healthcare reforms, the Hartz IV reform that merged unemployment assistance and social assistance, and the 2001 pension reform. For all these reforms, Stiller assesses to what extent 'ideational leadership' – 'leadership with the help of ideas' (p. 17) – is observable in the reform process and how this ideational leadership relates to the adoption of the reform. By carefully tracing the process of these reforms and, particularly, the role played by the minister involved in the reform (ideational leadership displayed or not?), Stiller shows that ideational leadership mattered for getting one of the health care reforms adopted but not for the other. In the pension reform and the Hartz IV reform, ideational leadership in combination with concession-making were important for getting the reforms adopted. By studying different reform processes in one country, Stiller employs a MSSD. An advantage of using this design within a single country context is that the context (e.g. institutional structure) is kept pretty much identical.

Lipset and Marks's (2000) analysis of why socialism – and social democracy more generally – failed in the United States (US) offers another example of a single case study that also includes comparative elements. Lipset and Marks assess a series of explanations given in the literature about why the Socialist party could not turn into a viable third party in the US, such as the impediments for third parties in the American two-party system and the split between the Socialist party and the trade unions. While thus not focusing directly on welfare state development, the absence of socialism is one of the factors explaining why the American welfare state is thus lean. The comparative part of Lipset and Marks's work comes in when they assess the hypotheses. Regarding the influence of the party system, they, for instance, argue that in countries with electoral systems similar to the American one, like Sweden up to 1907, Denmark until 1915, the United Kingdom (UK) and Canada, socialist or social democratic parties did become durable and often influential parties. This indicates that the party system by itself cannot account for socialism's failure in the US.

Conclusion

There are many approaches available for studying welfare state development, of which this chapter has discussed some of the most prominent ones. None of these approaches is 'best' in that it trumps the other ones in all respects. Which approach is most suitable, or best, rather depends crucially on one's research question and goal. When a researcher, for example, wants to get an in-depth understanding of how a process of welfare state development evolved in a particular country, a single case study seems the appropriate choice. If a researcher is interested more in how welfare states develops in general, i.e. if he or she wants to arrive at a (more) generalizable theory about the factor(s) influencing this development, a quantitative approach would be a better choice. Whether he or she in that case should opt for a cross-sectional design or a pooled time-series cross-sectional design depends in turn on the variation the researcher wants to explain (only across countries or also over time?) and on the available data. Researchers whose aims are somewhat in-between those of quantitative scholars and single case study ones in that they are interested in explaining welfare state development in a limited set of countries yet possibly with the ambition of arriving at a theory that is applicable to (a selected number of) other cases, too, are probably best of conducting a qualitative comparative study. Depending on the precise research question, hypotheses, available data and the number of cases, either a small-*n* comparative analysis or a configurational comparative analysis would be the appropriate choice. None of the approaches discussed has only strengths, and scholars need to be aware of the weaknesses of the approach they select. Sometimes these weaknesses can be reduced by employing different approaches into one study – although also this is not done without difficulties.

Further reading

Clasen, J. and Siegel, N. A. (eds) (2007), *Investigating Welfare State Change: The 'Dependent Variable Problem' in Comparative Analysis*. Cheltenham and Northampton: Edward Elgar.

Kenworthy, L. and Hicks, A. (eds) (2008), *Method and Substance in Macrocomparative Analysis*. London and New York: Palgrave Macmillan.

Pierson, P. (2004), *Politics in Time: History, Institutions, and Social Analysis*. Princeton, NJ and Oxford: Princeton University Press.

Rihoux, B. and Ragin, C. C. (2009), *Configurational Comparative Methods: Qualitative Comparative Analysis (QCA) and Related Techniques*. Los Angeles, CA: Sage.

References

Arts, W. A. and Gelissen, J. (2010), 'Models of the Welfare State', in F. G. Castles, S. Leibfried, J. Lewis, H. Obinger and C. Pierson (eds), *The Oxford Handbook of the Welfare State*, pp. 569–83. Oxford: Oxford University Press.

Beck, N. (2007), From Statistical Nuisance to Serious Modelling: Changing How We Think About the Analysis of Time-Series–Cross-Section Data. *Political Analysis*, 15(2), pp. 97–100.

Beck, N. and Katz, J. N. (1995), What To Do (And Not To Do) With Time-Series Cross-Section Data. *American Political Science Review*, 89(3), pp. 634–47.

Castles, F. G. (2004), *The Future of the Welfare State. Crisis Myths and Crisis Realities*. Oxford and New York: Oxford University Press

Clasen, J. and Siegel, N. A. (eds) (2007), *Investigating Welfare State Change: The 'Dependent Variable Problem' in Comparative Analysis*. Cheltenham and Northampton: Edward Elgar.

De Deken, J. and Kittel, B. (2007), 'Social Expenditure under Scrutiny: The Problems of Using Aggregate Spending Data for Assessing Welfare State Dynamics' in J. Clasen and N. A. Siegel (eds), *Investigating Welfare State Change: The 'Dependent Variable Problem' in Comparative Analysis*, pp. 72–105. Cheltenham and Northampton: Edward Elgar.

Esping-Andersen, G. (1990), *The Three Worlds of Welfare Capitalism*. Cambridge: Polity Press.

Flora, P. and Heideheimer, A. J. (eds) (1981), *The Development of Welfare States in Europe and America*. New Brunswick and London: Transaction Publishers.

Garrett, G. and Mitchell, D. (2001), Globalization, Government Spending and Taxation in the OECD. *European Journal of Political Research*, 39(2), pp. 145–77.

Green-Pedersen, C. (2002), *The Politics of Justification: Party Competition and Welfare-State Retrenchment in Denmark and the Netherlands from 1982 to 1998*. Amsterdam: Amsterdam University Press.

Kittel, B. and Winner, H. (2005), How Reliable is Pooled Analysis in Political Economy? The Globalization-Welfare State Nexus Revisited. *European Journal of Political Research*, 44(2), pp. 269–93.

Korpi, W. and Palme, J. (2007), *The Social Citizenship Indicator Programme (SCIP)*, Swedish Institute for Social Research, Stockholm University, dspace.it.su.se/dspace/handle/10102/7 (accessed March 2011)

Lipset, S. M. and Marks, G. (2000), *It Didn't Happen Here: Why Socialism Failed in the United States*. New York and London: W.W. Norton and Company.

Pierson, P. (1996), The New Politics of the Welfare State. *World Politics*, 48(2), pp. 143–79.

Plümper, T. Troeger, V. E. and Manow, P. (2005), Panel Data Analysis in Comparative Politics: Linking Method to Theory. *European Journal of Political Research*, 44(2), pp. 327–54.

Ragin, C. C. (1987), *The Comparative Method: Moving Beyond Qualitative and Quantitative Strategies*. Berkeley: University of California Press.

——(2008), *Redesigning Social Inquiry: Fuzzy Sets and Beyond*. Chicago, IL and London: University of Chicago Press.

Rihoux, B. and Ragin, C. C. (2009), *Configurational Comparative Methods: Qualitative Comparative Analysis (QCA) and Related Techniques*. Los Angeles, CA: Sage.

Scruggs, L. A. (2004), Welfare State Entitlement Data Set: A Comparative Institutional Analysis of Eighteen Welfare States, version 1.1. sp.uconn.edu/~scruggs/wp.htm (accessed March 2011).

Siegel, N. A. (2007), 'When (Only) Money Matters: The Pros and Cons of Expenditure Analysis', in J. Clasen and N. A. Siegel (eds) (2007). *Investigating Welfare State Change: The 'Dependent Variable Problem' in Comparative Analysis*, pp. 43–71. Cheltenham and Northampton: Edward Elgar.

Stiller, S. (2010), *Ideational Leadership in German Welfare State Reform: How Politicians And Policy Ideas Transform Resilient Institutions*. Amsterdam: Amsterdam University Press.

Titmuss, R. M. (1958). *Essays on the Welfare State*. London: George Allen and Unwin.

Van Kersbergen, K. and Vis, B. (2012), *Comparative Welfare State Politics: Development, Opportunities, and Reform*. Cambridge: Cambridge University Press.

Vis, B. (2010), *Politics of Risk-Taking: Welfare State Reform in Advanced Democracies*. Amsterdam: Amsterdam University Press.

Wilson, S. E. and Butler, D. M. (2007), A Lot More To Do: The Sensitivity of Time-Series Cross-Section Analyses to Simple Alternative Specifications. *Political Analysis*, 15(2), pp. 101–23.

28

Drivers for change

Virginie Guiraudon and Claude Martin

Introduction

Since the late twentieth century European and North American scholars have mainly focused on welfare state retrenchment or 'restructuring', especially since Paul Pierson's *Dismantling the Welfare State* (1994). This book on reforms that were unpopular emphasized that welfare states were 'immovable or resistant objects.' Nevertheless, welfare states have actually changed drastically, whether through potential path-departing procedures and/or incremental change (Thelen, 2004; Streeck and Thelen, 2005). Jacob Hacker's contribution to these debates focused on 'policy drift' (2004). He argued that the lack of actual reform given demographic evolution and economic restructuring should in fact be considered as a major form of change masked by apparent inertia.

Other contributions have underlined other types of developments beyond the retrenchment/expansion dichotomy. These include transnational paradigmatic changes in what Jane Jenson has called 'citizenship regimes': who is in charge of welfare, the national, the local, the private sector, the individual (Jenson, 2008 and 2010)? Others focus on the redefinition of the welfare state as a guarantor against 'new social risks' (Bonoli, 2005) or as a 'social investment state' (Esping-Andersen et al., 2002). Many scholars have also highlighted shifts from general to targeted benefits, from public to private service delivery, from institutional care to cash benefits or fiscal subsidies, from passive to active social policies, from the welfare state to the 'enabling state' (Gilbert, 2004).

Beyond the Organisation for Economic Co-operation and Development (OECD) world, change is also occurring, drastic in Latin America, systemic in post-communist states, induced by the pressure of international financial institutions in developing countries, and unstable in states where the welfare state depends on the sharing of revenues from national resources or migrant remittances.

Change itself, let alone its determinants and mechanisms in the field of social policy, is bound to be complex and analytically challenging. As Jochen Clasen and Nico A. Siegel put it: 'Despite a growing availability and comparability of relevant data, the body of comparative welfare state research cannot be described as resting on a widely shared empirical basis or common understanding about how much change there is, what drives change, or how the nature of change should be understood or conceptualized' (Clasen and Siegel, 2007, p. 4). To find our way, we first have to clarify what can be considered as change, depending of the level of change and the time-scale of the analysis (section one). Change can be defined as a process (e.g. policy drift) or an actual moment where change is visible (e.g. reform, social pact) and is independent of the mechanism of change (e.g. a horizontal policy transfer whereby country A mimics country B).

Then we must distinguish the 'why?' question and the 'how and who' questions. Analytically, this means distinguishing variables such as demographic trends or macroeconomic policy trends that challenge existing welfare state arrangements from the policy process whereby actors' constellations frame these trends and call for change exploiting proximate facilitating factors such as mobilizations or electoral policy windows (section two).

In section three, we address the question of cross-national variation of these drivers of change and the role of transnational institutions, which also raises the question of hypothetical convergence.

Levels of change

Change is a main challenge for social scientists. Concerning social policy and welfare state, three initial questions have to be clarified: what is the point of reference and the time-scale? What is the level of change taken in consideration? What are the factors of this change and the key protagonists of this story (ideas, institutions and actors)?

From an historical-diachronic and long-term perspective, many current welfare state reforms could be viewed as marginal adaptations on the long run, when from a more synchronic, sociological or political point of view some of these reforms (and sometime the same ones) are presented as real or potential turning points. If the reference is 'the great transformation' observed by Karl Polanyi (1944), how can we consider the current reforms of the late twentieth and beginning of the twenty-first centuries?

Another issue concerns the indicators of change. For example, even in the middle of the neoconservative storm of the 1980s and 1990s where the rhetoric against expanding public sector and social protection was at its peak, the welfare state still expanded revealing the gap between ideological clashes and concrete consequences. Since then, at the aggregate level and against many expectations, expenditure on social protection has remained stable (see Table 28.1).

The level of change is therefore not necessarily proportional to the intensity of the controversies or rhetoric battles. Easily understandable as well, the fact that our diagnosis on the welfare state depends strongly of the current and ideological context. For instance, during the 1970s many social scientists following the theory of 'social control' were critical about the extension and controlling role of the welfare state. Thirty years later, others and sometimes the same scholars are much more cautious and, given the drastic consequences of current reforms, seem to defend the welfare state foundations against violent neoconservative attacks. This analytical reversal does not mean that social sciences are not objective enough, or that social scientists are just unpredictable, but that our categories to think changes also have to change when society as a whole has been deeply transformed over time (Castel and Martin, 2012).

A similar phenomenon is at stake when important social scientists like Pierson or Esping-Andersen were diagnosing the inertia of contemporary welfare regimes in the middle of the 1990s, while other academics argue after a decade that even the so-called 'frozen' welfare states are going through substantial, institutional and perhaps paradigmatic changes (Palier and Martin, 2008; Palier, 2010). One must understand that both interpretations are not contradictory but complementary. They just take pictures at different moments of the process of change.

Retrospective and comparative analysis of the welfare state reforms raises the question of the importance or the level of change (Hall, 1993). Many factors must be considered: the time period, the selected indicators, and the specific programs under study. For some sectors of social protection like pension schemes, for example, the evaluation of change needs an extended time-lag as the current reforms may have a dramatic impact many years down the road. But the

Table 28.1 Expenditure on social protection in Europe (1997–2008) (% of GDP)

time geo	*1997*	*1998*	*1999*	*2000*	*2001*	*2002*	*2003*	*2004*	*2005*	*2006*	*2007*	*2008*
EU27:UE (27 countries)	:	:	:	26.4	26.6	26.8	27.2	27.1	27.1	26.7 (p)	25.7 (p)	26.3 (p)
EA16:Zone euro (16 countries)	:	:	:	26.6	26.8	27.3	27.7	27.6	27.7	27.3 (p)	26.8 (p)	27.4 (p)
BE	27.4	27.0	27.0	26.2	27.2	27.9	29.0	29.2	29.6	30.2	26.8	28.2
BG	:	:	:	10.1	9.7	10.1	9.7	9.6	15.1	14.2	14.1	15.4
CZ	18.5	18.5	19.2	19.5	19.4	20.1	20.2	19.3	19.1	18.6	18.6	18.7
DK	30.1	30.0	29.8	28.8	29.2	29.7	30.9	30.7	30.2	29.2	28.8	29.6
DE	28.9	28.9	29.2	29.3	29.4	30.1	30.4	29.8	29.7	28.7	27.6	27.7 (p)
EE	:	:	15.4	13.8	12.9	12.6	12.5	12.9	12.5	12.1	12.3	15.0
IE	16.4	15.2	14.6	13.9	14.8	17.1	17.8	18.0	18.0	18.3	18.8	22.1
GR	20.8	21.6	22.7	23.4	24.3	23.9	23.4	23.6	24.6	24.6	24.5	25.9
ES	20.8	20.2	19.7	20.3	20.0	20.3	20.6	20.7	20.9	20.8	21.0 (p)	22.7 (p)
FR	30.4	30.0	29.9	29.4	29.5	30.3	30.9	31.2	31.3	30.7	30.4	30.7 (p)
IT	24.9	24.5	24.8	24.7	24.9	25.3	25.8	25.9	26.3	26.6 (p)	26.7 (p)	27.7 (p)
CY	:	:	:	14.7	14.9	16.2	18.3	18.0	18.3	18.3	18.1	18.4
LV	15.2	16.1	17.2	15.3	14.5	14.1	13.9	13.1	12.6	12.6	11.2	12.6 (p)
LT	13.6	15.0	16.3	15.8	14.7	14.1	13.5	13.4	13.3	13.4	14.4	16.1 (p)
LU	21.5	21.2	20.4	19.5	20.8	21.5	22.1	22.2	21.7	20.4	19.3	20.1
HU	:	:	20.3	19.5	19.2	20.3	21.2	20.6	21.9	22.4	22.3	22.7
MT	18.0	17.9	17.8	16.8	17.7	17.8	18.3	18.7	18.4	18.1	17.9	18.8
NL	28.6	27.8	27.0	26.3	26.5	27.5	28.2	28.3	27.8	28.8	28.3	28.5 (p)
AT	28.7	28.4	28.9	28.4	28.8	29.1	29.6	29.3	28.9	28.4	27.8	28.1
PL	:	:	:	19.6	20.9	21.1	21.0	20.1	19.7	19.3	18.1	18.5
PT	19.7	20.2	20.6	20.9	21.9	22.8	23.3	23.9	24.5	24.6	23.9	24.3
RO	:	:	:	13.0	12.7	13.5	13.0	12.8	13.4	12.8	13.5	14.2
SI	23.8	24.1	24.0	24.2	24.5	24.4	23.7	23.3	22.9	22.7	21.3	21.4 (p)
SK	19.8	20.0	20.1	19.4	18.9	19.1	18.1	17.2	16.5	16.3	16.0	16.0 (p)
FI	29.1	27.1	26.3	25.0	25.0	25.7	26.6	26.6	26.7	26.4	25.3	26.3
SE	32.1	31.1	30.8	29.9	30.4	31.2	32.2	31.5	31.1	30.2	29.1	29.3 (p)
UK	26.8	26.3	25.7	26.4	26.8	25.7	25.7	25.8	26.2	26.0	23.3	23.7 (p)
IS	18.4	18.2	18.8	19.2	19.4	21.2	22.9	22.6	21.6	21.2	21.4	22.0
NO	25.0	26.9	26.9	24.3	25.4	25.9	27.2	25.8	23.8	22.6	22.8	22.4

Notes: : =not available; p=provisional value.

Short Description: Expenditure on social protection contain: social benefits, which consist of transfers, in cash or in kind, to households and individuals to relieve them of the burden of a defined set of risks or needs; administration costs, which represent the costs charged to the scheme for its management and administration; other expenditure, which consists of miscellaneous expenditure by social protection schemes (payment of property income and other). It is calculated in current prices.

Source: Eurostat; © European Union, 1995–2012. Last update: 26.10.2011. Date of extraction: 27 Oct. 2011 12:01:58 CEST; General Disclaimer of the EC: europa.eu/geninfo/legal_notices_en.htm; Table: epp.eurostat.ec.europa.eu/tgm/table.do?tab=table&init=1&plugin=1&language=en&pcode=tps00098.

issue is: are these changes 'minor' or 'substantial', marginal or paradigmatic? Are they mere adjustments, adaptations or revolutions? Did they result from the traditional process of policy learning, characterized by the adjustment of policy measures and/or instruments and/or institutions according to their capacity to reach a given objective, or did the main goal of the policy change itself? Are we facing small cumulative changes in a 'muddling through' process? In other words, are these reforms accumulating over time, as the incremental layering of new provisions and instruments which can lead to subtle policy changes or major turns depending of this accumulation and its final direction? Thus, as Hinrichs and Kangas suggest, the important question is: 'when is a change big enough to be labelled as a system shift?' (2003).

According to Peter Hall, these different levels of change involve different levels of analysis. 'Paradigmatic change' suggests ideational transfers and shifts. Changes in policy instruments prompt to pay attention to institutional pathways and interest groups as well as the means to achieve change (e.g. incentive structures). Changes in policy settings get us closer to bureaucratic actors, implementation and policy learning. Another question to investigate concerns the respective roles of political actors, interest groups, and high civil servants.

Visible and invisible factors of change

In this section, we distinguish the visible part of the policy reform from the more invisible part of the iceberg. We first distinguish triggers and drivers of change and then visible and invisible drivers. What is driving change (e.g. ideas and ideology) and what explains policy outcomes (e.g. institutional configurations)?

As an outcome of a given political economy, welfare state is largely determined by external macroeconomic and demographic factors. In that sense welfare state changes seem less a result of drivers (which implies actors, interest groups, power struggles, decisions, strategies), but more expression of triggers of change, which refers to global and drastic changes of the global society, in terms of population trends, economic production, labour division, gender, and social inequalities, etc., which lead actors to unavoidable changes (Palier, 2008). That is the reason why sudden economic changes, like the Great Depression of the 1930s and the recent fiscal crisis, had considerable and direct impact on welfare state politics more than voluntary initiatives.

Taking triggers of change in consideration leads to a variety of macro demographic and economic trends which impact dramatically the interrelations between economy, social risks, and living conditions. Initially built to accompany an industrial economy and regulate its consequences on individuals and households, welfare state had been progressively adapted to new challenges. These macro-transformations modify the nature of the risks which have to be regulated. For many welfare systems (in particular Bismarckian ones), the initial question was to guarantee the level of resources of the male low-skilled blue-collar workers in case of a series of given risks (disease, work injury, disability, family responsibilities). The system was based on a salary replacement model regulated by explicit social norms and legislations that represented the 'supports' of the workers (Castel, 1995).

Compared to this configuration of the post-war period, the situation for the last four decades has changed drastically up to the definition of 'new social risks' (Bonoli, 2005; Armigeon and Bonoli, 2006). To mention the most prominent issues: deindustrialisation, de-standardisation of work and the rise of services sector employment, feminization of the labour force, and the increasing demographic weight of the elderly population. These macro-transformations in developed countries since the mid-1960s have changed the welfare state equilibrium. Among the main triggers of change, one could insist on the ageing of the population, a phenomenon Europe is particularly confronted with. As a ratio between age groups, ageing is in itself a result of many other social trends: the growth of life expectancy due to better healthcare systems goes hand in hand with the fall of the birth rate linked to new family configurations, and work – family imbalance in dual earner couples.

The picture is contrasted at the European Union (EU) level. Eastern Europe is confronted to the bigger ageing process, before Southern Europe. Western Europe (France, Benelux, the

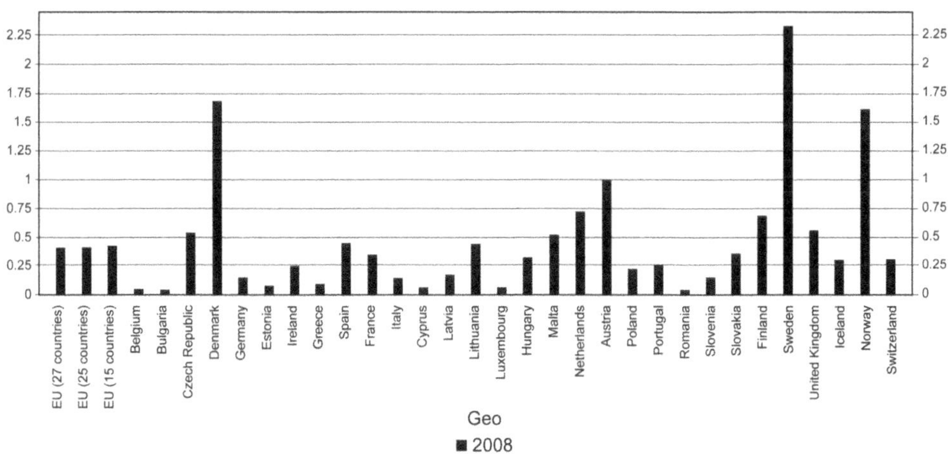

Figure 28.1 Expenditure on care for the elderly as percentage of Gross Domestic Product in 2008 in EU states
Source: Data from Eurostat.

United Kingdom and Ireland) as well as Nordic countries are in a better position. Nevertheless, confronted to these macro demographic trends, most European welfare states are adapting their respective systems at a different pace but with relatively similar agenda and instruments, either for their respective pension schemes or for the emerging long-term care systems. Long-term care policies represent a complete new set of instruments yet, except for some Scandinavian countries, with a very low level of funding (less than a half point of gross domestic product (GDP) at the European Union level, see Figure 28.1).

Second, as they require a combination of health and social care, but also a combination of public and private funding (public services, private insurance, but also private income and informal family support), long-term care has drastic consequences for the very old but also for their informal carers who are predominantly women. This means important challenges in terms of work – family balance, senior female participation on the labour market, gender equality issues and, for the caring workers, issues related to quality of work. This example reveals clearly how challenging these issues are for welfare systems which were configured with a vastly different set of needs and expectations in mind.

Welfare state actors (political, administrative actors, experts, but also professionals and lobbies) try to adapt their own discourses to these macro-economic and fiscal constraints. Ultimately, actors in the sector and governments must produce a coherent story to facilitate reforms by convincing publics that they are just inevitable. Yet this is no easy task. The process of change is inherently complex and uncertain and can be understood first and foremost as a power struggle between interacting actors. John Kingdon's multiple streams model may be heuristic here (1984). First, in the 'problem stream,' professionals, experts, and political actors may not agree on the diagnosis but also on what needs to be done. Second, in 'the policy stream,' their solutions may be seen as prohibitive from the point of view of bureaucrats and social partners. In the 'politics stream,' elected politicians are facing a dilemma. Credit claiming in addressing new social risks must go hand in hand with avoiding blame for fiscal restraint that is also necessary to tackle the costs of ageing in the age of structural unemployment. Delaying decisions or policy drift also has its costs. The key here therefore is to find a 'policy window' where the three independent streams meet.

Policy makers are in Kingdon's words 'surfers waiting for the big wave' (2004, p. 225). There are examples of such policy windows for welfare reform. For instance, experts believed that pension reform was necessary in Italy since the 1970s yet there was a first reform only in 1992 (the 'Amato' law) and the more comprehensive structural reform that took place in 1995 (the 'Dini law'). The domestic political dynamics are crucial to understand the timing of the reforms: the Amato and Dini governments worked closely with the trade unions and in 1995 the government waited for a unitary proposal from the unions. The 1992 reforms had shown that change was possible without massive strikes and the 1995 reforms included the main veto player (the unions). Yet international developments helped rein in the main actors: the Maastricht criteria allowed reform to be framed as necessary to join the eurozone given the high debt levels of Italy and thus reform could be enacted in spite of the political instability of the period. Twenty years later with the European debt crisis, the euro has again been linked to pension reform in Italy but this time the agenda is not set in Rome. Still, we can see that outside pressure can be used to merge different policy streams and make reform possible.

If one looks at the visible part of the iceberg, the policy process and actors' constellation, we will thus focus on how actors justify reform and which actors use which argument, identify who resists change and also study how they frame their arguments. If we look at the more invisible part of the iceberg, what is unsaid, what cannot be controlled necessarily by policy actors, we will look beyond reform itself and focus instead on the ways in which they make do. Let's stay in Italy and with the issue of elderly care that we have discussed in section one. Given fiscal constraints and political instability, institutional care is scarce and it is unlikely that the state can pay the price tag for developing such care given the age pyramid. While only about 1 percent of the Italian population over 65 is in public residential care, about 10 percent (a million persons) receive a flat rate subsidy to pay for continuous care and 27 per cent of those receiving it have a paid carer at home (known as a *badante*), almost all of whom are foreign *badanti* (Da Roit and Le Bihan, 2010; van Hooren, 2011). The driver for continuity here is immigration policy, whereby the Italian government regularizes illegal care workers and reserves immigration quotas for incoming migrant carers. They treat them differently in both speech and act than other migrants. Immigration policy serves as a palliative for policy drift in welfare policies. So they 'deal with a problem' rather than provide a solution (Brunsson, 2003). In the case of reform the 'problem' is the euro and in the case of policy drift the 'solution' is female migrants.

In any case, one focuses on very different actors and dynamics whether one looks underneath the lamppost at the means of change (mobilization, electoral dynamics, and international developments) or away from the light where day-to-day politics indeed resembles the arty 'science of muddling through' (Lindblom, 1959).

When one sees the success of cost-saving reforms such as 'nudge politics' (Thaler and Sunstein, 2008) with the UK Tory government after the Obama administration had embraced it to encourage the use of tax-free pension plans, one wonders if it is about reconciling talk, decision, and action (Brunsson, 2003), finding something that is both cheap and ideologically sound at that moment: 'libertarian paternalism', the idea that the state is steering the autonomous individual through what Thaler and Sunstein call 'choice architecture.' The ideas are put forward, while their low price may in fact be what makes them attractive (Borraz and Guiraudon, 2010). After all, if we could only just eat our five fruit and vegetables a day as the World Health Organization (WHO) thinks we should, wouldn't that help national healthcare budgets tremendously without state interference?

We have already evoked international organizations such as the European Union and the WHO and triggers of change that seem to be present cross-nationally. This brings us to an important question: do drivers of change and continuity vary cross-nationally?

Similar or different drivers for change?

Can we identify common drivers that seek to diffuse policy ideas and instruments regionally and globally? This is what we study next.

Just as in other fields of research, welfare state studies have not been immune to the 'globalization' pandemic. There has been a lot of focus on macro-level catalysts for change and also on the 'globalization' hypothesis (see Glatzer and Rueschemeyer, 2005). In this section, while avoiding 'globaloney,' we address two hypotheses related to this debate. First, there may be similar triggers for change: challenges that a number of countries face. It is thus interesting to study the activities of drivers for change at the transnational level: global elites such as the famous 'Chicago boys' of Chile, pace-setting countries exporting their models, and international organizations (on 'global social policy,' see Deacon 1997).

What is their role in driving change in various countries? The policy diffusion literature is useful here. Instead of simply predicting 'institutional isomorphism' (Powell and di Maggio, 1983) a form of mimetic replication of policy instruments, scholars focus on the processes whereby international ideas are appropriated, reinterpreted, or renegotiated by domestic actors and identify mechanisms of policy transfers (Dobbin et al., 2006). The same *solution* may in fact be used to solve different *problems* depending on the local context. Should ideas[1] propagate such as those associated with economic liberalism, they need to be translated in the vernacular, 'resonate' as viable frames for politicians, bureaucrats, and business and labor actors just as had been the case for Keynesianism (Hall, 1989).

Conversely, there is a large literature that dismisses the potential of transnational policy entrepreneurs and macro-trends to overcome national policy legacies. The latter comprise feedback from past political arrangements that have favoured particular social groups as well as sociocultural variables that are deeply embedded in existing welfare institutions. Think of the gender roles embedded in welfare state structures (Orloff, 1993) and the endurance of the single male breadwinner model that we have already mentioned. The question thus becomes whether different countries respond differently to common challenges or standardized messages.

Another example regards the WHO. While we can trace back to this international organization the need to develop new instruments to improve health, encouraging networking, best practices and more importantly to propose policies that are not only focused on medical care but also on income and nutrition. Yet, there is no direct transfer from the WHO to domestic actors. The ideas need to be circulated by intermediaries and, more importantly, health sector actors have to find it relevant in their local context, either because they believe prevalent diseases are indeed related to diet or that it is cheaper in times of austerity to communicate on the 'five fruit and vegetables a day' as part of aforementioned 'nudge policies' that are gaining ground in Europe also on ideational ground as focusing on individual responsibility and autonomy.

Yves Dezalay and Bryant Garth have shown that the introduction of neoliberal reforms depended on 'palace wars' – local struggles for power and legitimacy (2002). And we can surmise the same when it comes to the percolation of World Bank or International Monetary Fund recommendations. We would like to discuss current developments and wonder how we can explain what came next: the diffusion of the social investment state (Jenson, 2010).

We would like to rely on a South-South example: conditional cash transfers (CCTs) that have rapidly spread from Latin America since the late 1990s.[2]

CCTs seek to put cash in the hands of poor people to build human capital and prevent the generational transmission of poverty. Transfers were originally conditional on using education or health services. While there had been CCTs in Mexico and Chile in the 1990s, the programme considered as pioneer is the Brazilian unified Bolsa Familia programme of 2003 that relies on a unified federal registration system, consists in a single transfer, and imposes fewer conditions than its Latin American precursors. According to Ancelovici and Jenson (2011), the programme was framed as a social investment tool making families responsible for their children's future rather than a mere safety net or emergency relief and its success relies on the mobilization of its exporters and their capacity for standardization. The exporters included the World Bank but mainly the Brazilian government: The International Policy Centre for Inclusive Growth is a UNDP-Brazilian partnership that allows Brazil to act as a trendsetting Global South leader (Ancelovici and Jenson 2011). In the end, CCTs have been implemented in countries with less administrative capacity and others have shed the notion of conditionality and the discourse on responsibility so as to take on the policy instrument without the full paradigm and settings.

To conclude there are drivers for change that can be called international policy exporters and translators. They are successful once they shed any vernacular characteristic of the policy and are thus able to operate in countries that have different institutional capacities.

Conclusion

In this chapter, we have underlined that drivers of continuity remain strong inside or outside the state, whether they are bureaucrats or interest groups. There is the added fear in the North where austerity seems here to stay of opening up the Pandora's Box of new risks and issues such as dependent elders. Hard decisions are often delayed, or else reforms are piecemeal and changes incremental. Still, there have been a significant number of reforms all over the world.

There are differences in ex-ante socio-demographic situations, care traditions, policy legacies and of course institutional configurations (interest intermediation structures, electoral systems). This explains why reforms vary cross-nationally. Yet we have shown that there are cases of mimetism where global drivers of change play a role. What we hope to have underlined, however, is that the drivers for change need not be in the field of social policy and often have, in fact, different agendas: these include politicians that seek to avoid losing elections or want to gain international credentials as well as a whole range of experts and bureaucrats that seek to implement cross-sectoral reforms such as public management tools.

Ultimately what we have not factored into our analysis is the role of those on the front line of the welfare state and care practitioners. They are the ones that ultimately deliver care – to do more with less, and bestow benefits with tough guidelines, often in poor working conditions – and as Michael Lipsky said a long time ago, they are policy makers in their own way (1980) and thus can try to mitigate, or resist reform change or embrace it.

Notes

1 We are keeping the analytical distinction between paradigms or instruments from our above discussion of Hall (1993).

2 A North-North example of diffusion could be activation policies although the word has been used to describe radically different policies so that the literal 'translation' of the word in fact does not mean actual appropriation (see Barbier, 2002).

Further reading

Béland, D. (2010), *What is Social Policy? Understanding the Welfare State*. Cambridge: Polity Press.
Clasen, J. and Siegel, N. A. (eds) (2007), *Investigating Welfare State Change: The 'Dependent Variable Problem' in Comparative Analysis*. Cheltenham: Edward Elgar.
Gilbert, N. (2004), *Transformation of the Welfare State. The Silent Surrender of Public Responsibility*. Oxford and New York: Oxford University Press.
Hacker, J. S. (2006), *The Great Risk Shift. The New Economic Insecurity and the Decline of the American Dream*. New York: Oxford University Press.
Palier, B. and C. Martin (eds) (2008), *Reforming Bismarckian Welfare Systems*. Oxford: Blackwell.

References

Armingeon, K. and Giuliano B. (eds) (2006), *The Politics of Post-industrial Welfare States: Adapting Post-War Social Policies to New Social Risks*, London: Routledge.
Barbier, J.-C. (2002), Peut-on parler d'"activation' de la protection sociale en Europe? *Revue française de sociologie* 43(2), pp. 307–32.
Béland, D. (2010), *What is Social Policy? Understanding the Welfare State*. Cambridge: Polity Press.
Bonoli, G. (2005), The politics of the new social policies: providing coverage against new social risks in mature welfare states, *Policy and Politics* 33(3), pp. 431–49.
Borraz, O. and Guiraudon, V. (2010), *Politiques publiques. 2/ Changer la société*, Paris: Presses de Sciences Po.
Brunsson, N. (2003), *The Organization of Hypocrisy: Talk, Decisions and Actions in Organizations*, second revised edition, Copenhagen: Copenhagen Business School Press.
Castel, R. (1995), *Les métamorphoses de la question sociale. Une chronique du salariat*. Paris: Fayard.
Castel, R. and Martin, C. (eds) (2012), *Changements et pensées du changement. Echanges avec Robert Castel*. Paris: La Découverte.
Clasen, J. and Siegel, N. A. (2007), *Investigating Welfare State Change: The 'Dependent Variable Problem in Comparative Analysis*. Cheltenham: Edward Elgar.
Da Roit, B. and Le Bihan, B. (2010), Similar and Yet So Different: Cash-for-Care in Six European Countries' Long-Term Care Policies, *The Milbank Quarterly*, Vol. 88, no 3, pp. 286–309.
Deacon, B. (2007), *Global Social Policy and Governance*. London: Sage.
Dezalay, Y. and Bryant G. (2002), *The Internationalization of Palace Wars. Lawyers,Economists, and the Contest to Transform Latin American States*. Chicago, IL: Chicago University Press.
Di Maggio, P. and Powell W. (1983), 'The iron cage revisited' institutional isomorphism and collective rationality in organizational fields', *American Sociological Review* 48, pp. 147–60.
Dobbin, F., Simmons, B. and Garrett, G. (2006), 'Introduction: The International Diffusion of Liberalism,' *International Organization* 60, pp. 781–810.
Esping-Andersen, G. with D. Gallie, A. Hemerijck and J. Myles (2002), *Why we Need a New Welfare State*. Oxford: Oxford University Press.
Gilbert, N. (2004), *Transformation of the Welfare State. The Silent Surrender of Public Responsibility*, Oxford and New York: Oxford University Press.
Glatzer, M. and Rueschemeyer D. (2005), 'Conclusion: Politics Matter', in M. Glatzer and D. Rueschemeyer (eds), *Globalization and the Future of the Welfare State*, pp 203–25. Pittsburgh, PA: University of Pittsburgh Press.
Hacker, J. (2004), 'Privatizing risk without privatizing the welfare state. The hidden politics of social policy retrenchment in the United States,' *American Political Science Review* 98(2), pp. 243–60.
Hacker, J. S. (2006), *The Great Risk Shift. The New Economic Insecurity and the Decline of the American Dream*. New York: Oxford University Press.
Hall, P. (1993), 'Policy paradigms, social learning, and the state: The case of economic policymaking in Britain,' *Comparative Politics* 25(3), pp. 275–96.
——(1989), *The Political Power of Economic Ideas: Keynesianism across Nations*, Princeton, NJ: Princeton University Press.
Hinrichs, K. and Kangas O. (2003), 'When is a change big enough to be a system shift? Small system-shifting changes in German and Finnish pension policies,' *Social Policy and Administration* 37 (6), pp. 573–91.
Jenson, J. (2008), 'Redesigning Citizenship Regimes after Neoliberalism: Moving towards Social Investment', *La Rivista delle Politiche Sociali* (1), pp. 13–31.

——(2010), 'Diffusing ideas for after-neoliberalism: The social investment perspective in Europe and Latin America'. *Global Social Politics* 10(1), pp. 59–84.

Kingdon, J. (1984), *Agendas, Alternatives and Public Policy*, Boston, MA: Little Brown.

Lindblom, C. E. (1959), The Science of 'Muddling Through', *Public Administration Review* 19, pp. 79–88.

Lipsky, M. (1980). *Street-Level Bureaucracy: Dilemmas of the Individual in Public Services*. New York: Russell Sage Foundation.

Orloff, A. (1993), 'Gender and the social rights of citizenship: The comparative analysis of gender relations and welfare states,' *American Sociological Review* 58, pp. 303–28.

Palier, B. (2008), 'Drivers of change in the Welfare State: Understanding reform trajectory', Keynote speech at the Aarhus Summer School, July.

——(ed.) (2010), *The Long Goodbye to Bismarck? The Politics of Welfare Reform in Continental Europe*, Amsterdam: Amsterdam University Press.

Palier, B. and Martin, C. (eds), (2008), *Reforming Bismarckian Welfare Systems*. Oxford: Blackwell.

Pierson, P. (1994), *Dismantling the Welfare State. Reagan, Thatcher and the Politics of Retrenchment*. Cambridge: Cambridge University Press.

Polanyi, K. (1944), *The Great Transformation*. New York: Rinehart.

Streeck, W. and Thelen, K. (eds) (2005), *Beyond Continuity: Institutional Change in Advanced Political Economies*, Cambridge: Cambridge University Press.

Thaler, R. and Sunstein, C. (2008), *Nudge: Improving Decisions about Health, Wealth, and Happiness*. New Haven, CT: Yale University Press.

Thelen, K. (2004), *How Institutions Evolve: The Political Economy of Skills in Germany, Britain, the United States and Japan*. New York: Cambridge University Press.

Van Hooren, F. (2011), *Caring Migrants in European Welfare Regimes: The Politics and Practice of Migrant Labour Filling the Gaps in Social Care*. Department of Social and Political Sciences. Florence: European University Institute.

29

Real-typical and ideal-typical methods in comparative social policy

Christian Aspalter

During the past six years, international welfare state research has witnessed a revival of *ideal-typical welfare state theory and methodology* in comparative welfare state analysis (Gough et al., 2004; Wood and Gough, 2004; Aspalter, 2006a, 2011; Aspalter et al., 2009; see also Arts and Gelissen, 2002), while at the same time the growing number of real-typical welfare state studies (e.g., Lee and Ku, 2007; Kwon, 2005; Ramesh, 2004) has continued to leave its mark on the development of international comparative welfare state research.

In 2004, Ian Gough, Geof Wood and their colleagues (Gough et al., 2004; Wood and Gough, 2004) presented a new approach of how to classify different welfare state systems according to their degree of institutionalization, covering the entire world. In 2005, Aspalter classified East Asian welfare state systems (Japan, South Korea, China, Taiwan, Hong Kong, and Singapore) according to the ideal-typical method (as started by Esping-Andersen, 1987, 1990; and Titmuss, 1974). Following in this path, in 2009, Aspalter, Kim, and Park paid particular attention to the case of some Eastern Central Europe welfare state systems, focusing on Poland, the Czech Republic, Hungary, and Slovenia, classifying them as members of the continental group of welfare state systems after demonstrating their re-orientation towards the Corporatist/ Christian Democratic Model over the last one and a half decades, due to the historical, political and cultural affinity of their closest neighbors Germany and Austria. In 2011, Aspalter identified the ideal-typical nature of key welfare state systems in Latin America, particularly Brazil, Chile, Argentina, and Uruguay, determining their own regime-specific ideal-typical characteristics.

The new dichotomy between real-typical and ideal-typical welfare state research has re-energized the academic discussion in the area of comparative welfare state research (see also Aspalter, 2005, 2006a, 2006b; Meier Jæger, 2006; Arcanjo, 2006; Bambra, 2007a, 2007b).

This chapter will show why we must not confuse real-typical welfare state theory and methodology with ideal-typical welfare state theory and methodology. In fact, comparing real-typical studies with ideal-typical studies is like comparing apples with pears, or chickens with ducks. Both real-typical and ideal-typical are different breeds of study, designed for different purposes, each using a different methodological approach. Contrary to real-typical studies, ideal-typical studies go back to the methodology of identifying 'ideal types' as invented and developed by German sociologist Max Weber (which, to note, runs counter to the idea of any kind of 'perfect' state of affairs as in the sense of Plato). In the Weberian sense, ideal types are types with characteristics that are, by and large, shared by *most* members of a common group of research objects, societies, or in our case welfare state systems.

Comparing real-typical and ideal-typical methodology

One needs to pay attention to the definition of 'real-typical' and 'ideal-typical' in the context of comparative research. 'Real' here does not mean real, and 'ideal' here does not mean ideal, hence one must not confuse common language with scientific terminology. 'Real' here stands for 'in depth, in detail.' 'Ideal' here stands for 'average, by and large,' or in other words 'matching a certain yardstick or set of yardsticks.'

The use of both methods is bound to the purpose of each individual study. Those studies that look at a larger number of case studies, for example many dozens of case studies may use the ideal-typical approach, while others with only a limited number of case studies, may prefer to apply the real-typical method. Ideal-typical research analyses deliver the larger picture (looking over a wood from the sky, not looking while sitting on the branch of a tree) – they are 'ideal' in the Weberian sense, that is, they are *matching certain yardsticks* (for example, Hekman, 1983). Real-typical research on the other hand is detail-oriented, and hence subject to rather frequent changes.

Using different methodologies means looking at different levels of research. The view from a bird flying high in the sky will deliver a larger picture – less sharp, but more comprehensive and longer-lasting. A bird sitting on top of trees will look at the world differently, arriving at different conclusions. Both of which, however, are part of the reality of the world we live in, and hence necessary to better understand the very same world.

Table 29.1 highlights the fast growth in the area of real-typical welfare state studies shortly after the publication of Esping-Andersen's 1990 book *The Three Worlds of Welfare Capitalism*. It is interesting to note (see Meier Jæger, 2006) that the bulk of research did not focus on the ideal-typical nature of Esping-Andersen's study (Esping-Andersen, 1990; compare also Esping-Andersen, 1987), but nevertheless, ideal-typical research methodology found its way quietly into mainstream welfare state comparison (see Korpi and Palme, 1998; Gough, 1999; Abrahamson, 2003; Wood and Gough, 2004; Gough et al., 2004; Aspalter, 2005, 2006a).

The distinction between real-typical and ideal-typical welfare state analyses is vital since ideal types enable a greater degree of clarity on global or regional scale, and especially also when evaluating comparative studies. It is of little use to oppose ideal-typical studies based on the findings of real-typical studies and vice versa. It is very useful, on the other hand, to apply both methodologies when engaging in comparative analysis, since perspectives and insights from either methodology may strengthen and support findings of the other. It is paramount to understand that when using the ideal-typical method one is measuring completely different things, on a different level of observation, with a different analytical and theoretical purpose. Real-typical studies are employed best when the number of welfare state systems included in the analyses is kept low. Ideal-typical studies, however, may be applied when, for example, comparing half a dozen or dozens of countries. It may also be the case that a research study would like to check group membership of one or two countries or welfare state systems to an existing ideal-typical welfare regime.

Table 29.1 Advantages and disadvantages of ideal-typical and real-typical methodology compared

	Real-typical method	*Ideal-typical method*
Purpose	Focusing on the reality of welfare state institutions, their similarities and differences across nations; hereby researchers focus on the detail, on institutional differences rather than their similarities, for better clarity on 'micro cross-national' level.	Focusing on average features of each regime cluster, it is used as a 'yardstick' to facilitate broad cross-national comparisons; as a consequence, minor and some major differences are omitted for the sake of better clarity on the 'macro cross-national' level.
Theoretical basis	Researchers' own method of distinguishing system features	The theory of Max Weber on 'ideal types'*
Major advantages & disadvantages	*Advantages:* delivers the detailed picture, focuses on particular administrative and regulative set up, as well as legal and administrative technicalities, i.e. this methodology is more sensitive to programme-level and short-term developments, enables further analysis of welfare state institutions, also when building on knowledge derived from ideal-typical theories and models, enables greater clarity on national and policy level in welfare state comparison. *Disadvantages:* the grand picture at international level may be unclear or contradictory, some important similarities on international level, especially with regard to policy outcomes and strategies may be omitted (cf e.g. the importance of the principle of *functional equivalence*), the models set up change quickly over time, and often lack substance, i.e. a strong theoretical fundament.	*Advantages:* delivers the greater picture, focuses on *functional equivalences* (different systems or system structure deliver the same outcome, for example: housing ownership is *functionally equivalent* to pension income), provides a perfect starting point for further real-typical welfare state regime analysis, enables greater clarity on international and global level of welfare state, comparison, i.e. it is very helpful when comparing a larger number of welfare state systems. *Disadvantages:* details at national level may not appear, especially with regard to the institutional set-up of systems as well as administrative technicalities and legal provisions, some important policy levels and areas may not appear, the one or another country may not fit, or may not easily fit in an ideal-typical model (not every welfare state system has to be part of an ideal-typical welfare regime, some are atypical or simply drifting in between different welfare regimes, or changing from one to another).

Table 29.1 (continued)

	Real-typical method	*Ideal-typical method*
Representatives**	F. Castles and D. Mitchell (1991), E. Vogel (1991), F. Deyo (1992), S. Leibfried (1992), B. Deacon (1992), J. Lewis (1992), C. Jones (1993), A. Orloff (1993), E. Huber, C. Ragin and J. Stephens (1993), D. Sainsbury (1999), I. Ostner and J. Lewis (1995), J. O'Connor (1996), M. Ferrera (1996), F. Castles and C. Pierson (1996), G. Bonoli (1997), H. Kwon (1997, 2005), R. Goodman, G. White and H. Kwon (1998), E. Huber and J. Stephens (1999, 2009), P. Wilding (2000), I. Gough (2000a,b), I. Holliday (2000), C. Aspalter (2001a,b), C. Mesa-Lago (2003), M. Ramesh (2004), Y. Lee and Y. Ku (2007), C. Bambra (2007a,b), J. Martinez Franzoni (2008), G. Pascall (2008).	H. Wilensky and C. Lebeaux (1958), R. Titmuss (1974), G. Esping-Andersen (1987, 1990), W. Korpi and J. Palme (1998), I. Gough (1999), A. Hicks and L. Kenworthy (2003), P. Abrahamson (2003), I. Gough *et al.* (2004), C. Aspalter (2005, 2006a, 2011), G. Esping-Andersen and A. Hicks (2006), J. Weidenholzer and C. Aspalter (2008), C. Aspalter, J. Kim and S. Park (2009).

Note: *cf Esping-Andersen (1987), Hekman (1983), Burger (1978), Kalberg (1994), Eliæson (2002); ** demonstrative, not exhaustive list.

Ideal-typical welfare models

At this point, it is certainly most useful once more to look at the current state of ideal-typical welfare regime models. However, before we turn our attention to the world of Esping-Andersen and his three initial welfare regimes and further regimes identified in the process along the way, we shall focus on the most prominent, outstanding, and/or useful alternatives in classifying ideal types in welfare state comparison, one of which is the classification put forward by Korpi and Palme in 1998. Both Walter Korpi and Joakim Palme follow explicitly the method of constructing ideal types, which is also apparent in the lack of any welfare state system that would be attributed to the fifth model identified, the *Voluntary State-Subsidized Model.*

The *Basic Security Model*, according to Korpi and Palme (1998), is exemplified by the welfare state systems of Canada, the Netherlands, Switzerland, United Kingdom, and the United States. In all these countries entitlements are based on citizenship or contributions (see the role of functional equivalence!), and a flat-rate benefit principle is applied. On the other hand Sweden, Norway, and Finland match the yardsticks of the *Encompassing Model*, that is, entitlements are based on citizenship or labour force participation, while flat-rate and earnings-related benefits principles are dominant. Germany and France, in contrast, belong to the *Corporatist Model*, as entitlements are based on occupational category and labour force participation, while implementing the earnings-related principle. Another ideal-typical welfare regime was identified by Korpi and Palme: the *Targeted Model.* It is exemplified in the case of the Australian welfare state, where eligibility derives from proven need, and the minimum benefit principle is vigorously applied. The fifth model introduced by Korpi and Palme, the *Voluntary State-Subsidized Model*, is marked by eligibility based on membership or contributions, as well as flat-rate or earnings-related benefit principle.

In 2004, a group of analysts around Ian Gough developed another ideal-typical classification covering all countries on earth by looking on welfare state systems around the globe from a satellite perspective (see Gough et al., 2004; Wood and Gough, 2004; Gough, 1999) (see Table 29.2). The new classification is the broadest and the least detail-oriented of all comparative classifications so far, which result in both its advantages and disadvantages. As Wood and Gough (2004) state:

> the reality is more complicated than such a classification … in the sense that regions and countries within them can combine elements of all three 'families' within a single social formation. Thus different categories of a country's population can experience different primary regimes: some might be successfully incorporated into state protection; others reliant upon community and family arrangements; and others more excluded from formal or informal mainstream arrangements and reliant upon highly personalized politico-militia patrons, in which a sense of 'in/security' is prevalent. But within that complexity of hybrids, we are certainly clustering different countries of the world into a primary association with one of these three regime groups.

Since this particular classification is based on extremely broad ideal types, which in total include all countries of all development stages on earth, its actual purpose is to describe worldwide developments in social policy, including showing the relative absence thereof in the least-developed parts of the world. This classification – due to its catch-all strategy – is, however, not useful to describe or evaluate different kinds of social insurance programmes or different kinds of modern welfare state systems, or to compare them to one another. Rather, it is useful for the study of social development and developmental social policies (see Wood and Gough, 2004).

Table 29.2 Welfare regimes following Geof Wood and Ian Gough (2004)

Selected regime-specific characteristics	*The insecurity regime*	*The informal security regime*	*The welfare state regime*
Dominant mode of production	Predatory Capitalism	Peasant economies with peripheral capitalism, with uneven development	Capitalism, with technological progress plus exploitation
Dominant social relationship	Different forms of oppression	Different forms of exploitation, exclusion and domination	Exploitation and market inequalities
Dominant source of livelihood	Various forms of livelihoods with extensive conflict	Various forms of livelihoods	Access to formal labor market
Dominant form of political mobilization	Diffuse and fluid	Diffuse and particularistic (with patron-clientelism)	Class coalitions, issue-based political parties and political settlements
State form	Shadow, collapsed and criminal states with porous contended borders	'State' weakly differentiated from other power systems	Relatively autonomous state
Institutional landscape	Extreme negative permeability and fluidity	Broader institutional responsibility matrix with powerful external influences and extensive negative permeability	Welfare mix of market, state and family
Welfare outcomes	Intermittently extreme forms of insecurity	Insecurity modified by informal rights and adverse incorporation	Different degrees of decommodification plus health and human investment
Nature of social policy	Nonexistent	Less distinct policy due to permeability, contamination, as well as foreign actors	Countervailing power based on institutional differentiation and positive permeability

Source: See Wood and Gough (2004, p. 4).

Hence, every method, and every classification itself, may serve a different purpose – all of which help to bring forth new insights and developments in comparative analysis and theory-making.

A third alternative model derives from perhaps the oldest of any ideal-typical models in comparative welfare state analysis, that of Harold Wilensky and Charles Lebeaux's monumental work *Industrial Society and Social Welfare*, first published in 1958. Wilensky and Lebeaux created also ideal-typical classifications, i.e. the *Residual Model* and the *Institutional Model*, for which the United States and Sweden served as key examples. That is, the rudimentary welfare state model, with low levels of coverage and benefits and high levels of commodification on the one side, and the comprehensive welfare state model, with universal coverage of all people in all fields of social security, high benefits, and highest levels of decommodification on the other.

There were a number of classifications of social welfare models in the past, that also followed the notion of ideal types, though not explicitly (such as, for example, Estes, 1993). Thomas

Watts, to take one particular illustrative example, puts forward four models of social welfare (cited in Elliott, 2011), two of which are the original models as described by Wilensky and Lebeaux (1958), plus two additional models identified by Watts. Whereas Wilensky and Lebeaux classified welfare state systems, i.e. ideal types (in the Weberian sense) of welfare states, Watts identified ideal types of social policies and welfare provision. Apart from the *Residual* and the *Institutional Model*, which Watts has taken over from Wilensky and Lebeaux (1958), Watts described the main characteristics of the *Neoconservative Model*. The *Neoconservative Model* is following the principles of privatization of social policy and all of its welfare state institutions: market-principle in delivering social services, with emphasis on obligation instead of social rights of the individual or the welfare recipients.

Another major ideal-typical model of social welfare put forward by Watts is the *Developmental Model* (cited in Elliott, 2011; see also Midgley, 1995, 2008; Estes, 1993; Elliott, 1993), which also shares the pro-active approach of the *Institutional Model*, as well as a positive outlook on society, with the aim to create a better society by increasing public welfare wherever possible through social intervention, and employing a strategy of planned prevention and development. The *Developmental Model* also shares the importance of social justice, equality, and empowerment with the *Institutional Model*. A new feature of the *Developmental Model* is the emphasis on the positive outcomes of investment in human resources, i.e. social investment, to ensure the enablement of people and the development of their full potentials. The government and social welfare professionals further act as agents of change and advocates for more social welfare (see Elliott, 2011; Falk, 1984; Midgley, 1995, 2008; also Wood and Gough, 2004). In the development context, the eradication of illfare (i.e., diswelfare, oppression, dehumanization), precedes the development of welfare. Only when we rescue people who would otherwise die of thirst, starvation, disease, accidents, crime, terrorism, abuse and neglect – and try to prevent such incidences in the first place – can they effectively enjoy higher forms of social welfare, such as social insurance, legal protection, personal and group empowerment, social justice, etc.

We now turn to Richard Titmuss (1974) and his ideal-typical classification of types of social policy: *the institutional type*, the *industrial-achievement type*, and *the residual type*. Again, one may note the importance of the institutional and residual type as developed by Wilensky and Lebeaux (1958). The industrial-achievement type is heavily dependent on social insurance and a near all-inclusive, i.e. quasi-universal, coverage of the population with all major forms of social insurance systems, pensions, accident insurance, health insurance, unemployment insurance, as well as long-term care insurance, which only has relatively recently joined the rim of traditional areas of social insurance. On the contrary to Watts (cited in Elliot, 2011), Titmuss (1974) did identify so-called model countries, i.e. Sweden, Germany, and the United Kingdom, for the *Institutional*, the *Industrial-Achievement*, and the *Residual Model*.

Born out of this intellectual development, the tripartite classification of Gøsta Esping-Andersen (1987, 1990) conquered the stage of international comparative welfare analysis. The models, which have filled countless theoretical and empirical studies up to date, are, astonishingly, identical to that of Richard Titmuss (1974). However, Gøsta Esping-Andersen went a step further and not only classified (Weberian) ideal types of social policies, but ideal types of welfare state systems. Furthermore, another critical point of distinction between the two: Esping-Andersen went on to bring in the history of those welfare regimes, and, with it and central to the theory of Esping-Andersen, the political economy that caused and drove the development of welfare state regimes in the first place (see also Baldwin, 1990; Moore, 1969). Political and social class alliances, the size and timing of those alliances in particular, played a pivotal role in the development of the three welfare regimes, as identified by Esping-Andersen (1987, 1990) – these are: the Social Democratic Model (which he called the Socialist Model on several occasions throughout his 1990 book), the Conservative Corporatist Model, and the Liberal Model. Sweden, Germany, and the United States now served as model countries for these three ideal types of welfare regimes.

A number of studies, such as, Huber et al. (1993), Kersbergen (1995); Huber and Stephens (1999); Ebbinghaus and Manow (2001); Aspalter (2001c, 2006a, 2011); and Aspalter et al. (2009), identify the Continental European model as the Christian Democratic Model, since it was the Catholic social teachings of the 1850s (which preceded the establishment and the rise of the German social democratic movement) that shaped Continental European social policy up to date (Aspalter, 2001c), particularly with 1) the pivotal role of NGOs in service provision (health care, social work, education, etc.), 2) the self-governing role of social insurance bodies with the integration of labor unions, 3) the Federal structure (focusing on state level powers and diversity) of social policy and hence that of welfare state institutions, as well as 4 the occupational division of social insurance programs, which is central to the strategy of original Catholic social teachings (to create a better society while providing a strong alternative to pure Marxism or pure Neoliberalism on the far corners of the political spectrum, cf Aspalter, 2001c). This is supported also by the very clear findings of Woldendorp, Keman, and Budge (1998). In 1998, Woldendorp, Keman, and Budge found hard empirical evidence for the fact that long-term public social expenditures, and hence extensions of welfare state systems and institutions, are caused by the rule of a particular government party or parties (in case of coalition governments). They proved that the longer a party rules, the stronger is its influence on social policy, the formation and the development of welfare state systems. Social Democratic parties in government have been found to be correlated most with the highest degrees of welfare state extension. Not far behind were Christian Democratic parties when participating in government formation. Further behind we find social liberal parties, and then at last (pure) conservative parties. Christian Democratic parties support in general a large welfare state, though in recent years, both Christian Democratic and Social Democratic parties jointly set out to slash government expenditure and with it a great deal of welfare programs, entitlements, largely by reducing benefits, but also by tightening eligibility rules across the board.

Aspalter (2005, 2006a) added a *fourth ideal type* of welfare state systems, comprising welfare state systems in East Asia, particularly Japan, South Korea, Taiwan, Hong Kong, Singapore, as well as Mainland China. There is an array of characteristics that can be ascribed to the East Asian Welfare Regime, or the *Pro-Welfare Conservative Welfare Regime*, these include: the principle of universal benefits coexists with the principle of benefits based on performance and achievements; a strong focus on the principle of social investment in areas of education, healthcare, and housing; a concurrent extension of welfare state columns and institutions; generally medium benefit levels; dominance of employment-based social security and welfare benefits; a growing importance of mandatory individual savings accounts; dominance of social service provision by NGOs and families, as well as; a growing focus on active labour market policies and programmes.

In 2011, Aspalter integrated the case of Latin America into the existing stream of ideal-typical comparative studies in welfare state analysis, by identifying major characteristics of an ideal type of welfare state systems in Latin America, with Argentina, Brazil, Chile, and Uruguay as core members of this group of welfare state systems (Aspalter, 2011). Among the major characteristics of the Latin American *Anti-Welfare Conservative Welfare Regime*, we find: welfare states in Latin America regulate social inequality and have as a result been marked by 'regulated citizenship'; even though in some cases social spending is significant (as in the case of Brazil) social programmes are badly focused or ineffective; a dual legacy of Bismarckian social insurance systems and neoliberal privatization policies; partially universal elements of social welfare provision have been introduced (first implemented by autocratic regimes, recently by democratic governments), such

Table 29.3 Summary of key elements of five ideal-typical welfare regimes: following the footsteps of Richard Titmuss and Esping-Andersen

Regime-specific characteristics	*The social democratic welfare regime in Scandinavia*	*The Christian democratic welfare regime in continental Europe*	*The liberal welfare regime in Anglo-Saxon countries*	*The pro-welfare conservative welfare regime in East Asia*	*The anti-welfare conservative welfare regime in Latin America*
Dominant Welfare Ideology	Social Democratic	Christian Democratic	Liberal/ Neoliberal	Pro-Welfare Conservative	Anti-Welfare Conservative
Dominant Social Rights	Universal Social Rights	Performative Social Rights	Clientelistic Social Rights	Productive Social Rights	Regulative Social Rights
Dominant Mix of Welfare Institutions	Universal social security and welfare services	Bismarckian social insurance, NGO-based welfare services	Asset- and means-testing, limited social insurance, company-based welfare services	Universal social investment in education, health care, housing; Bismarckian social insurance and/or provident funds	Bismarckian social insurance and/or provident funds; universal and means-tested social assistance, health care services
Emphasis on:					
State	Strong	Strong	Weak	Increasing	Decreasing
Market	Weak	Weak	Strong	Decreasing	Increasing
Family	Weak	Strong	Weak	Strong	Strong
Individual	Strong	Weak	Strong	Weak	Weak
Degree of decommodification	High	Medium	Low	Medium-low	Medium-low

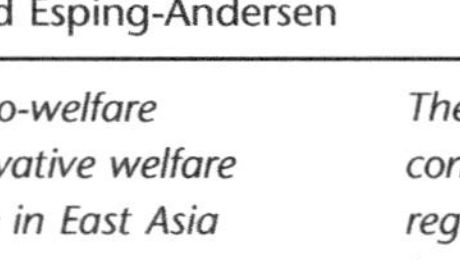
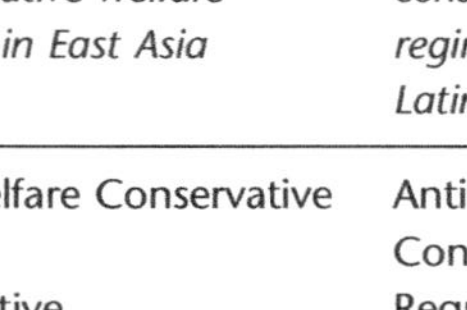
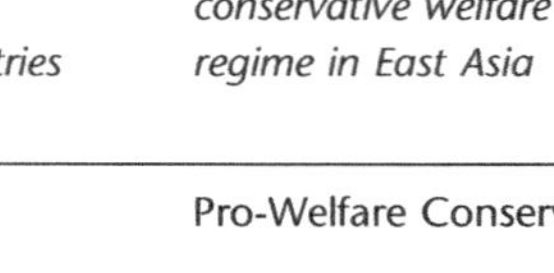

Table 29.3 (continued)

Regime-specific characteristics	*The social democratic welfare regime in Scandinavia*	*The Christian democratic welfare regime in continental Europe*	*The liberal welfare regime in Anglo-Saxon countries*	*The pro-welfare conservative welfare regime in East Asia*	*The anti-welfare conservative welfare regime in Latin America*
Degree of stratification	Low	Medium	High	Medium	Extremely High
Degree of individualization	High	Low	High	Medium	Medium
Countries/regions that belong to this general overall group	Sweden, Norway, Finland, Denmark, Iceland	e.g. Germany, Austria, Netherlands, Belgium, France, Switzerland, Portugal, Spain, Italy, Poland, Czech Republic, Hungary, Slovenia, among others	United States, Australia, New Zealand, Canada, United Kingdom	e.g. ML China, Hong Kong, South Korea, Japan, Taiwan, Thailand, Malaysia, Singapore, Indonesia, among others	e.g. Chile, Argentina, Brazil, Uruguay, among others

Notes: findings on the first five ideal-typical welfare regimes are particularly based on Titmuss (1974), Esping-Andersen (1987, 1990), Aspalter (2006a, 2011, forthcoming), Aspalter, Kim and Park (2009), Abrahamson (2003), as well as Kersbergen, (1995), Huber, Ragin and Stephens (1993), and Huber and Stephens (1999)

Table 29.4 Comparison of GINI indexes of family income distribution in five ideal-typical welfare models (selected countries)

The social democratic model		*The Christian democratic model*		*The liberal model*		*The pro-welfare conservative model*		*The anti-welfare conservative model*	
Sweden	0.230	Poland	0.349	USA	0.450	ML China	0.415	Brazil	0.567
Denmark	0.290	Italy	0.320	UK	0.340	Indonesia	0.370	Chile	0.542
Norway	0.250	Hungary	0.247	Canada	0.321	Japan	0.376	Argentina	0.414
Iceland	0.280	Germany	0.270	Australia	0.305	S.Korea	0.314	Uruguay	0.471

Source: CIA (2011).

as the recently implemented targeted cash transfer programmes; social security is a political instrument (which controls social insurance institutions) rather than in instrument of social policy; in Latin America social security systems and schemes work in favor of the rich, as they are to some extent regressive in nature and effect; highest levels of inequality among all welfare regimes identified so far; and a dominance of social service provision by NGOs (particular church organizations) and families.

Indeed, there may be more ideal-typical welfare regimes out there, which are yet to be identified by researchers, particularly interesting may be the case of the Middle East, the African continent, Central Asia, South Asia, and the many island states, especially in the Caribbean and the Pacific Ocean – with the possibility of arriving at one or more welfare regime clusters/groups in each of these regions.

Thus far, we count five ideal-typical welfare regimes within the original stream of ideal-typical welfare regime analysis, which began with the path-breaking works of Richard Titmuss (1974) and Esping-Andersen (1987, 1990). In Table 29.3, the major regime characteristics of each ideal-typical welfare regime (i.e. ideal types of welfare state systems) that has been identified so far have been displayed – these are the *Social Democratic Model*, the *Christian Democratic Model*, the *Liberal Model*, the *Pro-Welfare Conservative Model* and the *Anti-Welfare Conservative Model*. The last two models have both been classified as conservative, but, and this is important to stress, they are very different in terms of welfare ideology of the ruling elites and governments, and social policy strategy of governments, especially with regard to investment in human resources, such as healthcare, education, and in some instances public housing. Also, these two welfare regimes differ greatly with regard to welfare outcomes – particularly as a result of the active social investment strategy of East Asian countries – especially when looking at the Gini Index of family income distribution. Latin American countries achieve by far the worst results pertaining to income distribution among all welfare regimes examined (Table 29.4).

Conclusion

This article has discussed and analysed the particular advantages of the real-typical and ideal-typical methods in welfare state analysis, as well as referred to recent developments in the study of welfare state research. In doing so, the chapter clarified the methodological differences between identifying ideal-typical and real-typical welfare models.

Some major developments of ideal-typical welfare models that have been developed in the last decades have been looked at closer, starting from the early beginnings of Wilensky and Lebeaux in 1958 to new breakthroughs by Titmuss in 1974, Esping-Andersen in 1987, Korpi and Palme in 1998, Gough in 1999, Gough, Wood and their colleagues in 2004, and Aspalter in 2005 and 2011.

The business of comparing comparative welfare state analyses to one another is an interesting undertaking, with its very own rewards and pitfalls. All major classifications and methods discussed in this chapter have found to be of great use to the study of comparative social policy, be it in the field of social development studies, social security studies, social services in general or social work services in particular. For further contemplation the author recommends the reader revisit important studies of the past, each one of which has contributed to the development of comparative social policy, especially the welfare modeling business such as, for example, Francis Castles and Deborah Mitchell (1991), Stephan Leibfried (1992), Maurizio Ferrera (1996), Francis Castles and Christopher Pierson (1996), Martin Powell and Armando Barrientos (1998), Peter Abrahamson (1999), Robert Goodin et al. (1999), Bernhard Ebbinghaus and Philip Manow (2001), Wil Arts and John Gelissen (2002), Alexander Hicks and Lane Kenworthy (2003), Christopher Pierson (2003), Gøsta Esping-Andersen and Alexander Hicks (2006), Manuela Arcanjo (2006), Christian Aspalter (2006b, 2011), Clare Bambra (2007a, 2007b), as well as John Hudson and Stefan Kühner (2011).

Bibliography

Abrahamson, P. (1999), The Welfare Modelling Business. *Social Policy and Administration*, 33(4), pp. 394–415.

——(2003), The End of the Scandinavian Model? *Journal of Societal and Social Policy*, 2(2), pp. 19–36.

Arcanjo, M. (2006), Ideal (and Real) Types of Welfare State. *Working Paper*, No. 6, Department of Economics, Technical University of Lisbon, Lisbon.

Arts, W. and Gelissen, J. (2002), Three Worlds of Welfare Capitalism or More? *Journal of European Social Policy*, 12(2), pp. 137–58.

Aspalter, C. (2001a), Different Worlds of Welfare Capitalism. *Discussion Paper Series No. 80*, GPPP, The Australian National University, Canberra.

——(2001b), *Conservative Welfare State Systems in East Asia*. Westport, CT: Praeger.

——(2001c), *Importance of Christian and Social Democratic Movements in Welfare Politics*. New York: Nova Science.

——(2005), 'East Asian Welfare Regime', in N.T. Tan and S. Vasoo (eds), *The Challenge of Social Care in Asia*. Singapore: Eastern University Press.

——(2006a), The East Asian Welfare Model. *International Journal of Social Welfare*, 15(4), pp. 290–301.

——(2006b), New Developments in the Theory of Comparative Social Policy. *Journal of Comparative Social Welfare*, 22(1), pp. 3–22.

——(2011), Development of Ideal-Typical Welfare Regime Theory. *International Social Work*, 54(6), pp. 735–50.

——(forthcoming), *Ideal-Typical Welfare Regime Theory: The Cases of Thailand, Malaysia, and Indonesia*.

Aspalter, C., Kim, J. and Park, S.-J. (2009), The Welfare States in Poland, Czech Republic, Hungary and Slovenia: An Ideal-Typical Perspective. *Social Policy and Administration*, 43(2), pp. 170–85.

Baldwin, P. (1990), *The Politics of Social Solidarity*. Cambridge, MA: Cambridge University Press.

Bambra, C. (2007a), Sifting the Wheat from the Chaff. *Social Policy and Administration* 41(1), pp. 1–28.

——(2007b), Going Beyond. *The Three Worlds of Welfare Capitalism, Journal of Epidemiology and Community Health*, 41(1), pp. 1–28.

Bonoli, G. (1997), Classifying Welfare States. *Journal of Social Policy*, 26(3), pp. 351–72.

Burger, T. (1987), *Max Weber's Theory of Concept Formation*. Durham, NC: Duke University Press.

Castles, F. G. and Mitchell, D. (1991), Three Worlds of Welfare Capitalism or Four? *Discussion Paper No. 21, Public Policy Program*. Canberra: ANU.

Castles, Francis G. and Pierson, C. (1996), A New Convergence? *Policy & Politics*, 24(3), pp. 233–44.

CIA (2011), *World Fact Book*, www.cia.org.

Deacon, B. (1992), 'The Future of Social Policy in Eastern Europe', in B. Deacon et al. (eds), *The New Eastern Europe*. London: Sage.

Deyo, F. C. (1992), 'The Political Economy of Social Policy Formation', in R.P. Appelbaum and J. Henderson (eds), *States and Development in the Asia Pacific Region*. London: Sage.
Ebbinghaus, B. and Manow, P. (2001), 'Introduction', in B. Ebbinghaus and P. Manow (eds), *Comparing Welfare Capitalism*. London: Routledge.
Eliæson, S. (2002), *Max Weber's Methodologies*. Cambridge: Polity.
Elliott, D. (1993), Social Work and Social Development. *International Social Work*, 36(1), pp. 21–36.
——(2011), website, wweb.uta.edu/ssw/delliott/5303/SESSION%20TWO.doc.
Esping-Andersen, G. (1987), 'The Comparison of Policy Regimes', in M. Rein and G. Esping-Andersen (eds), *Stagnation and Renewal in Social Policy*. New York: M.E. Sharpe.
——(1990), *The Three Worlds of Welfare Capitalism*. Cambridge: Polity.
Esping-Andersen, G. and Hicks, A. (2006), 'Comparative and Historical Studies of Public Policy and the Welfare State', in T. Janoski, R.R. Alford, A.M. Hicks, and M.A. Schwartz (eds), *The Handbook of Political Sociology*. Cambridge: Cambridge University Press.
Estes, R. J. (1993), Toward Sustainable Development. *Social Development Issues*, 15(3), pp. 1–29.
Falk, D. (1984), The Social Development Paradigm. *Social Development Issues*, 8(4), pp. 4–14.
Ferrera, M. (1996), The Southern Model of Welfare in Social Europe. *Journal of European Social Policy*, 6(1), pp 17–37.
Goodin, R. E. and Headey, B. Muffels, R. and Dirven, H.-J. (1999), *The Real Worlds of Welfare Capitalism*. Cambridge: Cambridge University Press.
Goodman, R. White, G. and Kwon, H. (1998), *The East Asian Welfare State Model*. Routledge: London.
Gough, I. (1999), Welfare Regimes: On Adapting the Framework to Developing Countries. *Discourse: A Journal of Policy Studies*, 3(1), pp. 1–18.
——(2000a), Welfare Regimes in East Asia and Europe, paper delivered at the *Annual World Bank Conference on Development Economics Europe 2000*. Paris, June 27.
——(2000b), Globalisation and Regional Welfare Regimes, paper presented at the conference *Social Security in the Global Village*. Helsinki, September 25–27.
Gough, I., Wood, G., Barrientos, A., Bevan, P., Davis, P. and Room, G. (2004), *Insecurity and Welfare Regimes in Asia, Africa and Latin America*. Cambridge: Cambridge University Press.
Hekman, S. J. (1983), Weber's Ideal Type, *Polity*, 16(1), pp. 119–37.
Hicks, A. and Kenworthy, L. (2003), Varieties of Welfare Capitalism, *Socio-Economic Review*, 1, pp. 27–61.
Holliday, I. (2000), Productivist Welfare Capitalism, *Political Studies*, 48(4), pp. 706–23.
Huber, E. and Stephens, J. D. (1999), *Welfare State and Production Regimes in the Era of Retrenchment*. Institute for Advanced Study. Occasional Paper, No. 1.
——(2009), 'Successful Social Policy Regimes?', in S. Mainwaring and T. Scully (eds), *Democratic Governance in Latin America*. Stanford, CA: Stanford University Press.
Huber, E., Ragin, C. and Stephens, J. D. (1993), Social Democracy, Christian Democracy, Constitutional Structure, and the Welfare State. *American Journal of Sociology*, 99(3), pp. 711–49.
Hudson, J. and Kühner, S. (2011), Analysing the Productive and Protective Dimensions of Welfare, COMPASS *working paper*, No. 63.
Jones, C. (1993), 'The Pacific Challenge', in C. Jones (ed.), *New Perspectives on the Welfare State in Europe*. London: Routledge.
Kalberg, S. (1994), *Max Weber's Comparative-Historical Sociology*. Chicago, IL: University of Chicago Press.
Kersbergen, K. v. (1995), *Social Capitalism, A Study of Christian Democracy and the Welfare State*. Routledge: London.
Korpi, W. and Palme, J. (1998), The Paradox of Redistribution and Strategy of Equality. *American Sociological Review*, 63(5), pp. 661–87.
Kwon, H. (1997), Beyond European Welfare Regimes. *Journal of Social Policy*, 26(4), pp. 467–84.
——(ed.) (2005), *Transforming the Developmental Welfare State*. London: Palgrave Macmillan.
Lee, Y.-J. and Ku, Y.-W. (2007), East Asian Welfare Regimes. *Social Policy and Administration*, 41(2), pp. 197–212.
Leibfried, S. (1992), 'Towards a European Welfare State?', in Z. Ferge and J.E. Kolberg (eds), *Social Policy in Changing Europe*. Frankfurt a.M.: Campus.
Lewis, J. (1992), Gender and the Development of Welfare State Regimes. *Journal of European Social Policy*, 3, pp. 159–73.
Martinez Franzoni, J. (2008), Welfare Regimes in Latin America. *Latin American Politics and Society*, 050(2), pp. 67–100.
Meier Jæger, M. (2006), Welfare Regimes and Attitudes Towards Redistribution. *European Sociological Review*, 22(2), pp. 157–70.

Mesa-Lago, C. (2003), 'The Welfare State in Eight Latin American Countries', in C. Aspalter (ed.), *Welfare Capitalism Around the World*. Hong Kong: Casa Verde.

Midgley, J. (1995), *Social Development*. London: Sage.

——(2008), 'Developmental Social Policy', in S. Singh and C. Aspalter (eds), *Debating Social Development*. Hong Kong: Casa Verde.

Moore, B. Jr. (1967), *Social Origins of Dictatorship and Democracy*. Boston: Beacon.

O'Connor, J. (1996), Understanding Women in Welfare States. *Current Sociology* 44(1), pp. 1–12.

Orloff, A. S. (1993), Gender and the Social Rights of Citizenship. *American Sociological Review*, 58.

Ostner, I. and Lewis, J. (1995), 'Gender and the Evolution of European Social Policies', in S. Leibfried and P. Pierson (eds), *European Social Policy*. Washington, DC: Brookings Institution.

Pascall, G. (2008), 'Gender Models and European Social Policy', in P. Abrahamson and C. Aspalter (eds), *Understanding European Social Policy*. Casa Verde: Hong Kong.

Pierson, C. (2003), *Late Industrialisers' and the Development of the Welfare State*, paper, UNRISD, Geneva, Switzerland.

Powell, M. and Barrientos, A. (1998), An Audit of the Welfare Modelling Business, paper presented at *ESPAnet 2008 Annual Conference*. Helsinki, September 18–20.

Ramesh, M. (2004), *Social Policy in East and Southeast Asia*. London: Routledge.

Sainsbury, D. (1999), 'Gender, Policy Regimes, and Politics', in D. Sainsbury (ed.), *Gender and Welfare State Regimes*. London: Sage.

Titmuss, R. M. (1974), *Social Policy*. London: Allen & Unwin.

Vogel, E. (1991), *The Four Little Dragons*. Cambridge, MA: Harvard University Press.

Weidenholzer, J. and Aspalter, C. (2008), The American and European Social Dream: The Competition of Welfare Regimes. *Journal of Comparative Social Welfare*, 24(1), pp. 3–11.

Wilding, P. (2000), Exploring the East Asian Welfare Model. *Public Administration and Policy*, 9(2), pp. 71–82.

Wilensky, H. L. and Lebeaux, C. N. (1958), *Industrial Society and Social Welfare*. New York: Russell Sage Foundation.

Woldendorp, J., Keman, H. and Budge, I. (1998), Party Government in 20 Democracies. *European Journal of Political Research*, 33.

Wood, G. and Gough, I. (2004), Welfare Regimes: Linking Social Policy to Social Development. staff.bath.ac.uk/hssgdw/wood-gough.pdf.

30

Fiscal crisis, financial crisis, and the great recession

Kevin Farnsworth and Zoë Irving

There is an ongoing tension – some would argue contradiction – that goes to the heart of capitalist welfare states. On the one hand, states face ever-growing demands to provide more and better services. Some of these demands are made by citizens who desire better schools, hospitals, roads, and rail services. Some of these demands come from the corporate sector: for better educated workers; better funded public research facilities; more generous subsidies; public bailouts; and increased injections of public spending to increase macro economic demand. Few, however, appear to want to pay higher taxes to fund all this. Citizens of ordinary means are resistant to paying more, especially when the super-rich appear to be so reluctant to pay their fair share. Politicians also appear to have little appetite to tax the wealthy for fear of dampening their entrepreneurial spirit and causing them to flee to less punitive tax regimes, while increases in corporation tax are largely unthinkable. In any case, the wealthy and large corporations can employ various means to avoid paying even the tax levels laid down by law.

Governments, meanwhile, are caught in an uncompromising bind. Better services are vote winners, higher taxes are vote losers. They also face sophisticated and well-funded lobbyists, employed by the wealthy to represent their particular interests. And they are confronted by an overwhelming reality that, if they fail to create the right economic conditions to encourage new corporate investment and boost corporate profits, the revenues on which they depend will rapidly be depleted while demands on benefits systems and welfare services will rapidly increase as unemployment goes up.

This, in a nutshell, describes the roots of the fiscal crisis of welfare states. This chapter begins with a more detailed review of the nature and scope of fiscal crisis which is followed by a discussion of how economic globalisation, and more particularly its neoliberal transformation has contributed to shaping the conditions for the most recent financial crisis. The final section analyses the impact of the variety of crises evolving from the financial collapse and the implications for welfare states.

Understanding fiscal crisis

The spectre of the 'fiscal crisis' that lies at the heart of the welfare state was popularised in the 1970s by both left and right. The basic problem of the welfare state for neo-Marixsts and neoliberals alike was the fact that the public sector stifles private investment to the detriment of economic growth. The core of the arguments is different but the net result is fiscal crisis of the state.

To understand the basis of fiscal crisis, we have to first understand the relationship between state revenue (income) and expenditure. Government expenditure is usually based on three forms: taxation, borrowing, and any surpluses generated by government activities. The latter could include contributions from nationalised industries, money generated from the sale of state assets or charges levied on state provided services, but such contributions tend to be small. The most profitable nationalised industries have long since been privatised by many governments, and those that continue to be run by the public sector tend to bring low returns, or make losses. In some instances, state returns are deliberately reduced so that they can be used to effectively reduce prices to consumers or subsidise the costs of the private sector (O'Connor, 1973, pp. 7–8; Gough, 2000, p. 68).

Funding state expenditure through borrowing brings its own problems. To begin with, borrowing represents deferred expenditure with the addition of interest charges. This is not a problem if borrowing is used to fund exceptional expenditure, for instance, if it covers the short-term costs associated with a dramatic economic slowdown. Indeed, borrowing to boost consumption during a recession will help to reduce its depth and could stave off an economic depression. It can thus reduce its medium- and long-term costs. However, borrowing will squeeze budgets later on and is therefore unsustainable over the long term.

In the long run, taxation is the only sustainable way of funding government expenditure. Taxes are levied on individual and corporate incomes or expenditure. The key taxes paid by individuals include income taxes, national insurance contributions, property taxes and taxes on consumption. Business taxes include taxation levied on profits, capital gains, and employment (in the form of payroll taxes and national insurance contributions). The way in which taxation is levied is as important as state provision in determining final incomes. Taxes may be progressive (taking more as a proportion of income from the better off), flat-rate (taking an equal percentage of all incomes) or regressive (taking more from the poorest). Thus, how governments raise and spend tax revenues is a major determinant of final income distribution, consumption and access to essential services.

Fiscal crises occur whenever there is a structural gap between the revenues raised through these various measures and state expenditure (O'Connor, 1973, p. 221). O'Connor views this gap as inevitably arising from the endemic contradictions that confront capitalism, the key one being that governments have to fulfil functions: on the one hand they need to facilitate capitalist accumulation; on the other, they need to put in place programmes that legitimate capitalism. The struggle between these two is ongoing; spending on one limits the resources available for the other.

For Marxists, capitalist states are compelled by their existence within capitalist economies to ensure that public policies address (or at least do not harm) private economic activities, or, more specifically, private businesses. In the Communist Manifesto, Marx and Engels famously argued that the state manages the general affairs of the capitalist class or, to put it another way, it operates to satisfy capital's systemic needs (Wetherly, 2005). State activities are accordingly limited to those that promote, or at least do not undermine, the economic base; thus it is not the pressure brought to bear on policy makers by various actors that have the most impact on government, but the fact that the state's own interests are 'tied by a thousand threads' to the fortunes of capitalists (see Wetherly, 2005, p. 122). The capitalist state is, therefore, far from neutral; rather it acts as a factor of cohesion within capitalism, as Poulantzas (1973, pp. 291–305) put it, to satisfy the 'needs' of capital and stabilise otherwise unstable economic systems (Wetherly, 2005, p. 122). This argument does appear to be rather tautological at one level: the capitalist state is argued to preserve and protect capitalism because it is a capitalist state. But there are solid reasons why the capitalist state operates in this way. Elite Pluralists, led by Dahl and Lindblom (1976; Lindblom, 1977) and neo-Marxists, including Fred Block (1977, pp. 6–28) and Offe and Ronge (1984, pp. 119–29), emphasise the importance of future production, consumption, and investment by the business sector to ensure the strength and authority of governments as well as the continued sustainability of state revenues. Whether for sustainable economic growth, long-term financial stability, employment and political stability, or in order to acquire the resources to establish civil order or national defence, capitalist states ultimately depend on capitalists (see Farnsworth and Gough, 2000). But servicing the systemic needs of capitalism, including the specific needs of individual corporations and the needs of citizens, brings us back to the fiscal crisis problem. Higher taxes will undermine accumulation and require compensating measures (which will further undermine the fiscal balance), and the imposition of higher taxes risks a corporate and citizen-led tax revolt (O'Connor, 1973, p. 228).

For neoliberals, the argument is different. Although governments may feel compelled to intervene in economies, this compulsion is primarily motivated by the personal gains and/or objectives of politicians (political agency rather than structure) (Downs, 1957). The public sector is, according to this perspective, unproductive and inefficient compared with the private sector, and as a result of its inefficiencies, but also as a result of the motivations of politicians, the public sector will tend to grow and divert (or crowd out) increasing resources away from the private sector (Bacon and Eltis, 1976). Private investment and consumption will suffer and the knock-on effects will be that state resources will tend to decline over time. Revenues raised on the private sector will be squeezed as the pressures to increase public sector spending increase.

In reality, of course, policy solutions are not determined entirely by economics any more than politics can be divorced from economic context. Existing and past policy decisions shape and/or mediate crises, hence capitalism can exist and thrive with different balances between public and private. And in relation to the post-2008 crisis there are two factors that seriously challenge the thesis that high public spending leads to crisis. First, the size of the public sector did not determine the extent to which the Great Recession had an impact on economies and, if it did, it was precisely the states with larger public sectors that escaped the worst effects, even allowing for their lesser exposure to the effects of bank collapse. Second, the 'extent' of fiscal crisis within states does not appear to be determining the extent to which governments are cutting back on state spending. Large cuts in some economies are risking undermining recovery and weakening fiscal positions still further. Clearly, national politics and the local economics matter. But so does the global.

Globalisation and the seeds of crisis

Globalisation refers to the dramatic increase in the flow of goods, services, economic stocks and information between people, firms, and states, over increasingly large distances, since the 1970s. Political globalisation – the extension of political power and political activity across the boundaries of the nation state (Held et al., 1999) is of growing importance as international and supranational governmental organisations such as the European Union (EU), the World Bank, the International Monetary Fund (IMF), and the World Trade Organization (WTO) play increasingly important roles in national policy making. Economic globalisation – characterised by internationally mobile corporations and international industrial and financial trading environment – has transformed the ways in which governments and corporations engage with each other. Both elements are important here. Post-1970s globalisation has been as much about spreading neoliberal political ideas as it has been about economic integration. Neoliberal globalisation has promoted the ideas of smaller government – in particular fewer regulations on business, less public sector ownership, more private sector involvement in the running of public services, fewer trade restrictions, and more open economies. At the same time, economies have become more integrated, and more formally locked together if we include the rise of trading blocs in the equation. As a result of these changes, national economies have been transformed. High volume, low value production has moved in search of cheaper labour inputs and more specialised and technologically advanced production has flourished in developed economies. Capital mobility has increased exponentially and employment markets have been transformed. These developments have had several implications for welfare states and their fiscal positions therein. To begin with, governments have altered their tax bases in order to both encourage entrepreneurialism and to encourage free-floating transnational corporations to invest in their economies. Thus, corporate taxes and top-rate income taxes have been cut dramatically. Second, globalisation has placed downward pressure on workplace regulations. When coupled with broader economic structural transformations, the effect has been to increase unemployment levels and the significance of low wage jobs. Third, the effect of the first two forces combined has been growing economic inequality in most countries. Fourth, as regulations on financial capital have been reduced, so private borrowing and debt has increased.

In this context, the fiscal positions of states have been further undermined. The transformation in the tax base has dislocated the stability of government revenues and has made them more sensitive to relatively minor hiccups in the economy. Higher unemployment and greater instability for those in work have pushed up benefit claims. Governments have also sought to expand services that more clearly contribute to accumulation, including boosting tertiary education and training provision. And in political environments that appear to be increasingly hostile towards tax increases, many governments have come to depend more heavily on debt to finance spending (see Figure 30.1).

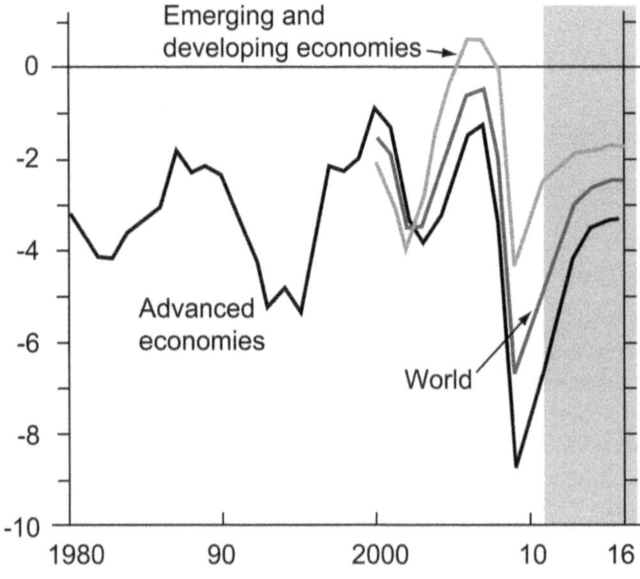

Figure 30.1 Fisical Balances
Source: IMF, 2011, 'General Government Fiscal Balances', www.imf.org/external/pubs/ft/weo/2011/02/c1/fig1_11.pdf.

The post-2008 economic crisis

The impact of the post-2008 'global' crisis was felt in almost every country, although not at the same time and not to the same extent. The response to it involved multilateral engagement to a degree that has not been seen since the Second World War. In terms of depth, as Figure 30.2 illustrates, events in 2008 were also more serious for the major economies than previous recent 'crises'. Nevertheless, in terms of its actual impact on nation states and its implications for social policy, the global crisis can best be understood as a series of consecutive international crises that were played out in various ways within different regions and different nation states. The international political response has also been variable: early on the crisis did promise a multilateral response, but entrenched national and economic interests have come to dominate at the expense of full international cooperation, and new differences and divisions have been created between and within states.

The economic crisis should also be seen as a series of crises that evolved over at least three separate waves. The first wave began with the initial banking crisis and the global credit crunch which originated in the US. In the wake of the US crisis, several economies faced the near-total collapse of their national banking systems and one economy – Iceland – effectively unilaterally defaulted on its foreign debts. The trigger was the contagion that spread from the collapse of the US sub-prime mortgage market. These 'high risk' mortgages were repackaged into financial products that were bought and sold in international markets – but the risks associated with them were undervalued or undisclosed. As the US economy slowed in 2007, it became apparent that banks and other financial institutions held a vast quantity of effectively worthless or heavily devalued securities that meant that they would, at some point, suffer huge losses. In simple terms, the stock they owned was worth a lot less than was previously thought. At the same time, it became clear that the companies that provided insurance against loan defaults would never be able to cover the level of risk they were exposed to. The relaxation of key regulations governing the amount of capital that banks were required to hold, bank lending arrangements and the internationalisation of national banks meant that the crisis was virtually invisible until it

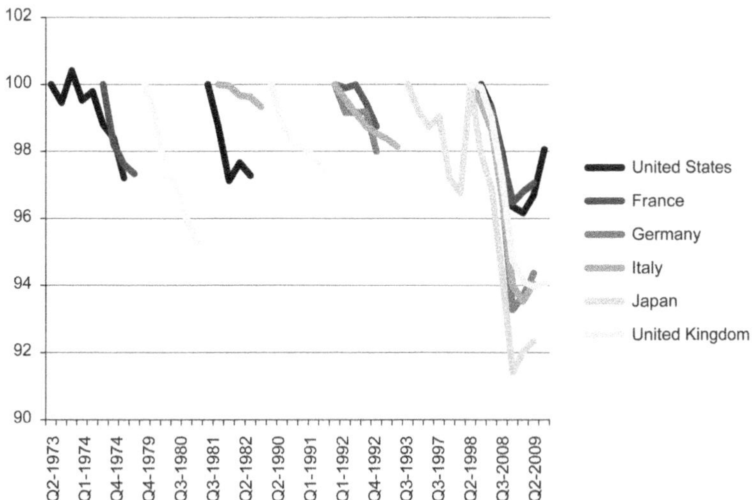

Figure 30.2 The depth of the 2008 crisis compared with others in recent past
Source: compiled from OECD data (stats.org.oecd.index.html).

was too late for states to reverse the damage. Not all nations had gone this route, but those that had – the US, UK, Iceland, Ireland – were hardest hit in this first wave of the crisis. Most economies, in fact, escaped the dire effects of this first wave. Most surprisingly perhaps, was the fact that the liberal economies – considered to have the most lax regulation of all – fared very differently. Canada and Australia, in contrast to the US, UK and Ireland, fared remarkably well in the first wave of the crisis (Béland and Waddan, 2011).

The response of the banks was to act to speedily to make up the shortfall in their losses and to attempt to recapitalise in order to protect themselves against bankruptcy. They closed down lending facilities to their customers, stopped issuing mortgages and stopped lending to each other. This had an immediate negative impact on economic growth and it precipitated the second wave of the crisis – the onset of the 'Great Recession'. How nations have experienced the recession depends, in turn, on the depth of their exposure to the banking crisis and the timing and relative size of the macro-economic interventions they instigated in order to protect their economies from falling demand. The spiral of falling demand for housing, plummeting consumer confidence and rising unemployment began to affect most, if not all, economies although the order of magnitude varied. This second wave of the crisis added to the financial woes of those hurt by the first wave, but it also had a heavy toll on the strong exporting nations. Whilst Finland, Germany, Sweden, and China escaped the first-wave 'crisis', they have suffered the effects of the global economic slump. Germany and China in particular suffered major downturns in export markets, but in both countries, pre-emptive measures to boost demand, including social policies, appear to have staved off deep recessions. Similarly, the Nordic countries appear to have survived the worst of the crisis and are dealing with recession rather than crisis management. These countries' crises in the early 2000s assisted in responding to the post 2008 period since they had already learned some of the lessons of rapid bank deregulations. They were also better positioned to forestall economic slowdown given their already large public policy infrastructure, not to mention their interventionist histories. For these reasons Germany, Finland, and Sweden have adjusted far more painlessly to the changed circumstance than countries that bore heavy costs during the first wave of the crisis. The role of past experience and the use of 'crisis' measures in informing and shaping the measures materialising in the post-2008 context are thus important. Indeed, for countries such as Iceland, Ireland, and the UK, there is much about the 2008 crisis that lacked precedent.

The third wave of the crisis began in 2009. It was caused by a combination of: 1) the huge costs borne by governments in their attempts to protect their financial sectors; 2) the costs associated with attempts to boost domestic demand and/or provide the growing number of unemployed with benefits; and 3) falling tax revenues. The extent to which economies have suffered in this third wave again depends on a number of factors, but the effects have been especially marked in the worst affected economies in the eurozone. Here, a combination of growing debt and an inability to control macro-economic policy, including monetary policy, have increased the likelihood of national bankruptcies. The cost of servicing government borrowing thus became prohibitively expensive for Ireland, Greece, Portugal, and Spain and only intervention by the European Central Bank and the IMF has saved these economies from total collapse.

From the global crisis to a new fiscal crisis of the welfare state?

The most recent crisis resulted in national interventions that were exceptional, not only in their scale but also their scope. Table 30.1 illustrates the enormous costs of the various measures borne by governments in their efforts to rescue *just* the financial sector. This does not include

Table 30.1 Headline support for the financial sector, upfront financing need and the cost of discretionary measures, 2008–2010 (% GDP)

	Finance and banking sectors							
	Capital Injection /	*Purchase of assets and lending by treasury /*	*Central Bank support provided with treasury backing /*	*Liquidity provision and other support by central bank /*	*Guarantees*	*Total*	*Upfront Government Financing*	*Non-targeted measures, Total (2008–2010)*
Argentina	0.0	0.9	0.0	0.0	0.0	0.9	0.0	1.5
Australia	0.0	0.7	0.0	0.0	8.8	9.5	0.7	5.8
Austria	5.3	3.5	0.0	0.0	26.6	35.4	8.9	
Belgium	4.8	0.0	0.0	0.0	26.4	31.1	4.8	
Brazil	0.0	0.0	0.0	1.5	0.0	1.5	0.0	1.1
Canada	0.9	8.8	0.0	1.9	13.5	25.1	9.8	3.6
China	0.0	0.0	0.0	0.0	0.0	0.0	0.0	6.2
France	1.4	1.3	0.0	0.0	16.4	19.2	1.6	1.5
Germany	3.8	0.4	0.0	0.0	18.0	22.2	3.7	3.6
Greece	2.1	3.3	0.0	0.0	6.2	11.5	5.4	
Hungary	1.1	2.2	0.0	4.8	1.1	9.2	3.3	
India	0.4	0.0	0.0	6.3	0.0	6.7	0.4	1.8
Indonesia 12/	0.0	0.0	0.0	0.0	0.1	0.1	0.1	2.0
Ireland	5.4	0.0	0.0	0.0	261.0	267.0	5.4	
Italy	0.8	0.0	0.0	2.5	0.0	3.3	0.8	0.3
Japan	2.4	11.4	0.0	1.2	7.3	22.2	0.8	4.5
South Korea	2.5	5.0	0.0	0.2	12.7	20.4	0.3	6.0
Netherlands	3.4	2.8	0.0	0.0	33.9	40.1	6.2	

Table 30.1 (continued)

	Finance and banking sectors							
	Capital Injection /	*Purchase of assets and lending by treasury /*	*Central Bank support provided with treasury backing /*	*Liquidity provision and other support by central bank /*	*Guarantees*	*Total*	*Upfront Government Financing*	*Non-targeted measures, Total (2008–2010)*
Norway	2.0	15.8	0.0	0.0	0.0	17.7	15.8	
Poland	0.0	0.0	0.0	0.0	3.2	3.2	0.0	
Portugal	2.4	0.0	0.0	0.0	12.0	14.4	2.4	
Russia	0.6	0.5	0.4	7.6	0.5	9.6	1.7	5.4
Saudi Arabia	0.0	1.2	0.0	0.0	...	1.2	1.2	9.2
Spain	0.0	4.6	0.0	0.0	18.3	22.8	4.6	4.2
Sweden	2.1	4.8	0.0	15.4	47.5	69.7	5.2	
Switzerland	1.1	0.0	0.0	7.2	0.0	8.3	1.1	
Turkey	0.0	0.3	0.0	0.0	0.0	0.3	0.0	1.1
United Kingdom	3.9	13.8	12.8	0.0	51.1	81.6	18.9	1.7
United States	4.6	2.3	0.7	41.9	31.4	81.0	7.5	4.9

Source: IMF (2010)

the costs of the subsequent slump. The actual costs of some of these measures are, as yet, unknown since governments will likely recoup some costs in due course. The amounts recovered from the sale of assets, such as shares, is unlikely to result in 100 per cent reimbursement of initial layout, let alone the costs of servicing that layout (when we consider interest charges). The IMF estimates that recovery rates from such 'crisis' interventions typically amount to around 51 per cent in developed economies and 13 per cent in emerging economies (IMF, 2009).

Guarantees may also bring with them zero or only marginal costs since, in most instances, corporations will remain solvent and governments will not have to make good the 'insurance' policies they have effectively put in place. However, there is a value to the private sector in both the purchase of assets and the guarantees issued by governments even if the eventual net costs to the state are negligible, just as any form of insurance or temporary loan has value.

Together, the value of the support packages that were put in place to rescue the financial sector range in cost from zero in several countries to 267 per cent of GDP in Ireland. The value of the packages in the US and UK is over 80 per cent of GDP. However, it is the upfront financing that is more meaningful in the short term. This represents actual amounts pumped into the economy by government. Again, in some countries the cost of upfront financing is negligible, but in the UK, it amounted to 19 per cent of gross domestic product (GDP). This does not include the costs of liquidity measures, including making short-term loans to the banking sector or buying up treasury bonds by printing money. Again, the former has value as a subsidy to the private sector equivalent to the difference between the 'market' rate of lending, and the state's rate of lending. At times during the crisis this latter was only a fraction of the equivalent retail lending rate. What this meant was that banks were able to borrow from the government at rates close to zero whilst lending to their customers at vastly inflated rates. These 'subsidies' are not costed in the OECD's figures and they may never actually be known.

The impact of the bailouts and the recession on the public finances has been huge. Fiscal balances declined sharply and are not set to recover for years, possibly decades. In 2010, Germany was spending the equivalent of more than 5 per cent more in GDP terms than it was raising in revenues; France in excess of 9 per cent more; Japan and the US in excess of 10 per cent; and the UK more than 13 per cent. Accumulated national debt (gross debt) has accordingly risen sharply. Average gross debt in the G7 countries in 2007 was 73 per cent of GDP, increasing to 99 per cent of GDP by 2009. This is projected to increase to over 118 per cent of GDP by 2018 (IMF, 2010). To put this into even starker perspective, gross debt to annual revenues is projected to increase to over 300 per cent by 2014 in the advanced economies as a result. In other words, if governments continued to raise revenues at the same rate as presently and devoted all of those revenues to paying back debt, it would take them three years to balance their books. In France, gross debt is projected to increase to almost 200 per cent of annual revenues, in Germany just over 200 per cent, in the UK, 267 per cent, and in the US 364 per cent (IMF, 2009).

To summarise, the post-2008 crisis and Great Recession has had at least three effects on welfare states. First, governments have poured huge amounts into trying to rescue their banking sectors. Second, the 'Great Recession' has stalled or reversed growth in many economies, leading to a massive reduction in government revenues. Consumption and income taxes (including taxes on profits) have both taken a huge hit. At the same time, increasing unemployment levels have increased government outlays. These 'automatic stabilisers' have helped to stave off even deeper levels of economic collapse, but they have also further undermined the fiscal positions of governments. Third, in order to try to stave off an even deeper recession, governments have implemented various stimulus measures, including tax cuts, new corporate subsidies and increases in social welfare provision.

These various initiatives have all further undermined the fiscal positions of states. Of course without them, the macro-economic environment would undoubtedly be worse. However, the pursuit of these various programmes is likely to have a negative, and in some countries a devastating, impact on welfare provision in the future. And here, two factors conspire to make the post-2008 situation worse than O'Connor could have predicted. First, the global crisis has had a dramatic impact on the availability of credit even to governments with relatively sound financial management. Second, the weaker eurozone economies face an even graver economic situation than other economies because their capacity to act in their national interest is limited by rules imposed by the European Central Bank. Thus, for a number of economies, the fiscal position is constrained by their inability to borrow. And this inability to borrow further reduces their economic stability, which further undermines their ability to borrow. In this context they face particularly intense fiscal crises.

Nor is it just the eurozone economies that have experienced difficulties in servicing their debts, however. During the third wave of the global crisis, governments have found it more difficult to obtain credit and its costs have increased – economically but also politically. Governments and political parties have formed new dependencies in order to try to resolve economic challenges and maximise support. The best example of this is the increasing dependence of the US and Europe on China which has agreed to buy up government bonds and large amounts of US dollars and Euros in order to stave off impending crises in the US and the eurozone. Moreover, the paradoxical position of state dependence on finance capital has also increased as governments continue to try to pay back the debts that many accumulated in their attempts to bail out financial institutions. Concentration in the banking sector in a number of OECD countries contributed to the too-big-to-fail problem and concentration has continued to increase since the crisis according to research by the OECD (2011). The contemporary fiscal crisis is therefore as much about trying to fund borrowing during a time when credit is more difficult to obtain, even for governments, since it is in the interest of finance capital to restrict credit and thus push up interest rates. The US, UK, and even Germany struggled to sell government bonds during 2011.

But what of the implications of the proposed cuts for welfare systems? Clear patterns are revealed in Figure 30.3. This plots average public expenditure levels between 2000 and 2008 in a number of countries alongside the prescribed 'IMF-adjustment' to spending levels that countries should, according to the IMF, make between 2000 and 2008. The initial prescriptions were made in 2009 and updated in 2010. The arrows illustrate the revised prescriptions between the two dates. Apart from clearly illustrating the different 'hit' that economies took between the first and third-waves of the crisis, Figure 30.3 illustrates clearly that, if pursued, the gap between the countries that pursue the most progressive social welfare models and those that pursue the most regressive is likely to increase. Based on the IMF's prescriptions, the higher spending welfare systems have to make the least cuts, the low spending ones the highest cuts.

This leads to consideration of the variety of responses that are available to states in times of economic uncertainty. While there are a limited range of options open to states that choose to cut expenditure in order to restore fiscal balance, reducing spending is only one of several strategies over the long term. Crises such as those emerging after 2008 can be viewed as opportunities for social investment as much as justifications for retrenchment and this has been the case in China for example (Cook and Lam, 2011). States may also focus their revenue-raising measures on increasing taxation, although in the post-2008 context this approach has been very mixed with only France targeting higher earners within these measures (Theodoropoulou and Watt, 2011). Economic growth is of course an obvious objective as far as accumulating surplus is concerned but the increase necessary (which would be greater than the rates of growth pre-crisis) to match

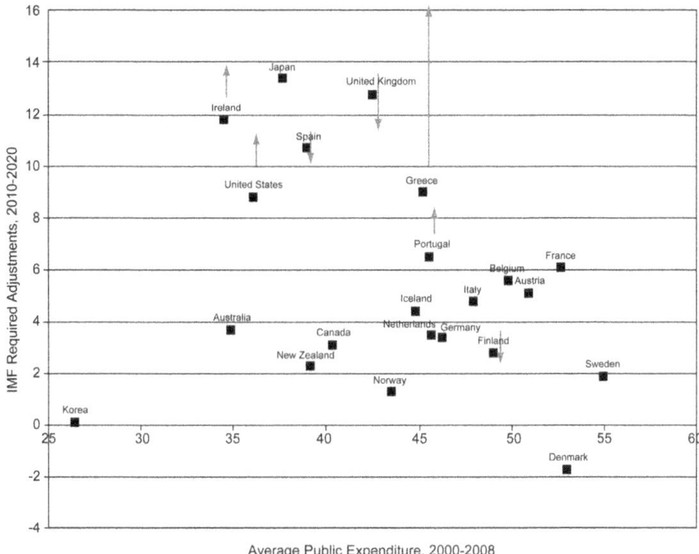

Figure 30.3 IMF prescribed adjustment and average public expenditure 2000–8

popular expectations in welfare expansion as well as generate extra income with which debts and interest payments can be settled, would require essential change, and more radical approaches to economic progress than governments are prepared to engage with, for reasons outlined earlier (Gough, 2011). Not least of alternative approaches is a reappraisal of 'debt' and the place of borrowing in national economies which from a far from radical Keynesian perspective is both necessary and legitimate.

In conclusion, it is clear that fiscal crisis as the enduring mismatch between a capitalist ideal and the real world inhabited by people with needs and capacity to make demands is as significant in the 2000s as it was in the 1970s. Globalisation has altered many of the processes through which social policies and the means to support them are played out, and has heightened and expanded the effects of crisis. Nevertheless, as actors, states make choices regarding the compromises and balances they seek in the economic and political spheres and it is these choices that determine social progress.

Bibliography

Bacon, R., and Eltis, W. (1976), *Britain's Economic Problem: Too Few Producers*. London: Macmillan.

Block, F. (1977), The Ruling Class Does Not Rule: Notes on the Marxist Theory of the State. *Social Revolution* 7(3), pp. 6–28.

Cook, S., and Lam, W. (2011), 'China's response to crisis: what role for social policy?', in K. Farnsworth and Z. Irving (eds), *Social Policy in Challenging Times: Economic crisis and welfare systems*, Bristol: Policy Press.

Dahl, R., and Lindblom, C. (1976), *Politics, Markets and Welfare*. Chicago, IL: University of Chicago Press.

Downs, A. (1957), *An Economic Theory of Democracy*. Upper Saddle River, NJ: Prentice Hall.

Farnsworth, K., and Gough, I. (2000), 'The Structural Power of Capital,' in *Global Capital, Human Needs and Social Policies,* edited by I. Gough. London: Palgrave.

Gough, I. (2000), *Global Capital, Human Needs and Social Policies*. Basingstoke: Palgrave.

——(2011), 'From financial crisis to fiscal crisis,' in K. Farnsworth and Z. Irving (eds), *Social Policy In Challenging Times: Economic crisis and welfare systems*. Bristol: Policy Press.

Held, D., McGrew, A. Goldblatt, D. and Perraton, J. (1999), *Global Transformations: Politics, economics and culture*. Cambridge: Polity Press.
IMF (2009), *The State of Public Finances*. Washington, DC: IMF.
—— (2010), 'Will It Hurt? Macroeconomic Effects of Fiscal Consolidation,' in *World Economic Outlook*. Paris: International Monetary Fund.
Lindblom, C. E. (1977), *Politics and Markets*. New York: Basic Books.
O'Connor, J. (1973), *The Fiscal Crisis of the State*. New York: St Martin's Press.
Organisation for Economic Co-operation and Development (OECD) (2011), *Bank Competition and Financial Stability*. Paris: OECD.
Offe, C., and Ronge, V. (1984), 'Theses on the Theory of the State,' in C. Offe (ed.), *Contradictions of the Welfare State*, pp. 119–29. London: Hutchinson.
Poulantzas, N. (1973), 'The Problem of the Capitalist State,' in J. Urry and J. Wakeford (eds), *Power in Britain*, pp. 291–305. London: Heinemann Educational Books.
Theodoropoulou, S., and Watt, A. (2011), *Withdrawal Symptoms: An Assessment of the Austerity Packages in Europe*. Brussels: European Trade Union Instutute (ETUI).
Wetherly, P. (2005), *Marxism and the State*. London: Palgrave.

Part III
Central policy areas

31

Social security

Frans Pennings

Introduction

Within the welfare state social security is a core element. It denotes the responsibility of the state for protection of its citizens from want and this is indeed essential, since only if basic needs are fulfilled are citizens able to access other public services, for instance going to public libraries, museums, or schools. This chapter will describe the core concepts of social security and how these have developed through time. It will then describe the forms of income protection used to realise social security. After that, it outlines the international dimension before giving some conclusions and addresses the main question: Is the definition of social security as developed at the beginning of the chapter still up to date?

The core concepts of social security

The following definition of social security will be used: social security concerns the income protection regulated in statutory schemes for the compensation of the loss of income due to materialisation of contingencies closely related to the physical (personal) situation of the persons concerned, loss of work by workers, and basic provisions to protect citizens from want. This definition will be discussed in the next part of the chapter. Discussions of core concepts can also be found in Pieters (2006) and Becker et al. (2010). There is, however, no general consensus on the exact definitions of the concepts, mainly since the field of social security can vary so much from country to country and from time to time, and continues to change. In this contribution a new attempt is made to define these concepts.

The following section will also discuss core elements: the extent of the obligation to provide social security, the forms by which this can be done, solidarity, and the responsibility of the insured.

Analysis of the core concepts

General

There may be large differences in how countries use the term social security. Sometimes 'Social Security Act' is the name of the Act that covers particular risks. In other countries the term is used to denote the administration of particular schemes or the responsible ministry. There may therefore be large differences in what is meant by the term, due to national differences and preferences. For the purpose of (comparative) research we need a general definition. For understanding the scope of the definition and better knowledge of core elements it is useful to first describe briefly the historical development of social security.

History

The establishment of employees' insurances

Centuries ago forms of mutual help could be found in various parts of the world; however, the adoption of the first statutory Acts is usually taken as a starting-point of what is later called social security. This was an important milestone, as it showed that the State began to take (though reluctantly) responsibility for the protection of income loss due to specific contingencies.

These first Acts were adopted in the last part of the nineteenth century, when in Germany statutory old age and disability insurances were established. Their purpose was to reduce dependency of workers in need on private organisations, such as charities and churches, or on local poor relief schemes. It was out of the fear of revolutions taking place at the time in several parts of Europe that Reichskanzler Bismarck decided to introduce these Acts.

The Acts were limited to workers and based on the insurance principle, i.e. only workers who had paid contributions were covered (employees insurance). Gradually also Acts for the risks of sickness, accidents at work, disability, and unemployment were developed.

The German Acts instigated also other European countries to make employees insurance Acts (Köhler and Zacher, 1982), as also they wished to reduce dependency of workers on the poor laws. The poor laws involved very strict means tests on income and capital including those of (even remote) family members. Relief recipients sometimes lost their citizen's rights and the administration deeply interfered with their personal affairs (see Checkland 1834 on the British situation). Therefore provisions with a better legal position were very much needed.

Insurance, equivalence, and solidarity principles in employees' insurances

Insurance was a very appropriate instrument for making such first schemes, since there was still large opposition and/or suspicion against State interference in social affairs. Insurance meant that only persons having paid a sufficient amount of contributions were eligible for benefit, thus both able to distinguish the deserving claimants from others and to serve as justification for State intervention, since recipients had also made their own efforts to reduce the income risk by contributing to the insurance. See Bruce (1961) on the British discussion on the Unemployment Insurance Act (1911).

Within insurance schemes the equivalence principle played an important role: this principle requires a relation between the level of contributions paid, the incidence of the risk and the level and/or duration of benefit payment. For instance, with each year of insurance, the level of the old age pension increases. The principle is not defined more precisely than this; the social security in question has to define the relation between the elements mentioned and that can vary from risk to risk and from country to country and through time it can also change. The equivalence principle is, however, useful to describe the various schemes, e.g. differences between public employees schemes, private insurance schemes and, mentioned below, national insurances (Beveridge-type schemes). From the equivalence principle it follows that employees insurance schemes have earnings-related contributions and benefits. In employees schemes the relation between contributions and level of benefit depends more on policy considerations than actuarial calculations. Persons with an over-average risk profile do not, for instance, have to pay higher contributions than others.

The extent to which proportional relations are loosened, i.e. that equivalence is less strict, shows the solidarity realised in the scheme. In periods of high unemployment, for instance, elderly unemployed are often entitled to a longer benefit period than younger ones with the same work record, since the older workers are presumed to have greater difficulties in finding work again. The equivalence relation between risk, contribution and level of benefit can vary from scheme to scheme, but the very influence of the solidarity principle is the reason to call the schemes social insurance schemes. Neither the equivalence nor the solidarity principle are defined in an absolute way, they are merely notions to describe provisions of concrete schemes.

From the solidarity principle also follows the compulsory character of the schemes: all persons within the personal scope of the scheme are compulsorily insured. Solidarity thus contributes to a certain redistribution of the effects of unequal impact of risks on persons.

The creation of residence insurances

During the Second World War in some countries plans were made for a better future after the War, which would solve some of the pertinent pre-War crises. An example was a blueprint for a new, general and comprehensive social security system, made by Lord Beveridge in the United Kingdom (Beveridge, 1942), whose purpose was to free all citizens from want. For this purpose it envisaged to no longer limit State protection to workers, since this left important parts of society (such as self-employed and non-working persons, including housewives) unprotected. Also the Beveridge proposal had the form of insurance, since in such a system it is easier to justify that persons receive benefit, on the grounds that they have been insured for the risk.

After the war, Beveridge's plan was implemented in the National Insurance Act. State protection of income was now extended to the whole population of Great Britain, although protection against some contingencies, for example unemployment, was limited to particular categories.

Residence schemes have specific characteristics. Earnings-related contributions do not fit well in these schemes, since not all insured have an income and some of them can to a large extent influence the level of their own income. Therefore Beveridge-type systems (often) have flat-rate contributions and flat-rate benefits. See also George (1968) and Gilbert (1966). As a result of this character the solidarity principle may have different effects than under employees insurance schemes.

Coining of the term social security

It seems that the term social security was first used in the 1930s, when the United States accepted obligations for income protection of particular groups by means of the Social Security Act (1935).

When, after the war, the Beveridge plan instigated governments, not only in the UK, to accept a general responsibility to protect the whole population from want, the term social security became used to denote this broad objective and the means to reach it.

Further development of the types of income protection schemes

After the Second World War many countries developed a social security system. Employees and residence insurance often served as examples, although the details of the schemes actually implemented vary considerably. Some countries have residence schemes only, other predominantly employees schemes, and still others have a mix of these schemes.

In addition subsistence schemes (social assistance) have been developed. Gradually they began to ensure a much better legal position than the old poor laws. However, since means testing remained an essential aspect of social assistance and this was found undesirable in case of some contingencies, schemes with minimum incomes (without means testing) were developed. Sometimes these were made for a particular category (e.g. the disabled) and sometimes for the whole population (e.g. old). These schemes are paid from taxes and therefore it can be said that the insurance character is losing ground within the social security system.

After the War in many Western countries family benefit schemes were introduced in order to compensate the costs of having children. Also healthcare schemes were made to ensure that persons have access to healthcare. These were initially often limited to workers, but were in several countries gradually extended to the full population. They began also to be considered as part of the social security system.

The definition of social security

Earlier in the chapter, social security was defined as the income protection regulated in statutory schemes for the compensation of the loss of income due to materialisation of contingencies closely related to the physical situation of the persons concerned, the loss of work by workers, and basic provisions to protect persons from want. This definition attempts to cover the provisions which were described above.

The contingencies covered are traditionally the following: old age, survivors, disability, industrial accidents, unemployment, sickness, and maternity. In the definition it is attempted to characterise these schemes: they are linked with the physical situation of the person that cannot work anymore (sickness, disability, old age) or personal situation that led to a loss of income (death of breadwinner). Unemployment is not related to the physical position, but often the result of economic development.

This definition does not mean that there is also an obligation to give protection in all situations which fall within this definition. For instance, self-employed persons are hardly ever protected against loss of income due to economic developments. However, if a scheme meets the definition, it is considered part of social security.

Family allowances and healthcare schemes were also considered as falling within the definition. Family allowances were considered necessary since the incomes of low-paid workers were otherwise insufficient to bear all the costs of living. Healthcare is considered necessary to ensure that everybody has access to healthcare provisions.

More generally, even though not addressed by an insurance scheme, meeting the needs of the poor is also part of social security.

The United Nations (UN) comment follows narrowly the contingencies mentioned in the previous paragraph and is not able either to give one single definition. Instead it needs a three-tier definition to include all the schemes: the right to social security encompasses the right to access and maintain benefits, whether in cash or in kind, without discrimination in order to secure protection, inter alia, from 1) lack of work-related income caused by sickness, disability, maternity, employment injury, unemployment, old age, or death of a family member; 2) unaffordable access to healthcare; and 3) insufficient family support, particularly for children and adult dependents.

The following sections will discuss criticism on this definition and approach, e.g. in view of the so-called new risks, for example the risk of divorce or the 'risk' of having to care for another person, for instance aged parents.

Another point of criticism is that the enumeration is the result of developments across, in particular, European countries. This means that the term social security has not a meaning independent from its context and as a result of demographic and economic developments it keeps changing.

The definition is sometimes adapted to fit with the actual question to be answered or research to be done, for instance if used to describe developments in government expenditure or compare budgets of countries. However, in discussions on the definition it is important to realize that the term social security also has a *normative* dimension. For this purpose delineation is useful or even necessary. We will discuss this in the next section.

The normative dimension of social security

Social security as a norm is laid down, in particular, in national constitutions and international instruments. For example, Article 22 of the Universal Declaration of Human Rights of the UN, provides that 'Everyone, as a member of society, has the right to social security' and the International Covenant on Economic, Social, and Cultural Rights recognises 'the right of everyone to social security, including social insurance' (Article 9). Although no enforceable rights can be derived from these provisions, Member States are given the obligation to elaborate this right (see also Riedel 2007) and therefore the provisions have indeed a legal meaning.

In order to be able to interpret the obligations following from the said instruments, it is necessary to limit the scope of social security to the protection for well-defined risks. Otherwise it is impossible to criticise a state for not fulfilling its obligations.

Contingencies in respect of which many states have already shown that they are willing to accept their responsibility for protection are very useful for the interpretation of the term social security in international instruments, such as mentioned in the previous paragraph.

Contingencies for which there is a widespread accepted responsibility are basically related to physical reasons for not being able to work and economic reasons affecting the depending working populations (including poverty). An example is, in particular, ILO Convention 102, the Social Security (Minimum Standards) Convention in 1952, which addresses the same contingencies as mentioned above. See also below and Dijkhoff 2011.

Also in other international contexts the term social security is used and also here a broad interpretation could lead to results unacceptable for states, so it has to be narrowed down for this purpose. For instance, Article 48 of the Treaty on the Functioning of the European Union (TFEU) requires that the European Parliament and the Council adopt such measures in the field of social security as are necessary to provide freedom of movement for workers. Examples of such measures are the export of benefits. If, for instance, the term social security is interpreted as also including housing benefits or study grants, these would have to be exported. This would be unacceptable for the European Union (EU) Member States. Regulation 883/2004 elaborating Article 48 solves this problem by giving a limitative list of benefits, corresponding with the benefits mentioned above. (See also Pennings, 2010.)

We can conclude that for the purpose of defining the extent of obligations of States and/or international bodies following from international instruments, it is necessary that the scope of social security is limited. The list of risks mentioned supra is generally accepted for this purpose. For other purposes the term social security may have another meaning. Basically, for the purpose of interpreting international standards, the definition of social security is rather narrow, focused on traditional risks.

Criticism on narrowness of the definition: 'new risks'

The definition given earlier in this chapter is sometimes criticised for being limited to so-called old risks, in particular those relevant to workers (see contributions in *EJSS Special Issue*, 2005). It is also argued that new risks have to be taken into account, for instance, the loss of income in case of divorce or the need to care for children or relatives, in particular if they are seriously ill.

While it is not the definition of social security which is being criticised as such, it is argued that state responsibility should extend to adopt a new risk under the definition. The State should also adopt compensation schemes for the loss of income in case of such a new risk.

In this discussion it is important to point out that the provisions recognised so far as social security (the 'old' risks) fulfil the requirement that their materialisation is not due to the initiative of the claimant. More precisely, it is possible to define precisely when a person is eligible or not, for example, between voluntary and involuntary unemployment. This criterion is closely linked with the insurance character of a large part of the schemes, but is also more generally still relevant, since the sustainability (financing) and legitimacy of the system depend very much on the possibility to control access and use. If one can claim 'at will' the system cannot survive. Therefore this principle that the materialisation of the contingency must not depend on personal choices is essential for distinguishing schemes as social security schemes.

The distinction between old and new risks on grounds of the possibility to influence one's own risk is not an absolute one. For instance, unemployed people can to a certain extent influence the duration of their unemployment depending on their willingness and activities to accept and find work. Also in case of illness there can be large variations in the work persons are still willing to do. Family benefits are only paid after a couple has taken the initiative to produce a child. If we compare this with a new risk: the obligation to care for a seriously ill child does not leave much choice, in some situations, to quit or reduce work.

The problem is, however, that for the old risks the legal conditions for benefit eligibility can be much more sharply defined and supervised than in case of the new risks. This makes it more difficult to control access to compensation for such new risks. For instance, in the example of the ill child, it can still be disputed whether the partner, or other family members, of a professional organisation is asked to provide the care. And in case of care for other family members, friends, relatives, the questions also arises if the person concerned has to undertake the task of caring or whether somebody else can be asked. Comparable discussions arise in case of a divorce insurance. The new risks make supervision difficult and would require to investigate the private situation of the claimant thoroughly.

Also study grants and housing benefits, which provide for income compensation, are for this reason not included in the social security concept.

This does not mean, of course, that States cannot make arrangements for such contingencies, but they fall outside the concept of social security generally used.

Is the concept too Europe-centred?

Another criticism on the social security definition is that it is too Europe-centred. Indeed, the history of European schemes was highly influential on the types of risks to be covered and the ways protection is ensured. Critics argue that in particular in developing countries the economies are still at a stage that is very far from being able to establish the 'Western-type' protection schemes against, for instance, unemployment and disability, in particular because of their large informal economies. Moreover, they argue that the most important risks which affect the lives of their people, such as drought, earthquakes and tsunamis, HIV/AIDS and large movements of refugees and other migrants, are not taken into account.

Although these are very valuable remarks, at this stage of discussion it is not possible yet to define more generally the measures to be taken to respond to these contingencies and to know what their long-term impact is. Therefore it is premature to incorporate such contingencies in the definition of social security. Further research on these issues is necessary; see Becker and Pennings (forthcoming).

The conclusion from the preceding part is: although the contents of the concept of social security are not fixed forever, the present definition is useful to elaborate obligations of States to ensure income protection of their citizens.

Type of schemes that can serve to realise social security

In the previous part I discussed the types of contingencies falling within the social security concept. The second question is which types of schemes can serve to realise social security. As we saw above, social insurance schemes were established to make workers less dependent on poor relief provisions. A first question is therefore whether the successor of poor relief, social assistance, is part of social security. This is particularly relevant in view of the question how states can fulfil their obligation to provide for social security.

In my view social assistance is part of the social security system. This does not mean that (international) obligations to provide social security can always be fulfilled by social assistance only. For instance, ILO Convention 121 does not allow means tested benefits as a way to provide income compensation for the victims of industrial accidents.

The view that social assistance belongs to social security is based on the fact that currently most, if not all, social assistance schemes do not essentially differ from other types of schemes, except from the fact that income of the claimants is taken into account for benefit eligibility (means test). Claimants have, however, a legally enforceable right to income if the conditions are satisfied. Also their legal position is often well-defined.

Moreover, means-testing is nowadays not limited to social assistance and the distinction between the traditional schemes and social assistance is declining. Insurance-type schemes sometimes have means tested elements, for instance for supplements to the benefit for dependents, or because of the nature of the benefit (e.g. in case of survivors benefits). Therefore there is no good reason to exclude social assistance from the concept.

Secondly, the question is whether social security is strictly limited to public schemes. As discussed in at the start of the chapter, acknowledgment of state responsibility for income protection was at the root of social security, thus stressing the importance of public responsibility. Of course, income protection can also be organised by other parties, including employers, family members, mutual funds, and private funds. This raises the question whether also such provisions are to be counted as social security. This question has become the more relevant, now in many countries the role of the State is being reduced and some public tasks are privatised, including parts of social security.

There is nothing against including such forms in the concept of social security, for instance for calculating expenditure on social issues or income redistribution. However, in view of the normative dimension the issue is different, since now again the question has to be answered whether the State has fulfilled its obligations. Because if the impact on the legal position of the persons concerned, it still makes a very important differences who is responsible for the income redistribution.

The normative dimension requires that the term social security is limited to those forms of income protection which are defined by statutory law giving the core obligations to be fulfilled. Within this context also private parties can be given the task to provide for an income. For instance, if the employer has the statutory obligation to continue to pay wages to ill employees, this obligation and payment can be considered as social security. If, however, the employer pays the employee money on the basis of an individual or collective employment contract, this is outside the scope of social security.

How is income protection organised within social security?

Types of benefit

Income protection can be organised in various ways. The current forms can be characterised as follows:

- Social insurance, where the insured receive benefits or services in exchange for contributions. There are two main schemes: employees insurance schemes, limited to workers and some assimilated categories; and residence schemes, covering all residents.
- The schemes are defined for specific contingencies and define the level and duration of benefit. In case of a low benefit and/or limited duration, recourse has to be made to schemes to supplement these schemes, which are often means tested (i.e. that they are paid only if a person has less than a certain amount of income).
- Employees' insurance schemes are often administered by organisations of social partners, but this is not necessarily the case. Also public bodies can have this task. Residence schemes are administered by public bodies.
- In some systems statutory law allows or obliges private parties (including employers) to take over part of the income protection (previously or still currently) organised by social insurance. This was discussed earlier.
- Universal benefits. These differ from the residence schemes mentioned above as the latter schemes are based on insurance and thus contributory. Universal schemes are non-contributory benefits without a means test for all residents. Examples are family allowances or public pensions. Strictly speaking, social assistance schemes can also be universal; however, because of their very important characteristic of being means tested, social assistance benefits are put in a separate category.
- Minimum benefits. These provide for a minimum income for particular groups with a low income – e.g. for disabled persons or the elderly – and are paid from taxes. The difference with public assistance is mainly that these benefits generally do not have a means test on the capital.
- Social assistance (means tested benefits). These benefits are paid to guarantee the subsistence level as defined in the country in question. For this purpose the income and capital of the person (and often also other family members) is taken into account.
- Social security may also be realised in the form of services, e.g. by means of accommodation special centres. Also healthcare schemes often provide care as services rather than in cash.

Activation

We mentioned already the obligation to limit recourse to social security to the minimum in order to keep the system sustainable. Although this general requirement has always been connected to social security, it is not automatically fulfilled. Benefit conditions are often not sufficient to limit recourse to the system, and persons are sometimes not able to leave benefit by their own efforts. Therefore active labour market measures are undertaken to help persons back to work. Examples are work experience measures and training activities. Sometimes also privatisation of parts of social security, and thus shifting the responsibility for income compensation to parties who feel the costs of their activities more directly, is a way to realising activation.

Because of the essential link of such measures with benefit schemes active labour market measures can also be seen as part of social security.

International aspects

International standards

Earlier we mentioned some international instruments which gave a general right to social security for 'everyone'. Much more fully elaborated and extensive are the international standards for social security set by the International Labour Organization (ILO).

The ILO was established after the First World War with the aim to promote social peace and to prevent a new war. Social unrest was considered a serious threat, and the Russian Revolution of 1917, which took place shortly before the creation of the ILO, confirmed the founders of this organisation in their view that measures had to be taken in order to raise the standards of living in the world. The ILO developed a large codex of standards in the form of conventions and recommendations giving minimum rules on the contents of the national social security legislation, including the persons covered, the content and level of benefits, conditions for entitlement to benefits and the administration. These standards are minimum standards; the conventions themselves explicitly allow higher levels of protection.

Alongside the ILO there are regional organisations also setting standards, including the Council of Europe, the States Parties to the American Convention on Human Rights, and Southern African Development Community (SADC). These have very different functions and instruments. We will here limit ourselves to ILO Conventions.

In the development of ILO standards two main eras can be distinguished. During the first era, which lasted from 1919 to 1944, most of the standards envisaged social *insurance* as the means for their application. This was the influence of the Bismarck-type schemes, discussed earlier.

The second era began after the Second World War and responded to the developments in the 1940s, when new concepts of social security were developed. A key element in these developments was the *Beveridge Report*, mentioned above. As we saw this report proposed universal and comprehensive coverage, guaranteed income security and medical care for the entire population. This concept was opposed to the pre-War schemes which covered particular risks and groups only and where poverty of the uncovered remained a large problem.

The Beveridge approach was laid down in Convention 102 of 1952. This convention covers nine main branches of social security in one single instrument, thus encouraging the establishment of general social security protection at a national level. The nine principal branches of social security addressed in this instrument are the same as mentioned earlier in the chapter.

Convention 102 encourages Member States to realise the protection mentioned and, since this is not easy to realise at once, offers the ability to ratify this convention by accepting at least three of its nine branches and subsequently accepting obligations under the other branches.

Some obligations which follow from the Convention are that benefits in cash have to be periodical payments; this excludes, for instance, in principle, lump-sum payments. Benefits have to replace previous income to a certain extent or to establish a guaranteed minimum. Thus, defined contribution schemes do not seem to be compatible with the conventions. Benefits and administration thereof have to be paid from insurance contributions or taxes; contributions paid by employees must not exceed 50 per cent of the total costs of the scheme. The state has to assume at least general responsibility for the due provision of the benefits and for the proper administration of the social security institutions. Representatives of the persons protected have to participate in the management of a scheme, or at least be associated with it in a consultative capacity in all cases in which the administration is not entrusted to an institution regulated by public authorities or a government department.

Later conventions follow these principles and lay down higher standards. For a description of these, see Pennings, 2007.

So far ratification of the Conventions on social security is limited (www.ilo.org) since States are reluctant to make their national powers in the area of social security subject to international supervision.

The Conventions give obligations to Member States, but sanctions in case of non-implementation are limited. After an ILO convention has been ratified, Member States have to report periodically on the convention concerned. These reports are examined by the Committee of Experts on the Application of Conventions and Recommendations (CEACR), which is composed of 20 independent persons, and which gives comments or asks further questions.

The EU and social security

We saw that relatively few ILO Member States have adopted social security standards. Also EU Member States are very reluctant to give the Union any power in defining the contents of their social security system – even more so because if such powers exist, supervision within the EU is much more powerful than in the ILO framework.

According to the Treaty of the Functioning of the European Union (TFEU), the Union shall support and complement the activities of the Member States in inter alia social security and social protection of workers, the combating of social exclusion and the modernisation of social protection systems. However, Article 153(2)(a) TFEU also provides that the Council must not take any measure which brings about harmonisation of the laws and regulations of the Member States. The Council may adopt minimum measures in the field of social security and social protection of workers but for these unanimity within the Council is required. So far no use is made of this possibility. Instead, soft law is used to encourage Member States to take, for instance, measures to reduce social exclusion and for the sustainability of pensions by means of the Open Method of Coordination (OMC) (see Berghman and Okma, 2002). Within the framework of the OMC Member States must make national action plans in which they make clear how they aim to realise the objective defined, thus not principally affecting the national autonomy to decide how this is realised. See also the Chapter on OMC in this book.

Conclusion

The main objective of social security is to ensure income protection, and social security is a core part of the welfare State. This chapter showed that its concept is to a large extent based on Bismarck- and Beveridge-type schemes, and discussed whether these origins mean that the concept has become outdated. Finally, it was concluded that, in view of the normative dimension, the concept as defined initially is still very useful, although it does not mean that it is unchangeable.

Bibliography

Becker, U. and Pennings, F. (forthcoming), *International Standard-setting and Innovation in Social Security*. Alphen aan/den Rijn: Kluwer Law International.

Becker, U., Pieters, D., Ross, F. and Schoukens, P. (2010), *Security: A General Principle of Social Security Law in Europe*. Groningen: Europa Law Publishing.

Berghman J. and Okma, K. (2002), The Method of Open co-ordination: Open procedures or closed circuit? *EJSS*, p. 331.

Beveridge, W. (1942), *Social Security and Allied Services*, London: Cmnd. 6404.

Bruce, M. (1961), *The Coming of the Welfare State*. London: Batsford.
Checkland, S.G. and E.O.A. (ed.) (1974 [1834]), *The Poor Law Report of 1834*. Middlesex.
Dijkhoff, T. (2011), *International Social Security Standards in the European Union – The Cases of the Czech Republic and Estonia*, Antwerp: Intersentia.
EJSS (special issue 2005), *Life Course Arrangements and Social Security – Papers from the EISS Conference 2005*.
George, V. (1968), *Social Security, Beveridge and After*. London: Routledge and Kegan Paul.
Gilbert, B. (1966), *The Evolution of National Insurance in Great Britain*. London: Joseph.
Köhler, P. and Zacher, H. (1982), *The Evolution of Social Insurance 1881–1981. Studies of Germany, France, Great Britain, Austria and Switzerland*, London: Pinter.
Pennings, F. (ed.) (2007), *International Social Security Standards. Current Views and Interpretation Matters*, Antwerp: Intersentia.
——(2010), *European Social Security Law*. Antwerp: Intersentia.
Pieters, D. (2006), *Social Security: An Introduction to the Basic Principles*. Alphen aan den Rijn: Kluwer law international.
Riedel, E. (ed.) (2007), *Social Security as a Human Right*, Berlin: Springer.

32
Housing, housing policy, and inequality

Gregg M. Olsen

Introduction

Housing is central to our lives and widely embraced as one of the most fundamental human needs. The United Nations (UN) acknowledged housing as an essential part of the right to an adequate standard of living in its 1948 *Universal Declaration of Human Rights* (Article 25), a position it would underscore almost two decades later in its *International Covenant of Economic, Social and Cultural Rights* (Article 11). Indeed, along with food and clothing, shelter is recognized as a basic necessity in even the most narrow and stringent 'absolute' definitions of poverty advanced by neo-liberal governments, agencies, and think tanks around the globe today. Yet, however routinely proclaimed as indispensable in official international and national documents, access to adequate and secure housing is far from universal, and a wide range of housing inequalities, including homelessness, can be readily observed across most countries today. Housing policy is a central means of addressing housing needs and inequalities and, despite being one of the more neglected policy areas in comparative, cross-national social policy/welfare state research, has generated considerable debate concerning its standing as either a 'cornerstone' or a 'wobbly pillar' of the welfare state in the broader and rapidly expanding 'housing studies' literature. After a brief account of the significance of housing and the character of housing markets and housing systems, this chapter addresses key dimensions of housing policy and goes on to consider its connections to social inequality.

The importance of housing

Housing is among the largest single consumer expenditures for most households and, for the majority of homeowners, it is their largest asset, comprising the lion's share of their wealth. Housing also serves a multiplicity of pivotal biological, social, economic, cultural, and legal functions. In addition to protection from the elements, including extremely hostile, life-threatening weather in many regions of the world, housing provides families with: a secure environment in which to conduct essential, if often taken-for-granted, quotidian routines (e.g., eating, resting, sleeping, washing, laundering clothes, doing homework); a retreat to recuperate from the daily grind; and a refuge from the outside world that permits a greater sense of control than in most other areas of life, largely free of external scrutiny. It furnishes them with personal space, a place to be with friends, an address where they can be reached, and a safe repository for their provisions, belongings and valued possessions. It fosters links to the community, can be critical to the construction of social identities and social status and, for most people, it is the acquisition most closely associated with the concept of a 'home'. Of course, the degree to which housing serves these functions varies markedly with the character of the social policies and family dynamics across and within nations. The dwellings of many residents of homeless shelters or other forms of inadequate or insecure housing, for example, or those of women and children who are victims of domestic violence, do not constitute safe, secure, tranquil, restorative havens that foster dignity and contentment. Moreover, for many women their residence is their workplace and the world outside it may provide a welcome escape from drudgery or isolation.

Housing markets and housing systems

Despite considerable variation in the specific ways that housing is allocated across the nations of the developed capitalist world, 'housing markets' play a central role in all of them. The number of households, their income levels, and their housing requirements are among the most salient concerns on the 'demand side' of housing markets, while the amount, type, quality, cost, and location of housing are key components of their 'supply side'. Housing markets actually comprise a series of overlapping submarkets, differentiated by location, dwelling type, tenure form, age, quality, and financing (Smith et al., 1988). Consequently, national economic and media reports indicating that *the* housing market in a particular nation is buoyant or in a slump during a given time period can mask notable contrary developments in some regions, localities, neighbourhoods, sectors, or other spatial and structural market segments. The state of housing markets – like that of stock markets – is routinely assumed to be a valid indicator of a nation's economic health. Depressed housing markets are often associated with downturns in consumer or business confidence and viewed as symptomatic of larger socio-economic problems. When unemployment rates are high the value of houses, and the demand for them, may decline further, rendering workforces less geographically mobile and stalling economic recovery. Increases in the construction of houses, townhouses, condos, and apartments ('housing starts'), in turn, are generally viewed positively because they can generate activity and jobs in various 'spin-off' industries, such as the manufacturing of building materials, furniture, and appliances, as well as in less directly related areas, such as finance, services, and entertainment, spurring economic growth. However, these standard economic indicators do not necessarily reflect the well-being of populations, or the character and level of inequality, including housing inequality, in a nation (Olsen, 2011, 2002).

Housing markets are strikingly similar to other markets in many respects. They have long histories of formal and informal restrictions or barriers to entry beyond ability to pay, including a range of discriminatory laws and overt, or more subtle, practices. More stringent screening measures, higher prices and rents, harassment, mistreatment and the denial of access to housing are among the various forms of discrimination endured by historically disadvantaged social groups in most housing markets. Ownership of many of the key 'inputs' required for the provision of housing, such as land, can be highly concentrated in housing markets. Housing markets offer two primary forms of commodities and services: homes for purchase and rental housing. Left on their own, housing markets may not provide sufficient quantities of affordable, quality housing in either form because developers, builders, landlords, and other housing producers or 'supply-side agents' typically look for the highest rates of return. In this context, poor and lower-income families often have to purchase or rent housing that is substandard and inadequately sized; housing that does not meet satisfactory standards of hygiene and comfort;

housing in neighbourhoods with fewer and inferior local amenities and services, and higher levels of pollution and crime. Indeed, in some of these areas even obtaining housing insurance can be considerably more difficult and, without vehicles or accessible public transportation, poorer families are often forced to rely upon more expensive local shops for food and other essentials (Williams, 1977). However, states may significantly modify housing markets to address the demand for affordable housing and mitigate many forms of housing inequalities.

Although most housing is distributed through the market mechanism across the capitalist world – with access to it, and its location and quality, largely based upon ability to pay – there is significant cross-national variation in the extent and character of state intervention in national housing markets and, consequently, in the ways that they function and their impact on inequality. Thus, as in the area of healthcare and other social policy domains, some housing researchers focus upon the broader 'housing systems' that exist across different nations, or groups of nations, highlighting the ways that states establish and enforce the 'rules of the game' in national housing markets through the unique packages of economic, fiscal, regulatory, social, and housing policies that they assemble (Hulchanksi, 2006; Malpass and Murie, 1999). Housing policies, like other social policies, are typically associated with the identification of salient social issues and problems, and with the formulation and implementation of specific programmes and 'courses of action' to address them. However, policies also include long-standing positions taken on these issues and problems and related 'courses of *in*action'. Thus, for example, while the US does not have a public universal healthcare programme like those in Canada and across Europe, it does have a healthcare policy; i.e., everyone who does not qualify for public Medicaid and Medicare should seek access to healthcare coverage in the private sphere, through their workplace or in the market. And it provides some fiscal incentives for some of its citizens to do so (Olsen, 2002).

Compared to many other countries the housing systems in some nations, such as Canada and the US, have placed considerably greater emphasis upon market dynamics, and they have become increasingly reliant upon them in recent years. This has actually required further state intervention to deregulate markets. In the US, for example, the state has stepped in to weaken longstanding government practices and rules and repealed 1930s 'New Deal' legislation that regulated the pivotal banking industry. This deregulation allowed the banks to engage in a much wider range of activities (such as selling securities and insurance), merge with other financial institutions, introduce new complex financial instruments (such as mortgage-backed derivatives), and greatly expand the subprime mortgage market, enabling large numbers of high-risk, marginal borrowers to purchase homes. All of this culminated in a major bust in the US housing market, with record numbers of defaults and delinquencies – including over 872,000 home foreclosures by 2011 – and a massive taxpayer-funded bailout of the financial industry (Dash, 2011; Hudson, 2009). But the roots of this financial/housing crisis go back much further, to the economic crisis of the 1970s and the dramatic reorientation toward neoliberalism, a multifaceted policy initiative that greatly extended the scope of the market via privatization, deregulation, greater corporate tax breaks, freer trade, and brutal attacks on welfare states, social security, and the public sector, seriously undermining or reversing many of the gains made in the first few decades of the post-World War II period. While virtually every capitalist nation experienced marked retrenchment during this era – not least in the housing sector – its severity and impact has been greatly attenuated in some nations. The character, patterns, and impact of state intervention into markets across the capitalist world, and the divergent nature and impact of national welfare states, has been a central concern in the social policy literature for over five decades.

Housing policy models and welfare regimes

Social policy researchers have attempted to impose order on the considerable cross-national variation in the size, shape, character, goals, and impact of national welfare states by grouping the ones that share some key features and orientations into policy clusters or models – see also Chapter 14. Studies have also identified and categorized approaches taken in some particular policy area or domain of the welfare state. Some of the first studies in the housing domain focused upon dominant forms of *housing tenure* across nations. Early functionalist accounts of housing policy had suggested that, with economic growth and increasing prosperity in the twentieth century, the predominance of private rental housing that characterized the previous century would soon give way to widespread home ownership. However, several housing policy analysts disputed the idea of a single, common trajectory of housing development. Despite the general trend toward owner-occupied dwellings, there were marked differences across the rich, developed capitalist world of nations. Anglo nations, they noted – such as Australia, Canada, New Zealand, the UK, and the US – had higher rates of home ownership than most other countries. And, the dominant ideologies and cultures in these 'home ownership societies', characterized as '*individualist*', advocated and privileged private solutions to housing problems and issues. In the US an almost fundamentalist devotion to the home ownership ideal has long been a central facet of the 'American Dream', and it was a central catalyst for the recent housing crisis there. Moreover, the high costs of home ownership, particularly in the early years, is said to have greatly limited the development of welfare states in Anglo nations because homeowners sought to avoid the heavy rates of taxation required to mount and maintain them. Various subsidies and fiscal measures favouring home buying were actively promoted in lieu of welfare states, and renting became stigmatized as an inferior, less secure, and less independent form of tenure in these countries. In contrast, wealthy capitalist nations with dominant *collectivist* ideologies and cultures, such as Denmark, Germany, the Netherlands and Sweden, had considerably lower rates of owner-occupied dwellings, more developed welfare states, significantly higher rates of social housing, and no stigma associated with renting in either its private or public forms (Conley and Gifford, 2006; Kemeny, 1981, 1992; Kurz and Blossfeld, 2004; Lowe, 2004; Ronald, 2008).

However, several housing policy researchers have disputed some central aspects of the models and arguments set out by theorists that grouped the national housing policies of nations on the basis of housing tenure and ideology. First, they argued that, even if it existed earlier, the strong inverse relationship proposed between home ownership and welfare spending weakened markedly over time. The growth of home ownership has not advanced more slowly in the more 'collectivist' nations; and public policy, in the form of fiscal and other subsidies, appears to have played a role in increasing aggregate home ownership rates across *most* nations (Castles, 1998a; Malpass, 2008). Moreover, the Anglo 'home ownership societies' did not have particularly high rates of home ownership during the period when welfare states were being developed, so the idea that their welfare states remained relatively undeveloped because of the great resistance to high taxes by financially strapped homeowners there is not very convincing. And, other Southern European nations, such as Greece, Italy, and Spain, have had very high rates of home ownership *and* more developed welfare states, with relatively generous pensions (Castles and Ferrera, 1996). Finally, the almost exclusive focus on housing tenure – with home ownership viewed as necessarily more market-oriented and public renting as necessarily less so and always more supportive – ignores myriad other ways that states might help families to access and secure housing (Andrews and Sánchez, 2011; Doling, 1999).

Other comparative housing studies went beyond the consideration of housing tenure alone, focusing on more inclusive networks of housing policies across nations. Housing policies in the

Nordic countries were identified as '*comprehensive*' because of their pronounced reliance upon state planning and regulation of their housing markets and their much greater emphasis on universality (Headey, 1978; Heidenheimer et al., 1990). 'Universality' in this context, however, referred to the creation of a single, general housing market for everyone, rather than to the provision of the same social service or income benefit provided as a right or entitlement to all residents as in other policy domains such as healthcare or education. Thus, despite marked differences in the specific institutional arrangements of their housing systems, the policies in Denmark, Norway and Sweden have been 'directed to all types of households and most segments of the housing market' (Bengtsson, 2008, p. 2). Housing policy in the Anglo nations, in contrast, has been described as '*selective*'. Private-sector industry and credit markets have played a much more central role here, with considerably less government regulation, and most state intervention – including the provision of social/public housing – has been largely targetted at poor households that can demonstrate need.

The most widely adopted welfare state typology is Gøsta Esping-Andersen's (1990) 'welfare regimes' approach. It sorts nations with broadly similar orientations into one of three policy families – liberal, social democratic, or corporatist/conservative. (Some researchers have proposed the addition of a fourth 'Latin Rim/Mediterranean', 'Antipodean', or 'East Asian', social policy family.) The central concepts Esping-Andersen used to distinguish these three ideal types was their varying capacity to 'decommodify' citizens, their impact upon existing systems of stratification and social solidarity, and the division of responsibility for welfare delivery between the market, the state and households (i.e., the 'welfare mix'). Decommodification is a *process* that advances as people become less reliant on markets for their well-being, usually through the provision of public services and other measures rendered by the state as a matter of right. Applied to housing it refers to the *extent* that people can obtain housing independent of their position or participation in the labour market.

Liberal regime welfare states, evident in the Anglo nations, are residual 'social safety nets' which leave citizens largely reliant on markets for their well-being. Because they tend to target low-income earners, both benefits and beneficiaries are stigmatized and social solidarity is undermined by a 'welfare/tax backlash'. *Social democratic* regime welfare states in the Nordic countries provide a mirror image of their liberal counterparts. They furnish generous income supports and a wide range of universal services as a right of residence, generating social solidarity. They also support a dual-earner family model. *Corporatist* regime welfare states, in turn, found in the Continental nations of northern Europe, are also highly developed and seek to displace market provision. But they emphasize separate income-related, status-maintaining social insurance programmes over encompassing universal services and benefits, thereby limiting their redistributive impact, and support the 'male breadwinner family model'.

Although broadly employed across several social policy domains, such as labour market policy and healthcare, the welfare regimes approach has only infrequently been used to address housing policy (for example, Barlow and Duncan, 1994; Hoekstra, 2003; Hulse, 2003). And the studies that have used it have often focused on only a few nations, or a single policy instrument – such as housing tenure (Kurz and Blossfeld, 2004), housing allowances (Kemp, 2007) or social/public housing (Priemus and Dieleman, 2002) – providing a more restricted form of comparison. Some researchers suggest that this relative neglect is partly because the housing policy area is anomalous and not as readily integrated into 'mainstream' welfare state research.

Housing policy: wobbly pillar or cornerstone of the welfare state?

In the 'Beveridge Report', and other social policy documents, the noted British economist and social reformer, William Beveridge (1942, 1943) sketched out his highly influential blueprint for the welfare state, identifying housing as a principal social policy pillar. However, several social policy analysts have suggested that, in practice, housing policy has rarely occupied such a central position. Qualifying Beveridge's metaphor, Ulf Torgersen (1987), for example, describes housing policy as a decidedly 'wobbly' welfare state pillar and highlights its institutional peculiarity. Other policy domains, he notes, such as healthcare and education, have fairly explicit standards that indicate when the institutions in charge are required to intervene, and specify the legal actions that may be taken if they fail to do so. They are also characterized by the presence of trained cadres of professionals, often divided into several occupational categories and specialities, and by the continuous delivery of services. Although these aspects are not entirely absent from housing policy, they are not nearly as pronounced there. For example, housing standards exist but, outside of critical, extreme cases, substandard conditions requiring action by public authorities, the nature of that action, or the repercussions for failing to act, are not very clearly delineated. Indeed, even very desperate circumstances, such as homelessness, may not be satisfactorily addressed or fully acknowledged via housing policy in many nations. Similarly, Michael Harloe (1995, p. 2), another housing policy analyst, points to housing policy's 'ambiguous and shifting status on the margins of the welfare state'. He depicts it as 'the least decommodified and the most market-determined of the conventionally accepted constituent elements of such states'. Unlike education and healthcare – two social services that are furnished for all citizens or residents by the welfare states in virtually every advanced capitalist nation – housing is not universally allocated by the state in *any* of them. Even the highly developed social democratic welfare states – including that in Sweden, the regime archetype – have been unable 'to manufacture a solidaristic housing policy' (Esping-Andersen, 1985, p. 246).

There are a number of reasons why states might opt to intervene in markets to provide housing for all residents or citizens in their nations. Compared to most other products on the market, dwellings are peculiarly complex commodities; each one is somewhat unique, spatially fixed, and must satisfy a bundle of specific needs, not just one. These characteristics and others, including attachment and transaction costs, create market imperfections that privilege sellers and landlords over buyers and tenants in housing markets. But there are many compelling arguments explaining why states have not provided universal housing and why housing is accessed via private markets right across the capitalist world. First, 'socialization' in the housing sphere constitutes a significantly greater threat to capitalists and capitalism than in most other policy domains. After all, it would require the state to gain ownership and control of a very significant amount of private property (real estate), impeding opportunities for profitability to a far greater extent than in other policy areas. Such public intervention would immediately mobilize intense resistance by powerful vested interests. Second, private housing markets have deep roots and long-established practices that militate against radical departures from existing traditions. Finally, because housing is a form of real property – an asset against which money can be borrowed – its cost can be met by relatively low payments over a long period of time. This situation enables larger numbers of people to purchase their homes instead of renting them, promoting greater 'commodification' (Harloe, 1995).

However, other housing policy analysts suggest that housing only appears to be a minor component, or 'wobbly pillar', of welfare states because there has been an undue overemphasis upon the level of social housing provided by the state. This orientation reveals little about the *quality* of housing provided but, more importantly, it incorrectly assumes that the provision of social housing is the only means of weakening market forces in housing markets, ignoring numerous other policy instruments and components of housing systems that may also serve to decommodify citizens (Malpass, 2008). In fact, most nations have introduced a wide range of supply side and demand side measures that can act as 'correctives' to housing markets and, to varying degrees, weaken people's dependence upon them (Bengtsson, 2001; Doling, 1999; Stephens and Fitzpatrick, 2008). *Supply side* measures are designed to address the level of the available housing stock in a nation, as well as its composition, quality, and price. States can correct deficiencies here in a number of ways beyond just providing or subsidizing social housing. They may furnish builders, developers, landlords, financiers and other producers or providers of housing with various forms of 'direct support', including grants, low-interest loans, public guarantees on loans, subsidized interest rates, and other 'bricks-and-mortar' benefits, and/or offer 'indirect support', including a wide range of tax relief measures. These producer subsidies may be available to both private and public providers of housing, including non-profit landlords, such as housing associations or local authorities (Kemp, 2007, 2000; Lujanen, 2004).

Demand side measures, in contrast, provide assistance directly to housing consumers (home buyers and home renters) to improve their position in housing markets. The most central and commonly employed type of consumer subsidies in most nations are housing allowances and other related forms of income assistance or cash benefits. But states may also provide a range of guarantees, subsidies, and tax exemptions to home purchasers, builders, and renovators. Access to housing can also be promoted by establishing and upholding rights to housing, or by introducing and enforcing rent controls and various other forms of regulations and protections for tenants and homeowners, including restrictions on evictions.

Housing policy networks and instruments

Welfare states comprise three distinct but closely interrelated networks of social support: 1) *income support* programmes (universal, non-contributory demogrants, social insurance, and means tested allowances, including housing allowances, as well as various forms of 'fiscal welfare'); 2) *social services* (such as education, healthcare, social housing, and related 'in-kind' provisions); and 3) *social legislation* (regulatory, protective and proactive social legislation, such as child protection laws, minimum wage laws, workplace health and safety legislation, rent controls, and protections against eviction, often collectively referred to as 'legal welfare'). Each of these three support systems is typically employed across a range of social policy domains, such as healthcare, family policy, old age policy, education, labour market policy, and housing policy, and each embraces a multiplicity of different policy instruments (Olsen, 2002). But their essence can vary significantly across national welfare states.

As noted above, there are numerous supply side and demand side housing policy instruments employed by states with varying impacts on inequality and decommodification. A brief overview of one central housing instrument from each of the three housing networks – housing allowances (an income support programme), social/public housing (a social service) and rent control (social legislation) is provided below. Their character, ability to decommodify, and impact varies markedly across nations, but some deviation from expectations generated by the welfare regimes typology is especially notable in the clustering of nations in some of the sub-areas of the housing domain.

Income support programmes: housing allowances

Most nations have introduced a variety of demand-side consumer subsidies to help households access housing, typically the single largest item in their budgets. The most common form of income supports are housing allowances. Housing allowances, and other housing supplements and 'top-ups', are usually means tested benefits provided to low-income families, and often targetted at particular demographic groups such as young people, families with children, people with disabilities, and pensioners. Housing allowance schemes may take varied forms, with different names, rules of eligibility, and levels of support across nations, but they are typically designed to help households access adequate housing, or reduce the share of their income devoted to housing expenditure (Åhrén, 2004; Ditch et al., 2001; Kemp, 2000; Lujanen, 2004). Many nations introduced them in the 1930s and 1940s and, in some of them, such as France, the UK and, especially, Sweden, they have markedly reduced the burden of rent for households living in poverty and promoted home ownership (Chen and Öst, 2005; Stephens, 2007). In many nations, such as Germany, France, and the Nordic countries, they are one component of the extensive packages of income benefits that are furnished. 'Implicit housing allowances', such as income-related rents and other forms of rent control, and a wide range of tax deductions, exemptions, and deferrals, are other measures that have been directed at housing consumers. Over the past few decades there has been a marked trend toward a greater reliance upon consumer subsidies, which have become the most central form of housing policy in many nations, and a corresponding movement away from the provision of social/public housing. At the same time, the accessibility and generosity of these allowances have become more restricted across most nations.

Social services: social/public housing

As noted above, evaluation of the housing policy domain as an undeveloped component of the welfare state is largely due to the observation that, unlike education or healthcare, no state provides housing for everyone. Nevertheless, 'social housing' has played a very important role in many of them. 'Social housing' is a broad term that refers to rental housing provided by the state, not-for profit organizations, or combinations of both. It is thus a more inclusive concept than 'public housing' which typically refers to rental housing that is owned and managed by the government at the central or local level. In the UK, social housing has been largely run by district and borough councils and referred to as 'council housing'. Although social rental housing existed earlier, most of the developed capitalist nations did not really begin to develop their social housing sectors until after World War II in an attempt to address severe shortages of affordable dwellings. Although it would never play more than a residual role in North America, it was central to post-World War II reconstruction in Europe, including the UK, where many nations faced substantial housing shortages due to the low levels of new construction and devastation caused by the war; in London alone, for example, over a million homes were destroyed or damaged by the Blitz.

Jim Kemeny (1995) identifies two forms of rental systems in industrialized capitalist societies, *unitary* and *dualist*. Nations with dualistic systems, have two very distinct rental markets, one that is 'open' and another that is 'protected'. The bulk of rental housing in these nations is provided in the open market, a private and largely unregulated sector. The protected market is a small, non-profit, state-subsidized public housing sector geared toward low-income households in need that does not compete with the large, open mainstream market. Dualistic systems exist in Anglo/'liberal' nations, such as Australia, Canada, the US, and the UK (a nation which has had a relatively large protected sector), as well as in the Mediterranean countries, and in some social democratic, Nordic countries, such as Finland and Norway (Kemeny, 1995, p. 66). Nations with unitary markets, in contrast, have single, integrated housing systems in which state-subsidized and not-for-profit housing compete directly with the private housing sector – a more encompassing and collectivist approach. Sweden, Germany, and the Netherlands are among the nations with unitary rental systems. Despite some overlap, Esping-Andersen's national clusters and the policy families that Kemeny identifies clearly do not entirely align here.

States have typically subsidized the provision of a certain quantity of housing at lower levels of rent than those available on the open market. While social housing sectors have always been 'supplemental' to the market, and have never accounted for more than a minor share of rental housing in any capitalist nation, they have been very significant in some nations. The way it has been organized, as suggested above, has differed markedly too. Sweden, for example, has never had the kind of targeted, residualized public housing and assisted housing sectors that exist in the US and other liberal nations. Instead, it created a non-profit housing sector after World War II. Its peak period was between 1965 and 1974 when a million dwellings were constructed via the 'million programme'. Like Denmark, Sweden has a 'unitary' rental market (Bengtsson, 2001, 2008; Kemeny, 2001). Virtually all its social housing is organized by municipal housing companies, with boards that are appointed by local authorities and, unlike in nations with 'liberal' or 'dualistic' housing markets that target the most vulnerable, it is open to everyone ('universal'). However, the municipal companies have long had a 'moral and political obligation' to cater to all types of households and, in practice, 'this has meant that socially-deprived households are over-represented in the municipal stocks' (Turner, 1999, p. 694; Magnusson and Turner, 2008). The past few decades have been marked by a stark decline in the state provision of social housing across most capitalist nations, reflecting a 'recommodification' of the housing market. In the Netherlands, the nation with the highest proportion of social rented housing, about 35 per cent of housing stock has taken this form. But in both Sweden and the UK, the nations with next highest proportions of social rented housing in the 1990s (at 24 and 22 per cent respectively), it has declined to about 18 per cent, approximately the same size as in Finland (17 per cent), one of the first nations to introduce public housing (Daly, 1999; Fitzpatrick and Stephens, 2007; Tähtinen, 2003).

Social legislation: rent control

Rent controls are based on an understanding that there is a significant power asymmetry between landlords and tenants. Tenants generally have less information about rental units and, once they have settled in, typically want to avoid the considerable costs of moving again. Rent controls provide some degree of protection from arbitrary and extortionate price-gouging and from retaliatory rent increases when tenants legitimately complain that the conditions of their home are grossly substandard. While a range of tax deductions and exemptions are typically available to landlords and home-owners, rent controls are often the only support tax-paying tenants can access. Rent controls also leave tenants with more money to spend to support local businesses and encourages them to renovate and improve their homes without fear that landlords will increase their rent because their units have increased in value.

Rent controls, which were introduced in some form in most nations across the developed capitalist world in an attempt to make housing more accessible and secure, have become more contentious in many jurisdictions in recent years. Opponents argue that they reduce the quantity and quality of available housing because they curtail incentives for builders to construct new housing and for landlords to maintain their existing properties. Their proponents, however, argue that even if the old post-World War II 'hard' rent controls had such an effect – and most vehemently dispute this – the newer 'soft' measures implemented since the 1970s do not. These 'second-generation' controls are much more flexible. They guarantee a fair return and allow landlords automatically to raise their rents with inflation, and when increases are justified by maintenance and improvement costs. Moreover, they typically exempt vacated units ('vacancy decontrol') and new rental housing, so they do not provide disincentives.

Nations with relatively large rental sectors, such as Sweden, the Netherlands, Germany, and Denmark, have strict rent controls in place, while those in Finland, New Zealand, the UK, and the US are much more lax (although some American cities, such as New York, have long histories with hard and soft rent controls). Other nations, including Canada, Italy, France, and Norway, fall between these two poles. Specific regulations regulating contractual aspects of tenant–landlord relations have also been much stricter in nations such as Sweden, Austria, and France, than in Norway, the UK, or the US. Many nations have eliminated or relaxed rent control legislation with the rise of neo-liberalism over the past two decades, leading to higher rates of evictions (Arnott, 1995; OECD, 2011; Stenberg et al., 2011).

Housing and inequality

With considerable cross-national variation, marked housing disparities are manifest across various facets, including housing access and ownership patterns, housing standards (the condition and security of dwellings, the presence or absence of basic amenities and services), and the character of neighbourhoods (including how safe they are and the accessibility of good schools and libraries, recreation centres and parks, grocery stores and shopping centres, and public transportation networks). These inequalities are closely associated with poverty, homelessness and numerous other imbricated dimensions of inequality, such as income, wealth, health, education, employment, social status, social exclusion and segregation, and other related social problems. For most families their homes are the primary form of wealth that they will possess, and there is tremendous variation in their value. Many families live in substandard, insecure housing, in homeless shelters, or on the streets. Substandard housing conditions have long been identified as a root of illness and disease. Mounting evidence amassed over the past two decades indicates that decent, affordable housing is not only critical to family health and well-being, it can also significantly improve educational outcomes for children (Lubell and Brennan 2007; Lubell, Crain and Cohen 2007).

Housing disparities are typically expressed across the same familiar fault lines and mutually embedded categories – including class, sex/gender, marital status, family size, race, ethnicity, national origin, religion, age, ability, and sexual orientation – evident with most other social inequalities. Certain groups are much more likely to be poorly or insecurely housed because of structured patterns of inequality and institutionalized power relations which foster conditions that render them much more vulnerable (Olsen, 2011). Women, for example, have both a heightened need for affordable housing, *and* more difficulty accessing it, because they have also had lower incomes than men and greater responsibility for children across virtually every nation. Evictions reflecting these and many other socio-economic disadvantages and conditions, including domestic violence, are among the most salient causes of their high rates of homelessness. Within this socio-economic context women have been much more reliant upon social/public housing, family and housing allowances, and other state supports, and they have been especially adversely affected by neo-liberal retrenchment over the past few decades (Kennett and Kam Wah, 2011; Somerville and Sprigings, 2005).

Housing disparities have also been closely linked to 'race', ethnicity, and nativity in most countries. Structural racism, formal and informal policies and practices in housing departments, institutions and agencies, and the discriminatory attitudes, assessments, preferences and practices of landlords, developers, real estate brokers and others in housing markets, have resulted in a wide range of housing inequalities and disadvantages for racialized groups, visible and ethnic minorities, new immigrants and refugees across much of Europe and North America. These inequalities include difficulties obtaining financing, lower rates of home ownership, a higher possession of old, substandard inner city properties that are costly to maintain, over-representation in dilapidated, overcrowded rental housing, exclusion from housing waiting lists, segregation in impoverished inner city neighbourhoods, and proportionately higher rates of evictions and homelessness. While ubiquitous, racial disparities in housing have been especially pronounced in some nations, such as the United States (e.g., Krivo and Kaufman, 2004).

The assumption that blacks and whites would live in separate neighbourhoods was long supported by Jim Crow laws in the South and, in large Northern urban centres, such as Chicago, Detroit, New York and Seattle, by 'racial restrictive covenants' – private, enforceable agreements between sellers and buyers of property not to sell, rent or lease property to specified minority groups, most commonly blacks (Jones-Correa, 2000–2001). These agreements, which became increasingly common after the US Supreme Court declared that existing city segregation ordinances were unconstitutional in 1917, allowed landlords, sub-division developers, and real estate operators legally to bar blacks and other groups from owning or occupying property in particular neighbourhoods. Moreover, because the covenants were frequently enforceable on subsequent sales and purchases of the same properties, their impact was enduring. It was not until 1948 that racial restrictive covenants were also declared unconstitutional. In 1968 the federal *Fair Housing Act* (Title VIII of the *Civil Rights Act*) more explicitly prohibited discrimination across a wide range of housing practices related to sales, rentals, the provision of insurance, and mortgage financing on the basis of race, colour and national origin, but racial steering, redlining and other entrenched discriminatory practices that long restricted access to loans, services, and neighbourhoods, helped to ensure that large numbers of blacks and other minority groups would continue to reside in slums, ghettos and segregated housing projects and have markedly lower home ownership rates and higher rates of homelessness.

Even in nations with much more developed welfare states and housing supports than those in the US, immigrants, refugees and minorities may reside in segregated mono-ethnic or multi-ethnic enclaves and exist on the economic margins. Focusing upon eight European nations, Koopmans (2010) suggests that it is the *interaction* between integration policies and social policies and welfare states that is pivotal here. He argues that in nations with developed welfare states and restrictive cultural policies (such as Germany, Austria, Switzerland and France) immigrants are, in effect, compelled by the state to desegregate and assimilate while in nations with multicultural policies but weak welfare states (such as the UK) it is markets that push them to do so. The combination of generous welfare states and multicultural policies in social democratic nations (such as Sweden, Belgium and the Netherlands) he somewhat counter-intuitively suggests, inadvertently fosters continued segregation among newcomers. Another cross-national study examining sixteen European nations found the highest degree of segregation in 'liberal' cities and the lowest levels in 'corporatist' cities and Latin Rim cities, with 'social democratic' cities occupying an intermediate position (Arbaci, 2007).

Homelessness

Homelessness is an extreme form of poverty, deprivation, and social exclusion, and one of the most momentous manifestations of housing inequality. Like other housing disparities, it is very closely linked to gender, race, and ethnicity, with disproportionately higher rates among the same familiar groups. There is no universal definition of homelessness and, as with poverty, nations can vary markedly in the ways that they define, measure and collect data on it. However, for a variety of political and technical reasons, most national studies tend to underestimate the levels of homelessness that exist.

The United Nations distinguishes two broad ways of conceptualizing homelessness, absolute and relative. *Absolute* homelessness refers to the absence of any shelter at all. This term encompasses people who live on the streets and in parks in the day and sleep on sidewalks, or in tunnels, abandoned buildings and vehicles or other public places at night. This narrow understanding fits the popular, often negative, image of 'acute' or 'literal' homelessness in the media, although the majority of people in this group typically try to stay out of sight. *Relative* homelessness is a much broader category that includes other forms of homelessness that may be hidden as well, including people who live in temporary accommodations, such as shelters, or who temporarily and involuntarily 'couch surf' or 'double up', living in the basements and sleeping on the floors and couches of friends and or family members. Strictly speaking, they are not without shelter but their residence is short-term and insecure, and it does not provide privacy. In some nations, such as the Nordic countries, people with insecure housing, including those without legal tenancy, those living under the constant threat of eviction, those in institutions (such as psychiatric hospitals or prisons), those subject to physical violence and abuse, and those living in substandard or inadequate housing conditions that are hazardous to their health, are also included among the homeless.

Although homelessness remains an urgent social problem in virtually every nation, there is notable cross-national variation in the ways that states have addressed it and in the impact of their policies and approaches. The incidence and severity of homelessness is much greater in nations with higher levels of poverty and less developed and inclusive welfare states, such as the Anglo nations. The welfare states in countries such as the UK, Canada and, especially, the US, are much less effective at reducing rates of poverty than those in the Nordic countries and most other European nations (Olsen, 2011, 2002; Smeeding, 2005). Finland in particular has effected a remarkable and steady decline in its level of homelessness since 1987, in part because of its commitment to 'housing first'. And while homelessness remains a very serious concern in nations such as Sweden and Finland, the position of the homeless there is strengthened through national constitutions and various other Acts, that indicate a 'right to housing'. These laws and principles may prove very useful in their fights against homelessness in the future (Helenlund 2008). In the Anglo nations, and many other nations, in stark contrast, the higher rates of homelessness encouraged by the rising levels of inequality and poverty, gentrification, social policy retrenchment, and the lifting of rent controls, among other neo-liberal measures, has been fortified by a raft of new laws criminalizing homelessness, denying public space to the most vulnerable members of society who already have no private space.

Conclusion

Debates about policy convergence or divergence have been a mainstay in the welfare state/social policy literature. Early accounts of housing policy suggested that, as in the other policy domains of the welfare state, economic development and growth and demographic change would be the central forces shaping it, gradually fostering policy convergence. However, 'politics' and culture have mattered a great deal more than anticipated, resulting in considerable variation across, and within, policy regimes in the housing domain. This chapter suggests that, despite some notable areas of convergence, such as the movement away from social housing toward consumer subsidies and a general rise in levels inequality including housing disparities and homelessness, significant cross-national variation can still be observed in the character and impact of housing policy.

References

Åhrén, P. (2004), 'Housing Allowances', in M. Lujanen (ed.), *Housing and Housing Policy in the Nordic Countries*, pp. 179–202. Copenhagen: Norden.

Andrews, D. and Caldera Sánchez, A. (2011), *Drivers of Homeownership Rates in Selected OECD Countries* (OECD Economics Department Working Paper No. 849). Paris: OECD.

Arbaci, S. (2007), Ethnic Segregation, Housing Systems and Welfare Regimes in Europe. *European Journal of Housing Policy* 7(4), pp. 401–33.

Arnott, R. (1995), Time for Revisionism on Rent Control? *Journal of Economic Perspectives* 9(1), pp. 99–120.

Barlow, J. and Duncan, S. (1994), *Success and Failure in Housing Provision: European Systems Compared*, Oxford: Elsevier/Pergamon.

Bengtsson, B. (2001), Housing as a Social Right: Implications for Welfare State Theory. *Scandinavian Political Studies* 24(4), pp. 255–75.

——(2008), 'Why so different?: Housing Regimes and Path Dependence in Five Nordic Countries', unpublished paper presented at the European Network for Housing Research International Research Conference, Dublin.

Beveridge, W. H. (1942), *Social Insurance and Allied Services*. London: HMSO.

——(1943), *The Pillars of Security and Other War-Time Essays and Addresses*. London: George Allen and Unwin.

Castles, F. (1998a), *Comparative Public Policy*. Cheltenhem: Edward Elgar.

——(1998b), The Really Big Trade-Off: Home Ownership and the Welfare State in the New World and the Old. *Acta Politica* 32(1), pp. 163–85.

Castles, F. and Ferrera M. (1996), Home Ownership and the Welfare State: Is Southern Europe Different? *South European Society and Politics* 1(2), pp. 163–85.

Chen, J. and Enström Öst, C. (2005), Housing Allowance and the Recipient's Home Ownership: Evidence From a Panel Data Study in Sweden. *Housing Studies* 20(4), pp. 605–25.

Conley, D. and Gifford B. (2006), Home Ownership, Social Insurance and the Welfare State. *Sociological Forum* 21(1), pp. 55–82.

Daly, M. (1999), 'Regimes of Social Policy and the Patterning of Homelessness', in D. Avramov (ed.), *Coping with Homelessness: Issues to be Tackled and Best Practices in Europe*, pp. 309–30. Aldershot: Ashgate.

Dash, E. (2011), 'As Lenders Hold Homes in Foreclosure, Sales are Hurt'. *The New York Times*, May 22.

Ditch, J., Lewis, A. and Wilcox, S. (2001), *Social Housing, Tenure and Housing Allowance: An International Review*, In-house Report no. 83, Department of Work and Pensions, York University, UK.

Doling, J. (1999), De-commodification and Welfare: Evaluating Housing Systems. *Housing, Theory and Society* 16(4), pp. 156–64.

Esping-Andersen, G. (1990), *The Three Worlds of Welfare Capitalism*, Princeton, NJ: Princeton University Press.

——(1985), *Politics Against Markets*, Princeton, NJ: Princeton University Press.

Fitzpatrick, S. and Stephens, M. (2007), *An International Review of Homelessness and Social Housing Policy*. London: Department for Communities and Local Government.

Harloe, M. (1995), *The People's Home: Social Rented Housing in Europe and America*. Oxford: Blackwell.

Heady, B. (1978), *Housing Policy in the Developed Economy: The UK, Sweden and the US*. New York: St. Martin's Press.

Heidenheimer, A. J., Heclo, H. and Adams, C. T. (1990), *Comparative Public Policy: The Politics of Social Choice in America, Europe and Japan*, 3rd edn. London: Macmillan Press.

Hoekstra, J. (2003), Housing and the Welfare State in the Netherlands: An Application of Esping-Andersen's Typology. *Housing, Theory and Society* 20(2), pp. 58–71.

Hudson, I. (2009), 'From Deregulation to Crisis', in J. Guard and W. Antony (eds), *Bankruptcies and Bailouts*. Blackpoint Nova Scotia: Fernwood Publishing.

Hulchanski, D. (2006), 'What Factors Shape Canadian Housing Policy: The Intergovernmental Role in Canada's Housing System', in R. Young and C. Leuprecht (eds), *Canada: The State of the Federation 2004: Municipal-Federal-Provincial Relations*, pp. 221–47. Montréal and Kingston: McGill-Queen's University Press.

Hulse, K. (2003), Housing Allowances and Private Renting in Liberal Welfare Regimes. *Housing Theory and Society* 20(1), pp. 28–42.

Jones-Correa, M. (2000–2001), The Origins and Diffusion of Racial Restrictive Covenants. *Political Science Quarterly* 115(4), pp. 541–68

Kemeny, J. (2001), Comparative Housing and Welfare: Theorising the Relationship. *Journal of Housing and the Built Environment* 16(1), pp. 53–70.

——(1995), *From Public Housing to the Social Market: Rental Policy Strategies in Comparative Perspective*, London: Routledge.

——(1992), *Housing and Social Theory*, London: Routledge.
——(1981), *The Myth of Home Ownership: Private Versus Public Choices in Housing Tenure*, London: Routledge and Kegan Paul.
Kemp, P. A. (ed.) (2007), *Housing Allowances in Comparative Perspective*, Bristol: The Policy Press.
——(2000), The Role and Design of Income-Related Housing Allowances. *International Social Security Review* 53(3), pp. 43–57.
Kennet, P. and Wah, C. K. (eds) (2011), *Women and Housing: An International Analysis*, London: Routledge.
Koopmans, R. (2010), Trade-offs Between Equality and Difference: Immigrant Integration, Multiculturalism and the Welfare State in Cross-National Perspective. *Journal of Ethnic and Migration Studies* 36(1), pp. 1–26.
Krivo, Kauren J. and Robert L. Kaufman (2004), Housing and Wealth Inequality: Racial-Ethnic Differences in Home Equity in the United States. *Demography* 41(3), pp. 585–605.
Kurz, K. and Blossfeld H.-P. (2004), 'Introduction: Social Stratification, Welfare Regimes and Access to Home Ownership', in K. Kurz and H.-P. Blossfeld (eds), *Home Ownership and Social Inequality in Comparative Perspective*, pp. 1–20. Stanford, CA: Stanford University Press.
Lowe, S. (2004), *Housing Policy Analysis*, Basingstoke: Palgrave.
Lubell, J. and Brennan, M. (2007), *The Positive Impacts of Affordable Housing on Education: A Research Summary*, Washington, DC: Center for Housing Policy and Enterprise Community Partners.
Lubell, J., Crain, R. and Cohen, R. (2007), *The Positive Impacts of Affordable Housing on Health: A Research Summary*, Washington, DC: Center for Housing Policy and Enterprise Community Partners.
Lujanen, M. (2004), 'Various Forms of Financial Support', in M. Lujanen (ed.), *Housing and Housing Policy in the Nordic Countries*, pp. 99–123. Copenhagen: Norden.
Magnusson, L. and Turner, B. (2008), 'Municipal Housing Companies in Sweden – Social by Default'. *Housing Theory and Society* 25(4), pp. 275–96.
Malpass, P. (2008), 'Housing and the New Welfare State: Wobbly Pillar or Cornerstone?'. *Housing Studies* 23(1), pp. 1–109.
Malpass, P. and Murie, A. (1999), *Housing Policy and Practice* (5th edn), Hampshire: Palgrave Macmillan.
Organisation for Economic Co-operation and Development (OECD) (2011), 'Housing and the Economy: Policies for Renovation', in *Economic Policy Reforms 2011: Going for Growth*, Paris: OECD.
Olsen, G. M. (2011), *Power and Inequality: A Comparative Introduction*, Toronto: Oxford University Press.
——(2007), 'Toward Global Welfare State Convergence?: Family Policy and Health Care in Sweden'. Canada and the United States; *Journal of Sociology and Welfare* XXXIV(2): 143–64.
——(2008), 'Labour Market Policy Convergence in the United States, Canada and Sweden'. *Social Policy and Administration* 42(4): 323–41.
——(2002), *The Politics of the Welfare State: Canada, Sweden and the United States*, Toronto: Oxford University Press.
Priemus, H. and Dieleman, F. (2002), 'Social Housing in the European Union: Past, Present and Perspectives'. *Urban Studies* 39(2), pp. 191–200 (special issue on social housing).
Ronald, R. (2008), *The Ideology of Home Ownership: Homeowner Societies and the Role of Housing*, Hampshire: Palgrave Macmillan.
Smeeding, T. M. (2005), 'Public Policy, Economic Inequality, and Poverty: The United States in Comparative Perspective'. *Social Science Quarterly* 86 (Supplement), pp. 955–83.
Smith, L. B., Rosen, K. T. and G. Fallis (1988), 'Recent Developments in Economic Models of Housing Markets' *Journal of Economic Literature* XXVI (March), pp. 29–64.
Somerville, P. and Sprigings N. (eds) (2005), *Housing and Social Policy: Contemporary Themes and Critical Perspectives*, London: Routledge.
Stenberg, S.-Å., van Doorn, L. and Gerull, S. (2011), 'Locked Out in Europe: A Comparative Analysis of Evictions Due to Rent Arrears in Germany, the Netherlands and Sweden'. *European Journal of Homelessness* 5(2), pp. 39–61.
Stephens, M. (2007), 'Necessary, Contingent or Independent? Exploring the Relationship Between Welfare Regimes and Housing Outcomes in Europe', unpublished paper presented at the European Network for Housing Research Comparative Housing Policy Workshop, Dublin, April 2007.
Stephens, M. and Fitzpatrick, S. (2008), Welfare Regimes, Housing Systems and Homelessness: How are They Linked?. *European Journal of Homelessness* 2, pp. 201–12.
Tähtinen, T. (2003), Financing Social Housing in Finland. *Housing Finance International*, June, pp. 22–26.

Torgersen, U. (1987), 'Housing: The Wobbly Pillar Under the Welfare State', in B. Turner, J. Kemeny and L. J. Lundqvist (eds), *Between State and Market: Housing in a Post-Industrial Era*, pp. 116–26. Stockholm: Almqvist and Wiksell.

Turner, B. (1999), Social Housing Finance in Sweden. *Urban Studies* 36(4), pp. 683–97.

Williams, F. (1977), *Why the Poor Pay More*, London: Macmillan Press.

33
Healthcare

Claus Wendt

Introduction

This chapter provides insights into one of modern society's most crucial arenas. Compared with other social policy fields, health policy concentrates less on benefits in cash and more on services (see also Chapter 9). Service provision is of great importance when analysing healthcare. Furthermore, governance and regulation in healthcare demonstrate major conflicts due to the presence of influential interest groups. While healthcare expenditure, financing, and provision can be assessed on the basis of quantitative data, analysing regulation and governance requires a combination of qualitative and quantitative data and methods. In this chapter, we first discuss core concepts of comparing healthcare policy and politics. We then assess developments in expenditure and healthcare provision. Finally, we discuss regulations in different healthcare systems and how regulation is related to patients' access to healthcare. We provide information for 32 Organisation for Economic Co-operation and Development (OECD) countries and reveal which countries are more successful in controlling costs as well as in translating monetary inputs into healthcare provision.

Core concepts in comparative health policy analysis

Comparative studies of health policy and politics can be distinguished by whether they focus on health policy actors and reform or on healthcare systems. The first group of studies concentrates on the role of political institutions, health policy decision-makers, and organized interests in health reform. The second group of studies analyses and compares institutions and characteristics of healthcare systems. In the following section, we discuss some of the most influential concepts in both clusters of writing.

Immergut's (1992) comparison of France, Sweden, and Switzerland still sets the standard for studying the role of political institutions and actors in healthcare reform. She focused on the veto potential of interest groups in different settings and showed that veto opportunities arise out of the specific features of political institutions. Her study suggests that the impact of physicians' organizations on health policy may have been much less decisive than was generally believed until the late 1980s. Immergut concluded that veto points in the political system are of greater importance than veto groups within society. Similarly, but with more emphasis on process tracing, Hacker (1998) analysed how political institutions systematically channel the way in which ideas and interests shape political debates and decision-making. His study of the historical sequence and timing of health policy change in Britain, Canada, and the United States clearly supports the policy importance of historical legacies and therefore the path-dependence thesis. A country's health policy path, he contended, is significantly influenced, first, by whether a sizable part of the population is enrolled in private plans before national health insurance is on the political agenda; second, by whether public health plans be targeted at residual populations from the outset; and third, by whether medical care be a substantial industry before the universal health insurance is politically salient. The United States fails on all three conditions, a fact that Hacker used to explain the much higher barriers to universal healthcare.

Other concepts have concentrated on governance and regulation. Tuohy (1999) provides the most theoretical approach to models of governance. She proposed that the dominant model of accountability in healthcare changed from agency to contract models and may currently shift toward complex networks. In the older, trust-based, principal–agent relationship, the state (the principal) delegated authority for the regulation and distribution of healthcare to the medical profession (the agent). As a result of better access to information, the medical profession dominated this model of governance until the end of the twentieth century. New information technologies, however, have provided governments with better information, reducing the information asymmetry between the state and the medical profession. Thus, a transformation from an agency to a contract model has taken place in many countries. In a contract model, the state's role is to purchase rather than to simply finance healthcare. The medical profession's loss of autonomy is due less to cost pressures than to the way in which the provision and verification of detailed medical information strengthens governments' power.

In his concept of 'the health care state', Moran (1999) classified healthcare systems according to three governing concepts: consumption, provision, and production. By consumption, Moran refers to patients' basis of eligibility for access to healthcare and to financing mechanisms. The provision dimension encompasses the control of hospitals and doctors, and the production dimension encompasses mechanisms that regulate medical innovation. Based on these dimensions, Moran constructed four types of healthcare states: the 'entrenched command-and-control state' (Scandinavian countries, Great Britain); the 'supply state' (United States); the 'corporatist state' (Germany); and the 'insecure command-and-control state' (Greece, Portugal). 'Supply states' are dominated by provider interests in all three dimensions, and this domination of suppliers, not the operation of market principles, is the primary problem with American healthcare. In 'command-and-control states,' on the other hand, the state is distinctive in all three governing concepts. Although they provide universal healthcare in legal terms, Southern Europe's 'insecure command-and-control states' lack the administrative capacities for guaranteeing universal coverage and equal access to care – principles that have characterized the Nordic countries and Great Britain for many decades. In 'corporatist healthcare states,' finally, public-law bodies and doctors' associations are dominant.

Wendt, Frisina, and Rothgang (2009) suggested a conceptual framework that simultaneously measures the role of the state in financing, service provision, and regulation compared with private and societal actors (see also Rothgang et al., 2010). Three ideal-type healthcare systems were identified: 'state healthcare systems,' in which the state is dominant in financing, provision, and regulation; 'societal healthcare systems,' in which societal actors such as social insurance funds are dominant in all three dimensions; and 'private healthcare systems,' in which all three dimensions fall under the auspices of private for-profit actors. Along with each category of ideal-type, six combinations of mixed types were identified for which state, societal, or private actors and institutions are dominant in two dimensions. Six additional combinations do not approach any of the three ideal-types. Comparative studies that apply this methodological framework or similar concepts may produce richer descriptive portraits. Germany, for instance, does not represent an ideal-type societal (or corporatist) model as suggested by Moran (2000) since healthcare services are mainly provided by private actors and institutions. According to this methodology, Central and Eastern European countries (CEE) that have replaced their former socialist healthcare systems with social insurance represent state-based health policy. The social insurance actors in these countries are weak, and healthcare services are in fact largely provided by public institutions.

Such studies of health policy decision-making need to be distinguished analytically from the analysis of healthcare systems (Marmor and Wendt, 2011). While studies of health policy decision-making focus on political institutions, actors, and reform, comparative studies of healthcare systems concentrate on financing and expenditure, regulation, health employment, and the provision of healthcare (Figure 33.1). The focus in the analysis of healthcare systems is on the institutional setting of different types of healthcare systems, and some studies link the analysis of healthcare institutions with the analysis of outcomes such as access to healthcare, satisfaction with healthcare systems, and health inequality. Due to the explicit or implicit focus on the living conditions in different institutional settings, the comparative study of healthcare systems is closer to the general welfare state debate than research of health policy decision-making (see Chapters 1 and 2 of this handbook).

Traditional models of healthcare comparison have mainly used the official labels of existing healthcare systems and have contrasted a social health insurance (Bismarckian) type with a National Health Service (Beveridgean) type, Germany being an example of the former and Great Britain of the latter. Analytically, however, it does not make much sense to use these terms for healthcare system comparison. First of all, they do not measure healthcare system change. Despite great changes, the German health insurance system (SHI) of 1883 and the British National Health Service (NHS) of 1946 still carry their labels from the time of origin. Second and more importantly, the labels suggest a certain mode of financing combined with a certain mode of governance: In SHI, healthcare is financed by social health insurance contributions and regulated by social insurance institutions through mutual self-governance; in NHS, tax financing and hierarchical state regulation are used. For empirical comparative studies, however, the labels SHI and NHS are not a useful tool. In Central and Eastern Europe, for instance, SHI schemes have been established in the early 1990s but lack a system of self-governance that is typical for the German model. Southern European countries have established NHS systems that, as Moran (2000) correctly observed, lack the administrative capacities of the British

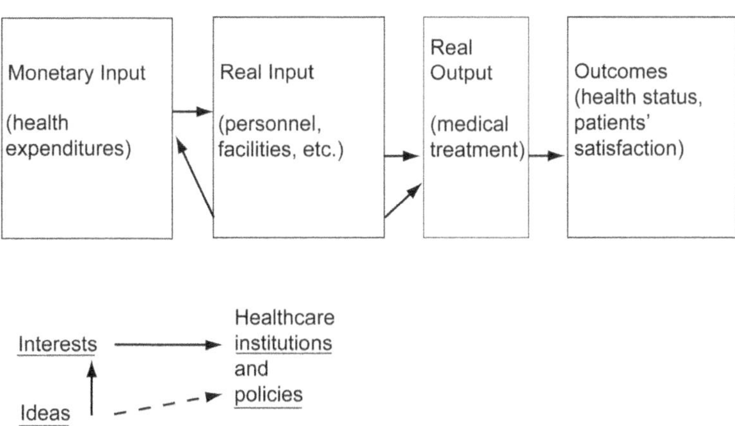

Figure 33.1 Ideas, interests, and institutions in healthcare
Source: Marmor and Wendt, 2011: xxv.

archetype. The Scandinavian countries set up NHS schemes that typically endowed the regional and local levels with much greater responsibilities than was the case in the hierarchical British system.

Only recently have concepts for comparing healthcare systems been suggested that do not imply a certain type of governance. Instead, these concepts have introduced a particular focus on patients' access to healthcare (Wendt, 2009; Reibling, 2010). According to Reibling (2010, p. 5), 'putting access at the centre of a health typology strengthens a patients' perspective and thereby the impact of health services on individual health.' The patient-oriented concepts aim at providing a better understanding of the relationship among healthcare systems, access to healthcare services, and health outcomes. They do not, however, directly measure the effects of healthcare systems on health status or other outcomes.

Wendt (2009) used the following criteria for classifying healthcare systems: total healthcare expenditure; the public–private mix of healthcare financing; private out-of-pocket payment; out-patient healthcare provision; in-patient healthcare provision; entitlement to healthcare; remuneration of medical doctors; and patients' access to healthcare providers. Based on these criteria, three types of healthcare systems were distinguished by cluster analysis: a 'health service provision-oriented type,' characterized by a high number of healthcare providers and free access for patients to medical doctors (Austria, Belgium, France, Germany, and Luxembourg); a 'universal coverage-controlled access type' in which healthcare is a social citizenship right and equal access to healthcare is of higher importance than freedom of choice (Denmark, Great Britain, Sweden, Italy, and Ireland); and a 'low budget-restricted access type,' with limited financial resources for healthcare and in which patients' access to healthcare is restricted by high private co-payments and through the regulation that patients have to sign up on a general practitioner's (GP) list for a longer period of time (Finland, Portugal, and Spain).

Reibling (2010) focused even more on patients' access to the supply of healthcare services and used the criteria of gatekeeping, cost-sharing, provider density (GPs, specialists, and nurses), and medical technology (magnetic resonance imaging units/MRI, computed tomography scanners/CT). Classifying European healthcare systems by these criteria, she arrived at four types: 'financial incentives states,' which regulate patients' access to medical doctors mainly by cost-sharing (Austria, Belgium, France, Sweden, and Switzerland); 'strong gatekeeping and low supply states,' with no cost-sharing but extensive gatekeeping arrangements for doctor's visits, low numbers of healthcare providers, and little medical technology (Denmark, Great Britain, the Netherlands, Poland, and Spain); 'weakly regulated and high supply states,' with weak gatekeeping and a high supply of healthcare providers (the Czech Republic, Germany, and Greece); and 'mixed regulation states' that combine gatekeeping and cost-sharing arrangements (Finland, Italy, and Portugal).

The concepts discussed in this section provide a sample of ways to comparatively analyse health policy and politics (see also Marmor and Wendt, 2011). Conceptual frameworks have been designed that, relative to a specific research question, capture either the relevance of political institutions and political and corporate actors in healthcare reform or the main institutional differences of healthcare systems. Cross-border learning requires fundamentally theoretical comparisons with an analytical framework that captures the relevant institutional characteristics and healthcare reforms on the basis of a standardized set of indicators. However, such sophisticated studies have often covered only a small set of countries and a limited time span (Marmor, Freeman, and Okma 2005). The typologies of health policy and politics presented in this chapter may provide a tool for the inclusion of a greater number of countries in comparative studies. They may also provide the basis for better combining macro- and micro-research in comparative studies on both the consequences of health policy decision-making and healthcare systems.

Healthcare expenditure, financing, and service provision

Conceptual frameworks and studies facilitate the understanding of developments in modern healthcare systems. The important developments described in this section are related to healthcare expenditure, financing, and provision.

Healthcare represents a particularly costly part of the welfare state. From 1970 to 2009, total healthcare expenditure (THE) as a percentage of the gross domestic product (GDP) increased at average from 5.2 to 10.0 per cent in OECD countries (OECD Health Data, 2012, p. 26; see Figure 33.2). When including countries from Central and Eastern Europe (CEE), the 2009 average is somewhat lower at 9.7 per cent (OECD Health Data, 2012; not shown).

Turkey has been the country with the lowest level of THE for almost the entire period but has seen a steep increase since the mid-1990s up to a level of 6.0 per cent of GDP in 2009. The other side of the spectrum is represented by the United States, with a level of 17.4 per cent of GDP in 2009. The distance between the United States and the OECD average has grown dramatically from 1.9 percentage points in 1970 to 7.4 percentage points in 2009. In Figure 33.2, three additional countries are presented that are often taken as exemplary cases in welfare state and healthcare system research. Great Britain remained below the OECD average for the entire period under study. However, the expenditure level increased to a greater extent compared with the OECD average since the implementation of market principles in the early 1990s. Later, the British government even announced to increase healthcare expenditure with the goal

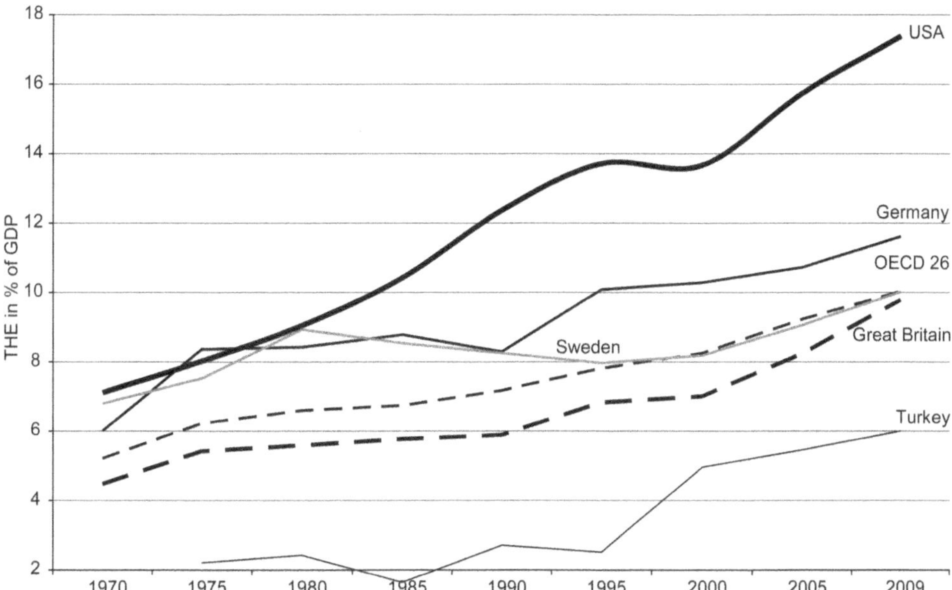

Figure 33.2 Total Health Expenditure (THE) as a percentage of GDP, 1970–2009

Notes: OECD 26: OECD countries excluding Chile, Mexico, and CEE countries; USA: country with highest THE; Turkey: country with lowest THE.

Source: OECD Health Data, 2012.

of reaching the average of OECD countries, which the country almost achieved in 2009 (Mays, Dixon, and Jones, 2011). In Germany, on the other hand, THE has always been above the OECD mean and was even higher than that of the United States in 1975. The period between 1975 and 1990, however, was one of cost containment reforms Germany, and only following its reunification did the country again face a steep expenditure increase. Other countries have been more successful in stabilizing healthcare costs. THE as a percentage of GDP was even reduced from 1980 to 2000 in Sweden, Denmark, Ireland, and Israel, partly related to a prosperous economic development (OECD Health Data, 2012). Sweden joined the group of high-cost healthcare systems in the 1970s and reached the OECD 26 average by the 1990s. Rothgang et al. (2010) have observed a catch-up of low-spending nations and therefore a convergence of OECD countries with respect to THE and to public health expenditure (PHE).

Healthcare is mainly financed by public money, which mirrors high public responsibility in the field of healthcare. Despite scarce resources, the state is not on the retreat in real terms. More public resources are invested in OECD healthcare systems every year (measured per cent of GDP and in US$ per head). However, since public financing has been increased to a lower extent than private financing, a relative retreat of the state from almost 80 per cent in 1980 to 75 per cent in 2005 has taken place (Rothgang et al., 2010).

More specifically, the sources of healthcare financing can be categorized into taxes, social insurance contributions, private insurance contributions, and private out-of-pocket payments. Thirteen OECD healthcare systems are financed mainly out of taxes, led by Great Britain, Sweden, and Denmark with tax financing of more than 80 per cent. Eighteen countries are mainly financed out of social insurance contributions, with the Czech Republic, France, and the Netherlands having the highest share, more than 70 per cent. Among OECD countries, the United States represents the only example in which private insurance is the financing instrument of first choice, and Mexico is the only example in which healthcare is predominantly financed out-of-pocket by patients (no data are available for Chile) (OECD Health Data, 2012). The overall share of public financing has slightly decreased in tax-financed systems and increased in social insurance-financed systems since the early 1980s (Rothgang et al., 2010). Direct private payments have remained quite stable on average. Most CEE countries, however, have increased direct private payments to a large extent since 1990. In Hungary, the Slovak Republic, and (outside the CEE) also in Switzerland, private out-of-pocket payments represent about a quarter of the total healthcare budget and arguably have a negative effect on access to healthcare, particularly for low-income groups and frequent users such as the chronically ill. Other countries, such as South Korea and Turkey, have reduced out-of-pocket payments. Despite wide public debates over user charges, we do not see a considerable individualization of social risks in most OECD healthcare systems. However, there is also no evidence that user charges successfully reduce costs without establishing barriers to necessary healthcare, as is often claimed (Marmor and Wendt, 2011).

In times of retrenchment, it becomes evident that healthcare systems with a strong role of the state, not user charges, are more successful in stabilizing healthcare costs. The role of the state can be estimated by measuring the public share of healthcare financing (Moran, 2000). In the 1970s, there was no correlation between the public share in healthcare financing and the level of THE in per cent of GDP. Countries both with a low share and with a high share of public expenditure increased the overall healthcare budget. Since the 1990s, however, countries with a higher involvement of the state have been much more successful in cost-containment, and we find a strong negative correlation between public financing and total healthcare expenditure in the early twenty-first century (Figure 33.3; see also Wendt and Kohl, 2010). The relative retreat of public responsibility in healthcare financing therefore potentially reduces

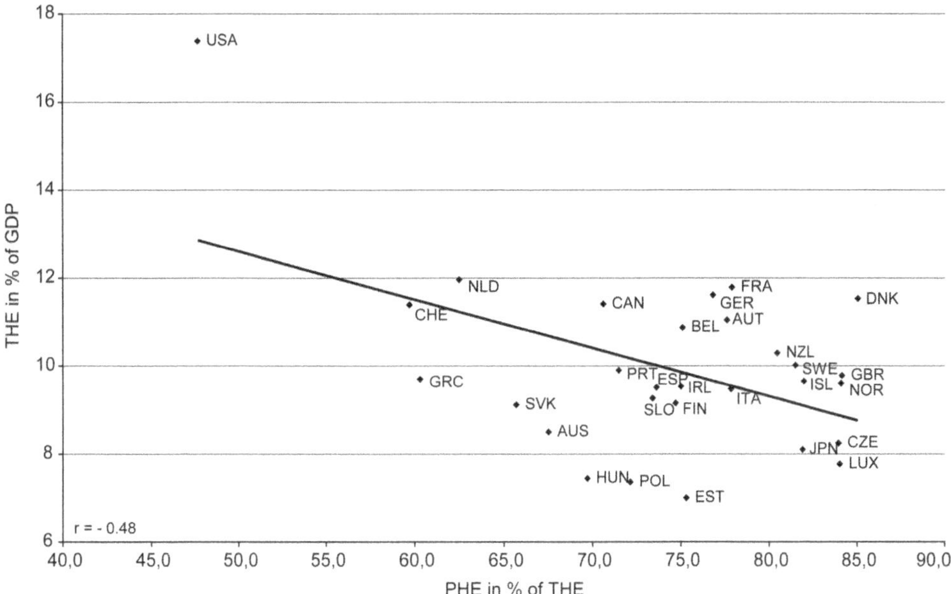

Figure 33.3 Public financing and level of total healthcare expenditure, 2009

Note: AUS: Australia; AUT: Austria; BEL: Belgium; CAN: Canada; CHE: Switzerland; CZE: Czech Republic; DNK: Denmark; ESP: Spain; EST: Estonia; FIN: Finland; FRA: France; GBR: Great Britain; GER: Germany; GRC: Greece; HUN: Hungary; IRL: Ireland; ISL: Iceland; ITA: Italy; JPN: Japan; LUX: Luxembourg; NDL: Netherlands; NZL: New Zealand; NOR: Norway; POL: Poland; PRT: Portugal; SLO: Slovenia; SVK: Slovak Republic; SWE: Sweden; USA: United States.

Source: Wendt and Kohl, 2010, p. 20; OECD Health Data, 2012.

the state's capacity to successfully control costs, as is shown most prominently by the US example.

Today, cost containment is the main focus of reform in most countries. Healthcare provision, in contrast, is often neglected in the health policy debate. Focusing exclusively on healthcare expenditures, however, misses the point of what health policy is all about. Neither maximizing nor minimizing expenditures is a reasonable policy goal in itself. High levels of expenditure only make sense under the assumption that these monetary inputs will be efficiently converted into real inputs (such as personnel and medical facilities) and eventually into real output (such as medical treatment). Likewise, containing or reducing expenditure would not make much sense if it resulted in cuts in real resources, the quality of services, or both. Expenditure containment (or reduction) only makes sense if it is not accompanied by a proportionate reduction of quality or quantity (Wendt and Kohl, 2010). Therefore, the real challenge of health policy is to make effective use of resources in order to meet the patients' needs and demands.

The number of healthcare providers increased in all OECD healthcare systems from 1970 to 2010 (measured in total health employment, medical doctors, and nurses; not shown; see OECD Health Data, 2012). Growing demand due to demographic changes and higher expectations by patients has resulted in continuous expansion of healthcare provider numbers per 1,000 population. However, not all countries have been equally successful in translating monetary resources into high healthcare provider numbers. As shown in Table 33.1, countries like Germany, France, Belgium, and Austria have invested an above-average share of the GDP

Table 33.1 Health expenditures and healthcare providers, 2003

Relative Le Expenditures (in % of GDP)	*Index of healthcare providers*					
	Above average (>100)			*Below average (<100)*		
Above average (>9.08 %)	Germany	10.9	111.4	United States	15.2	96.9
	France	10.4	131.4	Switzerland	11.5	98.3
	Belgium	10.1	148.8	Greece	10.5	93.7
	Norway	10.1	103.2	Canada	9.9	98.1
	Austria	9.6	118.7	Portugal	9.8	84.7
	Australia	9.2	117.0	Sweden	9.3	97.1
				Netherlands	9.1	74.7
Below average (<9.08 %)	Italy	8.2	117.6	Denmark	8.9	80.3
	Luxembourg	7.7	115.5	Hungary	8.3	91.4
	Czech Republic	7.5	100.9	New Zealand	8.0	84.6
	Finland	7.4	113.0	Spain	7.9	94.7
				Great Britain	7.9	85.8
				Ireland	7.2	96.7
				Poland	6.5	70.4
				Slovak Republic	5.9	80.3

Source: Wendt and Kohl, 2010, p. 26.

in healthcare and achieved an above-average level of healthcare providers (for the calculation of the healthcare provider index, see Wendt and Kohl, 2010). On the other hand, countries that have placed higher value on cost containment (such as Denmark, New Zealand, and Great Britain) have achieved healthcare provider levels below the OECD average. Some countries, in particular the United States and Switzerland, share the unfavourable combination of high costs and low provider levels, and few countries seem to be able to build up a high level of healthcare providers with below average healthcare expenditures.

When focusing on the public–private mix in healthcare provision, we find that most countries rely to a great extent on private providers. Healthcare providers in the out-patient sector are often self-employed, whereas in-patient healthcare is offered by public, private for-profit, and private non-profit hospitals. If specialist healthcare is mainly provided at hospitals and a private hospital market does not exist or holds a very limited market share, public healthcare provision is dominant (more than 60 per cent in Finland, Iceland, and Great Britain). However, if both GPs and specialists are allowed to open up their own practice and private hospital chains have entered the healthcare market, we find a large share of private for-profit healthcare provision (more than 60 per cent in Austria, France, Germany, Switzerland, and the United States). The private share of healthcare provision has increased in eleven out of fifteen OECD countries analysed by Rothgang et al. (2010).

Few comparative studies have related healthcare systems directly to outcomes such as healthcare utilization (Reibling and Wendt, 2011) and health inequities (Beckfield and Krieger, 2009). Van Doorslaer and colleagues most prominently pointed toward pro-rich inequity in specialist visits and slight pro-poor inequity in GP visits. Inequity in medical specialist visits is found in nearly all countries, irrespective of healthcare system characteristics (see, for instance, van Doorslaer and Koolman 2004). Measuring the effect of regulating patients' access to healthcare providers in European countries, Reibling and Wendt (2011) also found no country differences in inequities among income groups. However, access regulation, such as gatekeeping, affects patients' decision to see a doctor and reduces the extent of specialist healthcare used. At the same time, gatekeeping has favorable effects on reducing inequities among educational groups. Countries with stricter access regulation show lower levels of inequality in specialist visits among groups with different levels of education. Other studies have analysed outcomes such as trust and satisfaction. The experience of dealing with cost barriers when one is in need of medical care, for instance, reduces a population's trust that necessary healthcare will be provided when one is seriously ill (Wendt et al., 2012). Furthermore, both high levels of healthcare providers in the outpatient sector (but not in the inpatient sector) and the impression that doctors spend enough time with their patients increase the satisfaction with the overall healthcare system, while the level of public healthcare expenditure and the degree of access regulation (gatekeeping) have no effect on satisfaction (Gelissen, 2002; Wendt et al., 2010).

Findings indicate that healthcare reforms would win public support if they concentrated on the provision of outpatient healthcare and that most people would accept reforms that introduce gatekeeping. Over the last three decades, however, healthcare reforms have focused on other, partly opposite, issues. Pro-market reforms have been on the political agenda in many countries, and patients' choice of healthcare providers has been extended. Moreover, new financing models, such as diagnosis related groups (DRGs), have strengthened competition among hospitals. The Netherlands and Germany have also introduced and strengthened choice among sickness funds and thereby also competition on the financing side. In most cases, however, market elements are quickly diminished.

> Competition … , perhaps the signal term in the international discourse of reform, may well turn out to have been one of the more transient. In the U.K., where it was promoted most vigorously, and in Sweden, competition has turned relatively quickly into collaboration between larger units with more clearly defined functions of planning and providing care.
>
> *(Freeman and Moran, 2000, p. 55)*

More importantly, Marmor (2000) pointed to a fundamental theoretical weakness in the concept of market competition:

> Ironically, procompetitive advocates propose a variety of detailed government programs, laws, and regulations designed to address and eliminate the 'market failures' that occur in any unregulated medical environment. This points to the dilemma that has not been faced in most American discussions of competition in medical care markets. What is one to make of the logic of procompetitive proposals when government incompetence makes impossible the effective reform of medical market failures?
>
> *(Marmor, 2000, p. 165)*

If governments are capable of organizing a healthcare market, why should they lack the competence to organize a non-competitive healthcare system?

Another important issue in health reform is the improvement of information technology (Gauld, 2009). Healthcare information technology greatly impacts on the relationship between policy makers, funders, healthcare providers, and patients who have been empowered via better access to information. Interestingly, the tax-funded British NHS seems to be particularly innovative with regard to information technology. New forms of governance with more clinician and patient involvement in healthcare decision-making and planning have been developed as a result of better information technology. These new forms of governance, most visible in Great

Britain and New Zealand, are seen by Gauld (2009) as a social-democratic response to preceding neoliberal arrangements.

Conclusion

This chapter has revealed the continuous increase of healthcare expenditure in OECD countries. At the same time, however, the countries covered in this chapter offer various examples of successful cost containment. For instance, the Scandinavian countries of Denmark and Sweden reduced total health expenditure as a percentage of GDP in the 1980s and 90s. The United States represents the only healthcare system that has great difficulties in bringing healthcare costs under control. Since the US system is mainly based on a private insurance market, it contradicts the assumptions of politicians who still believe that privatization may serve as a solution for stabilizing healthcare costs. On the contrary, data in this chapter indicate that healthcare systems with a higher share of public funding are more successful in bringing healthcare costs under control. Studies on the role of the state, however, show a relative retreat of the state in healthcare financing, indicating that public cost containment capacities may decrease in the future. When analysing the relationship between healthcare expenditure and healthcare provision, it becomes evident that some countries are more successful at translating monetary resources into high levels of healthcare provision than others. Countries with a high market percentage of private health insurance share the unfavourable combination of high costs and below average healthcare provider levels.

Recent studies demonstrate the potential when bridging the macro–micro divide in healthcare research and analyze the importance of the institutional set-up for healthcare utilization and health outcomes. Regulating patients' access to healthcare providers (gatekeeping) has the potential to reduce both the utilization of healthcare services and inequalities in specialist visits among higher-educated groups with better access to specialist care than those with lower education (when controlling for health status). These studies see state regulation, not market-based reforms and financial incentives, as the solution for modern healthcare systems and as a method to increase patient involvement (through the use of improved information technology). For some studies, concepts are still required that would allow for measuring and classifying not only specific regulations but the overall healthcare system. For instance, we still need to learn more about health policies and healthcare systems that successfully translate healthcare expenditure into high healthcare provision levels, not to mention those countries that are better at achieving equal access to necessary healthcare services.

References

Beckfield, J. and Krieger, N. (2009), Epi + demos + cracy: Linking Political Systems and Priorities to the Magnitude of Health Inequities – Evidence, Gaps, and a Research Agenda. *Epidemiologic Reviews*, 31 (1), pp. 152–77.

Freeman, R. and Moran, M. (2000), Reforming Health Care in Europe. *West European Politics* 23 (2), pp. 35–58.

Gauld, R. (2009), *The New Health Policy*. Maidenhead: Open University Press.

Gelissen, J. (2002), *Worlds of Welfare, Worlds of Consent? Public Opinion on the Welfare State*. Leiden: Brill.

Hacker, J. S. (1998), The Historical Logic of National Health Insurance: Structure and Sequence in the Development of British, Canadian, and US Medical Policy. *Studies in American Political Development*, 12 (1), pp. 57–130.

Immergut, E. M. (1992), *Health Politics. Interests and Institutions in Western Europe*. Cambridge: Cambridge University Press.

Marmor, T. (2000), The Ideological Context of Medicare's Politics, in *The Politics of Medicare*, 2nd edn, pp. 151–69. New York: De Gruyter.

Marmor, T. and Wendt, C. (eds) (2011), *Reforming Healthcare Systems.* Two Volumes. UK and Northampton, MA: Edward Elgar Publishing.

Marmor, T. R., Freeman, R. B. and Okma, K. (2005), Comparative Perspectives and Policy Learning in the World of Health Care. *Journal of Comparative Policy Analysis*, 7 (4), pp. 331–48.

Mays, N., Dixon, A. and Jones, L. (2011), *Understanding New Labour's Market Reforms of the English NHS.* London: The King's Fund.

Moran, M. (2000), Understanding the Welfare State: the Case of Health Care. *British Journal of Politics and International Relations,* 2(2), pp. 135–60.

——(1999), *Governing the Health Care State. A Comparative Study of the United Kingdom, the United States and Germany.* Manchester: Manchester University Press.

Organisation for Economic Co-operation and Development (OECD) (2012), *OECD Health Data*, Paris: OECD.

Reibling, N. (2010), Healthcare Systems in Europe: Towards an Incorporation of Patient Access. *Journal of European Social Policy,* 20 (1), pp. 5–18.

Reibling, N. and Wendt, C. (2011), Regulating Patients' Access to Healthcare Services. *International Journal of Public and Private Healthcare Management and Economics*, 1 (2), pp. 1–16.

Rothgang, H., Cacace, M., Frisina, L., Grimmeisen, S., Schmid, A. and Wendt, C. (2010), *The State and Healthcare. Comparing OECD Countries.* Basingstoke: Palgrave Macmillan.

Tuohy, C. H. (1999), *Accidental Logics. Thy Dynamics of Change in the Health Care System in the United States, Britain, and Canada.* New York: Oxford University Press.

van Doorslaer, E. and Koolman, X. (2004), Explaining the Differences in Income-related Health Inequalities across European Countries. *Health Economics*, 13 (7), pp. 609–28.

Wendt, C. (2009), Mapping European Healthcare Systems. A Comparative Analysis of Financing, Service Provision and Access to Healthcare. *Journal of European Social Policy*, 19 (5), pp. 432–45.

Wendt, C. and Jürgen, K. (2010), Translating Monetary Inputs into Health Care Provision: A Comparative Analysis of the Impact of Different Modes of Public Policy. *Journal of Comparative Policy Analysis*, 12 (1–2), pp. 11–31.

Wendt, C., Frisina, L. and Rothgang, H. (2009), 'Health Care System Types. A conceptual framework for comparison'. *Social Policy & Administration,* 43 (1), pp. 70–90.

Wendt, C., Jürgen, K., Mischke, M. and Pfeifer, M. (2010), How Do Europeans Perceive Their Healthcare System? Patterns of Satisfaction and Preference for State Involvement in the Field of Healthcare. *European Sociological Review*, 26 (2), pp. 177–92.

Wendt, C., Mischke, M., Pfeifer, M., Reibling, N. (2012), Confidence in Receiving Medical Care when Seriously Ill: A Seven-Country Comparison of the Impact of Cost Barriers. *Health Expectations*, 15 (2), pp. 212–24

34

Old age and pensions

Karl Hinrichs

Introduction

In modern societies old age is synonymous with retirement. It describes a third stage in the life course which is no longer bound to gainful work because earned income is replaced with pensions and accruals from former savings. Ongoing increases in life expectancy have extended the retirement period, and while a lengthened life span is regarded as a blessing for the individual, a concomitantly prolonged average period of pension receipt poses substantial challenges for public and private pension schemes. Public pensions account for the largest spending item of most developed welfare states and, in view of the demographic ageing process, measures to moderate the growth of pension expenditures rank high on Organisation for Economic Co-operation and Development (OECD) countries' political agenda since about the 1990s. Old age not only means pension payments; the elderly are also the main consumers of health and long-term care, thus, further increasing the old-age bias in welfare spending. Along with their rising electoral weight, reforms that attempt to contain the growth of social expenditure relating to the elderly may become an ever more difficult exercise in democratic polities.

In this chapter we will first glance at the changed meaning of old age, centrally shaped by the development of pension systems. The subsequent section deals with the different functions and designs of pension systems, with a focus on developed welfare states. We then discuss the outcomes of pension policy, in particular the economic situation of the elderly. All welfare states are confronted with similar challenges resulting from ageing populations. After briefly looking into the results of demographic projections, the main part of the fifth section will deal with reforms of pension systems and the problems for present or future retirees that may arise from the (non-)adjustments. Giving private pensions a larger weight in the public–private mix of retirement income has been an important element of recent reform activities. These pre-funded components are exposed to fluctuations of financial markets which possibly threaten income security in old age. The final section reviews the impact of the global crisis of financial markets in 2008 and its aftermath on present and future pensioners.

The changing face of old age

During the pre-industrial era, 'old age' was hardly a separated phase of individuals' life in Europe. There was no such thing as retirement, rather, one worked until death or disability. However, really old people, understood as above 60 years of age, were very few. In England,

Germany, and Austria, until the end of the nineteenth century their share always amounted to far less than 10 per cent (Ehmer, 1990, p. 206; Laslett, 1995, p. 13).

An ordered, tripartite life course, organized around gainful employment and separated by chronological markers, emerged not before the state intervened into the labour market and, next, introduced public pension schemes (Kohli, 1986). Prohibition of child labour and compulsory schooling created a childhood/youth phase, preparing for employment, whereas access to (initially meagre) public pensions relieved the pressure to continue working under all circumstances. A true 'third age' – a post-employment phase free from work obligations – had two preconditions. First, the definitive withdrawal from the labour force requires sufficient means for maintaining the accustomed standard of living or, at least, for not becoming impoverished. In Western welfare states, this precondition for universal retirement became realized only after World War II when coverage and generosity of pension systems were expanded. Second, a 'third age' anchored in the plans for life of individuals presupposes a high probability to actually live well beyond a fixed retirement age.[1] Improved hygienic conditions, better nutrition, more effective safety at work, and general access to healthcare have contributed to a survival curve becoming ever more 'rectangular', i.e. reaching old age is no longer an exception but rather an expectable phase of one's life (Laslett, 1989, Ch. V and VI, 1995, pp. 22–5 and 50–5).

The gradual institutionalization of the life course with regularized transitions and events related to chronological age can be read off from the declining labour force participation rates of men aged 65 and older – in the 1920s, between 50 and 60 per cent of male over-65s were economically active in France, Germany, the UK and the United States (Ehmer, 1990, p. 137), while in 1970, when the expansion of pension systems was largely completed in all but a few countries, the rate had fallen to (far) less than 30 per cent in most developed welfare states (Table 34.1).

The return of high unemployment in Western welfare states in the late 1970s and 1980s, and the shift towards post-industrial economies, however, implied a de-standardization and differentiation of the tripartite life course, showing up in more varied ('fuzzy') pathways into retirement and, on average, a lowered age of exit from the labour market. It is indicated by the decreased labour force participation rates in the age bracket 60 to 64 years of age between 1970 and 1990 (Table 34.1). Additionally, further gains in life expectancy, predominantly occurring after age 65, have resulted in a prolonged third age. For example, a male Australian who actually stopped working at official retirement age (65) in 2009 can expect 18.7 further life years (plus 6.2 years compared to 1960), and a Spanish women, 21.8 years (plus 7.1 years – OECD, 2011a, p. 163). The advancing disconnection of biological and social age has led to proposals for differentiating between a 'third' and a 'fourth age' (Laslett 1989, pp. 152–4). An ever longer retirement phase is regularly spent in good health up to the 75th or 80th birthday. Here we find the 'new old' or 'best agers' endowed with the potentials for 'active ageing' and self-fulfillment, whereas the subsequent 'fourth age' is characterized by increasing frailty and dependence. It is only after age 80 when the need for long-term care increases steeply (OECD, 2011a, pp. 163–5).

Such realistic perspective of a long life nevertheless implies a challenge for individuals in 'work societies' meaningfully to structure everyday life for twenty or more years of retirement. A further ageing population, which is the combined result of below-replacement fertility and declining mortality rates at higher ages, will also have grave societal consequences. Presently (2010), the population share of those 65 years and older is highest in Japan and Germany and, according to projections carried out by the United Nations (UN), this will be true also in 2030 and 2050 (Table 34.2). In the past (between 1950 and 2010) the growth was strongest in Japan, but in future the increase will be steepest in China where the share of elderly will triple from 2010 to 2050. This foreseeable development puts substantial pressure on social security schemes.

Table 34.1 Labor force participation rates in OECD countries, selected years (sometimes nearest)

	Men 60–64			*Men 65+*		
	1970	*1990*	*2010*	*1970*	*1990*	*2010*
Australia	77.4	50.6	61.6	22.2	9.2	15.4
Austria	44.9	19.5	30.7	8.0	6.3	7.7
Belgium		19.3	27.2		1.9	3.2
Canada	74.1	50.9	57.7	22.6	10.8	16.2
Denmark	78.3	51.2	49.4	22.2	13.0	9.9
Finland	67.0	29.9	44.4	41.0	9.2	11.0
France	68.0	22.8	20.2	19.5	3.7	2.4
Germany	71.9	33.6	53.7	17.2	4.7	5.7
Ireland	87.6	55.6	55.2	44.0	16.4	13.9
Italy	48.2	36.0	30.6	12.9	7.1	5.7
Japan	81.5	72.9	76.0	49.4	36.5	29.1
Netherlands	73.7	22.7	50.0	11.3	3.3	9.2
New Zealand	71.9	35.0	78.9	23.6	10.4	22.6
Norway	79.4	64.2	63.9	25.7	25.0	23.2
Sweden	79.5	62.4	70.8	28.9	12.6	16.7
Switzerland	87.3	76.3	70.2	32.2	26.0	14.1
UK	87.0	54.4	57.9	20.2	8.8	11.3
USA	75.0	55.5	60.0	26.7	16.3	22.1
Czechoslovakia/ Czech Republic	32.7	26.6	38.2	14.3	9.4	7.1
Hungary	43.8	17.6	17.6	40.9	10.4	4.8
Poland	83.0	36.6	28.4	56.4	19.1	7.7

Source: OECD, StatExtracts; Gordon 1988, pp. 86–7 (some 1970 data).

Table 34.2 Population ageing in selected countries (2030 and 2050 projections)

	Population share 65+				*Ratio inactive elderly to total labour force*		
	1950	*2010*	*2030*	*2050*	*2010*	*2030*	*2050*
France	11.4	16.7	23.4	26.2	37.9	56.8	65.0
Germany	9.7	20.4	27.8	31.5	40.3	62.1	73.9
Sweden	10.3	18.4	22.8	24.6	35.5	47.1	48.7
UK	10.8	16.6	21.1	23.7	33.2	51.1	58.1
USA	8.3	13.0	19.7	20.7	26.0	46.5	50.3
Japan	4.9	23.1	31.8	39.6	46.8	68.6	94.9
China	4.5	8.4	16.2	23.7	13.9	30.2	48.0

Source: Population Division of the Department of Economic and Social Affairs of the United Nations Secretariat, *World Population Prospects: The 2010 Revision*, esa.un.org/unpd/wpp/index.htm (1950 data); OECD, 2009, p. 19 (all other data).

In order to cope with rising social expenditure, almost all developed welfare states have already legislated and partly implemented reforms of their public pension schemes (see Section 5). The increasing proportion of elderly people will also change the appearance of societies (in the streets, in enterprises) and, moreover, shift political power along the age axis. Voting power of the elderly will increase inexorably, and the rising age of the median voter has raised fears that, eventually, reforms violating vested interests of the older part of the population are no longer enforceable in democracies (Bovenberg, 2008). Others have disapproved the notion of a coming gerontocracy and argued instead that the elderly are not outright greedy, rather, are responsive to the needs of the young generation and support political attempts aiming at intergenerational equity (see contributions in Vanhuysse and Goerres, 2012).

Functions, designs, and development of pension systems

Fully developed national pension systems perform four different functions (Barr and Diamond, 2008, 25–33). First of all, they aim to *alleviate poverty* when flat-rate benefits are paid to all individuals above a certain age or are targeted at those with insufficient resources. In a number of countries state responsibility is limited to this function. *Income smoothing* is a further objective in order to avoid a steep decline of resources after withdrawal from the labour market and, thus, to keep up the attained standard of living during retirement ('earnings replacement'). Furthermore, pensions *insure against biometric risks.* As annuities they protect retired individuals from above average longevity so that they do not run the risk to outlive their savings. Survivors' pensions insure against the (premature) death of the main breadwinner or retiree, and disability pensions cover the risk of work incapacity before reaching regular retirement age. Finally, linked to poverty prevention is the objective of *redistributing income.* Pension systems may redistribute vertically (e.g. by means of a progressive benefit formula that replaces a higher percentage of previous earnings for low-wage workers than for higher earners), or horizontally when certain facts or events produce higher entitlements (e.g. redistributing towards families through a spouse supplement, as in the US Social Security system) by granting caregiver credits and between males and females when applying unisex mortality tables.

Basically, all four functions may be performed by only *one* public scheme – a social pension insurance (Table 34.3, 2nd tier of 1st pillar). In reality, however, national pension systems are more complex and consist of several components which are assigned different functions and display different properties. For example, most national pension systems have separate schemes

Table 34.3 Design of pension systems

Pillar		*Type*	*Membership*	*Financing*	*Management*
3rd		Individual savings	Voluntary	Fully funded	Private
2nd		Occupational pension	Voluntary or (quasi-)mandatory	Fully funded	Private
	3rd tier	Earnings-related	Mandatory	Fully funded	Private/Public
1st	*2nd tier*	Earnings-related	Mandatory	PAYG (contributions)	Public (self-administration)
	1st tier	Universal/ targeted basic pension	(citizenship right)	PAYG (taxes)	Public

Source: Author's elaboration based on European Commission, 2009, p. 8.

for basic security (1st tier of the 1st pillar) and earnings-related pensions (2nd and/or 3rd tier of 1st pillar). Moreover, one finds arrangements with functions divided between public and private components whereby the private pension schemes aim at income smoothing (3rd tier of 1st pillar, 2nd and 3rd pillar). 'Private' means that pension schemes are administered by non-governmental organizations, but are state-regulated in order to protect employees' or savers' claims. Actually, all old-age pension systems feature a 'public–private mix'. However, the mix ratio varies between countries and changes over time. Private components are usually *fully funded* which means that they are backed by assets, invested in pension funds. In contrast, the *pay-as-you-go* (PAYG) principle applies to public pensions (1st and 2nd tier of 1st pillar): benefits are paid out of current revenues (taxes or contributions). Furthermore, the components differ as to how pensions are calculated – either they are determined by a benefit formula that somehow takes into account past earnings and length of insurance/service (2nd tier of 1st pillar and, to a lesse extent, 2nd pillar) (*defined benefit* – DB) or they are dependent on the value of assets accumulated in individuals' accounts at retirement, i.e. assets accruing from contributions and the performance of their investment (3rd tier of 1st pillar, 3rd pillar and, increasingly, employer-sponsored occupational pension plans) (*defined contribution* – DC). Regularly, private schemes contain no redistribution beyond actuarially fair risk balancing

Today's pension systems in developed welfare state evolved from two different starting points – either the Bismarck or the Beveridge approach. The former is characterized by a public contributory social insurance scheme being the central institution for providing earnings replacement in old age. This approach is employment-centred, links benefits to previous earnings, and implies a priority of status maintenance ('consumption smoothing') over poverty relief. Germany's pioneering legislation of 1889 was followed in a number of countries of the European continent (e.g. Austria, France, and Belgium) at the end of the nineteenth or early twentieth century and in the United States in 1935 and 1939. A larger number of countries embarked on a different path, mostly around the same time (e.g. Denmark in 1891). They followed the *Beveridge* approach, so named after the architect of a universal, basic security welfare state in post-World War II Britain had presented his plan in 1942. These were the Anglo-Saxon nations (minus the US) and all of the Nordic countries. Here the focus is on poverty alleviation via universal flat-rate pensions based on citizenship and financed out of taxes or tax-like contributions. These pension schemes were generally means tested when first introduced, with some, but not all, later developing into universal 'people's pensions.'

Except for the Netherlands, all countries starting from the social insurance approach stayed on their path, at least until the most recent reforms (Hinrichs, 2000; Weaver, 2010). They expanded their public schemes within the original framework: coverage was broadened to almost the entire (working) population, eligibility criteria for enjoying a pension became liberalized (e.g. flexible retirement), the range of PAYG benefits was expanded (e.g. survivors' pensions) and, most importantly, the generosity of benefits was substantially increased and facilitated true retirement without additional private pensions. Significant changes occurred since the late 1950s in countries that followed the *Beveridge* model. Their pension systems became more complex when they supplemented their basic pension schemes in two main ways. In light of favourable economic and demographic conditions at that time, Sweden (1959), Finland (1961) and, somewhat later, Canada (1965) and Norway (1966) topped up their 'people's pensions' with a second *public* tier that displayed all features of a defined-benefit social insurance scheme (Gordon, 1988, pp. 44–55). *De facto*, these countries joined the traditional Bismarck countries during the course of the early 1960s.

In contrast to these *early birds*, countries that provided only a basic flat-rate pension as late as the early 1970s were the *latecomers*. They took a different route to achieving status maintenance in old age on a large scale. An earnings-related topping-up and, hence, an expansion of the system, was accomplished via *occupational* pension schemes that were either mandated by law (Switzerland in 1985, Australia in 1992) or arose through collective agreements and eventually achieved almost universal coverage (Netherlands, Denmark). In any case, in *latecomer* countries, the second pillar is private, fully funded and, regularly, it enjoys certain tax privileges ('fiscal welfare'). The UK pension system represents something of a unique 'hybrid' case with employees either entitled to (meagre) public earnings-related pensions or, supplementary retirement income from occupational and/or personal schemes, but still leaves many retirees reliant on the basic state pension and additional means tested benefits. The 2007/08 reforms attempt to broaden coverage with supplementary private pensions through soft mandate ('auto-enrolment' – Bridgen and Meyer, 2011). In Ireland and New Zealand, the remaining countries that followed the Beveridge approach, provision for supplementary pensions is still left to voluntary action of private actors, but also encouraged through automatic enrolment in newly founded pre-funded schemes.

During the last decades, a number of low-income countries has followed the Beveridge model and provided easy-to-administer universal flat-rate pensions to their elderly population. Among others, those schemes have been established in Namibia, Botswana, Nepal, Brunei, Bolivia, and Mauritius (in 1958) (Willmore, 2006). In a number of South East Asian countries (e.g. Singapore, Hong Kong, Malaysia, Sri Lanka, and the Fiji Islands) but also in Swaziland, an alternative to both the Bismarck and Beveridge model has been established: provision for old age works via *provident funds*. These are (mostly) state-run compulsory savings schemes to which the employees and employers contribute. After retiring from employment the funds accumulated in individual accounts are paid out as a monthly withdrawal, life annuity or, sometimes, also in part as a lump sum.

Pension systems in developed welfare states: outcomes

The expansion of pension systems in developed welfare states up to about the 1980s has substantially improved the income situation of the elderly population. Table 34.4 (column 3) shows the ratio between the median disposable income of persons aged 65 or over and all younger persons. In 2010, it varied between 0.8 and 1.0 in most European countries. Exceptions are Denmark where occupational pension schemes have not yet matured and Belgium whose pension system is comparably less generous. Regularly, among the older population those below age 75 are better off than people of higher age (OECD, 2011b, p. 147) because in the upper age brackets (widowed) women in single households are overrepresented who mostly dispose of lower own pension entitlements. Moreover, indexing of pensions at less than wage growth increasingly cuts the very old ones off from real income gains the working-age population experiences.

A somewhat different picture emerges if one looks at the poverty risk rates (Table 34.4, columns 1 and 2). In about half of the countries a higher percentage of the elderly population is at risk of poverty compared to people at working age. In Switzerland the difference is most extreme, and no other European country shows such a high share of elderly people with a disposable income of less than 60 per cent of the median. Apart from the Netherlands, the poverty risk rate is lowest in Hungary and the Czech Republic where the present generation of retirees is not (much) affected by pension reforms that have been legislated. The latter point is quite important because the income situation of today's elderly results from institutional arrangements and individual behaviour oriented to those rules, incentives or obligations as well as from the employment situation when they were at working age. Thus, figures presented in Table 34.4 (columns 2 and 3) do not inform about future pensioners' income situation which for many will be shaped by atypical employment careers and the effects of past and ongoing

Table 34.4 Income situation of the elderly population, net pension replacement rates and pension expenditure in selected OECD countries

Country	*At-risk-of-poverty rate (60% of median)*		*Relative median income ratio, 65+/<65 years (3)*	*Net replacement ratio (average earnings)*		*Pension expenditure, % of GDP (2007)*	
	age 18–64 (1)	*age 65+ (2)*		*2006 (4a)*	*about 2053 (4b)*	*Public (5a)*	*private (5b)*
Australia					58.9	3.4	3.4
Austria	10.7	15.2	0.91	83.9	89.9	12.3	0.3
Belgium	12.1	19.4	0.75	69.5	64.1	8.9	2.8
Canada					57.3	4.2	2.2
Denmark	12.9	17.7	0.71	71.3	89.9	5.6	3.3
Finland	12.3	18.3	0.78	69.0	65.2	8.3	0.5
France	12.8	9.7	1.0	79.4	60.4	12.5	
Germany	15.6	14.1	0.89	63.0	57.9	10.7	0.1
Ireland	15.5	10.6	0.86	82.0	35.8	3.6	
Italy	16.9	16.6	0.92	89.0	75.3	14.1	0.2
Japan					39.7	8.8	
Netherlands	10.1	5.9	0.87	91.8	99.8	4.7	3.6
New Zealand					41.5	4.3	1.3
Norway	10.8	12.0	0.85		62.2	4.7	2.0
Sweden	11.9	15.5	0.79	67.3	53.6	7.2	1.3
Switzerland	11.2	27.4	0.8		64.1	6.4	5.4
UK	14.9	21.4	0.81	74.6	41.5	5.4	2.8
USA					50.0	6.0	3.3
Czech Rep.	8.1	6.8	0.82	79.3	64.4	7.4	0.3
Hungary	11.9	4.1	1.01	100.4	106.0	9.1	0.2
Poland	16.9	14.2	0.93	77.7	68.2	10.6	0.0

Source: EU-SILC database (columns 1, 2, 4); European Commission, 2009 (column 4a); OECD, 2011b, p. 125 (column 4b – the entitlements include benefits from mandatory public or private and 'quasi-mandatory' [coverage ≥85%] private pension schemes – OECD, 2011b, pp. 116–7); OECD, 2011c, p. 245 (columns 5a, 5b).

pension reforms, endangering their income security after retirement in several European countries (see contributions in Hinrichs and Jessoula, 2012).

Another way to grasp the impact of pension systems on retirees' income position is to look at the percentage of former earnings that is replaced with (public) pensions. The European Commission (2009) has calculated the net replacement rate for workers who retired in 2006 after an employment career of 40 years at normal pensionable age (Table 34.4, column 4a). The figures show quite considerable variance between European countries: Hungary and the Netherlands top the list while Germany and Sweden rank lowest. Both the European Commission (2009) and the OECD (2011b) have also modeled the net replacement rate for future retirees who started employment in the 2000s and included the rules of the respective pension (and tax) system valid in 2008 or becoming implemented over the next decades. The figures presented in Table 34.4 (column 4b) are based on a single male worker entering the labour market in 2008 at the age of 20 and then always earning an average wage. The replacement rates vary widely between the countries and where it is possible to compare the figures in columns 4a and 4b, the effects of already legislated retrenchments show up (e.g. for Germany, Italy, or the Czech Republic) as well as improvements due to the maturing of second-pillar schemes (Denmark, the Netherlands). However, the calculated replacement rates tell nothing of how representative the average earner pursuing a standard career actually is in their respective country. Further estimations for workers earning a multiple of the average wage (0.5 or 1.5) and different career profiles (e.g. breaks in employment or early/delayed retirement) show the progressivity and other distributive effects of the pension and tax system (European Commission, 2009; OECD, 2011b, pp. 116–31).

Finally, the different design of pension systems shows up in the figures on pension expenditure (Table 34.4, columns 5a and 5b). Public spending is very high in countries with a mature and (still) generous PAYG pension insurance scheme and a comparatively large share of people aged 65 and older, such as Italy, Austria and France. In contrast, Australia, merely providing resource-tested basic security, spends much less. Private expenditure on second-pillar pensions was already on the same level in 2007 and will grow further in the course of these occupational schemes maturing. The same is true for other latecomer countries.

Challenges and recent reforms of pension systems

Population ageing poses the most important challenge for all developed welfare states. Increasing old-age support ratios creates problems of financial sustainability and generational equity as more elderly will have to be supported by fewer people of working age. The rising share of the population aged 65 and older (Table 34.2) appears even more dramatic if it is put in relation to the total labour force: For example, in Japan there are presently about three elderly for ten members of the labour force. The OECD estimates that in 2050 it will be an almost one-to-one ratio between elderly people and gainfully employed. In other countries listed in Table 34.2 the change will be somewhat less severe; the old-age dependency ratio will roughly double between 2010 and 2050, except for China where it quadruples. Only a steep increase in the employment ratio (mobilizing more women and elderly), massive immigration or a reversal of declined birth rates could moderate this development. This foreseeable development has triggered pension reforms in all OECD countries. The timing, patterns and intensity of reforms, however, are not directly related to the magnitude of imminent population ageing. Rather, these features vary with the structural attributes of a given type of the pension system and the established (or changed) politics of pension policy.

The latecomer countries (plus Ireland and New Zealand) have pursued reforms within the given structures of their pension system (Table 34.5). Here the pressure on their public schemes is less pronounced because they are regularly on a smaller scale than in Bismarckian countries. Nevertheless, they attempt to contain the rise of expenditure on basic pensions by introducing an eligibility age above 65 (e.g. in Denmark, the UK, Ireland, and Australia), gradually lowered and – sometimes – more targeted benefits, and less fiscal support for private pensions. In order to still ensure adequate earnings replacement, these countries bank on further broadened coverage of private pensions (in particular for employees with fixed-term contracts, working part-time, or holding other atypical jobs) and the maturing of these funded schemes which means higher private pensions.

Adjustments of Bismarckian pension systems may be divided into *parametric* and *structural* reforms. The latter are systemic changes that move established systems 'off path', while the former constitute incremental adjustments to the system's 'parameters'. They aim to stabilize or contain a further rise of pension contribution rates by altering the worker/pensioner (system dependency) ratio, the wage replacement (benefit) ratio, or by adding new sources of funding.

Table 34.5 Pension reform measures

Reform action	*Countries with Bismarckian pension schemes*	*Countries with Beveridgeian basic pensions*	*Objectives of reform*
Higher retirement age; foreclosing early retirement	X	X	Financial sustainability; equal treatment
Strengthened contribution-benefit link	X		Financial sustainability; eliminating distributive distortions
Changed indexing formulae	X	X	Financial sustainability
Build-up of reserve funds	X	X	Financial sustainability
New/improved caregiver credits	X		Social adequacy
Improved minimum protection	X		Social adequacy
New/extended private pension schemes	X	(X)	Maintaining earnings replacement

Source: Author's elaboration.

One can distinguish five main types of parametric reforms that occurred beginning in about 1990 (Table 34.5).

1 A higher retirement age limits the implicit expansion of pension systems due to lengthened life expectancy. Closing pathways into premature retirement (e.g. special pre-retirement schemes, granting disability benefits for labour market reasons) attempt to reverse the former early exit trend and will lower the system dependency ratio. Furthermore, legislation lifting the standard retirement age has been brought underway in a number of countries (e.g. the US, Germany, and Italy), and where women and public employees enjoyed a lower eligibility age before it will be aligned to the one of men and/or private sector employees. In addition, a number of countries has introduced or extended options for flexible retirement. Claiming a public pension before reaching the standard retirement age regularly implies permanent (and more or less actuarial) benefit deductions, while working beyond the standard age is rewarded with a corresponding bonus.
2 The *contribution/benefit link* has been tightened in various ways. Where previously a certain number of years in covered employment sufficed to attain a 'full' pension, and the benefit level was determined by earnings achieved during a number of 'best years' or 'last years' prior to retirement, benefit formulae have been changed so that earnings over the entire employment career are taken into account (e.g. in Austria or Finland). The strictest (and most transparent) link between lifetime contributions and benefits, which eliminates all internal redistribution, was established in so-called *notional defined contribution* (NDC) schemes (e.g. in Sweden or Poland), which mimic fully funded plans (with the growth rate of covered wages defining the 'interest rate') but actually operate on a PAYG basis. Other variants to scale down redistributive features were to abolish entitlements not earned out of contributions on own earnings (e.g. in Germany).
3 In almost all countries *indexing formulae* have been modified. Past earnings, which determine the level of the first claimed pension entitlements, are less often valued in line with average earnings growth, and increasingly adjusted to match the inflation rate (e.g. in France). Elsewhere, demographic parameters – further life expectancy at retirement age, as in all Nordic

countries and Austria, or the changing contributor/pensioner ratio in Germany – have been incorporated in the formula by which the benefit level is determined at the time of retirement. Finally, pensions in payment are increasingly adjusted to consumer prices instead of previous wage development. This programmatic retrenchment yields a substantial long-run savings effect.

4 *New sources of funding*, meant to contain the contribution rate, have been injected into public pension schemes. Tax-financed subsidies cover redistributive features like caregiver credits or (improved) minimum pensions. Moreover, public schemes normally operate on a pay-as-you-go basis, holding reserve funds of varying amounts. In a number of countries these reserves have been temporarily augmented through a variety of means: by charging a higher contribution rate than is necessary to meet current expenditures (the US, Canada, and Finland), by setting aside revenues from privatising public enterprises or state budget surpluses in earmarked funds to be incorporated in the pension system at a later date (Belgium and France), or by drawing on other publicly owned funds (Norway).
5 The only expansionary type of reform that has occurred in Bismarckian countries since the 1990s is the insertion of *caregiver credits* into the benefit calculation. Unpaid family work, like raising children or taking care of frail elderly, may now result in (higher) pension entitlements and, thus, improve benefit adequacy for women in particular. The procedures for crediting care work and the benefits that accrue from it vary widely across countries. A few countries have also improved *minimum protection* in old age, either inside the pension insurance or as a separate scheme, in order to cope with lower earnings-related benefits in future.

Beyond these incremental changes, *structural reforms* have been implemented in almost all Bismarckian countries that previously relied on earnings-related public schemes as the sole or predominant source of retirement income. International organizations the International Monetary Fund (IMF), the OECD and notably the World Bank, have pressed for such changes. The World Bank's seminal publication (1994) founded the 'new pension orthodoxy', and the Bank became a most influential player in pension reform worldwide. In particular, it pushed for a new (or extended) mandatory, employment-related, and funded component within the pension system (the 3rd tier of the 1st pillar in Table 34.3) that was supposed to be less vulnerable to population ageing than PAYG schemes. The strengthened role of pre-funding was also meant to increase national savings as a vehicle for enhanced economic growth in emerging welfare states, and the World Bank became directly involved in the reform process in some Latin American and Central and East European transition countries which set up mandatory funded second-pillar schemes (Müller, 2003; Orenstein, 2008).

Although the World Bank's advice was less directed towards welfare states with mature PAYG schemes it, nevertheless, contributed to weakening the prevailing pension policy paradigm in Bismarckian countries. Until about the 1990s, this paradigm had rested on cognitive and normative beliefs about the superiority of the social insurance approach vis-à-vis multi-pillar arrangements. It was widely shared among political and social actors. The apparent exhaustion of this single-pillar approach in light of long-term financial problems, however, has allowed the competing multi-pillar approach to gain ground in these countries. Real path departure took place when privately funded pillars were introduced or substantially expanded in order to compensate for lower replacement ratios caused by the parametric reforms mentioned above. Participation in those supplementary schemes is now either mandatory (Sweden, Norway, Poland, and further transition countries) or voluntary but stimulated by tax advantages (Germany, Belgium, France) and auto-enrolment (Austria, Italy). By embracing the multi-pillar approach, pension systems in almost all Bismarckian countries have come closer to the structure implemented in *latecomer* countries.

Both parametric and paradigmatic pension reforms have proved to be difficult, and often involve serious political conflicts (Hinrichs, 2000; Myles and Pierson, 2001; Schludi, 2005). Because pension systems bridge extended time spans – from the start of an earning career until the receipt of the final pension payout – and because the capacity of individuals to adjust to institutional changes decreases with proximity to retirement age, reforms regularly include long phasing-in periods. Moreover, public schemes have created large constituencies for whom pensions are of vital significance, and governments' reform efforts may be risky undertakings if they aim at cutbacks of vested rights of current and future pensioners. In order to mitigate the political risks of pension reform, governments have chosen a variety of strategies including forming coalitions with opposition parties to create oversized majorities in parliament, seeking out cooperation with major stakeholders, notably labour unions and interest organizations of seniors, and/or forming expert commissions to furnish advice that can help legitimize painful decisions.

The world of pensions after the financial market crisis

The general trend of pension reforms in all developed welfare states has been a shift from defined-benefit (DB) type schemes towards a larger role of defined-contribution (DC) schemes. The partial privatization of pension provision and stronger reliance on pre-funded pension schemes goes along with a 'risk shift' (Hacker, 2006): future pensioners will bear as individuals the risks of exposure to financial markets and increasing longevity because accumulated assets have to be 'stretched' over a longer period of retirement and imply a lower annuity. Additionally, in countries that have created or expanded those *welfare markets* for retirement income, the retreat of states from the responsibility to ensure social security and social justice leads to different outcomes: welfare markets for private pensions serve the same purpose (income smoothing), but being void of redistributive features and accruing pensions depending on the performance of investments, they rather increase income inequality in old age.

The risks of private, funded DC schemes became painfully clear in 2008 when financial markets (almost) collapsed. Pension funds in OECD countries, on average, lost almost one quarter of their assets in 2008. This event was preceded by a smaller although substantial global downturn of stock markets during the early 2000s in the wake of the 'dotcom crisis'. The pension funds recouped some of their losses in 2009 and 2010, but it was a 'lost decade' for participants in welfare markets and meant a setback for states which increased their public pension reserve funds. In view of the public debt and euro crisis, starting in 2010, financial markets still remain volatile. The financial losses implied serious consequences for pension savers close to retirement if they were unable to postpone their withdrawal from the labour market or received no tax-financed bailouts. Future pensioners might see their old-age security thwarted as (real) interest rates are at a trough so that, ultimately, fewer than expected assets will be available for conversion into a monthly pension payment.

The recent financial market crisis meant a serious backlash for the protagonists of pre-funded pensions. It 'fed the perennial debate about the suitability of funded schemes as a mechanism for funding old-age security and […] brought to the fore the risk that pension systems face when cash benefits of individuals are linked to the fluctuations of financial markets' (Pino and Yermo, 2010, p. 7). In contrast, contributory PAYG pension schemes have only been affected by the economic recession in the wake of the financial market crisis when lower wage growth and higher unemployment meant lower revenues. Despite the 'perfect storm' for the protagonists of funded pensions, they are anxious that individuals and policymakers 'overreact' and dismiss the idea of diversification, or concede to demands for abrupt policy change. Instead, they ask for better governance, improved regulation, portfolios that increase conservative investments with the individual proximity to retirement (life-cycle funds), and better minimum protection (World Bank, 2008; European Commission, 2010, pp. 136–39).

The declined appeal of the shift towards funded pensions has nevertheless triggered a next wave of pension reform. Some countries which envisioned funded schemes as a core component of a modernized pension arrangement have completely abolished this pillar (Argentina, Hungary), shifted to voluntary participation (Slovakia), or (temporarily) reduced the contribution share diverted for individual accounts (Poland, Latvia). For the same reason, a number of Bismarckian and latecomer countries have put a new emphasis on a higher retirement age. Working longer, if employees are actually able to stay on, generates higher entitlements to a public or private pension and a shorter period of benefit receipt.

Note

1 In Germany, when it compulsorily insured almost all employees against income loss due to disability and old age by legislation of 1889, the declining abilities of older workers were the main social problem. Thus, disability pensions predominated (even until the early 1960s). A statutory retirement age (initially 70) served as a marker for generally assumed disability at which an old-age pension was granted without a medical examination of the fitness for work. It already embodied the concept of a work-free phase of 'retirement', becoming true only decades later.

References

Barr, N. and Diamond, P. (2008), *Reforming Pensions: Principles and Policy Choices*. Oxford: Oxford University Press.

Bovenberg, A.L. (2008), Grey New World: Europe on the Road to Gerontocracy? *CESifo Economic Studies*, 54(1), pp. 55–72.

Bridgen, P. and Meyer, T. (2011), 'Britain: Exhausted Voluntarism - The Evolution of a Hybrid Pension Regime', in B. Ebbinghaus (ed.), *Varieties of Pension Governance: Pension Privatization in Europe*, pp. 265–91. Oxford: Oxford University Press.

Ehmer, J. (1990), *Sozialgeschichte des Alters*. Frankfurt a.M.: Suhrkamp.

European Commission (2010), Joint Report on Pensions: Progress and Key Challenges in the Delivery of Adequate and Sustainable Pensions in Europe. *European Economy, Occasional Papers* 71 (November). Brussels.

European Commission (Social Protection Committee, Indicator Sub-Group) (2009), *Updates of Current and Prospective Theoretical Pension Replacement Rates, 2006–2046 (Annex-Country Fiches)*. Brussels.

Gordon, M.S. (1988), *Social Security Policies in Industrial Countries: A Comparative Analysis*. Cambridge: Cambridge University Press.

Hacker, J.S. (2006), *The Great Risk Shift*. Oxford: Oxford University Press.

Hinrichs, K. (2000), Elephants on the Move: Patterns of Public Pension Reform in OECD Countries. *European Review* 8(3), pp. 353–78.

Hinrichs, K. and Jessoula, M. (eds) (2012), *Labour Market Flexibility and Pension Reforms: Flexible Today, Secure Tomorrow?* Houndmills, Basingstoke: Palgrave Macmillan.

Kohli, M. (1986), 'The World We Forgot: A Historical Review of the Life Course', in V.W. Marshall (ed.), *Later Life: The Social Psychology of Ageing*, pp. 271–303. Beverly Hills: Sage.

Laslett, P. (1989), *A Fresh Map of Life: The Emergence of the Third Age*. London: Weidenfeld and Nicolson.

——(1995), 'Necessary Knowledge: Age and Ageing in the Societies of the Past', in D.I. Kertzer and P. Laslett (eds), *Ageing in the Past: Demography, Society, and Old Age*, pp. 3–77. Berkeley: University of California Press.

Müller, K. (2003), *Privatising Old-Age Security: Latin America and Eastern Europe Compared*. Cheltenham: Edward Elgar.

Myles, J. and Pierson, P. (2001), 'The Comparative Political Economy of Pension Reform', in P. Pierson, (ed.), *The New Politics of the Welfare State*, pp. 305–33. Oxford: Oxford University Press.

Organisation for Economic Co-operation and Development (OECD) (2009), *OECD Factbook 2009. Economic, Environmental and Social Statistics*. Paris: OECD.
——(2011a), *Health at a Glance 2011: OECD Indicators*. Paris: OECD.
——(2011b), *Pensions at a Glance: Retirement-Income Systems in OECD and G20 Countries*. Paris: OECD.
——(2011c), *OECD Factbook 2011–2012: Economic, Environmental and Social Statistics*. Paris: OECD.
Orenstein, M.A. (2008), *Privatizing Pensions: The Transnational Campaign for Social Security Reform*. Princeton, NJ: Princeton University Press.
Pino, A. and Yermo, J. (2010), The Impact of the 2007–2009 Crisis on Social Security and Private Pension Funds: A Threat to Their Financial Soundness? *International Social Security Review* 63(2), pp. 5–30.
Schludi, M. (2005), *The Reform of Bismarckian Pension Systems: A Comparison of Pension Politics in Austria, France, Germany, Italy and Sweden*. Amsterdam: Amsterdam University Press.
Vanhuysse, P. and Goerres, A. (eds) (2012), *Ageing Populations in Post-Industrial Democracies: Comparative Studies of Policies and Politics*. London and New York: Routledge.
Weaver, R.K. (2010), Paths and Forks or Chutes and Ladders? Negative Feedbacks and Policy Regime Change. *Journal of Public Policy* 30(2), 137–62.
Willmore, L. (2006), Universal Age Pensions in Developing Countries: The Example of Mauritius. *International Social Security Review* 59(4), 67–89.
World Bank (1994), *Averting the Old Age Crisis: Policies to Protect the Old and Promote Growth*. New York: Oxford University Press.
——(2008), *The Financial Crisis and Mandatory Pension Systems in Developing Countries*. Washington, DC: World Bank, Pension Reform Primer Note.

35

Disability

Bjørn Hvinden

The right to live a life in the same way as others has been the principle cornerstone of disability policy. The question is whether this objective has been fulfilled in contemporary welfare states, what the possible barriers are, and how persons with disabilities live in different welfare states. Possible instruments to promote the objective include redistributive measures (e.g. income transfers, other cash benefits and provision of services) and social regulatory measures (e.g. non-discrimination and accessibility legislation).

Introduction

This chapter gives an overview of the main issues related to the situation of persons with disabilities in society, including key concepts, perspectives, and empirical facts related to the diverse life courses of persons with disabilities, and the main types of efforts by various actors, including disabled people themselves, to achieve social recognition, equal participation, and the material conditions for independent living and personal fulfilment for persons with disabilities.

Core concepts, perspectives, and some basic facts

Until recently perceptions of persons with disabilities and the provisions to assist them have been dominated by a *bio-medical understanding of disability*. According to this understanding, disability is basically and mainly caused by a medical condition or *impairment*, i.e. a reduced functioning of the person's bodily, mental, or intellectual capacity. Individual- and deficiency-oriented understandings of disability have for a long time played a key role in defining eligibility for cash benefits and services, often with the stated purpose of compensating for the effects of reduced individual functioning.

In this context it is notable that some scholars have argued that historically the notion of disability was invented to mediate the ways in which traditional poor law rather harshly distinguished between the deserving and non-deserving destitute (e.g. Stone, 1985; de Swaan, 1988). By defining or categorising destitute persons of working age as 'disabled' (usually other more derogatory terms were used), local authorities could legitimately exempt these persons from the general duty to work and be economically self-sufficient. In this way, some destitute persons escaped the brutal treatment and compulsion that the non-deserving poor were exposed to.

With the advent of the welfare state and social security provision from the end of the nineteenth century and onwards, the use of a medically oriented disability categorisation was refined and developed further. Often disability has been assessed in an absolute and binary way; a person has been deemed either disabled or not. The authorities have given the main emphasis to how the person's impairment influenced his or her capacity for paid employment and being economically self-sufficient, to avoid that the persons become 'a burden for society'.

In other words, the concept of *diminished work capacity* (or earnings capacity) is synonymous with neither the concept of disability nor the concept of impairment. A person's ability to perform in a given job or occupation depends on a number of factors, including whether the person has relevant and sufficient vocational qualifications for the job, command of the language(s) to be used in the job, the extent to which the person has an impairment or disability affecting his or her ability to perform in this particular job, and whether an actual or potential employer provides the appropriate workplace accommodation or adjustments allowing the person to use his or her qualifications, experience and capacity.

Significantly, a second approach to conceptualising disability originated from the experience of large-scale war, especially after the First World War (Amos, 1943; Obermann, 1967; Grahame, 2002; Ross, 2008; Linker, 2011). The great number of persons wounded and injured in war action tended to be fairly young, male, with or without work experience before they were mobilised. Widely regarded as 'national heroes', the war injured were a highly legitimate group and representing an important labour potential in reconstruction after war. Alongside privileging war-injured servicemen by providing better financial support and services than for those who had been injured in work, these factors led to the invention of vocational rehabilitation services and workplace adjustments to accommodate veterans' injuries.

After having first been introduced for injured servicemen, the aim of offering vocational rehabilitation and workplace accommodation were later generalised to encompass all who had been born with or later acquired an impairment affecting their prospects of finding or continuing in work.

For instance, in order for a person with an impairment to be able to fill a job he or she is best qualified for, practical changes in the work situation or improved accessibility to the workplace or other premises may be required (Häikiö and Hvinden, 2012). In other cases, persons with impairments may need flexible working time arrangements, the modification of equipment, training procedures, reference manuals, procedures for testing or assessment, an assistant (reader or interpreter) or supervisor, reorganisation of work tasks, or the reassigning of non-essential duties to other employees.

Gradually two different approaches combined; on one hand vocational rehabilitation services provided by work medicine, physiotherapy and occupational therapy, and on the other hand systematic analysis of work operations to achieve a good fit between job demands and workers' capacities – 'ergonomics' – carried out by engineers and technicians. This combination contained the germ of what was eventually codified as *the relative understanding of disability* (Tøssebro, 2004; Shakespeare, 2006). Here disability has been perceived as 'a mismatch between the person's capabilities and the functional demands of the environment or in terms of a gap between individual functioning and societal/environmental demands' (Tøssebro, 2004). According to this understanding, bodily, mental, or intellectual impairments do not in themselves determine how disabled or incapacitated a person will be, but the interaction or relationship between the person's impairment and the person's social, cultural, and physical context.

If governments are to build their policies on this understanding of disability, their task become two-fold:

- To reduce the gap between the individuals' capacities and the demands of the environment, both by improving the individuals' qualifications and capacities through education or retraining and other relevant provisions (technical aids, adjusted housing, transport, personal assistance, etc).
- Requiring employers to modify the demands of jobs and the work environment to achieve accessibility and various forms of social and organisational accommodation, and if necessary, to contribute to employers' costs related to such accommodations.

While governments' policies have given different relative emphasis to the two forms of interventions, it is still notable that many governments have moved towards adopting a relative understanding as the framework for their disability policies more generally.

A third conceptualisation of disability originated within the international social movement of persons with disabilities and was first codified by scholars who themselves had experience from living with a disability. This *social-contextual understanding* frames disability in terms of oppression, systematic discrimination, exclusion, and segregation, i.e. redefining disability as socially and culturally created (Oliver, 1990; Barnes, 1991). The social-contextual understanding is set in clear opposition to bio-medical understandings of disability and involves a strong criticism of conventional welfare arrangements building on such understandings, claiming that these arrangements contributes to the margin position, passivity, segregation or even exclusion of persons with disabilities.

Proponents of this social-contextual understanding – often referred to as 'the social model' – call for broad social changes to enable persons with impairments to participate in society on equal footing with others, live independently in the community and exercise self-determination. Key demands include removing barriers for participation by making accessibility legally required and combating discrimination and exclusion through legal and other instruments. A distinct strand of disability studies and research in the United Kingdom and a number of other countries has elaborated the social-contextual understanding and the related demands for social change (Barnes et al., 1999; Barnes and Mercer, 2003; Campbell and Oliver, 1996; Oliver and Barnes, 1998). Inspired by the social-contextual understanding, broad alliances of organisations of persons with disabilities have successfully mobilised and campaigned for the adoption of accessibility and non-discrimination legislation at both national and supranational levels.

In their turn, both the relative and social-contextual understandings of disability have been criticised (Shakespeare, 2006). For instance, one of the objections against the relative understanding is that it gives indeterminate or insufficient guidance for decision-making and therefore has had limited practical effect. The relative understanding advocates a reduced mismatch between the individual and the environments but it does not tell how to calibrate overall public efforts on strengthening the individual's qualifications and capacities *versus* putting pressure on employers to provide accessibility and other forms of on-the-job accommodation. Cynically one may predict that governments will follow the road of least resistance; mainly try to change individuals' qualifications and capacities while being more reluctant when it comes to confront employers and challenge their traditional prerogatives. Similarly, criticism of the social-contextual understanding observes that the distinction between impairment and disability tends to become reified, denying the impact of bodily difference and the ways in which not only disability but also impairments may be socially created or shaped (ibid.; Thomas, 2007).

Other writers have criticised the simple binary division between persons with and without disabilities. These writers have outlined what they call a *universalist perspective* on disability, claiming that everyone is – or will at some point be – confronted with limitations in his or her physical and mental capacity (e.g. Zola, 1989; Bickenbach et al., 1999). According to this perspective, to have an impairment or chronic illness is a matter of degree rather than a dichotomy. Rather than being stable and fixed categories, we are talking about highly changeable characteristics locating all of us at diverse and variable points of our life courses on a continuum from disabled to non-disabled. Inspired by cultural analysis and queer analysis, crip theory has highlighted these flexible boundaries between disability and 'non-disability' (McRuer, 2006; Siebers, 2008).

Finally, the great diversity of specific impairments and their practical impact on everyday life is hidden behind the term disability. The heterogeneity of the adult population living with more substantial impairments is illustrated by the different degree of participation in economic life. According to a study carried out in 51 countries across the world the average employment rates were 53 per cent for men with disabilities and 20 per cent for women with disabilities, compared to 65 per cent for men without disabilities and 30 per cent for women without disabilities (WHO and World Bank, 2011). Largely for the same reason, across the world persons with disabilities tend more often than persons without disabilities to live in economic hardship, poverty, and bad health, being denied basic human rights and security (ibid.).

The Organisation for Economic Co-operation and Development (OECD) stipulates that the average employment rate of persons with disabilities was just above 40 per cent while the average rate of persons without disabilities were close to 75 per cent in member states in the mid-2000s (OECD, 2009).

However, these and other studies show that persons with mental or intellectual impairments tend to have considerably lower employment rates than persons with other impairments. For a long time persons with mental or intellectual impairments were also more often than other persons with impairments placed in large institutions, isolated and hidden from the rest of society, and in many cases exposed to demeaning and degrading treatment and abuse. While many Western countries have carried out a programme of closing down the large institutions and seeking to integrate people in the community, other countries, for instance post-communist societies, are still lagging behind with this deinstitutionalisation.

According to current estimates more than one billion people in the world live with some form of disability, of whom nearly 200 million experience considerable difficulties in functioning (WHO and World Bank, 2011). These and similar estimates must, however, be interpreted and used with caution for reasons related to the challenges of conceptualising and measuring disability in a valid, consistent and comparable way.

Despite the wider acceptance of relative or social-contextual conceptions of disability, social surveys aiming to measure the proportion of a given population that has a disability, and how this disability impacts on the situation and well-being of the persons, tend to be oriented toward individual impairments or restriction in functioning. This is partly because surveys are usually using probability samples of individuals in order to estimate the distribution of characteristics in the whole populations, rather than trying to interview all members of these populations. This procedure means the individual's replies to a set of questions about whether he/she has an impairment or experiences a restriction in everyday life are used as a screening device to identify him or her as a person with a disability. Moreover, information about the individual's relationships to his/her physical, social or organizational environments has to be gained through the replies of the individual.

Unfortunately we still have fairly little comparative, representative and reliable data about the prevalence of disability and the consequences of living with a disability. Attempts to collect or compile such data have, for instance, been made by Eurostat, International Labour Organization (ILO), OECD and the European Social Survey programme. The European Community Household Panel (ECHP) study, the Labour Force Survey (LFS) Ad Hoc Module 2002 of the Eurostat, and the current European Union Statistics on Income and Living Conditions (EU-SILC) surveys have all included disability-related questions. These attempts to produce comparative data have faced the fundamental issue of how to define disability for the purpose of official statistics and research. Unlike demographic characteristics such as age and gender, whether a person has a disability or not is a characteristic which national statistical authorities cannot rely upon existing registers. Knowledge about whether a person has a disability or not has to be collected through statistical surveys, based on interviews or questionnaires and large scale representative samples of the whole population. Since this approach is based on screening and self-identification, a source of error is the reluctance of some respondents to disclose to a stranger that they are a person with an impairment or disability.

Another complicating factor is that, despite the goal of producing strictly comparable data from different countries and translating terms as precisely as possible between different languages, it is unavoidable that the terms used might have somewhat different associations or connotations for respondents in different countries. Possibly the availability and scope of a country's disability provisions – both of the redistributive and social regulatory kinds (see later) – influence respondents' inclination to identify themselves as having an impairment or disability. Moreover, different demographic structures of countries will affect their proportion of citizens with disabilities.

Attempts to collect comparative data have been compounded by the striking and surprising difference in the proportion of respondents from different countries who reported that they had a disability. For instance, in the 1996 wave of the ECHP this proportion varied from 8 per cent (Italy) to 23 per cent (Finland), whereas in the 2002 LFS Ad Hoc Module this proportion varied from 7 per cent (Italy) to 32 per cent (Finland).

Presentation and analysis of these elements

A basic and general mechanism behind the overrepresentation of persons with disabilities among groups experiencing disadvantage and hardship is the tendency of human beings to favour the normal, ordinary, conventional, familiar, and recognisable. The more narrow and strict notions of normality are, the more exposed to separation and exclusion will be persons who are perceived to be different or deviating. More specifically we tend to have fairly clear standards of how one should look and present oneself. In our culture we have a long tradition of celebrating facial and bodily beauty and idealising the young, well-trained and perfect body. Generally, this idealisation tends to put persons who look, talk, walk and behave differently than others at disadvantage and risk of being neglected, disparaged, stigmatised, excluded, or segregated from the rest of society.

A second mechanism is the general necessity of human beings to work in order to live and the related norm that one has to contribute in order to enjoy the gains of work. While the necessity and social duty to work is modified and mediated in modern and highly differentiated societies, the perceived ability to perform and carry out one's part of the work is still an important criterion for our judgment of fellow human beings (and ourselves) and a significant source of social recognition and respect. The elaborate differentiation of our societies means that performance expectations are particularly strong and dominant in the economic sphere, the market, and the work organisation. Broadly speaking, this performance orientation puts persons with reduced work capacity at disadvantage in economic life, especially if the reduction is of a long-term nature.

A third mechanism is our tendency to make untested assumptions about other people, what they are like, or what they are able to do or achieve. Often our knowledge is more limited than we like to admit and we make judgements on the basis of weak or flimsy evidence or limited experience. As a result persons with disabilities are often exposed to prejudices, stereotypes, or unwarranted generalisations. Thus an employer may disregard a well-qualified job applicant with a particular impairment on the basis of the untested belief that the person would be less able to carry out the job, even if the impairment is completely irrelevant for the person's ability to undertake the tasks of the job. This disregard would represent a case of (direct) discrimination on the part of the employer. Whereas we in everyday life tend to talk about discrimination as if it involved dislike, bad will, or deliberate adverse intention towards another person, the legal concept of discrimination is broader, encompassing both intended and unintended effects of human action.

Modern welfare states have partly tried to prevent the operation of these and similar mechanisms putting persons with disabilities at a disadvantage, partly sought to ameliorate or diminish the mechanisms' impact. Broadly speaking, these efforts have taken the form of *redistributive* or *social regulatory* provisions. While redistributive provisions seek to equalise life chances through tax-financed cash transfers and services, social regulatory provisions involve efforts to influence the behaviour of non-governmental actors, especially actors operating in the market, in ways that promote social objectives – or at least ensure that the behaviour of these actors can be reconciled with such objectives (Majone, 1993). In relation to disability, redistributive provisions appear for a long time and in most countries to have played a more dominating role than social regulatory provisions. One indicator of this dominance is that most adult citizens seem to be aware of the availability of cash benefits and services in the event of acquiring a disability or health-related incapacity, while relatively few seem to know about the legal protection against inaccessibility or discrimination related to disability, or how to file a complaint should they experience inaccessibility or discrimination. A second indicator some governments appear to have been ambivalent introducing such legal protection, and if they have introduced such legislation, create conditions for effective implementation and enforcment, for instance by providing easily accessible information about the legal right not be exposed to inaccessibility or discrimination and where and how to file complaints. Third a number of studies have found that it is difficult to find any clear impact of the introduction of non-discrimination legislation or other forms of social regulation instruments related to disability (e.g. Clayton et al., 2011a).

Redistributive provisions have offered income maintenance or replacement for persons who have been unable to find work or who had to give up working. Such cash benefits have for instance been called disability or incapacity benefit (pension). The exact construction of disability-related cash benefits has varied considerably between countries (or over time within countries) in terms of eligibility criteria, associated training requirements, generosity (replacement rates) and duration. Despite this huge variation in design, both national governments and supranational organisations like the OECD have been worried about increasing numbers of disability-related beneficiaries and the associated burden on public budgets. A recurring concern has been whether the availability of such cash benefits creates discentives to work (meaning that 'work does not pay'), especially for people who are likely to find themselves at the lower end of the income distribution. Although there is some evidence for such discentive effects, there are disgreements abut how great and significant they are, for instance compared to the strictness of medical and work-capacity testing, the frequency of and efforts invested in reviews of granted benefits, the amount of resources spent on vocational rehabilitation, training, active job guidance, and monitoring of job-seeking efforts. Some scholars have argued that the availability of disability benefits has contributed to ease the restructuring and modernisation of economic life, by providing fairly acceptable avenues for those who become redundant and are unlikely to find new jobs. While this (ab)use of disability provisions may appear convenient for the directly affected (including the employer), some observers maintain that this effectively means 'purchasing the absence of the other' (Quinn, 2005) and creating an additional mechanism for excluding persons with disabilities.

As already suggested, many governments spend substantial amounts of resources on measures to strengthen the capacities of persons with disabilities by improving their qualifications, and through this, their labour market prospects. Evaluations of such welfare-to-work measures have, however, revealed mixed findings about effects (e.g. Clayton et al., 2011b). Some fear that such measures removes participants from the labour market for too long or that having participated is stigmatising the person in the eyes of potential employers. It is worth asking whether some of these resources might have been put to better and more effective use by ensuring that young people with disabilities succeed in completing their education as planned and with sufficiently solid results to make them competitive in the labour market. Several studies have found that persons with disabilities on average have lower educational achievements than persons without disabilities and that this difference has contributed to the gap in employment rates.

Some redistributive provisions are particularly targeted at persons with disabilities involving more long-term or permanent reduction of work capacity. Such provisions include various forms of financial incentives for employers to hire these persons (wage subsidies, tax deductions, etc.) and the possibilities to combine a part-time job with a graded disability pension. In some countries, companies over a certain size are obliged to have a certain quota of employees with reduced work capacity, serving some of the same function as wage subsidies. While wage subsidies and quotas appear relatively successful in promoting employment for persons with permanently diminished work capacity, some observers argue that they distort the normal functioning of the labour market through displacement of other jobseekers or redefinition of already employed persons. Such unintended effects could probably be avoided if one improved arrangements for assessing the extent to which a person's work capacity is actually diminished, and possibly, reviewing whether this is still the case after a certain period of time.

In most OECD countries redistributive provisions include social services to assist persons with disabilities. The nature, quality and scope of these services have changed considerably over time, e.g. from placement in large total institutions to services provided in the local community and aiming to create conditions for the privacy, independence, and self-determination that citizens generally expect to have in modern societies. Even if the enjoyment of these goods are defined a basic rights under international human rights conventions, they are not a matter of course in all societies. In some countries we still find large institutions, whereas in other countries family and kin are still main providers of care for persons with disabilities. Meanwhile, in countries where deinstitutionalisation has almost been completed one can see worrying signs of re-institutionalisation through the establishment of large 'group-homes', driven by efforts to cut public expenditure. Similarly, the provision of personal assistance, vouchers or direct payments to enable persons with disabilities to hire assistance is threatened in local cost-cutting exercises, undermining or reducing possibilities for independent living.

As already indicated, new *social regulatory provisions* first of all involve giving employers, public, and private actors operating buildings, transport, communication, and information systems the legal duty to ensure full accessibility (i.e. preventing and removing barriers to equal access, use, and participation). Second, such provisions generally seek to promote equal treatment by prohibiting discrimination of the ground of disability or impairment, for instance in relation to employment and occupation. Third, the provisions give employers the duty to offer reasonable accommodation to job applicants or employers with disabilities who may require such accommodation. In this context 'reasonable' means that the accommodation should be appropriate and relevant in relation to the person's requirements but not representing a disproportionate burden for the employer. Some countries have public arrangements covering some part of the costs related to accommodation, making it harder for employers to claim that accommodation would represent a disproportionate burden.

In 2012 most European countries had introduced accessibility and non-discrimination laws as a consequence of their membership or association with the European Union (EU). The EU includes accessibility requirements in its legal regulations for the internal market. All Member States had to transpose their national legislation in accordance with the EC Directive 2000/78 on equal treatment in employment and occupation (EC, 2000) while associated countries have decided to introduce shadow legislation to match the Directive.

In the broader international context, equal treatment, accessibility and non-discrimination have been given a strong boost through the adoption of the United Nations (UN) Convention on the Rights of Persons with Disabilities (UN, 2006), brought into force 3 May 2008. In February 2012 the Convention had 153 signatories and 110 entities across the world, including the EU, had ratified it.

Researchers disagree on what impact the new social regulatory provisions have had in terms of improving the situation for persons with disabilities. So far the practical impact appears to be greater in relation to accessibility than in relation to non-discrimination, for instance in employment. Even in countries that introduced non-discrimination legislation relatively early, for instance the United States (1990) and United Kingdom (1995), the evidence on impact is mixed. Overall the legislation appears to have been most successful in preventing discrimination of persons who are already employed than in preventing discrimination of persons outside work seeking to get a job.

Some early studies indicated that the Americans with Disabilities Act (ADA) led to diminished employment rates for persons with disabilities These studies suggested that employers sought to avoid litigation by not hiring persons with disabilities or that the obligation to provide reasonable accommodation deterred employers from recruiting jobseekers with disabilities. Other researchers questioned these findings, arguing that the work disability measure used did not accurately reflect the coverage under the ADA. Later studies have found that while the employment rate of persons with disabilities diminished in the early 1990s, the cause was not the introduction of ADA but a new definition of disability in the income maintenance system.

Research in the United Kingdom indicates that the Disability Discrimination Act (DDA) did not have any impact in the first period after its introduction and that it even contributed to a decrease in the employment rate of persons with disabilities. The DDA may have influenced employers to avoid firing employees who had acquired an impairment but to less extent had a positive impact on recruitment practices. The employment rates of persons with disabilities have increased recently but observers have offered competing explanations; a delayed impact of DDA or the effects of the Blair government's New Deal for the Disabled.

There may be additional reasons to the lack of positive and robust effects of non-discrimination legislation. One reason may be methodological; for instance, with the data that researchers have had access to, it may not have been possible to account for the effects of potentially counter-acting factors. Another reason is that researchers may lack data of the extent to which non-discrimination legislation is effectively implemented and enforced in the sense mentioned before; through a system of awareness-raising, information, supervision, and enforcement, aiming at a combination of preventive measures and sanctioning of actual cases of discrimination. This aspect may be particularly important when comparing the effect of non-discrimination legislation in different countries.

Anyway, non-discrimination legislation has some limitations. For instance, there is a case of direct discrimination only if a person with a particular disability is equally qualified and able to perform the core tasks of a job (with appropriate accommodation) as a person without that particular disability, and the person with this disability is treated less favourably on the grounds of having this disability. There is no case of discrimination if the person with this disability, for instance, is turned down for a job because he or she has less relevant education, training, or work experience than another applicant without this particular disability, and the latter gets the job. In addition, persons with disabilities on average have less education, training, and work experience than persons without – this difference may explain a considerable part of the employment gap between the two groups.

For these reasons policy efforts to improve the employment prospects of persons with disabilities need to *combine* elements of regulatory and redistributive provisions, rather than seeing these as alternative approaches.

Conclusion

Despite governments' stated aims of ensuring that persons with disabilities enjoy the right to live in the same way as others, the daily reality for a great number of persons with disabilities is different. While we find large variation in the living conditions of persons with disabilities across different countries and kinds of impairment, neglect, ignorance, stereotypes, prejudice and discrimination are still preventing too many people with disabilities from enjoying a life in security, dignity, respect, independence, and self-determination. Most countries' provisions to address the situation of persons with disabilities appear insufficient or misdirected, or both. Significantly, the adoption of UN Convention of the Rights of Persons with Disabilities has created a new optimism and belief in change across the world, in rich, emerging, and poor economies. The Convention is likely to stimulate a change from different national and regional points of departure but pointing in the same direction.

References

Amos, J. T. (1943), Vocational Rehabilitation during and after the War. *The Canadian Journal of Economics and Political Science*, 9. 2, pp. 164–74.

Barnes, C. (1991), *Disabled People in Britain and Discrimination: A Case for Anti-Discrimination Legislation.* London: Hurst & Company.

Barnes, C., Mercer, G. and Shakespeare, T. (1999), *Exploring Disability: A Sociological Introduction.* Cambridge: Polity Press.

Barnes, C. and Mercer, G. (2003), *Disability*. Cambridge: Polity Press.

Bickenbach, J. E., Chatterji, S. Badley, E. M. and Üstün, T. B. (1999), Models of disablement, universalism and the international classification of impairments, disabilities and handicaps. *Social Science & Medicine*. 48, 9, pp. 1173–87.

Campbell, J. and Oliver, M. (1996) *Disability Politics: Understanding our Past, Changing our Future.* London: Routledge.

Clayton, S., Barr, B., Nylén, L., Burström, B., Thielen, K., Diderichsen, F., Dahl, E. and Whitehead, M. (2011a), Effectiveness of return-to-work interventions for disabled people: a systematic review of government initiatives focused on changing the behaviour of employers. *European Journal of Public Health* (Electronic access from August 2011).

Clayton, S., Bambra, C., Gosling, R., Povall, S., Misso, K. and Whitehead, M. (2011), 'Assembling the evidence jigsaw: insights from a systematic review of UK studies of individual-focused return to work initiatives for disabled and long-term ill people', *BMC Public Health*. 2011, 11:170.

de Swaan, A. (1990), *In Care of the State: Health Care, Education and Welfare in Europe and the USA in the Modern Era.* Cambridge: Polity Press.

European Commission (EC) (2000), Council Directive (EC) 2000/78 establishing a general framework for equal treatment in employment and occupation [2000] O.J. L303/16.

Grahame, R. (2002), The decline of rehabilitation services and its impact on disability benefits. *Journal of the Royal Societies of Medicine*. 95, pp. 114–17.

Häikiö, L. and Hvinden, B. (2012), 'Finding the way between universalism and diversity: a challenge to the Nordic model', in A. Anttonen, L. Häikiö and K. Stefansson (eds), *Welfare States, Universalism and Diversity*. Cheltenham: Edward Elgar.

Linker, B. (2011), *War's Waste: Rehabilitation in World War I America*. Chicago, IL: The University of Chicago Press.

Majone, G. (1993), The European Community between social policy and social regulation. *Journal of Common Market Studies* 2 (1993), 31, pp. 153–70.

McRuer, R. (2006), *Crip Theory: Cultural Signs of Queerness and Disability*. New York: New York University Press.

Obermann, C. E. (1967), *A History of Vocational Rehabilitation in America*. Minneapolis, MN: T. S. Denison.

Organisation for Economic Co-operation and Development (OECD) (2009), *Sickness, Disability and Work: Keeping on track in the economic downturn*, High-Level, Forum, 14–15 May, 2009, Background Paper, www.oecd.org/els/disability/stockholmforum (accessed 11 July 2011).

Oliver, M. (1990), *The Politics of Disablement*, Basingstoke: Macmillan.

Oliver, M. and Barnes, C. (1998), *Disabled People and Social Policy: From Exclusion to Inclusion*. Harlow: Longman.

Ross, J. (2008), *Occupational Therapy and Vocational Rehabilitation*. Chichester and Oxford: Wiley-Blackwell.

Shakespeare, T. (2006), *Disability Rights and Wrongs*. London and New York: Routledge.

Siebers, T. (2008), *Disability Theory*. Ann Arbor: The University of Michigan Press.

Stone, D. (1985), *The Disabled State*, Philadelphia, PA: Temple University Press.

Thomas, C. (2007), *Sociologies of Disability and Illness: Contested Ideas in Disability Studies and Medical Sociology*. Basingstoke: Palgrave Macmillan.

Tøssebro, J. (2004), Introduction to the special issue: Understanding disability, *Scandinavian Journal of Disability Research*, 6, 1, pp. 3–7.

United Nations (UN) (2006), United Nations Convention on the Rights of Persons with Disabilities and Optional Protocol, adopted 13 December 2006, entry into force 3 May 2008, www.un.org/disabilities (accessed 13 July 2011).

World Trade Organization (WHO) and World Bank (2011), *World Report on Disability*, Geneva: World Health Organization, www.who.int/disabilities/world_report/2011/report.pdf (accessed 13 July 2011).

Zola, I. K. (1989), 'Toward the necessary universalizing of disability policy', *The Milbank Quarterly*, 67, Suppl.2, Pr. 2, pp. 401–28.

36
Family policies

Chiara Saraceno

Introduction

Family policies as a specific set of guidelines explicitly aimed at supporting socially desirable behaviours and relationships are relatively recent. An important exception is France, whose pro-natalist policies date back to the beginning of the twentieth century. Governments' intervention in family matters, regulating what constitutes a family and what obligations family members have to each other, however, dates back to the formation of nation states, when these started to compete with kin, churches, local communities, and traditions for the power to regulate this sphere of life and relationships. Social family policies, which constitute the focus of this chapter, are, while certainly important, only a manner of public intervention in family matters.

Family policy goals have changed and change over time and across countries (Gauthier, 1996; Saraceno et al., forthcoming), and so have the instruments. Kaufman (2002) and Bahle (2008) identify a variety of possible motives for family policy. Concern for ('too low' or 'too high') fertility and demographic reproduction is among the main reasons for states' intervention. Poverty among families with children has also traditionally been an important policy driver both in Europe and in the US, and it is becoming the main concern of both anti-poverty and family policies in many developing countries. A radical change of goal witnessed in many Organisation for Economic Co-operation and Development (OECD) countries concerns the role of women and more generally of gender relations. While at the origins of the welfare state social policies as well as legal norms directly or indirectly supported the male-breadwinner/family-carer model, in recent years family policies have been argued as a means to support the dual earner and in some cases also the dual-earner/dual-carer model, supporting both mothers' participation into the labour market and, although to a lesser degree, fathers' participation in child care.

In the following sections, first the concept of (social) family policies itself and the various dimensions of such policies will be analysed, with particular regard to the distinction between goals and outcomes, between different kinds of instruments and their possible interplay, and to whether it is possible to identify specific family policy patterns that distinguish clear country clusters. Then the main targets and instruments of family policies will be presented and discussed from a comparative perspective. The concluding section will synthesize the main issues discussed in the chapter.

Concepts and dimensions

Kamerman and Kahn (1978; see also Kamerman, 2010), propose to distinguish between explicit and implicit family policies. Explicit family policies are deliberately designed to achieve specific objectives with regard to individuals within families and/or the whole family. Implicit family policies include actions taken in various policy domains for non-family-related goals, but which nevertheless have important consequences for children and families. Kaufman (2002) uses this distinction to identify not so much policies as between countries that have an explicit family policy, i.e. those that explicitly formulate policies aimed at influencing how families are organized and behave, and countries that have no such explicit goal in mind when formulating their policies. In his view, France and Belgium are typically explicit family policy countries, while English-speaking countries are typically implicit ones. Boundaries between these two groups are not clearly cut, however, and many countries lie rather in between. Furthermore, some countries may shift from one group to the other, not so much changing its policies as redefining the already existing ones. It has occurred, for instance, when maternity and parental leave have been discursively moved from labour market to family policies (and back).

In this chapter, the choice is made to use an operational definition of family policies. Included are all those public policies that are explicitly designed to affect the situation of families or individuals in their, gender and intergenerational, family roles, and thus have clear, though possibly unintended, consequences for such families and individuals: direct and indirect income transfers designed to support the cost of children and/or of a dependent spouse, services, and cash transfers aimed at dealing with the caring needs of young children or other not fully self-sufficient family members. Financial and caring responsibilities within families, between generations, and between partners are, in fact, the main areas of family policy intervention, even if in different ways across time and space.

In analysing policies, sector, goals, and instruments must be kept analytically distinct. The caring needs of a small child (sector) may be, in fact, answered (measured) both by providing services and by supporting parents (usually the mother) to provide all necessary care, through various kinds of income transfers. Whether one or the other instrument is used depends on the specific goals of the policy and on the implicit or explicit behavioural norms it wants to promote.

Typologies of family policies differ depending on the criteria used as an identifying base as well as on the number and type of countries considered. Anttonen and Sipilä (1996) have clustered (Western European) countries according to the degree to which the state (at the time of their analysis) assumed care responsibilities for the welfare of children and the frail elderly. They have identified four distinct groups focusing on indicators that capture defamilialization: service coverage that is: generous to the frail elderly but not to children, as in The Netherlands, Norway and Great Britain; generous to children but not to the frail elderly, as in France, Belgium and Italy; generous to both children and the frail elderly, as in Denmark, Finland and Sweden; and generous to neither children nor the frail elderly, as in Portugal, Greece, Spain, Ireland and Germany. In a later work, however, the same authors, together with Baldock (2003), have concluded that it is not possible to construct a typology, since care policies are a mixed package and include services alongside leaves of differing length and levels of compensation. Bettio and Plantenga (2004) and Bettio et al. (2006) also develop a typology of what they define as caring regimes, which includes the market and pays particular attention to migrant care labour.

Gender arrangements are basis of numerous typologies of family policy. The concept of gender regimes was first developed by Orloff (1993), who elaborated on Esping-Andersen's concept of decommodification by including a gendered notion of social citizenship, that is, the degree to which policies support women to access paid work and balance it with family life, rendering them financially independent from a relationship with a man. Lewis (1992) based her classification on the degree to which policies support or, on the contrary, weaken the male-breadwinner model

Work–family reconciliation issues are at the basis of specific typologies, more or less loosely linked to gender-based ones. Gornick et al. (1996, see also Gornick and Meyers, 2004) have classified countries according to the degree they support employment for mothers of pre-school children. Bahle (2008) constructs his typology (which includes twenty-five European Union (EU) countries) on the basis of the degree of state support for the family–work relationship (in the form of maternity/parental benefits and childcare services) and family income (via family/child allowances). This results in five country clusters, ranging from the most generous and universal to the least. According to his interpretation, cross-cluster differences in the way in which the needs of families with children are addressed may be the outcome of historical differences in the relationship between states and churches in particular.

The well-being of children is at the basis of Bradshaw's (2006) typology, which includes fifteen European countries and focuses on the generosity of the provision of cash benefits, tax credits, and services for children in different family situations.

Daly (2010) distinguishes family policy profiles on the basis of the strength of particular underlining motivations and the diversity of national philosophical orientations, which shape distinct family–market–state relationships. Focusing on a selected number of countries, she therefore distinguishes between: 1 countries such as France and Belgium, with a pro-natalist and pro-family orientation, linking together fertility, family, and national interest; 2 countries such as post-war West Germany which on the contrary the state should interfere as little as possible in families and should support their autonomy mainly through income transfers; 3 states such as the Scandinavian ones, whose goal is egalitarianism between men and women, but also among children, and therefore underplay the role of the family as an economic and redistributive unit while assigning the state a role to support individual autonomy; and 4 states such the UK, the US, and Australia, where policies are intended not to support families as such, but to contrast poverty.

Kaufmann (2002) distinguishes four family policy profiles ('families of nations') within Western Europe on the basis of their overall generosity, that is, the level of financial (cash benefits) and infrastructural (services) support they offer to families, irrespective of the explicit or implicit goals. These profiles range from the most generous in terms of both benefits and services (the Nordic countries and France) to the least generous (Italy and the other Southern European countries).

Leitner (2007) and Saraceno (2010, with Keck 2010) have proposed to categorize policies on the basis of whether they relieve family members from some of their financial and caring obligations or support them in performing them by giving them money and/or time. They distinguish between: 1) familialism *de facto*, or by 'default', when supports are minimal or non-existent; 2) supported familialism, when policies, usually through financial transfers (including taxation and paid leaves), support (specific) family members in keeping up their financial and care responsibilities; and 3) defamilization, when policies reduce family responsibilities and dependencies, shifting them (more or less) partly to the public sphere. These different policy approaches also have a different impact on the gender division of labour in families. In particular, both familialism by default and supported familialism tend to crystallize the gender division of labour, while defamilization helps reduce it (Korpi, 2000). Yet, supported familialism may also be intended as an instrument to acknowledge the desire to care and to change the gender division of labour, as in the case of specific quotas of parental leave allocated to fathers (e.g. Leira, 2006). While single policies may be assigned to one or the other category in the familialization–defamilization continuum, the overall package of a given country's family policies results from a combination of all three approaches. Cross-country variation derives from the relative incidence of each in one or more areas. Based on the public/private divide and on the degree of institutionalization of policies, Hantrais distinguishes between four types of family policies. In particular, she distinguishes between 'traditional' familialism, which in her view is typical of Mediterranean countries, and re-familialization, which would be typical of the former communist countries.

This synthetic overview of attempts at developing typologies testifies to the different dimensions involved in family policies, as well as to the different goals they may be perceived to (have to) address. Within the EU and OECD countries, however, in recent years there has been a growing convergence in explicit goals, also because of the active role played by these two national organizations, and particularly the EU, through its directives (e.g. the 96/34 parental leave directive), recommendations, and jointly agreed targets (e.g. the target concerning women's labour force participation or that concerning child care coverage for pre-school children). In particular, the joint goal of increasing women's labour force participation and supporting work–family conciliation has taken first place, in a more or less coherent conjunction with that of supporting fertility and investing in children. In this perspective, in all countries, the family has become a more explicit target of policies, whether or not they are actually called 'family policies'. Country-specific policy packages remain different, however.

Areas and instruments of family policies

We may distinguish policies on the basis of their goal, their target, and of whether they are in income (financial transfers) or in kind (time/services). In the following, policies are grouped on the basis of their targets.

Policies for families with children

A first group of policies addresses the presence and cost of children. Children cost both as consumers of goods and as consumers of time. The first type of cost is usually addressed through direct or indirect (tax allowances) financial transfers. The second kind of cost is addressed both through time allowances and financial transfers, as in the case of paid maternity and parental leaves, and through services. In the first case we might speak of supported familialism, in the second case of – more or less extended – defamilialization, insofar as part of the caring time is provided outside the family.

In all EU countries, but not in all the OECD or the developing ones, we find all three instruments. But there is a wide cross-country variation in the generosity of direct and indirect income transfers aimed at relieving the cost of children as consumers of goods as well as in whether they are means tested – as in Italy, Spain, Portugal, and all the former communist Eastern European countries – or whether the amount differs with the rank and/or the age of the child or in particular household cases (e.g. lone parent, or disabled children). Given the complexity of these different rules and of their interaction with the taxation system, it is difficult to compare the overall generosity of child-related income countries. Some systems, in fact, are more generous towards lone-parent households, others towards poor households, and still others towards households with more than one child, and so forth. Substantial variation exists also in the second set of measures. Statutory in all EU countries and targeted to working parents, both maternity and parental leaves differ as to who among workers has access to them (exceptions may concern short term workers, the self employed as well as all irregular workers); their duration; and whether they (particularly parental leaves) are paid and with what degree of substitution of lost wages. A further difference concerns whether there are specific incentives for fathers to take up a portion of the parental leave. These incentives are present in all Nordic countries except Denmark, Belgium, Germany, Italy, Luxembourg, and Portugal. They usually consist in a 'take it or leave it' reserved quota, which appears to be efficacious only if the level of compensation is substantial (e.g. UNICEF, 2008). Important cross-country differences exist also in the coverage rate offered by publicly financed services for preschool children, particularly for those under the age of three.

Figure 36.1 offers a graphic description of how these different instruments are combined within the EU, as well as the degree of caring responsibilities left to the family. Where leaves are

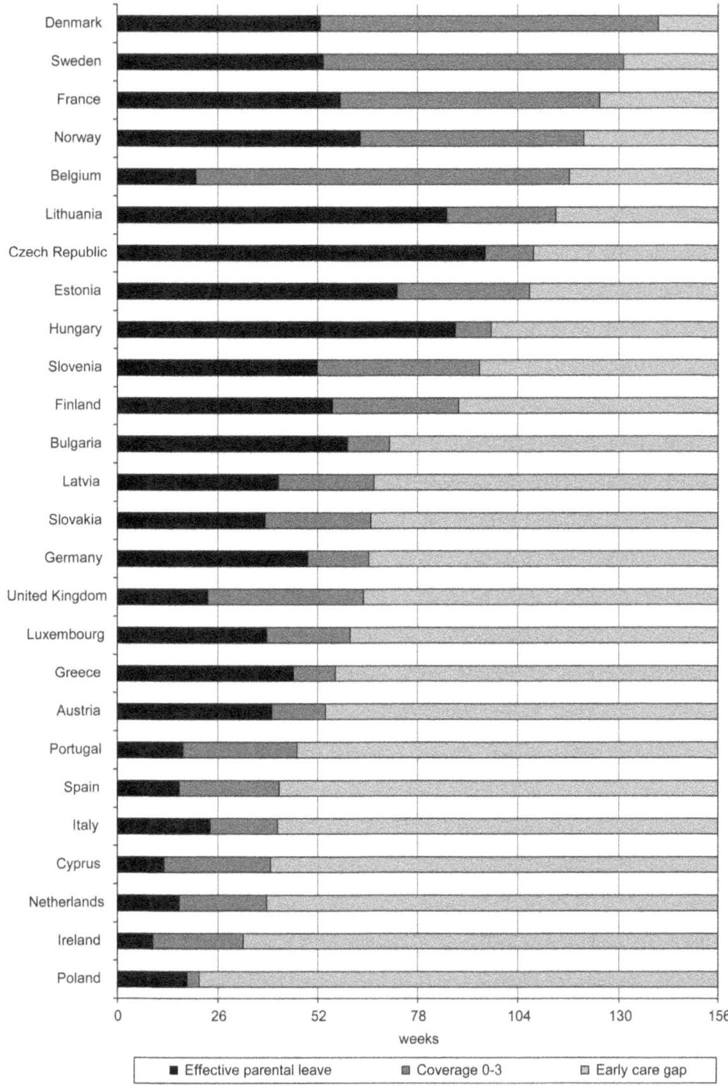

Figure 36.1 Effective parental leave time * and childcare coverage for children aged under three**
Notes: * Including the portion of leave reserved for mothers after childbirth, which in most, but not all, countries is often a separate kind of leave, usually defined as maternity leave.
** In weeks per child of the total population of children under three.
Source: Multilinks Database and Saraceno and Keck, 2010.

comparatively short and services scarce, as in Italy and other Southern European countries, the proportion of caring time and responsibilities left to the family, *de facto* mostly to the mother, is high. This also happens when leaves are long and well-compensated, but after they expire (typically a year), services are not available, as occurs in many Eastern European countries.

A growing literature has pointed out that early childcare and education is an important means of reducing social inequalities among children in cognitive development (Mahon, 2006). However, while services for children over three are generally defined as educational services, in many countries services for the under-threes are defined either as social assistance, health services, or both (Moss, 2010).

Policies supporting mothers' employment

Whatever the specific national context, policies addressing the caring needs of children increasingly overlap with those addressing a second policy aim, that of supporting mothers' labour market participation, insofar they may be framed also (if not prevalently) as 'work–family conciliation' policies. The policy goal to increase women's labour force participation through work family conciliating policies has multiple grounds. One is the concern for equal opportunities between men and women. Another is to increase the proportion of contributors to the social security system in ageing societies. Still another is that of reducing poverty among lone mother households and therefore also among children, reducing also their dependency on social assistance. Finally, since the turn of the century, work–family conciliation policies are often argued from the perspective of supporting fertility in the OECD countries, where fertility rates have become positively related to women's labour force participation rates, although the link with policies is far from being clear and univocal (OECD, 2011).

Whether simple participation by women in the labour market may be equated with gender equality or even equal opportunities is debatable and debated. From the point of view of family policies, however, promoting a family model where all adults are (also) in paid work represents a radical shift in the state's intervention in family and gender arrangements. For a long time, in fact, policies have, directly or indirectly, supported mothers to stay at home, either through supporting the male-breadwinner household (e.g. through a favourable taxation such as the splitting system in Germany or the family quotient in France, or generous tax allowances for a dependent spouse, as well as survivor pensions), or through acknowledging motherhood and mothers' caring responsibilities as an autonomous entitlement to benefits, particularly in the case of income support for the poor. Even where policies in favour of the male breadwinner were not particularly generous, as in the Southern European countries and the US, this normative model was the implicit legitimising ground for not providing services and for considering working mothers as an exception, and to be treated as such. The innovation is so radical that Daly (2011) has argued that family policy is becoming *de facto* mainly labour market policy and that policies have shifted from a 'maternalist' (but also wifely) focus to considering mothers (and wives) mainly as earners, with or without adequate service support (see also Orloff, 2006). Countries, however, differ not only by the degree in which they actively support this model through policies, but also in the radicality with which they try to implement it, particularly in the case of couples' households. Thus, in countries such as the Netherlands or Germany part-time social security protection (mainly for women) is actively supported as a way of balancing paid work and care, encouraging a one-and-a-half earner-and-carer household model, rather than a dual-earner one (e.g. Lewis et al., 2008).

Work–care conciliation policies are overall less generous and institutionalised in the non-EU OECD countries, where maternity and parental leaves have been introduced later, are generally shorter, and often unpaid. In the developing countries, the presence of a large informal economy sector renders it difficult not only to finance, but to implement a generalized system of leaves, since many women do not have formal contracts nor pay contribution (Beneria, 2008).

Family policies as anti-poverty policies

The shift from maternalism to considering mothers as breadwinners is particularly evident in the case of poor lone mothers asking for social assistance. Encouraging mothers to work while subsidizing low income earners, rather than simply providing income transfers, have become the most preferred policy choice in the case of poor lone mothers and generally of poor households since the turn of the century, through the 'activation rhetoric'. This approach configures an indirect family policy for the poor, through a mixture of incentives and deterrents (for an overview see OECD, 2011). Its extreme form is represented by the 1996 TANF reform in the US, where it is also explicitly coupled with attempts at 'normalizing' the moral behaviour of poor (and often black or Latino) lone mothers discouraging them from having further children and promoting marriage (see Smith, 2006). A similar approach with regard to 'making work pay', or 'welfare to work', stressing the breadwinning responsibilities of poor lone mothers may also be found in the New Labour 'new deal for lone mothers' approach in the UK, and even more in the working tax credit in the former French *prime pour l'emploi*, now substituted by the Revenue Social d'Assistance (RSA), and in the 2004 German Hartz reform of social assistance.

Family policies are being developed as explicit anti-poverty policies in various developing countries, with a specific focus on children (Fiszbein and Schady, 2009). In such diverse countries as Mexico, Brazil, Uruguay, South Africa, and others, minimum income transfers have been introduced for families with children below the poverty line, with the requirement that they attend school and have medical check-up regularly. Mothers, rather than fathers, are the recipients of the benefit as well as the parent held responsible for implementing the required behaviour. This choice has caused a debate on whether it represents an empowerment of women or rather a further crystallization of their role as mothers (e.g. Molineux, 2006). Another policy that is proving successful in developing countries in supporting poor households with children is the introduction of an old age pension, insofar as usually the old are embedded in extended, three-generational households and their access to a secure income becomes an asset for all household members and particularly children.

Policies for the frail old

Similarly to what happens for children, the ways and extent to which the caring needs of the frail old are addressed by public policies are largely based on implicit or explicit assumptions concerning individual entitlements and family responsibilities (e.g. Saraceno, 2010). Policies addressing the needs of the frail old, therefore, may be defined also as, at least indirect, family policies.

Three important dimensions of welfare state arrangements are relevant from this perspective. The first is whether support (not related to healthcare) is income-tested or universal. The second is the threshold of dependency above which one is entitled to receive support. The third is how much of the individual need is covered. These dimensions define who is entitled and under which conditions, and what is left to his/her own and family resources. Two other important dimensions of programme design must be added: whether support is offered in kind or in

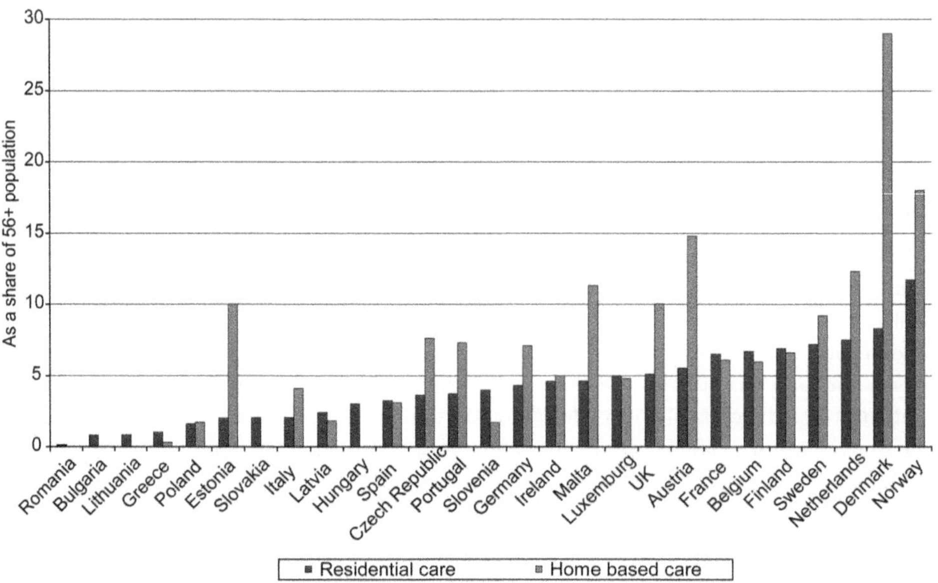

Figure 36.2 Coverage through care services for the frail old (residential, home-based)
Source: Multilinks Database; Saraceno and Keck (2010).

money or via a combination of the two; and, when monetary support is provided, whether there are specific rules as to how it should be spent. These two further dimensions allow distinguishing between defamilialization via publicly provided services, defamilialization via market services supported by public money, and supported familialism. Figure 36.2, based on different, unfortunately not always updated sources offers a very general idea of diversities in the degree as well as the composition of public efforts in the availability of publicly supported care services.

Only the Nordic countries and the Netherlands have comparatively high levels of both residential and home care, with Denmark and Norway being clear outliers in the degree of defamilialization, followed at a great distance by the Netherlands, Sweden, Finland, Belgium, and France. At the opposite, in most of the Central and Eastern European EU member states, but also in Greece, Italy, and Spain, coverage is minimal and therefore the degree of familialism by default, with or without recourse to the market, is high. The market solution is substantial in the US.

Cash-for-care allowances exist in several countries, although under different conditions. In some cases, they are meant to substitute services, in others to pay for services of one's own choice, or, as in the case of Germany, an option may be given between receiving cash or services. Allowances may be more or less generous, flat rate, or varying with the degree of dependence. In most countries, they are paid to the care dependent person, but in some (e.g., the United Kingdom) they are paid directly to the family carer (see, e.g. Pavolini and Ranci, 2008). While cash-for-care allowances are quite widespread, the traditional instrument of supported familialism in the case of childcare – leave for the carers – is also provided in most European countries for caring for a dependent person, but it is far less generous in terms of length and compensation. There is a great heterogeneity with regard to who is entitled, what kind and duration of leave is available, and whether it is paid. Generally, however, while short leaves of a few days are compensated, long ones tend not to be compensated. Finally, some country, but in a smaller number than in the case of children, acknowledges time spent in caring for a frail old relative through 'fictious contributions' towards the old age pension. Overall, however, spending time to care for a frail old relative, although often expected by the policy design, is acknowledged as a less deserving behaviour than caring for a small child.

Conclusion

Goals and instruments of family policies differ over time and across countries. The degree to which countries actively try to influence family-linked individual behaviour and family arrangements also varies. Furthermore, a large deal of policies addressing families is outside the realm of social policies and welfare state arrangements. They concern civil law and the way it regulates what is a family, what relationships create family ties and obligations and what these obligations are.

With regard to the social policies addressing families, within the EU and OECD countries, the ideal family model implicitly or even explicitly supported seems to have shifted over time from the male-breadwinner/female-carer model to the dual or one-and-a half-breadwinner/carer model. There has been, therefore, an increase in so-called work–family reconciliation policies, also with some timid effort at rebalancing the gender division of unpaid care in the case of small children, through a mixture of income transfers and services. The overall policy package, however, varies greatly across countries.

Most policies address the presence of young children through the combination of financial, time, and service transfers. Care for the frail old remains still largely unfocused within public family policies. Kinship aging, increasing women's labour force participation and raising of the pension age suggest however emerging risks of family overburden and caring deficit precisely in this area in the developed countries.

In the developing countries, with their much younger population and high poverty rates, child poverty is the main driver of family policies, which show distinct, and, to some degree, original characteristics, compared both to the European countries and to the US.

References

Anttonen, A., Baldock, J. and Sipilä, J. (eds) (2003), *The Young, The Old and the State*. Cheltenham: Edward Elgar.

Anttonen, A. and Sipilä, J. (1996), European social care services: Is it possible to identify models? *Journal of European Social Policy* 2, pp. 87–100.

Bahle, Th. (2008), 'Family policy patterns in the enlarged EU', in J. Alber, T. Fahey, and C. Saraceno (eds), *Handbook of Quality of Life in the Enlarged European Union*, pp. 100–126. London and New York: Routledge.

Beneria, L. (2008), The crisis of care, international migration and public policy, *Feminist Economics*, 13, 3, pp. 1–21.

Bradshaw, J. (2006), 'Child Benefit Packages in 15 Countries in 2004', in J. Lewis (ed.), *Children, Changing Families and Welfare States*, pp. 26–50. Cheltenham: Edward Elgar.

Daly, M. (2011), What Adult Worker Model? A Critical Look at Recent Social Policy Reform in Europe from a Gender and Family Perspective, *Social Politics*, 18, 1, pp. 1–3.

Fiszbein, A., and Schady, N. (2009), *Conditional cash transfers*, Washington, DC: the World Bank.

Gauthier, A. H. (1996), *The State and the Family: A Comparative Analysis of Family Policies in Industrial Countries*, Oxford: Clarendon Press.

Gornick, J. C., and Meyers, M. K. (2004), *Families that Work*, New York: Russel Sage Foundation.

Hantrais, L. (2004), *Family Policy Matters*, Bristol: Policy Press.

Kamerman, Sh. (2010), 'Child, family and the state: the relationship between family policy and social protection policy', in Sh. Kamerman, Sh. Phipps, and A.r Ben-Arieh (eds), *From Child Welfare to Child Well-Being*, pp. 429–37. New York: Springer.

Kamerman Sh. and Kahn, A. J. (1978), 'Family and the idea of family policy', in idem (eds), *Family policy: Government and Families in Fourteen Countries*, pp. 1–16. New York: Columbia University Press.

Kaufmann, F. X. (2002), 'Politics and policies towards the family in Europe. A framework and an inquiry into their differences and convergences', in F. X. Kaufmann, (ed.) *Family Life and Family Policies in Europe. Vol. 2: Problems and Issues in Comparative Perspective*, pp. 419–77. Oxford: Clarendon Press.

Korpi, W. (2000), Faces of inequality: gender, class and pattern of inequalities in different types of welfare states, *Social Politics* 7 (2), pp. 127–91.

Leitner, S. (2003), Varieties of familialism. The caring function of the family in comparative perspective, *European Societies* 5 (4), pp. 353–75.

Lewis, J. (1992), Gender and the development of welfare regimes, *Journal of European Social policy* 2 (3), pp. 159–73.

Molineux, M. (2006), Mothers at the Service of the New Poverty Agenda: Progresa/Oportunidades, Mexico's Conditional Transfer Programme, in *Social Policy and Administration* 40 (4), pp. 425–49.

Moss, P.R. (2010), 'Early childhood education and care', in Sh. B. Kamerman, Sh. Phipps, A. Ben-Arieh (eds), *From Child Welfare to Child Well-being*, pp. 371–84. London and New York: Springer.

Multilinks Data Base (nd), http://multilinks-database.wzb.eu.

Organisation for Economic Co-operation and Development (OECD) (2011), *Doing Better for Families*, Paris, OECD.

Orloff, A. S. (1993), Gender and the social rights of citizenship. The comparative analysis of gender relations and welfare states, *American sociological review* 58 (3), pp. 308–28.

——(2006), 'From maternalism to "employment for all": state policies to promote womens employment across the affluent democracies', in J. Levy (ed.), *The State after Statism*, pp. 230–71. Cambridge, MA: Harvard University Press.

Pavolini, E. and Ranci, C. (2008), Restructuring the Welfare State: Reforms in Long-term Care in Western European Countries, *Journal of European Social Policy* 18 (3), pp. 246–59.

Saraceno, C. (1997), 'Family Change, family policies and the restructuring of welfare', in OECD (ed.), *Family, Market and Community. Equity and Efficiency in Social Policy*, pp. 81–100, Social Policy Studies no. 21, Paris, OECD.

——(2010), Social inequalities in facing old-age dependency: a bi-generational perspective, *Journal of European Social Policy* 20 (1), pp. 32–44.

Saraceno, C. and Keck, W. (2010), Can we identify intergenerational policy regimes in Europe? *European Societies*, 12, pp. 5, 675–696.

Saraceno C., Leira, A. Lewis, J. (forthcoming), 'Introduction. Families and states', in C. Saraceno, J. Lewis and A. Leira (eds), *Families and Family Policies*, Cheltenham: Edward Elgar.

Smith, R. (2006), Family Caps in Welfare Reform: Their Coercive Effects and Damaging Consequences, *Harvard Journal of Law and Gender* 29, pp. 151–200.

United Nations Children's Fund (UNICEF) (2008), *The Child Care Transition*. Innocenti Report Card 8, Florence.

37

Risk and the management of crime

David Denney

There is now a well-established international consensus amongst criminal justice policy makers and practitioners that various forms of risk management can be used as predictive tools. Internationally governments identify crime as a major problem which needs to be managed through various forms of individualised actuarially based risk assessment. Risk management constitutes a significant paradigm change within criminal justice practice throughout Europe, the USA, Canada, Australia, and New Zealand.

In this chapter risk-based policies and practices will be placed within the context of a wider societal shift towards the 'risk society' in neo-liberal and social democratic states over the last twenty years. Although the contours of criminal justice policy have been shaped by a political preoccupation with risk, there are important differences in policy approaches to crime, personal, and collective security. It will be argued that 'problem, policy, and political streams' drive ever changing and frequently contradictory master risk narratives. Risk discourses are modified and recreated by politicians in an attempt to read and respond to public 'mood'. However, concentration on individualised risk assessment has diverted attention from the risks to public safety created by structural inequalities.

Moreover, an over-emphasis on risk appears in many instances to be accompanied by a more punitive approach, particularly to young offenders.

Core concepts

The emergence of risk has become a focus of interest within social science. In Beck's classic text Risk *Society: Towards a New Modernity* he describes changing patterns of values provided by social institutions as 'reflexive modernity'. Whereas in the traditional society political control is institutionalised through the state, law, and administrative procedures, political control in the post-traditional society becomes more fragmented and disjointed. Beck has argued that 'normal' linear biographies which characterised traditional societies have been transformed. Beck's work leads to a position in which calculating risk is part of a political rhetoric in which the state criminal justice system no longer gains its legitimacy through its capacity to rehabilitate offenders, but through its ability to identify and prevent offending. Beck describes risk as a '[s]ystematic way of dealing with hazards and insecurities induced and introduced by modernisation itself' (Beck, 1992, p. 21).

Risk now constitutes a guiding principle in societies where the:

> place of the value system of the 'unequal' society is taken by the value system of the 'unsafe' society. Whereas the utopia of equality contains a wealth of substantial and positive goals of social change, the utopia of the risk society remains peculiarly negative and defensive. Basically one is no longer concerned with attaining something 'good' but rather preventing the worst.
>
> *(Beck, 1992, p. 49)*

The prolific psychologistic research of David Farrington has been hugely influential internationally in establishing the risk factors associated with criminal behaviour. He and his colleagues have linked crime to large families, child rearing methods, low parental involvement, neglect, and disrupted families (Farrington and Welsh, 2007).

Within the criminal justice system risk factors are identified through the administration of various forms of risk assessment which can be seen at its most simplistic level as the 'process of identifying hazards which may cause an accident, disaster or harm' (Manthorpe, 2000).

The actuarial nature of these assessments within criminal justice systems bears remarkable similarities to assessments pursued in the commercial insurance industry. Such forms of risk assessment ostensibly calculate the regularity of criminal events and the likelihood of crime being committed in the future with respect to specific populations. Risk according to Ewald represents an attempt to master time and discipline the future (Ewald, 1991).

Risk factors are often identified in two forms. Static risk factors refer to the characteristics of the person and the nature of the offence for example sex, age, and criminal record. Dynamic risk factors are wider and incorporate risks associated with poor education, unemployment, dysfunctional families, and attitude towards the offence (Mair, 2001).

Many criminal justice systems now routinely classify offenders into levels of dangerousness using various actuarial risk prediction tools. A Canadian tool LSI-R (Level of Service Inventory) was one of the first risk assessment tools to be adopted by a number of probation services including the UK. In the UK this was replaced by the most recent tool OASys the Offender Management System which now constitutes the starting point for assessment and intervention of offenders. These tools identify static risk factors but frequently fail to take account of the significance of dynamic risk factors.

The development of risk-based criminal justice systems

Criminology has been neglectful of analyses which attempt to understand the relationship between political cultures and the formation of criminal justice policy (Jones and Newburn, 2005). Nowhere is this more the case than in discussions of the impact of risk assessment on the developments of criminal justice policy. Technologies of acturialised risk such as OASys have been shaped by different policy approaches.

O'Malley makes an important distinction between the anti-welfarist form of neo-liberalism most obviously present in the US and UK and the more welfare-based neo-liberalism of Australia, Canada, and New Zealand. O'Malley analyses the different trajectories of criminal justice policy making since the Second World War. In the US and UK a criminal justice system has developed upon a form of pragmatism expressed through exclusion and control of high-risk populations. The other less conservative traditions seen in Australia, New Zealand, and Canada have to some extent been shaped by experiences of colonisation. Criminal justice policies are conceptualised in terms of an attempt to correct the wrongs that have been done to oppressed people, thus aiming to create a more inclusive society. Inequality from this perspective creates the risk of a segregated and fragmented society which can possibly create the risk of social segmentation and division. In New Zealand and Canada for instance the development of restorative justice programmes in the 1970s represented an attempt to reintegrate offenders into the community whilst acknowledging the wrong that had been done to them and also recognising the heritage of indigenous peoples. In New Zealand restorative justice draws upon elements of Maouri justice which had been abandoned during the colonial period. Similarly 'circle sentencing' used as part of the restorative justice process in Canada bears some resemblance to 'First Nation' forms of justice.

Criminal justice policies in Australia have also been rooted in the need to acknowledge cultural heritage and individuals who have been made vulnerable to crime through circumstances which are located within structural inequalities and a history of colonialism. In the 1980s the Australian Labour Government adopted a policy with the specific intention of integrating aboriginal people and to right some of the wrongs perpetrated by colonialisation. By the late 1990s, however, Pauline Hanson's 'One Nation' Party had transmogrified previous policy approaches into an attack against the worst excesses of what she conceptualised as 'political correctness'. The risk for Hanson lay in the fragmenting impact of 'preferential treatment' given to any cultural group. Throughout this policy shift the need to remain one nation, avoiding the risk of segregation and Aboriginal exclusion, was emphasised. In her maiden speech in the Federal Australian Parliament, Hanson quoted from a speech made by Paul Hasluck to the Federal Parliament in October 1955 when he was Minister for Territories. Hasluck made the distinction between a 'social' and 'racial' problem. A 'social' problem was one that concerned the way in which people live together in one society. A 'racial' problem confronted two different races who live in two separate societies, even if those societies are side by side (Hanson, 1996). Australia has consistently sought to enable people to live together in one society, or, as O'Malley puts it:

> The social democratic tradition in Australia has generated distinctive responses which neo-liberalism has shaped in important ways – but the hybrid form of Australian politics is far more consistent with mentalities of categorical inclusion.
>
> *(O'Malley, 2004, p. 44)*

Risk-based policy developments which characterise criminal justice policy developments in the more conservative US aim to identify high-risk populations, and separate and exclude them in order to protect the law-abiding majority. Here risk is conceptualised as the dangers created by criminal acts, the central aim of criminal justice policy being public protection. Risk-taking assessment involves generating risk scores from a risk assessment tool and using such scores to justify inclusion or exclusion of offenders into various corrective programmes in the community.

Criminal justice policy has been based on the political need to create feelings of greater security and the belief that feelings of security will flow from targeting criminal populations.

> The management of risk has displaced rehabilitation as the central organisational aim of the criminal justice system.
>
> *(Garland, 2001, p. 177)*

This central rationality underpins policy objectives which are designed, as Castel has argued, to anticipate all possible manifestations of the future eruption of danger (Castel, 1991). The precautionary principle is a key justification for risk assessment since it is based upon the proposition that hazards can be identified before they occur and that appropriate precautions can then be taken to ensure that harm to the public is kept to a minimum (Denney, 2005).

A number of writers have analysed the shift from rehabilitation towards a risk-based form of punitive social control. Garland describes how during the second half of the twentieth century a shared 'culture of control' has arisen in neo-liberal states like the US and UK (Garland, 2001). In another seminal text published in the early 1990s Feeley and Smith described a 'new penology' developing in the USA. Criminal Justice is not concerned with rehabilitation or punishment, but the identification and management of unruly groups. Managerialised risk assessment processes form the basis for identifying dangerousness individuals who form a significant risk to public safety (Feeley and Smith, 1992).

In the US the risk-based technologies are dominantly incapacitative. Three-strike laws requiring courts to impose mandatory custodial sentences to offenders convicted of three serious offences now forms the basis for 'formulaic sentencing' and the reappearence of curfews (O'Malley, 2004). Other projects in the USA have concentrated on tackling the physical environment cleaning up rubbish and graffiti. The New York Police Department were given local goals on tackling local crime – the 'removal of beggars', 'shakedown artists', and 'squeegee pests' and other so-called incivilities (Wright, 2002, p. 13). O'Malley also regards the expansion of 'prison warehousing' and home detection as purely incapacitating.

Many of these strategies have proved to be of limited value. The 'three strikes and you're out' movement was largely symbolic and provided a tough message about Law and Order. In the US and the UK there was growing public and media concerns about crime and the 'leniency' of judges in sentencing. In the US system and most other states with the exception of California the impact of three strikes has been limited (Jones and Newburn, 2006).

Risk-based actuarial justice has gained less of a hold in countries with a more social democratic tradition such as Australia and New Zealand. In Australia in 1997 the federal Liberal National (conservative) government attempted to change the three strikes policies which had been adopted in the northern territories of Australia since it was regarded by the national government as having a racist effect on aboriginal people (O'Malley, 2004).

Impact of risk-based policies on offenders

Risk-based policies have had a profound impact on the development of criminal justice policy and practice which moves far beyond the processing of offenders into high and low risk. Emphasis on individualised risk is often associated with a more punitive approach to sentencing. Risk factors become reified entities used to identify those who posed danger to public safety. This is especially evident in the way in which 'high-risk' children and young people are treated in risk-based criminal justice systems. Children and young people can be seen as being both vulnerable whilst also being identified as a potentially risky group. Even the very young are not exempt from blame and the accusation that they are irresponsible and dangerous. The principle of *doli incapax* (literally meaning incapable of crime), meant that children under the age of 10 could not be considered criminally responsible. The abolition of this principle in 1998 in the UK came in the wake of the murder of two year old James Bulger by two other children. A media frenzy followed calling for more severe sentences for dangerous younger offenders (Muncie, 1999). The lowering of the age of criminal responsibility in 1998 drew criticism from the European Commissioner for Human Rights and the Commission on the well-being of children. It is not consistent with most other European countries where the age of criminal responsibility is between 12 and 15 years (Tony and Doob, 2004).

In Trondheim Norway in 1994 a five-year-old girl was murdered by two six-year-old boys to some extent mirroring the murder of James Bulger one year previously. Here the murder was seen as a tragedy and a collective sense of shame and responsibility emerged. The boys were never named and returned to school within two weeks of the murder (Muncie, 2002). This response was in marked contrast to the reporting and public response in the UK to the Bulger case which suggested that new level of degeneracy had been reached (*The Times*, 24th November 1994 in Muncie, 1999).

The use of drug therapy has also been used to treat those deemed to be at high risk of disorderly conduct. There is as Walsh argues a tendency to treat conduct disorders therapeutically. The enthusiastic use of Ritalin to treat children designated as suffering from ADHD (Attention Deficit Hyperactivity Disorder) is now well established (Walsh, 2011).

One of the most significant responses to risk-based criminal justice has been the increased use of mass incarceration. Muncie notes a reversal of policy in the Netherlands from the mid-1980s onwards with a major prison-building programme being linked to a tendency towards pre-trial detention and longer sentences (Muncie, 2004). Between 1995 and 2009 the prison population in England and Wales increased by 32,500 (66%). On the 8th April 2011 the prison population stood at 85,361 (Ministry of Justice, 2011). When Kenneth Clarke was Home Secretary from 1992 to 1993 the average prison population was 44,628. Over 2 million individuals are incarcerated in the US representing 724 prisoners per 100,000 of the general population (BBC, 2010). Although as Muncie points out that there has been a move towards the greater use of imprisonment across Europe, the UK incarceration rates are higher than in neighbouring EU countries (Muncie, 2004). In France (with the same population as the UK) the prison population is 59,655, and in Germany (with a population of 20 million more than the UK) the prison population is 72,043. Some 74% of children released from custody in the UK in 2008 reoffended within one year (Bromley Prison Briefings, 2010). However, the increased costs involved in mass incarceration now form part of an all-encompassing national debt risk narrative.

Knepper has argued that around 1973 or so the United States began its experiment in 'mass imprisonment'. Rates of imprisonment climbed annually peaking in 2000. At the same time as crime rates fell some suggested that mass incarceration had reduced risk to the public from criminal acts. Knepper argues that crime rates fell for a number of possible reasons in the US including changes in gun laws, illicit drug markets, economics, and demographics (Knepper, 2012). Thus as the risk of crime declines there would appear to be a concomitant rise in the use of imprisonment.

Problems, policies, and politics: a case study of emerging risk agendas

The use of mass incarceration as a crime reduction strategy carries with it as Knepper further argues 'externalities' which in themselves constitute a risk. In crime policy, externality describes the situation when measures undertaken to fight crime create unforeseen (but foreseeable) demands on social welfare (Knepper, 2012).

One such such externality is cost. In a time of economic turbulence the cost of incarceration could impact on spending elsewhere in the welfare system since budgets are being cut across the welfare spectrum.

However, policy strategies are as Stenson points out, not just responses to external problems. The 'problems' that they address are given shape and recognition by emerging policy discourses (Stenson, 2002). The implementation of criminal justice policy change should not necessarily be regarded a rational response to any particular problem. Jones and Newburn argue that:

> We need to examine how and why certain ideas arise and are promoted and the circumstances in which they become linked with particular problems.
>
> *(Jones and Newburn, 2005, p. 67)*

Jones and Newburn draw on the work of Kingdon (1995) who described 'streams' which lead to the development of criminal justice policy. A variety of policy ideas float around in what he terms the 'policy primeval soup' (Kingdon, 1995 in Jones and Newburn, 2005). Problems which need to be dealt with by policy makers tend to stream rather than appear in sequential stages. Policy 'streams' can be seen as the complex changing and often contradictory responses to streams of problems. Consequent political responses shape and modify policy in response to streams of events (Kingdon, 1995, in Jones and Newburn, 2005). New problems will often occur as policy is being implemented, resulting in the modification of political responses. In the risk society criminal justice 'problem' streams can more accurately be regarded as 'risk streams'.

Problem streams and risk

Criminal justice policy is now shaped by competing and contradictory demands which frame events in terms of threat or danger. At any one time there will be competing constituent elements running through a risk stream. Individuals (e.g. serial killers), groups of individuals (e.g. high risk populations in areas of social deprivation), and events (e.g. economic crises) form part of the risk stream. At the time of writing, the hybrid discourse of risk and criminal justice has become enmeshed within wider problem streams relating to the global economy. Current political rhetoric across Europe warns of the risks associated with global economic crisis and high levels of public expenditure which take precedence over the impact of criminal behaviour. There is a risk that the cost of mass incarceration could impact on other areas of spending in the criminal justice system which are less punitive aiming to include offenders rather that isolate and exclude. Recent events in Europe have demonstrated that public expenditure cannot be allowed to stunt economic growth or economic recovery. The fearful image of the chaos created by unrestrained public spending, cheap lending, and the tenuous position of the euro against the dollar has given rise to an urgent call for public expenditure cuts. The risks associated with uncontrollable borrowing have become the global 'dread' risk. This comes at a time when the US has massive debt repayment problems. At the time of writing the US is struggling with a $14 trillion debt crisis which has added to the sense of impending economic doom (BBC, 2011a).

Ken Clarke the current Lord Chancellor and Secretary of State for Justice in the UK linked the need for rapid deficit reduction with expenditure cuts in the criminal justice system in order to avoid impending economic doom. He warned that Western nations are 'not out of the woods yet' and that Western economies are 'in grave danger of financial collapse' (*Guardian*, 2010).

The global economic crisis of 2008, combined with financial chaos in Greece, Italy, and the need for International Monetary Fund (IMF) intervention in the Irish fiscal crisis of 2011 defines, shapes, and reinforces the new discourse of economic risk dominating risk streams in a number of European countries. Concerns about the Spanish and Portuguese economies have added to the sense of crisis within the eurozone. Rapid deficit reduction and high levels of incarceration are part of the same problem stream in the risk society. Radical solutions to these problems carry political risks, whilst policy often has to be redirected in order to accommodate changing perceptions of the political impact of the risk stream. As a response to these problems in the UK in May 2010 Ken Clarke expressed his intention to radically reduce the prison population from its unsustainable current levels.

Risk and political streams

Political systems and political cultures present constraints and opportunities for criminal justice policy makers, whilst as has been suggested earlier, policy development should not be seen as rational response to a particular problem (Jones and Newburn, 2005). Political responses are often shaped by unfolding events and political perceptions of the public acceptability of policy proposals.

In the UK one possible way of reducing the prison population was the extension of sentencing discount for early guilty pleas. This effectively meant that any individual pleading guilty at an early stage could receive a 50% discount on sentencing compared with the 30% which had been put in place by New Labour. This policy was designed to cut court costs and reduce the prison population.

However, this policy was thwarted by the unpredictability of the political impact of a constituent part of the risk stream. In May 2011 Clarke took part in a radio interview in which a victim of rape described various aspects of the many ordeals associated with rape. Clarke in his response suggested that there were levels of seriousness of rape which could in some circumstances justify differential sentencing (BBC, 2011b).

The public media and political reaction which followed the interview forced Clarke into an apology. On 21 June 2011, UK Prime Minister David Cameron announced a reversal in policy when the new Justice Bill was launched.

Clarke had been forced into a defensive posture in that he was presented by the media as minimising the risk to the public posed by the early release of dangerous prisoners. He had underestimated the centrality of risk within popular consciousness. 'Lenient' sentences for rapists and other serious offenders were an intrinsically important part of the criminal justice 'risk stream'. This was compounded by the fact that during the radio interview risks associated with discount sentencing were being described by an individual who had herself been a victim of a serious crime. The lack of recognition of victims of crime is also a significant part of the 'problem stream'.

There are significant consequences or what could be referred to as externalities in the political decision to change direction as is evidenced here. Introduction of the 50 per cent discount would have significantly reduced the prison population and the decision to abandon it will result in significant budget cuts elsewhere in the system. These could occur in the police, probation service, courts system, the limiting of legal aid, and restricted use of remand in custody (*Guardian*, 21st June 2011). However, in this case risk formed a central part of the problem 'streams' which ultimately shaped criminal justice policy taking political precedence over pressing economic national and global policy imperatives.

Discussion

One of the most common criticisms of Beck's position is that he fails to take account of the specific complexities of risk situations. Also Beck has been accused of failing to recognise the continuing existence of inequality regarding poverty in absolute rather than relative terms (Dingwall, 2000). Other commentators have pointed to the danger of focusing too heavily on risk which is one aspect of the social world (O'Malley, 2000).

Notwithstanding these criticisms it has been argued that conflicting discourses of risk are at the centre of political processes and the formulation of criminal justice policy. A 'risk factor prevention paradigm' has now replaced more traditional criminological concerns with crime causation (Muncie, 2004). Yet risk assessments only tell part of the story. Over-reliance on individualised risk assessments can be politically pragmatic by providing a justification for an unpopular policy whilst risk factors related to the commission of crime constitute a relatively narrow set of questions. Moreover, concentration on risk factors individualises the causation of crime drawing attention away from the underlying inequalities social conditions and historical context which give rise to the risk factors in the first place. The instruments used for assessing risk are also of questionable value, diverting funds from other parts of the criminal justice system. Bullock in recent research into the operation of risk tools in the UK Probation Service has described some level of subjectivity in the way in which probation officers can score for failing to fully complete OASys risk assessments. Risk assessments generally make poor indicators of future criminal behaviour, whilst failing to take sufficient account of exceptional circumstances, and individual characteristics which are less predictive for young offenders. The tests also fail to take sufficient account of the socio-economic circumstances of the offender (Bullock, 2011).

Ideas about risk assessment in criminal justice will change in the future. One possible future scenario is technologically led, marking a return to a variation on biological determinism reminiscent of early criminologists, most notably Lombroso (Lombroso and Ferrero, 1893). It is claimed by some researchers that neuro-imaging techniques could reveal bio markers for conduct disorders. Such a development is potentially within the realms of neuro-scientific possibility and would add a further dimension to risk prediction. There is a growing belief among some neuro-scientists that there are characteristics which could be used to identify and aid in the management of psychopathy (Walsh, 2011). In the US context Rutherford has described juvenile justice as being caught between 'The Exorcist' and 'A Clockwork Orange'. Children are portrayed as being demonic or as potential subjects for reprogramming (in Walsh, 2011).

This raises the critical question as to how any criminal justice system balances the need to protect the public and prevent crime with the rights of the offender and the appropriate role of risk assessment within the due process of law. Human rights should form the basis for the balance between crime control and due process (Ashworth, 1995). Over-emphasising risk has made justice synonymous with punishment, whilst risk-based policies have in some cases resulted in due process being given less emphasis that the politics of safety. It is worrying that there is little to suggest a person designated a risk to public safety by a specific population group is owed justice (Hudson, 2001).

Conclusion

A theme which seems to run through criminal justice policy is that state intervention encourages bureaucratic waste and offender idleness. Although there has been a recent rekindling of interest in rehabilitation within the research community (Robinson and Crow, 2009) this has not been reflected in policy. Policy makers appear to have become engulfed in a wider search for security in a battle being waged against invisible and unknowable global dangers. Problem streams are characterised by conflicting discourses of risk associated with global economic crises, over-incarceration, risks associated with rapid deficit reduction, and the political need to look tough on serious crime. The balance between the need to maintain confidence in the criminal justice system and keep control of public expenditure is a recurring dilemma in social policy and will no doubt be a continuing theme with criminal justice policy for this and future governments. However, individual responsibility does not automatically preclude state-centred welfare institutions (Taylor-Gooby, 2000). There needs to be a redefining of risk-based research, which takes into account 'socially' mediated risks rather than simply placing responsibility on the individual offender to address their level of risk (Garside, 2009). There is no doubt that absent parents, childhood abuse, drug and alcohol addiction, mental illness, and poor education are closely associated with crime, but they describe and reflect deep-seated socio-economic inequalities which divide society. Risk technology systems used in the criminal justice systems can only provide snapshots upon which to base judgements. The effectiveness and practicability of implementing risk-based policies seems highly questionable whilst there remains no consensus as to what constitutes a risk. Risks are often invisible, complex, and based upon interpretation, and have been exaggerated, dramatized, and minimised by policy makers. The proliferation of risk management in criminal justice systems has yet to be fully justified.

Further reading

Kemshall, H. (2002), *Risk Social Policy and Welfare.* London: Sage.
Newburn, T. and Sparks, R. (2004), *Criminal Justice and Political Cultures.* Cullompton: Willan.

References.

Ashworth, A. (1996), 'Principles, Practice and Criminal Justice', in P. Birks (ed.), *Pressing Problems in the Law: Criminal Justice and Human Rights.* Oxford: Oxford University Press.

BBC (2010), *World Prison populations*, online: news.bbc.co.uk/1/shared/spl/hi/uk/06/prisons/html/nn2 page1.stm.

——(2011a), *Is the US in denial over 14 trillion dollar debt*, online: www.bbc.co.uk/news/world-13906274.

——(2011b), Clarke interview, online: www.bbc.co.uk/news/uk-

Beck, U. (1992), *Risk Society: Towards a new Modernity*, London: Sage.

Bromley Briefings (2010), *Prison Fact File December*, London: Prison Reform Trust.

Bullock, K. (2011), The Construction and Interpretation of Risk Management Technologies in Contemporary Probation Practice, *British Journal of Criminology* 51, pp. 120–135.

Castel, R. (1991), 'From Dangerousness to Risk', in G. Burchell, C. Gordon and P. Miller (eds), *The Foucault Effect: Studies in Governmentality*, Chicago, IL: University of Chicago Press.

Denney, D. (2005), *Risk and Society*, London: Sage.

Dingwall, R. (2000), '"Risk Society" The Cult of Theory and the Millennium', in N. Manning and I. Shaw (eds), *New Risks, New Welfare: Signposts for Social Policy.* Oxford: Blackwell.

Ewald, F. (1991), 'Insurance and Risks', in G. Burchell, C. Gordon and P. Miller (eds), *The Foucault Effect: Studies in Governmentality.* Chicago, IL: University of Chicago Press.

Farrington, D.P. and Welsh, B.C. (2007), *Saving Children from a Life of Crime: Early Risk Factors and Effective Intervention*, Oxford: Oxford University Press.

Feeley, M. and Simon, J. (1992), The New Penology: Notes on the emerging strategy of correction and its implications, *Criminology, 30, 4 449–474.*

Fleissig, A. Jenkins, V. Catt, S. and Fallowfield, L. (2006), Multi disciplinary teams in cancer care: are they effective in the UK? *Lancet Oncology* (7) 935–43.

Franklin, J. (2006), 'Politics and Risk', in G. Mythen, S. Walkgate (eds), *Beyond the Risk Society.* Maidenhead: Open University Press.

Garland, D. (2001), *The Culture of Control: Crime and Social Order in Contemporary Society.* Oxford: Oxford University Press.

Garside, R. (2009), *Risky People or Risky Societies? Rethinking Interventions for Young Adults in Transition, Transition to Adulthood*, Centre for Criminal Justice Studies, Kings College, www.crimeandjustice.org.uk/opus1736/T2A1risk.pdf.

Guardian, (2010), *World in grave danger of financial collapse, says Ken Clarke*, 14 October. www.guardian.co.uk/politics/2010/oct/14/britain-danger-collapse-ken-clarke.

——(2011), *Cameron Shelves parts of Clarke's Sentencing Reforms*, 8 June.

——(2011), *Ken Clarke forced to abandon 50% sentence cuts for guilty pleas*, 21 June, online: www.guardian.co.uk/law/2011/jun/20/ken-clarke-abandon-sentence-cuts.

Hanson, P. (1996), Pauline Hanson's maiden speech in Australian Federal Parliament, Tuesday, 10th September 1996, online: www.australian-news.com.au/maiden_speech.htm.

Hudson, B. (2001), 'Punishment Rights and Difference: Defending Justice in the Risk Society', in K. Stenson and R. Sullivan (eds), *Crime, Risk and Justice*, Cullompton: Willan.

Jones, T and Newburn, T. (2006), 'Three Strikes and You're Out, Exploring Symbol and Substance in American and British Crime Control Politics', *British Journal of Criminology* 46 (781–802).

Jones, T. and Newburn, T. (2005), 'Comparative Criminal Justice Policy Making in the United States and the United Kingdom – the case of private prisons', *British Journal of Criminology* 45 (58–80).

Jordan, B. (1998), *The New Politics of Welfare*. London: Sage.

Kingdon, J.W. (1995), *Agendas, Alternatives and Public Policies* (2nd edn). New York: Addison, Wesley Longman.

Knepper, P. (2012), 'An International Crime Decline: Lessons for Social Welfare Crime Policy', in H. Kemshall (ed), *Crime and Social Policy Special Issue, Social Policy and Administration*, 46 (4).

Lombroso, C. and Ferrero, G. (1893/2004) *Criminal Woman, the Prostitute and the Normal Woman*, translated with a new introduction by N.H. Rafter, and M. Gibson, Durham: Duke University Press.

Mair, G. (2001), 'Technology and the Futures of Community Penalties', in A. Bottoms, L. Gelsthorpe, and S. Rex (eds), *Community Penalties, Change and Challenges*. Cullompton, Willan.

Manthorpe, J. (2000), 'Risk Assessment', in M. Davies (ed.), *The Blackwell Encyclopaedia of Social Work*. Oxford: Blackwell.

Ministry of Justice (2011), *Population Bulletin* 8th April. Online: www.hmprisonservice.gov.uk/resourcecentre/publicationsdocuments/index.asp?cat=85.

Morgan, R. and Newburn, T. (2007), 'Youth Justice', in M. Maguire, R. Morgan and R. Reiner (eds), *The Oxford Handbook of Criminology*. Oxford: Oxford University Press.

Muncie, J. (1999), 'Exploring Demons: Media Politics and Criminal Justice', in B. Franklin (ed.), *Social Policy, the Media and Misrepresentation*, London: Routledge.

——(2002), Policy transfers and what works: some reflections on comparative youth justice. *Youth Justice*, 1 (3): 27–35.

——(2004), 'Youth justice globalisation and multi modal governance', in T. Newburn, T. and R. Sparks (eds), *Criminal Justice and Political Cultures National and International Dimensions of Crime Control*. Cullompton: Willan.

O'Malley, P. (2004), 'Globalising risk? Distinguishing styles of neo liberal criminal justice in Australia and the USA', in T. Newburn and R. Sparks (eds), *Criminal Justice and Political Cultures*. Cullompton: Willan.

Powell, M. and Hewitt, M. (2002), *Welfare State and Welfare Change*. Buckingham: Open University Press.

Prison Reform Trust (2010), *Prison Fact Files December*. London: Prison Reform Trust.

Robinson, G. and Crow, I. (2009), *Offender Rehabilitation, Theory Research and Practice*. London: Sage.

Rutherford, J. (2002), *Juvenile Justice, Caught Between The Exorcist and Clockwork Orange*. De Paul Law Review 51: 715–42 in Walsh, C. (2011) Youth Justice and Neuro Science: A dual use Dilemma, *British Journal of Criminology 51 21–39.*

Stenson, K. (2002), 'Community Safety in Middle England: The Local Politics of Crime Control', in G. Hughes and A. Edwards (eds), *Crime Control and Community*, Cullompton: Willan.

Taylor-Gooby, P. (ed.) (2000), *Risk Trust and Welfare* London: Macmillan Press.

Tonry, M. and Doob, A.N. (eds) (2004), 'Youth Crime and Youth Justice, Comparison and Cross National Perspectives', in R. Morgan, and T. Newburn (eds), *Youth Justice The Oxford Handbook of Criminology*, Oxford: Oxford University Press.

Walsh, C. (2011), Youth Justice and Neuro Science: A Dual Use Dilemma, *British Journal of Criminology 51, 21–39.*

Wright, A. (2002), *Policing*, Cullompton: Willan.

38

Financing the welfare state and the politics of taxation

Nathalie Morel and Joakim Palme

Introduction

In an era of 'permanent austerity' (Pierson, 2001) and financial crisis, the issue of financing welfare state provisions is topical. Moreover, the future of welfare state funding in countries with ageing populations is no doubt raising increasing interest in scholarly as well as policy circles. Yet the financing side of welfare provision has traditionally been given little attention and remains somewhat of a black box of the welfare state. The fact that some of the financing mechanisms have remained 'hidden' has added to the confusion about existing policy alternatives.

In developed countries, the demands on welfare state financing have been driven by the fact that, on average, gross public social expenditure across Organisation for Economic Co-operation and Development (OECD) countries has increased from 7 per cent in 1960 to 19 per cent in 2007 (SOCX, 2011). In the European Union (EU), this figure reaches as much as 26 per cent of gross domestic product (GDP) (Eurostat, 2011). As such, the financing of social policy is a highly salient economic and political issue, marked by continued conflicts regarding to what extent and in what ways social policies should be financed and how the cost should be distributed. The financing and institutional mechanisms that have been put in place for the extraction of resources and their redistribution thus provides a direct insight into the different kinds of social contracts that underpin each and every welfare state, reflecting different conceptions of solidarity and different redistributive ambitions (Sjöberg, 2000).

The different financing mechanisms that support social protection systems not only have an impact on the redistributive outcomes of social policy, but also on the political legitimacy of social systems and social benefits and therefore on the willingness to pay. They also have an impact on the economy, not least in the way it affects the cost of labour but also, potentially, economic growth and competitiveness. The question of the economic impact and financial sustainability of the different modes of financing social policy has increasingly come to the fore since the 1980s, and even more so now in a context of increased economic globalisation and of financial crisis. Despite the crucial economic, political and social issues that are involved, the sociological and political scholarship on the financing of the welfare state remains surprisingly underdeveloped, even if there now seems to be a renewed interest in the field of fiscal sociology, including in relation to the welfare state (see Howard, 1997; Swank and Steinmo, 2002; Campbell, 2009; Manow, 2010; Béland, 2011).

In this chapter we start by discussing the main determinants of the financing needs of welfare systems. We then turn to the different sources of revenue and patterns of welfare state funding in the advanced industrial nations. This is not to deny the importance of funding social protection systems in development contexts but rather reflects the fact that most research has been focused on the rich part of world and the emerging development-oriented research has given a lot of attention to the experience of industrialized nations (see Hujo and McClanahan, 2009; Barrientos, 2008). The third section analyses the politics of taxation and financing trends in the mature welfare states. In particular, we address the impact of the different financing techniques on employment and economic growth and on the political legitimacy and reform possibilities of the different social protection systems. The fourth section addresses the issue of the redistributive impact of the different financing techniques and underlines the importance of analysing the dynamics between how the financial resources are raised and spent. Finally, the chapter discusses the current and future challenges to welfare state financing in the face of increased globalisation and ageing populations. In the conclusion, we summarize the key lessons to be learnt from the analysis of welfare state financing.

The cost of the welfare state: determinants of social expenditure

The current demands on funding for modern welfare states are the outcome of a century-long development, where various social policy programmes have emerged, expanded and matured. This expansion can be related to two different types of factors: the extension of social rights, on the one hand, and the growth of needy populations, on the other (Kangas and Palme, 2007). The entitlement structure to social benefits, that is to say the social citizenship rights codified in national laws or collective agreements, determines the number of beneficiaries (by setting the eligibility criteria, for instance by specifying the age at which people can retire) as well as the level of benefits and thus impacts on the cost of a given programme. The demographic context has an impact on the social protection system's dependency ratio, that is to say on the number of beneficiaries in the system compared to the number of people financing the transfers. But demographics only explain a portion of the financing needs and financing possibilities of a given welfare state. How many people receive benefits and how many people there are to finance these benefits depends on economic factors such as employment levels. The number of unemployed people affects both the financing needs for unemployment insurance schemes and social assistance and the earning and taxing capacity of the country.

The demands on the financing systems are, to varying degrees, possible to influence by reforming the entitlement structure, for example by raising the legal retirement age, by reducing the level of benefits or lengthening the contribution period necessary to become entitled to a given benefit (such as unemployment benefits for instance). But there are also other ways in which governance could modify the dependency ratio and the fiscal sustainability of the welfare state. Increasing the tax base by boosting employment levels, raising taxes and/or social contributions to finance social expenditures, but also increasing family benefits to affect the birth rate and thus improve the demographic old-age dependency ratio in the long run, are other ways that can modify the financing needs and capacity of a given welfare system.

Sources of revenue and modes of financing

As Richard Titmuss had pointed out more than a half-century ago, social welfare, understood as the formal publicly financed and provided social programmes, only constitutes one part of the welfare state. Occupational welfare (see Chapter 4) and fiscal welfare (see Chapter 3) constitute other important sources of welfare provision. This chapter is, however, focused on the analysis of the statutory social protection schemes.

Social protection systems rely on different sources of income, of which taxes (in the form of a share of general revenues or taxes earmarked for social protection purposes) and social contributions (paid by employers and/or employees) form the main part. Other sources of revenues such as returns on funding exist but ordinarily play only a marginal role.

The source of financing is usually related to the characteristics of the benefits (Cichon et al., 2004, p. 232). Universal benefits are normally funded from general tax revenues but they can be funded from mandatory contributions, possibly including contributions from the unemployed and non-workers. Means tested social assistance benefits are typically funded from general tax revenues because the low-income recipients of these benefits might not qualify on the basis of accumulated contributions. Social insurance systems are usually financed through contributions from employers (payroll taxes) and workers/insured persons, sometimes complemented by government contributions. Here it is important to note that while the formal share of state funding is mostly low, large deficits in insurance programmes are typically covered by general revenue funding (Sjöberg, 2000). Finally, provident funds and individual account defined contribution plans are financed by workers' contributions withheld from wages, often without a corresponding contribution from employers.

Social protection systems and individual social protection schemes are generally categorized according to whether they are predominantly tax-financed or contribution-financed, but most systems actually combine different types of revenues. Nonetheless, core differences between welfare regimes reflect the diversity of tax instruments used to fund the different types of welfare states.

The patterns of welfare state funding in Europe and the other advanced industrial nations have to be seen in the light of the different social policy models that have emerged over the past century. The Bismarckian countries of Continental Europe follow the insurance principle, with social contributions as the main source of funding (over 65 per cent of social protection receipts, the main part being paid by employers) and a historically small role for taxation. Taxation has, however, been of increasing importance in this model in more recent years (Manow, 2010). While the Beveridge system initially placed a strong emphasis on contributions as a mode of financing, the importance of general taxation has increased in Beveridgean countries, to about 50 per cent of social protection receipts in the UK. In the Nordic countries, social protection systems were predominantly tax-funded, but the post-war expansion was made possible by increased employer contributions. Yet general government revenue still accounts for over 60 per cent of social protection receipts in Denmark and Norway. Social contributions paid by employees, while still comparatively low, have been on the rise in recent years in the Nordic countries, notably in Finland and Sweden.

Thus, while there are still clear differences in the funding structure of different welfare states, these differences have gradually become less pronounced, not least amongst the European countries. There are still significant cross-national differences in levels and patterns of public social spending and taxation, however. For instance, public spending and taxation levels are comparatively low in the English-speaking countries, and much higher in the Nordic welfare states (Obinger and Wagschal, 2010).

Looking at public spending levels and types and levels of taxation does not, however, give a full picture of welfare provision in the different welfare states. Indeed, fiscal welfare, in the form of tax expenditures (i.e. tax exemptions, deductions, allowances, or credits to targeted groups or specific activities), constitutes a sometimes important element of welfare provision, not least in the English-speaking countries where public social protection expenditure is relatively low

(Adema and Ladaique, 2009). Because tax expenditures, which can serve to subsidize different private schemes such as health or pension insurance as well as family policy (such as the Child Tax Credit in the US and the UK, or the tax splitting system in France or Germany to support families with children), do not involve monetary transfers, they do not appear in traditional social protection accounting systems, but they do represent income foregone by the government and should in fact be counted as part of overall public social protection expenditure. As Howard (1997) has shown for the US, tax expenditures represent important sums of government revenue foregone and very much constitute some sort of 'hidden welfare state' (see also Hacker, 2002 and Chapter 3). In recent years, fiscal welfare measures have been on the increase in all welfare states (De Deken, 2009), which constitutes another element of convergence in the financing techniques used across welfare regimes. This is the case particularly in the field of pensions, but other measures such as tax deductions for child care and for household services have been introduced, both in Continental European countries as well as in the Nordic countries.

The politics of taxation and financing trends in the mature welfare states

The reforms and progressive convergence in the financing techniques used can be understood in light of the relative strengths and weaknesses of the different modes of financing as well as of the changed demographic and economic contexts which all welfare states are facing. However, the importance of politics should not be underestimated either with regard to maintaining the existing order or for changing it.

In the case of tax-financed systems, the main issue has to do with the increasing fiscal and budgetary constraints that have been placed on governments (linked to increased unemployment and ageing, along with economic globalisation and tax competition), making social policy expenditure a more salient issue, and one on which there is pressure to cut back. In times of budgetary constraints, resource allocation between social policy and other fields of expenditure (such as defence or education for instance) becomes a more contested process, making benefit levels more subject to annual budget decisions and thus less stable than in contribution-based systems. The growing political resistance to tax increases in all countries puts a further strain on funding possibilities. On the plus side, general revenue financing provides greater flexibility and overall government control over public sector financing, giving governments greater leeway in defining spending priorities.

Contribution-financed systems or schemes, which are funded and most-often administered by bipartite or tripartite governing bodies independently of the government budget, have historically tended to be more generous and less susceptible to retrenchment than tax-funded schemes since contributions are earmarked for specific benefits and thus do not depend on overall government budget decisions. As such, there is evidence of greater willingness to contribute wherever there is earmarking and the use of funds is known, and the political legitimacy of contribution-financed systems thus tends to be high, especially if benefits are attractive and income-related (Manow, 2010). Indeed, contributors feel they have a stake in the system and that the money they pay in will come back to them in the form of a 'deferred wage' and an earned social right.

Contribution-financed schemes are for the most part based on a pay-as-you-go (PAYG) system, which means that the benefits paid out (for pensions, sickness, unemployment, and maternity leave) are paid directly from current workers' contributions. The financial sustainability of such systems, at least in the case of defined-benefit schemes, thus very much depends on the dependency ratio between the number of people receiving benefits and the number of people paying in contributions. In this context, it has been suggested that funded pension systems could be a solution. But this is only partly true: the effect of the changing age structure will be the same in funded and PAYG systems, unless pension funds are invested internationally – which involves other kinds of risks. In the case of short-term benefits (sickness, unemployment, maternity) contributions can be adjusted relatively quickly to changing economic and demographic realities, but pensions require much more long-term planning (Cichon et al., 2004). In Europe, where defined benefit contribution-financed pension schemes largely predominate, population ageing, combined with a shrinking workforce due to rising unemployment and a strategy of labour-shedding in the Continental welfare states in the 1980s and 1990s (Esping-Andersen, 1996) have put considerable strain on contribution-based PAYG schemes, especially in the field of pensions which suffer huge deficits and which therefore have been the site of (often very contested) reform attempts. The picture is slightly different where tax-financed schemes play a larger role, e.g. in the UK, Ireland, Denmark, and the Netherlands. The introduction of defined contribution systems in Sweden and Italy should be seen in a context of strong political ambitions to control expenditure developments.

Budget deficits are also found in the field of contribution-financed healthcare systems where financers and providers of care are separate, and where there is thus little control over the demands placed on healthcare providers. In tax-financed healthcare systems, on the other hand, the state is often also the provider of care and can exercise more control over spending (Palier, 2004).

Yet the problem that has appeared in contribution-financed systems that has perhaps become of most concern has to do with the way social contributions, and especially employers' contributions, affect the cost of labour thus making firms potentially less competitive in the global economy and reducing the demand for labour in countries where employers' contributions are high. As different scholars have argued, high fixed labour costs have constituted an obstacle to private job growth, and especially for low-skilled jobs and in the low-productivity service sector, more so than in countries relying predominantly on income taxation (Scharpf, 2000; Kemmerling, 2002; Manow, 2010). High social contributions may also provide incentives for informal sector activity rather than formal employment for both employers and workers. This negative impact on labour demand and supply may exacerbate the deteriorating dependency ratio between the number of people paying in and the number of people receiving benefits of contribution-financed welfare systems.

This issue was exacerbated in the 1980s and 1990s when raising social contributions was perceived as the most politically viable solution. Indeed, as Manow (2010) has argued, governments essentially could respond in three ways to the fiscal stress caused by diminished growth combined with increased welfare spending demands: they could cut costs, run a higher debt, or increase revenue. According to Manow, these basic strategies were associated with varying political costs depending on how the welfare state is financed in a given country and depending on how easy it was to run a higher public debt. Increasing social contributions proved politically less problematic, not least as such measures are less visible. Manow gives several reasons for this. One is that while most tax increases have to be legislated, social insurance contributions often rise automatically whenever revenue falls short of expenses. Moreover, such automatic increases can be attributed to secular trends like demographic ageing or costly medical progress, which dilutes direct political responsibility for increases. Another reason is that earmarked social insurance contributions are not formally part of the government's budget but go into the fiscally independent and more autonomous budgets of the social insurance schemes. Thus, if the government budget is not directly affected, the government has no or little political interest in preventing contribution hikes. In other words, a government's political capacity to cut costs as well as its political interest to do so are generally much less developed in contribution-financed welfare states.

This explains why there was a general trend towards increasing the role of social contributions in continental European welfare states, and also why tax-financed welfare states started to introduce social contributions that did not weigh directly on the state's budget.

However, such an increase in social contributions in the continental welfare states also exacerbated the problem of high non-wage labour costs and hampered job growth, thus contributing to high and persistent unemployment. By the mid-1990s, this detrimental impact on employment and growth was widely recognized and became one of the main reasons for attempting to reform and restructure the way these welfare systems are funded. Various measures have since then been taken to reduce non-wage labour costs, especially by relieving employers from paying social insurance contributions for certain groups of workers such as the low-skilled, low-paid workers, but also for young people to help them access the labour market, as well as for the disabled or the long-term unemployed. Social contribution exemptions have also been introduced in specific sectors, especially the service sector (e.g. for home care and household services) in order to encourage the creation of jobs in this sector, but also to provide incentives for such jobs to operate within the formal economy rather than on the black market (Morel, 2007). The long-term risk of giving rebates to low paid jobs is that old and inefficient structures are cemented (Palme et al., 2009).

Another issue that has appeared in relation to contribution-based systems is that given the deteriorating economic environment and employment conditions, more and more people do not qualify for social insurance benefits due to a lack of sufficient and continuous attachment to the labour market. In the 1990s, the increasing cost of non-contributory social assistance benefits paid out to the long-term unemployed, along with other flat rate social minima such as those for the elderly or the disabled, became an increasing problem for contribution-financed welfare systems, as governments were tempted to pass off these costs to the social insurance funds. There was an increasing feeling amongst the social partners that these costs should not be paid out of social contribution funds but rather out of tax-financed social solidarity (Palier, 2010).

This growing discontent of the social partners combined to the above-mentioned dominant interpretation at that time of the negative impact of high payroll taxes on job growth have led governments to seek to expand the range of funding sources, especially through general revenue taxes and/or earmarked taxes. These new sources of funding are used to finance specific benefits and/or to improve the financial equilibrium of different schemes. There has been a substantial increase in the use of earmarked taxes (these represented 2.17 per cent of GDP in 2008 for the EU15 against only 0.55 per cent in 1997 – Eurostat, 2011) as these present the double advantage of enjoying the same kind of political legitimacy as social contributions while introducing more equity in social protection systems by broadening the tax base instead of having the funding rest on the working population alone.

Redistributive impact of the different financing techniques

Other trends that span all welfare regimes include a shifting of costs to the private sector and to individuals. We can thus observe a general increase in the use of user fees in the areas of service provision such as childcare, care of the elderly, and healthcare. Another important method, as previously discussed, has been the increasing use of fiscal measures to encourage the development of voluntary and mandated private insurance schemes in areas such as healthcare, sickness benefits and old-age provision (De Deken, 2009).

While it is fairly clear that this latter trend towards shifting the costs to the private sector affects the redistributive profile of welfare systems negatively due to the fact that tax expenditures benefit the wealthier segments of the population in a way that has been shown to be highly regressive (see Howard, 1997), and while this is likely to hold true also in the case of increasing user fees, it is more difficult to assess the redistributive impact of the other trends.

The move towards more tax funding in continental Europe could improve the redistributive profile of these welfare states by taxing all forms of income, including capital income. Taxes also tend to be more progressive than social contributions. Indeed, social contributions are often regressive because they do not have a basic tax allowance, which reduces the relative tax burden on low-income earners, but do have ceilings on contributions, which reduce the relative tax burden on high-income earners. They are also levied from a much smaller proportion of the population than taxes. Consumption taxes have a more ambivalent impact. On the one hand, these are hard to avoid even for the owners of highly mobile assets. But on the other, if applied at a uniform rate, their distributive impact tends to be regressive since poor people have to spend a larger share of their income. Split tax rates (one for luxury goods and one for basic needs) have a less negative impact.

The past decades have seen a trend towards less progressive tax scales, which could suggest that the income tax systems have become less redistributive. However, this may not necessarily hold true. Firstly, the flattening of the tax rates has been accompanied by a broadening of tax bases. Secondly, the redistributive effect is also affected by the level and structure of social expenditure, which implies that any serious analysis of the redistributive effects of the welfare state has to analyse the combined effects of revenues and expenditures (Korpi and Palme, 1998). It is furthermore important to underline that social insurance systems tend to be redistributive because the risk of getting sick or unemployed falls unevenly on the shoulders of low-income people. This effect tends to be much stronger than some of the 'imperfections' on the contribution side.

Current and future challenges

New challenges have called into question present financing arrangements and raise questions regarding the future financial sustainability of welfare states. Economic globalisation is imposing constraints on national tax policies and can lead to tax competition and a race to the bottom, while increased migration sets pressure on welfare states to harmonise welfare policies and their financing. High unemployment in many European countries has further reduced the possibility to raise revenue. In addition, many countries will have to deal with the consequences of the financial crisis (see Chapters 20 and 30).

The future of the welfare state is likely to hinge on the ability for nation states to levy taxes and social security contributions on their populations. Yet, also the most economically advanced nations are experiencing shrinking workforce, eroded tax bases, population ageing, and increased demands on social services from increasing parts of the populations. Faced with these new challenges, some countries have reduced budgetary deficits by not only modifying the structure of the financing of their social protection systems, but also by transferring some of the costs to the private sector, with important economic, social, and political implications. Not only are such tax expenditures regressive in terms of distributional outcomes, they also deprive the state of the resources to make the necessary investments in the current and future workforce and tax base of the nation.

Economic globalisation and the resulting tax competition appear to have conditioned the role of political parties and other domestic factors (Ganghof, 2008). Hence, not only have the corporate tax rates converged, the relative strength of political parties appears to have had no effect on the changes, although this does not hold true for all forms of taxation. The EU-context adds some issues with regard to welfare state funding and this despite the fact that both the taxation system and the welfare state by and large are outside EU competencies. One important exception is the protection of migrant workers. Given the differences with regard to financial structures this introduces certain tensions when migrants move between different kinds of systems, or, in the case of cross-border work, work and live in different systems/countries. The growing importance of the European Court of Justice also opens up for an increased significance of the EU-context, for example when it comes to the healthcare systems and the rights of EU citizens to get publicly funded care provided in another EU Member State than that he or she resides in.

Conclusion

The future funding of the welfare state is about increased demands under obvious constraints, and hence about increasing the tax base and about policy reform and innovation. The alternative is a future with more modest entitlements. As such, the transformation of the fiscal structure is part and parcel of welfare state transformation and restructuring.

The European populations have a lot to gain in terms of securing the future tax bases by pursuing social investment policies that broaden the tax base, improve the skills of the population, and improve the gender balance in paid work (Morel, Palier, and Palme, 2012). Combating unemployment, and especially long-term unemployment, is crucial both for increasing the tax base and securing receipts, and for diminishing expenditure, while augmenting the skills of the population is likely to reduce the risk of unemployment and to increase the quality of jobs and wages, and thus of revenues. Finally, the presently low female labour force participation rates in many countries represent something of a reserve army of potential taxpayers.

There also appears to be room for innovation with respect to financing mechanisms. An example is the French CSG (General Social Contribution) introduced in 1991 and levied on all forms of income, including capital and property income, which suggests that, even in an era of supposedly 'permanent' austerity, the state can find new ways to actually expand its fiscal capacity instead of simply attempting to reduce and control social policy costs while cutting or stabilizing tax levels.

Yet tax competition and global governance issues are also on the agenda for the future financing of the welfare state. The fact that the deregulation of capital markets has increased the freedom of movement of tax bases, notably capital, has had repercussions on financing mechanisms. Corporate taxes are showing a downward trend, not least in Europe. While labour is the primary tax base in terms of funding the welfare state, the erosion of other tax bases may still have repercussions on welfare state funding. The effects of an increased mobility of labour in terms of tax/welfare state competition are not straightforward because low taxes and high benefits may be equally attractive.

References

Adema, W. and M. Ladaique (2009), 'How Expensive is the Welfare State? Gross and Net Indicators in the OECD Social Expenditure Database (SOCX)', *OECD Social, Employment and Migration Working Papers*, No. 92, OECD Publishing.

Barrientos, A. (2008), 'Financing Social Protection', in A. Barrientos and D. Hulme (eds), *Social Protection for the Poor and Poorest: Concepts, Policies and Politics*. London: Palgrave.

Béland, D. (2011), Taxation and the Politics of Social Policy paper presented at the Annual Meeting of the Research Committee 19 of the International Sociological Associated, Seoul, South Korea, 25–27 August.

Campbell, J. L. (2009), 'Epilogue: a renaissance for fiscal sociology?', in I. Martin, A. Mehrotra and M. Prasad (eds), *The New Fiscal Sociology: Taxation in a Comparative and Historical Perspective*. Cambridge: Cambridge University Press.

Cichon, M., Scholz, W., van de Meerendonk, A., Hagemejer, K., Bertranou, F. and Plamondon, P. (2004), *Financing Social Protection*. Quantitative Methods in Social Protection Series. Geneva: International Labour Office/International Social Security Association.

De Deken, J. (2009), Depoliticising the financing of the welfare state? Financial profiling and the hidden costs of privatised retirement provisions, paper presented at the 2009 ESPANET Conference in Urbino, Italy, September 17–19.

Esping-Andersen, G. (1996), 'Welfare states without work: the impasse of labour shedding and familialism in Continental European social policy', in G. Esping-Andersen (ed.), *Welfare States in Transition*, London: Sage.

Ganghof, S. (2008), *The Politics of Income Taxation: A Comparative Analysis*. Colchester: European Consortium for Political Research Press.

Hacker, J. (2002), *The Divided Welfare State: The Battle over Public and Private Social Benefits in the United States*, Cambridge: Cambridge University Press.

Howard, C. (1997), *The Hidden Welfare State: Tax Expenditures and Social Policy in the United States*. Princeton, NJ: Princeton University Press.

Hujo, K. and McClanahan, S. (eds) (2009), *Financing Social Policy: Mobilizing Resources for Social Development*. Palgrave/Macmillan.

Kangas, O. and Palme, J. (2007), 'Social Rights, Structural Needs and Social Expenditures', in J. Clasen and N. Siegel (eds), *Investigating Welfare State Change*, pp. 106–29. Cheltenham: Edward Elgar.

Kemmerling, A. (2002), 'The Employment Effects of Different Regimes of Welfare State Taxation: An Empirical Analysis of Core OECD-Countries', Max-Planck-Institut für Gesellschaftsforschung, Discussion Paper 02/8, Cologne.

Korpi, W. and Palme, J. (1998), The Paradox of Redistribution and Strategies of Equality: Welfare State Institutions, Inequality and Poverty in the Western Countries. *American Sociological Review*, 63, pp. 661–87.

Manow, P. (2010), 'Trajectories of Fiscal Adjustment in Bismarckian Welfare Systems', in B. Palier (ed.), *A Long Goodbye to Bismarck?*, Amsterdam: Amsterdam University Press.

Morel, N. (2007), From subsidiarity to 'free choice': child- and elderly-care policy reforms in France, Belgium, Germany and the Netherlands, *Social Policy & Administration*, 41(6): 618–37.

Morel, N., Palier, B. and Palme, J. (eds) (2012), *Towards a Social Investment Welfare State? Ideas, Policies and Challenges*. Bristol: Policy Press.

Obinger, H. and Wagschal, U. (2010), 'Social Expenditure and Revenues', in F. Castles, S. Leibfried, J. Lewis, H. Obinger and C. Pierson (eds), *The Oxford Handbook of the Welfare State*, Oxford: Oxford University Press.

Palier, B. (2004), *La réforme des systèmes de santé*. Paris: PUF, Coll. Que sais-je?

——(ed.) (2010), *A Long Goodbye to Bismarck? The Politics of Welfare Reform in Continental Europe*. Amsterdam: Amsterdam University Press.

Palme, J., Nelson, K., Sjöberg, O., and Minas, R. (2009), *European Social Models, Protection and Inclusion*. Stockholm: Institute for Futures Studies, Research Report 2009/1.

Pierson, P. (ed.) (2001), *The New Politics of the Welfare State*. Oxford: Oxford Univerity Press.

Scharpf, F. (2000), 'Economic changes, vulnerabilities, and institutional Capabilities', in F. Scharpf and V. Schmitd (eds), *Welfare and Work in the Open Economy. From vulnerability to competitiveness*, Oxford: Oxford University Press.

Sjöberg, O. (2000), *Duties in the Welfare State. Working and paying for social rights*. Swedish Institute for Social Research Dissertation Series No. 42.

Swank, D. and Steinmo, S. (2002), 'The new political economy of taxation in advanced capitalist democracies', *American Journal of Political Science*, 46: 642–55.

39

Social OMCs

Ideas, policies and effects

Caroline de la Porte

Introduction

European Union (EU) welfare states face common challenges of ageing populations, low fertility rates, and insufficient labour market participation, especially among low-skilled workers. Furthermore, the criteria associated with Economic and Monetary Union (EMU) constrains manoeuvre in fiscal policy, especially during economic recession. Given this context, the 'social OMCs' (European Employment Strategy (EES) and OMC in social policy – social inclusion, pensions, healthcare, and care for the elderly) were developed to support welfare reform through multi-lateral ideational exchange. For each area where the open method of coordination (OMC) is applied, the policy cycle is iterative, though its frequency varies. First, policy objectives (sometimes accompanied by quantitative benchmarks) are proposed by the European Commission. Then Member State representatives, first in Council formations and then at the yearly meetings of the Spring European Council, decide upon which objectives the Member States will pursue. Next, efforts to meet the objectives agreed for any given OMC process are reported by Member States, after which they are reviewed by peer Member States and by the EU level (Commission-Council) with assessments of performance, and (very) soft recommendations in the case of non-compliance. In addition, a wealth of information is produced in the specific peer review programmes on the exchange of best practices, designed to provide more in-depth information about a specific aspect of an OMC for practitioners.

The OMCs are the EU's tool for developing and diffusing ideas and policy solutions in a broad range of areas, in particular in labour market and social policy. OMC ideas are particularly relevant for member states with rigid labour markets, low levels of labour market participation and/or for countries having difficulties to sustain social protection systems. As it is applied in areas of national sovereignty – fiscal policy and social policy – it operates through voluntary learning. However, it is difficult to measure the role of the OMC in the process of ideational change, not to mention its role in policy change. In addition, domestic actors (re)interpret the ideas and objectives of the OMC considerably, making the task even more difficult. Nonetheless, much headway has been made recently in this area, and this involves determining from which aspect of the OMC learning takes place (de la Porte and Pochet, 2012) and through which mechanisms (Weishaupt and de la Porte, 2011).

This chapter first provides an analysis of the (shifting) ideas about welfare reform developed within the OMCs. Secondly, it identifies how the impact of social OMCs can be analysed. Thirdly, it discusses the empirical findings about influence of the social OMCs in different welfare state configurations. Finally, it draws conclusions about how to consider the social OMC in future comparative welfare state research.

The ideational foundations of the social OMCs

One objective of the social OMCs has remained stable throughout time: the ambition to maximize labour market participation in order to sustain economic growth. Other aims, related to the quality of social protection services and gender equality, depend more on the EU's economic situation and its political priorities. In the following, an overview of the ideational and political-party origins of the key objectives will be presented, as well as how they have altered over time. A reflection will be made about the implication that this has for the analysis of the impact of the OMC.

The early literature on the OMC has highlighted its social-democratic and socialist ideational origins. Karl Johansson (1999) has traced the origins of the EES objectives to a social-democratic coalition that originated around the labour movement in Sweden in the early 1990s, preceding that country's membership of the EU. Ideas about activation, training, a comprehensive public employment service, and reconciling work and family life were brought to agenda of the party of European socialists by Allan Larsson, finance minister and head of the Swedish social democratic party from 1991 to 1995 (Party of European Socialists, 1994; de la Porte, 2011). Parallel to this, ideas about high labour market participation and supply-side policies were also being discussed in the European Commission, initiated by Jacques Delors, President of the European Commission from 1985 to 1994 (Delors, 1993; European Commission, 1993; Goetschy, 1999). The ideas adopted at the EU level in this period were to enhance labour market participation through supply-side policies: job-creation, activation, and training initiatives, as well as labour market flexibility and the reduction of non-wage labour costs (European Council, 1994). We shall see in the following that these ideas have remained stable throughout the alterations made to the EES.

Full political commitment to these ideas was developed in the European Employment Strategy, adopted formally in the Amsterdam Treaty in 1997. The policies initially promoted in the EES (and later in the other social OMCs) resonate with the (positive) normative notion of a 'European social model' (Jepsen and Serrano Pascual, 2005). The objective of the EES is to achieve a high level of employment through the promotion of ' ... a skilled, trained, and adaptable workforce and labour markets responsive to economic change'. Employment growth is clearly the backbone of the Strategy. The first set of more specific objectives – the 'European Employment Guidelines'– was agreed in November 1997, where seven (out of a total of 19) guidelines were devoted to activation (termed 'employability'). Some objectives were devoted to adaptability (to the labour market), to entrepreneurship, and to the promotion of equal opportunities between men and women. In 2000, the role of public employment services for placing individuals in various types of employment schemes was emphasized in the EES (de la Porte, 2008). At the same time, the EU agreed on a quantitative benchmark, to reach an average employment rate of 70 per cent for the EU by 2010 (and 60 per cent for women as well as 50 per cent for older workers) (European Council, 2000, 2001).

In 2000, the OMC was adopted for social inclusion policy. It is to be noted that the European concept of exclusion which provides the building blocks for the social inclusion strategy joins two seemingly contradictory notions of poverty: targeted anti-poverty strategy that has been dominant in the Anglo-Saxon tradition; and the preventive universalistic rights-based approach that is characteristic in the Scandinavian countries (Armstrong, 2006; Esping-Andersen, 1990). The core of this ideologically-merged European conception of poverty is contained in the four objectives for social inclusion. These are, first, to facilitate access to employment for all citizens; second, to provide universal social rights and services; third, to target actions for groups at the risk of social exclusion; and fourth, to boost the involvement of a wide range of stakeholders in policy development and implementation. In addition, a European threshold for monetary poverty was adopted at 60 per cent of the median income. This is higher than the Organisation for Economic Co-operation and Development (OECD)'s poverty threshold, at 50 per cent of the median income, distinguishing the EU's position. While not a quantitative benchmark, it is a numerical point of reference with which to comparatively assess poverty across the EU, and has instigated some debate about poverty assessment in some member states. In the area of pensions the aims are to combine social adequacy and financial sustainability of pensions systems while modernizing them in response to changing employment, household, and demographic patterns. In healthcare and care for the elderly OMC the aims are to ensure access and quality in healthcare services and care for the elderly. Contrary to social inclusion, pensions and healthcare are core aspects of national social protection systems, implying that member states are defensive with regard to the EU's intervention in these areas.

After 2005, when there was a conservative-liberal majority in the Council, the policy aims of the EES and the social OMCs became more focused around 'jobs, jobs, jobs'. Expert groups under the leadership of the Dutch politician Wim Kok were instrumental in this altered strategy (Kok, 2003, 2004; Armstrong et al., 2008). The objectives of the EES became concentrated more narrowly around investment in human capital, the development of skills, and the improvement of education systems. Furthermore, the EES became integrated with economic policy coordination, with the hope of enhancing its salience in Member States. This increased the influence of DG ECfin and national finance ministries in focusing more on objectives related to economic growth and less on objectives related to gender equality. There were also changes to the other OMCs: prior to 2006, the social inclusion, healthcare, and pensions OMCs had been autonomous, with independent reporting cycles and procedures, while after 2006 these three processes were merged together, implying a decrease of their visibility. At the same time, a benchmark to eliminate child poverty by 2010 was agreed in 2005.

In 2010, an even narrower 'Europe 2020' replaced the Lisbon Strategy within which the EES and social OMCs were embedded. Within the new arrangement, there are a total of ten guidelines of which two are in employment policy: to increase labour market participation (to 75 per cent by 2020) and to enhance human capital development. There is one aim in social exclusion, which is to decrease poverty, with a rather loosely defined benchmark: to 'lift at least 20 million people out of the risk of poverty and exclusion' by 2020 (European Council, 2010). The pensions and healthcare OMCs will continue in parallel, but their political salience is low (de la Porte and Weishaupt, 2011). Europe 2020 clearly mirrors the economic recession that emerged in the aftermath of the 2008 global financial crisis, where fiscal austerity packages have changed the welfare reform agenda drastically.

Throughout the last two decades, some objectives of EU's social and labour market strategy have been strengthened: to increase labour market participation (also seen as the only sensible way out of social exclusion), to make labour markets more flexible, and to enhance human capital development. However, other aims are on the agenda only temporarily, in particular those related to gender equality and to comprehensive social protection. The fact that the OMC's aims change over time makes its long-term impact difficult to analyse. Nevertheless, some progress has been made in analysing its effects, and it is possible to differentiate the effects of the OMC according to welfare state regime, as will be discussed in the next two sections.

Analysing effects of the social OMCs

Since the OMC is a soft mode of governance, promoting specific policies, but with no mechanism of coercion, it functions via soft ideational exchange, in turn inducing policy learning. In some instances, learning from the OMC is direct and can be identified through careful process-tracing. In other instances, it can be indirect, where learning about ideas from the social OMC occurs in conjunction with European Social Fund (ESF) funding or other fora, such as the OECD, that has recommended labour market flexibilization and activation for several decades.

Recent research has made headway in analysing the mechanisms of change associated with the OMC. One mechanism through which ideas can be transferred is socialization, which involves exposure to new information about an issue (problem and/or solution) in a forum associated with the social OMC (such as the social protection committee or the peer review programme). It is during socialization that learning can be initiated (de la Porte et al., 2008). A second mechanism is reflexivity, which is learning about one's own policies and institutions – strengths but also weaknesses – on the basis of information produced in or discussed/deliberated within the OMC process (Zeitlin, 2005; Trubek and Mosher, 2003). A third mechanism is the broader diffusion of an idea, which presupposes that the information of the OMC has multiple channels through which to be diffused. The OMC can also be used in other ways: actors can use the OMC as 'leverage' vis-à-vis their respective governments, political parties, or EU institutions (Ehrel et al., 2005). It is to be noted that socialization, reflexivity, diffusion, and using the OMC as leverage are not mutually exclusive. In addition, the OMC may or may not lead to policy change: in order for change to materialize, it is crucial to transform policy ideas associated with specific frames (of problems and solution) and new knowledge into initiatives and strategies. This necessarily involves some degree of transformation or 're-interpretation' as has been highlighted in the Europeanization literature (see Martinsen, 2005). For example, the notion of 'activation' has been interpreted differently in the various member states, ranging from comprehensive up-skilling to workfarism (de la Porte and Jacobsson, 2012). In the following section, the learning effects of the OMC in welfare reform will be presented according to (five) different types of welfare state configurations: universal, liberal, conservative, Meditteranean and Post-socialist (Esping-Anderson, 1990; Ferrera, 1996; Aidukaite, 2009).

Exploring the results

For the Nordic countries, the main effect of the social OMCs has been reflexive learning, i.e. learning about the strengths of their own universal welfare state model, and in the case of Denmark, its own 'flexicurity' model (Kvist, 2007). Governments and politicians have not used the OMCs to reflect upon weaknesses of the universal model, particularly gender segregation on the labour market, discrimination against immigrants (Jacobsson, 2005), and creeping problems of poverty and exclusion (de la Porte and Al-Gailany, 2011). As a contrast, non-governmental organizations (NGOs) have drawn extensively on the OMC to frame problems and solutions (obtained through socialization and reflexivity) such as child poverty. They insist on adopting an official poverty threshold, which does not exist in the Scandinavian universal welfare state tradition. Furthermore, NGOs benefit from the peer review programme which has not only led to new ideas, but has been transformed to new initiatives, such as the development of a homelessness strategy in Denmark (de la Porte, 2011). Trade unions, on the other hand, did not learn from the policy ideas of the EES, as they already have strong channels through which to impact labour market policy. Concerning other policy changes in the Scandinavian countries – the integration of immigrants on the labour market and pension reform – these were initiated due to domestic reforms, where the OMC was but one (weak) channel through which policy ideas related to these issues were raised (Jacobsson, 2005; Jacobsson and Johansson, 2009; de la Porte, 2011; Saari and Kangas, 2007; Jacobsson and Schmid, 2002; Lopez-Santana, 2009).

For liberal countries, the social OMCs have had more potential to contribute to policy reform, since the liberal welfare states have high labour market participation, but a workfarist approach to enhancing labour market participation, a high proportion of low-skilled workers, and intergenerational transmission of poverty. The OMC in social exclusion, in particular, has been utilized for conceptualizing and debating child poverty among governmental actors and NGOs, because it was in line with national priorities. However, when issues such as up-skilling were not framed according to the domestic agenda, the OMC was largely ignored by governments. In the UK and even more in Ireland, civil society has used the OMC and its policy agenda as leverage, to gain support for combating poverty, exclusion, workfarism and child poverty. This has led to some dialogue between government and non-state actors, but not to many new initiatives (Büchs and Friedrich, 2005; Armstrong, 2005, O'Donnell and Moss, 2005; 2006; Büchs, 2007; Kröger, 2008; van Gerven, 2008; van Gerven and Beckers, 2009; Mailand, 2009). Governmental actors mainly re-interpret OMC objectives in line with domestic priorities, rather than reflexively learning about weaknesses in existing policy solutions, while social partners and NGOs engage in learning from the EU level as well as reflexive learning in order to attempt to obtain commitment to new policy aims, which has only in some cases been successful.

The learning potential of OMC goals in conservative welfare states is considerable. Concerning the influence of the EES in Germany, one set of researchers concludes that the influence on policy change in labour market and social exclusion policy is minimal, an effect that is captured by the concept 'surface integration' (Büchs, 2007; Büchs and Friedrich, 2005). According to Büchs (2007), the landmark Hartz reforms were driven by domestic concerns, and were barely informed by ideas associated with the OMC. Another set of researchers (Preunkert and Zirra, 2009) consider that the EES guidelines were an important lever for the initiation of the Hartz reforms (Preunkert and Zirra, 2009, p. 194). They conclude that there was a strong and direct effect of the EES on labour market reform in Germany, where it had a decisive role in shaping policies, thus leading to 'paradigmatic change' (ibid.). In the French case, the ideas of the social OMCs have supported new reform initiatives in labour market policy, although the role of the EES in this process is disputed (Ehrel et al., 2005; Barbier and Samba-Sylla, 2004; Barbier, 2008). The EES and OMCs represent one channel through which ideas for policy responses are developed.

For the welfare state countries of the Mediterranean rim, as for the countries of continental Europe, the EES and the OMC in social policy addresses key challenges. These countries traditionally have low rates of labour market participation of women and older workers, few and underdeveloped care structures, as well as many low-skilled workers. Most of the literature highlights that concepts associated with social OMCs have been diffused widely in this group of countries. Activation, female labour market participation, life-long up-skilling, flexicurity, and social inclusion were novel ideas introduced through the social OMCs (Adao and Silva, 2009; Ferrera and Sacchi, 2005; Mailand, 2009). For the Spanish case, Mailand (2009, p. 163) argues that the 'the preventive approach would not have been introduced without the existence of and pressure from the EES,' while Lopez-Santana argues that ideas about activation were already present in national thinking due to the ESF. Ideas about activation have been diffused broadly and quite consistently over time via the EES, but also the ESF. In addition, empirical analyses in

Italy and Spain show that the EES was used as a political opportunity structure. However, the EES was used as a scapegoat by the governments to enhance the development of precarious contracts and labour market flexibilization. Furthermore, availability of affordable and high-quality child care institutions remains a problem in the southern European countries (Lopez-Santana, 2009; Ferrera and Sacchi, 2005). Thus, ideas developed within the EES and OMC have been reinterpreted entirely. This points to the importance of analyzing how ideas from the OMCs have been used.

The social OMCs have had a major potential for being used constructively in the new member states. They have framed problems, such as inadequacies of education, which has been addressed in recommendations to most CEE (de la Porte and Jacobsson, 2012). The national OMC reports prepared by the CEE reveal that there is an awareness of this and other issues. On the surface, the ideas developed in the OMCs, such as flexicurity and lifelong learning, resonate with key reform responses of the CEE in recent years. However, a closer analysis reveals that the terms associated with the OMCs are used broadly, without the intended connotation. Flexicurity has most often, apart from some exceptional cases such as in Slovenia (Lajh and Silaj, 2010) been interpreted as deregulation by governmental actors and politicians in these countries (de la Porte and Jacobsson, 2012). Social partners are weak, while civil society actors are even weaker, neither having benefited from the potential of the OMC as leverage. In fact, even if these actors are opposed to some government reforms as stated in the national reports to the EU, they rarely have enough leverage to make themselves heard (de la Porte and Jacobsson, 2012). Overall, there has been no real desire by governments to engage in reflexive learning, partly because, as pointed out by Orenstein (2009), many of the CEE aim to 'out-liberalize' the EU-15, which involves welfare state retrenchment rather than a more balanced approach to reform, which is behind the social OMCs. Those actors that do want to use it are too weak to be able to have a strong influence.

The OMC's main effect across welfare states has been socialization for governmental actors but, ironically, they are the ones that are the least willing to use it to reflect upon how to alter problem and/or solution framing. Governmental actors (re)interpret EU concepts in line with their own preferences, exemplified by labour market deregulation being identified as flexicurity. Reflexive learning is strongest for non-state actors, particularly large NGOs linked to an EU umbrella organization, because they have fewer institutionalized channels for voice compared with social partners. NGOs are also the most active in using the OMC as leverage, although the extent to which they are successful varies considerably.

Conclusion

In analysing OMC, it is important to take account of the continuity and changes of the EU's socio-economic agenda, now coined Europe 2020, in which OMCs are embedded. Policy coordination is a fundamental mode of EU policy making that does provide member states with ideas about reform solutions in the process of labour market and welfare state re-structuring. Furthermore, it is crucial to consider a reform process comprehensively in which the OMC is but one soft and highly politicized mechanism through which ideas about policy reforms and solutions could be introduced. Research on the OMC at national level should include analysis of pressures for reform not only from the domestic level, but also from the EU and international levels.

More than a decade of research on the influence of the OMC shows that its ideas are used (and interpreted) selectively and politically by actors. Governmental actors mostly seek to defend their policies to convince the EU level that their reforms have been following EU's agenda. NGOs, on the other hand, are more likely to use the OMC as leverage vis-à-vis governmental actors. The potential of the OMC to provide ideas of added value is greatest in welfare state configurations with most distance from EU objectives, but it is also in these countries that governments stretch the meaning of the OMCs concepts the most, and where governments have used the EU as a scapegoat for unpopular reforms.

While the interest in the OMC has led to a particular strand of Europeanization scholarship, involving detailed analysis of how the OMC leads to new ideas and solutions, comparative welfare state researchers focus on national reform processes and they barely, if at all, consider the effect of the OMC. By considering policy coordination within the process of domestic reform, the scholarship on Europeanization and comparative welfare state reform should come closer. Researchers interested in reform processes from a domestic or a European perspective should have similar objects of study – how can a particular reform be understood, what are the ideas behind it, and how did it come about? – and comparable analytical frameworks, even if they are still likely to differ slightly in what they concentrate on.

Bibliography

Adão e Silva, P. (2009), Il Portogallo come caso di studio dell'europeanizzazione delle politiche sociali. *La Rivista delle Politiche Sociali*, (4), pp. 229–60.

Aidukaite, J. (2009), 'Old welfare state theories and new welfare regimes in Eastern Europe: Challenges and implications'. *Communist and Post-Communist Studies* 42 (1), pp. 23–39.

Armstrong, K. (2006), The 'Europeanisation' of Social Exclusion: British Adaptation to EU Co-ordination, 8, *British Journal of Politics and International Relations*, pp. 79–100.

——(2005), 'How open is the United Kingdom to the OMC process on social inclusion?', in J. Zeitlin et al. (eds), *The Open Method of Coordination in Action: The European Employment and Social Inclusion Strategies*, pp. 287–310. Brussels: PIE-Peter Lang.

Armstrong, K., Begg I. and Zeitlin J. (2008), EU governance after Lisbon. *Journal of Common Market Studies*, 46 (2): 413–50.

Atkinson, A. et al. (2004), Indicators and targets for social inclusion in the European Union. *Journal of Common Market Studies*, 42(1), pp. 47–75.

Barbier, J.-C. (2008), *La longue marche vers l'Europe sociale*, Paris: PUF.

Barbier, J.-C. and Sylla, N. S. (2004), 'La stratégie européenne pour l'emploi: genèse, coordination communautaire et diversité nationale', Report for the French Labour Ministry, Noisy-le-Grand; Centre d'études de l'emploi.

Büchs, M. (2007), *New Governance in European Social Policy: The Open Method of Co-ordination*. Basingstoke: PalgraveMacmillan.

Büchs, M. and Friedrich, D. (2005), 'Surface integration. The national action plans for employment and social inclusion in Germany', in J. Zeitlin and P. Pochet (eds) *The Open Method of Coordination in Action: The Employment and Social Inclusion Strategies*, pp. 249–86. Brussels: PIE-Peter Lang.

de la Porte, C. (2011), 'Principal-agent theory and the Open Method of Co-ordination: the case of the European Employment Strategy'. *Journal of European Public Policy*, 18(4), pp. 485–503.

——(2008), 'The Evolution and Influence of the Open Method of Coordination: The Cases of Employment and Social Inclusion', unpublished PhD thesis, Social and Political Science Department, European University Institute, Florence, Italy.

de la Porte, C. and Pochet, P. (forthcoming 2012), 'Why and how (still) study the OMC?' *Journal of European Social Policy*.

de la Porte, C. and Jacobsson, K. (2012), 'Social Investment or recommodification? Assessing the employment policies of the EU member states', in N. Morel, B. Palier and J. Palme (eds), *Towards a Social Investment Welfare State? Ideas, Policies and Challenges*, Bristol: Policy Press.

de la Porte, C. and Al-Gailany, Y. (2011), 'The social inclusion OMC: capable of addressing structural challenges in welfare state reform? The case of Denmark', paper prepared for the 9th annual Espanet conference, Valencia, Spain.

de la Porte, C., Natali, D. and Pochet, P. (2009), 'Self-Governance in EU employment and social policy through the Open Method of Co-ordination', in E. Sørensen and P. Triantafillou (eds), *The Politics of Self-Governance*, Farnham: Ashgate.

Delors, J. (1993), Entering the 21st century: orientations for economic renewal in Europe, Policy Paper submitted to the Copenhagen European Council, June.

Erhel, C., Mandin, L. and Palier, B. (2005), 'The leverage effect. The open method of coordination in France', in J. Zeitlin, P. Pochet and L. Magnusson (eds), *The Open Method of Coordination in Action. The European Employment and Social Inclusion Strategies*, pp. 217–47. Brussels: Peter Lang.

Esping-Andersen, G. (1990), *Three Worlds of Welfare Capitalism*, Cambridge: Polity Press.

European Commission (1993), White Paper on growth, competitiveness, and employment: The challenges and ways forward into the 21st century, COM (93) 700 final of 5 December 1993.

European Council (1994), Essen European Council, *Presidency Conclusions*, pp. 9–10 December.

——(2000), Lisbon European Council, *Presidency Conclusions*, 23–24 March.

——(2001), Stockholm European Council, Presidency Conclusions, 23–24 March.

——(2010), Brussels European Council, Presidency Conclusions, 25–26 March.

Ferrera, M. (1996), 'The Southern Model of Welfare in Social Europe'. *Journal of European Social Policy* (1), pp. 17–37.

Ferrera, M. and Sacchi, S. (2005), 'The open method of co-ordination and national institutional capabilities. The Italian experience', in J. Zeitlin et al. (eds), *The Open Method of Coordination in Action: The European Employment and Social Inclusion Strategies*, pp. 137–72. Brussels: PIE-Peter Lang.

Jacobsson, K. (2005), 'Trying to reform the "best pupils in the class"? The open method of coordination in Sweden and Denmark', in J. Zeitlin and P. Pochet, with L. Magnusson (eds), *The Open Method of Coordination in Action*, pp. 107–36, Brussels: PIE Peter Lang.

Jacobsson, K. and Schmid, J. (2002), 'The EES in Denmark and Sweden', in C. de la Porte and P. Pochet (eds), *Building social Europe through the Open Method of Co-ordination*, pp. 177–221. Brussels: P.I.E.-Peter Lang.

Jacobsson, K. and Johansson, H. (2009), 'The micro-politics of the open method of coordination: NGOS and the social inclusion process in Sweden', in M. Heidenreich and J. Zeitlin (eds), *Changing European Employment and Welfare Regimes: The Influence of the Open Method of Coordination on National Reforms*, pp. 173–91. London: Routledge.

Kröger, S. (2008), *Soft Governance in Hard Politics. European Coordination of Anti-poverty Policies in France and Germany*. Wiesbaden: VS Verlag.

Kvist, J. (2007), 'Denmark: from foot dragging to pace setting in European Union policy', in J. Kvist and J. Saari (eds), *The Europeanisation of Social Protection*, pp. 195–210. Bristol: Policy Press.

Lajh, D. and Silaj, T. (2010), 'Slovenian employment policy: from self-management to common (international) goals and paradigms', in D. Fink-Hafner (ed.), *The Open Method of Coordination: A View from Slovenia*, pp. 35–58. Ljubljana: Faculty of Social Sciences.

López-Santana, M. (2009), 'Soft Europeanization? The differential influence of the European employment strategy in Belgium, Spain and Sweden', in J. Zeitlin and M. Heidenreich (eds), *Changing European Employment and Welfare Regimes. The Influence of the Open Method of Coordination on National Labour Market and Social Welfare Reforms*, pp. 134–53. New York: Routledge.

Mailand, M. (2009), 'North, South, East, West: the implementation of the European employment strategy in Denmark, the UK, Spain and Poland', in J. Zeitlin and M. Heidenreich (eds), *Changing European Employment and Welfare Regimes. The Influence of the Open Method of Coordination on National Labour Market and Social Welfare Reforms*, pp. 154–72. New York: Routledge.

Martinsen, D. (2005), 'The Europeanization of Welfare-the Domestic Impact of Intra-European Social Security'. *Journal of Common Market Studies*, 43 (5), pp. 1027–54.

O'Donnell, R. and Moss, B. (2005), 'Ireland: The very idea of an open method of coordination', in J. Zeitlin et al. (eds), *The Open Method of Coordination in Action: The European Employment and Social Inclusion Strategies*, pp. 311–50. Brussels: PIE-Peter Lang.

Ornestein, M.A. (2008), 'Out-liberalizing the EU: pension privatization in Central and Eastern Europe'. *Journal of European Public Policy*, 15(6), pp. 899–917.

Party of European Socialists and European Parliament (2000), 'Putting Europe to Work 1994 – 1999' Programme of the PES (Party of European Socialists) for the European Parliamentary Elections of 1994, A review: what has been achieved in the last five years? Hughes, S., Chair of the EP committee on social affairs and employment and Tuyttens, B., PES secretariat.

Preunkert, J., and Zirra, S. (2009), 'Europeanization of domestic employment and welfare regimes: the German, French, and Italian experiences', in M. Heidenreich, and J. Zeitlin (eds), *Changing European Employment and Welfare Regimes: The Influence of the Open Method of Coordination on National Reforms*, pp. 192–213, London: Routledge.

Saari, J. and O. Kangas (2007), 'Finland: social protection reform', in J. Kvist and O. Saari (eds), *The Europeanisation of Social Protection*, pp. 153–74. Bristol: Policy Press.
Trubek, D. and Mosher, J. (2003), 'Alternative approaches to governance in the EU: EU social policy and the European employment strategy'. *Journal of Common Market Studies*, 41(1), pp. 63–68.
van Gerven, M. (2008), The broad tracks of path dependent benefit reforms: a longitudinal study of social benefit reforms in three European countries, 1980–2006. *Studies in Social Security and Health* 100, Helsinki: Social Insurance Institution Finland.
van Gerven, M. and Beckers, M. (2009), 'Unemployment protection reform in Belgium, Finland, the Netherlands and the UK: policy learning through the OMC?', in J. Heidenreich and J. Zeitlin (eds), *Changing European Employment and Welfare Regimes: The Influence of the Open Method of Coordination on National Reforms*, pp. 61–83. London: Routledge.
Weishaupt, T. and de la Porte, C. (2011), 'State of the Art. OMC in social and employement policy: theory, methods, substantive outcomes and new directions' paper prepared for the 9th annual Espanet conference, Valencia, Spain.
Zeitlin, J. (2005), 'Conclusion: The open method of coordination in action: theoretical promise, empirical realities, reform strategy', in J. Zeitlin et al. (eds), *The Open Method of Coordination in Action: The European Employment and Social Inclusion Strategies*, pp. 441–98. Brussels: PIE-Peter Lang.
——(2009), 'The open method of coordination and national social and employment policy reforms: influences, mechanisms, effects', in J. Heidenreich and J. Zeitlin (eds), *Changing European Employment and Welfare Regimes: The Influence of the Open Method of Coordination on National Reforms*, pp. 214–45. London: Routledge.

40

Evaluation, evidence, and review

Ian Greener

Introduction

We live in an era when politicians are anxious to claim that their policies are not based on ideologies, or simple opinions, but instead on evidence. Despite the claims of the more post-modern theorists that attempts to examine evidence in a rationalistic manner are futile, the claims of policymakers have never been more modernistic, or more concerned to show that they are implementing 'what works' (Davies, Nutley, and Smith, 1999).

However, in practice, evaluating whether existing policies or programmes work, or presenting evidence that reforms are based on the best available research to achieve evidence-based policy, have proven difficult to achieve. In the UK, the claims by Secretary of State Andrew Lansley that the 2011 health reforms were evidence-based were met in some quarters of the informed media with derision (Goldacre, 2011). This suggests that policymakers' understanding of what counts as evidence might be very different from those engaged in research, and points to important questions about both what should count as good evidence in policymaking, and how we should evaluate existing research to the end of producing better policy.

When considering evidence, there is an obvious appeal in claiming to be taking a scientific approach to the construction, assessment and evaluation of data. The problem is working out exactly what this means. Economists advocate cost-benefit approaches as a scientific approach, but such appraisal exercises have become parts of evaluation packages rather than being the entire approach. Instead, the foundation of evaluation studies has become based on experimental methods derived from natural science, and especially from the most applied of the scientific disciplines, medicine.

This chapter considers the questions of what counts as evidence in evaluation, exploring three approaches that attempt to provide a method for the synthesis of research, with each either attempting to provide an underpinning for the way that either interventions can be evaluated, or existing research synthesised for policy purposes (or both). It considers the strengths and weaknesses of each, as well as the assumptions they hold about what counts as good research. It concludes by suggesting that the realistic approach suggesting by Ray Pawson has the greatest potential for informing policy through research because of its more sophisticated consideration of the problems of applying social research to policy ends, but that its application and widespread usage will require a new mind-set from both policymakers and academics that recognises the limitations of what research can achieve, and which gives a greater role for creativity in social research.

The chapter proceeds as follows: first it considers what many social researchers regard as the gold standard in terms of evidence in evaluation, the randomised controlled trial (RCT), and assesses the extent to which research outside of the hard-science paradigm meets the preconditions necessary for the application of RCT-based ideas. It then moves on to attempts by social researchers, especially those who are often engaged in asking questions with both clinical and qualitative elements, to make use of frameworks inspired by the RCT, adapting the criteria, often to try and include qualitative data, before finally moving onto a third approach presented by Ray Pawson and his collaborators which is based on very different assumptions to the RCT. Having considered the strengths and weaknesses of each evaluation approach, the chapter then moves on to its conclusion.

Randomised controlled trials, evaluation and evidence

Many social researchers regard the randomised controlled trial (RCT) and systematic review as representing a gold standard for the creation, assessment and evaluation of evidence. It is not hard to see why. RCTs originate in medicine, which represents a paradigmatic case of the application of scientific ideas to a social context. The idealised view of medicine combines rigorous research with informed professionals able to interpret that research for the specific individual before them to the end of alleviating their illness or improving their health. The achievements of medical research in the twentieth century, as even its critiques accept (Le Fanu, 1999) are truly astounding.

However, the extent to which what we might call the RCT model of evidence collection and assessment evaluation outside of medical textbooks is more of an open question than is often assumed (Greenhalgh, 1998). In medical practice itself, critics point the often significant gaps between evidence and practice, and the problem that relatively few existing treatments meet the high evidence standards applied to new ones. Even so, the RCT model represents an ideal against which researchers in other disciplines have often compared themselves in order to try and improve the standards of their research, as well as hoping by conforming to its scientific tenets they might improve the standing of their work amongst policymakers.

In medical science, RCT methods aim to produce systematic and robust knowledge through the application of a demanding series of methodological requirements. In order to meet these, scientists undertake large-scale trials making use of double-blinded groups (so neither those administering the tests not those taking part know whether they are part of the control or treatment groups), with participants of the research selected on a random basis. These three elements (random sampling, large-scale trials, double-blinding) are attempts to capture the effects of treatments or other interventions in the most rigorous possible manner. Random sampling, especially in combination with large trials, means that individual differences in reaction to treatments should be averaged out, and the effects of extreme results reduced. Large-scale random sampling means that results aim to be as generalizable as possible in relation to their population.

When several RCTs in the same area have been conducted, provided their methods are seen to be robust enough, they can then be carefully combined to form a systematic review of the research regarding the intervention or treatment under consideration, to effectively combine the trials into a single, large-scale synthesis. This requires a great deal of care, with existing trials being closely scrutinised in terms of their reported methods especially, and with only those trials meeting the highest standards (in terms of their reported compliance with the large-scale, randomised, double-blinded approach) being incorporated in full into the review. Clear inclusion and exclusion criteria are drawn up to aid those conducing the evaluation in deciding which studies should and should not be incorporated, and if they are to be included, on what basis.

The assumptions underlying the RCT and systematic review approach

The RCT approach, and the systematic reviews that synthesise it, carry with them a range of ontological and epistemological assumptions that need to be considered carefully to assess whether they apply outside of medial contexts, to see if those principles can be translated into social research. In terms of ontology, the methods treat the existence of an objective world as, perhaps a little paradoxically, both straightforward and problematic.

The use of double-blinded methods means that both researchers and participants are acknowledged as potentially having an impact on research outcomes should they become aware of whether they are participating in control or intervention group, and so implicitly acknowledging that mental constructs about the assumed efficacy of treatments or clinical interventions can influence the success of the research.

At the same time as acknowledging subjectivity in relation to treatment through double-blinding, however, the RCT approach treats the measurement of clinical outcome relatively unproblematically. The extent to which the efficacy of the intervention being assessed by research will undoubtedly be affected by a range of factors outside the control of scientists, as humans go about their everyday lives doing a range of things that can improve or reduce the efficacy of the treatments under consideration (even in the relatively controlled circumstances of a hospital this holds true), and so a constant conjunction model of cause and effect is largely in place that measures the results of treatments or interventions as following relatively straightforwardly from them.

The RCT-method attempts to get around the problems of not dealing with closed systems, and of variation in both intervention and subjects through the robustness of its method, by applying large-scale random sampling to try and reduce confounding factors, and by using its double-blinded methods in an attempt to reduce subjectivity. The aim is to produce an approach that creates objective knowledge in that it is independent of the particular participants or researchers within the trials, and which is at a level which is abstracted from particular cases (where confounding may occur) to a level where it is generalizable to the population as a whole. RCTs methods are epistemologically geared to favouring knowledge that is generalizable, objective, and independent of our individual conceptions of it.

What these assumptions lead to is a view of evidence that suggests (in a normative way, as well as constructing it through its method) that it should be context-independent, and achieved through methods which by putting in place controls. RCTs attempt to, as far as possible, achieve a closed system, and to compensate for any problems with this through large sampling to reduce the effects of environmental variables, and isolating the effects of an individual intervention or treatment so that they can be measured as rigorously as possible through a constant conjunctive model in which cause and effect can be measured statistically. This approach is generally also shared by social science disciplines like economics, which attempt to present themselves as scientific. The key question is the extent to which these methods and ideas can be applied in social research more generally, or are specific to areas such as medicine where scientific methods can be applied (albeit imperfectly).

Problems with applying RCT methods in social science

The application of context-independence, closed systems, and constant conjunction cause and effect measured by statistical methods, all have significant problems when transferred without adaptation into social science.

Context-independence raises profound questions for social research. This is because many contemporary methodologists (for example Flyvbjerg, 2001) suggest that the key to functioning in social systems is the acquisition of knowledge that is context-sensitive, or even context-specific. Some everyday examples illustrate this – even for professionals doing ostensibly the same job, moving to another place of work will mean learning new rules, new ways of doing things, and a range of new social practices, in order to be effective.

Context specificity occurs because (to bring in the second point above), we do not operate and live in closed systems where experimental controls can be applied, but often in radically open ones. The impact of our environments upon our lives is profound. This creates something of a paradox in biomedicine because whereas RCTs incorporate double-blinding to attempt to avoid subjective influences on interventions and treatments, biomedical knowledge then attempts to operate largely independent of subjectivity in practice. Subjectivity can be reduced (or at least standardised) in the case of surgeries where patients are rendered unconscious (but even then will play a significant role in patient recovery), but for the vast majority of treatments, the patient's social subjectivity and social context will have a profound effect on their clinical outcome.

The third (and again related) point is that, in social systems, measuring cause and effect statistically does not take any account of reflexivity (Giddens, 1993), or of the possibility of more complex relationships between cause and effect. If I tell a colleague they are doing a good job today, it may have an effect on raising their morale (albeit one that is difficult to measure and subject to all the vagaries of open systems so that it may be countered by the many other things that happen in his/her day). That effect, however, will be different if someone else tells them exactly the same thing. If I tell my colleague they are doing a good job tomorrow as well, the effect might be reduced, but still occur. If I tell them every day for the next week, the effect might be diminished to almost nothing. If I continue to do it long enough, the effect might be close to zero or even negative. That might suggest that we should not tell our colleagues whenever they are doing a good job, but this would methodologically be a mistake because it does not take account of human interaction – we are not machines or microbes, and respond in different ways at different times to different people, and repeating the same intervention is likely to produce a different result on different occasions (even where the intervention is identical), specifically *because* of the previous interventions. Simple statistical measurement may fail to take this into account. It is therefore extraordinarily difficult to evaluate the success of interventions in organizations that are primarily inter-personal – it will depend on who is attempting the intervention, and who is on the receiving end of it.

Equally, a constant conjunction model of causation fails to capture any relationships where causes and effects do not occur in a straightforward, repetitive manner. In the social world, cause and effect may take years to work through and be contingent on a range of factors, but with causes still having important effects. Social class, for example, does not determine someone's social mobility, but will lead to either the addition or subtraction of barriers in a person's life in a way that is causally significant, even if it plays out differently for different people (Sayer, 2005).

RCT research tends to presume that interventions lead to outcomes in relatively straightforward ways, where patterns between the causes and effects can be accurately and straightforwardly measured. Again, a moment's thought suggests that most social problems aren't like this – a new policy intervention will often affect different groups in different ways, and at different speeds and times. Increasing unemployment benefits, for example, may have complex effects on different groups of people, on the labour market more generally, as well as on incentives to work or remain on benefits. These effects may take months or even years to work through, and impact upon different regions of the economy in entirely different ways (they may not affect affluent areas at all, for example, but completely change the dynamic in areas where minimum wages prevail).

If, in social research, it is not possible to treat context as independent, to approximate a closed system in order to isolate the effects of an intervention, or to measure the result of interventions unproblematically, then it is not clear how it is possible to claim to have demonstrated whether something 'works' or not through the application of methods derived straightforwardly from science.

Finally, applying the experimental methods upon which RCTs are based to interventions related to policy issues raises difficult ethical issues. On the one hand, it may not be regarded as ethical to introduce an intervention policymakers believe will improve the lives of a particular group, but for that intervention to take the form of an experiment initially so that only a trial group only receive it. If policymakers believe that their intervention will make things better (or why else would they be making the change?), then it can be considered unethical for that improvement not to be generalised to the entire population. At the same time, however, introducing an experimental policy change without it having been evaluated risks that group receiving an intervention that isn't as good as what is presently in place, raising a different kind of concern.

In countries such as the United States or Australia, different states may take different approaches to particular policy interventions, making some kind of comparison between those interventions possible, and so some policy writers suggest they form 'natural experiments'. There is some truth in this, but even then, the different interventions in different states occur in different social contexts (it would be hard to compare the results of different interventions in two US states, no matter how closely matched, without also taking account of their different histories, ethic, gender, and age make-ups, as well as other differences that exist across a huge range of other variable factors and may influence the success or otherwise of a new policy). In the UK is has become fashionable to argue that the increasing devolution between England, Scotland, and Wales creates opportunities for cross-boundary learning as each can be regarded as participating in a kind of experiment, but this is to ignore the very different historical, socio-economic and cultural contexts in those countries.

As such, despite their importance in biomedical research, the RCT-based approach has considerable problems when applied to the evaluation of social research, and to the construction of evidence-based policy advice. What alternatives are there?

Adapting RCT approaches for social research

A second approach to the problem of evaluating and synthesising social research comes in work that attempts to set quality standards through which studies might be excluded or included from evidence syntheses, but which accept that social research is often carried out in a different way, and with different aims, to RCT-research.

There are several examples of work in this vein, not least from qualitative health researchers (Dixon-Woods, Fitzpatrick, and Roberts 2008). These approaches, while being inspired by RCT research, attempt to adapt both their criteria for inclusion as well as their synthesis method to take account of methodological differences. The first problem they often have to face is how to incorporate qualitative research into their evaluation, and tends to lead away from an attempt to combine all research into one, large study as in a systematic review, but instead to find the best available evidence from the studies conducted. This means trying to find some means of applying statistical techniques to explore quantitative research then using qualitative research findings to 'triangulate' with the quantitative synthesis to give an evaluation of the available research as a whole.

One approach for attempting to achieve the goal of combining qualitative and quantitative research for synthesis has been pioneered in the work of Harden and Thomas and the research teams they work with, and has led them to creating what they call a 'mixed method' approach for 'combining diverse study types' (Harden and Thomas, 2005).

Harden and Thomas acknowledge the importance of systematic reviews for practitioners and policymakers in presenting a summary of the most important evidence as a means of saving time, but also because it enables readers to access the findings of a wider range of research than they would otherwise be able to achieve. They present what they call the 'standard stages of a systematic review' (p. 259), in which 'user-driven' questions and boundaries are set for the study, a review protocol developed, a comprehensive search carried out, inclusion criteria are applied and research quality assessed, after which data is extracted from papers for inclusion in the review, and findings synthesised, according to complex, usually statistical, procedures.

Harden and Thomas go on to explain how their own research centre has developed a mixed approach to systematic reviewing in which the focused review question is answered both by trials (which largely follow the procedure outlined above), but also by incorporating what they call 'view' studies (p. 262), and which aim to produce a qualitative (rather than quantitative) synthesis. Synthesis is achieved by reviewing qualitative work through similar stages as for quantitative research, going through the application of inclusion criteria, quality assessment, data extraction and then producing a synthesis of the qualitative findings.

Whereas quantitative assessments tend to use statistical techniques, the qualitative synthesis element is based on the development of analytic themes, which can then be compared to the quantitative synthesis to seek matches, 'mismatches and gaps' (p. 264) towards a complex end result that blurs the distinctions between the two types of research in the synthesis, and instead leads to (according to the authors) a means by which more diverse research questions can be answered to gain a better understanding of the phenomena. The researchers adopt what they call a 'half-way house' (p. 268) between the two different forms of data.

This approach appears, in many ways, an ideal way of dealing with the problems we identified above in relation to the applicability of RCT-type research to investigate social phenomena. In asking a diverse range of questions, some of which might be answered through quantitative data, and some through qualitative, a more rounded synthesis can be produced that can attempt to find the best that both types of research can produce. However, significant problems will remain with the approach.

First, Harden and Thomas's approach to synthesis tends toward the view that there is one right answer to the phenomena under investigation. This is, in many respects, something of a relic of the authors' own research interests, which are mostly about assessing the efficacy of interventions that combine the social and the clinical. By assuming that the product of a research synthesis can produce a single right answer, there is an implicit assumption that interventions can be assessed in an acontextual way. However, as we have already seen, in social research this may be a significant problem – it may well be that context is all in such a situation. It is difficult to imagine a policy intervention that will not be significantly contextually affected in implementation. Equally, there is a real need to acknowledge the conflicting and complex nature of social life, and so that policies will be interpreted, understood, and implemented in completely different ways (Stone 2012) – assuming that there is one right answer seems extremely hopeful.

Second, by putting in place selection criteria for the inclusion of qualitative research the review method depends on there being consensus about what counts as good research, and that methods are clearly and consistently reported in social research publications – and neither is the case. Especially in policy research, often relatively little space is given in journal articles to reporting research methods, and because there is less of a tradition of using such research for synthesis, work is not reported with a view to being included in syntheses later. It may well be that existing research would be excluded from syntheses not because it was poorly conducted, but because, when written up, the authors preferred to spend time on reporting the results of the research rather than explaining their methods according to criteria against which they did not envisage being assessed. There is no single methodological paradigm in social research, and so it is extremely difficult to draw up criteria against which we can review methodological validity – instead we have to assess work in the terms of the research tradition it attempts to position itself. There are very few criteria that would apply in every research tradition, and each piece tends to need us to assess it in relation to its own goals and standards.

It is also the case that qualitative research is not geared to an experimental method that attempts to assess the result of a particular intervention, but instead generally aims to understand the complex social context within which actors are living and working – it tends to be inductive rather than deductive. Harden and Thomas themselves admit that they are 'very dependent on the descriptions of the interventions supplied by the authors' (p. 268), but this does not really cover the complexity of the issue, which is that qualitative research is often simply not geared to trying to assess whether particular interventions work or not, and is instead engaged in trying to interpret complex social systems.

These concerns suggest that it may well not be possible to apply what seem like scientifically based selection criteria to qualitative research in the same way as research syntheses do for medical research. Social research does not present methods in a consistent manner that allows comparison, there is no single accepted 'right way' of doing things, and the research itself is not often directed at trying to evaluate a particular intervention, but instead to understand it in an entirely different way through a view of the world in which actors' interpretations and understanding are at least as important as what is actually taking place in that world (if it even makes sense to make that distinction, which writers such as Law would attack as being naive (Law, 2004)).

Finally, it is not clear what would happen in Harden and Thomas's model if the quantitative findings produced answers that were directly at odds with the qualitative research. What then? The authors are at pains to say that what they are attempting from their approach is not triangulation (answering the same research question using different methods), but investigating parallel or overlapping questions using different methods has the potential to produce potentially conflicting results. Because the assumptions underlying their synthesis approach appear to treat the social world as existing independently of our conceptions of it in a relatively unproblematic way – that we can straightforwardly measure the results of interventions in social contexts and work out which is the best, it is not clear what would happen if the results of their two different syntheses end up contradicting one another.

All in all then, Harden and Thomas's work looks promising in trying to break down the barriers between quantitative and qualitative research to produce policy-relevant findings, but instead end up treating qualitative research as being synthesisable through a similar means as quantitative work, being quality assessable and reviewable using the single method they call thematic review. This seems to go against the grain of the standard justification for carrying out qualitative research (to 'get close' or produce contextually-sensitive understandings of the social world), and so to end up treating it on terms different to those that that carried out the work in the first place would have envisaged.

Realistic evaluation and review

A third approach to both evaluation and review comes from the work of Ray Pawson and his collaborators (Pawson, 2006; Pawson et al., 2005; Pawson and Tilley, 2001). Pawson has applied his ideas to a range of research problems, first coming to international attention in relation to his work on evaluation (Pawson and Tilley, 2001), but since moving on to a range of other insights, especially in relation to considering evidence in policy research (Pawson 2002a; Pawson 2002b). Pawson's work presents an extended critique of conventional approaches to evaluation and systematic review which share many of the same concerns offered above (and from which the work above draws) – and from which he concludes that in attempting to adapt a method derived from the scientific, experimental paradigm to social systems there is a risk of making a number of methodological errors that carry the risk of misunderstanding the phenomena under investigation.

Rather than attempting to apply RCT principles so social research, Pawson suggests that it is necessary, when considering social systems, to explore complex inter-relationships between contexts, mechanisms, and outcomes. In order to achieve this, a comparative approach needs to be taken which looks at the way the same or similar mechanisms are introduced in differing contexts to different outcome effects. This is a different causation logic to experimental methods (which have in place a constant conjunctive model, where cause and effect are tightly coupled and statistically measured), but instead through a generative model where causes and effects are far more difficult to ascertain, and require a careful and creative unpicking of data in order to unearth.

One of Pawson's classic examples of exploring causality in this more complex way comes in his explorations of 'naming and shaming' policies, where different contexts produce entirely different outcomes (Pawson and Tilley, 1997). Naming and shaming is based on the idea that publishing the names of individuals who are deemed to be falling short of the behaviours generally accepted in society will lead to communities censuring those individuals, as well as preventing individuals from wanting their offences publicised. This is what we might call the 'programme theory' for the policy. In the case of the use of Anti-Social Behavioural Orders (ASBOs), for example, attempting to 'name and shame' offenders led to ASBOS not being seen as a potential source of community censure, but instead as a kind of badge of honour, with some people even competing to see who could get an ASBO at the youngest age, or who could receive the most ASBO notices. In the case of paedophile registers, however, naming and shaming led to an entirely different outcome.

What this points to is that policies based on the same programme theory can have very different results because different social contexts will shape their effects in very different ways. Instead of assuming that interventions are acontextual and that one policy intervention will work in all circumstances, the approach leads to more nuanced understanding of what works for whom in what circumstances, and to the idea that we must explore the outcome effects of different contexts to evaluate a programme.

To understand the implications of Pawson's approach it is perhaps best to consider what might have happened if a more standard approach to evaluation has been applied to the above research on naming and shaming. In that case we might have come to the conclusion that, on average, it doesn't work, or even that it has a negative effect on outcomes. But this would miss the point – naming and shaming may work in some circumstances – where those being named are genuinely embarrassed by it and so are likely to change or regulate their behaviour, but not to the extent that they are driven into hiding or where those who are the target audience of the data are likely to engage in vigilantism (as might be the case with naming and shaming paedophiles) or even come to regard those that have been shamed in esteem (as was the case with ASBOs). Evaluations need to take careful account of the complex relations between outcomes and contexts, finding creative ways of exploring how the same programme theories have been implemented through similar mechanisms in different contexts.

What this suggests is that Pawson's approach attempts to directly deal with the problems and concerns of RCT-based approach to social research explored above – that RCT-based approaches to evaluation and review attempt to produce acontextual knowledge when social systems are almost inherently contextual in terms of the knowledge required to navigate and understand them, that whereas RCT-type work tends to try and approximate closed systems through the use of controls, such an approach is not possible in social systems, and that causality in social systems needs a different model to the statistically measured constant conjunctive model. All this means, in Pawson's approach, is that it is necessary to be focused on trying to achieve a comparative, pattern-seeking approach that looks for similar interventions across a range of cases to try and find out what they have in common and difference in terms of both context and outcome, rather than trying to find statistical regularities amongst cases of a similar type.

Pawson's approach, however, is not without its problems. One issue that it can be extremely difficult to define what is meant by 'context' within the approach. This is because it appears to require the researcher or reviewer to be able to understand the range of occurrences within which the particular phenomena under investigation (the mechanisms) occurs, and then to work back and find differences between those occurrences in order to work out a system for differentiating them. This requires, in turn, that we are able to define a programme theory which is suitably abstracted in order to find a range of cases to compare (as in the case of naming and shaming above), but not so general that we end up comparing mechanisms that don't have very much in common.

To take a very topical example, evaluating 'nudge' policies is extremely difficult as they cover such a wide range of potential interventions designed to engineer decision-making to encourage individuals to choose the 'right' outcome for themselves. Nudge interventions range from putting fruit next to tills in supermarkets rather than chocolate, to try and encourage healthier snacking, through to requiring smokers to re-register annually with their doctor in order to have a licence that allows them to purchase cigarettes, as suggested by the former UK government health policy adviser Julian Le Grand.

Evaluating nudge represents a potentially fascinating research project, but would have to include a very wide range of interventions that might appear to have little in common, and so require a creative process of comparison. It is striking that the House of Lords' attempt to evaluate nudge programmes (House of Lords Science and Technology Select Committee 2011) failed really to get to grips with these challenges, and so reached the conclusions that 'non-regulatory measures used in isolation, including "nudges", are less likely to be effective' (p. 5). However, this is because the nudge programmes were assessed in a largely atheoretical and acontextual way – a more theoretically-driven approach that too much greater account of context might have come to a different answer, and provided us with a much richer understanding of nudge interventions as a result.

What this shows is that it is necessary to take a contextual, programme-driven view of what is relevant in terms of context, to be careful in defining programme theories so that they are not so abstracted to be meaningless, and yet not so concrete that they do not allow comparative cases to be considered, and that, finally, we are able to assess and compare the patterns of context, mechanism, and outcome across a range of related activities to understand better how they illuminate the phenomena under investigation. In short, in Pawson's approach, context, programme theory (mechanism), and outcome are necessarily interrelated, and it can be difficult to break into these inter-relationships at an appropriate level to conduct the evaluation or review.

Pawson's approach also involves a degree of creativity that is rather greater than in conventional approaches to evaluation and review. It requires the researcher or reviewer to be able to find programme theories that have been applied in different contexts, and to be able to find the relevant contextual elements that appear to cause differences in outcomes. This will not be the same in each programme, and often requires trial and error before the best 'fit' is found (an example of a 'retroductive' research strategy). This may mean that different reviewers or evaluators have the potential to produce different evaluations. This is entirely understandable when we consider that the research is taking place in complex social systems whose workings may be open to different interpretations, but can be alarming for policymakers and research-funders who may prefer the apparently more concrete answers that RCT-based research can lead to. The key question, however, is whether such research is over-simplifying the social because of its (relatively uncritical) use of experimental scientific understandings about the world in contexts where they may not apply.

Conclusion

Looking across the three approaches to evaluation and review explored above, all have their problems. The RCT-approach makes assumptions about the world that may not apply in social research as they assume a 'one-best-way' approach to methods and inquiry, along with a relatively closed environment and constant conjunction model that simply doesn't reflect the reality of conducting doing research in other settings. It is certainly difficult to argue from a philosophical basis that experimental methods hold much traction in complex social environments (Byrne 2003) – and even where experiments can be adapted for use in social research, they need to be handled with extreme care to make sure their assumptions can stand up to the very different research context rather than being assumed to be the only right way to do work.

The approach exemplified by Harden and Thomas is pragmatic in suggesting that that RTC-type methods can be adapted to become more multidisciplinary and incorporate qualitative research findings, but in doing so they appear to attempt to assume a standardisation of the reporting of methods in qualitative research that is unsustainable. They end up treating qualitative data in a standardised way that seems to assume standards in the reporting of methods and which ignores the standard philosophical justification of their use in achieving legitimacy through their closeness research contexts, rather than through claiming to produce objective results and generalisable findings. The end result is a standardised process that may appear to be multi-disciplinary, but has perhaps made rather too many concessions to the experimental, RCT-approach without taking sufficient account of research contexts or the complex, open systems within which social research often has to be conducted.

Pawson's approach is both the most intellectually coherent in terms of its account of the social world, but is also potentially the most variable in use in that it requires a great deal of imagination and care in its use to find programme theories at the appropriate level to test, and to be able to isolate the appropriate contextual factors making the different to outcomes in those theories across a range of cases. The need for creativity is likely to lead to differences in interpretation between researchers, and appears odd to researchers grounded in the standardised methods adopted by the other two approaches explored here. Pawson's approach requires us to place more faith in the researchers conducting the review or evaluation, but also for them to earn trust by being clear and transparent about the method choices that they have made.

This chapter has argued that, in order for social research engaged in evaluation and review for policy purposes to have the best chance of being intellectually coherent, its method must take account of the different demands that social research has in terms of the complexity of the phenomena under investigation, the degree of openness of the system under investigation, and the type of causality social systems have in place. Adapting methods which assume linear, constant conjunction causation based on assuming a relatively closed system in which interactions are relatively simple, seems to be misplaced for most social research. Attempts to adapt methods that start from these assumptions, as Harden and Thomas do, seem destined to fall short as they do not start with a range of assumptions that match the worlds we are investigating.

Of the three approaches explored here, Pawson's has the best chance of succeeding, but requires us to think of the role of the researcher or reviewer rather differently. Instead of asking them to be neutral, objective, independent observers who gain their legitimacy from an almost technical application of a particular method to their data, Pawson's approach requires us to understand the complexities of social systems are open to different interpretations that require creativity to explore, and intellectual honesty to explain which understandings were chosen as the best and why. We have to put our trust more in the researcher and reviewer, and accept that any interpretation they come up with will be open to contestation – but that should actually be a part of the process of deciding which policies our politicians follow, rather than being merely a response to what they have already decided. Pawson's work is both a response and a challenge to conventional approaches to evaluation and review, and should be treated as such, but in turn open to challenge from researchers coming up with different interpretations of the evidence.

Following Parson's ideas require us to accept that it is unlikely, in most social contexts, that there is a one, best answer. Instead there are multiple possibilities that are constrained by resources, ideology, social inheritances, and a range of other factors. Policy debates should not be about pretending in such complex environments we can find technical fixes, but instead exploring the interrelationships which new and existing research appears to highlight, and to engage both communities and policymakers with our findings to try and make things better.

Many researchers will be unhappy with these conclusions, but they do follow from a careful exploration of the implications of dealing with the complex, open-environment context into which policies and social interventions appear. It seems that we can either find new ways of thinking about evaluation, accepting its limitations and that there is necessarily an element of creativity and subjectivity in their interpretation, or we can simply conclude that it is impossible to evaluate anything. Accepting the latter course of action is to give way to a passive form of postmodernism in which it becomes impossible to know anything for sure. We can accept the limits of our knowledge, but at the same time present findings not as definitive answers, but as our best attempts to understand the complex phenomena we are investigating, and as a basis for dialogue rather than as fact.

Evaluation needs to grow up beyond its assumptions about the social world which are simply not viable, and deal with the messy, complex, open systems into which policies are introduced. In such circumstances there are no final answers, but that does not mean we shouldn't be trying to put forward, honestly and openly, the best answers we can, accepting that they will always be theory-laden, but being transparent about our assumptions rather than attempting to conceal them behind a cloak of objectivity which is ontologically and epistemologically unsustainable.

References

Byrne, D. (2003), *Interpreting Quantitative Data*. London: Sage.

Davies, H., Nutley, S. and Smith, P. (1999), What Works? The Role of Evidence in Public Sector Policy and Practice. *Public Money and Management* 19(1), pp. 3–5.

Dixon-Woods, M., Fitzpatrick, R. and Roberts K. (2008), Including qualitative research in systematic reviews: opportunities and problems. *Journal of Evaluation in Clinical Practice* 7(2), pp. 125–33.

Flyvbjerg, B. (2001), *Making Social Science Matter: Why Social Inquiry Fails and How it Can Succeed Again*. Cambridge: Cambridge University Press.

Giddens, A. (1993), *New Rules of The Sociological Method*. Cambridge: Polity Press.

Goldacre, B. (2011), Evidence supporting your NHS reforms? What evidence, Mr. Lansley? in *Guardian*.

Greenhalgh, T. (1998), Narrative based medicine in an evidence based world. *British Medical Journal* 318:323.

Harden, Angela, and James Thomas. (2005), Methodological Issues in Combining Diverse Study Types in Systematic Reviews. *International Journal of Social Research Methodology* 8(3), pp. 257–71.
House of Lords Science and Technology Select Committee (2011), *Behaviour Change*. London: The Stationary Office.
Law, J. (2004), *After Method: Mess in Social Science Research*. London: Routledge.
Le Fanu, J. (1999), *The Rise and Fall of Modern Medicine*. London: Abacus.
Pawson, R. (2002a), Evidence-based Policy: In Search of a Method. *Evaluation* 8(2), pp. 157–81.
——(2002b), Evidence-based Policy: The Promise of 'Realist Synthesis'. *Evaluation* 8(3), pp. 340–58.
——(2006), *Evidence-based Policy: A Realist Perspective*. London: Sage.
Pawson, R., T. Greenhaigh, G. Harvey, and K. Walshe. (2005), Realist Review - a new method of systematic review for complex policy interventions. *Journal of Health Services Research and Policy 10* (Supplement to Issue 3), pp. 21–34.
Pawson, R., and N. Tilley. (1997), *Realistic Evaluation*. London: Sage.
——(2001), Realistic evaluation bleedlines. *The American Journal of Evaluation* 22(3), pp. 317–24.
Sayer, A. (2005), *The Maoral Significance of Class*. Cambridge: Cambridge University Press.
Stone, D. (2012), *Policy Paradox: The Art of Political Decision Making*. London: Norton.

Part IV
Future

41

Future of the welfare state?

Bent Greve

Introduction

The welfare state has said to be in crisis several times since what was labeled the its golden time of expansion from 1960 to the first oil crisis in the early seventies. Welfare states have been recalibrated, recast, dismantled, restructured – in fact, many other words have been used to describe the various changes in what and how the welfare states finance, and whether they deliver welfare services in cash or kind. How the balance has and is being changed between state, market, and the civil society is also continuously open for scrutiny. However, it seems that the many and varied incremental changes in welfare states on the one hand follow the historical path, (i.e. there is some path-dependency) however on the other hand the welfare states change in such a way that they are no longer the same type and model as they used to be. The question is therefore: will there still be a future for the welfare states? Or will we be moving towards a more market-based type of state where distribution of income and wealth, welfare, and various types of objective and subjective elements traditionally being part of the welfare state will be left to the market and civil society to organize and structure.

Still, people have previously argued that the time of the welfare state is over. However, before reaching such a conclusion one needs to go into why we have a welfare state, e.g. the core reasons for the welfare states as they still exist, and, therefore why there will still be a need for them in the future. This is not necessarily informing us about the optimal size, how to choose a good institutional structure, or the splitting of financing and delivery in the different welfare states. It is as if the welfare state is a piggy bank (Barr, 2001), helping increase society's efficiency and intergenerational distribution of consumption possibilities.

This last chapter will, given the topic is the future, be more speculative in its approach, although it will draw upon the existing knowledge of the welfare states and their historical development, and how they can and have had an impact on everyday life and societies' development.

The chapter will first recapitulate why we have a welfare state, discuss the challenges for welfare states and recent developments, and then conclude on the prospects and ideas of the welfare state in the future. Given that the analysis is not about one specific country, but more general, this also raise the question whether we will be witnessing continuously very different types of welfare states (see chapters on typologies and methods), or if welfare states will converge so that their differences are mainly the priorities made between different sectors (e.g. health, elderly, transfers, social services, families etc. – see chapters on central policy areas).

Is the present economic and fiscal crisis new?

Industrialization and risk of being unemployed, having a work accident, being sick, or having no-one to support one during old-age can be argued to be the first reasons for development of welfare states, such as, the development in Bismarck's time and social insurance stemming from this period. These old risks still prevail.

Given that the economic crisis seems to have, and will be important for, the welfare states' future it is important to look into whether this is a new issue.

There have been economic, bank, and fiscal crises many times in the economic histories of all types of society. Crisis in development of prices of raw materials, notably oil prices in the seventies, and many years with high levels of unemployment. Stagflation and recession has thus been part of welfare states' earlier developments.

There was a bank crisis in the US in 1907, the famous crash at Wall Street in 1929, and a change away from gold standard, which was given up in 1931. The crash in 1929 led to a long period of low economic growth and a very high level of unemployment. Part of the reason being that the public sector at that time had a limited use in order to cope with the recession, for example, by an expansive fiscal policy

Fewer fiscal automatic stabilizers were thus built into the societal models for steering the economies.

Still, the crisis in the 1930s has been seen as one of the reasons for the development of social policy in the US – Roosevelt's New Deal – setting the scene for combating the economic crisis while at the same time coping with the high level of unemployment and economic depression. Keynes' arguments for intervention in the economies and trying to handle business cycles also stems from this time. Look out for the employment and the economy will look after itself has been a key message from this time.

The way to solve the world's economic and political problems after the Second World War was inspired by the famous Beveridge report, and also being a core reason for the development of the British welfare state. When the world settled and more free movement of goods and services developed, welfare states in Europe advanced rapidly in what has since been called the heyday of the welfare state in the sixties and seventies, until the oil price crisis took over and showed the clear contradictions of varieties of welfare capitalism and contradictions between growth and economic management. Despite this, many welfare states, especially in Europe, continue to grow and are measured by spending as proportion of gross domestic product (GDP) – a spending level in the more mature welfare states was around 25–30 % of GDP when the last crisis started.

There have been several other times of economic crisis, such as the crisis starting in Asia in 1998, and the international fiscal crisis starting in the US in late 2007, which has ended up in what has been labeled the first crisis of globalization (Brown, 2010). These all indicate a need for concerted international economic action, however it has proven difficult, when the crisis seemingly ebbs out, to agree upon international co-ordination or common initiatives to cope with the economic impact of the crisis. There is on both theoretical as well as a political level a conflict between the understanding and acceptance of a Keynesian argument of the need for intervention to cope with economic imbalance and a more market-based approach requiring non-public sector intervention, e.g. a free market economy, perhaps with an acceptance of monetary policy. This conflict still seems to prevail.

Every economic crisis has had an impact on the economic growth, and after a financial crisis the business cycle seems to take longer to recover. However, the net impact might be lower due to the higher level of economic growth before the crisis. The crisis has further had repercussions on the level of unemployment and the ability to sustain welfare benefits. Economic crises of the magnitude we have witnessed in recent years could thus be argued to be a new social risk, whereby the welfare state will have a new role by ensuring that the necessary economic stabilizers are at place reducing the impact on core welfare issues by changing economic climate.

There is a need for an international co-ordination of economic development. This is important also due to the fact that the market will presumably not clear by itself. A problem being that 'the global capital flows and global sourcing of goods and services that characterize globalization are not complemented by the institutions and culture of a global market that functions sufficiently well for us to gain all the benefits of market disciplines' (Brown, 2010, p. 89). Besides, if the need is an increase in demand only coordinated actions can ensure this without negative impact on individual countries. Growth in one country can spread to other countries, as also a downturn in the economy can.

The economic crisis and the impact on nation states are seemingly spreading further and faster around the world than before. The interconnectedness of the economies has increased implying also new roles for the welfare states. Given the size of the welfare states today, on the one hand they have an option to positively influence the economic outcome for families of the crisis, while on the other hand they are more economically restricted than earlier also due to several countries having had many years with public sector deficit and increased levels of debt. This has been going on without trying to finance the welfare state by, for example, demanding the necessary level of taxes and duties or reduction in spending or increase in the economic growth.

The many years with deficit also reflects that there is at the same time a risk that the welfare states will be used as scapegoat and cuts in welfare spending will be the outcome. This is because the welfare state is only looked upon to a limited extent as a social investment. Naturally, there is a need for having public sector income to cover expenditures, but as long as the tax system is presumed to be the burden instead of part of the solution, then this can be difficult.

This is furthermore because the recent crisis will presumably be implying a need for a larger type of economic buffer in nation states and at a global level. Buffers can be expected in the public sector as well as in the financial sector and other important economic institutions. There will presumably also be a more reluctant stance to increase spending as this might be difficult to change in the future. The need for larger buffers is also because there will be new crisis or at least economic downturns in the future. The learning of agents as a reaction to bubbles in the economy is seemingly only more limited (Taleb, 2010), for example when new options for speculative profits arise people will still believe they are able to win and speculate better than other people in the market. Therefore there will be a need for a society who is able to counteract bubbles and economic crises. The implication being that there is a need for some kind of national or international reserve fund, but before they have been built up there is a risk that the pressure on welfare states will be immense.

A specific problem is that within the financial system, and, presumably also other markets for goods and services where a high and speculative income is possible (such as the housing system), there will be a tendency that some will try to get their 'part of the cake' and make risky investments that might have a negative impact on other members of society. How to regulate this will be difficult, but the suggestion to 'inject morals into markets and empower individuals in society' (Richardsson, 2011, p. 209) seems less likely to be the right solution. Morals are always good, but how to ensure they remain and that all citizens abide by them is less obvious. Thereby, also an indication of that normative solution to the crisis is less likely to have long-lasting effect, as they can be difficult to implement, implying a need for a state or a concerted type of state action.

There have already been several responses to the fiscal crisis and deficits in welfare states. In principle they need to use a variety of responses: higher taxes and duties that also can imply less hidden economy, ensure economic growth and prioritize public-sector spending. In this sense this is also at the core of why we have a welfare state.

Why we have a welfare state

This section will be dealing with core reasons for having a welfare state, such as market failure and the common pool argument, but also how criticism of the welfare state has been argued – especially from a liberal perspective. We will then consider whether these reasons continue to be relevant for retaining a welfare state.

Markets left to themselves will imply a risk of market failure. The implication is that certain goods and services will not be provided and some people will not be able to gain access to welfare and welfare services. This is, as just one example, often the case with old age care as it is difficult for the individual to foresee the need for it. A further implication of a complete free market can be that unemployment will be high, and the degree of inequality is higher than what individuals are willing to risk if having to decide in ignorance, e.g. not knowing their position in society, in a Rawlsian understanding. Furthermore, in some areas the welfare state is more efficient than either an insurance market (Barr, 2010) or leaving the issues to the free market.

In some areas there are thus efficiency arguments for the welfare states' intervention, and in others there are reasons of equality, at least in access or options for choosing, to supply certain types of services. Hospitals are, for example, in most countries a service with universal access and often free of charge. Efficiency argument has to do with the common pool argument: that adding resources together is cheaper than all having to save money, for example, to be taken care of in old age, given that we do not know beforehand whether we will need this service. In addition, recent years have seen arguments revolving around whether the welfare state can be understood as a social investment state (Esping-Andersen, 2002), given that certain types of services will not be delivered, or at least not sufficiently, by the market. This perspective has, at least to a certain extent, also been followed by a common European employment strategy in relation to affordable and high-quality day care for children. This strategy has had the impact and intention to create both an option for more equal access to the labour market for men and women, but also an increase in the labour force to ensure a growth in the economies. In this way the welfare state is in line with investment in infrastructure and education enabling countries to compete with other countries.

Understood in this way, without the welfare state societies will not be able to prosper as they are a core part of societal investment in the future. This has further been used as an argument for supporting especially very young children as a good start in life will ensure higher labour market participation, lower levels of crime, and more trust in others. Societies with higher levels of welfare, if measured by GDP per inhabitant. Furthermore, inhabitants have a higher level of happiness (Greve, 2011), and more equal societies tends to be more cohesive, more healthy, and with less crime (Wilkinson and Picket, 2010).

The other viewpoint is that a welfare state needs to be financed, and taxes and duties will imply distortions in the way the economy is working and by this reduce the utility of the citizens. The financing of the welfare state in this view has a negative impact on economic development, and a reduction of public sector spending and lowering of taxes and duties can by dynamic impact imply a more positive economic development for welfare states. This is a continuation of an older debate on the impact of public sector growth on economic performance. A theoretical discussion is including whether or not there exist a so-called Baumol's disease in the public sector service provision. However, measurement of productivity is not easy, one argument being that service provision has a lower productivity level than private industrial production.

However, the overall goal and need to have a stable societal development points toward the core reasons for having a welfare state persisting. This includes the need to correct market failures such as monopolies, ensuring public goods, and regulating with regard to externalities. Furthermore, a wish to ensure a decent living standard and access to key types of goods and services, such as healthcare, seem likely to be part of welfare state development.

Changes in recent years

Recent years have seen many and very diverse changes in the welfare states. Discussion on transformations and changes in welfare states are not new.

The expected demographic changes, especially in the more affluent societies around the globe, but also in China in just 15–20 years' time, with a growing number of elderly compared to those on the labour market, has raised discussions on the sustainability of the welfare state. Demographic changes are putting pressure on public sector spending and the possible increase in production due to lack of labour. Therefore changes in pension systems, retirement age, and more targeting of welfare state expenditure – services as well as income transfers – has for a long time been on the agenda. In several countries reforms of the pension system have taken place in the last 10–15 years, and have been on the way since before the economic crisis. These changes create a higher reliance upon occupational and private pensions, and a more clear link between contribution, return on investment, and actuarial calculations in relation to average life expectancy and risk of being in need of an early retirement pension.

The last 10–15 years have also in contrast to changes mentioned above, in Europe at least, seen a development towards more services provided or supported by the welfare state, in areas such as child care, education, healthcare and care for the elderly. These changes of welfare states, from its historical central perspective of providing mainly cash benefits with regard to social risk, to a move towards more benefits in-kind, can also be attributed to different perspectives on the welfare states role, for example an increased focus on the welfare state as having an investment role. Still, the intergenerational perspective is still there implying that the welfare state helps in leveling out consumption possibilities over the lifetime in an effective way.

However, the impact of the latest fiscal crisis of the welfare states – with many governments in Europe and the US having high levels of public-sector deficit and high levels of public sector debts put forward – reinforces a liberal perspective, alongside a strong focus on reduction in the size of the welfare state. A reduction in welfare spending from the public sector, with more focus on what the private sector and families can deliver, implies that the welfare state's ability to deliver welfare will be reduced. It further reduces the welfare state's ability to be responsible in times of economic crisis to reduce the impact of the economic development on private households – it will be less able to reduce the impact of the business cycle.

At the same time the desire and need for welfare services has been increasing in countries with growing living standards. This is following traditional economic analysis that there is an income-elasticity above one in relation to this type of goods and services, and, therefore with increasing levels of disposable income more services are in demand – public as well as private. Occupational welfare and welfare through the tax system has thus to a larger degree been complementary, instead of a substitution, to the public welfare. There has also been a role for the civil society and voluntary organizations, and an ongoing debate about their role in providing welfare services. The welfare mix is thus under constant changes, and boundaries needs not to be fixed over time.

Migration within economic areas, between the North and South, might also imply a pressure on the welfare states, due to the risk of increased spending on those arriving unable to support themselves by getting a job on the labour market. However, at the same time this increases the opportunities to augment production by having a larger labour force than previously possible.

Despite earlier economic and political crises in many welfare states, especially in Europe, as also argued above, the society has taken over a larger part of the responsibility in relation to care for children and the elderly. This shows the welfare state has a larger role in relation to services than historically, and that the boundaries between state, market, and civil society seemingly are under constant change. How the boundaries will be in the future is it not possible to foresee, but it is obvious that there will be a role for the state in order to ensure welfare, at least for the most vulnerable, but also in a broader sense in helping to ensure societal development.

Focus in the years to come will presumably be on sustainability both in relation to financing the welfare state, but also the way in which new initiatives will be enacted, as the willingness to try new things is likely to decrease in times of economic difficulty (Thelen, 2004). If this diagnosis is correct the implication is that the coming years will presumably have a clear and more structured focus on the role of the welfare state. Less likely is that the welfare state will be involved in and taking many new types of initiatives. It will be more of the same and with a strong and continued focus on the overall level of spending and to which groups this spending will be directed. Focus presumably will also be on long-term sustainability, both with regard to economic options, number of jobs, and impact on the environment. However, economic growth and societies becoming more affluent might cause increased demand for services, and thus also for welfare services from the public sector.

The efficiency of the welfare state can be argued to relate to the ability, with as little money as possible, to reduce the degree of inequality resulting from the outcome of the markets' way of working. Therefore there has also been a focus on how the welfare state can redistribute between rich and poor, and how the welfare state can redistribute consumption possibilities over the life cycle. Furthermore, more equally societies with higher levels of equality see better health, less crime, etc. (Wilkingson and Picket, 2010). This focus of redistribution, besides that reduction of poverty, has also historically been one of the welfare states' core issues, stretching back to the poor laws in many countries. How to combine reduction of poverty and ensuring a certain degree of equality while at the same time being able to finance the welfare states is one of the challenges for the welfare states ahead.

In the same vein lies a constant discussion of whom the welfare state should help. Should it only be those very poor and/or deserving/non-deserving dependents that are eligible for benefits? This also includes debates on whether income transfers should be universal or means tested, and how the means test should be carried out.

Conclusion

The welfare state is here to stay, regardless of the size, structure and its ability to reach goals of equality and full employment. The impact of nation states on welfare in an evermore global and regionalized world is open for discussion.

We have in the last few years witnessed, in some ways, a retrenchment in the classical welfare states' activities, such as income transfers, while at the same time have seen an increase in the welfare states' role in relation to new social risk and delivery of services, implying a welfare state bridging the intergenerational gap and being more in line with a social investment welfare state approach. There has also, at least among some nearby countries, been a tendency towards convergence, not necessarily in the sense of structural convergence, but more in the sense of the economic effort used in relation to welfare issues. At the same time welfare states have moved from mainly providing income transfers to specific groups, to having a larger role in providing welfare services, including care for children and the elderly, and providing an educational system and universal healthcare provision in most countries.

The welfare state will also have a central role as the one with the options and power making it possible to reduce the negative impact on employment and equality from the large up- and downturns in the economies. Whether it is possible on a global scale to agree upon measures to reduce the variation is more doubtful.

This also implies that welfare states in the future presumably to a lesser degree can be put into typologies or welfare regimes, except perhaps more divided into a few geographically based regimes, for example Europe, the US, Asia, Southern America, and Africa. Still, this does not imply that they will be without differences or national diversities given the varied historical traits, but more that the outcome and impact of welfare states, including the size of the economy and the need for financing, will be around the same level in at least regional-based geographical areas. The national variations can have an impact on who gets what and under what conditions, and by this also an impact on the degree of equality in consumption possibilities and access to different kinds of goods and services. Boundaries and understanding of who is deserving and who is not deserving different kind and types of benefits can also change, and these changes might have an impact on the way the welfare states will be structured and who they will support.

We will presumably also need welfare and demand welfare in the future, notwithstanding how we define it (see Chapter 1). However, the balance between actors, who will benefit and who will pay, and the varieties across countries can be expected to prevail in the future.

References

Barr, N. (2001), *The Welfare State as Piggy Bank: Information, Risk, Uncertainty, and the Role of the State.* Oxford: Oxford University Press.

Brown, G. (2010), *Beyond the Crash. Overcoming the First Crisis of Globalisation.* London: Simon and Schuster.

Esping-Andersen, G. (2002), *Why We Need a New Welfare State.* Oxford: Oxford University Press.

Greve, B. (2011), *Happiness. A Key Text.* Oxford: Routledge.

Richardson, J. (ed.) (2011), *From Recession to Renewal. The Impact of the Financial Crisis on Public Services and Local Government.* Bristol: Policy Press.

Taleb, N. (2010), *The Black Swan.* London: Penguin Books.

Thelen, K. (2004), *How Institutions Evolve: The Political Economy of Skills in Britain, the United States and Japan.* Cambridge: Cambridge University Press.

Wilkinson, R. and Pickett, K. (2010), *The Spirit Level. Why Greater Equality Makes Societies Stronger.* New York: Bloomsbury Press.

Index